INTERVIEWING
Speaking, Listening, and Learning for Professional Life

Rob Anderson
Saint Louis University

George M. Killenberg
University of South Florida, St. Petersburg

Mayfield Publishing Company
Mountain View, California
London • Toronto

To our families, Dona, Eric, Neil, and Penny,
Andrew, Kristen, Anne, and Mark, for their support

Library of Congress Cataloging-in-Publication Data
Anderson, Rob.
    Interviewing : speaking, listening, and learning for professional
life / Rob Anderson, George M. Killenberg.
        p.   cm.
    Includes bibliographical references and index.
    ISBN 1-55934-956-5
    1. Interviewing.   I. Killenberg, George M.   II. Title.
BF637.I5A53   1998
158'.39—dc21   98-44466
                                                    CIP

Mayfield Publishing Company
1280 Villa Street
Mountain View, California 94041

Manufactured in the United States of America
10 9 8 7 6 5 4 3 2 1

Sponsoring editor, Holly Allen; production editor, Melissa Kreischer; manuscript editor, Judith Brown; design manager, Susan Breitbard; text designer, Anne Flanagan; cover designer, Claire Seng-Niemoeller; art editor, Amy Folden; photo researcher, Brian Pecko; cover art, © Sandra Dionisi; manufacturing manager, Randy Hurst. The text was set in 10½/13 Adobe Garamond by Thompson Type; and printed on acid-free 45# Highland Plus by Malloy Lithographing, Inc.

Photo Credits

CO-1, © Bob Daemmrich/The Image Works; **CO-2,** © Bob Daemmrich/The Image Works; **CO-3,** © Sven Martson/The Image Works; **CO-4,** © Spencer Grant/The Picture Cube, Inc; **CO-5,** © Michael Newman/PhotoEdit; **CO-6,** © Billy E. Barnes/PhotoEdit; **CO-7,** © Tony Freeman/PhotoEdit; **CO-8,** © Mark Antman/The Image Works; **CO-9,** © Amy Etra/PhotoEdit; **CO-10,** © Rick Scott/The Picture Cube, Inc.; **CO-11,** © Nita Winter/The Image Works; **CO-12,** © AP/Wide World Photos; **CO-13,** © Bob Daemmrich/The Image Works.

 This book is printed on recycled paper.

✥ Preface

We've learned a lot from our students about interviewing.

Mainly we've learned that students react to interviewing in dramatically different ways. Some students are almost pathologically nervous about asking or answering questions, especially if they're videotaped. They find an interviewing class similar to a public speaking class in that it asks them—they think—to perform. They overestimate the difficulties of interviewing because they interpret it as a tense performance situation. Other students, however, underestimate its difficulties, figuring an interviewing class ought to be a breeze. After all—they think—talking is easy, and talkative people should have no trouble exchanging information in conversational, informal settings.

More than twenty-five years of teaching interviewing to students, managers, and career journalists have convinced us that interviewing is one of the most practical skills a professional communicator can develop. But it isn't necessarily as intimidating, or as automatic, as some people assume.

Interviews as Opportunities

Interviewing is not a simple behavioral skill or procedure that can be practiced over and over until it's done "right." As authors and teachers, we cannot prescribe exactly what students should do or say, because we can't anticipate the specific people or contexts they will encounter. Experienced interviewers and interviewees discover that each interview is brand new, with a fresh and different set of invitations and challenges. A class, and a textbook, shortchanges students if it doesn't encourage flexibility and creativity in a variety of interviewing concepts. An effective interview isn't a collection of techniques, carefully practiced and skillfully orchestrated beforehand. It is often a mutual improvisation between two or more people who probably have different ways of seeing the world. It is an opportunity for learning through dialogue.

While interview talk can be unpredictable, it isn't random, either. Learning baseline communication tendencies along with new behavioral skills will put interviewing tasks in context, allowing interviewers and interviewees to be far more creative. So, in reading this book, we suggest that students

- think about current professional goals and future career possibilities;
- relate interviewing tasks to previously learned concepts;

iii

- consider the interviewing class in relation to other classes taken in college;
- understand how this class is integrated into "real life" situations (assignments in such a course will not involve throwaway practice interviews, but real ones with family, acquaintances, and professional people);
- don't just read about skills, but try them out at every opportunity;
- understand that the basic motivation for interviewing is *learning*.

Boiled down: People are unlikely to be good interviewers if they're not curious about learning new things; people are unlikely to be good interviewees if they're not knowledgeable. And each role boosts the other.

Features of This Book

Interviewing is a book for students who want to build practical skills, and for students and faculty who also want the interviewing course to be interesting, thoughtful, and engaging. A practical course does not simply ask students to learn how-to performance skills; it also starts them thinking about the process and demonstrates the relevance of interviewing for daily life. Here, then, are the key features of this book:

- **"Skills-plus" orientation:** Throughout, we describe essential skills and place them in conceptual context. With an effective blend of skills, appreciations, and knowledge, interviewing easily can be linked to other courses in the major, such as communication theory, research methods, interpersonal communication, listening, mass communication, journalism, organizational communication, and intercultural communication. We want to help students understand the concepts supporting behavioral advice, but this book is selective in the research it cites. Long footnotes of specialized research studies aren't essential for beginning students, although instructors may choose to supplement assignments with additional resources found in the *Instructor's Resource Guide*.

- **Helpful and flexible organization within chapters:** Each chapter includes "The Basics" and "Beyond the Basics" sections, allowing instructors more choice in making assignments and adapting the text to their courses.

- **Helpful and flexible overall organization of chapters:** Part 1 develops basic skills and appreciations, and Part 2 describes specific basic interview contexts and strategies (for employee selection, organizational evaluation, journalistic information gathering, research, helping, and persuasion). Part 3 places interviewing in a wider analytical context and includes Chapter 12, "Understanding and Analyzing Interviews in Popular Media Culture," a unique contribution of this book.

- **Clear division of basic interviewing skills into three interrelated types—listening, questioning, and framing:** Listening is the skill that enables interview-based learning in the first place; questioning is the skill that focuses learning; and framing is the skill that interprets and places learning in appropriate context.

• **Student-friendly writing:** A narrative style featuring many stories and anecdotes, often about everyday college life, is supplemented by clear summaries. We describe how and why interviewing styles work for participants through numerous examples. Exercises involve students in interviewing as an avenue to organizational success and, more broadly, as an opportunity to learn more about their campuses, about their families and friends, and about themselves.

• **Emphasis on how interviewing contributes to the quality of public dialogue:** Effective interviewing skills and appreciations support democratic action. Perhaps more than any other interviewing textbook, this one stresses that ethical interviewing creates better citizens, whose rhetoric will become more civil, sensitive, and attuned to other voices in the political process.

• **Integrated approach to both interviewer and interviewee roles:** This book prepares students to be more responsive and effective interviewees, in addition to becoming more successful interviewers. Unless they understand the interdependence of these roles, students may learn to approach professional tasks in selfish or fragmented ways.

• **Integrated ethics approach:** Ethics, we stress, is not a separate concern for interview communicators; it is involved in all message choices. Incidents with ethical implications illustrate concepts in each chapter and challenge students to articulate their own responses to ethical choices inherent in interviewing.

• **Integrated cultural approach:** Straightforward discussions, examples, and analyses of multicultural issues are included within each chapter.

• **Integrated treatment of employment interviewing:** We treat the goals and problems of interviewer and interviewee as interrelated in the selection process, in one chapter, instead of separating these closely linked issues into different chapters.

• **Innovative boxed supplements:** A series of highlighted examples help students enrich their learning. "Interviewers/Interviewees in Action" boxes offer first-person accounts of interviewing successes and failures. "Reminders" boxes develop important ideas and help students organize and remember key skills. "Trying Out Your Skills" boxes provide practical ways to examine the depth of learning, often by analyzing brief interview excerpts. End-of-chapter "Making Your Decision" boxes present hypothetical situations, often oriented toward ethics, that encourage students to apply insights creatively in ambiguous contexts sure to stimulate class discussion. In addition, each chapter includes "The Interview Bookshelf," an annotated section recommending books students would find helpful for further reading or future interviewing-related assignments in other classes.

• **A thorough *Instructor's Resource Guide* for the teacher:** The Guide supplements the textbook materials with suggestions for class activities, resources, and assignments. It also explores the many practical decisions involved in teaching with a skills-plus approach.

Where a Book Comes From

Textbook authors do a lot of thanking because they, better than anyone else, know their debt to the support and ideas of others.

Without our families, including Dona, Eric, and Neil Anderson, and Penny, Andrew, Kristen, Anne, and Mark Killenberg, we wouldn't have had the spark or the support to want to write. Somebody who cares about you needs to say something like, "Sure, that's important, too—spend a lot of time cooped up in a cluttered office without me and get it done." Although we think they know how much we love them, we want to say it again here.

Without our students, we wouldn't have been able to test-drive many of the ideas that made it into the book, and some that didn't. They have been delightfully willing to share what works for them, and what broke down.

Without our friends and colleagues, we would have missed conversations that stimulated what we hope are some of the book's special strengths. Nobody gets many good ideas sitting around alone, but in conversations we come alive: "Oh, yeah! I'd never thought of it that way before. Tell me more. I wonder if I can use that in Chapter 6?" Specifically, we appreciate the contributions of Daniel Nelson in helping with library research, Sherry Lillie in sharing materials and experiences teaching interviewing skills to professionals, Bob Krizek in counseling us about the intricate issues of research interviewing, and Kerry Kirkland in sharing her expertise in employment interviewing. And, as we have been since 1972, the authors were indispensable friendly critics for each other's work—nitpicking, admiring, arguing, and, most often, agreeing.

Without editors and staff at Mayfield and reviewers at various colleges across the country, we would have missed a variety of excellent teaching and learning options we'd never have considered on our own. We appreciate their assistance immensely. Communication editor Holly Allen gave us the opportunity to publish our ideas and moved the project along efficiently, with the help of editorial assistants Devra Kupor and Star MacKenzie. Production editor Melissa Kreischer coordinated the multiple tasks and decisions that turn a manuscript into an attractive, readable book. Thanks also to the rest of the book team, including Judith Brown, manuscript editor; Susan Breitbard, design manager; Brian Pecko, photo researcher; and Amy Folden, art editor.

In addition, the backstage work of reviewers—all experienced teachers—deserves recognition. We accepted much of their advice, but in the final analysis we had to trust our own instincts and experiences. The following reviewers provided excellent feedback, and the book is vastly improved because of their careful attention: Peggy Yuhas Byers, Ball State University; James A. Gilchrist, Western Michigan University; Sandra L. Herndon, Ithaca College; Sherry Holladay, Illinois State University; R. Bruce Hyde, St. Cloud State University; Elizabeth Kizer, University of Missouri; Mary Y. Mandeville, Oklahoma State University; Rebecca Parker, Western Illinois University; Russell F. Proctor II, Northern Kentucky University; Nathan P. Stucky, Southern Illinois University; and Dudley B. Turner, University of Akron.

 Contents

❀ 4   Skillful Questioning   80

⌘ 7   Interviews in Organizations   208

�֍ 10   Interviews in Helping Professions: Diagnostic, Therapeutic, and Counseling Contexts   316

✿ 11   Interviews in Persuasive Situations   346

1 Beyond the Q & A Presumption

Interviewing with a Listening/Learning Perspective

Interviews can be like a warm bath or a cold shower, verbal massage or medieval torture. Interviews can motivate or they can alienate, push, or pull, join or separate you from those you interview.

—FRANK MacHovec,
Interview and Interrogation

LEARNING GOALS

After reading this chapter, you should be able to

- Understand the implications of an "inter-view" perspective
- Discuss the three complementary facets of interviewing: listening, speaking, and framing
- Recognize the major qualities of effective interviews
- Know the various ways interview types are used in professional and personal lives
- Approach interviewing with an ethical orientation

A young married couple, Ronald and Rae, spend their Saturday afternoon driving around town to visit three different day care centers. They want to talk to the directors and get a feel for the atmosphere of each place. They are appropriately careful about researching the centers, as they know how important this decision can be for the education and safety of their daughter. They have prepared a list of questions to ask and concerns to check out; in other words, they have become interviewers whether they have had formal training in interviewing or not.

After visiting the directors at the three centers, Ronald and Rae stop at the mall to grab a bite to eat. Just outside the food court, a nicely dressed man with a clipboard asks for their cooperation in responding to a brief marketing survey. Which stores do they usually visit? How often do they eat at the mall? What draws them to the mall? Advertised sales? Special events? Wide selection of products? Ease of parking? Down the aisle, a volunteer for a local politician wants their opinions about the school district. The couple take three or four minutes to talk over their shopping habits and their attitudes about education; they have become interviewees.

Returning home, Ronald and Rae thank and pay the baby-sitter and ask a series of questions about their daughter's day. Did she like the sitter's games? Was she fussy? Did she eat well? Though this conversation feels informal and spontaneous, it serves many of the same functions as a formal interview. Persons who don't have the information they want or need use a focused conversation to obtain that information.

Conversation and interviews are alike in that both, if done right, lead to knowledge and understanding. Not all conversations are interviews; not all interviews have the tone of conversations. But they share a common goal of helping people learn. Raymond Gorden (1969), author of a classic book on interviewing, observes, "Just as interviewing cannot be divorced from other methods of gaining understanding of human behavior, neither can it be separated from the basic skills of ordinary conversation. Any two-way conversation involves many of the same skills and insights needed for successful interviewing. The main difference is in the *central purpose* of interviewing as opposed to other forms of conversation" (p. 30).

Interviewing's central purpose is assisted learning, to satisfy the need for information and insight. Gorden goes on to warn about the dual dangers that confront beginning interviewers and interviewees: first, the notion that interviewing is "just talking to people in a spontaneous social way" and, second, the belief that interviewing is "a magical and mysterious formula" that is directed by known techniques. It is neither. Interviewing is conversational, to be sure, but it is a specialized form of creative conversation that can't be learned by memorizing a repertoire of handy techniques, gimmicks, or formulas. The rest of this book is an elaboration of this basic but elusive theme.

✤ THE BASICS

The Interview as "Inter-View"

In a formal sense, an **interview** is an interpersonal or public communication situation in which one or more persons seeks information and insight from another or others. Most interviews therefore must rely on questions and responses, but it's limiting if not misleading to think of interviews only as occasions for asking and answering questions.

Although interviews at times appear to be conducted for the primary benefit of one or the other parties, most effective interviews lead to mutual understanding, giving participants knowledge and insight as they make decisions affecting their own lives and the lives of others. In presenting the many realistic and practical decisions communicators must make in interviews, we'll remind you often of this ideal of mutuality to challenge you to make as few compromises as necessary in your interviews.

Consider what the word suggests—"inter-view," a sharing of views (Killenberg & Anderson, 1989; Kvale, 1996). In this sense, an interview becomes a partnership in which interviewer and interviewee realize that more can be gained, for both, with a genuine atmosphere of collaboration. Success in interviewing comes from thorough and reciprocal exchanges, not from a concern for who wins and who loses. An interview conducted as a partnership isn't a tea party with phony polite talk; although civility is usually expected, words such as *challenging, confrontational, intense, exhausting,* or *angry* appropriately describe certain types of interviews.

Interviews are indispensable occasions for many types of routine collection of data. Beyond the routine, however, interviews constitute important turning points for us individually and collectively. Although some interviews seem far more important than others, everything is relative. To a supermarket manager hiring a minimum-wage clerk, the employment interview is no big deal; to the young mother who has spent weeks looking for work, it's a crucial moment. Interviews often involve high personal stakes—hiring decisions, medical diagnoses, marriage counseling, crash investigations, to name a few. The potential for error and misunderstanding is great, even when the interview participants seek a partnership.

Much of the time, interviews are framed and conducted as data accumulation, not as an opportunity to go beyond the data to achieve understanding or shared learning. Social science researcher Steiner Kvale (1996) uses the metaphors of the miner and the traveler to illustrate the difference between mere collection of facts and a search for understanding. The miner acquires information by extracting previously hidden nuggets of fact or meaning, digging and scraping and treating the interviewee like so much ground. Mining has its place in interviews, but it's a method with limitations. The interviewer-as-traveler, unlike the miner, understands that interviewing is not something one person does to another; it is something done together. The traveler, eager to explore, searches for knowledge in the company of the interviewee; they move about, learning from each other, perhaps changing each other. The partnership model stresses attitude over process; it offers no guarantee of success. But it does, we believe, offer far more promise for effective learning.

Anyone can imagine many legitimate, necessary exceptions to partnership styles of interviewing. Police questioning witnesses to an abduction need accurate, truthful information quickly; a social worker investigating child abuse cannot leisurely negotiate information from an uncooperative relative. Exceptions aside, the gap between the norm and the ideal remains sizable. Interviewers and interviewees often work at cross-purposes, playing roles that may encourage individual or even selfish objectives over mutual ones. Certain expectations follow, as well. Interviewers assume a superior, controlling position; interviewees act accordingly. The interviewer questions, the interviewee answers, rarely achieving anything like the spirit of an "inter-view."

Common Stereotypes of Interviews

The interview as *partnership?* We're more likely to picture someone in a suit sizing up a job prospect with a gruff opening question, "Tell me why *my* company should hire *you*," or Sam Donaldson or Diane Sawyer boring in with questions that leave a corporate representative squirming before a TV audience of millions. Influenced by stereotypes, many prospective interviewers and interviewees brace for an uncomfortable, even painful, experience. The word *interview* suggests a formal, structured, controlled inquiry at the hands of a stranger who asks penetrating questions while we sit consumed with anxiety about the outcome. Or we're the stranger, trying to be tough and tender at the same time. For most people, interviews are associated with the *Q & A presumption*—the belief that questions and answers are the only important factors. To some, the prospect of an interview is about as appealing as visiting a dentist for a root canal. No wonder a popular book on the subject is titled *Sweaty Palms* (Medley, 1992).

Unfortunately, the stereotypes about interviews too often hold true. Interviewees do often assume a subservient, vulnerable role, or they are expected to. Interviewers exert power and control; their objectives and interests often seem to come first. As a result, many interviewees are taken for a ride, with little say in how they travel, much less the destination. Limiting, limited views of interviewing prevail, and some originate from the way the subject was learned or taught.

An education in interviewing based on a study of communication research and practice isn't part of the average person's schooling. Even those perceived as skilled at interviewing, such as police and journalists, seldom receive more than a cursory exposure to the literature and research of interviewing. Most of us go through life experiencing interviews here and there, perhaps knowing less about the subject than we do about microbrewing or Michael Jackson's family life. What we've learned has been through snippets of experience or the anecdotal advice of self-help books. The average interviewee's sparse repertoire probably consists of basic survival skills: what to be nervous about, what not to say, how to behave, how to protect him- or herself. A so-called trained interviewer may have a slight advantage—perhaps a three-hour company workshop on interviewing. But as a rule, few people are prepared to make the most of an interview.

Don't assume, either, that those exposed to a formal, textbook-driven communication curriculum possess a broad perspective on the potential of interviewing. Some textbooks are written primarily from the interviewer's perspective, an approach that overlooks several important considerations. When teachers and students focus so intently on the interviewer, they're likely to miss or underestimate the potential value of an interview as a collaboration. An emphasis on the interviewer also reinforces a misconception that the interviewer's role is paramount and encourages interviewers to exert their perceived dominance. That, in turn, ultimately encourages countertactics by interviewees. Interestingly, the self-help books and articles published for laypeople, not students, usually stress the interviewee's perspective, as in a recent article titled "What You Need to *Ace* Today's Rough-and-Tough Job Interviews." In other words, it's perhaps too easy for interviewees to experience the meeting only as a test.

Even in the helping professions, such as medicine and counseling, the interviewer is emphasized. A doctor or health-care specialist isn't likely to see the interview as a cooperative venture with patients. The interviewee may be the beneficiary, but the approach might be perceived as paternalistic even when the specialist is sincere and helpful. The patient or client is treated as someone to be probed, inspected, analyzed, assessed, and—ultimately—helped.

Although some people wind up as formal interviewers, almost everyone is interviewed at one time or another. All of us could benefit from an education in interviewing, not just the professionals who regularly conduct interviews in their work. The key

BOX 1.1   I N T E R V I E W E R S   I N   A C T I O N

James G. Goodale

M anagement consultant and author James Goodale warns against the assumption that effective interviewing is intuitive:

"Many of us have known people who appear to conduct effective interviews almost by intuition and seem to have the knack to say the right thing at the right time. We are inclined to attribute their success to personality and intuitive feel and therefore conclude that a good interviewer is born not made.

"This conclusion, however, is simply not true.

". . . Just as the ballet dancer, the professional athlete, and the professional comedian have planned and practiced each individual action we observe in their seemingly effortless performance, successful interviewers have worked very hard to perfect their art. As with any other art form, interviewing must be grounded in sound principles and excellent technique."

Source: Goodale, 1982, pp. 1–2

components of interviewing, such as listening, choosing our words, interpreting people's spoken and unspoken words, and assessing information, are valuable qualities for all of us, at work and at home. This book defines the topic broadly enough to encompass a host of situations and activities, recognizing that an interview, in whatever form it takes, is a fundamental form of human communication none of us should take for granted (see Box 1.1).

Characteristics of an Interview

No one can offer a definition of an interview that is universal or comprehensive—one you'd find in every textbook or article on the subject. Too many variables and exceptions make that task impossible. However, most interviews have certain key characteristics, functions, and qualities in common.

Let's extend our earlier definition a bit. Considered at its most basic level, an interview is a form of communication, usually between two people, talking face-to-face, in a more or less organized way. The participants in an interview assume complementary roles, usually with the interviewer initiating and sustaining the talk that occurs. The interview has a purpose, usually understood by all parties. And the purpose usually is to learn something useful in making a decision or planning a course of action. Occasionally, the interview is a step in the further communication of ideas to audiences that would not have had access to them otherwise. The qualifications are a necessary part of our description because no two interviews are alike. At times, for example, the interview has no immediately discernible plan; at times it has clearly conflicting plans or purposes. Our description is also simple—deceptively so. There's nothing simple about most interviews, because communication is rarely simple. See Box 1.2 for characteristics of an interview.

As communication theorists and researchers will attest, the term *communication,* which seems so straightforward at first glance, is remarkably complex and dense. Although **communication** usually refers generally to the development of shared meaning between persons in a relationship, that shared meaning can never be completely or exactly understood the same way by all participants. Although much of the meaning is shared symbolically through language (verbal messages), significant aspects of human life also are influenced directly by the nonverbal messages we interpret in each other's behavior and in the contexts for our talk.

Communication between people can be as unadorned as a good-bye wave or a casual greeting, such as "Good morning. How are you?" Beyond the basics, communication becomes more convoluted. Even routine communication can go awry, with unanticipated consequences. A shrug can be misinterpreted as a sign of disrespect; an offhand joke can cost someone a job. Interviews, too, have a hierarchy of significance. Some are brief, matter-of-fact, no-risk encounters, such as a survey researcher asking shoppers to rate detergents. Others can be serious business, with implications and consequences that sometimes extend beyond the immediate participants.

As a form of human communication, the interview consists of three fundamental processes: listening, speaking, and framing. That's simple enough, too, but only if we believe listening, speaking, and framing will come naturally to anyone with ears, a mouth, and a brain. Don't underestimate what is involved, especially if the goal of communication, in interviews and other forms of talk, is to understand and be understood. *Listening* involves the essentially internal, but still active, means of focusing on the messages of interviewing. *Speaking* involves the active questioning and responding that constitutes the "out loud" experience of interviewing. *Framing* indicates a different kind of activity—the complex inner process of interpreting and evaluating messages in context. Although we'll discuss them in sequence, try to imagine their overlaps. Listening and speaking are not separate processes, but interwoven at every level; listening and framing are both interpretive processes that create meanings; speaking is possible because of humans' abilities to frame meanings. The more each participant knows about complexities and subtleties of communication, the more likely the interview will serve as a path toward learning—one that ultimately guides participants in their actions and attitudes.

At a minimum, competent communicators should be aware of the potential contributions of effective listening and its attendant nonverbal messages, the power of the spoken word, and the differences in styles of attaching importance to messages. Subsequent chapters will address communication issues and problems in more detail, but here we'll present nontechnical introductions for the three basic components of interviews: listening, speaking, and framing.

Listening

We start with listening as the first of our three processes because of a simple fact. Talk tends to occur only when speakers presume that the potential for attentive listening is already present. The interesting implications of this for interview partners will be examined later, but for now, let's look at a few defining characteristics of effective listening.

Merely hearing something is not the same thing as listening, although it is perhaps too easy to equate the two. **Hearing** is a physiological or biological process by which sounds are perceived by the human ear and auditory apparatus. Listening, on the other hand, is much more important for communicators to understand. A more thorough definition will be presented in Chapter 3, but for now, consider **listening** as the holistic process of attending to, comprehending, and interpreting oral messages. It is holistic because people listen with their eyes, body, minds, and hearts in addition to their ears. Listening involves effort, commitment, and concentration.

The ability to listen is tested at times by occupational, personal, and psychological distractions. Ringing phones, a nagging headache, problems at home, or personal biases, for example, can impede listening. Everyone must occasionally work in conditions where he or she has little control, but whenever possible, participants in an interview should position themselves physically and attitudinally to listen at their best. A willingness to listen, and the skill to do it well, is under your control even in the most trying circumstances.

Listening is important as a means of enhancing the relationship between interview partners. An attentive, responsive interviewer says nonverbally, "I'm with you," if not verbally, "I hear you." Listening becomes a message in itself, confirming the identities of the speakers and the importance of the occasion. It can inspire more revealing, more complete discussion because people tend to speak more earnestly and more often to others who listen carefully. Those who mishear us or are easily distracted receive less of our attention.

Listening is important, too, for creating an accurate record of the interview. Listening, then, requires questions and probes to double-check what we hear—or what we think we hear—such as saying, "Could I rephrase what you just said to be sure I've got it right?" Interviewers, in particular, must guard against becoming so absorbed with recording the results of an interview that they listen narrowly, only to words, and not for the meanings that are often found in nuances or unspoken messages. Skillful interviewees will probe to ensure they are in fact addressing the issues the interviewer raises. Careful listening also helps interviewees, such as medical patients, to keep their own record of the interview.

Finally, listening is not only receptive; it is also interpretive. What people say, even when expressed in simple terms, can be far more complicated than it first sounds. Interviews require discriminating, evaluative listening that can detect inconsistencies, improbabilities, evasiveness, doubts, ambiguity, half-truths, metaphors, and other subtleties of speech, verbal and nonverbal, between two people. Listening interpretively enables the interview to reach its fullest potential.

Speaking

Interview participants frequently give little thought to exactly what they'll say, letting the talk that transpires take its natural course. Indeed, some interviews built and sustained by spontaneous speech can work quite well. On the other hand, a totally free-form interview can be an exasperating experience of conversational mishaps and dead ends, which, when it's over, leaves little evidence of accomplishment. A carefully scripted interview might work well, too. But an interview that marches in lockstep with someone's predetermined conclusion is likely to be exasperating for its rigidity and lack of accomplishment. Somewhere between those extremes is the middle ground that balances preparation with spontaneity.

The choice of words used in an interview isn't inconsequential by any means. Questions, responses, and other verbal components of an interview can potentially energize talk or stifle it; inspire eloquence or prompt monosyllabic grunts; build trust or raise suspicions. Both participants in an interview should be aware of the power of language to advance or damage communication. Although most people take language for granted, we'll challenge you to do the opposite in many sections of this book. We ask you to sensitize yourself to what your language might be saying in addition to what you *mean* it to say.

Preparing for the interview involves a combination of information gathering and reflection. Knowing what to say depends on a multitude of considerations, such as the context of the interview, the personalities of the people involved, and the subjects to be broached. Before each interview, participants should commit themselves to assessing the situation and to seeking background information and insights necessary to facilitate understanding.

Ideally, most speakers would like their speech to be clear, eloquent, and provocative so that what they say generates further speech. Communicators like conversations to flow smoothly, without a hitch. Failing to meet that goal at times doesn't mean the interview won't be successful. Mumbling and stumbling occur fairly often in effective conversations and interviews just because we're human. However, skilled interview participants become reasonably mindful of their speaking as it is shaped by the conversation; without obsessing about it, they can monitor and regulate their speech to accomplish flexible objectives. Questions, answers, observations, and disclosures can be naturally related to each other. In other words, participants can be guided by speech in addition to using it. For that step to occur, the next component of the interview plays a central role—the ability to frame information well.

Framing

Speaking and listening are inextricably linked to our ability to **frame**, that is, to interpret what we think is really going on in social situations. Sociologist Erving Goffman (1974) established one type of frame analysis to illuminate how communicators themselves define their experiences with others. One way to think of framing is that it is like a picture frame—something that defines the boundaries of something else and creates its context. (That photo of Mom, you might think, would look better in a wood frame or a gold one, rather than silver. The frame tells a perceiver in a sense how to "take" or interpret the picture.) But you might also want to think of a frame as a pattern made of parts fitted together for mutual support, as in the wood frame that supports a house as it is being constructed or a car's frame that gives it strength and stability. (Carpenters know that a subpar frame causes huge construction dilemmas later.) Finally, in another connotation, think of concocting a story to frame someone else for a crime—that's a kind of patterned deception designed to be interpreted in a certain way. ("He framed me" means he created a coherent story that falsely implicates me in something.) Some sort of supportive pattern is fundamental to all these definitions. All the meanings depend on something being interpreted within a context governed to some extent by a frame. It's a useful concept for interpersonal communication researchers, too.

For example, what one person intends as a friendly series of questions showing sincere curiosity will perhaps be framed by a respondent as a personal attack or cross-examination. Examples of what Paul Watzlawick, Janet Beavin, and Don Jackson (1967) termed "punctuation" problems abound in interviewing. **Punctuation** is the mental act of taking a complex series of events and attributing causes and effects, starts and stops, to it, much like punctuation marks in writing (periods, question marks, commas, and so forth) tell a reader how to identify a coherent unit of language. The problem is that different people punctuate differently, and this can become a framing dilemma. Therefore, when a politician answers a reporter's question curtly, it may be because he perceives the question as an extension of last month's contentious give-and-take in a press conference. The reporter, on the other hand, punctuates differently by seeing this interview as a new event, thinking, "This is my first question and I'm being nice. Why is he so mad already? That's not fair." The tone of the interchange sours from there, becoming more strained, while neither interviewer nor interviewee considers that there may be different frames for the "same" sequences of interaction. Yet they both think they know what's going on.

Anthropologist Michael Agar (1994) also discusses framing as a basic human style of handling similarities and differences: "A frame, as the name suggests, sets a boundary around the details and highlights how those details are related to each other" (p. 130). But Agar goes on to say that frames are holistic (they disclose interrelationships and patterns); comparative (they tell us how to move knowledge and insight from old situations to new, from known to unknown); and based on fieldwork (they're understood and changed through direct experience in the "field" of everyday communication). This is a good, brief model of everyday learning: (1) be alert for patterns, (2) compare situations in which you find those patterns, (3) try out what you think you know to see if it works.

Something similar undoubtedly happened when experts programmed Deep Blue, the IBM computer that grabbed headlines in the spring of 1997 for beating the human chess champion, Gary Kasparov. Deep Blue had to acquire certain frames for interpreting Kasparov's moves; although chess proceeds one move at a time, success depends upon seeing the moves not singly but as components of larger intricate patterns of strategies. Chess has many terms (gambits, ploys, sacrifices, for example) that refer to these complex sequences of moves and the intentions that motivate them. Despite recognizing all relevant rules of the game, no computer could beat Kasparov until it could be programmed (until it could "learn") to interpret the champion's moves in the context of his larger tactics and strategies. In other words, the computer had to refer to frames for Kasparov's openings, his endgames, his patterns of making sacrifices, and so on, in addition to developing creative and untransparent frames for its own best moves. Deep Blue may lose a rook; is this a real loss or a net gain (of position, perhaps)? Only a frame for the concept of what a sacrifice is or can do could answer that question. Not rule knowledge but pattern knowledge was paramount.

To understand framing's effect in human communication is to understand how persons engaged in the same activity (objectively speaking) can believe they are doing very different things. The interview ultimately allows us to confirm what we know and identify what we don't know; to separate, as best we can, truth from untruths and facts from myths; to confront the ambiguity of conflicting frames; and to obtain clarification, elaboration, or amplification (see Box 1.3).

Sometimes communication can be seen as a series of alternating steps: The interviewer asks a question; the interviewee listens and, presumably, mulls over what's been heard, then answers. The interviewer now listens, thinks about the answer, and responds, usually with another question. The steps and countersteps continue until the interview ends.

There is another way of seeing an interview—the *transactional* model. Much is happening all at once in an interview; it's one of life's activities that cannot be easily understood or appreciated without seeing it as a pattern of complementary, mutually supportive activities. This is what a **transaction** is to philosophers (Dewey & Bentley, 1949)—a behavioral relationship in which each participant simultaneously and mutually defines itself and its counterparts. All persons in a human system, for example, are influenced and defined by all other persons who are components of that same system. Each has an identity that depends not only on its unique characteristics but also on how others in the system react. We speak so that others might listen. We listen so that others might speak. Each activity depends on and is affected by the other. If we say that speaking and listening are defined transactionally, that means that what we call speaking cannot be defined except by reference to the process of listening and vice versa. A leader cannot be defined except by referring to followers.

BOX 1.3   REMINDERS

Connotations of the Framing Metaphor

- The picture frame (reminds us that framing is a way of establishing the limits, definitions, or boundaries of an idea)

- The frame for structural support (reminds us that a good frame—such as in a house or a car—bolsters and strengthens interpretations)

- The frame-up in which someone is implicated in another person's story (reminds us that frames are narratives and that persons are all interwoven in each other's "stories")

Framing enters the equation because of the need to organize the experience of what is said and heard. Framing also influences the quality of speaking and listening by fine-tuning, with mutual feedback, the communication taking place. The transactional model is a way of picturing the interview; it is also a way of conducting it. A transactional view of interviewing acknowledges the blizzard of messages being sent in an interview. Once we understand that the interview is not a merely mechanical process of alternating packages of questions and answers, the ideal of an interview as a learning and understanding experience seems more attainable.

Qualities of Interviewing

Every interview has an emotional climate, and its participants will be changed by its conversational weather. Perhaps too often it's an inhospitable climate, marked by tension, suspicion, anxiety, and other draining, counterproductive qualities. A supportive climate enhances the ability to communicate, reducing or eliminating concerns that characterize many encounters between strangers. The common qualities of emotionally satisfying interviewing—whatever the context—are empathy, honesty, respect, and validation.

Empathy

In the behavioral sciences, **empathy** means the attempt to sense someone else's world accurately, as she or he senses it, without leaving your own. In part, it's the ability to detect and appreciate another person's feelings, emotions, and concerns. Empathy is not sympathy, which involves two people in agreement or harmony in feelings or beliefs. It's not a full identification with the other, in which someone loses a separate sense of self. Empathy doesn't necessarily signal approval or disapproval, either. But it does say, "I understand" or, at least, "I'm trying to see things your way." It's a quality ideally needed by both participants in an interview: "I'm trying to understand your position. You're trying to understand mine. Let's hope we can reach a point where what comes out of this interview is basically 'ours.'"

Honesty

Nothing reassures like candor. Conversely, in the interview setting, nothing undermines a relationship more quickly than the perception of dishonesty. In some settings, withholding information or adopting a role is warranted and perhaps expected. A doctor, for example, interviewing a patient with symptoms of a potentially serious illness, might hide some of her suspicions until tests confirm a tentative diagnosis. In negotiating a real estate sale, both sides might hedge as they measure their relative interests in buying and selling the property. But with a few exceptions, honesty is, indeed, the best policy. Various shades of dishonesty—hidden agendas, deception, half-truths—might go undetected and even produce results in the short run. In more cases than not, however, people can sense when someone is not forthright or honest. Even when full disclosure by interview partners is unrealistic—due, for example, to prior commitments, ethical constraints, or time limits—an attitude of honesty should guide interviewer and interviewee. Here is one test that might help interview participants: All parties, whatever their goals, should enact a *presumption toward candor* wherever possible. In other words, occasional compromises of total honesty or full disclosure should not undermine the fundamental expectation that communicators will be direct and honest; exceptions to candid communication should be clearly justifiable as exceptions, not as reasons to be dishonest as a matter of course. (We will discuss this further in a later chapter as one of the common "conversational maxims" that guide interpersonal talk.) The fullest appropriate disclosure, by both parties, allows the interview to move into substantive talk and past a suspicion-laden contest of thrust and parry. Empathy can encourage and support honesty in interviews. And an honest, empathic approach helps demonstrate respect.

Respect

Respect in an interview goes beyond pleasantries, beyond politeness and cordiality. It means authentic concern for differences in status, gender, age, race, ethnicity. It means honoring essential human qualities, such as dignity, self-esteem, courage, humor, determination. Without respect, we are likely to see what we expect to see. A job interviewer, for example, meets an applicant who is young, shy, socially awkward, and nervous. With an attitude of respect, the interviewer discovers a fresh side of the young person—one of previously suppressed maturity. Interviews are occasions for both respectful listening and speaking. In many instances, the interviewer holds the power cards, such as when to stop, what to discuss, when to point the conversation in new directions. Cutting an interview short, showing impatience for someone's halting speech, and glancing at the clock are easily experienced as signs of disrespect. Respect in an interview means making an appropriate investment of time and effort. Everyone has a life that needs attending to; interview partners present opportunities to learn and make a difference. Far from being impositions on your life, these are occasions of potential significance for you personally, if respect for each other prevails.

Validation

Empathy, honesty, and respect blend in an interview, helping set the stage for validation. **Validation** essentially means acknowledging that there has been a sincere, cooperative exchange of views. Perhaps the outcome remains unsatisfactory—you didn't get the job or promotion, for example. But the interviewer acknowledges your position; you've been given a fair, full opportunity to be heard. Validation cuts both ways. Interviewers appreciate validation, too. Validation, in its fullest sense, means the interview reached a plateau of understanding. An interview, even one conducted as a partnership, still has elements of yours, mine, and ours. Participants cannot will or guarantee the outcome they desire. Without validation, however, the interview probably will feel incomplete and unsatisfactory for all concerned. Validation is a somewhat more general term for what we call confirmation in Chapter 3.

In the chapters that follow, the qualities of empathy, honesty, respect, and validation will resurface in similar ways in particular interviewing contexts (see Box 1.4). Keep in mind that such supportive attitudes always complement the skills employed in interviews. If you focus only on practicing behavioral skills, you'll overlook crucial ways that attitude changes can also improve interviews.

Traditional Types of Interviews

Identifying interview categories helps explain how one interview differs from another. The categories, while not entirely arbitrary, vary, depending on how broadly *interview* is defined. Parents and children practice interviewing, especially when talking through problems. A popular guide from a few years ago, *Parent Effectiveness Training* (Gordon, 1975), stresses active listening through nonjudgmental inquiries—conversational family interviews in a sense—about a child's anger, poor grades, or withdrawal, for example. Police and social workers regularly use interviews as investigative tools. Despite these examples, we don't label a category "family" interviews and another "investigative." Interview objectives and participants differ, of course, but all interviews overlap considerably. Our category "helping interviews" relates to parenting, among other situations where helping is the primary objective. The "journalistic" and "research" categories cover investigative methods, including those applicable to police work.

The categories also overlap because interviews sometimes have multiple purposes. A selection interview generally covers hiring decisions, but certainly there is also an element of persuasion, as a company hopes to recruit a top prospect and an applicant may hope to impress the personnel manager. The six categories listed and summarized here suggest nearly every possible type of interview. Each category will be addressed in detail in subsequent chapters.

Selection Interviews

Our first category of interviews, the selection interview, typically involves hiring decisions. Personnel experts or managers in corporations rely upon job interviews for screening and selecting employees, from office clerks to CEOs. Most job interviews involve a "yea" or "nay" choice. The interviewer holds power that can be abused in a variety of ways, especially when the interviewee is vulnerable. Most employment-selection interviews are conducted face-to-face, usually on the interviewer's turf. Other types of selection interviews include screening for membership in groups, determining who among a group of bidders gets a contract, and deciding among plans or courses of action by asking their advocates to present and defend them. Each of these selection settings involves weighing pros and cons, sometimes between individuals vying for a job and sometimes between organizations competing for business.

Organizational Interviews

Selection interviews occur most often within organizations, but other interview forms also support and advance organizations' goals and needs. Today's organizational environment demands greater emphasis on teamwork and decentralized decision making. Instead of bosses dictating from on high, employees increasingly have a say in plotting the course and implementing strategies and procedures. Interviews help uncover problems and find solutions. They also are used to generate ideas and cost-saving innovations. On another level, appraisal interviews assess the performance of individuals or groups within the organization, while other interviews might occur at a point of crisis or intervention in order to discipline, correct, or even fire an employee. The methods used might range from a narrative evaluation of an employee's work record and goals or a discussion with a quality-control focus group that represents a larger contingent of employees.

Journalistic Interviews

The most prominent professional informational interview is the news interview. Its assumptions, appreciations, and skills are broadly applicable to the interviewing process, whether or not you will ever become a reporter. In addition, understanding the dynamics of the journalistic interview gives citizens an entirely new perspective on how the public sphere works and how it might work better.

The news interview is the basic vehicle of journalists. Interviews enable so many journalists to gather information, verify facts, elicit quotes, clarify conflicting accounts, and reconstruct events that it's hard to imagine journalism without interviews. The news generated by interviews is shared with an audience that might number in the millions. Because we rely on journalists for our perspectives on the world, news accuracy is crucial. Rumors, reckless accusations, and erroneous information conveyed by journalists can do tremendous damage. News interviews require careful listening and confirmation of information. The quality and depth of the news depends largely on the joint conversational efforts of reporters and the people they sometimes call their "sources."

Research Interviews

Research interviews generally focus on collecting data or information that is essential for a larger task of learning about, or deciding about, something. Such research takes many forms. Social scientists gather both quantitative and qualitative data in their work, such as geographers studying population shifts and sociologists investigating perceptions of crime in an inner city. Marketing firms working for corporations use surveys and focus group interviews to determine consumer preferences and needs. Political consultants interview citizens to measure voter attitudes and the salience of social issues; this research helps candidates and parties settle on policies and campaign strategies. Research interviews are usually more important to interviewers than to interviewees, although there are clear exceptions. For example, interviewers doing oral history research may help a group become more familiar with its own cultural narratives; thus the "researched" may be enriched immeasurably by the shared research experience. The researcher's work depends on the cooperation of other participants, who might need to be convinced that they will profit as well.

Helping Interviews

Doctors, teachers, counselors, therapists, and ministers, among others, structure helping interviews that typically involve such tasks as diagnosis, therapy, and problem solving. Candor is important in all interviews, as we suggested earlier, but it becomes especially crucial when helping is the objective. In helping interviews, talk may center on personal feelings and issues that are painful or embarrassing to disclose. The path toward helping may require a series of interviews, each progressing from building rapport to defining the problem, exploring answers, and diagnosing possible solutions. Clearly, issues of trust, relationship duration, credibility, and openness are more important in helping situations than in most other forms of interviewing.

Persuasive Interviews

What has traditionally been termed the persuasive interview involves tasks like closing a business deal, such as a product sale or a contractual agreement. Monetary considerations are at the center of many persuasive interviews, and while money isn't everything, it

BOX 1.5   **R E M I N D E R S**

Major Types of Interviews

- *Selection* (to develop information/insight necessary for making a decision, usually about matching a person or group to a position or task)

- *Organizational* (to develop information/insight necessary for coordinating or appraising people and policies within companies and other complex organizations)

- *Journalistic* (to develop information/insight necessary for providing news to public audiences)

- *Research* (to develop information/inight necessary for developing better theories and practices of human behavior)

- *Helping* (to develop information/insight necessary for assisting people in meeting their own psychological and health goals)

- *Persuasive* (to develop information/insight within situations of direct interpersonal influence)

certainly is weighed heavily as people move toward a decision about signing on the dotted line. Another form of persuasive interviewing entails bargaining or negotiating sessions in which issues of basic fairness, convenience, safe working conditions, and other factors may be just as central as financial gain.

The persuasive dimension of interviews also arises outside business settings. Candidates for political office, for example, appear before the editorial staffs of newspapers or the officers of a workers' union seeking endorsements; and therapists engaged in helping clients often use persuasive techniques to overcome resistance to treatment.

For a summary of major types of interviews, see Box 1.5.

Getting Started on a Basic Informational Interview

As you build your skills and knowledge, you will develop ideas for conducting interviews in various professional and personal contexts. You'll be able to adapt what you know to getting and keeping a job, conducting organizational interviews, reporting the news, researching social issues, helping others diagnose problems, persuading others responsibly, and completing other specialized tasks. Most people will not be expected to participate in all these interview forms in each job, but then most people will not know while taking college classes exactly what shape their careers will take. In addition, each professional context, if studied and practiced, will enhance almost any career. This book will build on the foundation of skills and appreciations you're now beginning to construct.

What about perhaps the most straightforward and broadly practical interviewing task—your need to learn something specific that another person knows well? In a sense, almost all specialized interviewing tasks are variations on this theme. Sometimes called the information-gathering interview, this is the prototypical form for most interviewers and interviewees. It most closely resembles the journalist's task, although the metaphor of gathering is somewhat misleading; skillful journalistic interviewers know that information (or news) is never simply lying around ready to be gathered. Information worth its salt is rarely prepackaged and ready for consumption.

Often the people who are most able to inform you aren't even fully aware of what they know, such as the laboratory scientist who has a voluminous knowledge of a new drug but has given scant thought to the social or political changes its legalization might bring. You engage information experts, talk with them, let them know why you're curious, convince them you will listen carefully. Then—if you're skilled or lucky—you begin to find they will open up to you. They'll even surprise themselves with what they are able to articulate. This is the true excitement of interviewing: coming up with what neither person expected. The scientist who knows about the chemical nature of a drug that counteracts male impotence, or one who fully understands the science of cloning, discovers she or he has an estimate of the social consequences of such innovations.

Before moving further into the finer points of interviewing, which will include a study of how interviews can be analyzed as communication, let's forget about jargon and red tape and reduce **informational interviewing**, defined as one person's (or group's) desire to learn something specific from another person or group, to its basic elements: the stimulus, the participants, the relationship, the content, the process, and the outcome.

- The *stimulus* (why does an interview happen?): In informational interviewing, someone has an informational itch that needs to be scratched. There is a knowledge gap, a crisis, or a problem someone wants solved.

- The *participants* (who participates in an interview?): The interviewer wants to obtain information or insight not already possessed. He or she identifies someone ideally knowledgeable or qualified enough to provide guidance—a responding interviewee.

- The *relationship* (how are participants connected?): Interviewers who need information or insight usually must rely on the goodwill and responsiveness of respondents. Informational interviews are usually requested by interviewers and arranged at the convenience of interviewees if at all possible. In a different sense, interviewers are those people who help interviewees talk about things they might not have articulated before. Each party performs a service for the other.

- The *content* (what do participants say and do?): As guided conversations, interviews generally are propelled by questions and answers. However, don't assume that all the questions must be the interviewer's nor all the answers necessarily the interviewee's. Each will probably ask, answer, and need to clarify at various times.

- The *process* (how do speech and action develop in interviews?): Generally, the primary responsibility for "maintenance" in interview situations lies with the interviewer, and the question—or, in some cases, an inquiry implied by a comment or observation—is the prime way to move things forward. Interviewing is a conversation that is managed and pointed in certain directions, to make certain outcomes more likely than others. Interviews that aren't limited by external commitments (such as, "I have to leave by 5:30 to pick up my daughter") usually last as long as the parties perceive progress toward getting the interviewer's question(s) answered or problem(s) solved.

The informational interviewing process is often relatively <u>directive</u>. In other words, an interviewer may lead with a brief statement of task, then introduce a fairly general and open-ended question. He or she would quickly move to requests for specific details, phrased in <u>relatively closed ways</u>. Interviewers must signal clearly what is needed in order for respondents to reply efficiently. Then, each <u>topic change</u> thereafter could be noted with a general question. For example:

LUCAS (interviewer): In order to project a budget for student government this coming year, I need the final figures on the Spring Fling promotion. You and Monique handled that, right?

SERENA (interviewee): Well, yes and no. I did most of the planning, but then after I got sick Monique took it over. We both handled PR and ads, but she was much more responsible for the leg work.

LUCAS: I just need the final figures. Should I ask her, or do you have that information, too?

SERENA: I've got them right here, but they're just copied down in pencil in my notebook—I don't have the official report. Is that OK?

LUCAS: Right. No problem. All I need is ballpark estimates for the different parts of the Fling. How much for equipment rental?

SERENA: Looks like about $250. Much less than we'd thought, by the way.

LUCAS: How about ads—print and radio both?

SERENA: We did only print this year, but we did both the *College News* and the *Herald-Instigator* in town. Quite a chunk. Total came to just over $500.

LUCAS: Do you think the lack of radio ads hurt the attendance? Maybe we should go back to them next year.

SERENA: Not a problem, I'd say. Attendance was actually up. Monique and her group did a great job on banners and fliers.

LUCAS: They cost next to nothing, right?

Compare Lucas's systematic information-seeking approach with a second way he could have approached his task:

LUCAS: Hi, Serena. You were involved in the Spring Fling, right? What could you tell me about it?

SERENA: Yeah, I was. What do you want to know?

LUCAS: I've got to get some figures together. I wish someone else could get this together, but they asked me to do it.

SERENA: For what?

LUCAS: Why'd they ask me?

SERENA: No, silly. What are the figures for?

BOX 1.6   R E M I N D E R S

Basic Informational Interviewing Steps

- Describe needed information or purpose
- State general question for this interview
- Listen by probing with specific questions about details

- Probe subtopics and other issues by recapping second and third steps
- Check for accurate understanding

Six turns into their discussion, Serena still doesn't know exactly why they're talking together. She likes Lucas, perhaps, but is wondering, "What is he talking about? Are we just passing the time here, or does he need something more specific from me?"

The second example shows Lucas and Serena enjoying a conversation, but Lucas is not efficiently matching his need to know something with Serena's ability to share information. There's nothing wrong with this second conversation as conversation, but there will be times when its tendency to waste time will not be appreciated. A more focused interview style might be necessary. Note that in the first example, Lucas and Serena are also talking informally; being focused and systematic doesn't mean being stuffy or excessively formal. And you can be sure that in most professional contexts, efficient informational interviewing is a skill much appreciated by colleagues.

- The *outcome* (what is learned?): In many interviews, both interviewer and interviewee will learn something new; the interview process can be seen usefully from both perspectives. However, it's probably fair to say that most people think about interviews from the vantage point of the original inquirer, and they assume an effective interview is one that helps the interviewer learn what is necessary.

Therefore, in seeking basic information, think of your inquiry strategy as variations on just a few steps. Although these five steps look like a prescriptive procedure in a textbook, they develop quite naturally in friendly interview situations (see Box 1.6):

1. State what you need, based upon prior consideration of your task and the other's information.

2. Phrase a general question about the respondent's ability (or willingness) to provide information.

3. Listen to the response well enough to follow up with specific questions that clarify, extend, and test the information you are gaining.

4. Revisit steps 2 and 3 when probing subtopics or further issues.

5. Check to ensure you've understood the information accurately, showing your appreciation to the respondent who helped you.

Now reverse the roles; you're being interviewed. Imagine a situation in which you have information you suspect an interviewer needs, but you don't know quite how to provide or package it. From an interviewee's perspective, simply mirror the steps: (1) Make

- Pair up with a partner from your interviewing class, or let your teacher match you on the basis of *dissimilar* interests.

- Talk for five minutes, each of you disclosing some basic, not-too-personal facts about hobbies, politics, school activities, and family life.

- Decide on one specific aspect of your partner's life that you'd like to know more about ("You're a concert pianist? What kind of practice schedule do you have to keep?"; "I've heard a lot of students try to get into the physical therapy major, but I've never understood what jobs you might be aiming for. What are the most common career goals?"). Each of you should have time to play the interviewer role.

- Each should interview the other for five to ten minutes. When you are the interviewer, start by phrasing a general question that indicates your interest in that aspect (see examples above). Use the reply to that question to suggest other, perhaps more specific, directions. Be sure to *help your partner talk* by phrasing your curiosity as clearly as you can and by following up as specifically as possible on the details. (Your general question we will later call a primary question, and the follow-ups we'll later term probes; for now, though, don't worry about the distinctions.)

- Your teacher may ask you to use the information obtained in these mini-interviews as material to help you introduce your partner to the class. This is often a good way to let class members sense, early in the semester, what they have in common and what is unique about them.

sure you clarify what the interviewer needs and what he or she needs it for. This will suggest how you might phrase the information or, in some cases, whether you might even want to avoid discussing the matter. For example: "You want to discover who did what in the Tompkins incident?" (2) Clarify the general question the interviewer is asking you. For example: "You want to know whether I was primarily responsible for hiring Tompkins?" (3) Ask if your specific responses are providing the information the other person needs: "I recommended Tompkins, but you may know that two other people did, too. And The Big Guy was really pushing for her. So I was in on it, sure, but I wouldn't say I was responsible 'primarily.' Does that make sense?" (4) Continue to check on the other person's listening as the conversation progresses. You have at least as much concern for accurate and effective messages as the interviewer does. (5) Conclude the interview with a summary of what you think you've told your partner.

BEYOND THE BASICS

Ethical Implications and Dimensions

An emphasis on ethics is fast becoming an integral component of the image and behavior of complex organizations. Ethics is stressed through advertising, sensitivity training, in-house workshops, written rules and policies, ethical "audits," and lofty mission statements. Moreover, most professional organizations, such as the Society of Professional Journalists and the American Psychological Association, have formal codes of ethics, some with recommended sanctions for violations. But the ethics of interviewing is still too often found at the periphery of study, discussion, and practice, if it's considered at all.

Ethical Orientations

Understanding ethics in an interviewing context begins with understanding ethical orientations. We can start by examining two major types—teleology and deontology—although other orientations are also possible and will be discussed later. **Teleology** comes from the Greek *telos,* meaning "end" or "goal." It looks at ethical behavior from the perspective of outcomes or consequences. Teleology is often referred to as *consequentialist* ethics. An example of consequentialist ethics is **utilitarianism,** which itself takes several forms. One of those forms promotes a noble ethical objective: Do what is most likely to produce the greatest good for the greatest number. Another consequentialist approach puts individual interests first: ethical **egoism.** An egoism-based ethics, while consequentialist in orientation, would result in doing what is most likely to produce the greatest good for the deciding individual, not for the greatest number.

Applied to an interview, a utilitarian approach taken by one participant and egoism by another *could* result in an acceptable outcome for both—but probably won't. The manager of a security firm, for example (putting the overall good of the company first), decides it's too risky to hire an ex-convict, so he simply goes through the motions of an interview, never revealing or discussing his knowledge of the applicant's police record. The job applicant, guided by egoism, withholds his criminal past, figuring he'll never get hired and have a shot at straightening out his life if he comes clean. In a narrow sense, both are being ethical according to their separate codes, based on a weighing of possible consequences. Is a middle ground possible? Perhaps, but unless the two are able and willing to explore the issue that keeps them locked on individual objectives, it's unlikely they will find it. As we've said before, the idea of partnership ought to guide interviews, but that is usually not the case. If there is an ethical orientation to an interview, it's usually based on individual objectives and outcomes: *My* ethical view dictates, not what is best *overall* in the interview. Of course, as this hypothetical instance demonstrates, one or both participants may be reluctant to address an issue openly that could be resolved satisfactorily for all concerned.

Deontology, the second major ethical orientation, comes from the Greek *deon,* meaning "duty." Deontology stresses strict adherence to rules or duties, often regardless of the consequences. A strict deontologist probably would argue that anticipated consequences should have no bearing in determining what is ethically right or wrong. For example, if we have an obligation to tell the truth, there would be no justification for lying, even if people might be spared harm as a consequence. Attempting to practice an unbending form of deontology can tie you in ethical knots. But generally, ethical behavior based on moderate forms of deontology will not completely reject the relevance of anticipated consequences; rather, it simply places greater emphasis on the consistency of duties and principles. Sometimes, though, general duties, such as the doctor's dictum "do no harm" and other guidelines such as "tell the truth" will clash. Journalists often find that publishing truthful stories can hurt people. Balancing duties might be necessary, based on possible consequences. That teleological-deontological balancing might result in telling the truth in ways that minimize the harm done.

Whether schooled in philosophical frameworks of ethics or operating from an intuitive sense of right and wrong, ethical interviewers typically consider both duty and consequence as they decide how to behave. As our ethical behavior moves into particular situations or professions, we're influenced by the circumstances or norms that apply. In ethics, as in life, there is no single, certain, absolute path to follow. Often we face ethical dilemmas that must be addressed one way or another. Being ethical requires deliberation and discussion, which enable us to justify the path we *do* follow.

Deliberation, Discussion, Decision Making

Ethical considerations should start at the beginning of the process, which seems to state the obvious. But what is the beginning? Sometimes, ethical deliberation and discussion are *ex post facto*—coming after the deed is done. The fallout of the decision sends the decision makers into an ethical huddle, as they ask, "Where did we go wrong?" Trying to figure out what is ethical at that stage is not pointless, but it's certainly too late for the victims. An understanding of what it means to be ethical in a given situation must come before the first step is taken. Interview participants would do well to develop an ethical SOP—standard (or standing) operating procedure—to provide a touchstone of acceptable behavior in the ever-changing contexts of work or relationships. This touchstone could be a personal guide; it could be based on professional or organizational norms; it could be a combination of both. Ethics isn't mathematics, with set formulas and axioms to follow, so we must be prepared for the unexpected. Interviews differ for many reasons but largely because they are human enterprises, subject to the vagaries of being human.

Ideally, each person in an interview will act ethically. Realistically, however, setting the ethical tone is a responsibility that usually falls, first and foremost, to the interviewer. That responsibility begins with an ethical grounding and a commitment to abide by it. From there, the ethical person works from an implicit checklist of sorts, asking at each stage, "Have I been ethical?" Here is a sample:

- What is the purpose of the interview? Is there a shared understanding of the purpose? If not, is there a justifiable reason to withhold or disguise the real purpose of the interview? Full disclosure should be the rule, with rare exceptions.

- What preparation has been done? Have I done enough reading, study, and deliberation to conduct a fruitful interview? Has the interviewee been given comparable opportunity to prepare?

- Who will be interviewed? Can the *selection* of the interviewees be justified as fair and appropriate? Are any of the interviewees emotionally vulnerable or in need of special care or consideration?

BOX 1.7   R E M I N D E R S

The Ethical Ground of Interviewing—A Checklist

- Is there a shared understanding of the interview's purpose?
- Has preparation been appropriately thorough?
- Have interviewees been selected and treated with fairness and respect?
- Are there safeguards against exploitive use of the interview information?

- Does the listening of each person create an open space for dialogue and choice making?
- Has the interview created harmful conditions for others?

- What will be the substance and impact of the questions asked? Are the questions well intentioned? Honest? Will they upset, disturb, or cause harm in any way? Is the information sought essential to the purpose of the interview? How will the information acquired be used? Is there any reason to believe that the information might be misused? What safeguards might be necessary?

- Am I listening well? What distractions or listening difficulties might arise? Have I tried to create a listening environment conducive to open communication? Have I listened with the interviewee's interests in mind in addition to my own?

- What is the outcome? Has the interviewee been given ample time and opportunity to be heard and understood? Could others be harmed by interview outcomes? Is my behavior at every stage ethical and justifiable if subjected to public scrutiny? Have I been true to the duties binding my conduct, and have I weighed the consequences for all who might have a stake in the outcome? What has been accomplished in this interview? Has mutual learning and understanding occurred? If roles were reversed, would I feel I'd been treated fairly, honestly, and respectfully?

The context for each interview will vary, so don't consider this a one-size-fits-all checklist (see Box 1.7). To act ethically, each person must accept individual responsibility and accountability for her or his behavior and decisions. Blindly following someone else's path rarely leads to truly ethical behavior. That said, finding our ethical bearings isn't something we do alone. Discussion with coworkers, friends, family, and mentors helps us uncover flaws in our thinking, find alternatives, fine-tune our duties, and identify the consequences. The ultimate ethical act is a commitment to ethical decision making itself, even if that means saying no when under pressure or orders to bend those beliefs. People have quit jobs rather than act unethically. Such a sacrifice may not be necessary; ethical people often prevail by the strength of their convictions. An experienced organizational consultant once said that the most radically powerful member of an organization is usually the person who is both effective and nonmanipulative.

Some ethical concerns include a legal dimension. Federal and state statutes, for example, legally restrict inquiries in interviews about sexual orientation, age, race, and personal matters. There is an ethical foundation to the law, but law and ethics are not the

23

same thing. Law generally sets a minimal standard—a bottom-line guide to behavior. Privacy laws limit disclosures of confidential academic records of individual students; a teacher's personal ethical code regarding a student's rights to confidentiality may encompass far more than the law protects.

Public Dialogue

Studying interviewing brings rewards that extend far beyond participating in interviews. It emphasizes a research sensibility, an openness to listening, a respect for diverse voices, an ability to be introspective, and a willingness to be thorough. These are characteristics that some critics increasingly believe we're losing in our society's entire structure of public discourse. Have we lost track of civil ways to talk with each other? Does a preoccupation with advocacy and a habit for dismissing arguments of others deplete our public life? In this book, you'll find essentially a dialogic model for interview communication, one that can be translated readily into larger spheres of family and public life. As you listen, question, and frame messages responsibly in one-on-one interviews, you're practicing the same basic skills that will help you manage relationships and meanings in other life contexts. Interviewing skills are directly applicable in many work, home, and public interactions.

Interviewing Skills in the Workplace

Look around an office, school, factory, or any place where people work together, and you'll find too many examples of communication glitches. These misunderstandings and misperceptions result in costly mistakes, morale problems, lost business, reduced productivity, or disruptive behavior. (Of course, even effective communication can create morale problems and lost business, but that is another story.) The list of negative consequences is long enough to underscore the point that poor communication creates mistrust, detachment, lack of purpose, and dissatisfaction. Those conditions are far less common in workplaces where people generally listen and talk things out. People aren't robots who leave their pride, convictions, ambitions, and feelings in the parking lot. Most of us want a voice in our fate; most of us want to be appreciated for our talents and efforts; most of us want to make a difference in what we do. The workplace challenges our communication ability, to be sure. It is here that people with different experiences, different expectations, and different needs come together. Recognition of these differences must be an integral part of communication programs on the job. But differences, remember, energize relationships and help us frame our lives effectively.

Increasingly, companies and institutions are encouraging communication, sometimes from the bottom up, through groups and teams that readily acknowledge differences. Such groups discuss, listen, and seek solutions, often improving organizations in tangible ways and building a sense of mutual ownership.

Interviewing Skills at Home

At some point in the recent history of American families, carryout meals eaten on the run replaced leisurely conversations around the dining-room table. On the other hand, the nostalgic, middle-class picture of father holding sway at the head of the table, with mother and the children speaking in turn, isn't ideal, either. In general, communication at home, as with communication elsewhere, wasn't very good then, and it may be worse now.

Many of us aren't comfortable communicating at home, which isn't surprising. Formal education doesn't often provide instruction and practice in communication skills. But in many homes, conflicts over finances, discipline, and relationships strain the family to the breaking point. If there has been a breakdown of the family, it's been partly a radical shift in communication. Relations tend to improve when parents and children set aside time and commit themselves to asking thoughtful and nonjudgmental questions, phrasing reasonable answers, understanding one another, and working toward solving problems. Of course, there is no shortage of pop culture gurus willing to tell us all exactly how to live. That is not the goal here. This book simply suggests that good interviewing skills can be applied at home to raise the quality of family life, too. Practicing interviewing is practicing for enhancing your quality of life.

Interviewing Skills in Public Life

With work and home life dominating the lives of most Americans, the responsibilities of citizenship probably seem low on personal priority lists. With fewer than 50 percent of the electorate voting in presidential elections, and even fewer in local elections, political observers are not surprised to find a corresponding decline in civic, face-to-face activities and associations, such as churches, parent-teacher organizations, and fraternal groups.

Ours is a republic, which means supreme power rests in the citizenry. Without an informed, involved public, the ideal and practice of republican government will die a slow death. What grows in its place may not be a totalitarian system, but it may well be one that is far less of, by, and for the people. Passive, inactive citizens surrender their authority and power by default. Special-interest groups and political operatives quickly fill the void.

Public life exists through our ability and willingness to communicate; public life suffers and withers when communication fails. Through civic talk at all levels of public life, people settle problems, set priorities, and establish policy. At least, that is the way it should work. Today, though, diatribes, sloganeering, harassment, threats, and, when all else fails, fire bombs often take the place of civic discourse.

The interview is a useful model for communication throughout society. It stresses ability at language, at listening, at analyzing. It is based on the principle of cooperation, even collaboration. It also is based on honest, respectful communication. It recognizes the complexity and layers of human communication. Its goal is mutual understanding.

We hope *Interviewing: Speaking, Listening, and Learning for Professional Life* proves of value well beyond its applications in interviewing situations. A broadly based education in interviewing will mean that, for example, more citizens may feel comfortable questioning

Unplanned, informal interviews happen frequently in the course of our lives, and we usually participate in those interviews as matter-of-fact occurrences. We help friends talk out personal problems; ask questions about issues affecting us; share feelings and thoughts with family members. But as you become more aware of the meaning and practice of interviewing, you'll see these occurrences as opportunities to apply what you've learned. At the end of each chapter are "Making Your Decision" boxes like this one. As a warm-up exercise, consider several fairly typical "interviews" from everyday life and determine how you'd address each one.

- **Helping a friend:** Over coffee, a friend asks you, "I'm having trouble at work. I can never seem to please my boss. Frankly, I'm worried about losing my job. What do you think I'm doing wrong?" You're not a trained counselor, but friends often play this role. What would you say? You could change the subject and reply, "Gee, I don't know what to say." But assume you want to help. How would you go about it? Would you mostly listen and clarify rather than inquire and advise? Would you ask questions, seeking information about your friend's behavior and attitudes at work? What types of questions? Would you go the next step and offer advice? Would you be frank, indirect, noncommittal? What about consequences of your talk? For you? For your friend? For your relationship?

- **Questioning the candidate:** A flyer stuck in your door handle announces a neighborhood forum with a candidate for city council. You decide to attend; it's a small gathering of fewer than a dozen people. The candidate introduces herself, states her plans in general terms, then asks for questions. Here's your opportunity to become informed as a voter—an opportunity for face-to-face dialogue. What would you want to learn? Why? Qualifications? Issues? Character? Family and personal life? What questions would elicit information that would help you assess whether the candidate warrants your vote? What would you do if you feel the candidate is being evasive? How persistent or aggressive should you be in your questions and reactions?

- **Making a sale:** It's time to sell your 1985 Toyota, a dependable car that is past its prime. A nervous young man answers your classified ad. He's looking for his first car, and he has a list of questions to ask you. To some extent, this is a moment of truth. You're not going to lie about the car's condition, because it does have some problems. But it's safe and runs. Do you volunteer information? Would you sidestep some questions? What might they be? Could you justify withholding information? Would you try to maneuver the conversation away from the negatives about the car? How far would you go in using your powers of persuasion to make a sale?

Try to imagine these episodes playing themselves out. Raise questions of your own and try answering them, as well. The objective is not to test whether you have the "right" answers, because there aren't any. The exercise is meant to reinforce the notion that interviews are both common and uncommon. They're common because so many of our communication encounters involve elements of interviewing. They're uncommon because the unique dynamics of a particular interview can be incredibly complicated. There is no prior knowledge that guarantees how an interview will turn out. But with knowledge and commitment, you will be able to say, "I've tried to make the most of this interview, acting wisely and responsibly."

mayoral candidates at public forums and assessing their performance; parents may be more likely to attend conferences with their children's teachers; officers in neighborhood organizations may be better prepared to research the preferences of other residents. Nearly everyone can benefit from being a better interviewer and interviewee.

Summary

This chapter has introduced many of the basic ideas and issues that will reappear throughout the book. We view interviews as conversations focused on information and, ideally, guided by a sense of mutual involvement. Although popular stereotypes often make the process sound like unpleasant competition, the best interviews are more likely to resemble partnerships.

Interviews can be analyzed by emphasizing their characteristics, qualities, and types. We have defined the three characteristic subprocesses of interviewing as listening, speaking, and framing. Effective interview partners find qualities such as empathy, honesty, respect, and validation extraordinarily practical in a variety of communication settings. In this book we'll focus on six interview settings: selection, organizational, journalistic, research, helping, and persuasive.

In "Beyond the Basics" we place the interviewing process in larger context by discussing ethical implications and the contributions of interviewing to dialogue at work, at home, and in civic life. Interviewers and interviewees can contribute significantly to democratic discourse, but only if they remain sensitive to questions of interpersonal ethics.

References

Agar, M. (1994). *Language shock: Understanding the culture of conversation.* New York: William Morrow.

Dewey, J., & Bentley, A. (1949). *Knowing and the known.* Boston: Beacon Press.

Goffman, E. (1974). *Frame analysis: An essay on the organization of experience.* Cambridge, MA: Harvard University Press.

Goodale, J. G. (1982). *The fine art of interviewing.* Englewood Cliffs, NJ: Prentice-Hall.

Gorden, R. (1969). *Interviewing: Strategy, techniques and tactics.* Homewood, IL: Dorsey Press.

Gordon, T. (1975). *P.E.T.: The tested new way to raise responsible children.* New York: New American Library.

Killenberg, G. M., & Anderson, R. (1989). *Before the story: Interviewing and communication skills for journalists.* New York: St. Martin's Press.

Kvale, S. (1996). *InterViews: An introduction to qualitative research interviewing.* Thousand Oaks, CA: Sage.

MacHovec, F. J. (1989). *Interview and interrogation.* Springfield, IL: Charles C. Thomas.

Medley, H. A. (1992). *Sweaty palms: The neglected art of being interviewed.* Berkeley, CA: Ten Speed Press.

Watzlawick, P., Beavin, J. H., & Jackson, D. D. (1967). *Pragmatics of human communication: A study of interactional patterns, pathologies, and paradoxes.* New York: Norton.

✿ 2 Before Skills

Appreciations and Habits of Dialogue

Dialogue is not merely a set of techniques for improving organizations, enhancing communications, building consensus, or solving problems. During the dialogue process, people learn how to think together—not just in the sense of analyzing a shared problem or creating new pieces of shared knowledge, but in the sense of occupying a collective sensibility, in which the thoughts, emotions, and resulting actions belong not to one individual, but to all of them together.

—BILL ISAACS,
The Fifth Discipline Fieldbook

LEARNING GOALS

After reading this chapter, you should be able to

- Describe the difference between a skills approach to interviewing and this book's skills-plus approach
- Discuss the characteristics of a dialogic appreciation of interviewing and be able to point to examples from everyday life
- Begin to analyze your personal interviewing style in terms of such skills-plus concepts as credibility, resource and structure factors, content and process knowledge, multiculturalism, communication reticence/apprehension, and empathic ways of being
- Build on your basic knowledge of interviewing to understand how the more theoretical notions of conversation—such as communication rules, the cooperative principle, and conversational maxims of quantity, quality, relevancy, and manner—can help interviewers and interviewees make better decisions

Cassaundra, a recent college graduate, encounters trouble landing the job that will get her started in public relations. Her solid if not sparkling work in classes, along with excellent experience doing volunteer service for several local nonprofit agencies, helped her construct an impressive resume and earned her several interviews with good companies. Yet no job offer has materialized, and she fears that if things don't turn around soon, she'll have to give up her apartment and ask Mom and Dad if she can return home to live until she gets full-time work. But now she's after a position she really wants, for the organization she has admired for years—a breakthrough job, she thinks. As she approaches the door of the interviewer's office, she thinks, "Everything rides on this interview."

Loren, a freelance writer, has tried for several years to break into the major magazine market with articles on important social issues. He's sold a few pieces to industry publications and smaller magazines, but although some of these supplemented the family income with extra spending money, none was likely to establish his reputation or open new doors for Loren. He has recently discovered that an attorney from his hometown, a woman he knew as an acquaintance in high school, was on the defense team for a high-profile celebrity who has been charged with murder in an eastern state. The trial has just ended, and while on a visit to East Baileyville to see family, the attorney agrees to talk with Loren about the case. He's driving to her parents' home thinking of his big opportunity and how, "Everything rides on this interview."

Kathryn, a community organizer, has become committed to getting a comprehensive youth program started in her city. For two years she's worked tirelessly to provide services to teenagers from troubled families in tense, sometimes violent, neighborhoods. Most of her work, and most of its benefit, has occurred behind the scenes. Yet several days ago, a news story broke that threatens the entire project: two youth counselors were arrested on charges of selling cocaine to minors. Public suspicion about her program is now mounting, and its very existence is threatened. Somehow she must explain—without defensiveness—that the two counselors, even if they are guilty, should not be allowed to taint an otherwise successful and needed program. "Everything," she says to herself as the newspaper's most cynical investigative reporter knocks on her door, "rides on this interview."

These sincere but ego-involved interview participants are all probably wrong on one count—rarely does "everything" hinge on a single interview. Yet they can be forgiven for their emotional involvement, because interviews so often seem like pivotal incidents in life. People feel nervous, and naturally so, because in interviews they know something important is likely to happen. Someone is on the spot; something is being listened to, or for, especially carefully. The interview, considered as a focused occasion for direct talk, can put interaction under the magnifying glass and occasionally expose its imperfections. The potential for miscommunication is high. The potential for embarrassment is high. The potential for manipulation is high. And the personal and professional stakes are typically just as significant, as interviews can lead to significant decisions. Who gets the job? Who gets the story? Whose impressive accomplishments might be dismissed unfairly because of a single misstatement in an interview?

It is easy to think of interviews as tests for individuals. In fact, it is easiest, perhaps, for most people to think of interviews as occasions either for personal crises or for personal crisis management; they often are. In this chapter, however, we want to remind you of the extent to which successful interviews are not merely the result of individual successes, and disappointing interviews, likewise, are not simply caused by individual failures. Rather, the quality of an interviewing experience is more fundamentally based on specific expectations and habits of dialogue that the participants enact in the interview.

A Skills-Plus Approach

Most of this book will concentrate in one form or another on describing the skills necessary for effective interviewing. **Skills,** often defined as the behavioral ability to adapt to the demands of different contexts, create much of the foundation for competent communication. Most interviewing classes in colleges or universities, or interviewing workshops and seminars in organizations, are conceived by their sponsors as skills courses. Participants learn new ways of acting and speaking, as they should. Yet, as Rebecca Rubin (1990) suggests, the competent communicator goes beyond mere skills to consider them in a wider context. She defines **communication competence** in these terms:

> . . . [It is] knowledge about appropriate and effective communication behaviors, development of a repertoire of skills that encompass both appropriate and effective means of communicating, and motivation to behave in ways that are viewed as both appropriate and effective by interactants. This definition implies that communication competence can be taught through enhancing this knowledge, these skills, and this motivation. (p. 96)

Rubin's definition stresses three components of competence—components that are not separate in any real sense when we are communicating. Translated into the context of this book, her definition suggests that interviewers and interviewees be knowledgeable, skillful, and motivated. *Knowledge* means concepts, vocabulary, ideas, facts, research findings—the issues communicators need to understand. With *skills* we put into practice the behavioral how-to choices of communicators. We can't hope to improve in any situation by relying only on techniques; we have to understand how technical skills work and have enough background to understand when to employ them. Skills depend upon knowledge and vice versa. The ability to behave differently will not be very valuable unless we know when to do so, but the fullest possible knowledge of situations will not increase our competence unless we have a wide repertoire of behavioral alternatives available. And neither knowledge nor skill will be sufficient for effective communication without the motivation to use them. *Motivations* are inner predispositions or choices that lead us in certain directions but not in others. They are influenced by what we value and what we expect from the interview.

As you concentrate on skill development in reading this book and in practicing listening, questioning, and framing behaviors, you will also be building a framework of knowledge that supports your efforts. This skill and knowledge, however, will not be worth much unless you want to improve and reinforce or develop the kinds of motivations that fuel successful interviews. Therefore, we advocate a **skills-plus approach** to interviewing, which emphasizes skills in the context of the values and motivations of the people who use them. In skills-plus interviewing the "plus" part must involve a consistent motivation toward dialogue and an appreciation of its power. In the remainder of this section, we will describe several attitudes of a dialogic interviewing perspective—attitudes that help communicators become motivated to achieve high-quality interviews (see Box 2.1 for an example of skills-plus thinking).

THE BASICS ⌘

BOX 2.1   INTERVIEWERS IN ACTION

Richard Farson

Richard Farson, psychologist and management consultant, wrote the recent best-seller *Management of the Absurd*. In it, he describes his interview research into how people function effectively as parents and as managers in organizations. Interestingly, he decided to study effectiveness from the standpoint of what children and employees remembered and were influenced by, rather than from the perspective of what parents and supervisors actually did. He asked children and employees what they remembered about significant moments in these relationships with their supposed leaders and role models. Perhaps surprisingly, he found that it was almost never techniques that mattered, but people's responsiveness to concrete and immediate situations. Farson concludes from his interviews and a variety of other social science evidence that mere techniques and skills are not central to effective communication; instead, the core requirement is the personal presence of a perceptive "other" who wants to keep the relationship going. Farson values communication deeply, even as he expresses equally deep suspicion of a skills- or technique-centered assumption about communication:

> "In both parenthood and management, it's not so much what we *do* as what we *are* that counts. . . . Each new human relations technique always promises to make the leader more effective. Managers who are taught to listen nonjudgmentally or to reward certain behaviors in others may initially feel that they have found the answer. At last, something that works! But the feeling seldom lasts. Over time, they usually discover that their newfound techniques are actually working to prevent closer human relationships—just the opposite of their intended effect. The most obvious reason is that any technique loses its power when it becomes evident that it is a technique. 'Don't listen to me that way.' 'Don't treat me as if you were my therapist.' 'I see what you're doing.' 'Are you rewarding me now?' "

Source: Farson, 1996, pp. 34–35

Appreciations of Dialogic Interviewing

Although people sometimes associate the word *dialogue* with warm, cuddly friendships among people who intimately know each other's emotional needs, that everyday sense is, at best, a limited, narrow slice of a large, complex subject. Far from presuming a full union or merging of souls, most uses of dialogue in contemporary philosophy and social science actually acknowledge the inadequacy of our knowledge about others. We attempt dialogue not because we already love others or already know who they are but because, most assuredly, we do not know what we are "getting into." Dialogue partners, however, are convinced that the sustained attempt at communication and connection is worth the effort.

What is dialogue? One way to answer the question is to twist it a half turn and ask—as Robert Grudin (1996) does in a recent book—what *happens* in dialogue? The key ingredients, he believes, are "reciprocity and strangeness":

> By reciprocity I mean a give-and-take between two or more minds or two or more aspects of the same mind. This give-and-take is open-ended and is not controlled or

limited by any single participant. By strangeness I mean the shock of new information—divergent opinion, unpredictable data, sudden emotion, etc.—on those to whom it is expressed. Reciprocity and strangeness carry dialogue far beyond a mere conversation between two monolithic information sources. Through reciprocity and strangeness, dialogue becomes an evolutionary process in which the parties are changed as they proceed." (p. 12)

To philosopher Martin Buber (1965), dialogue was a complex process whose essence could nevertheless be distilled to an easily understood principle: Genuine dialogue is "where each of the participants really has in mind the other or others in their present and particular being and turns to them with the intention of establishing a living mutual relation . . ." (p. 19). Considering Grudin and Buber in the context of our skills-plus approach, we define **dialogue** as a mutually interactive relationship, not based in technique or deception, that is open to continual change over time. The attitude of dialogue, in turn, creates the opportunity for a series of moments of insight through which communicators are changed in new and surprising ways.

Opposed to dialogue is an experience of *monologue,* in which one person seeks to establish a single voice as the dominant one and treats the partner as an object rather than a person. Monologic speakers transform the other person into a mere source of reward, or into someone they conceive as an "objective" by which their success is gauged. Interviewers can fall easily into the monologue trap. As psychologist Edward Sampson (1993) puts it, "When I construct a *you* designed to meet my needs and desires, a *you* that is serviceable for me, I am clearly engaging in a monologue as distinct from a dialogue. Although you and I may converse and interact together, in most respects the you with whom I am interacting has been constructed with me in mind. Your sole function has been to serve and service me" (p. 4).

If you doubt whether such selfishness happens often in the vibrant give-and-take world of interviewing, think of the journalist who interviews the grieving parents of a child killed in a plane crash, leaving immediately after eliciting the most harrowing emotional disclosures but getting good quotes for a story that must be filed fast, before the other media catch up to the parents. Think of the retired mayor who appears on a local television talk show only to plug a book, while ignoring inquiries about how the current mayor, her handpicked successor, is doing. Think of the research interviewer at the university who schedules interviews with students to investigate their study habits but gets angry with one who leaves early with an upset stomach. Think of the magazine writer who, while interviewing a celebrity just recovering from the depths of alcohol addiction, seems interested only in the lurid and sensational aspects of the drunkenness rather than the calm satisfaction with which the star currently regards his life. Or imagine the perfunctory way a press secretary for a politician or a public information spokesperson for a corporation answers questions at a press conference; are the questions likely to be interesting after the questioners have become cynical about hearing anything genuine?

All these situations feature interviewers and interviewees who are interested in others only to the extent that other people can supply immediate rewards, and no further. If

Farson is right that skills aren't as important as who we are, such behavior is ironically counterproductive; the attitude of objectifying others to get more information results in *less* information sharing. All these interchanges have been crippled by monologue when they needn't be. Even in the most monologic of interview contexts, the survey interview, respondents often can tell whether the interviewer genuinely cares to hear their answers. With interview participants who exhibit a monologic attitude, partners share only the most superficial of insights or ask only the most mundane questions.

Communication scholars (for example, Cissna & Anderson, 1994; Johannesen, 1996) have created lengthy lists of characteristics by which dialogue could be recognized in social, cultural, and political contexts. But for the purpose of understanding effective interviews, consider five basic appreciations and habits of effective dialogue, phrased in simple, every-day words: curiosity, knowledge, diversity, flexibility, empathy. Any interviewer or interviewee would profit by paying careful attention to such factors and by acting in ways consistent with them whenever possible.

Curiosity

Effective interviews, especially from the standpoint of interviewers, are characterized by *embodied curiosity*. Although it is probably easiest to think of interviewing as a systematic search for certainty, actually a fundamental recognition of ambiguity more commonly fuels the interview. Those who are absolutely convinced of what is desired or necessary, or know exactly what they must "get" from the other person, will never be consistently good interviewers or interviewees. Every interview, in other words, should begin with some assessment of what is *not* understood, is *not* known, is *not* certain.

Curious interviewers, for example, approach the conversation with a healthy respect for what they don't know and a burning desire to fill that gap (see Box 2.2). No amount of technical skill will make up for an absence of fundamental curiosity on the part of interviewers. Respondents will notice "I don't care" attitudes, even if they accompany slick techniques, and probably will react negatively. How would you respond to an interviewer who asks a series of otherwise appropriate questions but approaches the conversation with a bored demeanor and does not appear especially interested in your answers? Effective questions from interviewers are not just effective because of a formula; they have to be genuine, and they have to be sincere. A few of the questions that emerge from an interviewer's healthy curiosity might include: What motivates the other person? What does he or she know? What can I discover that helps explain my world, solve my problem, educate my readers, improve my company, or meet my goals?

Interviewees, too, are rewarded by demonstrating their curiosity in a variety of circumstances. Curiosity is based in questions and is demonstrated in them as well. What is the perspective of the other, and how can I find out more about it? What is the basis for these questions and the assumptions behind them? What motivates the interviewer's curiosity? Who needs this information, and how will it ultimately benefit them? The moment people become convinced that they know "exactly where the other person is coming from," they quit listening carefully. This complacency will lead to missed opportunities for clear explanations.

BOX 2.2   **INTERVIEWERS IN ACTION**

Jeannette Batz on Claudia Dreifus

Jeannette Batz, columnist for the *Riverfront Times,* an award-winning weekly alternative paper in St. Louis, features unusual perspectives on public people and issues in her column "Conversations." Here's her account of an interview with someone she held in awe:

> "It hit me the night before the interview. I'd seen Claudia Dreifus' new collection of Q&As, read her in the *New York Times,* knew she'd been one of *Playboy*'s best serious interviewers, heard her compared to the near-inimitable Oriana Fallaci. So I was happily reading up, preparing to—oh, my God!—interview *her.*
>
> "How do you subject the consummate professional to her own craft, done slap-dash? You don't. You cheat and ask her what she'd ask herself.
>
> "'I think I'd ask what moves me to do it,' she begins thoughtfully, and my relief swells like a bubble-gum balloon. This isn't so hard. What does move her to interview people as diverse as Arthur Schlesinger, Benazir Bhutto, Susan Sarandon and the Dalai Lama? 'A desire to have adventure in my own life, to have a front-row seat on history,' she muses. 'And to ask deep questions that I want the answers to.'
>
> "This rings such a bell, I find myself asking her what I won't ask myself: Is the adventure real? 'It's not vicarious,' she answers quickly. 'I'm really in a taxi traveling through the Jordanian border without a visa, and the Palestinians on the bus saying, 'That woman's going to jail!'
>
> "'I think it's a very noble thing to provide people with good information,' she continues."
>
> *Source:* Batz, 1997, p. 10

Knowledge

Both interviewers and interviewees prepare for successful interviews. Although preparation often involves behavioral rehearsal—as job applicants surely understand—the most crucial aspects of preparation involve how participants acquire relevant knowledge or fail to do so. Because interviews are such focused occasions for communication, and because they usually involve sharing information along one or two dimensions, doing preparatory research is especially important.

As described more fully in Chapter 11, all communication contexts involve some kind of persuasion; people, intentionally or not, constantly influence each other. This is true not only when a salesperson from Don's Ford Country is asking you about your driving habits while standing in the middle of the lot on a Friday evening but also when the boss asks you after two weeks on the job how you like it. Even in the simplest interviews, participants are rarely, if ever, completely unconcerned with how they're seen or what effects they'll have on the other person. Persuasion is pervasive. One of the most important determinants of persuasive success, **credibility,** is composed primarily of listeners' estimates of speakers' *expertise* (how much they think the speaker knows) and their *trustworthiness* (how much they can rely on the speaker). In the interview both basic aspects of credibility, but especially expertise, depend upon knowledgeable preparation for the interview.

35

Interviewers, who are usually responsible for initiating the action, ought to begin interviews with curiosity and a certain willingness to tolerate ambiguity. But this is far from saying they should begin with a lack of knowledge. Indeed, successful interviewers in any field find that while they still are willing to be surprised, the more they interview, the less they are blindsided by completely unexpected responses. Their knowledge base has familiarized them with the likely language, background, values, and motivating interests of their conversation partners.

Such a knowledge base is equally important for interviewees, though for different reasons. They are wise to anticipate the interviewer's focus in regard to content—not an easy task. They are also wise to anticipate what kind of interview structure the interviewer has in mind.

It's best to think of interviews in terms of *resource factors* and *structure factors*. Resources are those considerations that are valuable for the interview participants or audiences, while structure refers to the way the interaction is organized. The primary focus for most interviews is the information resource, largely controlled by the interviewee; that is, the respondent usually can decide how much information to share and how much to withhold. Other resource factors are possible, including entertaining stories that a broadcast interviewee, for example, might share if the interview is stimulating or involving enough. Yet that primary focus on resource factors must be maintained within the context of structural variables largely controlled by an interviewer; the interviewer usually chooses the questioning strategies, timing decisions, topic changes, and the like. Both resource factors and structure factors depend on knowledge—*content knowledge* (what-is-known understanding) for resource factors and *process knowledge* (how-to understanding) for structure factors. For example, Sandra Fish (1990) analyzed crisis-line telephone communication between callers and counselors. Callers, she found, retain control over content and initiation/termination choices. The counselor, however, has a different kind of power, largely over the process (structure) of the call—"length, timing, and duration of probing questions, the degree to which the caller needs to be supported . . . ," (p. 161), and other factors of what we're calling structure.

But any conclusions about who controls knowledge can only be generalizations with many exceptions. Box 2.3 summarizes the relationships between knowledge variables in interviews.

Diversity

Appreciating diversity means that interview participants can use cultural and social differences to energize their talk and make it meaningful in unexpected ways. Some interviews involve persons who know each other quite well, may have come from similar social, cultural, or economic strata, and may have developed an easygoing familiarity with each other. A reporter, for example, might be assigned to interview a famous journalist at a competing paper, when the two have known each other for many years. But this is a relatively rare occurrence. More commonly, interviewers and interviewees are unfamiliar

BOX 2.3   R E M I N D E R S

Knowledge Factors in Interviewing

	Knowledge type	*Kind of understanding*	*Who controls*
Resource factors	what is known	content	interviewee
Structure factors	how-to	process	interviewer

or barely familiar with each other's lives before they begin researching how they want to handle the resource and structure variables discussed in the previous section. This gap gives the interview a special character of discovery that involves implications far beyond basic curiosity and the will to know.

A particularly challenging characteristic of most interviews is that they depend upon people's willingness to talk across a variety of differences—differences of culture, ethnicity, gender, power, age, status, sexual preference, and other ways communicators invest their identities. Later in this book we will present specific suggestions for improving your communication skills in cross-cultural interview settings; here, simply consider how certain relatively narrow cultural or social habits will hinder you as an interviewer or interviewee.

No textbook authors can tell you what kind of personality or what kind of person is "best." Therefore, this book will not try to manipulate you into a cultural or political position with which you are uncomfortable. Yet the research into communication effectiveness suggests that a certain style of interviewing tends to provide the best results and tends to leave participants with a higher level of satisfaction. Although the word *multicultural* has become politically charged in recent years with a variety of meanings, no other term better describes what is necessary for interview communicators who confront others very different from themselves.

Stated simply for the interview context, **multiculturalism** is an appreciation for the fact that other people's cultural habits and expectations appear as normal and reasonable to them as yours do to you. "Multi-" suggests that there are many such cultural systems; "-ism" suggests that you might profit from developing a generalized reminder for yourself that these other systems are not necessarily wrong, dysfunctional, evil, or inefficient for interview partners culturally different from yourself. In other words, effective interview participants tend to develop a pluralistic worldview in which a wide range of behavior is possible and functional (see Box 2.4). With an appreciation of multiculturalism, you acknowledge and value diversity instead of being intimidated, frustrated, or frightened by it.

Interviews are usually brief communication contacts with highly focused purposes that extend beyond the encounter. Most interviews, with exceptions such as counseling and certain types of ethnographic research, aren't concerned with deep relationships involving personality analysis or intense emotional involvement. You're not going to effect radical changes in each others' lives in most cases. Your goals will usually involve understanding other persons much more than attempting to change them (see Box 2.5). Acknowledging and respecting diversity is not the same as agreeing artificially with the

BOX 2.4   REMINDERS

Problems of Avoiding or Ignoring a Pluralistic Worldview

You will be frustrated with the results of your interviews if

- You believe you already know what someone thinks or should think.
- You think you should use the interview to persuade others not to be who they are.
- You can justify avoiding certain interviewers or interviewees because they are too different from you—you'll never understand each other.
- You are convinced that only your religion, your view on social controversies, or your own ethnic culture holds a patent on some kind of essential truth. (This does not mean you must abandon all your own beliefs in interviews, only that you must check constantly to ensure you are not using them to dismiss the possibility of others' beliefs.)
- You believe it is your duty to moralize publicly about others' behavior.
- You hold grudges, not only against persons but against the groups they supposedly represent.
- You depend upon relatively static or frozen evaluations of groups and people to carry you from situation to situation.
- You believe you represent a substandard or inadequate culture or group whose voice does not need to be heard.

specific people who are different from yourself or adopting a kind of banal toleration in which you think you must always love everybody. You can still be effective in interviews if you disagree with some differences you encounter, but you will likely not be as effective if you don't appreciate the fact that other communicators have built worlds of meaning that are just as important to them as your values are to you.

Flexibility

Most people have developed habits of communication that are comfortable for them, and they begin to rely upon those habits in most of their relationships. For example, some are comfortable speaking up in a group of strangers; others try to avoid such behavior. Some share their emotions readily and don't care who knows what they feel; others maintain a sense of privacy in which their personal experience is customarily not disclosed. Some people tell jokes loudly and laugh readily; others' sense of humor tends to be more subtle.

A difficulty faced by many beginning interview participants is that it takes a certain amount of courage on the interviewer's part to make the social requests necessary to interview others and, perhaps, equivalent courage on the interviewee's part to be listened to carefully and seriously. Interviewing involves social risks of embarrassment, vulnerability, and the possibility of your mistakes being observed and made public. It is not a

BOX 2.5   INTERVIEWERS IN ACTION

Hugo Slim and Paul Thompson

Hugo Slim, senior research officer for Save the Children Fund in Great Britain, and Paul Thompson, professor and director of Britain's National Life Story Collection, have practiced their craft of narrative, oral history, and life stories interviewing in a variety of world cultures. Their book is a rich resource in cross-cultural interviewing that describes problems they and similar researchers have faced and, often, surmounted.

"While the interview is now a common form of enquiry and communication in the West—where the job interview is a prerequisite for most employment, the media feature endless interviews, both informative and entertaining, and few people escape having to take part in polls and questionnaires—this is by no means a universal experience. . . . In some societies the interview is not an established type of speech event, and there can often be an incompatibility between standard interview techniques and indigenous systems of communication. This incompatibility can create problems for people who, as interviewees, are forced to express themselves in an unfamiliar speech format. In particular, the interview form has a tendency to put unnatural pressure on people to find ready answers, to be concise and to summarise a variety of complex experiences and intricate knowledge. It may also mean that researchers and interviewers unwittingly violate local communication norms relating to turn-taking, the order of topics for discussion or various rituals attached to storytelling. In some societies, individual interviews are considered dangerously intimate encounters. In others, the recounting of group history can be a sacred ritual and certain people must be consulted before others. Sometimes, a number of clearly prescribed topics should be used to start proceedings, while other topics may be taboo, or should not be introduced until a particular level of intimacy and trust has been achieved."

Source: Slim & Thompson, 1995, p. 62

comfortable experience for many persons, and therefore a certain amount of reticence is normal. However, for many people, other personality difficulties create further roadblocks. The literature in communication and psychology concerning interaction apprehension, shyness, and reticence is directly relevant here (for example, Daly & McCroskey, 1984; Phillips, 1981, 1984, 1991; Zimbardo, 1977). For many people, the appreciation of flexibility is more a mental reality than a behaviorally realistic option. Gerald Phillips's research (1984) notes that few people are reticent across the board, consciously avoiding almost all communication interchanges because they lack confidence. Virtually all people feel very confident about selected communication contexts in their lives. However, Phillips reports, the following are the most common situations that people who identify themselves as reticent avoid because they feel uncomfortable. Reticent communicators experience

- Inability to ask and answer questions at work or in school
- Inability to present connected discourse in public
- Inability to make social conversation and small talk
- Inability to make the kinds of talk associated with the development of friendship and intimacy
- Inability to interact with the opposite sex
- Inability to participate in group activities
- Inability to get the attention one thinks one deserves
- Inability to talk with authority figures, parents, teachers, bosses, people with prestige (p. 60)

Consider how many of these situations apply to successful interviews. Extremely reticent, shy, or apprehensive people who avoid such situations are unlikely to be as flexible as interviewers and interviewees need to be, even if they try to force themselves to perform the "correct behaviors." Interviewing involves questions and answers, coordinated in specific ways that often depend upon small talk and development of rapport. Interviews typically involve persons of different genders and gender orientations and often occur in public or semipublic settings in which participants must draw attention to themselves. Finally, interviews often cross lines and boundaries of prestige as those who have comfortable jobs talk with unemployed applicants, a rookie reporter interviews a governor, a world-renowned brain surgeon is asked a series of possibly naive questions by a patient about to have an operation. Perhaps almost as much as in public speaking contexts, interview participants must deal with nervousness and apprehension. Most people do so, with practice, and a sense of coping or even mastery develops; but others might need additional assistance, such as specific training programs in coping strategies or desensitization that are available at many universities and other institutions.

Although most so-called inflexible behaviors appear to relate to personality characteristics and traits, other behaviors experienced as either comfortable or uncomfortable could have cultural roots. Take eye contact, for instance. Some people are comfortable maintaining consistent eye gaze at close quarters, while others are not. Yet this is not only a personality variable but also a cultural one. Some cultures train young people to avert direct eye contact from those of perceived higher status, no matter who is speaking. Touching is another example. Some people regard as perfectly normal a high incidence of touching during conversation, while others expect conversants to maintain a clear distance. Different cultural groups appear to mandate certain kinds of behaviors relatively predictably: these behaviors are likely to be employed by their members unless they consciously choose to do otherwise.

Empathy

Psychologist Carl Rogers (1959), one of the most famous of counseling interviewers, defined *empathy* as the ability "to perceive the internal frame of reference of another with accuracy and with the emotional components and meanings which pertain thereto as if

Trying Out Your Skills

Write a brief one- or two-page history of your interviewing experience, giving special attention to the degree of reticence, nervousness, or apprehension you experienced. Be sure to describe any occasions in which you avoided an interview (for example, seeing a teacher to discover what was wrong with your paper, not applying for a job you knew you were qualified for) just because you wanted to avoid the feelings you knew you'd experience. Then:

- Share your essay with someone whose feedback you value. Interview this person to determine whether the self-image expressed in the essay coincides with your partner's image of you.

Then turn the tables: Have your partner ask you questions about when you have been most comfortable in one-on-one communication situations.

- Research what counseling or continuing education services are available on your campus. Are there programs, workshops, or counseling opportunities designed to assist reticent, apprehensive, or shy students in becoming more flexible communicators? (*Note:* This exercise provides valuable skill development and insight even if you are already a highly flexible and comfortable communicator.)

---

one were the person, but without ever losing the 'as if' condition" (p. 210). Interestingly, although empathy has often been taught and learned as if it were a simple skill of peering into another's experience and understanding it almost as if the perceiver were a mind reader, Rogers saw it less as a skill and more as a "way of being." His attempts to understand clients often took the form of tentative restatements of others' comments, to ensure he was understanding them, as well as offering out loud his tentative verbal "explorations" of others' experiences. His partner could correct the interpretations if necessary. Rogers became frustrated that his genuine curiosity about the distinctive "otherness" of the other person came to be taught as a simplistic technique of "reflective listening" in which the listener only tries to mirror exactly what the speaker just said.

To Rogers, however, being empathic was this more inclusive way of being a person. It could be expressed in conversations by a certain kind of active listening we will explore in other chapters, but the basis of empathy is an attitude of respect, an attitude that links several of the other appreciations in this chapter. In an essay in his 1980 book *A Way of Being*, Rogers notes these "profound consequences" of empathy that are supported by research in interpersonal communication:

> . . . Empathy dissolves alienation. For the moment, at least, the recipient finds himself or herself a connected part of the human race. (p. 151)
>
> A second consequence . . . is that the recipient feels valued, cared for, accepted as the person that he or she is. . . . It is impossible to accurately sense the perceptual world of another person unless you value that person and his or her world—unless you, in some sense, care. (p. 152)
>
> . . . A third impact of a sensitive understanding comes from its nonjudgmental quality. The highest expression of empathy is accepting and nonjudgmental. This is true because it is impossible to be accurately perceptive of another's inner world if you have formed an evaluative opinion of that person. (pp. 153–154)

Respect

Trying Out Your Skills

Read the following interview excerpt. Using the concepts and ideas of this chapter, can you make the case that this is an example of dialogic interviewing? Or is there more evidence here that these communicators do not appreciate dialogue?

Delores Wilson, an African American student with a history of campus activism, is talking with her 60-ish white male political science professor, Michael Van Allen. This is one of a series of interviews conducted by a small group of students to determine whether faculty and administration would support the establishment of an African American Studies interdisciplinary major. Many students, black and white, support such a program, but others on campus, incluing many faculty, believe there are already too many majors and too many interdisciplinary programs as well. Some faculty, also, wonder if diversity-oriented programs may not "water down" traditional education. Wilson and Van Allen meet in Van Allen's office late one afternoon.

DW: Thanks, Dr. Van Allen, for meeting with me. I know you're busy.

MVA: This isn't a problem, Delores. I'm happy to help. What can I do for you?

DW: Well, there are a lot of us who feel . . .

MVA: A lot of you? Who do you mean?

DW: A lot of students, and a lot of black students especially, who feel that the campus just kind of, well, doesn't give us many options.

MVA: At last count, there were at least twenty-five different majors in Arts & Science alone. Now that I think about it, there was a faculty council meeting last Wednesday, and that number may be in the hundreds by now.

DW: (smiles) I know. There are a lot. Well, I didn't know there were that many, but I knew there were quite a few. That counts sciences, doesn't it? But what I mean—we mean—by "not many options" is that so many of the humanities and social science majors seem like just different ways

Empathy is not only a phenomenon of therapeutic communication; Rogers thought that it characterized all effective relationships as a way to free effective and honest talk. Few insights could be more functional for developing interviewers and interviewees. But this is because empathy suggests a basic respect for persons and their experience, not because it is a handy technique for unlocking someone's thoughts or for keeping them talking.

❦ BEYOND THE BASICS

A skills-plus approach to interviewing, as we have seen, must depend on more than the techniques of asking and answering questions. Success will come not only when certain techniques or tactics are used but also when interviewers and interviewees fully recognize the complexity of their interactions. Over the past thirty years or more, many researchers have explained the subtle ways conversants appreciate this complexity—or the ways they fail to appreciate it. Here we will be especially concerned with baseline concepts of communication rules and the cooperative principle.

to look at the same traditional things like elections, politics, great books, and so on. But you think that the twenty-five majors give enough choices to all students?

MVA: Doesn't sound so bad to me. Those things you mentioned are the core issues of society—things all citizens need to come to grips with. No matter what color they are. The article in the paper made it seem like black students want to do their own thing, read only minority authors. I very much liked your performance in my class last semester, Delores, but I have to admit I'm not in favor of an African-Americans-only major. Why not stick with doing well in traditional majors like English, political science, or even business?

DW: Thank you for the compliment, Dr. Allen. I do work hard in school. The article in the paper was misleading, though. Rasheed got misquoted, and it did sound like the new proposal might be for African Americans and minorities exclusively. It's not designed that way at all. Has anyone shown you the proposal itself?

MVA: No. I've heard people refer to it but haven't seen it.

DW: I can get you a copy tomorrow morning, OK? I could be wrong, but to me it seems like it would attract a lot of students from all cultural groups. It's not just a club kind of atmosphere. One of the things that's different about it is that it would be a *second* major for any student who declared it; it'd be a substitute for a minor, not a major.

MVA: I didn't know that. How many hours would be included? What departments and faculty have expressed interest? How are the courses going to be coordinated? There are a lot of questions.

DW: That's true. Would you still like to see the proposal? It answers some of those things, but—I have to admit—maybe not all of them. Teachers have different ways of looking at these things than students do, I know.

MVA: Sure. I'd like to read it. Drop it by during my ten o'clock office hours, if you can. . . .

Communication Rules

Discussions about communication "rules" generally refer to the complex set of guidelines that help communicators make their behavioral choices and adjustments with each other in various contexts. A **communication rule,** to the interpersonal communication researcher Susan Shimanoff (1980), is a "followable prescription that indicates what behavior is obligated, preferred, or prohibited in certain contexts" (p. 57). In other words, many times in conversations, we accommodate ourselves to each other in predictable ways—but in ways that no one specifically dictated or necessarily taught. In fact, most of our interactions with each other are governed in these kinds of subtle ways, by implicit "rules" that are never codified but constantly affirmed in our mutually developed understanding of what is right to do in a given situation.

Of course, not everyone will agree with or enact the rules in the same ways. Rules are broken all the time. Your conversation partner is edging toward the door as you talk, and has looked at her watch twice in the past few minutes, but you continue to press new questions, unaware that she needs to leave. Your ignorance of the implications of her behavior are, in effect, rule violations; you should have noticed. But significantly, these everyday rules governing talk are broken less often by interviewers and interviewees who make themselves aware of the cultural contexts of communication and the kinds of diversity required in them (see the discussion of diversity earlier in this chapter). The rules are broken less often, too, by communicators who have developed a high degree of behavioral flexibility and adaptability.

Interviewing demands what we call **high-flex communicators**—those who are aware of not only the content stream but also the process stream of conversational rules and can adjust their behaviors accordingly. They are not chameleons, changing their behavior constantly to fool others, but—ideally—highly ethical speaker-listeners who know how to adapt in a variety of situations to help others communicate in the best way they can. High-flex communicators can infer the language and nonverbal rules that seem to guide their partners and, when necessary, adapt their own talk to those rules. This is more than a skill; it is an inherent appreciation for the complexity of communication and the flexibility it demands.

The Cooperative Principle and Its Maxims

H. P. Grice (1975), a researcher specializing in analyzing conversational talk, suggested that speakers and listeners, at least in the Western world, are bound together by what he calls an overall "cooperative principle" and, further, by four other "maxims" that—other factors being equal—will help conversants decide when and how they need to be flexible. These insights (pp. 45–47), paraphrased here, will help explain the importance of a skills-plus approach.

The Cooperative Principle

Each speaker should contribute in ways that are appropriate to the seemingly mutually accepted stage, purpose, and direction of the conversation that engages the persons. We don't begin to talk with others assuming they will try to undercut us, interfere with our talk, or otherwise work against understanding.

The Conversational Maxims

Quantity: Speakers should not provide more or less information than is required by the type of conversation being conducted.

Quality: Speakers share only those observations and statements they believe to be true and supportable by external evidence.

Relevancy: Speakers concentrate on providing information and commentary pertinent to the situation.

Manner: Speakers avoid expressions that are likely to confuse the other person, to be misunderstood, or to be unnecessarily ambiguous or obscure.

As an active member of your campus's Student Activities Board, you are asked by the president of student government to investigate why international students and their organizations are less active in campus governance and in planning activities. To supply this kind of information, you decide to interview the most important and active members of each international student group (for example, the Korean Student Association, the African Student Alliance, and so forth).

1. How would you decide whom to interview from each group?

2. What would you do if a significant population of students on campus was not represented by a formal organization? Would you attempt to interview someone anyway? If so, how would you decide whom to interview?

3. It's possible that interviewees could feel they were being singled out or blamed for not participating on campus. You want to avoid this impression, because you are genuinely interested in facilitating increased learning between cultures. (In other words, though you may be a skillful interviewer, you want the appropriate attitude to be apparent to interviewees.) How would you seek to convince students of different cultures that you are sincere in your curiosity and desire to help? Would you have a specific plan for how to establish this kind of rapport early in each interview?

4. Would you want to do research to discover any special communication rules that characterize cultural assumptions? Where would you go to discover some basic rules that would help you avoid potential situations in which you unintentionally insult or offend the interviewees, or just avoid significant misunderstandings? *Hint:* You might want to think about coursework in cross-cultural communication and Internet research capabilities. See the current edition of *Communication Research: Strategies and Sources* (Rubin, Rubin, & Piele, 1996) or one of the many guides for interviewers on information collection, such as *The Reporter's Handbook: An Investigator's Guide to Documents and Techniques* (Ullman & Colbert, 1991).

It is hard to overestimate the importance of Grice's insights for interviewers and interviewees. Several examples from the standpoint of interviewees' experiences illustrate the point, although we could as easily give examples of the interviewer's role. An interviewee who filibusters in answering a question violates the maxim of *quantity.* (See Sunday morning news interview programs for many intentional examples of this, although most instances are probably unintentional.) The interviewer is well advised to consider polite and effective ways to nudge the speaker back toward pointed, streamlined, and more efficient discussion. An interviewee who misleads listeners on purpose, who lies, or who tells a half-truth violates the maxim of *quality* and, depending on the context, might expect an alert interviewer to call attention to the violation either in immediate interaction or later, perhaps in a story written about the interview. A political science professor who, when asked pointedly by a reporter for an opinion on the mayoral election, responds with a long discussion of how qualified he is to assess the charisma and policies of the two candidates has probably violated the maxim of *relevancy* in this context. Finally, a scientist trying to explain the greenhouse effect in a broadcast interview launches into a long discussion of reactivity and stability in fluorocarbon chemistry; she has certainly violated the maxim of *manner,* even though the information's relevance, quality, and quantity may be sound.

Summary

When interviewing is done well, it employs many of the most practical communication skills in professional life. In later chapters, we divide various skills into three major categories—listening, questioning, and framing—before surveying a series of contexts for interviewing in your career and personal life.

It is a mistake, we believe, to study interviewing in terms of a collection of skills, as if they can be used as tools at our disposal. This chapter has placed interviewing skills in a broader context of communication competence in which certain appreciations and communicative habits can guide your choice of skills. Our skills-plus approach emphasizes five basic appreciations that can guide effective interviews: persistent curiosity, thorough knowledge, sensitivity to diversity, behavioral and attitudinal flexibility, and a willingness to be empathic.

The Interview Bookshelf

On the appreciation of dialogue and conversation in interviewing

Schumacher, M. (1990). *Creative conversations: The writer's complete guide to conducting interviews.* Cincinnati, OH: Writer's Digest Books.

This practical book is by an interviewer experienced in writing human interest profiles. Schumacher avoids the trap of trying to make a formula of interviewing and urges that interviewers should rely on curiosity, habits of dialogue, and—as the title implies—the creative experience of a conversational approach.

On multicultural interviewing

Fetterman, D. M. (1989). *Ethnography step by step.* Newbury Park, CA: Sage.

Ethnography is the qualitative research approach in which the researcher attempts to "get inside" a culture or cultural group in order to experience and describe its inner workings. In addition to various styles of interviewing, it usually involves participant observation methods and a series of assumptions on the part of investigators that the culture studied will be "strange," different, and new in yet-to-be-discovered ways.

On communication competence and rules theory for interviewers

Cushman, D. P., & Cahn, D. D., Jr. (1985). *Communication in interpersonal relationships.* Albany, NY: State University of New York Press.

This book examines how important it is to understand the influence of rules in face-to-face situations. The authors include many applications, direct and indirect, to interviewing, such as employment, appraisal, and assessment interviewing; negotiation and persuasive interviewing; and cross-cultural interviewing.

On conversational dynamics

Nofsinger, R. E. (1991). *Everyday conversation.* Newbury Park, CA: Sage.

Probably the best brief explanation of conversation yet to come out of communication studies. Interviewers and interviewees who read this book will be well prepared to deal with a variety of problems.

References

Batz, J. (1997, September 10–16). Inquiring mind. *Riverfront Times,* p. 10.

Buber, M. (1965). *Between man and man* (R. G. Smith, Trans.). New York: Macmillan.

Cissna, K. N., & Anderson, R. (1994). Communication and the ground of dialogue. In R. Anderson, K. N. Cissna, & R. C. Arnett (Eds.), *The reach of dialogue: Confirmation, voice, and community* (pp. 9–30). Creskill, NJ: Hampton.

Daly, J. A., & McCroskey, J. C. (Eds.). (1984). *Avoiding communication: Shyness, reticence, and communication apprehension.* Beverly Hills, CA: Sage.

Farson, R. (1996). *Management of the absurd: Paradoxes in leadership.* New York: Touchstone.

Fish, S. L. (1990). Therapeutic uses of the telephone: Crisis intervention vs. traditional therapy. In G. Gumpert & S. L. Fish (Eds.), *Talking to strangers: Mediated interpersonal communication* (pp. 154–169). Norwood, NJ: Ablex.

Grice, H. P. (1975). Logic and conversation. In P. Cole & J. Morgan (Eds.), *Syntax and semantics, Vol. 3: Speech acts.* New York: Academic Press.

Grudin, R. (1996). *On dialogue: An essay in free thought.* Boston: Houghton Mifflin.

Isaacs, B. (1994). Dialogue. In P. M. Senge, A. Kleiner, et al. (Eds.), *The fifth discipline fieldbook.* New York: Doubleday.

Johannesen, R. (1996). *Ethics in human communication* (4th ed.). Prospect Heights, IL: Waveland.

Phillips, G. M. (1981). *Help for shy people.* Englewood Cliffs, NJ: Prentice-Hall.

Phillips, G. M. (1984). Reticence: A perspective on social withdrawal. In J. A. Daly & J. C. McCroskey (Eds.), *Avoiding communication: Shyness, reticence, and communication apprehension* (pp. 51–66). Beverly Hills, CA: Sage.

Phillips, G. M. (1991). *Communication incompetencies: A theory of training oral performance behavior.* Carbondale, IL: Southern Illinois University Press.

Rogers, C. R. (1959). A theory of therapy, personality, and interpersonal relationships, as developed in the client-centered framework. In S. Koch (Ed.), *Psychology: A study of a science, Vol. III. Formulations of the person and the social context* (pp. 184–256). New York: McGraw-Hill.

Rogers, C. R. (1980). *A way of being.* Boston: Houghton Mifflin.

Rubin, R. B. (1990). Communication competence. In G. M. Phillips & J. T. Wood (Eds.), *Speech communication: Essays to commemorate the 75th anniversary of The Speech Communication Association* (pp. 94–129). Carbondale, IL: Southern Illinois University Press.

Rubin, R. B., Rubin, A. M., & Piele, L. J. (1996). *Communication research: Strategies and sources* (4th ed.). Belmont, CA: Wadsworth.

Sampson, E. E. (1993). *Celebrating the other: A dialogic account of human nature.* Boulder, CO: Westview Press.

Shimanoff, S. (1980). *Communication rules: Theory and research.* Beverly Hills, CA: Sage.

Slim, H., & Thompson, P. (1995). *Listening for a change: Oral testimony and community development.* Philadelphia: New Society.

Ullmann, J., & Colbert, J. (Eds.). (1991). *The reporter's handbook: An investigator's guide to documents and techniques.* New York: St. Martin's Press.

Zimbardo, P. G. (1977). *Shyness: What it is, what to do about it.* New York: Jove/HBJ.

✼ 3 Skillful Listening

A listening atmosphere is not improvised. It is, on the contrary, the product of a strenuous process of conception, growth and devoted attention.

—Gemma Corradi Fiumara,
The Other Side of Language

LEARNING GOALS

After reading this chapter, you should be able to

- Describe the process of listening and distinguish it from the more physical process of hearing
- Develop effective strategies that will prepare you to listen with more focus and sensitivity
- Identify five major types of listening skills and discuss how different interviewing contexts depend upon these types
- Practice the verbal and nonverbal skills of active listening, a style that confirms communicators and allows listeners and speakers to verify the extent of their mutual understanding

Readers might expect a chapter on listening to start with a discussion of listening, with good reason. But that may not be the most helpful way to introduce the subject. Instead, consider the times when you feel comfortable speaking. Ask yourself these questions:

- When faced with a decision that is important to talk through, whom do I call?
- Are there certain topics I won't bring up with certain people or in certain situations?
- Do I have friends who are nice people, but after a conversation with them I never seem to feel understood?
- When giving directions to some people, do I have to repeat things two or three times, and they still don't get it?
- Do I look forward to talking with people who show little interest in what I have to say?

Your answers should give you a preliminary idea of why we think it's important to study listening as a fundamental step in improving your interviewing effectiveness. If you are like most people, you may appreciate poor listeners for their other qualities (they may be generous or wise or witty), but you aren't likely to trust them with sensitive information, with dilemmas you're trying to sort out, or with decisions they'll make on the basis of nuances of information. Simply put, there are people you want to talk to and others you will avoid because you're pretty sure you'll be misunderstood somehow.

Consider the possibility that friends or coworkers sometimes find you the kind of listener they will want to avoid. You're the one who mixes up messages; the interrupter; the one who always finds a way to turn the topic selfishly back to yourself when your partner is talking about her or his own problem; the one whose own opinions about a topic engulf the other person's; or the one whose judgments about others stifle them.

If you're a poor listener, chances are people in your life have not told you about the problem and would never want to hurt your feelings by lecturing you about your listening limitations. More likely, they'll just end conversations prematurely or not call you when certain occasions arise. Remember, these are friends and acquaintances; what could strangers be expected to do? Similarly, if you are interviewing others in professional or public settings—or being interviewed by them—and you display poor listening habits, they aren't likely to explain the real reason when a discussion suddenly ends with remarks like these: "I have a meeting I have to go to now" or, "I can't think of anything more that needs to be covered."

This chapter will help you inventory your habits and skills to diagnose how your own listening style can make or break your interviews. The first part of the chapter surveys the basics of what experienced interviewers know about listening and introduces research that supports that knowledge. You will see how this knowledge can be turned into insights and behavioral skills that, in turn, translate directly into improvements in your communication. You'll learn how listening is not a separate process from speaking and how it's not the same thing as merely hearing something either. You'll read about hints for preparing to listen before you ever encounter any interviewee or interviewer partner. Knowing the types and functions of different listening goals will further help you adjust your style to the demands of each interviewing challenge. Finally, you'll understand how listening in interviewing is an intensely active process, far from the passive receiving experience most people associate with it.

In "Beyond the Basics" you'll move past fundamental skills to a wider philosophical appreciation of how better listening can improve the communication between interviewer and interviewee.

THE BASICS

Defining Listening

Although most people associate conversations primarily with talking and think about interviews only in terms of questions and answers, we want to start in a slightly different place in attempting to define the importance of listening: the assumption that interpersonal talk will be *heard* and *responded to*. After you learn that a customer in your store is a German tourist with little skill in English, you change your speech patterns and word choices. After you learn that your roommate's brother is hearing impaired, it's natural to avoid speaking to him when he can't also see you. In a less obvious but equally real example, you don't ask friends for favors unless they are able to hear the request, and you usually don't ask for a favor unless you believe the friend is at least somewhat able to understand the basis for the request. This doesn't mean that you know beforehand whether the friend will comply or even if the request will be understood in the same way you intend it. It only means that you have some reason to assume that people you talk to will not be on a completely different wavelength. In short, you act on the assumption we're highlighting here: Talk is based on the presumption of listening.

We Not Only Listen to Others' Speaking, We Also Speak to Their Listening

Effective communicators in sensitive situations (mediators, therapists, diplomats, parents, and others) know that people don't just decide to "say something"; speakers decide to say a particular thing to somebody and to say it in a certain way. Their assessment of the other's listening skill, or lack of it, influences that speech. Listeners, in other words, are not only hearing the other person's speech, but they are also hearing the kind of speech the other person believes is appropriate for the skill or style of the listener.

If this sounds obvious, you might be surprised at the thousands of interviewers who constantly forget this fact, perhaps believing that the "interviewee was a nervous person" or "the governor doesn't want to talk about the budget." In reality, the interviewee may have been a usually calm person who was agitated only when talking with you (because of your poor eye contact and habit of interrupting). Or maybe the governor wanted to avoid fiscal topics with you because of previous interviews in which you showed your unwillingness to follow the ins and outs of statistical reasoning. To good communicators, no message can be understood out of its context. In this sense, many interviewers and interviewees aren't good communicators because they fail to understand the influence of listening on speaking. It's true that we constantly listen to other people's speech; it's equally true that we constantly speak to other people's listening.

We can define **listening,** therefore, as the active process through which communicators process aural (sound) stimuli, interpret them as messages, and use them to construct meanings of speech, speakers, and contexts. This definition should explain why we chose to present the topic of listening before the topic of questioning. Listening is not the effect caused by speaking; it is the very condition within which speaking becomes relevant at all. The experience of understanding and being understood, as Earl Koile stresses in Box 3.1, is a primary avenue to personal growth, as well as to everyday sanity. While listening, we create the conditions within which others can feel more human. Beyond that, listening creates a space in which speakers find they have more and better things to say. Our listening is not simply a way of receiving effects from others; listening creates effects of its own if it is focused and helpful enough.

Speech has to be defined in terms of its relationship to listening, because the latter is the ground on which talk can develop in the first place. This centrality of listening is also

BOX 3.1   INTERVIEWERS IN ACTION

Earl Koile

Therapist and teacher Earl Koile comments on how productive it can be for an interviewer to listen carefully:

"Almost always we listen to ourselves as we listen to others. We seldom by-pass ourselves. The echoes of our thoughts and feelings reverberate within us and influence what we hear and how we respond. To know what we are saying to ourselves is a prelude to listening and hearing someone else. But sometimes we cannot listen clearly—either to ourselves or to someone else—until we are heard by someone who can play back what we are saying and help us to find out what is going on inside. When we are heard we hear better. A chain reaction of sorts may be set in motion.

"Years ago a college senior in one of my classes came for a conference. She was working part time as a dorm advisor to freshmen, and, after talking about the class, she stayed to talk about how weighted down she felt listening to so many girls with seemingly insoluble problems. For an hour she described their problems and her worries about them. The next day she stopped by to announce that she had discovered something quite wonderful. 'When you listened to me without taking over my worries,' she said, 'I found out that I could listen better to them.' Then she asked, 'I wonder if I might come by once in a while to let off a little steam when hearing their problems gets me down?' As she was walking out she looked back over her shoulder and then stopped. I was struck by her appreciation for what it is like to be heard, when she asked, 'But is there someone who will then listen to you?'"

Source: Koile, 1977, pp. 122–123

why we stressed in Chapter 1 that interviewing has to be conceptualized as a process much more complex than just asking and answering questions. Effective listening is what links the question to the answer for the interviewee; beyond this, effective listening is what makes the answer useful and accurate for the interviewer.

Listening Is Not Hearing

Recall in our definition, we stressed that listening involves the active processing of aural stimuli. The word *processing* is important because another misconception about listening is that it's primarily a matter of accurately remembering or registering the details or facts of what the other person said. "Yes, I was listening," you might say, "you just asked if you could borrow my car." Or, "Yes, I listened in ethics class; the lecture yesterday was about Rawls's theory of justice." However, does either of these comments, which are based on retrieving facts, tell us much about how well the person listened?

Researchers who study listening typically distinguish between hearing and listening. *Hearing,* they believe, is primarily a physiological process by which various stimuli are perceived as present or absent. Although we can, by force of will, make ourselves hear something, most of the time hearing occurs relatively automatically, and at least some of what we hear will stick. For example, hearing is what happens when you turn suddenly to try to figure out what caused that loud noise outside your window. Hearing is the act of recognizing as soon as you pick up the phone that this is Anita calling you and not Marquita. Hearing is noticing that Mark is talking louder now that he's excited about Melville in American Literature, compared with the first week or two of the semester. *Listening,* though, as you've seen, involves processing the information gained through hearing sounds, to make more and more sense out of it. If hearing is physiological, listening is more reasonably understood as a psychological process that uses what is heard in the person's attempt at making sense.

Another implication of our definition is that the listening process does not involve simply getting the other person's message "right." Accurate understanding of auditory stimuli is important, of course. Interviewees, for example, who consistently misunderstand interviewers' questions and intentions are unlikely to be sought for subsequent interviews and may pay other prices, too, such as a damaged public reputation. Interviewers who consistently misunderstand or misquote interviewees will usually fail in achieving their own goals, too. Yet effective listeners go beyond simply registering the basic messages to imagine the deeper or wider meanings that accompany the talk. The effective listener is a verbal detective, using the conversational choices of the partner as clues to other meanings that might not be spoken or demonstrated overtly. Effective listeners can get things wrong, and they might not have a full enough context to understand people and their motives completely, but like other detectives, they follow their leads doggedly.

Preparing to Listen

Effective listening is not something you can make yourself do by force of will. If you've just been fired from your job, the meeting you've scheduled for the Student Government Association will probably not receive your full attention. Despite wanting to listen carefully to your friends, your state of mind will tend to interfere. This extra set of stimuli will create what communication theorists call noise—a condition in which messages you don't need or want to attend to will distract you from more important messages. **Communication noise** is any message that interferes with message(s) to which you want to attend. Noise can be psychological, such as fear about losing a job, or physiological, such as the jackhammer outside your window that interferes with all but the most superficial and trivial conversations. Noise is a problem because it is composed of competing stimuli that limit not just hearing but listening, too. In other words, the conditions for listening can be all wrong. Although the specific challenges brought up by the problems of listener

preparation and distraction are dealt with more specifically in the descriptions of professional interviewing contexts we examine in Part 2, we should discuss several general issues
of preparation here. These reminders apply to virtually all interviewing contexts.

In their book on listening, Carol Roach and Nancy Wyatt (1988) include real-life reports
of listening difficulties. One in particular illustrates distracted listening in interviews:

> It was an awful interview. After we introduced ourselves and shook hands, he said to sit
> down anywhere. There were only two sorts of couches, so I sat down on the nearest one.
> There were no arms and when you sat back you were practically lying down. So I had to
> sit hunched forward resting my arms on my knees. The interview lasted half an hour,
> and when I tried to stand up I practically fell down. I had a cramp in my leg and my
> neck was getting stiff. I can't remember anything that was said in that interview. (p. 24)

If conditions become that disruptive, then controlling them (and your reaction to them)
should become a part of your listening skill. To the extent possible, effective listeners learn
to choose conditions and occasions when interferences are minimal. Moreover, they look
for ways to minimize the noise of daily life. Box 3.2 summarizes some practical ways to
plan your listening for an interview. Not all of them will be practical or even possible in
all situations, but they should remind you of the control you could exercise over these
conditions.

Preparing to listen in systematic ways helps counteract a pervasive problem in all face-
to-face communication situations—what behavioral researchers call the **self-fulfilling
prophecy.** In this phenomenon, people encounter a new situation with old perceptual
habits, ultimately finding what they expect to find or creating conditions that would not
have occurred if not for the expectations. In fact, what they "find" exists largely as a
product of their prophecies and expectations. One study of interaction is particularly
interesting in this regard. Researchers (Snyder, Tanke & Berscheid, 1977) set up experimental conditions that placed pairs of communicators in separate rooms and asked them to
talk and listen over an intercom as a way to become acquainted. Each was given only
sketchy information about the other, but that information did include a snapshot of the
partner. It might not surprise you to learn that the photos did not match the actual
partners at all, although the participants weren't told this. The researchers were interested
in whether communicators would talk differently to people they presumed were attractive.
They did. (Separate tests, conducted before the main experiment, validated the attractiveness of the photographed subjects.) Independent judges listening to recordings thought
that speakers talking with visually "attractive" partners were more social, more humorous,
more interesting, and that they enjoyed the process more than other speakers.

However, something just as interesting occurred with the partners: When recordings
of those assumed to be attractive were evaluated, they were found to exhibit more animation, interestingness, enthusiasm, and confidence. When they were treated as someone
attractive, their speech began to match that assumption, and they started to act more
"attractive." In other words, speakers' presumptions about whom they were talking with
influenced (in this case, positively) others' behaviors, even when those presumptions were

BOX 3.2   R E M I N D E R S

Preparing to Listen in Interviews

Effective interview partners prepare to listen by

- *Doing a listening self-assessment.* Each person has unique listening strengths as well as particular problem areas. For example, some people are skilled at personality-based listening and use subtle cues to develop accurate impressions of others' personalities. Others, who have trouble listening for personality patterns, are instead particularly effective at remembering relevant facts, or listening for inconsistencies, or reading emotional messages. Do your best to become self-aware as a listener by being introspective and open to feedback.

- *Reviewing and acknowledging immediate sources of personalized psychological noise, such as nervousness or a toothache, and, if necessary, attempting to clear the mind.* For example, some skilled communicators set aside a half hour or hour before important interviews to review notes and immerse themselves in the topics most important to the other person. Interviewees and interviewers both might therefore be able to get their minds off entirely idiosyncratic types of noise and be better able to enter the new spaces of the conversation.

- *Imagining how psychological noise might affect your ability to understand and interpret the other person's questions, answers, and intentions.* For example, if you are interviewing a school board candidate whose positions you personally abhor, prepare yourself to give every benefit of the doubt to your interviewee. Otherwise, your own feelings could function as unwanted noise. On the other hand, if you're the interviewee and your experience tells you that this reporter has written unflattering stories before, remind yourself that this interview is a fresh opportunity to discuss your views.

- *Anticipating possible sources of physiological noise in the interview situation and, if necessary, attempting to alter those conditions or change the interview site.* For example, if you know a professor is distracted and busy dealing with student questions right after a class, you might want to wait until her more leisurely office hours to ask about her new assignment as advisor to the school newspaper. Or if you're being interviewed by a questioner who is not sufficiently aware of how complex your responses might be, you'd be wise to suggest rescheduling the meeting for a time when you'll be able to "stretch out" your ideas more effectively.

- *Predicting the specialized kinds of language or jargon the interview partner is likely to use and preparing yourself to "enter" the new vocabulary readily or explain your own vocabulary succinctly.* For example, if a popular professor has been denied *tenure* (a status attained by faculty who are no longer on probation and can't be terminated without extreme cause), an interviewer would not want to ask the dean about the proceedings without first reviewing the definition of tenure and the institution's particular guidelines; and the dean would want to anticipate the possible misunderstandings of tenure outside academic life.

- *Clarifying the major goals of the interview.* For example, if both partners know that a series of interviews is planned, they may find a somewhat unfocused and even meandering first conversation to be satisfying in setting the stage and introducing the participants to each other. That same conversation could be seen as a waste of time if one or both have not thought carefully beforehand about their listening goals.

One informal way to do a listening self-assessment is to take the following exam, adapted from an exercise in *Effective Listening* (Steil, Barker, & Watson, 1983, pp. xi–xii). (See the "Trying Out Your Skills" box at the end of the chapter for answers.)

Listening Beliefs Quiz

1. Speaking is a more important process than listening. T ____ F ____

2. Listening is relatively easy to do, because it is so automatic in human communication. T ____ F ____

3. When people hear something well, they can be said to be listening. T ____ F ____

4. When something is important, people can force themselves to listen well. T ____ F ____

5. Speakers are primarily responsible for ensuring successful communication. T ____ F ____

6. Listening is a natural process, so academic training in it is likely to make people too self-conscious. T ____ F ____

7. Listening competence is developmental, so people tend to become better listeners as they get older. T ____ F ____

8. Listening and reading are basically the same process. T ____ F ____

9. Listening is a process of paying attention to the words of speakers. T ____ F ____

10. People who remember things well are good listeners. T ____ F ____

never verbalized. Our expectations for listening and speech may create the very conditions under which people say more things, or fewer things, or different things, or have different feelings about the interaction.

If you decide to listen to others as if they are interesting, or attractive, or important, or insightful, they are more likely to rise to those expectations. Both of you are much more likely to regard the interchange as important and much more likely to experience satisfying results.

Types of Listening

Clearly, listening at some level occurs almost constantly when people are together in social situations. Humans are meaning-making creatures who are constantly trying to use the speech of others to interpret what is going on, what others might mean, what they might want to say but are unable to say. Yet this meaning-making occurs in very different ways in different contexts. Effective interviewers and interviewees know they must vary their strategies from context to context not only to accomplish their own goals but also to allow their partners to develop their own intended meanings appropriately.

Andrew Wolvin and Carolyn Coakley (1996) identify several basic forms of listening (see Box 3.3). Although their typology is not specifically applied to interviewing, it is well suited for interview partners who want to analyze and diagnose their own behavior. Whether they find themselves primarily asking questions or answering them, communicators must anticipate themselves as listeners accomplishing various tasks. At times a listener's goal is to pay careful attention to distinguish one type of message from another or, perhaps, distinguish sincerity from deceit in speakers. Wolvin and Coakley call this **discriminative listening** because the listener discriminates among different types and subtleties of messages. At times, in a process called **comprehensive listening,** a listener wants to ensure that he or she "gets it"—understands and processes as many messages as possible according to a speaker's intention. On other occasions, listeners must use their relational skills to help the speaker accomplish his or her own goals by supportive listening styles; this is **therapeutic listening.** Listeners also often find themselves responsible for judging the worth of communication and evaluating—perhaps for a distant audience—the quality of messages through a process known as **critical listening.** Finally, in **appreciative listening,** people listen simply to appreciate the particularly interesting, creative, or aesthetic features of a message. We'll consider each type of listening from the standpoint of interview participants.

Discriminative Listening

Discriminative listening is the most basic type of listening because through it the interviewer or interviewee gains access to the range of messages the other has to offer. Moreover, the good discriminative listener can also then become a good listener in the comprehensive, therapeutic, critical, and appreciative modes. Interviewers who are not effective at distinguishing messages carefully will be unsure about what they are hearing, about what notes to take, about what to remember; and they won't have the raw materials to accomplish any more sophisticated listening tasks. Interviewees deficient at discriminative listening will find it difficult to understand the inquiries of their interviewers and likely will miss such things as the subtle vocal cues by which interviewers often signal their intentions.

Any interaction involves a variety of skills. Yet in discussing each of the listening types, it may be useful to identify and stress—in each type—two basic skills interviewers and interviewees should build to monitor and improve their effectiveness. Although we use Wolvin and Coakley's overall typology of listening, the labels we use here are not necessarily theirs. In addition, such a brief chapter cannot present the full richness of the issues involved in interpersonal listening skills. We encourage you to look into other sources, such as Wolvin and Coakley (1996), Purdy and Borisoff (1997), Brownell (1996), Roach and Wyatt (1988), and Stiel, Barker, and Watson (1983), for more detail.

The key skills of discriminative listening are **recognition skills** (attentiveness to verbal, vocal, and behavioral cues of meaning) and **regulation skills** (sensitivity to cues that guide

BOX 3.3   REMINDERS

Wolvin and Coakley's Types of Listening

- *Discriminative listening:* Listening to discriminate among, or distinguish, different auditory stimuli, ideas, and meanings. *Discrimination* in this sense is a positive phenomenon that allows more sophisticated listening tasks to be conducted on the basis of solid information.

- *Comprehensive listening:* Listening to *comprehend* by attempting to match one's understanding of a message with the intention of the speaker. The goals of comprehensive listening are accurate reception and retention of information.

- *Therapeutic listening:* Listening to "provide a troubled speaker with the opportunity to talk through a problem" (p. 277). Effective therapeutic listening encourages the speaker to continue talking in an atmosphere of helpful and suppor-

tive communication. Such listening usually does not focus on evaluation of the person, nor does it concentrate on offering advice or disagreement.

- *Critical listening:* Listening to evaluate the quality or importance of messages, perhaps by applying criteria while listening. By using critical listening skills, listeners can keep themselves from being victimized by persuasive or potentially manipulative messages.

- *Appreciative listening:* Listening to "obtain sensory stimulation or enjoyment through the works and experiences of others" (p. 377). In this form, the listener engages in the experience for its own sake, not usually to lead to some other instrumental goal.

Source: Wolvin & Coakley, 1996

the process). Examples of recognition skills include your familiarity with the language used by your partner, recognition of how the partner signals irony or sarcasm or kidding by tone of voice, understanding how verbal context can affect which meaning of a word is actually intended, and so forth. Simply put, a listener has to recognize that there is something to which he or she needs access and must be willing and able to catch on at some level, even if it's impossible to get everything right. Examples of regulation skills include your ability to recognize—and act on—the nonverbal cues governing how conversational turn taking is managed (for example, How do you know it's your turn to speak? How do you know when you've spoken too long? How do you know when it's OK to overlap another's speech and not have it interpreted as an interruption?).

Comprehensive Listening

A prime goal of information-gathering interviewers, such as those doing detective work or investigative journalism, effective comprehensive listening emphasizes the accurate reception of messages and the accurate recall of the responses given by interviewees. Clearly, too, it is the responsibility of the interviewee to comprehend the full implications of questions and issues brought up in the interview, because he or she must decide how to address each question. Although the ability to remember and reconsider the results of the interview usually is more crucial for interviewers, interviewees will also profit by an accurate memory and comprehensive understanding of the content of the interview—when quotations are remembered differently by each party, for example.

Trying Out Your Skills

Read the following diagnostic interview between doctor and patient and identify the times when recognition skills and regulation skills are used effectively or could have been used more effectively.

PATIENT: Hello (fidgeting, looking away).

DOCTOR: How are you? It's been a long time since I've seen you. I guess that's a good thing, huh? You must have been healthy. What brings you in today? What a great day!

P: Hi, Doctor Payne. I'm here because of my leg. It's a rash or something, but I can't figure out why it begins to get sensitive in the afternoons. By evening it hurts so much that I have to sit down.

D: Hmmm. How long have you had it?

P: (Fidgeting) I don't remember. Long time. I thought it would go away, but it never did.

D: You said it was a rash "or something." You think it's not like the rash you had on your arm last year? Let's have a look (rolling up leg of jeans).

P: The arm rash went away in a week or so. Besides, it didn't swell up like this.

D: Ah . . . swelling, too? How much?

P: Some. It's not swollen now, much. There are times when it is and times when it isn't. Gets redder, then less red, then real red again, then . . .

D: (Interrupting) How much swelling is "some"? Enough to keep you from your evening jog? I used to see you chugging down Elm Street. Have you changed your route?

P: Actually, no. Haven't been running since mid-March. Maybe that was when the swelling started. Really, Doctor Payne, I don't know what to think. This isn't just a rash, is it? I'm scared.

D: I know you are. I'll bet it swells quite a bit. How much?

The key skills of comprehensive listening are **full mental focus**, which means being able to capitalize on "listening spare time" (taking advantage of the difference between the rate of speech and the rate of thought), and **paraphrasing** (repeating the speaker's ideas and facts in your own words to verify that you've heard them accurately. (An allied skill, recording details of the interview, is discussed in Chapter 5.) Many technically capable interview participants who know how to ask and answer questions glibly find themselves curiously bogged down in details, or unable to make smooth transitions between points, or unable to recognize internal contradictions in the speaker's assertions. With practice, your listening spare time will allow you to listen well to others while you engage in an active inner dialogue about the implications of the conversation. The most rapid speaker you know, for example, probably speaks no faster than 180 words per minute in everyday conversation, and most of us speak 125–150 words per minute. Yet studies of compressed speech, in which talk is electronically "squished" by eliminating silences without changing vocal pitch, show that most people can understand speech at twice the normal rate without sacrificing comprehension. Most texts on listening describe how such resulting spare time allows listeners to compare, analyze, add examples, paraphrase, and in a variety of other ways augment the speaker's content. Of course, paraphrasing is not only an inner skill but also an interpersonal method of checking the accuracy of a listener's perception. Listeners should develop the habit of reflecting or paraphrasing significant aspects of the message smoothly back: "Your office will cut back workers by 50 percent, you say?" Or, "You said you have no plans to run for Congress; I take this to mean you will not campaign under any circumstances?"

Therapeutic Listening

Far from being the exclusive province of psychiatrists, therapists, and counselors, therapeutic listening can occur in any context where the listener takes on the prime responsibility for helping the speaker meet his or her own goals, disclose difficult or personally involving material, solve interpersonal problems, or establish emotional equilibrium. Therapeutic listening can also occur when it is to a speaker's or interviewee's advantage to be understood as fully on several rational or emotional levels at the same time; in other words, it is a style of listening that offers innumerable advantages for many complex interview situations. Many listeners who are especially effective at discriminative or comprehensive listening are not necessarily good at therapeutic listening because, unlike discriminative or comprehensive listening, a therapeutic style must be—at least to some extent—demonstrable externally. That is, the person being listened to must see and hear that they are being supported, that their partner's listening is, in fact, taking place. They must not only *be* understood but also must *feel* understood.

The key skills of therapeutic listening are emotional sensitivity and nonjudgmental response. **Emotional sensitivity** is an ability to infer, from the words and behaviors a speaker displays, the emotional state of mind that lies behind the overt messages. There are few if any guarantees or precise measures that the listener can rely on in accomplishing this task, but some guidelines within a culture can help. For example, consider your past experiences with your own nervousness and with nervous people. The outward signs of the inner feelings, while not inevitable, are at least common enough to allow generalizations. Nervous people tend to speak faster, make verbal slips, fidget, perspire, suffer from dry mouth, and find it hard to maintain eye contact with conversation partners. You can use such information directly in diagnosing how to help an interviewee who is going through personal turmoil. Knowledge about others and what they are feeling will always be a matter of educated guesswork. Still, the observant and sensitive listener will be better able to infer what it is like to live life from the other person's perspective. Professionals in the helping professions call this kind of insight empathy, a concept we discussed in Chapter 2.

Similarly, a listener using **nonjudgmental response** avoids attacking or judging the essential humanity of the other person, even when the other person's actions might be negative. Further, the nonjudgmental listener not only listens more supportively but also, in responding, speaks for herself or himself instead of putting words or ideas into the other's mouth. For example, instead of the **you-messages** typical of blaming responses ("You should have taken more control over your life years ago"; "You made your wife unhappy"), the nonjudgmental response opens the door for more speech, and more expansive explanation, by supplying an **I-message:** "I'm unsure of your point about your home situation" or even, "I don't know why, but I'm feeling sad hearing this." Whereas judgment tends to increase defensiveness and shut off disclosure from conversational partners (Gibb, 1961), I-messages—if they don't inappropriately shift the spotlight to the listener—tend to encourage more verbal exploration. It may seem paradoxical that a brief message about the listener's personal response can keep the spotlight on a speaker, but it appears that speakers feel safe when confronted with personalized, yet nonjudgmental, listening. Therefore, it is no accident that this form of listening is often found in those who do anthropological research or who facilitate cross-cultural communication in groups and organizational training programs (see Box 3.4).

Critical Listening

Interviews often are for the express purpose of selecting which persons or messages are the most important or valuable in meeting the needs of the listener. In buying a car, for example, shoppers typically ask a series of questions to determine the willingness of the dealership to service and stand behind its product. Few salespersons or dealers will express any reservations whatsoever about their company's ability to service automobiles or treat customers fairly, but experience shows that not all dealerships are alike. Critical listening provides answers to these questions: How do I use interview information to make the right decisions? How do I keep from being misled or deceived by others, or simply victimized by my own temptations?

The key skills of critical listening are testing and clarification. **Testing** skills involve a constant willingness to make comparisons (using your listening spare time) between (1) what you're hearing and what you've known before to be true, (2) what you're hearing and fallacies of reasoning (see Box 3.5), or (3) what you're hearing and previously formulated criteria for making certain decisions (such as which applicant to hire, which candidate to vote for, which lawn mower to buy).

In certain cases, interviewers and interviewees must be willing to discuss openly the problems exposed by tests of critical listening. Some journalistic interviews, for example, are purposefully confrontational; the reporter might confront the school board president about the *ad hominem* attack on her opponent or the inconsistency between her recent reference to budget cuts and the budget flexibility she touted just last spring. Often, however, as in selection interviews, both parties are expected to leave the encounter politely pretending that they had not been engaged in intensive critical listening designed to assess the suitability of the applicant for the job or, conversely, the company's culture and reward system for the applicant. In no sense does this kind of strategic avoidance of topics

BOX 3.4   INTERVIEWERS IN ACTION

Elizabeth Bird

Interviewers in professional contexts sometimes fail to appreciate or employ therapeutic listening because they believe they must be more direct, and, after all, they aren't therapists or counselors. They overlook, however, a potentially significant opportunity to understand the worlds in which those they interview live. Journalists, we can report from years of firsthand experience, can be especially disdainful of therapeutic-type methods. We will consider specific approaches to journalistic interviewing in a later chapter. Here, however, consider the experience of anthropologist and journalist Elizabeth Bird, who has found empathic listening very practical:

"... The empathetic approach may in the end be more effective than the confrontational approach in reading a deeper understanding, and professional journalists may be guilty of fostering the idea that only adversarial, '60 Minutes' style reporting is really effective in discovering the 'truth.' I have certainly been struck by the pervasiveness of this attitude among my journalism students, eager as they are to rush out into the 'real world' and expose evil. Many seem reluctant to accept the possibility that a deeper understanding could result from building relationships with sources, rather than setting out to expose them.

"In discussing this point in class, I use my own experience, including one instance in which I had the opportunity to interview a local Ku Klux Klan leader. I found the use of a wide-ranging, non-confrontational approach to be extremely effective in encouraging the source to expand his ideas, and even to seek me out for further interviews when he recalled other topics he wished to develop. The final picture that emerged was more complete and informative than would have been painted using an adversarial approach. It was certainly more useful than a quick round-up of phone calls to local official sources asking standard questions on Klan activity.

"The problem of over-identification with sources is shared by journalists and anthropologists. Nevertheless, while it is not an easily resolved problem, its existence is not enough for journalists to reject the deeper understanding that [such anthropological approaches as empathy] may offer."

Source: Bird, 1987, p. 9

invalidate the importance of listening critically. Participants still need and must use the insight gained from such tests in making decisions based on the interview.

The second major skill of critical listening, clarification, comes in handy when you suspect you may disagree with the other person, but you aren't sure. **Clarification** is similar to the skill of paraphrasing, described earlier in the chapter, but clarifying is more proactive. Listeners cannot evaluate the worth of a course of action, a candidate, or a product without ensuring that the speaker's definitions of claims and future benefits match the listener's definitions. An interviewer who is a critical listener will ask a job applicant, for

BOX 3.5   R E M I N D E R S

Listening for Potential Lapses in Reasoning

Remember that a small flaw in logic does not necessarily invalidate a person's entire argument or point, and be generous enough to recognize that your estimate of the quality of someone else's reasoning might be due to your own idiosyncratic or flawed perception or analysis. However, prepare yourself to recognize the following types of faulty reasoning and fallacies you're likely to encounter in interviews.

- *Hasty generalization:* The speaker seems to reason that a whole class or group of things will necessarily exhibit a characteristic observed in a single instance or a few examples. ("I was treated very rudely at MagicMart this afternoon; they're always so obnoxious there.")

- *Ad misericordium:* Instead of demonstrating why a given action should be taken, the speaker appeals to pity, sympathy, or some other strong emotional attachment of listeners to the speaker's topic. ("I deserved that higher grade; even though the teacher was against me, I worked harder than anyone in that class. It's not fair.")

- *Ad hominem:* The speaker attacks the person who advocates an idea rather than refuting the idea itself. ("My opponent wants to represent you in the Senate in debating our country's social policies. Yet he's already been divorced twice, and his wife was just arrested for drunk driving. You can see where his values are. Vote against him.")

- *Tautological reasoning:* The speaker argues in a circle. ("I'm against extending equal legal rights to gay people." [Why?] "Because the Church says homosexuality is wrong." [Why does it say that?] "Because so many people regard it as wrong, and the Church guides people in decisions of right and wrong.")

- *Post hoc, ergo propter hoc:* The speaker argues that conditions that came after an event were actually caused by the event when there may have been no cause-and-effect relationship whatsoever. ("See what confidence we have in the president? Right after the state of the union speech, unemployment fell by some 15 percent!")

- *Non sequitur:* The speaker reasons in a way that the conclusion does not follow from the premises on which it is supposedly based, such as suggesting that one of two unrelated things automatically explains the other. (Sarcastically: "You're not interested in computers? Well, of course, you're from that technologically sophisticated state of Iowa!")

- *Ad populum:* The speaker suggests that because many people like something or do something, it must be a good thing. ("I must be doing a good job as mayor after all; my poll numbers are way up.")

- *Ad novarum:* The speaker suggests that a policy, issue, person, or thing is better just because it is newer than its alternatives. ("Why would you want to preserve the old post office building downtown when you could have a gleaming new metal and glass showplace in the county?")

example, to define what a previous job title of "Office Assignments Coordinator" means. The applicant in the same situation will be sure to get a clear definition of what the personnel manager calls the organization's "state-of-the-art benefits package." Clarification can come from direct questions. ("What do you mean by 'assignments coordinator'? Were you responsible for assigning duties, or did a supervisor ask you to check up on other people's projects?") Or the strategy might be less direct. ("I assume from your description that your benefits package is at least equivalent to Gomez & Martino's benefits on the health insurance, vacation and leave package, and retirement fronts.") What you want as a critical listener is not only to get raw information but also to build a picture or pattern of information upon which to base a decision.

Appreciative Listening

Most people do not participate in interviews to exercise their skills in appreciative listening; interviewing is usually more instrumental than that. Interviewers and interviewees generally have a goal in mind. Appreciative listening emphasizes a relatively goal-free enjoyment of the beauty of a message, such as when a listener can acknowledge and be inspired by the creativity of planning and execution that goes into a symphony performance or an intricate sax solo in an improvisational jazz group. Such appreciations enhance the experience, but they hardly seem to be at the core of listening within face-to-face interviews. You might, however, consider the ability to be transported by the beauty of improvisation especially helpful in interviewing, for what else is effective interviewing but improvisational verbal jazz, a collaborative performance that has essentially artistic elements as well as technical or instrumental goals?

The key skills of appreciative listening are clearing and concentration. Of the five listening types, interviewers are probably least likely to discover practical applications for appreciative listening. Yet many enjoy the artistic challenge of interviewing and look forward to interviewing because they are able to give themselves completely to the experience. Larry King (1989), who interviews celebrities on television and radio, finds that his time on the air with an interviewee is the time of least pressure in his day, because "every day of my life, from Monday to Friday, I meet the most interesting people in the world—writers, politicians, film directors, historians, surgeons, lawyers, athletes, comedians, singers, psychiatrists—and ask them anything I want. And I get paid for it" (p. 5). Such interviewers are probably able to immerse themselves in their work completely because of two interrelated skills: clearing and concentration.

By **clearing,** we refer to the psychological and physiological process of eliminating extraneous objects of attention, so you can participate without distraction. Sir Yehudi Menuhin (1992), the renowned violinist and conductor, once wrote, "Until we can create a still centre within ourselves we will be unable to attune the 'third ear' to the messages that are broadcast to us, loud and clear for the most part, but rendered futile due to our incapacity to listen" (p. 7). Some people clear themselves by clearing their environments and situations of stimuli that act as psychological noise. Some audiophiles will never put on a CD of a symphony, a jazz group, or a singer as background music, but instead will listen only when they can sit directly between the speakers, preferably in the dark or with their eyes closed, and give all their attention to the music. Many interviewers, too, prefer a nearly isolated environment for the occasion, in which interruptions will not detract from the miniature world cocreated by the participants. Other communicators, before an important event like an interview, will clear their minds by physiological techniques such as breathing and centering exercises, guided imagery, or creative visualization. Such exercises can combat nervousness and at the same time create a receptive psychological space for new insights.

By **concentration,** we refer to a listener's ongoing ability to create a focal awareness on the messages and ideas that are most important to the communication while filtering out or diminishing the effects of distractions by the skill of clearing. For most of us, the process of concentrating is not an automatic state of interest that maintains itself in some stable or predictable way; rather, it is a constant process of perceptual adjustment and change by which we constantly remind ourselves of the reasons for listening and the centrality of the message(s) for us. In a sense, appreciative listening comes from concentration that is persistently achieved and reachieved from moment to moment. This is why, after following closely a long speech or lecture by one of your favorite politicians or professors on one of your favorite subjects, you are not relaxed but are in some ways tired. You may be energized, too, and excited, but your involvement and appreciation have been deep enough that you've participated in the talk, not just received it passively.

Responsive and Active Listening

Many skills of listening and attitudes about listening can be helpful to those in interview situations, but is there one essential habit of listening for interviewers and interviewees? The answer, we believe, is yes. If, in a workshop that brought together interviewees and interviewers from all walks of life, we only had thirty minutes to practice an activity, that activity would be what Carl Rogers and Richard Farson (1957) call **active listening:** the willingness on the part of the listener to test his or her emerging interpretations by verbalizing them, by reflecting essential elements back to the speaker, and when necessary, by going beyond what the speaker has said in order to verbalize inferences about additional meanings that might motivate the other's words.

Active listening can take different forms in different contexts, but the general pattern usually resembles one or more of the following comments:

"Your brother let you all down" (your response after your partner complains about her brother not doing his part in supporting the family). Or, "You really want the new highway as a first priority" (a reporter's response after the mayor in a press conference stresses how important it would be to redesignate a new business route for the city's major highway). These are *paraphrases* or **mirror responses.** Their use is an attempt to verify for the speaker that he or she has been heard accurately.

"Let me see. What seems to be bothering you is . . ." or, "Although you haven't said so directly, you seem to emphasize the values of a public school education over a private school experience. Is that true?" These are **content inference responses.** They attempt to show the speaker not only that he or she has been heard but also that the listener has attempted to understand something beyond the overt or obvious message.

"When you speak about your family, I hear a lot of anger and your body tightens up." This is a verbalized inference that notes a behavioral or nonverbal interpretation rather than focusing directly on content. Such responses are termed **affective/behavioral inference responses.**

Note that not all of these responses are questions; nor is it necessary that the interviewer's inferences be correct. An inference, after all, is an educated guess. Good listeners must be willing to be wrong if high-quality communication is their goal. A valuable service is still performed if the active listener is corrected by the speaker (for example, "No, that wasn't my point at all"); both parties then know what kind of conversational work must be done to repair the previous misunderstanding. This is a positive outcome, not a failure. You're not trying to read the mind of the speaker; instead, you're trying to make sure the speaker doesn't have to read yours in order to know the quality of listening that is developing.

Nor is active listening only the province of interviewers. Savvy interviewees know that they often must say things like, "I want to be sure to answer the question you're most interested in. I think you mean to ask me . . ." or, "When you ask about 'health-care providers,' I think you're interested in my opinion about hospital and clinic doctors and nurses. But you may mean administrators, too. Do you mean both?" Although the simplest level of active listening is the direct mirroring or basic paraphrase of the other's actual words, most active listening involves more educated guesses and often a demonstration of the state of the listener's interpretation.

Active listening depends upon the basic assumption that people disclose more and are more comfortable disclosing when they feel understood. They are apt to feel understood when the listener demonstrates actively and openly the quality of listening. If you are a tax lawyer, for example, explaining the intricacies of corporate taxes, you might use gross generalities and clichéd metaphors with your interviewer, until, that is, your listener convinces you through active listening that she or he is following your explanation well and can handle more detail. Then and only then will you be willing to explain the more knotty concepts of internal corporate decision making. Of course, active listening doesn't guarantee understanding. It only sets the stage for increased levels of trust and accuracy in listening to develop. Active listening skills also serve as excellent follow-up questions or probes in most interviews, as you'll see in several other chapters, including those on questioning, journalistic interviews, and counseling interviews.

 BEYOND THE BASICS

Deeper Issues of Listening

The study of listening and how to improve listening is a burgeoning area within the communication research tradition, and the private sector increasingly is realizing the importance of such research and applying its results (Purdy & Borisoff, 1997). Like any research area, its complexity is daunting; the sophistication of what specialists know about

Trying Out Your Skills

An activity teachers call "listening triads" is helpful for practicing active listening skills. You can do the experiment with two partners by yourselves, or your teacher may want the class to try it during a class session.

1. Think of an emotionally involving experience that you're willing to tell as a story to an acquaintance or stranger—not one that is too private or would embarrass someone else in your life (examples: your anger when you were treated badly at the bookstore the other day; your disappointment and sadness when your best friend moved away; your joy when you found out you received a scholarship).

2. Divide your available time into three equal parts. (The minimum time for the exercise to work well is thirty minutes; forty-five minutes or more will be better.)

3. For each segment of time, decide on three different roles: speaker, listener, and monitor. The speaker will tell the story, the listener will practice active listening, and the monitor will not participate except to discuss (after the conversation) the effects of the active listening on the story. The monitor should take notes to highlight especially striking instances of active listen-

ing or places where it could have been used more effectively.

4. The basic rule of the exercise is that the listener cannot comment on, add to, or shift the content of the story until the conversation is over. During the conversation, he or she can only use active listening responses such as paraphrasing, content inference, or affective/behavioral inference.

5. After the conversation (which could last five or ten minutes), the monitor should discuss the listener's strengths and how the story was affected.

Note: Don't expect a full conversation emphasizing active listening to sound entirely natural or normal. One problem of interviewing—and everyday conversations—is that listeners often don't care enough to ensure that they understand fully, so this exercise might seem artificial at first for participants. Unfortunately, it's often experienced as abnormal for listeners to be fully present for a speaker's story. However, the proof is in the results: did the story emerge with more detail, more vivid detail, and more comprehension? Keep in mind that you are practicing a skill so that you can choose to use it more naturally when it's appropriate.

---

listening is impossible to summarize in a brief chapter. So far, we've only scratched the surface of what this topic means for professional interviewers and interviewees. Among the deeper issues of listening, we've chosen two especially interesting ones for more intensive review: the literature showing that effective listening within any culture carries certain behavioral expectations, and the literature showing how practical some philosophical approaches to listening can be.

Listening is a fundamentally cognitive, psychological process. But as you will see consistently in the chapters of Part 2—where we explore interviewing skills relevant to various professional contexts—the behavior of listeners, as perceived by speakers, appears to be an integral part of the process. Another way of suggesting this is to observe that a systematic look at effective listening reveals it is not only a cognitive process occurring inside someone's head, but it also has a certain appearance and can be recognized from the outside. At least, speakers believe they know when they're being listened to, and they adjust their speech accordingly. To understand listening in this way, consider two research traditions within communication—research into nonverbal immediacy and research into interpersonal confirmation/disconfirmation.

Immediacy

Albert Mehrabian's (1981) **immediacy theory** investigated how face-to-face communication tends to be experienced as successful and satisfying when participants engage in behaviors that increase two basic factors—perceived *directness* and perceived *intensity*. To grasp the concept, think of immediacy as something "im-mediate." That is, think of "media" as channels that are placed between people, and remember that "mediators" are third parties who attempt to negotiate interests between primary communicators. With these meanings in mind, think of "im-mediacy" as connoting the absence of needing such intermediaries. Mehrabian found communication that increases immediacy reduces distance and barriers for people in order to increase their presence for each other.

Although immediacy can be verbal as well as nonverbal ("the death of a parent is upsetting to anyone" is less immediate than "your father's death has naturally upset you, LaVerne"), many relationship-defining moments occur at times when someone nonverbally reduces the distance between self and other. One partner might increase eye gaze or eye contact, remove a barrier, lean toward the other to indicate interest or fascination with the topic of conversation, reach out to touch the other person appropriately (as when consoling someone after the passing of a family member), or in any number of ways make it clear that the speaker is the unique and valuable person to whom the listener wants to give attention and energy.

Researchers of communication rules (Pearce & Cronen, 1980; Shimanoff, 1980; Smith, 1984) and other interpersonal communication issues have provided good clues about how interviewers and interviewees demonstrate their listening nonverbally. Communication rules, as you've discovered, are those implicit social agreements that tell communicators what behaviors are "obligated, preferred, or prohibited in certain contexts" (Shimanoff, 1980, p. 57). Communicators usually cannot articulate the rules that guide how they talk in their own cultures and subcultures in everyday life, because the rules are rarely taught explicitly. They are usually learned informally in the course of mundane and even trivial interaction with others. For example, you've probably never had a class in how to know when someone is interested in your stories, but you would typically be irritated when, during an emotional account of your argument with your supervisor, a listener begins to watch television. Although it's technically possible for the listener to track much of your story, listeners to important messages—at least in general North American culture—are expected not just to give attention but to show attention overtly.

Unfortunately, because interviewing is a specialized task that many people don't do every day, because many beginning interviewers and interviewees are naturally nervous, and because many interviews involve touchy topics or high-prestige partners, people may

BOX 3.6   **R E M I N D E R S**

Immediacy Behaviors Associated with Listening

- *Eye contact:* Speakers expect that listeners will look at them—not all the time, as in staring, but at especially important moments in the development of ideas or when emotional topics are discussed.

- *Appropriate distance:* Speakers expect that listeners will neither be too distant nor too close considering the topic and context at hand. Anthropologist Edward Hall's (1966) research into *proxemics* (the study of how people send messages by their choice of distance in communication) shows that most conversations about nonintimate social topics occur in a zone from about four feet to about twelve feet. Obviously, a generalized set of expectations guides how far apart people are as they communicate.

- *Forward lean:* Speakers tend to associate an inclined posture, especially when seated, with interest and involvement in listening. This does not mean listeners get sore backs from constant leaning, but the leaning moments are appropriately matched with the times speakers emphasize especially important meanings.

- *Nodding and other interest indicators:* Speakers tend to assume that listeners who are "connected" in conversations will be nodding up and down (as opposed to nodding off) as a nonverbal signal affirming the reception of verbal messages. This behavior is often coupled with vocal encouragements such as, "Uh-huh" or, "Hmmm," which indicate, "I'm still with you" to speakers. Although we also nod when agreeing with a speaker, most head bobbing in conversation is not experienced as agreement as much as simple recognition.

- *Removal of barriers:* Speakers expect that serious listeners will introduce no unnecessary barriers between them. Thus, listeners should ask themselves what behaviors or artifacts could be interpreted by the other person as a barrier. Dark glasses, large notebooks, baseball caps with low brims, and large tape recorders placed directly between interviewer and interviewee could all impede communication through introducing artificial barriers. Notice that we do not mean to judge whether someone has the right to wear sunglasses, for example. You may have the right to do a lot of things and it might be unfair for the other person to judge you for them, but that doesn't change the fact that when communication rules are violated, efficiency and satisfaction suffer.

---

lose sight of things they do naturally in other situations. Because rules might be broken or ignored inadvertently under such circumstances, interview participants should probably train themselves to build immediacy messages into their listening behavior (see Box 3.6).

Confirmation

Being aware of immediacy rules becomes important for both interviewers and interviewees because of people's desire to be confirmed. In communication, **confirmation theory** (Cissna & Keating, 1979; Cissna & Sieberg, 1981) examines the interactions in which people experience acknowledgment and recognition by others—both verbally and nonverbally—and the ways our messages encourage or discourage such reactions in others. To think about confirmation concretely, consider what it's like to walk into a small party at someone's home and have not just your host but a couple of other people come up to you

Watch a videotape of yourself in an interview situation, either as interviewer or interviewee. Using the immediacy behaviors described in Box 3.6, rate yourself from one to ten on each behavioral area. Decide on one thing in each area you will either be sure to do again or be sure to do differently next time you interview someone.

to start conversations. Whether they like you or not, whether you all agree about the topics of conversation or not, the fact remains you are noticed and you make a difference in the gathering. Confirmation of this sort is widely thought to be important in establishing people's self-esteem and, at deeper levels, their very identities and concepts of self.

Conversely, imagine walking into the party and, although people might notice the fact of your entrance, no one makes eye contact to acknowledge or welcome your presence, no one makes any effort to start a conversation, and everyone remains busily engaged in tasks that do not include you. This unfortunate but fairly common (at least for some) experience is a disconfirming one. But interpersonal disconfirmation extends beyond not being noticed to a variety of other messages with which we diminish each other. Confirmation researchers analyze three general categories of disconfirmations: indifferent responses, impervious responses, and disqualifying responses (Cissna & Sieberg, 1981). For purposes of illustration, first examine the major forms of disconfirmation from an interviewer's standpoint; then we will specify positive suggestions for how any interview participant can increase confirmation (see Box 3.7).

- **Indifferent responses:** When interviewers are *indifferent,* they are suggesting that the interviewee, for all practical purposes, either isn't fully present or isn't worth communicating with. Common examples of indifferent responses are lack of eye contact, rapid cutting off of the interview without explanation, not calling back to verify information after promising to do so, and monotonic vocal style indicating the interviewer is bored.

- **Impervious responses:** When interviewers are *impervious,* they may acknowledge presence and communication but fail to perceive interviewees accurately or carefully. This can take the form of implying the speaker doesn't know his or her own mind as well as the interviewer does. Common examples of impervious responses are statements like, "You don't really mean that" or, "I know you're going to come out of this a better person" when the interviewee has suggested otherwise—some listeners' habit of creating a false front for the interviewee and then speaking only to that role or front, or constantly reinterpreting the other's stated experience. (Understanding these potential problems should remind interviewers of some dangers of so-called active listening and paraphrasing styles. These skills are effective only when they do not intrude upon the respondents' speech or seem to be putting words in their mouths.)

BOX 3.7   REMINDERS

Confirmation in Interviews

Interviewers and interviewees should not just avoid indifference, imperviousness, and disqualification. Stated more positively, they should exhibit *recognition, acknowledgment,* and *endorsement* in their messages. In effect, these approaches say to your partner, "I'm fully present with you," "I'm trying to see and hear you accurately," and "I'm accepting you as you are," respectively (Cissna & Sieberg, 1981). These behaviors can be described in clusters that work together to reinforce these confirming relational messages.

- **Recognition cluster:** "I'm with you." Direct engagement in a clearly defined space and time; nonverbal behaviors suggesting focused attention and increased immediacy (eye contact, inclusive distance and posture, and so on).

- **Acknowledgment cluster:** "I see you and hear you." Willingness to follow the train of thought and remain engaged; direct response to the other's topics and roles whether that response is agreement or disagreement.

- **Endorsement cluster:** "I accept you." Statements and behaviors that suggest acceptance of the other person's messages as important or OK ("I see what you mean," "That's a point I hadn't considered," various kinds of vocal and visual "encouragers," such as "Uh-huh," or nodding when important points are made).

- **Disqualifying responses:** When interviewers are *disqualifying,* they adopt an attitude of dismissing, blaming, or disparaging the other person, or reacting as if the topics brought up by the interviewee are trivial, irrelevant, too obvious to pay close attention to, or not as important as the contributions the interviewer could make on the same subject. Common examples of disqualifying responses are derisive sighing as the interviewee explains a point, inappropriate or unexplained interruptions or rapid topic shifts, attempts to place the interviewer's own stories in center stage and deflect attention from interviewees, and judgmental comments like, "Don't you think that's a naive thing to say?"

Being asked to participate in an interview is itself a confirming message for most people. The request itself sends a message: You're important or What you have to say is worth listening to. Yet within the interview itself, the listening styles of both interviewer and interviewee might function either to confirm or disconfirm the persons. Certainly, not all disconfirmations are intentional or evil; in fact, most are probably unplanned and rooted in interpersonal habits that the participants don't realize will be experienced as disconfirmations. Similarly, not all confirming messages are sure evidence of genuine warmth or sincerity; many people in certain roles (salesclerks, customer relations personnel, and others) have trained themselves to display such messages without necessarily experiencing warm and positive feelings about the person they're with. Both sides of this coin—the potential for unintentional disconfirmations when interviewers are trying to be sincerely helpful and the potential for phony or tactical confirmations when interviewers are trying to be deceptive—underscore the importance of videotaped analysis of your own behavior in various interviewing contexts. Many students are surprised at what they see, saying, "I didn't know I did that!"

BOX 3.8   **R E M I N D E R S**

Practical Advice from Philosophers of Listening

- Listening well is the basis for creative communication. You are not listening just for the purpose of gauging another's intentions accurately. He or she may not even have a well-formed idea that you are supposed to "get," so let listening be an experience you share.

- Listening and speaking are interdependent; if you are bored by someone's talking, consider the possibility that your listening style might have contributed to that boredom too. And consider that more *interested* listening from you can stimulate more *interesting* speech from others.

- Understand the relationship between listening and questioning. Remember, try to discover what led your interviewee to be the kind of listener she or he has become, or, if you are the interviewee, try to figure out what kinds of listening your interviewer believes is important.

- Use your listening style and even your silence to create a space for dialogue, in which something unexpected and surprising is likely to be said.

- Listen not *to* words, but *through* the words to the larger issues your interview partner must be motivated by, or to his or her existence as a person. Try not to concentrate so hard on getting the words right that you miss the real message of the other person's talk (or life). In other words, philosophers support our earlier insight that listening is much more than just hearing the words correctly.

A Brief Philosophy of Listening for Interviewers

Students taking an interviewing course probably are more concerned with being effective than with pondering deep philosophical issues. They want and need extensive practical experience and ways to speak, listen, and frame ideas more skillfully when they are face-to-face with others, and that is an understandable and appropriate concern. However, don't forget how practical your other humanities, liberal arts, or general education courses might be in helping you understand interviewing in a wider context. To illustrate, consider how the insights of several philosophical traditions provide practical reminders for how to listen in interviews (see Box 3.8).

Philosopher Martin Heidegger found listening to be a centerpiece concept in understanding what it is to be human. In an essay for his book *On the Way to Language* (1982), Heidegger wrote

> Speaking is known as the articulated vocalization of thought by means of the organs of speech. But speaking is at the same time also listening. It is the custom to put speaking and listening in opposition: one man speaks, the other listens. But listening accompanies and surrounds not only speaking such as takes place in conversation. The simultaneousness of speaking and listening has a larger meaning. Speaking is of itself a listening. Speaking is listening to the language which we speak. Thus, it is a listening not *while* but *before* we are speaking. This listening to language also comes before all other kinds of listening that we know, in a most inconspicuous manner. We do not merely speak *the* language—we speak *by way of* it. We can do so solely because we always have already listened to the language. What do we hear there? We hear language speaking. (pp. 123–124; emphasis in original)

Thus our first point toward an informal philosophy of listening is that without listening, we don't know what to say or how language can, in a manner of speaking (!), create new futures for us. When humans speak, it is from the standpoint of a *listening* consciousness; no one who fails to listen well can expect, therefore, to have much to say. What lesson in communication could ultimately be more practical than this?

It is not as easy as most people think to separate listening from speaking. Russian philosopher and literary theorist Mikhail Bakhtin stressed that human life, being dialogic, depends upon a "double-voicedness" and a "surplus of seeing" in which humans together become partners in completing each other. To Bakhtin, the concept of **surplus of seeing** means that each person sees or hears—and thus contributes—something the other partner(s) cannot. Each becomes an active "other" without whom communication would be impossible. Bakhtin (1986) writes that ". . . when the listener perceives and understands the meaning (the language meaning) of speech, he simultaneously takes an active, responsive attitude toward it. He either agrees or disagrees with it (completely or partially), augments it, applies it, prepares for its execution, and so on. And the listener adopts this responsive attitude for the entire duration of the process of listening and understanding, from the very beginning. . . . Any understanding of live speech, a live utterance, is inherently responsive" (p. 68).

Other more contemporary philosophers have contributed to a practical understanding of listening as well. Philosopher Hans-Georg Gadamer (1982) believed that listening was closely tied to the questions persons are able to ask. Every genuine question arises in listening, and each statement made in response to some question or other can be thought of as an answer. Any topic we want to study, Gadamer thought, could be thought of as a group of answers to questions that previous thinkers have asked. To understand their "texts"—their books, speeches, poems, or interviews, for example—we have to understand how they listened well enough to question the world in new ways. Therefore, if you are unsure of what Picasso's paintings mean, one way to approach them is to assume they are ways for Picasso to answer questions he had about art, the world, loving relationships, and so on. An interviewer who wants to know how General Colin Powell got interested in social action and political life could profit by considering that Powell's life has not been a random series of acts and events, but instead a series of answers to questions he has had. What are those questions, and how did he listen to them? Ask him! Interviewers may want to file away this practical insight for future reference: When perplexed about what to ask next, think of ways to ask about your interviewee's listening habits. Whom does he ask for advice? To whom does she turn for inspiration? How did an author's last book try to answer new questions raised by other authors? Try to relate such choices and habits to the essential questions in their lives.

Gadamer and the Austrian philosopher Martin Buber (1965) were both interested (although in different ways) in how listening and questioning enhanced dialogue—that experience of creative communication only possible when two or more people interact with the full expectation that they will be changed and surprised by the encounter. In dialogue the meanings emerge not from the psyches of communicators but from their meeting and their relationship.

Think back over any courses you may have had in philosophy, literary criticism, history, or other areas of the humanities that seem fairly far away from the practical concerns of business executives or other professional communicators.

- What did you learn from these courses that seemed practical to you? Make a list of practical points. If the courses seemed to empha-

size impractical topics and concerns, make a list of the points you found impractical.

- Ask two professors of philosophy or literary criticism or a similar area for an interview. Ask them only one primary question, and listen for their response: "How do you define the 'practicality' of what you teach?" See what they have to say about what is and what isn't "practical."

Two other philosophers familiar with the phenomenological tradition, Gemma Corradi Fiumara (1990) and Don Ihde (1976, 1983), have emphasized that listening creates an experienced "space" in which dialogue can develop. Listening is an immediate experience, one that potentially immerses the listener in what is happening here and what is happening now. As such, it demands the kind of total attention that makes others feel safe investing their own creative thoughts. To Fiumara (1990), "The highest function of silence is revealed in the creation of a coexistential space which permits dialogue to come along" (p. 99). Effective listeners, in other words, not only hear more in the moment of listening but also enable their conversation partners to think of newer, better, and more creative things to say. Ihde relates dialogue to a curious experience you may have had, in which you were listening so hard to something that you understood the words but couldn't connect with the meaning or the sense behind them. This often happens when people are nervous or when they're trying to understand unfamiliar topics in important situations. In explaining such a phenomenon, Ihde (1983) writes

> When I listen to an other I hear him speaking. It is not a series of phonemes or morphemes which I hear, because to "hear" these I must break up his speech. I must listen "away" from what he is saying. My experiential listening stands in the near distance of language which is at one and the same time the other speaking in his voice. I hear what he is saying, and in this listening we are both presented with the penetrating presence of voice language which is "between" and "in" both of us. (p. 153)

Phrased in terms of the practical demands of interviewing, Ihde suggests that interviewers and interviewees not listen "hard" to each other and that they not listen so carefully to the words themselves that the meaning and the person might seem harder to grasp. Instead, when possible, listen "soft" and holistically for the larger sense that is available in any conversation. Listen *through* the words to the person, to put it another way, not just *to* the words for their separate meanings.

- You are writing a personality profile of the president of your college for the student newspaper, and she has been extremely generous with the time spent with you. Not only has she granted an interview of over an hour, but she's invited you to follow her around as she moves from meeting to meeting throughout the afternoon. This is a rare opportunity.

  Around midafternoon, however, you overhear her in a phone call telling a board of trustees member that there is nothing to worry about in the school's transition from Division I sports programs to Division II, that alumni are clearly supportive of this move. But you've heard from her best friend, the academic vice president, that the president is quite concerned that annual giving from alumni might in fact diminish if there is no major conference football and basketball program to energize the campus in the public eye. Although these two perceptions aren't exactly contradictory (she may in fact believe rationally that there is "nothing to worry about" while she feels an unavoidable "concern" personally), your critical listening skills have exposed what may be a contradiction. But the matter must be handled delicately to avoid the appearance of accusing her of lying or deception. At the end of the day, President McLish gives you a chance to ask a few final questions.

  Would you use what you've learned to phrase a new question? If not, why not? If so, phrase a diplomatic but clear "active listening" response (reflecting words, paraphrasing, imagining the perspective of the other, and so on) that would give her a chance to explain her position.

- Reread Elizabeth Bird's account of how she interviewed a Ku Klux Klan member by using an empathic style of listening. She chose to get a fuller story by letting the Klan member talk out his feelings and perceptions, without stimulating judgment, argument, and disapproval from her. She decided that a confrontational approach—even though she implies she felt negative about him—would have been counterproductive.

  Consider the implications of Bird's choice. What if she had advertised her disapproval? Would that have been fair? Should she have assumed she already knew enough to disagree with the interviewee, or is that part of what the interview is for? We've suggested that empathy is not the same thing as agreement, but could it deceptively imply that the interviewer is on the side of the interviewee? Are ethical dilemmas, perhaps of misrepresentation, involved here? On another front, would you be able to put aside your personal prejudices when interviewing someone you disagree with and proceed to listen in this way—perhaps having therapeutic effects on the other person? Remember that Bird not only got a story but also, if we are to believe her account, helped the Klan member develop his ideas with more thoroughness and detail. The interview may have helped him just as much as it helped her. How would you handle such a situation?

Summary

In this chapter we've defined listening as the active process through which communicators process aural stimuli, interpret them as messages, and use them to construct meanings of speech, speakers, and contexts. Listening is a vastly more complex process than most interviewers and interviewees conceive it to be and one that, if understood fully, can enhance every other aspect of interviewing.

In our examination of basic concepts, we've shown how listening and speaking appear to regulate each other. We listen when someone else speaks to address us, but the process is not just a matter of receiving their meaning as if listeners were blank slates. Your manner as a listener often regulates how others will speak with you and what they will decide to say. Perhaps no other single insight is more valuable for, but more often overlooked by, beginning interviewers.

In this chapter, too, you have discovered how listening transcends the physiological process of hearing, how you can eliminate some of the unwanted effects of noise and distraction by preparing to listen systematically. You've learned about Wolvin and Coakley's five basic types of listening—discriminative, comprehensive, therapeutic, critical, and appreciative—and how each of them offers slightly different skills to interview communicators. And you've read about how all interviewing tasks inherently involve an active, responsive style of listening. Active listening is a basic attitude of inquiry much more than it is a group of behavioral skills or neat, tidy ways of phrasing reflective responses.

Finally, in "Beyond the Basics" we introduce, and link to listening, two topics often treated in advanced courses in interpersonal communication—rules theory and philosophy of communication. In each topic, we concentrate on the pragmatic challenges faced by interviewees and interviewers rather than on introducing the ideas in theoretically sophisticated ways. Still, students should know, we believe, that theory and practice, the abstract and the concrete, the philosophical and the everyday, are not that far apart.

The Interview Bookshelf

On a general appreciation of listening

Berendt, J.-E. (1992). *The third ear: On listening to the world* (T. Nevill, Trans.). New York: Henry Holt Owl Books.

An entertaining and literate appreciation of how listening contributes to the quality of human life. Berendt, an internationally recognized jazz critic, has integrated amazingly diverse research and stories, covering the full range of listening concerns from physiology to literature, philosophy to music, personal growth to social science.

Trying Out Your Skills: Answers and Discussion

Answers to the Listening Beliefs Quiz, from this chapter's first "Trying Out Your Skills" box: All answers are *false*. But people who believe some of them to be true are likely to have developed ineffective habits that interfere with effective interviewing.

1. Speaking and listening are interdependent processes that can't be separated.

2. Listening is neither automatic nor easy, because it is based upon a commitment to interpret messages accurately and creatively.

3. Hearing is a physiological process that is relatively automatic (see question 2), but listening involves a complex set of psychological choices.

4. When people confront important issues, they tend to fall back on their ingrained habits of listening, not shift to a higher level of functioning.

5. Speakers can't ensure good communication because listening sets the stage for speaking and more or less determines the criteria for effectiveness. Ineffective listening has discouraged many speakers from even attempting to be effective.

6. Academic courses sensitize students to the problems of listening so they can take more control over solving them. The goal is to become appropriately conscious without being overtly self-conscious.

7. Most adults simply solidify their previous listening habits instead of improving them.

8. Despite some similarities, listening is a far more complex interactional process.

9. Listening also must involve sensitivity to a speaker's nonverbal cues and the listener's own way of expressing interest.

10. Effective listeners may or may not have precise memories. Memory is a long-term or short-term process of storing and accessing information, whereas listening is an active and immediate process of obtaining or interpreting it.

On the research into listening behavior

Wolvin, A., & Coakley, C. G. (1996). *Listening* (5th ed.). Dubuque, IA: Brown & Benchmark.

This textbook combines the best features of a how-to approach with the knowledge and background research necessary for comprehensive learning. Here you'll read not only about what to do but also why it should be done and whose research says so. Probably the leading text in the field of listening.

On applying listening to professional interview settings

Purdy, M., & Borisoff, D. (Eds.). (1997). *Listening in everyday life: A personal and professional approach* (2nd ed.). Lanham, MD: University Press of America.

A collection of essays designed to show how high-quality listening is a practical requirement within a variety of professions. After several essays about the concept of listening, you will read how listening contributes to careers in education, training, service industries, helping professions, law, health-care professions, and journalism.

On listening's relevance to democratic decision making

Levin, D. M. (1989). *The listening self: Personal growth, social change, and the closure of meta-physics*. London: Routledge.

Levin's primary concern is to justify the contributions that improved listening can make to the quality of democratic decision making. Through mindful attention to listening processes, he argues, we become reciprocal beings—better able to cooperate with others and help them help us.

On placing listening and interviewing in a philosophical context

Fiumara, G. C. (1990). *The other side of language: A philosophy of listening*. London: Routledge.

One of the best syntheses of philosophical approaches to listening. Probably most readable for those with some philosophical background, Fiumara's book is nevertheless surprisingly accessible. Interviewers and interviewees will develop useful perspectives from her ability to place listening in the context of a "tradition of questioning."

References

Bakhtin, M. M. (1986). *Speech genres & other late essays* (V. W. McGee, Trans.; C. Emerson & M. Holquist, Eds.). Austin, TX: University of Texas Press.

Bird, S. E. (1987). Anthropological methods relevant for journalists. *Journalism Educator, 41,* 5–10, 33.

Brownell, J. (1996). *Listening: Attitudes, principles, and skills*. Boston: Allyn & Bacon.

Buber, M. (1965). *The knowledge of man: A philosophy of the interhuman* (M. Friedman & R. G. Smith, Trans.; M. Friedman, Ed.). New York: Harper.

Cissna, K. N. L., & Keating, S. (1979). Speech communication antecedents of perceived confirmation. *Western Journal of Speech Communication, 43,* 48–60.

Cissna, K. N. L., & Sieberg, E. (1981). Patterns of interactional confirmation and disconfirmation. In C. Wilder-Mott & J. Weakland (Eds.), *Rigor and imagination* (pp. 230–239). New York: Praeger.

Gadamer, H. G. (1982). *Truth and method* (G. Barden & J. Cumming, Trans.). New York: Crossroad.

Gibb, J. R. (1961). Defensive communication. *Journal of Communication, 11*(3), 141–148.

Fiumara, G. C. (1990). *The other side of language: A philosophy of listening* (C. Lambert, Trans.). London: Routledge.

Hall, E. T. (1966). *The hidden dimension*. Garden City, NY: Anchor.

Heidegger, M. (1982). *On the way to language* (P. D. Hertz, Trans.). New York: Perennial Library.

Ihde, D. (1976). *Listening and voice: A phenomenology of sound*. Athens, OH: Ohio University Press.

Ihde, D. (1983). *Sense and significance*. Atlantic Highlands, NJ: Humanities Press.

Killenberg, G. M., & Anderson, R. (1989). *Before the story: Interviewing and communication skills for journalists*. New York: St. Martin's Press.

King, L. (1989). *Tell it to the king*. New York: Jove.

Koile, E. (1977). *Listening as a way of becoming*. Waco, TX: Regency.

Laing, R. D. (1971). *Self and others*. New York: Pelican.

Mehrabian, A. (1981). *Silent messages: Implicit communication of emotions and attitudes* (2nd ed.). Belmont, CA: Wadsworth.

Menuhin, Y. (1992). Foreword. In J.-E. Berendt, *The third ear: On listening to the world* (p. 7). New York: Henry Holt Owl Books.

Pearce, W. B., & Cronen, V. (1980). *Communication, action, and meaning*. New York: Praeger.

Purdy, M., & Borisoff, D. (Eds.). (1997). *Listening in everyday life: A personal and professional approach* (2nd ed.). Lanham, MD: University Press of America.

Roach, C. A., & Wyatt, N. J. (1988). *Successful listening*. New York: Harper & Row.

Rogers, C. R., & Farson, R. E. (1957). *Active listening.* Chicago: University of Chicago Industrial Relations Center.

Shimanoff, S. (1980). *Communication rules: Theory and research.* Beverly Hills, CA: Sage.

Smith, M. J. (1984). Contingency rules theory, context, and compliance-behaviors. *Human Communication Research, 10,* 489–512.

Snyder, M. Tanke, E. D., & Berscheid, E. (1977). Social perception and interpersonal behavior: On the self-fulfilling nature of social stereotypes. *Journal of Personality and Social Psychology, 35,* 656–666.

Stiel, L. K., Barker, L. L., & Watson, K. W. (1983). *Effective listening: Key to your success.* Reading, MA: Addison-Wesley.

Wolvin, A., & Coakley, C. G. (1996). *Listening* (5th ed.). Dubuque, IA: Brown & Benchmark.

✤ 4 Skillful Questioning

Almost everything of moment reaches us through one [person] asking questions of another. Because of this, the interviewer holds a position of unprecedented power and influence.

—DENIS BRIAN,
Murderers and Other Friendly People

LEARNING GOALS

After reading this chapter, you should be able to

- Appreciate the role of questioning in everyday life and in interviews
- Understand how questions serve several purposes in fueling conversation and eliciting answers
- Know the various types of questions and how they are used in different settings and situations
- Recognize the advantages and disadvantages of different forms of questions
- Construct better questions, knowing the importance of wording and delivery
- Understand the role of context in answering and asking questions
- Ask questions ethically, with consideration for informed consent and confidentiality

Edna Buchanan (1987) received a Pulitzer Prize in journalism for her coverage of mayhem and murder in Miami. She quickly learned the importance of asking the right questions after missing an unusual detail in a homicide investigation. "The case seemed routine—if one can ever call murder routine. But later I learned that at the time the victim was shot he was wearing a black taffeta cocktail dress and red high heels" (p. 265). She tracked down the detectives and asked why they hadn't told her about the dead man's wardrobe. Their response? *You didn't ask.*

"Now I always do," she said.

Questions are versatile, powerful tools of communication for anyone seeking answers. They are versatile because they enable us to learn everything from the mundane ("What time is it?") to the complex ("Why do you say you hate your mother?"). They are powerful because they can uncover buried truths and even alter lives. (Q: "Will you marry me?" A: "Gee, let me think about that.") Used wisely and properly in interviews, questions help us acquire vital information by which to assess relationships, identify problems, find solutions, make decisions, and gain insights. Beyond simply requesting answers, questions kindle candid, comfortable talk by their ability to challenge, amuse, flatter, and entice us.

81

An interview is not exclusively an exercise in questioning; nonetheless it often succeeds or fails on the ability to ask and answer questions. Used carelessly or thoughtlessly, questions can easily extinguish communication. Skilled professional interviewers know this, and they consider such important aspects as the tone, timing, sequence, and wording of their questions.

Although asking questions is more art than science, even interviewers who seem to have inborn talent can profit from a fuller knowledge of how questions function as stimulants of further communication. Too much is at stake in most interviews to take the question-and-answer interchange for granted. Edna Buchanan learned a fundamental lesson of questioning early in her career. But her success as a journalist suggests she continued her education in both the art and science of asking questions.

The first section of this chapter itself opens with a question: Why do we ask? From there, the common uses of questions are discussed, followed by a catalogue of question types, including the advantages and limitations of each. In "Beyond the Basics" we discuss the complex motives behind questioning and the ethical and emotional complications of questions and answers. We won't address every facet of skillful questioning in this chapter because the goals and methods of questioning depend on the type of interview. Each chapter in Part 2 will consider questions in particular contexts and circumstances. Here, we focus on spoken questions; Chapter 9 describes criteria for wording questions precisely in standardized surveys and written questionnaires.

A caveat before moving on: Questioning cannot be divorced from the complementary skills of listening and framing. So as you read this chapter, remember that questioning itself is not an independent process. It is part of the intricate, dynamic enterprise of human communication. Even an interviewer's "best" questions will fail if they are not accompanied by an ability and commitment to listen and understand.

❦ THE BASICS

Asking Questions: Why?

Before determining *what* to ask and *how* to ask, interviewers first need to ask themselves: Why do I ask? Answering that question isn't simple or easy. At least it shouldn't be.

Interviewing is a purposeful communication activity, with explicit or implicit objectives or goals. The questions at the core of most interviews should be carefully crafted and designed to serve those objectives or goals. Despite how obvious this sounds, many professionals overlook such a simple insight. A personnel manager who has conducted thousands of interviews over a twenty-year career might operate with only the vaguest purpose to guide her: "I want to hire a good person." Although that could be called a purpose, does it provide the foundation for a series of focused, effective questions? Interviewers ideally want to stimulate accurate, helpful answers, so one answer to the question Why do I ask? is *interviewers ask to learn*. But learn what? An interview with a vague or generalized purpose might succeed, but it is more likely to flounder.

Establishing a purpose for interview questions requires careful consideration of what needs to be learned—a target. An interviewer who asks questions without a target in sight is like a pitcher throwing blindfolded. Take the analogy another step: Try batting against a blindfolded pitcher. Interviewees need to understand the relevance of questions in order to provide effective responses.

A Starting Point

Where do you begin in establishing a purpose—the *why* behind interview questions? J. T. Dillon (1990), an expert on questioning, suggests beginning at the end. "A smart way to proceed is to plan right away in terms of answers rather than questions," he advises (p. 167). Identifying the type of answers needed ought to help interviewers and interviewees devise focused and clear questions. That advice, however, like most advice, should be qualified by an important consideration: Questions frequently explore the unknown. Dillon is not suggesting you frame questions to get the answers you've already decided you want or expect. Rather, he's recommending that you preconsider what kinds of answering best fit your needs and then approach the task of phrasing questions from the perspective of how they will sound to the interviewee.

The specific answers you need may not come into focus until the interview is well under way. Basing questions on anticipated or desired answers without being flexible artificially forces an interview toward a predetermined destination. Flexibility, on the other hand, allows for discovery of unexpected but rewarding alternatives. Individual personalities and circumstances influence why we ask. Even though we frequently ask questions without knowing *all* the answers, it is unwise to question without knowing *something*. These observations also apply to the interviewee, whose questions will, in part, be preconsidered and, in part, spontaneous, based on the ebb and flow of the interview.

To provide an example, consider how a university selects its faculty. Metro State advertises for a new English professor with an announcement in the *Chronicle of Higher Education:*

> Metro State University seeks an assistant professor of English to teach American literature and advise the campus literary magazine. Ph.D. required. Candidates should expect to teach four classes a semester.

In job searches, one answer looms above all others: matching a strong person to the position. The advertisement (streamlined here for purposes of illustration) outlines the bare-bones expectations and requirements and suggests a few generic questions about a candidate's credentials and professional experience. But what else? The faculty, administrators, and students conducting the interviews cannot expect much progress toward an answer without specifics to guide them. Usually a set of standards, expectations, or criteria defines the initial parameters of the questions asked and answers sought.

Using our example, we'll see how Dillon's advice of first determining what answers you seek can help determine the questions asked. (To streamline our example further, we'll focus only on questions likely to be put to the teaching candidate and dispense with sample questions the candidate might ask of the interviewers.) You're on the selection committee, and it's time to interview the first prospect, Dr. Mary Stinson. As a student representing the interests of other students in the department, your perspective, and the answers you seek, may differ from those of a professor or dean. Your focus is on Dr. Stinson, the teacher. So how do you go about finding answers? What questions would help?

You'd probably explore Dr. Stinson's classroom experience, such as the courses she's taught, the student evaluation scores she's earned, and the instructional workshops she's attended, to collect tangible *information*. But you'd also want to know about her demeanor, relationship with students, and reasons for becoming a teacher; you'd then be exploring important intangibles of *values and attitudes*. Finally, you'd likely seek insights into her teaching, classroom management, and grading methods, moving into the area of *behavior*. In other words, your questions originate from who she is, relative to who you are and whom you represent. Given your focus, you'd probably be interested in answers to questions like these:

- How much experience do you have in teaching freshman composition?
- What are your grading criteria on essays or other written papers?
- How do you involve students in class discussion?
- Why did you become a teacher?
- What do you like best about teaching?
- Have you ever caught a student plagiarizing? What did you do?
- If you could describe the ideal student, what would be his or her characteristics?
- If your superior asked you to change the grade of a student-athlete to avoid academic suspension, what would you do?

Answers to these questions would form the basis for additional questions, by you and others participating in the interview. Pursuit of the ultimate decision—whom to hire—could generate hundreds of questions as various interviewers attempted to determine which candidate would fit best within the educational milieu of students, colleagues, campus, and community. The process, according to Dillon (p. 168), resembles a *pas de deux*—a dance with answers and questions in constant motion.

Sound a bit daunting? Interviews can be, especially if you haven't prepared with a clear purpose and plan for seeking answers and asking questions.

Clarity of Purpose

The foundation for effective interview communication is clarity of purpose. Participants ought to know what is going on and what is at stake in virtually all interviews. Ideally, the questions asked and answered serve a shared, clearly understood purpose. Realistically, we

Trying Out Your Skills

Analyze the following interview between a newspaper reporter and a cancer researcher; decide what the interviewee might assume about the purpose of the interview. Could she develop a clear perspective on why she's being interviewed? What could the reporter—and the doctor—have done differently to help the interview progress with more clarity?

REPORTER: I'd like to talk with you today about your work. OK?

DOCTOR: That's fine. About how much time do you think we'll need? I have a meeting in thirty minutes.

R: Oh, it's not going to take anywhere near that long.

D: All right. Let's sit down here, in the conference room. . . . Now, how can I help you?

R: I just wanted to ask a few questions.

D: I see. What do you want to know?

R: I was told by my editor that you were in the forefront of a new cancer initiative. Is that right?

D: Well, I've been involved in basic research since 1978, and our team has come up with some remarkable findings. There have been two breakthroughs in the past three years. I'm wondering which one you might have in mind.

R: Uh . . . Could you tell me about them?

D: I don't know where to begin. One of them concerns the physical exercise habits of women who discover breast lumps in early middle age. The other is a new approach to chemotherapy. But maybe I'm not the best person to discuss these things. Do you know why your editor asked you to interview me in particular?

R: Well, it probably has something to do with the *USA Today* article last Friday. Did you read it?

D: Yes. But that article was only about breast cancer generally and about some faith-centered treatments. You don't want me to comment on those, do you?

R: Are we going to run out of time? Do you want me to call back when we have more time to talk? . . .

---

cannot expect a common purpose—a partnership—in every interview. People sometimes act in selfish, deceitful, or misguided ways. Occasionally, it won't occur to them to state the purpose or to seek common ground. But even the most self-serving interviewers should be concerned about the dangers of clashing purposes or hidden agendas. Even though a commonality of purpose may be impossible, clarity of purpose is quite attainable. An auto salesperson interviews a potential buyer about driving habits and price range; they are both focused on a midnight blue four-door sedan, but for different reasons. The salesperson's questions might serve one prime purpose: get a signed contract. The buyer's response serves another purpose: don't get ripped off. They may find cooperation difficult for understandable reasons. The salesperson may ask aggressive questions in an exasperated manner, bordering on insulting "What do I have to *do* to earn your business?" The buyer, wary of high-pressure tactics, responds in kind "Do you think I just fell off a turnip truck?" The goals of interviewer and interviewee in such a persuasive interview will likely never be the same. Still, it might be worthwhile to clarify a mutual purpose toward which both could work: a satisfying purchase of a good product at a fair price.

BOX 4.1   **R E M I N D E R S**

Common Uses of Questions

Preparatory
- Establish rapport or break the ice
- Screen information
- Acquire background

Primary
- Collect data or factual information
- Confirm the truthfulness or accuracy of information
- Explore attitudes, values, and beliefs

- Identify a problem
- Arrive at an outcome—a solution or decision, for example
- Predict behavior
- Persuade

Supportive
- Control, direct, or regulate communication
- Clarify ambiguous or uncertain information
- Provide transitions

Uses of Questions

Questions help accomplish particular information-seeking goals, such as encouraging disclosure or acquiring accurate information. Teachers, for example, use questions at times to determine what their students know or how well they can recall what they are supposed to know "Which American president developed the U.S. space program?" On a higher cognitive plane, teachers use questions to encourage learning by challenging students to integrate and build on the facts they know "What do you think President Kennedy considered as he decided to invest American resources in space exploration?" On still another level, teachers will probe attitudes or assess values "Do you think President Kennedy was right or wrong to lead us into space in an era of social turmoil?"

Fundamentally, questions seek answers. Their range varies from basic fact gathering to far more complex incursions into the mind and emotions. Participants in interviews often draw on a variety of question types, a subject covered later in this chapter. First, though, consider an inventory of common uses that fall under three broad categories: preparatory, primary, and supportive (see Box 4.1). Through sample questions, we'll see how these uses apply in a typical job interview.

Preparatory Uses

It's natural for most people to be nervous or tense at the beginning of an interview. As a result, interviews often begin with questions used to establish a comfort level before embarking on substantive matters. **Preparatory questions,** then, prepare communicators to accomplish other tasks later by establishing rapport or screening information in a nonthreatening atmosphere. The most common preparatory questions include ones of hospitality or housekeeping:

"How was your trip here?" (Interviewer)

"Would you like a cup of coffee or soft drink?" (Interviewer)

"Are you comfortable talking in my office, or would you like to go down to the coffee shop?" (Interviewer)

"Did you get my message that I won't be needing a ride to the airport? My aunt will be picking me up." (Interviewee)

In another stage of preparatory use, questions build goodwill; they also help everyone ease into the interview gradually. These questions can pop up spontaneously, usually prompted by surroundings or situations:

"That's a very handsome briefcase. Did you buy it locally? (Interviewer)

"I saw the Orioles memorabilia outside your office. Is Baltimore your hometown?" (Interviewee)

Simple research can provide material for questions, such as looking over a list of references attached to a resume and finding a familiar name:

"We know someone in common—Virginia Matthews of Acme Construction. How's she doing?" (Interviewer)

To use their time together efficiently, interviewers and interviewees both should study background information in advance. A portfolio, job application, or company report can provide answers, but they also suggest questions about missing details. Common background questions include

"I see you graduated from Midwest College with a bachelor's degree in English. Did you specialize in any particular area or field?" (Interviewer)

"Who actually founded the company? There wasn't a history in the material I looked at." (Interviewee)

Other preparatory questions accomplish screening tasks, such as determining whether an applicant meets minimum requirements for the job. These questions might be asked as part of a separate process, such as a telephone interview, test, or questionnaire:

"Because you applied for our training slot, I'm assuming that you probably conducted orientation training while you were at Electronic Systems. Am I right?"

Preparatory questions and the answers they elicit can be crucial. They might readily reveal a charming personality or a boorish one. Even casual inquiries warrant careful attention by interviewer and interviewee alike.

Primary Uses

With a comfortable climate established and other preparatory steps completed, interviews usually progress to **primary questions** whose purpose is to uncover basic information or problems, search for solutions, or test or confirm attitudes. They also move the interview into more challenging terrain that calls for even greater care and alertness. Questions used for preparatory purposes rarely address sensitive subjects overtly; primary questions frequently do. Moreover, the consequences of primary questions loom larger. The following sample questions illustrate the functions of primary questions associated with job interviews.

No company wants unhappy employees, so one line of questions might serve to explore working environment or identify potential problems:

> "How do you feel about working for a company that's known for its civic involvement? Many employees take on extensive volunteer duties." (Interviewer)

> "What is the company's policy on a father taking days off to care for an ill child?" (Interviewee)

A question that explores a problem might ultimately lead to follow-up questions that, in turn, find a solution or compromise:

> "My family supports a move to another city. But we hope to see this as a long-term commitment, too. Is there a possibility of being transferred in a couple of years or less? (Interviewee)

> "What if I could almost guarantee that you'll be assigned here for at least five years? Would that work for you?" (Interviewer)

Behaviorally based questions have become common in job interviews. Proponents find them valuable for assessing future performance under trying conditions. Behavioral questions often ask the respondent to relate a story or anecdote about previous experiences: "Tell me about . . ." or, "Describe a situation . . ." are typical openings for this type of question.

> "Tell me about a time when you showed enterprise in solving a customer's complaint." (Interviewer)

Interviewees occasionally use behavioral questions in return:

> "Could you tell me about an occasion when the company dealt with a factory worker who reported a safety hazard? I'm especially interested in what happened next, after the first report." (Interviewee)

Certain qualities of a good employee aren't evident on resumes or samples of an applicant's work products. That is why primary questions cover such areas as attitudes about communication with coworkers, consensus building, loyalty, or work ethic:

> "Have you had the experience of delegating authority?" (Interviewer)

> "How often do managers sit down with the staff to discuss how things are going?" (Interviewee)

Some of the toughest primary questions address issues of integrity:

"Your resume doesn't reveal this, but we learned you were dismissed from your previous job. Would you please explain why that position isn't mentioned anywhere in your application material?" (Interviewer)

"Last year, your company was investigated by the Securities and Exchange Commission for alleged price fixing. How has the company answered those allegations?" (Interviewee)

Primary uses of questions move both participants forward. They define the central topics motivating the communicators and in many ways determine the ultimate success of the interview.

Supportive Uses

Our final category consists of **supportive questions**, which are used to direct and advance interviews by bolstering, setting up, or following up primary questions. They can be as simple as, "Tell me more," "What happened next?" or, "I'm going to switch gears now, with some questions about your first job. OK?"

Supportive uses include questions or communication that show respect and attentive involvement. In a supportive approach, an interviewer (or interviewee) sometimes summarizes the other participant's statements, thereby ensuring that what has been said by one participant is understood by the other. The interviewer would ask, for example, "Let me see if I fully understand what you mean by the term 'educationally challenged.'" The interviewee, in turn, would either confirm, correct, or modify with a response.

Often, supportive questions seek amplification or provide encouragement. In this role, they bring primary questions to fruition through expanded responses, a point developed later in the chapter when probes are discussed. Supportive questions also act as barometers of the climate, or condition, of the interview:

"Are these questions meaningful for you?" (Interviewer)

"Am I fully answering your questions?" (Interviewee)

Periodic inquiry into the impact or reception of primary questions guards against unnecessary misinterpretations and can head off hurt feelings or other negative reactions that arise during an interview.

Finally, some questions help you make transitions from one subject to another. Maintaining a smooth pace of questioning helps keep everyone in focus, while a sharp change of direction can be disruptive. A simple question can serve as both a turn signal and a sign of consideration for your interview partner.

"I don't want to cut short our discussion on this point, but if you're ready, would you mind if we move to another subject?" (Interviewer)

These examples have been tailored to job interviews. However, with modification, they would apply in many other interview contexts. Now that you've seen how questions are used, we can examine particular types of questions and learn how they work.

Types of Questions

Part of choosing questions is picking the best tool for the job, and you wouldn't use a pipe wrench for carburetor adjustments. On the other hand, questioning is not auto repair; sometimes a question that seems perfect for the situation won't work, and one that seems ill suited will succeed. Nonetheless, we need to know the strengths and limitations of the questions we ask. While no question comes with a warranty or a foolproof set of instructions, we can expect certain results from particular types.

In the family of questions, two general forms illustrate opposite ends of a continuum: open-ended and closed questions.

Open-Ended Questions

By letting respondents choose their own directions and context as much as possible, **open-ended questions** invite talk. "Could you talk for a while about the South as a place to live?" opens up a wide array of response choices and thus is relatively open. By contrast, a more closed approach narrows the field of possible responses. Information about self-concept, for instance, could come from a sequence of more directive questions, such as, "What honors and awards have you earned?" followed by, "Which ones have been most important to you?" Open questions reduce the interviewer's role as questioner and intensify the interviewer's roles of listener and observer. Moreover, with open-ended questions, respondents are freer to roam; there is also loss of interviewer control over the structure factors of interaction (see Chapter 2). Interviewees might produce meandering answers that lead, at one extreme, to panoramic vistas or, at another, to fruitless dead ends.

Open-ended questions have these advantages:

- They allow people to communicate in their own words as they determine the content and depth of answers.

- They help reveal the importance of the question to a respondent, which some call the *salience* factor. (Salience also can be measured by a pattern of closed questions.)

- They reveal a respondent's priorities.

- They uncover a respondent's feelings, attitudes, or behaviors.

- They gauge the depth of a respondent's knowledge, insight, eloquence—or the absence of such qualities.

- They can encourage a conversational flow to interviews, which helps diminish a feeling of being interrogated.

- They can help someone talk through a problem.

Open questions can backfire, though. Among their disadvantages:

- They can encourage rambling, disorganized answers.

- They take time—and possibly waste time.

- They put pressure on people who aren't comfortable or skilled at answering questions that require them spontaneously to marshal thoughts, feelings, or experiences.

- They complicate recording and analysis of interviews by producing more "data" than might be needed for a given purpose.

These observations about open-ended questions should not suggest absolutes. The success of an open question depends on a willingness and ability to answer. In some respects, they afford perhaps too much freedom—freedom to filibuster, freedom to obscure, freedom to evade.

An open question needn't be long or complex. A simple question can prompt a well-developed response (see Box 4.2). Open questions, however, should be specific enough to elicit a significant answer, not merely a bulky one. "Tell me about yourself" could touch off an avalanche of personal details, or it could stump a respondent into saying, "I don't know where to begin." The question probably is too vague, unless it really means, "Just talk about any aspect of your life for as long as you'd like."

Closed Questions

At the other end of the continuum, **closed questions** seek specific information and limit the range of an interviewee's answer. They discourage unwanted answers and mark the boundaries of the interview. They are particularly useful and effective for gathering, confirming, or screening factual information, which is why market researchers rely on closed questions. But these questions are not particularly good for tapping feelings or examining meanings, which is why counselors don't rely on them. Among their advantages:

- They allow accurate comparisons and analysis among answers from a large number of respondents, a result usually most helpful in social science surveys.

- They give interviewers greater control, especially with inexperienced or uncooperative interviewees.

BOX 4.2   INTERVIEWERS IN ACTION

David Fetterman

David Fetterman, a cross-cultural researcher, discusses the importance of open questions in his projects:

"An open-ended question allows participants to interpret it. For example, in studying an emergency room, I asked a regular emergency room nurse, 'How do you like working with the helicopter nurses?' This question elicited a long and detailed explanation about how aloof she thought they were and how unfair it was that the helicopter nurses did not pitch in during the busy periods. She said she could list five or six activities that emergency room and helicopter nurses did together during the week, but said these activities were all superficial.

"This response opened new doors to my study. I followed up with questions to helicopter nurses, who indicated that they did wait around a great deal of the time waiting for a call to rush to the helicopter. They explained that they could not pitch in during regular emergency room busy periods because they might be called away at any time, and leaving in the middle of a task would be unfair to both the regular nurses and the patients. Thus an open-ended question helped to illuminate the conflicting world views these two sets of nurses held about the same emergency room experience—information that a closed-ended question, such as, 'How many times do you interact with the helicopter nurses each week?' might not have elicited."

Source: Fetterman, 1989, p. 54

- They are efficient, saving time and energy for more productive tasks.
- They help provide focus for people who find it difficult to express themselves.
- They reduce the effort of answering.
- They confirm an agreement or understanding.
- They discourage unnecessary equivocation.

Be aware of these serious disadvantages, however:

- They frustrate people who prefer to explain and develop their answers.
- They reduce the possibility of discovering the unexpected in an interview.
- They discourage a partnership approach to interviews.
- They impede an interview from becoming a conversation.
- They discourage necessary and appropriate equivocation.

The most common closed questions seek no more than a yes or no, either-or choice, or a select-from-one-of-the-following type of answer, for example:

"Do you drive a car?"

Other closed questions offer a choice, but within limits:

"What make of car do you drive?"

"How many miles do you estimate that you drive each work day?"

"How often has your car needed repair in the past six months?"

"Would you describe yourself as an aggressive, moderate, or timid driver?"

Notice that while the questions elicit answers, the usefulness of the answers remains primarily limited to data collection. It's possible to explore complex areas such as motives and attitudes through closed questions (see Foddy, 1993), but closed questions do not capture individual, personalized responses well.

Both closed and open questions are common in interviews. Which form to use, and in what ways, should be based on the circumstances of the interview. But as we learn to communicate, habits develop—some influenced by our personalities, others by our environment. Without implying that openness is entirely a gender issue, Deborah Tannen (1994) and other researchers have detected differences between male and female communication, with men being generally more control oriented and direct than women in their questioning behavior. Note the word *generally;* clearly many people are exceptions. Still, most people naturally emphasize one communication style over another, at least by temperament and by cultural influences. Knowing that, interviewers can adjust their style to the context and break away from habits or tendencies. Many interviews, too, will profit from a mix of questioning approaches.

Probes

Probes support previous communication by following up, extending, amplifying, or clarifying topics raised in primary questions. Probes belong to the family of questions in that they seek an answer or response, even though they don't always sound or look like questions. Some amount to silent questions; they nonverbally ask, by a nod of the head, for example, "Would you please go on?"

Three types of probes do heavy lifting in interviews: clarification, amplification, and confirmation.

Clarification probes assist understanding and resist misunderstanding. They enable interview partners to test perceptions and listening. A typical clarification probe takes this form:

"To be sure I understand you, let me restate your response: Did you mean . . . ?"

Here, the probe acts as insurance against errors by reflecting, or paraphrasing, what the respondent has said. A variation on this strategy is to summarize longer, complicated answers and ask for the respondent's reaction to your summary.

More directly, some clarification probes simply state, "I'm not sure I understand your answer." People appreciate your efforts to understand facts and, perhaps more important, meanings as accurately as possible.

Amplification probes are follow-up questions that ask for an expansion of a response to a primary question. They acknowledge that full answers rarely emerge immediately from a single question. Usually a nudge or two provides missing details or fills gaps. Respondents often don't know what a questioner might be most interested in knowing, so an amplification probe helps establish the parameters of the interview. An interviewer might ask a primary question, such as

"You were injured in an accident last year. What happened?"

After a reply, the questioner could still want to learn more. Amplification probes might include

"Would you tell me what happened right after the accident?"

"How did you feel when that occurred?"

"Why do you think the accident happened?"

Silence acts effectively as an amplification probe. It not only encourages fuller answers but also allows time for them. When a questioner is silent and does not move on immediately to the next question, many people will return to their previous answer to provide an example, a reservation, a qualification, or other bits of extra information. Nonverbal cues, such as a smile, a nod, a quizzical expression as encouragement, work well to provide amplification. Even a long, "Hmmmm . . . ?" delivered with a questioning inflection, serves as an amplification probe.

Confirmative probes test the accuracy or completeness of information. At times, they serve to raise doubts or challenge answers to ensure that those answers can be trusted. Of all probes, they are most likely to apply uncomfortable but necessary pressure. Here are several examples and their intended effects:

"Are you *certain* that figure is correct?"

In this instance, the confirmative probe puts the respondent on notice that you're concerned about accuracy. People tend to generalize or guess when recalling dates, figures, and other types of factual data. Your probe gives your partner reason to pause and question the accuracy of a disclosure; it might also lead him or her to retrieve documents or records that provide confirmation. At times, a probe meant to confirm a point can sound like a clarification probe, perhaps because you don't want to put undue pressure on your partner:

"I'm not sure of what you just said because it sounds different from your earlier comments. Are you saying you didn't get dismissed from your job?"

Sometimes journalists and others must address internal contradictions in an interview. People contradict themselves for many reasons; usually, it's a memory problem or verbal slip, not an intentional act of deception. Contradictions also arise in the form of external information that differs from that provided by the respondent:

Brian Lamb

Brian Lamb, host of "Booknotes," an author-interview program on the cable network C-SPAN, describes the art of asking simple questions:

"'Where do you write?' 'Do you use a computer?' 'How did you research this?' 'Why are these folks in your dedication?'

"After nearly eight years and 400 author interviews, these basic questions still yield interesting, sometimes surprising answers. Forrest McDonald writes history on his rural Alabama porch—naked. Richard Ben Cramer interviewed 1,000 people for his landmark 1992 biography, *What It Takes: The Way to the White House.* Clare Brandt explored Lake Champlain and the Hudson River in small boats for her biography of Benedict Arnold. Robert Caro read through 650,000 pages from the LBJ Library for the second book in his Lyndon Johnson series. Cheryl Wudunn dedicated the book she and her husband, Nicholas Kristof, co-authored on China to the sister she lost in the KAL airliner downing."

Source: Lamb, 1997, p. xvii

"Information I have from other sources differs from your account of what happened. Can you provide evidence?"

Interview participants must remain alert for contradictions, which is another reason to stress the relationship of listening and framing to questioning. Before you can ask about a contradiction, you must listen alertly and frame the different facts as at least a potential contradiction.

Confirmative probes, finally, help keep everyone in focus by seeking to establish relevance.

"I'm not sure your answer addresses my question. How does it relate to the subject?"

In a related use, questions help interview participants who stray off course return to the subject through a friendly reminder, such as, "Let's get back to what you were talking about a few minutes ago."

Questionable Questions

Certain questions should come with a warning label. Don't automatically avoid them because they're risky, but understand their possible side effects, and then handle them with care. (See Box 4.3 for an interviewer who specializes in simple, basic questions.)

Stress Questions These are questions expressly designed to make respondents uncomfortable, so the questioner can observe how that discomfort affects the other. Of course, most interviews induce some form of stress; is it necessary to add more? Perhaps. In certain interviews, particularly in the selection of employees who must work under trying conditions, certain questions *might* reveal a problem. The emphasis is on *might*. Critics (Kanter, 1995, pp. 63, 64) contend that stress questions give interviewers unfair power and often impose an artificial situation that won't apply to the job.

Stress questions vary in intensity and purpose, as these examples demonstrate:

"As a new employee of Smithton Enterprises, you discover by accident that our chief financial officer and two members of the board have invested in a company you know has produced many films of child pornography. Only you possess this information, which is potentially damaging to the company's reputation but unlikely to be made public. Whom, if anyone, do you tell, and why?"

"What would you do if you had to dismiss one of two equally effective employees, and one of the employees was your best friend at work?"

Imagine facing difficult questions like these, which are calculated to make you squirm. How would you answer on the spot? In some cases, interviewers actually expect a thoughtful answer; in other instances, the answer is secondary to the reaction. At times, stress questions test glibness and communication agility more than on-the-job potential. Stress questions can, of course, disclose a flaw or accomplish something positive. Be wary of them, however, as they might prompt a defensive reaction that infects the rest of the interview.

Hypothetical Questions   This form of question creates a dramatic situation and asks respondents to react as if they were participants. Practical, logical respondents likely will bristle, "I don't deal in hypotheticals." Creative types might relish the opportunity to speculate and ponder. Hypothetical questions usually begin with, "What if . . . ?" Some seem outright silly, such as this one:

"If you had to go through life as a golf club, which one would you be and why?"

If you choose to phrase hypothetical questions, be aware that the quality of your interviewee's answer will vary widely according to a psychological frame over which you have no control and about which you have virtually no information. For example, you may congratulate yourself on the cleverness of your golf question. But how clever are you, really, if the person answering knows next to nothing about golf and responds, "Putter," because it's the only club he or she knows a name for? What have you really learned? Other hypothetical questions seek useful information and encourage respondents to think through possible scenarios:

"Professor, what if a Category 5 hurricane hit New Orleans head-on?"

Such a question may help the expert place knowledge into a framework with more human dimension. Instead of referring to meteorological descriptions of a hurricane's magnitude, the interviewee is forced to think of a phenomenon the way everyday people do, yet with added technical expertise.

Personal Questions   These questions ask for disclosures of information normally shared only among friends and family, if it is shared at all. Questions can venture into private zones, and at times with good reason, such as a physician dealing with a patient's impotence. Personal questions are appropriate when clearly justified and with the promise of confidentiality. In other instances, personal questions raise hackles. Aside from medical conditions (illness, medications, mental health), private zones usually include sexual behavior, finances (debt, investments, salary), and family relationships (husband-wife, parent-child). In fact, most questions with no obvious relevance to the context of the interview could be construed as personal. Consider these examples:

"Are you a liberal or a conservative?"

"How would you describe your style of driving?"

"Are you a pet lover or not?"

Would you consider them personal? Can you imagine circumstances that would warrant such questions? Perhaps. A veterinarian hiring an assistant might be justified in asking about pets, but it's not a suitable inquiry in other job searches.

Although some interviewers consciously misuse their power by prying into others' private lives, occasionally people stumble innocently into private zones, such as asking a parent about a child's progress in school and opening an emotional wound. Be aware that people differ in what they consider appropriate or taboo. A sociologist interviewing exotic dancers shouldn't expect blushes or outrage over sexually explicit topics. But what about gray areas? Relevance remains the central criterion. Do the questions serve the purpose of the interview? If not, or if you're in doubt, dispense with questions that enter personal realms. A single misplaced query could offset the benefits of a dozen judicious questions.

Illegal Questions   Certain questions are forbidden by law, largely in employment contexts where employees might be vulnerable to employers' power. Government regulations attempt to make the employment playing field more level by restricting employers' ability to elicit information that could be used for unfair discrimination or prejudicial treatment. Relatively few interviewers intentionally ask illegal questions, but this is not a reason to avoid learning appropriate legal stipulations found in state or federal statutes, such as the Americans with Disabilities Act (ADA) or the Civil Rights Act, both of which protect against discrimination in hiring, housing, or other areas. Illegal interview questions arise most often in selection interviews (see Chapter 6 for more details).

Loaded Questions   These are questions that plant the questioner's emotional presumption within the wording of the question. Loaded questions come in two varieties—those loaded in the sense of judgmental, potentially offensive language and those that spring an accusatory trap. In the first instance, loaded questions take these forms:

"Are you bothered by cheap foreign imports?"

"Do you think the principal is too macho?"

Including the words *cheap* and *macho* in these questions will affect respondents in a variety of ways, many of which are unpredictable. What if an interviewee wasn't particularly bothered by imported cars until your credibility momentarily convinced him or her of their "cheap" (not just inexpensive) qualities? Or what if an interviewee was bothered by import policies but doesn't consider the cars themselves to be "cheaply" made? Will this loaded question accurately probe either of these attitudes? It's better to stay away from language that will polarize respondents or affect their emotions unnecessarily. Many words and phrases can be called loaded in that they carry connotations that might be offensive or judgmental to some.

The second instance is the type of classic loaded question that pins someone in a corner:

"When did you stop cheating at cards?"

"How did you come to be an apologist for the lunatic fringe of this country?"

If you ask questions like these, expect a defensive counterpunch or an abrupt end to the interview. In practice, few interviewers deliberately ask loaded questions. Those who do usually ask them for effect—such as a talk show host seeking a tasty sound bite—not to promote understanding. That's why the word *baited* is associated with loaded questions intended to torment or incite.

Accidental loaded questions are more common. They could reveal someone's biases or insensitivity instead of malice. Stay alert for loaded questions, and avoid them unless you are convinced it's the only way left to break through a logjam in the interview. Never use questions maliciously.

Leading Questions   These questions suggest or make much more likely a certain kind of answer. One kind of leading question encourages disclosure; another suggests answers. Questions that lead toward disclosure do so by aiding or priming an answer, and parents, counselors, and therapists find them helpful when talking to a reticent respondent or when entering into a sensitive subject:

"It sounds as if you're upset about your grade in history class."

Leading questions or statements of this kind often are demonstrations of active listening, and they encourage disclosure by a nonjudgmental statement of what's being heard and interpreted. This kind of implied question is only effective if it's clear to the respondent that he or she has the option of denying the statement if it's not true.

Other questions lead, however, in overly manipulative ways, and they resemble loaded questions in that they rely on charged words or phrases. As a result, some experts on questioning use *leading* and *loaded* interchangeably (Payne, 1980). We make this distinction: Loaded questions, whether deliberate or accidental, land with a noticeable blow. We usually know a loaded question when we feel it. Leading questions rely on the power and emotional impact of language, too, but in subtler ways. In their suggestive form, leading questions, whether deliberate or accidental, influence answers by verbal appeals or sleight of hand. The following examples illustrate how leading questions work.

"With the rising number of DUI-related fatalities, wouldn't you say that state officials ought to crack down with random sobriety checkpoints?

"Then, you'd say that the company could do a better job of rewarding its employees for meritorious service?"

"Do you think the United States should allow public speeches against democracy?"

In the first example, the reference to a growing social problem invites a positive response. After all, who isn't concerned about accidents associated with drunk driving? In the second example, the question all but provides a yes answer. The third example comes from a classic study (Rugg, 1941) that found respondents reacted in significantly different ways when the word *forbid* replaced *allow.* Faced with the question, "Do you think the United States should forbid public speeches against democracy?" 54 percent of the respondents said yes—that is, the government should "ban antidemocratic oratory." However, 75 percent answered no when asked, "Do you think the United States should allow public speeches against democracy?" In this case a much higher percentage of respondents seemed willing to let the government ban antidemocratic oratory.

Discriminating listeners won't be fooled by a leading question. They'll pick one apart and uncover its weaknesses. An undetected loaded question, however, might result in an invalid answer. In any event, questions that intentionally trick or maneuver someone into answers will undermine the legitimacy of an interview.

Threatening Questions   Threatening questions state or imply punishment or retribution if an appropriate response isn't forthcoming. Many questions could be called threatening either for their way of presentation or their content.

"Do you want to lose your job over this?"

"Do I have to call your parents to get to the bottom of your bad grades?"

Threatening questions are associated with scenes like a police interrogation, but even under adversarial conditions, a less aggressive approach generally holds greater promise for disclosure. Many threatening questions have power because they operate as **rhetorical questions,** ones for which the answer is so obvious that the question doesn't literally need to be answered at all.

In a few cases, a threatening question serves as a form of shock therapy. For example, a doctor dealing with a patient's unwillingness to treat a medical condition might threaten as a final step of intervention. If used at all, a threatening question should be asked without frustration or anger.

Blindside Questions   These are questions the interviewer knows to be unexpected by the interviewee. Questions like these can hit like a sucker punch. They come seemingly out of nowhere, unexpected and unprovoked. A blindside question doesn't seem fair, and many of them aren't. In rare instances, a blindside question can offset a rehearsed answer or alibi and therefore is a tactic used in investigative journalism, law enforcement, and courtroom interaction. A blindside question could be the first one asked, or it could come after a series of soft set-up questions:

> "Reverend Skyler, you have been a persistent critic of the mayor's marital background, including his two divorces. Am I correct?"

> "And your position is that a leader loses all moral authority if he or she has been unable to keep marriages together, is that right?"

> "Specifically, you don't like the ways that welfare mothers have been—in your words—'rewarded in the past for their sins.' True?"

> "Then Reverend Skyler, as a leading advocate of family values, why have you hidden the fact that you're the father of a child born out of wedlock?"

Blindside questions land dramatically when asked in a public forum, such as a news conference.

Often, those who spring surprises are more interested in the reaction than an answer. Does a question cause the interviewee to go ballistic or melt under pressure? In that sense, a blindside question functions as a stress detector.

No matter how they're used, blindside questions rarely achieve worthwhile results. Public figures are usually well prepared for surprise questions; less experienced interviewees might collapse when blindsided. But what is gained in either case? Blindside questions deserve a warning: Use them only as a last resort and then only when you've fully resolved their ethical and practical dilemmas.

Side Effects of Problem Questions   Our list of problem questions isn't exhaustive, nor is it neat and tidy. For example, some questions can exhibit multiple personalities—combining a stress question, personal question, and hypothetical question. CNN reporter Bernard Shaw asked a devastating question of Massachusetts Governor Michael Dukakis, the Democratic presidential candidate in 1988. Dukakis and Vice President George Bush met in a nationally televised debate seen by 50 million households, where Shaw, as moderator, asked Dukakis the first question: "Governor, if Kitty Dukakis were raped and murdered, would you favor an irrevocable death penalty for the killer?" Reporters in the pressroom gasped, but Dukakis answered without hesitation, "No, I don't, Bernard. And I think you know that I've opposed the death penalty during all of my life." Instead of answering with emotion or attacking the question, Dukakis stuck to his principles, but coldly and mechanically in the eyes of critics (Simon, 1990, pp. 291–295).

The question launched a debate. Was Shaw grandstanding, or did he do his job of asking questions not to be found in candidates' briefing books—questions that reveal important issues of leadership? Should Dukakis have said, "I'd want to kill him," showing he's emotional and committed to his wife in a fundamentally human way? Or was his relatively bloodless answer justified, as a reasoned response that showed his commitment to principles? Under scrutiny, both question and answer defy easy classification. Who did the right thing? Who was wrong? In some cases we'll never be sure of what to ask or how to answer.

Organizing Questions

The organization of questions in an interview is in some ways like a musical arrangement: It displays sequence and timing and can have elements analogous to a prelude or a crescendo. Questions can follow a detailed "score," like a symphony, or spring from disciplined improvisation, like a jazz group's jam session. Interviewers call their plan or sequence of questions a **schedule.**

A structured, standardized interview, such as a survey, typically follows a set of prepared questions, asked in sequence, with no deviation. Professional interviewers often call this a **highly scheduled interview** because the question sequence is completely decided ahead of time. But most other interview forms vary in organization from an **unscheduled interview** format (used, for example, by a reporter who discovers an "interview of opportunity" when a celebrity unexpectedly agrees to a conversation in the lobby of a hotel). In some counseling interviews, a **moderately scheduled** set of standardized "intake" questions can set the stage for improvised and individualized questions later in the session.

Assuming you have an established, clear purpose for an interview, you'll have to decide whether the following guidelines fit your interview:

- *Progress from relatively simple to relatively harder questions.* A warm-up period helps everyone get comfortable and mentally stretched for more demanding communication. Saving tough questions for last minimizes the possibility that a tough question might end the interview prematurely. Don't, however, deliberately soften someone with easy questions only to zap them with the tough one you were afraid to ask directly. Honesty, as the cliche goes, usually is the best policy.

- *Order questions typically from general to specific—or specific to general.* Think of the choice in terms of a funnel. At which end do you start? Imagine starting at the wide end: What interview professionals call **funnel organization** begins with general, open-ended questions, tapering down to increasingly specific questions. For example:

"What have you heard about the city's plan to build a new jail?"

"What do your friends and neighbors think about the plan?"

"What's your opinion about the proposed location?"

"Will you vote against the jail plan?"

Interviewing citizens about a proposal charged with political, economic, and social implications probably would stir a reaction from almost anyone in town. As a questioning strategy, however, the funnel approach is best suited for well-informed, articulate interviewees. The introductory question doesn't hint of an answer; it provides the inter-viewee ample room to explore the issue. It's the type of question a politically active citizen would eagerly answer, even though it's general. A funnel sequence, however, might seem perfect for the interview and turn out a bust. As we've said before, asking questions requires that you remain nimble enough to adjust on the run.

inverted funnel organization

If you adopt the **inverted funnel organization**, you will progress from narrow, specific questions in the opening to broader, more general ones later (imagine turning the funnel around). For example:

"Have you read the editorial in the paper supporting the proposed new jail?"

"Have you heard Alderman Jackson speak against the jail?"

"Do you plan to vote when the proposal is on the next ballot?"

"What are your friends and neighbors saying about the jail plan?"

"Is the city's plan to build new buildings reasonable?"

The inverted funnel may coax information from someone who is not accustomed to being asked questions about government policy or politics. It's also effective as a quick assessment of a respondent's knowledge on a subject. In some cases, interviewers will provide background information to refresh memories. The respondent answers with a question: "Is that the jail that's supposed to go up near Central Elementary?" Once that's confirmed, the questioning can continue.

• *Finish a line of questioning completely before moving to another.* Inexperienced interviewers often ask a question, get an answer, then move on to the next question on the list. They fail to flesh out answers adequately. Continue asking and re-asking questions, using probes as well, until you're convinced a complete answer has emerged. This advice, however, must be qualified. Watch for an interviewee's willingness to come back to prior topics, even if the issues seem to be closed. Remember the advice from Chapter 2 about allowing your interviewee to retain a significant control over resource factors such as content knowledge, even while you will tend to have more control over structure factors.

• *Listen and watch for a natural conclusion to your questioning.* Interview partners prepare for the heart of the interview with questions and answers. They're less apt to prepare for an ending. Common interview-ending questions often tie up loose ends, summarize, and check one more time for understanding and accuracy. If you've pro-gressed through your schedule and can think of no further issues to raise, give your partner the final word by asking a **wrap-up question**, also known as a **clearinghouse question.** For example, you might ask, "Do you have anything else you'd like to discuss or tell me?" Made as a sincere offer, not a polite gesture, the question might surprise you with its results. People sometimes hold important questions and comments until they feel the interviewer is finished, or they might be reminded of additional important ideas by the overall experience. If there's an encore, let it be the interviewee's.

Wording of Questions

People don't communicate with computerlike precision. We struggle, at times, to express ourselves. Sharing a common language doesn't ensure that the words we offer to others will connect as intended. We may think we're clear and direct and discover the opposite. Misunderstandings abound, even among people with years of experience talking to one another, like spouses or old friends. Misadventures multiply when communicating with strangers, and cultural differences further complicate the process.

The difference between effective and ineffective questions often depends on choice of wording. Four areas are particularly important: vocabulary, connotation, ambiguity, and directness versus indirectness.

Vocabulary

Competence in communication is aided by a well-stocked vocabulary. Questioners draw from their vocabularies to construct questions, assuming that others will be familiar with the words they use. Unfortunately, for a variety of reasons, people may miss each other's meanings. Regional differences, age, culture, education, and other social factors affect how people use and understand words. In wording your questions, try to avoid using technical, unfamiliar, or out-of-context words.

Technical or Specialized Words   Complications can arise when using **jargon,** the language of particular fields, professions, or interests. For example, the term *ADD* (attention deficit disorder) may be far more familiar to teachers than to laypeople. If the clarity of a question depends upon using jargon, try to insert a brief, informal definition when it's first said. Audience analysis is also necessary when using **euphemisms,** which are presumably inoffensive words designed to replace unpleasant words—as in saying "downsized" instead of "fired." Although many euphemisms are helpful in taking the edge off certain touchy questions, some listeners may find euphemistic expressions distracting; "downsized" may sound like a ludicrous substitution for the experience of losing a job to the out-of-work spot welder, if not to the CEO.

Pretentious or Unfamiliar Words   Overblown, pretentious words deflect listeners' attention from the inquiry itself. Showing off your vocabulary won't impress most people—for example, saying "parsimonious" when "stingy" would be more widely understood. Questions can contain multisyllabic words, especially when a precise meaning can be achieved only by the nuance of a particular word. But simple, commonplace words generally work best. When there is doubt about use of an uncommon word, a definition can be embedded in the question. Rather than admit their unfamiliarity with words, some people pretend they know and try to discern the meaning, searching the rest of the question for clues. A job applicant, then, might successfully figure out an unfamiliar word without asking for help. (Q: "Would you say it's justified to prevaricate when someone asks you an extremely personal question?") Then again, the applicant might only come close to the meaning, figuring *prevaricate* means "withhold" or "delay." (A: "Well, yes, that happens pretty often. Though I'm open, other people don't need to know my business.") Without meaning to, the applicant has admitted to lying almost as a matter of course.

A related problem arises with words that sound like ones we know, such as hearing the word *taught* when the speaker is saying "taut." These are problems that a collaborative approach to interviews might overcome. The interviewer, working with the interviewee, remains alert for any signs of misunderstanding.

Out-of-Context Words   The vocabulary of teenagers, for example, differs vastly from that of most adults. Attempts to communicate in a language outside our own experience can backfire. A middle-aged white male using "dis" or "crib" in questions might be seen as condescending or totally out of touch. Talking down to someone, by use of simplistic words and examples, can be another turnoff and result in diminished returns in an interview. A scientist would likely expect and welcome intellectually challenging questions—but so would a factory supervisor. This isn't strictly a matter of using challenging words, of course. It means asking questions that stimulate and channel constructive thinking about the subject. But finding the appropriate vocabulary for questions involves weighing factors like these.

Connotation

Through usage and association, words and phrases acquire a reputation. The literal meaning follows the dictionary; the connotative meaning is a shadow. With some words, the connotative meaning closely follows the literal definition. The dictionary, for example, defines *timid* as "lacking in courage or self-confidence." In connotative meaning, it implies a weak, fearful, ineffectual person. Most of us wouldn't consider *timid* a complimentary word. But connotative meaning sometimes varies; in another connotative sense *timid* implies "shy" or "bashful." These, too, aren't terms of endearment, but they help illustrate the shades of gray in connotative meaning. When dealing with **denotation,** you acknowledge the literal, official definition of words; **connotation,** on the other hand, refers to the range of informal meanings a word acquires in everyday usage.

The shades of gray extend to words that, depending on circumstances, carry *either* positive or negative connotations. According to the dictionary, *shrewd* means in one sense "clever and keen" but "wily" or "tricky" in another. Applied in a corporate setting, the word implies an admirable quality. Would *shrewd,* though, positively describe the director of a charitable organization?

Precision with words should characterize all communication (see Box 4.4). But questions present a higher imperative for precision because they invite an interchange ideally leading to cooperative meaning. We ask to obtain answers, and if we want effective answers, the words we use should be chosen with care. Accounting for the impact of connotative meaning is part of that care.

BOX 4.4   INTERVIEWERS IN ACTION

Seymour Sudman and Norma Bradburn

Sudman and Bradburn, experts on asking questions, offer this story about the importance of precise wording:

> "Two priests, a Dominican and a Jesuit, are discussing whether it is a sin to smoke and pray at the same time. After failing to reach a conclusion, each goes off to consult his respective superior. The next week they meet again. The Dominican says, 'Well, what did your superior say?' The Jesuit responds, 'He said it was all right.' 'That's funny,' the Dominican replies, 'my superior said it was a sin.' Jesuit: 'What did you ask him?' Reply: 'I asked him if it was all right to smoke while praying.' 'Oh,' says the Jesuit, 'I asked my superior if it was all right to pray while smoking.'"

Source: Sudman & Bradburn, 1982, p. 1

Ambiguity

Ambiguous words or phrases make it hard to distinguish between two or more meanings. Sometimes people correct one another in situations of obvious ambiguity. At other times, we talk over and around ambiguity, with neither side recognizing a glitch.

Stanley Payne's 1951 classic, *The Art of Asking Questions,* provides a rogue's gallery of ambiguous words (pp. 158–176). *You,* for one, can confuse because of its potentially ambiguous mix of singular and collective meanings.

"How many cars do *you* repair in a week?"

A mechanic might say, "Twenty," referring to a personal count. Another mechanic might interpret *you* as applying to all the mechanics working at the shop. Such a misunderstanding obviously could affect an answer to a question that appears to be clear at first glance.

Abstract words present another problem of ambiguity. When you use *fair,* for example, does it mean "average," "just," or "unbiased"? To avoid misunderstanding, it might be necessary to either use an explicit word or provide a definition of the word in your question.

It's easy to fall into hidden traps. The simplest of questions can be ambiguous, such as, "How do you get to school?" You might answer, "Well, I take Central Avenue to Interstate 40, then exit at 33rd Street, and follow that to campus." But the question wasn't precise. The interviewer meant to say, "What kind of transportation do you take to school?" When the ambiguity reveals itself as readily as in this example, the problem is easily corrected, although it wastes time. When ambiguity isn't this obvious, the subsequent misunderstanding could derail an interview, with neither party understanding why.

Direct or Indirect?

Wording of questions also requires us to consider whether our approach will be direct or indirect. **Direct questions** usually are blunt, streamlined, and uncompromising. A doctor trying to stop someone's self-destructive behavior might say, "Do you want to die?" That's about as direct as it gets. **Indirect questions** frequently are marked by introductory phrases, related issues, or qualifiers, allowing the respondent to infer the question rather than hear it directly. Instead of a blunt question, the doctor says, "I know you love your family, so what do you think they want you to do about this problem?"

The choice of direct or indirect questions isn't always clear cut. The choice, though, ought to be guided by the circumstances, not by the temperament of the interviewer. If your personality is by nature more direct, it's important to consider whether the situation might call for indirect questions. If you're more comfortable with asking indirect questions, you might have to adapt in an interview with someone who prefers a direct style.

Direct questions, while valuable in some contexts, can put people on the defensive. ("How dare you ask that?") Conversely, an indirect approach might prevent the interview from reaching a crucial juncture because the interviewer tiptoes around sensitive areas. Once again, flexibility should be your guide.

Presentation

Except for some standardized, pencil-and-paper, or self-administered survey interviews, presentational style profoundly influences how questions are perceived and answered. Delivery of a message counts. If you've driven twenty minutes to the mall to return a defective toaster, you're not going to show much patience with a clerk who asks, in a sneering voice, "What *seems* to be the problem?" In interviews, we are likely to be even more sensitive to tone, and when put off by what we hear, see, or *sense* in the questions put to us, successful communication becomes that much harder.

Four aspects of presentation play especially important roles in how the interview progresses: tone, inflection, rhythm, and pace.

Tone

Tone refers to how the manner or style of speech presumably reflects inner emotional states. Whether baritone or soprano, we're all capable of a wide range of nonverbal implications, moving, by tone of voice, from icy detachment to dripping sweetness. We aren't robots, so tone of voice, while controllable, will be dictated in part by our emotional or physical condition. People who know you well can tell, even over the telephone, if your tone isn't normal. "You don't sound like yourself," a friend might say, meaning there's something in your voice that suggests you're distracted or tired or sad. Tone might also be influenced by how we perceive our conversational partner. For example, a nurse might interview an older person as if addressing a child, or a boss might evaluate a subordinate in a condescending tone. Interviewers and interviewees should conduct what amounts to a sound check: Is my tone justified and appropriate for the interview at hand?

Tone can also be affected by other forms of nonverbal expressiveness. A question delivered without much discernible facial expression of interest or involvement sends a confusing message, at best. On the other hand, simple eye contact, a smile, or other form of reinforcement makes a big difference in people's willingness to answer. Nonverbal messages, however, can be misunderstood, a point developed more fully in Chapter 5. A nod might be construed as agreement rather than acknowledgment, for example. Moreover, if a nonverbal message seems staged, it could do more harm than good in the delivery of questions.

Inflection

Related to tone of voice but in a particular way, **inflection** is how we emphasize or stress certain words over others by raising the volume or pitch of our voice. Stanley Payne (1980) again helps us understand how inflection affects the meaning of a question. He uses a sample question, "Why do you say that?" and advises repeating the question aloud, accenting each word, one at a time (p. 204):

"*Why* do you say that?"

"Why *do* you say that?"

"Why do *you* say that?"

"Why do you *say* that?"

"Why do you say *that*?"

Do you detect a difference in each accent? For each example, inflection carries a shade of meaning. In the last, the emphasis suggests incredulity on the interviewer's part.

Inflection can have its place in questions, but it should be used with a purpose. Inflection also relates to body language. A raised eyebrow, smirk, or frown can provide inflection as effectively as raised pitch.

Rhythm

By **rhythm**, we mean a comfortable, harmonious order and progression of an interview. Interruptions, in particular, can break the rhythm of an interview, so be patient and give your partner ample time for a complete response before offering another question or comment. Questioning often takes on a give-and-take intensity, and a badly timed interruption spoils the mood and chemistry. Some people interrupt because they lack listening discipline. Others interrupt because they incorrectly sense the speaker has finished a thought. Remember that answers don't always gush out; they may take time to percolate.

BOX 4.5   **REMINDERS**

Asking Questions Comfortably

- *Rehearse your interview questions and pretest them on friends or colleagues.* Read the questions aloud and then consider each: Was it clear? Fair? Could it be improved? Ask, too, about your delivery. What would a listener hear in your pacing or tone of voice?

- *Keep your questions as simple as possible.* Use concrete, everyday language whenever possible. Avoid any **suitcase question**—one crammed to overflowing with implications. Avoid, as well, **double-barreled questions,** with two or more parts to them. They leave respondents trying to decide which part to answer first, provided they can remember one part from another. For example, are you tempted to ask, "Where did you grow up, and how did you like the kids you played with there?" If you ask two different questions instead, you'll let a respondent answer each comfortably.

- *Monitor the impact of questions, being alert for verbal or nonverbal signs of misunderstanding or hostility.* Watch the respondent's eyes. They reflect

boredom, confusion, anger, and many other reactions. Body movement and gestures also can be quite expressive. Ask about the question if you detect any sign that it's not being interpreted as you expected.

- *Give room and encouragement to answer.* Don't rush through your list of questions. Give yourself and your partner enough space to accomplish goals. Unless it's clearly necessary because of time constraints, don't cut short an answer. Closed questions don't allow conversation to energize the interview; relatively open primary questions are advisable in all but standardized, highly scheduled survey interviews. Then you can probe to flesh out the details and specifics of the interviewee's perspective.

- *Remain calm and professional as you question and listen.* That doesn't mean you must maintain a totally neutral, detached demeanor. Intensity and engagement demonstrate that you're committed to the interview. But anger, frustration, or defensiveness are unlikely to advance your goals.

Pace

Pace describes the timing and tempo of questions. It's related to rhythm, because bad timing and discordant tempo will affect the flow of the interview. But proper pacing has more serious implications for the quality and quantity of information and insight elicited. To rush through questions or move abruptly from one question to the next can affect the outcome; people differ in their pace of answering. One person's normal rate of speech might sound as slow as molasses to someone else. Be sensitive to differences in pace and the reasons for them, such as culture or age. Interviewers should adjust their questioning to maintain a pace that is comfortable for both partners (see Box 4.5).

Answers without Questions

There can be a judgmental aspect to questions. Often, questioning begins with the basics—who, what, where, when.

Trying Out Your Skills

Find a published interview in a magazine, newspaper, book; or tape one from a broadcast interview. Using the criteria discussed in this chapter, identify and analyze

- Types of questions
- Order of questions
- Effectiveness of questions

"Do you recycle?"

"What do you recycle?"

"When and where do you recycle?"

Questions usually aren't viewed negatively, however, until they cross a threshold into the realm of motivation and values. The questions may follow a logical progression from fact-finding to exploration, but clearly they are different from the preceding ones.

"You said you seldom recycle. Why not?"

The threshold has been crossed, although tentatively. Then a bolder question: "Do you feel you have an obligation to be environmentally responsible?" Judgmental inferences continue with the line of questioning. "What about future generations? Do you want them to inherit a country of landfills?"

The judgmental quality of these examples is obvious. However, seemingly benign questions can also seem judgmental or accusatory, particularly in their cumulative effect, as they pile on, one after another. A relentless question-and-answer cycle can depersonalize communication and limit dialogue, according to Alfred Benjamin, author of *The Helping Interview* (1987). (See Box 4.6 for suggestions on how to answer questions comfortably.) Information can emerge from verbal and nonverbal statements and forms of encouragement that "ask" without the introduction of a question mark. A neutral request for information or a comment can succeed where a question, with its judgmental qualities, fails. "Why" questions, in particular, demand explanations, which, in turn, can compel people to incorporate excuses or justifications as part of an answer. Consider the differences between the following two alternatives:

Question: "Why did your marriage end in divorce?"

Comment/request: "I'm curious about your interpretation of the divorce. Tell me about it from your perspective."

Either approach could produce an answer. Which, though, would you prefer? The neutral request puts the interviewee in control of the substance of the answer (unless it is said in a demanding tone) and tends to reduce the possibility of defensiveness.

The request approach might include using a comment to elicit a response. A comment-as-question could take a variety of forms so long as stimulating an answer is still the objective.

BOX 4.6   R E M I N D E R S

Answering Questions Comfortably

- *Prepare for an interview by anticipating the questions likely to be asked.* Remember that the prepared interviewer has thought about the questions, perhaps even to the point of mentally drafting possible answers. Anticipating questions obviously helps in formulating a thoughtful response instead of a spur-of-the-moment one. If the question doesn't come up, don't consider your efforts wasted. You still have acquired additional insights.

- *Don't rush to answer questions.* Although certain questions can be dispatched quickly, reduce your speed at times. It's not bad form to ponder for a moment or two, perhaps saying, "Let me give that a little thought, please." Studies show that students tend to produce fuller, richer answers when allowed **wait time**—a significant pause of several seconds in which a questioner indicates a willingness for respondents to think through the implications of a point (Rowe, 1987). But because not all interviewers are used to offering wait time, you might claim it comfortably for yourself. With complex questions, simply pause to collect your thoughts before answering. And don't hesitate to say, "Would you

please repeat the question?" if necessary. Often, the interviewer takes this as a cue to reconstruct or clarify the question.

- *Make sure you have enough information to understand* and *answer the question.* There are two parts to this reminder. First, if the language or terminology isn't familiar, it's better to ask for definitions than to answer based on a flawed understanding. Second, ask for additional information or background if you're not sure you know enough about the subject. A memory nudge might be all you need.

- *Discuss questions you don't feel are appropriate or relevant to the interview.* In most cases, you're not obligated to answer all questions. Dodging a question with an evasive answer generally exacerbates the situation. It's better to confront a problem directly.

- *Follow up to ensure the question was answered, or that the questioner hasn't misinterpreted your response.* Mistakes are inevitable when people communicate. Check things out before moving on to another line of answers or before ending the interview.

Comment: "You didn't make it to today's committee meeting. You must have been busy with something else."

The comment is another way of asking, "Why weren't you at the meeting?" but without a judgmental or accusatory implication. Of course, if it's essential to obtain an overt explanation of what happened and it isn't forthcoming, a direct question might be required.

BEYOND THE BASICS

Why People Want to Answer, Why They Don't

Questions can flatter. When someone asks us about ourselves, it's an invitation to speak and be heard. Yet questions sometimes cause us to demur, "Oh, you don't really want to know about my childhood, do you?" Do we doubt the sincerity or motives of questioners? Do we doubt our ability to provide a bright, original answer? Our reaction may depend on how we see our stake, for answering questions carries ramifications. Do the questions reflect a sincere interest in me? Or do I feel patronized? Can I trust the person asking me questions? Or do I feel exploited? In answering a question will I suffer no harm? Or will I put myself in jeopardy? Will my best interests be served? Or will I live to regret ever opening my mouth?

We're questioned in depth as we apply for insurance, rent a car, take out a home loan, open a checking account, fill out a patient's form, or seek financial aid for school expenses. Our habitual role of answerer explains why strangers can ask questions, even personal ones, and many of us respond without hesitation. With an interview, however, the stakes increase, and, often, so does our wariness. Interview questions put us on the spot because they demand a response, even if that response is a refusal to answer.

"Did you ever get caught shoplifting?" (Interviewer)

"I refuse to dignify that question with an answer." (Interviewee)

Questions can intrude or unsettle. They may force us into revealing part of ourselves we'd rather keep private.

Here is a fundamental truth about the act of answering: *When questioned, people want to feel safe more than anything else.* If they sense danger in a question, the defenses go up. Indeed, it can be perilous to provide answers. That is why empathy should accompany interviewers' questions. When questioning, try assessing each question as the other person might experience it from his or her perspective. In addition, you might use your own experience as a criterion: Would I find the question invasive? Hurtful? Insensitive? Empathy, supported by honesty of purpose on the part of the questioner, should help encourage comparable behavior by respondents. Sometimes, though, we must abandon certain questions or qualify what we ask if we want a complete, honest answer. Questioning doesn't have to be a hand-holding sensitivity session. Difficult situations may call for difficult questions. Empathy and honesty, however, can make it possible to ask tough questions and get answers. A collaborative, supportive environment encourages disclosure.

Questions aren't more important than answers, although the emphasis given them in interviewing textbooks suggests this is the case. A saying goes, "Judge people by their questions, not their answers," but clearly people reveal themselves by their answers, too. Another saying advises, "There are two sides to every question." Certainly that's true when considering that a question may have different meanings for the interviewer and the interviewee. That applies to answers as well. Constant monitoring of questions and answers, often by questions *about* what's being said and perceived, helps keep interview participants on the same frequency. A two-way question-and-answer pattern, however, usually promotes communication and safeguards against misunderstandings.

For various reasons, people don't always answer in ways that satisfy the questioner. Think of your own experience in questioning. You ask someone about her ill father ("How's your dad doing, Sarah?") and get a clipped response ("Oh, he's OK"). It seems apparent that Sarah is uneasy or unwilling to say more, so you might decide to abandon the subject or ask a series of less direct questions. To you, her answer suggests another level of meaning. That happens often enough as we process answers, although perhaps not as starkly as Sarah's reticence about her father's illness.

Herbert Blumer (1969) coined the term **symbolic interactionism** to identify a way of explaining how humans interact. Symbolic interactionism applies to question-and-answer behavior. Summarizing Blumer's work, William Foddy (1993) says people don't react in a simple stimulus-response model; they ascribe meaning to one another's acts in an attempt to construct a symbolic world they both will inhabit verbally. When meaning isn't clear or openly discussed, then both interviewer and interviewee typically search for clues in their interpretation of their questions and answers, taking into account presumptions and knowledge of each other and the situation facing them (pp. 21, 22).

Symbolic interactionists suggest that personal and social processes are inevitably intertwined, and that symbols, including language use, are the key to understanding both. Through language, people internalize social processes and imagine others' evaluations and reactions to them, developing along the way a sense of self by comparing personal experiences and larger social patterns. The hidden or multiple meanings of answers underscore the importance of listening and interpreting as a companion skill to questioning. If we want questions and answers to work in harmony and, ultimately, lead to mutual understanding, we must do our best to understand the truest meanings of answers from the perspective of those who offer them. Don't let assumptions distort your ability to discern answers. What you find evasive might not constitute an underhanded tactic; rather, it could be a justifiable attempt to protect the interviewee's privacy or emotional health. Analyze answers with an open mind, recognizing that no interviewer possesses omniscience. You'll make mistakes in exploring what an answer says or doesn't say, but you'll make more mistakes by neglecting to analyze and account for the meaning of answers.

If you've considered an answer carefully and still can't figure out why it seems deficient or unhelpful, evaluate the quality of your question. Answering questions constitutes an act of giving that can never be taken for granted.

Ethics of Questioning

Asking questions must include a consideration of values, biases, motivations, consequences, duties, and alternatives. Inescapable ethical implications accompany questioning. Let's start with *values* that influence our everyday communicative behavior. For example, do we respect the words and feelings of others? Do we believe in truth telling? Do we appreciate collaboration and dialogue? Raising these points involves introspective examination of our questioning orientation and motivation. Interviewing can be a heady, ego-gratifying experience. Interviewers should inquire of themselves with questions like these: Do I ask to win? To rationalize my biases? To prove my toughness? To see others squirm or cry? Early in his career, Mike Wallace (1984) sharply questioned cartoonist Al Capp, creator of

"Li'l Abner," fixing on Capp's nervous giggle. "Why do you laugh that way, Mr. Capp? It seems compulsive, doesn't it?" Capp began to sweat and squirm, which spurred Wallace on. "Capp's distress had a mesmerizing effect on me and I persisted; I didn't let up because I felt we were getting close to the bone" (p. 34). Wallace's reaction hints at the addictive power of questioning and underscores the advice that interviewers look deep into their motives.

Of particular concern are questions distorted by *biases*. We all see the world in some-what different ways. By looking hard at our questions for signs of bias, we have an opportunity to compensate. Biases exist in many forms, and if we're not diligent about resisting their pull, they'll become part of our conventional way of thinking and acting. Among your biases might be a belief that females cannot manage male factory workers or that teenagers cannot be trusted to follow directions. Biases also include assumptions about personality types, business procedures, and communication styles. Without ac-knowledging your biases, you'll find it hard to be fair and, in turn, ethical, in asking questions *and* interpreting the answers.

Further examination of our questioning orientation leads to another ethical crossroads: Whose interests are served by my questions? My own? The interviewee's? The company's? The profession's? A combination of interests? A TV reporter could say with conviction that his aggressive questions are meant to produce a fair, honest story that serves the public interest. His *motivation,* the reporter says, "is the pursuit of truth." This is a justification for questioning that most journalists would say sounds reasonable. A district manager might conduct an appraisal interview to weed out average-performing salespersons and advance the company's mission. That, too, sounds reasonable. But what about people who ask questions without regard for the *consequences* to others who have a stake in the outcome? Can you justify a purely self-serving rationale for your questions? Success in an interview can be measured in various ways. It's possible for everyone to "win" when an interview is a collaboration instead of a contest. An exercise in teamwork asks participants to pair up and arm wrestle, with the instruction to "win" as many times as possible in fifteen seconds. Most people square off against each other, struggling to pin the opponent. But those who don't define winning as one person defeating another use the time to flip their arms in a back-and-forth exchange, without resistance.

In Chapter 1 and elsewhere we've covered two principal ethical orientations—teleo-logical (consequence based) and deontological (duty based). As we practice ethics in our lives, we usually account for both duties and consequences. Not every situation allows us, however, to meet all our duties, for they sometimes compete. Moreover, duties and con-sequences clash, leaving us with difficult decisions.

After reviewing our questioning values, biases, and motives, the next stage involves establishing our personal and professional *duties* to ask, and there can be a tug of war between the two. In some fields, among them medicine and counseling, conflicting schools of thought complicate ethical decision making. Physicians, for example, might decide a paternalistic approach to communication best serves particular patients, and therefore they withhold or disguise the purpose of the interview and their questioning.

Instead of saying, "I'm interviewing you to decide whether you're a good candidate for a liver transplant," the doctor allows the patient to assume the questions are part of a standard medical history. You might say an interview of such import should keep all information strictly above board. But the doctor decides an oblique approach is both ethically and medically justified, even though she personally would prefer directness.

The general goal of questions is to seek the truth. But there must be limits to asking questions, even in pursuit of the truth. Who could condone torture as a truth-detection method? Obviously, the ends cannot always justify the means, especially if the questioning, by intent or recklessness, hurts someone through, for example, embarrassment, humiliation, ridicule, or bullying. Asking questions involves consequences as well. In balancing duties versus consequences, it's necessary to identify the stakeholders and consider how they might be affected by your action. The consequences of seeking the truth, for example, might result in emotional distress for the interviewee, but are larger interests at stake? The interviewer's obligation to protect an interviewee from harm may have to yield to the consequence-based concept of utilitarianism—the greatest good for the greatest number.

Ethical interviewers not only weigh duties and consequences, they also factor in *alternatives* to asking questions and obtaining information. Usually, there are several possible routes to a destination. It might be safer and more effective to take a roundabout path than race down Main Street. Ethical decision making should not be done in haste. Question and justify your actions with acute ethical sensitivity.

Informed Consent

When police question crime suspects, they're required to issue a *Miranda* warning. The language of the warning varies by locale, but essentially it covers four points: "You have the right to remain silent. If you waive your right, anything you say may be used against you. You have the right to an attorney. If you can't afford an attorney, one will be provided without charge." The U.S. Supreme Court devised the warning as a procedural safeguard against abuse by police interrogators skilled at getting people to talk without the benefit of legal representation.

Skilled interviewers, like skilled detectives, know how to get answers. When asking sensitive questions, a standard ethical approach calls for **informed consent,** the Miranda warning for interviewers. Informed consent involves telling participants about the risks and benefits of answering questions. It also can include a reminder that participation is voluntary and consent can be withdrawn at any time.

Informed consent usually arises in interviews conducted by researchers on human subjects. Grant guidelines and other rules governing the research, set by institutions or universities, often require a signed informed-consent form from participants as a condition for approval of a project. Informed consent, however, isn't considered a requirement in interviews conducted by journalists, job recruiters, managers, or counselors, for example. In these situations, it's frequently assumed that the interviewee knows what is at stake. An ethical interviewer won't accept that assumption.

When is informed consent appropriate? In general, informed consent fits any interviewing situation posing risks that for one reason or another aren't obvious to the interviewee. Certain interviewees warrant extra care, mainly children and the mentally or emotionally impaired, when there is concern about either their answering ability or vulnerability.

Informed consent invariably includes an explanation of how the information will be kept confidential or made public. Confidentiality is a serious ethical issue.

Confidentiality

Confidentiality in questioning usually covers two conditions—that the private information collected won't be made public and/or that the source of the information won't be identified. Of course, many interviews are conducted without a formal pledge of confidentiality. But lack of a written agreement doesn't free interviewers of a responsibility to keep confidences. With the exception of published or broadcast interviews by journalists, interviews aren't public events, and, as a result, interviewees expect that what they say won't end up as office gossip or cocktail talk. People may voluntarily answer quite personal questions, but they also do so with a tacit understanding that the information will be used discreetly and properly. People, though, sometimes act carelessly about the information obtained by questioning, and they blab it to others or fail to ensure the security of notes and other recorded material. Besides being bad form, it may be a violation of a confidence. When interviews go well, it's often because the provider of information trusts the recipient to act responsibly.

A pledge of confidentiality—formal or informal—should not be taken lightly. It obligates you to protect that confidence, no matter what happens. You should be sure of your position before agreeing to safeguard information. Pressure, including litigation, might force you to disclose what you've collected from a subject. Journalists have been jailed for refusing to identify anonymous sources. Ethics, however, isn't an exact science. The balance can tip in favor of disclosure over confidentiality when circumstances warrant, such as a teacher who concludes her higher ethical duty, based on weighing the consequences, is to report a child's confidence that "Mommy's boyfriend hurt my brother."

Deception

Deception in questioning takes three forms: false identification, pretense, and devious behavior. Interviewers who hide their identity do so usually because they feel deception gives them an advantage. People tend to conduct themselves in ways that seem appropriate for the situation, and that includes how to answer questions. We are different from one communication context to the next. A job applicant, for example, who is told he's going to talk to some prospective coworkers, might assume a casual demeanor, making light of some questions that he might answer more seriously if asked by a boss. In truth, several of the people he chats with are managers who want to observe the "real" person. Certainly, the interviewee suffers a disadvantage, denied the opportunity to adjust his communication style to the situation. It's difficult to justify masquerades or disguises as ethical. But

Asking

In your role as president of the campus chapter of a professional organization for accountants, you're investigating reports that the group's treasurer has been pocketing money from sales of sweatshirts instead of depositing it in a scholarship fund. You discover that an inventory of sweatshirts and receipts shows a $150 discrepancy. You cannot account for the missing funds despite repeated review of the facts as you know them.

Here is a situation that would challenge anyone's questioning acuity, but you conclude that questions must be asked to uncover the truth, which includes the possibility there has been no wrongdoing.

- *What would you do before questioning the treasurer?*
- *What answers would you seek?*
- *How would you begin the interview?*
- *How would you frame and order your initial questions? Try devising a list.*

Let's hope a plausible explanation emerges before you reach the ultimate question about theft of the funds. But what would you do if the answers aren't satisfactory or suggest the treasurer isn't telling the truth? What next? What are your ethical concerns?

Answering

You're making plans for finding a job in law enforcement after graduation. As a preparatory step, you schedule an interview with the college placement director for advice. Let's assume you've encountered someone who is not known for tact, and you find yourself facing these questions:

- *Why is a petite thing like you planning a career in law enforcement?*
- *Some police agencies do thorough background checks of applicants. Have you or any of your relatives been in trouble with the law?*
- *What satisfaction would you get out of carrying a gun and handcuffs and locking people up?*
- *Have you thought about less dangerous work?*

What is your reaction to these questions? How would you answer them?

they're also questionable as a useful learning tactic. Above all, deception breeds distrust, and that includes its effect on those who practice deception because they assume others will deceive them.

Interviewers who resort to pretense to camouflage the actual purpose of an interview may not lie outright, but they certainly aren't being truthful. Deception about the purpose of an interview borders on entrapment, and people who engage in that tactic usually rationalize that they won't gain the interviewee's cooperation by being forthright. Once again, the deception denies the interviewee freedom of choice. Moreover, it undermines both the credibility of the interviewer and the validity of the information collected. Communication should be conducted on as equal footing as possible, but there are always exceptions.

Occasionally, something less than full disclosure may be acceptable. Researchers and other interviewers sometimes walk an ethical tightrope when they withhold details about interview objectives. At times, it's in the best interests of the interviewee to withhold certain details. At other times, it's a matter of simultaneously serving the specific interests of the interviewee without jeopardizing the important, broader interests of the interview. In a few instances, the greatest-good theory might prevail.

Finally, deception can take the form of tricks and exploitation, such as an interviewer who feigns empathy in asking questions. Getting answers by posing as a confidant or friend amounts to betrayal. Those who pretend engage in acting, and unless they are exceptionally good actors, eventually they'll be exposed. It's far better to rely on ability than guile.

Toughness versus Courage

Conscientious interviewers work hard to devise the "right" questions, which often means "tough" questions. In fact, by male standards mostly, interviewers get high marks for throwing "hardball" questions and are demeaned for lobbing "softballs" or "marshmallows." Tough doesn't necessarily equate to good, although there are certainly effective, tough questions. However, concentrating on the zinger, bomb, or coup de grace elevates the negative question over those that, while less dramatic, hold greater potential for beneficial results.

Courage in questioning is another matter. Professional interviewers assume a responsibility to do their duty, even when it might be uncomfortable or painful. Avoiding that duty usually means avoiding a problem—the interviewer's or the interviewee's. Eventually, the problem must surface. For example, a supervisor who values his popularity avoids questioning an employee about alleged safety violations. The supervisor lacks the courage to put the safety of workers over his personal interests.

The perfect ethical decision doesn't exist. But we meet our responsibilities best when we reflect as thoroughly as possible about our questioning ethics. Asking and answering questions requires an ethical guidance system.

Summary

You've learned from this chapter that the ability to ask questions is at the heart of effective interviewing. Questioning, though, cannot be divorced from its companion skills of listening and framing.

Focusing on a purpose and a plan for questioning is an essential first step. Without clarity of purpose, shared, ideally, by interviewer and interviewee, the interview may drift without direction.

Questions help fuel conversation and elicit useful answers. Particularly important are questions, called probes, that serve to bring answers to their fullest potential. The wording of questions is also important. Misunderstandings are common in interviews, so questions should be as clear and focused as possible. Both interviewer and interviewee have responsibilities to check and recheck the condition of the interview and the questions and answers that arise.

In "Beyond the Basics" we note that the ethics of questioning involves a range of considerations, including the interviewer's communication orientation and biases. A thorough ethical audit helps reveal potential problems and conflicts. The responsibilities to gather information and safeguard the interests of the interviewee might conflict. An ethical grounding helps interviewers make justifiable decisions and avoid causing harm.

The Interview Bookshelf

On a general understanding of questions in human interaction

Dillon, J. T. (1990). *The practice of questioning.* New York: Routledge.

Loaded with advice and insights into questioning under various conditions. Especially good sections on the notions of questioning and the alternatives to questioning. Well supported by research and theory.

On the difficulties of phrasing effective questions

Foddy, W. (1993). *Constructing questions for interviews and questionnaires.* Cambridge, UK: Cambridge University Press.

Technical in places but useful for its insights into how memory affects the quality of answers and what steps you can take to ensure that your questions work as intended.

Leeds, D. (1987). *Smart questions.* New York: Berkley Books.

Pitched to managers, but it's filled with good ideas about the why and wherefore of asking questions in various situations. Particularly good is a section on making questions fit certain personality types, among them the "convincers" and the "calculators."

The classic work on questioning

Payne, S. L. (1951/1980). *The art of asking questions.* Princeton, NJ: Princeton University Press.

This readable classic provides a catalogue of question pitfalls. Payne also suggests questions to ask about our questions, with clever, useful examples throughout.

References

Benjamin, A. (1987). *The helping interview.* Boston: Houghton Mifflin.

Blumer, H. (1969). *Symbolic interactionism: Perspective and method.* Englewood Cliffs, NJ: Prentice-Hall.

Brian, D. (1973). *Murderers and other friendly people.* New York: McGraw-Hill.

Buchanan, E. (1987). *The corpse had a familiar face.* New York: Random House.

Dillon, J. T. (1990). *The practice of questioning.* New York: Routledge.

Fetterman, D. M. (1989). *Ethnography: Step by step.* Newbury Park, CA: Sage.

Foddy, W. (1993). *Constructing questions for interviews and questionnaires.* Cambridge, UK: Cambridge University Press.

Kanter, A. (1995). *The essential book of interviewing.* New York: Times Books.

Lamb, B. (1997). *Booknotes: America's finest authors on reading, writing and the power of ideas.* New York: Times Books.

Payne, S. L. (1951/1980). *The art of asking questions.* Princeton, NJ: Princeton University Press.

Rowe, M. B. (1987, Spring). Wait time: slowing down may be a way of speeding up. *American Educator,* 38–40.

Rugg, D. (1941). Experiments in wording questions: II. *Public Opinion Quarterly 5,* 91–92.

Simon, R. (1990). *Road show.* New York: Farrar, Straus, Giroux.

Sudman, S., & Bradburn, N. (1982). *Asking questions.* San Francisco: Jossey-Bass.

Tannen, D. (1990). *You just don't understand: Women and men in conversation.* New York: Ballantine.

Wallace, M., & G. P. Gates (1984). *Close encounters.* New York: Morrow.

✿ 5 Skillful Framing

The frame around a picture, if we consider this frame as a message intended to order or organize the perception of the viewer, says, "Attend to what is within and do not attend to what is outside. . . ." Psychological frames are related to what we have called "premises." The picture frame tells the viewer that he is not to use the same sort of thinking in interpreting the picture that he might use in interpreting the wallpaper outside the frame. . . . The frame itself thus becomes a part of the premise system.

—Gregory Bateson, *Steps to an Ecology of Mind*

LEARNING GOALS

After reading this chapter, you should be able to

- Define framing and discuss its importance relative to the other two basic skills of interviewing: speaking (including questioning) and listening
- Employ in interviews the four basic skills of framing: metacommunicating, contextualizing, offering accounts, and reframing
- Make informed choices about when, how, and whether to use note taking, delayed note taking, and tape recording to document interviews
- Articulate your own position on a contemporary controversy about language and group identity, and use acceptance-oriented language in interviews

M any interview participants act as if their communication is entirely about speaking and listening. Yet speech is not automatically meaningful, and listening is not always focused. What makes communication in an interview meaningful and focused enough for participants to believe they each have been understood?

Interaction, as anthropologist and communication theorist Gregory Bateson claims throughout his writing, becomes meaningful to the extent that humans perceive it as *patterned.* You can never simply "have" a conversation with someone else in the same sense that you "have" a car or "have" a cold. It can't be possessed, because conversations are not things but mutually coordinated action that belongs to no one. To participate in conversation means that you and your partner are constantly constructing an overall pattern of meaning into which each of the various messages will seem to fit—if you are successful. Bateson (see, for examples, 1972, 1980, 1991) believed that persons never know what is going on "in" their lives unless they can perceive the larger patterns *between* their lives that participants are creating.

In a sense, these patterns form part of the meaning of talk. Unfortunately (or perhaps fortunately), communicators rarely articulate or even indirectly refer to these larger patterns, in part because they don't think they need to do so and in part probably because they can't articulate the frames fully. Martina notices that her younger brother Mitch forgot about their father's birthday and has heard from a friend that he's missed quite a few classes lately at the university, too. Adopting her usual lighthearted attitude of kidding, she calls to express her concern, asking if everything is all right: "Hey, Bub. Where have you been? Dad asked about you at the birthday party. You sick, or what?" Mitch, however, replies, "Why do you always have to check up on me? You're always grilling me. Let me live my own life." This takes Martina aback, and she is shocked. What Mitch evidently interpreted as prying she had intended as an expression of loving concern. How could this happen between reasonable people? Prying and loving concern are very distinct, perhaps even contradictory, categories in most people's minds. It never occurred to Martina that Mitch would take her question as an example of interrogation, and it never occurred to him that Martina didn't intend her inquiry as a criticism. Yet as they talked, their two different frames for the communication became more decisive than the actual words themselves.

Linguist Deborah Tannen (1986, 1990) has explored some of the dimensions of interpersonal security and insecurity that arise from different patterns of talk. As an example, she observes that ". . . if you talk to others as if you were a teacher and they were your students, they may perceive that your way of talking frames you as condescending or pedantic. If you talk to others as if you were a student seeking help and explanations, they may perceive you as insecure, incompetent, or naive. Our reactions to what others say or do are often sparked by how we feel we are being framed" (1990, pp. 33–34). Perhaps this helps explain why Mitch reacted as he did with Martina, despite her assurance that her question was motivated by love. More to the point of this book, such alignment of interpretive patterns explains why it's such a delicate balancing act for a job applicant to come across as appropriately deferential and appropriately assertive at the same time. Does the applicant frame herself or himself as a "learner" (seeking knowledge) or a "teacher" (offering expertise)? Or is it possible to do both simultaneously? In Chapter 6 we offer a series of suggestions for dealing with this issue head-on.

Bateson, as an anthropologist attempting to understand others' experiences across cultural differences, recognized that cultures themselves were made up of these larger patterns for making experience and action meaningful. Stated another way, you know you are communicating in a different culture, subculture, or coculture when you are often surprised at how others take things and at how they react seemingly unpredictably to your behavior. To them, the reactions aren't unpredictable; they perceive your behavior from within their own frame of experience. You experience unpredictability because you're applying a different framework. As we shall see later in the chapter, some of the most striking examples of communication conflict and misunderstanding come from trying to apply intracultural frames cross-culturally. Yet the basic phenomenon Bateson identified extends far beyond cross-cultural communication, essentially to all human interaction.

In Chapter 1 we introduced framing in general terms as the ability "to form interpretations of what we think is really going on in social situations." In addition, we discussed Michael Agar's (1994) notion that a frame "sets a boundary around . . . details and highlights how those details are related to each other" (p. 130). Only by understanding the concept of a frame is it possible to understand how people who seem to be doing the same thing together (such as conducting an interview) are each actively engaged in doing something else. His frame for a comment is "playful joke," but hers is "unfair put-down." In this chapter we will build on that fundamental problem of pattern recognition. In "The Basics" we discuss three issues: (1) we define the process of framing more specifically in the context of interviewing, (2) we describe a set of skills and appreciations that can help interview participants sharpen their understanding of these larger patterns of meaning, and (3) we suggest practical approaches for taking notes and recording interviews. Then, in "Beyond the Basics," we return to Bateson's cultural motivations more directly. We'll ask you to grapple with framing problems introduced by our language habits. If naming and renaming things changes people's experience of those things, as frame theorists claim, then such matters as gender-neutral and other forms of bias-free language are extremely important. In this section you will be challenged, perhaps, to think of the political correctness controversy in different terms. We hope to remove the controversy from a narrowly political liberal versus conservative context, to reframe it as a matter of clear communication.

Definitions of frame and framing vary somewhat from researcher to researcher, although most seem to trace a lineage from Gregory Bateson (1972) through Erving Goffman (1974). It might be helpful to bring the concept down to earth with a practical example from the world of interviewing. Think of this as a definition in motion.

THE BASICS ⌘

What Is Framing? Knowledge Interpreted in Pattern

Consider the task of Barbara, a personnel manager interviewing an applicant whom, from the first minutes of their meeting, she likes enormously. She discovers a ready rapport developing, and Barbara and Rose genuinely appear to enjoy each other's company. In a seemingly effortless way, interviewee and interviewer quickly shed certain more or less official aspects of their roles and engage in banter about different organizations and bosses for whom they have worked. Barbara shares a couple of minor irritations that, she realizes too late, could be thought to apply to her own company as well as to others. By the time Rose starts to answer the standard schedule of questions originally planned for each interview, she has gained much more information and insight about the organization than most interviewees are likely to have.

Suddenly, Barbara recognizes that this experience is different from the previous twelve interviews she's conducted for this position, and for the same reasons, it's likely to be different from the next several. It's going smoothly, but something is faintly troubling, too. It's not going to be easy to compare these responses with those of the other twelve applicants. Some questions have not been asked at all, because Barbara thought their answers might be inferred reasonably from the conversation early in the interview. Barbara heard how some topics elicited elongated stories, as if from friend to friend, and she reveled in their telling. She found herself, also, subtly trying to "sell" the company by phrasing even restrictive personnel policies in their best light. A faint, but real, warning buzzer sounds inside Barbara, telling her that while this conversation feels right in many ways, there might be something wrong as well. Will the tone and presumption of friendship affect her ability to make an effective recommendation on which candidate to hire? Are there aspects of her role as employment interviewer that require her to maintain some distance between her and interviewees, at least for a while?

Nervously, Barbara clears her throat, sits up straighter, and announces, "Well, let's move more directly now to a series of job-related issues. We want to know how you've interceded in conflict situations in your previous leadership positions. Could you elaborate?" Barbara's language and demeanor suddenly become much more formal, and Rose takes the cue even without fully understanding what is happening, mirroring by making her own comments sound more official: "Yes. I directed a great many projects at the National Endowment. When tempers rose, I tried to establish a buffer zone between the parties." At one level, Rose—as a skilled communicator—is alert enough to see that something has changed. But inside, at another level, Rose is upset. What has she done wrong? Has she offended Barbara unintentionally? Why the sudden turnaround just when things have been going so smoothly? What are the new ground rules? Off balance and tentative, she stumbles through the rest of the interview, offering opinions without much confidence.

There are many ways to analyze what is going on here. The human resources department, whose members trained Barbara in equal employment opportunity, affirmative action, and fair hiring practices, might see an excessively friendly and informal conversational tone as a breach of fairness to other applicants and applaud Barbara's change of heart. Rose might think, at least initially, it was her good fortune to have had a personality so compatible with the interviewer's. Others in the company might suggest that Barbara's conversational impulse was not wrong at all, because it successfully discovered an excellent interpersonal "fit" between worker and organization. Barbara might see the whole incident as a lapse in professionalism or a regrettable fact of an interviewer's life that she can never really be "herself." However, from the standpoint of this book, we want to understand the event simply as an example of how different frames—ways of organizing and interpreting the situation—have consequences for common action.

One particularly good way to analyze this situation is through the actors' own definitions of the situation. Both parties arrived expecting their communication to conform to their expectations for the social event called "job interview." They had, in sociologist Erving Goffman's (1974, p. 338) words, a clear frame—one in which all participants have a similar definition. Roughly stated, these expectations for employment interviewing usually involve a relatively high degree of formality, a clear differentiation of power between interviewer and interviewee, heightened emotional tension, and reliance upon a series of well-defined questions and answers. Based upon Barbara's initial positive impressions and perhaps Rose's successful **impression management skills** (her ability to shape her talk and nonverbal messages successfully to the demands of a situation), the definitions each held of the situation began to melt, to be replaced by new expectations—ones that more nearly characterize informal chats between friends, for example. The formality decreased, the mood was decidedly egalitarian and nonthreatening, both felt more relaxed, and interchanges depended more on spontaneous statements and observations than on questions and answers. A new frame emerged, one that could be called "friendly chat," perhaps. In this instance, the new frame seemed to be a mutual creation that was formed by the talk itself as each person let herself break out of previous assumptions. Both frames were conversations, but the expectations and rules guiding them were decidedly different.

Yet, after the informal friendly conversation was established, Barbara found it necessary to shift gears abruptly, back to a formalized interview tone. In Goffman's (1974) terms again, she was **breaking the frame;** that is, she violated the evidently shared assumptions that regulate interaction. Rose was taken aback, not knowing how to respond. How could she? In this communicator's roller-coaster ride, she understood all the words, all the sentences, and even the main nonverbal messages of the interview. Yet she still didn't "get it." Despite the idea of framing being a bit abstract, it is indeed the missing part of the puzzle for both Rose and Barbara.

Goffman took Bateson's concept of frame and ran with it. "I assume," he wrote, "that definitions of a situation are built up in accordance with principles of organization which govern events—at least social ones—and our subjective involvement in them; frame is the word I use to refer to such of these basic elements as I am able to identify. That is my definition of frame. My phrase 'frame analysis' is a slogan to refer to the examination in these terms of the organization of experience" (1974, pp. 10–11). This chapter may widen Bateson's and Goffman's idea of framing somewhat, but the basic elements remain the same.

Framing Skills in Action

Although skills are commonly discussed only in terms of individual psychological attributes or behaviors, the concept of framing implies that communicators work together to produce and adjust frames that then guide their choices. Communication is a we-phenomenon; an "I" never "communicates" by itself, although "I" certainly contribute skillfully or less skillfully to "our" communication. Yet no one can perceive another's framing choices or framing errors directly. As R. D. Laing (1967) reminded us long ago, we can experience someone else's behavior, but we can never experience someone else's experience. Some aspects of dealing with frames have to be considered as personalized (and we will deal with them that way), but try to keep in mind the fact that if they are effective, these approaches exist in concert with what others are doing, too. With that simple qualifier, consider the following as especially important skills and insights that can help you become more effective in interviews.

Framing Skill 1: Metacommunicating

Metacommunication is a term from communication research that describes the process of communicating about our communication. One form of metacommunication is the inevitable mix of verbal messages with nonverbal messages. In any comment you make, both how you act while saying it and how you say it (body movements or tone of voice, for example) can be perceived as a silent commentary on how the verbal message should be interpreted. However, here we want to concentrate on the second metacommunicative form—the more overt process of metacommunicating verbally about verbal statements.

Many people go through life believing that communication is such a natural process that they never need to pay special attention to it, and, much of the time, they are right. Most everyday interchanges are best done with little attention to analyzing our conversations directly. We want to be aware of the immediate consequences of what we say and do without becoming obsessed. One of the most famous therapist-interviewers of the twentieth century, Carl Rogers, emphasized that theorizing is important but that within interviews the therapist's experience must be essentially atheoretical (1967). What he meant was that the time for theorizing—for puzzling out what something might mean in the context of a prior hypothesis—is after an interaction. It was a mistake, in Rogers's way of thinking, to be responding theoretically in the moment of encountering another person. Listeners need to focus on what is said and done in that moment. It's possible to overthink the situation so much that you outsmart yourself.

However, metacommunication does not need to involve high theorizing. It can exist in the moment, too, as a perception check or an aid to listening. In this way, it averts or troubleshoots frame problems effectively. For example, as a selection interviewer, you could announce a frame shift:

> "Up to this point, I've asked you about your experience working with kids at the special school district. Now, I'd like you to imagine we've already hired you for this position. Your descriptions were interesting and relevant, but let's switch gears. Here are several situations that have arisen lately around here. Give me your first impressions of how you'd respond to them, OK? It's not past experience I'm interested in, but what you'd do in new situations."

Or you could check out what you perceive as an interviewee's nonverbal discomfort:

> "You looked a lot more comfortable when we were discussing your qualifications, which are excellent. Since we started talking about our department here, you seem . . . I don't know . . . more reserved. I'm wondering if this is beginning to sound less like an interview to you and more like a gossip session or something. If so, it's OK that you feel that way; we can take a different direction with this."

Or if you were an interviewee, you might metacommunicate to find out if an interviewer is in fact interpreting your answers from within the frame you suspect:

> (After discussing a series of hypothetical actions, triggered by interviewer questions) "Well, I've gone on quite a long time here, but it might not be my storytelling skill

you're interested in. Some of my answers, I guess, were pretty personal. Was this the kind of thing you had in mind?"

In metacommunicating, remember, you are explicitly bringing up what is not usually explicit in conversation. You are making the process of communicating become the content too. If you do this all the time, it will likely sound phony and stilted. Yet as an intervention during crucial moments of a conversation—those moments when the partners are most likely to misinterpret each other—metacommunication can be a powerful skill.

Framing Skill 2: Contextualizing

An allied skill to metacommunication (in fact, it could take the form of metacommunicating at times) is contextualization. **Contextualizing** means acknowledging for yourself, and maybe for the other person, the full context in which a statement is made. As an example, think about what makes certain words offensive in sensitive matters of cross-cultural assumptions, gender, race, class, sexual preference, or disability. People often believe readily that certain words are automatically offensive, almost as if the word directly delivers the offense. But in everyday life, that's not how we act. Typically, we give the benefit of the doubt whenever possible. We take into account who is saying the word, her or his capacity for knowing the potentially offensive effect, and an entire range of other considerations. African Americans who object with good reason to being called "colored" or "Negro" often report that they are not offended in the same way when the speaker is an eighty-five-year-old white man who may not be up on contemporary dialogue about the cultural implications of language use. He may, in fact, be sincere and careful in avoiding what he considers to be the much more offensive word that his friends used in his youth.

Contextualizing does not mean you must condone the use of such words or blithely accept a variety of offending actions or misinterpretations. It only suggests that understanding context expands your range of choices for doing so. As the discussion of assertiveness in the next section suggests, you may want to reply to, or correct, the other person directly. Generally, skillful communicators cut each other reasonable slack or, stated another way, give others interpretive room to move. Context matters so much in communication that the same words can be said to the same person in different situations, resulting in anger and frustration one time and amusement and entertainment the next.

For another example related directly to interviewing, imagine yourself in the position of a female job applicant who is asked a question that you consider to be illegal: "You seem to love your children very much. Who knows what the future will bring?" (Is this a direct inquiry about whether you plan to become pregnant in the near future? It could be interpreted in this way.) A skillful contextualizer—rather than leaping to a conclusion—might consider when in the interview this question/comment was uttered. Was it toward the end of the interview after the interviewer had become obviously interested in your qualifications and seemed enthusiastic about bringing you into the company? Or was it in the context early in the interview, perhaps in an opening interchange of small talk about the interviewer's family pictures on her desk? If the latter, an alert contextualizer might interpret it as a benign comment about common concerns, laced with friendly feeling. The interviewer's, "Who knows what the future will bring?" could even have been her way of referring to her own family, not a ploy to invade your privacy or trick you into divulging personal decisions with your husband. Are you sure you want to assume the worst?

Another form of contextualizing is to identify and use the contextual frame most comfortable for an interviewee. You could ask an entrepreneur about the difficulties of running a small clothing store in a strip mall and get clear answers about those problems. But a skillful contextualizing interviewer will understand that a richer version of the problems will emerge if the interview occurs at work, during a Friday afternoon and evening full of sales, returns, customers' complaints, and creditors' calls. On the owner's turf, you hear the answers within the interviewee's frame of reference, and your understanding will deepen.

An excellent example of entering an interviewee's frame is in sportswriter Ira Berkow's book, *To the Hoop* (1997), which chronicles his lifelong passion for pickup basketball. Berkow, the consummate professional, is not against using basketball as a pretext for interviewing, as we see in his relationship with Earvin "Magic" Johnson, the former NBA star turned AIDS activist. While talking with Johnson and some of his barnstorming teammates one day, Berkow writes, "At some point I also mentioned that I still play pickup basketball games—again, to try further to gain their confidence about my basketball acumen. It wasn't just ego on my part; I knew that if they trusted my knowledge of the game, they might give me better stuff. They nodded when I mentioned my basketball playing, and nothing more about that was said." Berkow continues

> The following day, while waiting to board the plane for Paris, I was sitting with Magic, and I again recalled that pass he made to Conner.
> "Shooters like to get the ball in their rhythm," said Magic.
> "I know," I said. "I'm a shooter."
> I smiled. He smiled. I had interviewed Magic on several occasions over the years, and I had never mentioned anything to him about my playing basketball. They are, after all, two different worlds, his ball and mine. (p. 92)

The next morning in Paris, in a long interview, Johnson told Berkow several intimate details about the personal moments immediately following his disclosure to his wife that he'd tested positive for the HIV virus. Later that same morning, the team Johnson had assembled to play exhibition games in Europe was warming up. Berkow was standing off to the side of the court holding his notebook when Johnson indicated he wanted to throw the ball to the writer. Jamming the notebook in his hip pocket, Berkow took the pass in the corner of the court at the three point line. Was this still interviewing, or was it now basketball? The line blurs:

> Obviously, Magic was curious, as were the rest of the players. Could I in fact shoot a basketball? I was a middle-aged sportswriter, after all. But Magic would be able to tell, of course, whether I was "a shooter" by how I took the shot. This seemed a test—light-

hearted, but a test nonetheless. And something wholly unexpected. The players stopped to watch. . . .

"You want to put big bucks on this shot?" I said to the players. Somehow I thought the moment called for a bit of goofy bravado. Locker room stuff, I guess. Magic laughed.

"I'll bet two thousand dollars that you don't make the shot," said Long [another player on Johnson's team].

A look of concern flashed across Magic's face. "Why don't you move in for a warmup?" he suggested kindly.

"I don't need to move in," I said. Magic's eyes widened. I knew that I just had to show good form—and hit the rim. An air ball would have been embarrassing. . . .

I looked up to the basket. I reminded myself to get a good arc on the shot to assure distance. And I let the ball go. It felt good as it left my fingertips, lofted nicely and dropped right through the hoop. All net!

Magic shrieked. He ran over and threw me a high five. "I trust you now!" he exclaimed. "I trust anything you say!" He turned to John Long. "You owe the man two thousand dollars, J. Long," said Magic. . . .

"Let the money slide," I said. "No problem." I played it cool as could be. Like I make this shot in my sleep. . . .

I absently took the notebook out of my pocket—it remained unopened—and sat down in a chair beside Lon Rosen, who still looked surprised.

No one suggested I try another shot, and I wouldn't have. Not for all the money in the world. (pp. 93–94)

Framing Skill 3: Offering Accounts

In many interpersonal situations that seem like miscommunication, people assume that other communicators should be able to understand them almost transparently. The point is "already clear," or "painfully obvious," we hear people say. Or there are appeals to something called common sense: "I shouldn't *have* to tell you not to do that," a parent might say; "Everybody knows better than to do *that*!" The trouble with interviewing is that it often brings together people who have trouble saying such things to each other. Interviewers and interviewees are naturally concerned with saving face, or appearing smart, or maintaining their credibility in addition to being understood. Interview partners usually don't hear parental messages or appeals to common sense, or assertions that a particular point is already so clear that it shouldn't have to be explained further. Rather, those are the things interviewers and interviewees think but won't say aloud. It might help for someone to break delicately into this cycle of suspected misunderstanding.

One way out of a potential framing dilemma is to more or less announce the frame you're employing. This clarifies the interaction for your partner and gives him or her good evidence about whether the two of you are generally on the same wavelength or talking about two quite different things. Although the word *account* means various things in different forms of communication research, here, **account** refers to making your own frame explicit in response to a possible misunderstanding or incongruence of frames. As John Heritage (1988) observes, "To make sense, the overt descriptions and explanations (or accounts) which actors provide for their actions must articulate with . . . already established implicit understandings" (p. 128). Not all of us are equally aware of our own frames, but we know whether we're speaking in a given conversation as a friend, a family member, an expert, a boss, a woman, or a man. For example, consider a defense lawyer (L) interviewing a client (C) who has been charged with income tax evasion. The lawyer assumes her client knows she is speaking in terms of legal strategy, although the two are also friends living in the same neighborhood:

L: "What caused you to withhold those other sources of income?"

C: "I didn't withhold them. I only forgot them. There are so many little, piddly things, I can't keep track of them all."

L: "I don't like that explanation."

C: "What do you mean? You want me to lie? I did forget them. I can't lie about that. You'll get me into a lot of trouble!"

L (calmly): "No, I don't want you to lie. When I say, 'I don't like that explanation,' I mean that *when I think about your case as a lawyer*—not as your friend— I think your style of explaining things would be pretty hard to sell. That's because the prosecutor will explain everything as withholding and hiding and greed. Also, a jury won't be very sympathetic to someone who's annoyed at having a lot of different sources of income. Sounds like you're annoyed at being rich. See what I mean?"

In her last statement, the lawyer has offered an *account* aimed at clarifying not only the statement in question but also her overall stance or position as a communicator. She suggests that in this interview, the client shouldn't think of what is said as coming from a friendship frame but instead should assume the talk will reflect the wider frame of advocacy (ethical, we hope). Of course, not all occasions for offering accounts will be this obvious, so you'll have to play detective at times and ferret out when it might be necessary to announce your frame for clarification. Our common vernacular has an apt phrase for this. We want to know not only what someone said but also "where they're coming from." To understand persons' accounts of their own frames is to understand where they're coming from more comprehensively.

At times, offering accounts effectively depends upon other skills. Interpersonal communication teachers and trainers often distinguish among the terms aggressiveness, acquiescence, and assertiveness (see Smith, 1975, for one treatment of assertiveness). Although there are undoubtedly appropriate times and places for all three, assertiveness is the most transferable and useful response in situations of frame conflict or frame misinterpretation. **Aggressiveness** is the attempt to prevail in a situation (get what you want, have your say, define the outcomes as you wish) with little regard for the rights or feelings of others. It is a form of communicative selfishness. If aggressiveness is one end of a continuum of communicative respect, acquiescence is the other. **Acquiescence** is when communicators passively accept whatever comes, as though they couldn't possibly have control over the situation; thus, acquiescence is the process of letting others prevail with little regard for your own rights. The midpoint, the skill that permits communicators the most flexibility, is **assertiveness.** Assertive communicators do not dominate situations inappropriately, nor do they automatically retreat from them, but they are unafraid of acting or expressing themselves when that is called for. They respect the rights of others but also respect themselves; in doing so, they affirm how self and others are intertwined. Assertiveness blends the most helpful features of aggressiveness and acquiescence while avoiding the characteristics that make those styles frustrating to fruitful conversation.

To offer an account assertively is not the same as claiming that your frame is the best or the only one possible. You simply are attempting to clarify for yourself and others why the messages could make more sense when understood in context. Both interviewers and interviewees will find many occasions for offering accounts. Some will require delicate tact, because interviews can become threatening, ego involving, and emotional on other levels, too.

Interviewers and interviewees sensitive to frame problems face a series of subtle dangers in choosing whether to offer accounts. If framing is signaled primarily by nonverbal **metamessages** (messages about how to interpret other messages, such as winks, clothing choices, and tone of voice), then making nonverbal context verbal by offering an account introduces powerful changes. As many communication researchers (for example, Tannen, 1986) have pointed out, naming a frame changes it. In a job performance appraisal interview, for example, you may want to accept your supervisor's invitation to make the occasion one for mutual feedback. You enjoy your work and particularly appreciate all the things the boss has done to help you in the past two years. You want to communicate this appreciation but don't want it to be framed as insincere schmoozing or, in the popular semicrude vernacular, "sucking up." If the two of you are both sincere in wanting to exchange honest and, let's say, appreciative feedback, then attempts to name that frame and distinguish it from other alternatives could actually be counterproductive: "I know this sounds like I'm buttering you up, and I don't want to be seen as bringing apples to the teacher, but I really think you're doing a great job managing the unit. I want you to know that." Such an account, paradoxically, could actually introduce the "schmoozing frame" inappropriately into the relationship, creating ambiguity, when a simple direct compliment would suffice. In other words, remind yourself that most frames don't need to be named. In some situations, it is downright risky to name them.

Framing Skill 4: Reframing

At times, a dominant frame can create unhealthy effects for communicators. Therapists Paul Watzlawick, John Weakland, and Robert Fisch (1974, pp. 94–95) tell the story of a man who, out of necessity, took a job as a salesman despite being a lifelong stutterer. His speech difficulties when dealing with customers were so unsettling and embarrassing to him that he felt his life careening out of control. Yet he needed the job. The excruciating dilemma was real: What he *must* do was what he *couldn't* do while maintaining his self-esteem. What can we do when we see no options for doing anything?

The therapists' suggestion involved **reframing,** in which the person "change[s] the conceptual and/or emotional setting or viewpoint in relation to which a situation is experienced and to place it in another frame which fits the 'facts' of the same concrete situation equally well or even better, and thereby changes its entire meaning" (Watzlawick, Weakland, & Fisch, 1974, p. 95). What the salesman experienced as an inevitable occasion of embarrassment was not the only way to frame the persuasive interviews (see Chapter 11) he had to conduct. He was asked, for example, to name some of the worst criticisms of salespeople, and he came up with such things as how ordinary people mistrust the "slick, clever ways of trying to talk people into buying something they do not want" and how customers dislike salespersons who deliver an "uninterrupted sales talk" by using an "offensive barrage of words." The therapists asked if he noticed how carefully people listen to someone who stutters; and they suggested if he could mentally compare the worst image of "slick salesman" with his particular persuasive advantage, he would never come across as slick. He would enjoy a certain level of attention and listening that other sales professionals couldn't muster. "As he gradually began to see his problem in this totally new—and, at first blush, almost ludicrous—perspective, he was especially instructed to maintain a high level of stammering, even if in the course of his work, for reasons quite unknown to him, he should begin to feel a little more at ease and therefore less and less likely to stammer spontaneously" (pp. 94–95). By reframing, he gained a sense of mastery over his situation, instead of the reverse. Instead of framing his stuttering as an embarrassing defect, it became a frame of unique advantage.

Studs Terkel (1967), the radio interviewer and author of many books collecting the insights of ordinary people, had to tape his interviews, but found himself hampered by being a bit of a technological klutz. Was this a huge problem for him? No—he reframed it into an advantage. He discovered that if he mentioned at the beginning of an interview how awkward he was with tape recorders, and made jokes about how alien and mysterious they seemed, interviewees began to loosen up. In this way he demystified the experience of being tape recorded by positioning himself on the interviewee's side with respect to this potentially intrusive (although necessary) technology. Fumbling with the recorder was transformed from an embarrassing problem to an opportunity for Terkel to identify personally with the interviewee (p. xxii). His approach is another version of skillful reframing.

In reframing lies a powerful lesson for interview participants, whatever their role. Our attitudes about things can determine subsequent actions. If we're not careful, they can even narrow alternatives unnecessarily and lock us into patterns of failure.

Freeze-Frame: Note Taking and Recording in Interviews

Throughout this book we stress the crucial role of listening in interviews (see Chapter 3 especially, but all chapters spotlight listening). A discussion of framing is a good context

Trying Out Your Skills

Read the following interview excerpt and apply the concepts and skills of framing to help you understand how the partners are relating to each other. The campus director of counseling services (C) is meeting a student (S) for the first time. What are the different frames for the two? Do the participants seize or miss opportunities for contextualizing and offering accounts, in order to be understood? What are the possibilities for the student's reframing the problem here? In your opinion, should the counselor suggest a way for the student to reframe the situation? Should the counselor help the student to adapt to the realities of college life? Or should the counselor simply be a good listener?

S: Here I am, right on schedule.

C: I'm glad you came by. Our conversation on the phone the other day reminded me of some interesting things about how we make decisions here about students. I'm hoping we have the time to get into those again, if not today, then maybe next time.

S: We need to talk again? I got the impression you were just going to hear me out about this problem of professors demanding a lot of class participation and then basing your grade on it. That's not right. I know as much about Shakespeare as anyone in class, and scored higher on every exam, but because I'm shy and don't like to pop off in class, I get a B, and some people with lower scores got As!

C: Well, no, we don't need to talk again if you don't want to. But maybe you'll want to. You're really angry.

S: Damn right I am.

C: It doesn't seem fair that class discussion can make such a big difference in how someone evaluates your learning.

S: The way I look at it, my role is to learn, and the teacher is supposed to tell me how well I'm doing that. What difference does it make how much I talk?

C: So the talk seems extra, an add-on to the class, and the real content of the class is in the plays and the sonnets. You're mad enough to take out that insulting ad in the campus paper. What do you suppose Dr. Smith was trying to accomplish by requiring attendance and class participation?

S: That's what I don't understand.

C: I can't speak for him, but I do know that when I plan a course, I think about how students don't just want to listen to me lecture all the time. They learn a lot, it seems, by testing out ideas themselves in class. I try to encourage that, too.

S: I knew you'd take his side.

C: It doesn't feel like I'm taking his side. I'm trying to understand part of what might have motivated him. Let me hear more about your side, too, OK? What makes a class a "good class" for you? . . .

BOX 5.1   I N T E R V I E W E R S   I N   A C T I O N

Lewis Anthony Dexter

Lewis Anthony Dexter explains the task known as "elite and specialized interviewing," in which experts and specialists in a field share their insights with each other and with larger audiences. The following statement is from an essay in which Dexter summarizes his work interviewing lawyers (evidently, in this sample, all men).

"For our purposes it is generally more important to record during the interview itself the style of a man's responses than the substance. To give one very simple example: if several judges always refer to courts in general as 'they,' not as 'we,' to 'them,' not to 'us'—this may be a significant clue to attitudes. Yet an interviewer could very well get down the substance of answers on many problems without noting this 'little' point."

Source: Dexter, 1970, p. 87

in which to consider how an interviewer, listening effectively, chooses to record, retain, and interpret information. Effective listening, remember, goes far beyond merely being silent and paying attention. Any listener is actively framing and interpreting information, considering it in alternative contexts, while ensuring that after the interview ends, the ideas and insights will somehow endure. When it is time to make a decision, write a story, present a report, or schedule another interview, the interviewer has to rely on some method of recall. (See Boxes 5.1 and 5.2 for two interviewers' experiences.)

The heading of this section is both illustrative and misleading. It's useful to think of methods of recording interviews as choices for how to "freeze" previous communication so we can remember it better. Not all interviewers need to record their interviews, but many do so for good reasons. Journalists and celebrity interviewers listen for quotes, because these are considered the nuggets of meaning that capture the speaker's personality. In a way, we recall the quote as a vivid symbol of the person's excitement, skill, commitment, intelligence, ideology, or emotion. Psychotherapists and psychiatrists need to refer back to the exact words with which a client or patient expressed a personal problem; embedded in the language are many clues to the larger framework of a person's lived experience. To capture exact language for later reconsideration seems like freezing the frame. However, it's also a bit misleading to think communication can be frozen. It is constantly in flux and can never be fully captured or described. If, in taking notes, you write down the words "exactly," you don't preserve the exact words at all. Your notebook omits the volume, rate, and passionate inflection that were part of the spoken words. Even if you audiotape the speech, you omit as much as you capture; the words, tone of voice, and other features are there but without the visual cues that formed a context (a frame) for their interpretation. A videotape omits or distorts a whole range of cues as well, such as odor, touch, and many micromovements of facial expression. Further, in no sense can

BOX 5.2   **INTERVIEWERS IN ACTION**

Jack Mendelsohn

In his book on Unitarian religious philosophy, Jack Mendelsohn recounts his interview with the renowned philosopher of dialogue, Martin Buber:

"As he began to talk, I scribbled furiously. Suddenly there was silence, and when I looked up, Buber was smiling. 'Mr. Mendelsohn,' he said, 'either you can take notes without really listening, or you can really listen without taking notes.' It was said with no trace of harshness. Firmly, I closed my notebook and 'really listened.' He said, 'Throughout the world, there is a spiritual front on which a secret, silent struggle is being waged between the desire to be on life's side and the desire to destroy. This is the most important front of all—more than any military, political, or economic front. It is the front on which *souls are moulded.*'

"My question was the obvious one: 'What can individuals do to tip the balance?'

"Buber gazed out the window for a moment; then he turned to me and said: 'No one can chart a day-to-day course for anyone else. Life can only be determined by each situation as it arises. We all have our chances. From the time we rise in the morning until the time we retire at night we have meetings with others. Sometimes we even meet ourselves! We see our families at breakfast. We go to work with others. We meet people in the streets. We attend gatherings with others. Always there are others. What we do with each of these meetings is what counts. The future is more determined by this than by ideologies and proclamations.'"

Source: Mendelsohn, 1985, p. 48

Interestingly, Buber's response to Mendelsohn's substantive question also can be read as a response to the interview situation, in which we must always live for the immediate meeting. Although Mendelsohn surely did not hear Buber's comment as an instruction that an interviewer should never take notes, he received a forceful reminder about this interviewee, on this occasion, on this topic.

you ever freeze and keep the relational or psychological frames that made the interaction uniquely immediate for participants while it was occurring.

Still, many interviewers want to remember as much of what was said as possible. What are some of the practical ways of doing that? In our book on journalistic interviewing (Killenberg & Anderson, 1989), we surveyed the advantages and disadvantages of three general methods—note taking, delayed note taking, and tape recording. Except for a number of examples and applications, this discussion borrows heavily from our previous survey.

Note Taking

Taking notes is obviously an aid for an interviewer, yet few people realize how it also aids the interviewee in significant ways. Speakers whose listeners note their words pay close attention to their own speech. They focus on a topic in especially careful ways. They can observe which parts of their message are interesting or relevant for the listener. They are encouraged to take themselves seriously. (Of course, these factors can make people nervous as well, if they are insecure about their credibility or footing.)

Because of the many advantages to speakers, effective listeners in interviews won't generally consider note taking to be a negative message or a compromise at all, with one significant reservation we'll expand later—writing too much, or becoming obsessed with preserving voluminous quotations, deflects a listener's attention. Consider, however, the following advantages of an optimum level of note taking in an interview:

- Note taking is a way for interviewers to key themselves, within the frame of the conversation, to how this interaction connects to previous ideas, statements, or factors.

- Note taking can capture pithy comments from speakers relatively unobtrusively and easily.

- Reviewing notes is easier and quicker than reviewing an entire taped interview.

- Notes can remind the listener of probes to be used later in the interview and can be a cumulative record of impressions, not just a series of quotes and claims by the interviewee.

- Note taking is a constructive task that reminds interviewers to keep the focus on the interviewee, curbing the temptation to talk too much or interrupt.

- Writing notes provides a reliable signal to speakers about what interviewers consider important, and this can encourage interviewees to elaborate more (Gorden, 1980, pp. 222–223).

- Keeping notes can document an interview in case of a later dispute, legal or otherwise; a record of the conversation can explain subsequent actions, if necessary.

Despite its advantages, note taking can present problems, too:

- Done awkwardly or too extensively, note taking interrupts the flow of a conversation, as Martin Buber suggested to writer Jack Mendelsohn (see Box 5.2).

- Inexperienced note takers may become so enmeshed in the mechanics of their task that they neglect to listen for basic or central ideas, or to interpret accurately the frames from which the other speaks.

- Trying to record too much results in a stenographic role in which the interviewer essentially becomes passive, limiting the potential for fresh or surprising insights that a more active or constructive approach might facilitate.

- The interviewer's words (and therefore the interviewer's interpretations and framing habits) can become mixed in with the interviewee's words, producing inaccurate quotations later. One study comparing reporters' attributed quotes in a courtroom to the actual trial transcript found that nontrivial errors occurred in at least 50 percent of cases. One paper misquoted 45 percent of the time, with 39 percent of these misquotes

BOX 5.3　　　REMINDERS

The Nuts and Bolts of Note Taking for Interviewers

- Cue your interviewees on why you're taking notes, and let them know that this is to their advantage also. For example: "Would you mind if I jot some of these things down? I want to be sure I remember all your points later."

- Smaller notebooks are generally better than legal pads or full-sized tablets, especially when you don't have a table to write on.

- Write only in those moments when the speaker has already clarified the main point and might simply be rephrasing or adding examples. It frustrates interviewees to get to the nub of an idea just when a listener is concentrating on writing what they said a minute or two ago.

- Be alert to what it might suggest to the interviewee if you *stop* taking notes for a long time. Does she or he think you're less interested now? That you've gotten what you wanted already and are only biding your time until you can leave?

- Avoid full sentences, except for quotes. You're writing reminders to yourself, words to jog your memory, not an essay. Although the teaching of formal systems of shorthand appears to be fading from the educational scene, you can develop your own shorthand. For example:

& (and)

cd, wd, sd (could, would, should)

w/, w/o (with, without)

(amount, number)

$ (money, dollars, cost)

pos, neg (positive, negative)

pol (politics, politician)

- Be especially alert to figures of speech and adjectives the interviewee returns to often in the conversation; make a note of these. They indicate the person's values and priorities.

- Make sure you get names and titles right. Double-check the spelling of someone's name or the exact title of an article or report, for example, with the interviewee. In spite of an occasional interruption, this attention to recording accurate detail will reassure almost all interviewees.

- In closing the interview, don't stop your note taking too soon. Ask something like, "Before I put away my notebook, is there anything specific or especially important that you're afraid I won't remember? I want to be sure to jot it down now."

major errors of interpretation; another paper published misquotes 71 percent of the time, with 67 percent of those defined by researchers as exhibiting significant errors.

- Notes, if allowed to get "stale," can become virtually undecipherable to interviewers because they are so dependent upon the immediate interaction.

Notice that many of the so-called problems of note taking are simple warnings and not reasons to forsake taking notes. With the occasional exception of some persuasive interviewers and broadcast interviewers, virtually all other interviewers who care about accurate and helpful communication work hard to polish their note taking skills (see Box 5.3). Interviewees are advised to take notes as well, despite the fact that it is usually only interviewers who are expected to take them. As an interviewee—for instance, in an employer's disciplinary interview—note especially those comments that you'd be likely to forget because of your emotional involvement.

Delayed Note Taking

Writer Truman Capote was reputed to possess an exceptional memory, which allowed him to interview an unusually wide range of people, from small-town Kansans to Hollywood celebrities, simply by engaging them in spontaneous conversation (Nelson, 1979, p. 149). Afterwards, he would cloister himself in an apartment or motel room and spend hours reconstructing how his partners told their stories, complete with fine detail and emotional nuance. Without notes or audiotape, Capote claimed he could achieve 97 percent accuracy in these narratives. Perhaps he did. Most listeners, however, including experienced professional interviewers, couldn't come close to that mark. Contemporary life simply doesn't tune our ears or minds to listen in that way. Capote was on to something, though. To a lesser extent, his approach can be seen in the styles of many active, creative, and conversational interviewers.

Experienced interviewers know that in sensitive situations respondents may be reluctant to speak at all, much less speak openly to someone hanging on every word with scratching pencil or the infallible technological memory of a cassette recorder. Every overt reminder that an interviewer wants to "capture" the words feels like a threat to fence in the person and may be met with resistance. Some interviews, therefore, call for a trade-off: The notebook is left in the car with the tape recorder so the interviewee will feel more comfortable and communicative. Without notes and without tapes, however, how does the interviewer keep a record of the conversation? With difficulty. Yet it is possible.

The interviewer's technique in this situation, which we call **delayed note taking**, involves (1) scheduling a block of time, preferably at least thirty minutes, immediately after the interview; (2) ensuring that this time will be uninterrupted; and (3) reconstructing the interview in as much detail as possible. For some interviewers, such a task can be accomplished effortlessly, because they have trained their minds to remember details and register their importance. For the rest of us, it is a difficult task of reminding ourselves systematically of what was likely to have been important:

- How did the interview begin? Who initiated the talk? What was the other's mood? What were opening comments in conducting small talk?

- What were relevant details of the physical setting? If the interview took place in a room, what were its distinguishing features? If the interviewee made any choices that affected the nonverbal setting, such as chair placement or conversational distance, note them. Did the interviewee welcome interruptions or forbid them?

- What behavioral aspects of the interaction seemed meaningful? Fidgeting or nervous tics? Steady eye gaze? Locked jaw? A ready smile? Note all that you can think of. Develop tentative statements about how these behaviors might reflect the framing process of the other person and how you and your task might have affected these outcomes.

- Note what you considered to be the "critical incidents" of the interview. What were the high points? The low points? The turning points? The misunderstandings? The obvious points of agreement? What surprised you and what didn't?

- What was vivid (or not) about the interviewee's choice of words? Even though you weren't taking notes on the spot, some comments may have made such an impression that you believe you can recall them exactly. Write them down, but be wary of your ability to remember exact wording; use quotation marks in your delayed notes only for quotes that you remember absolutely accurately. For example, do you have much confidence that Mendelsohn's quotes from Martin Buber are exact after you discover he took no notes? (See Box 5.2.) If in doubt, write a paraphrase (you might write, "She talked about how frustrating it was for PR directors to feel torn between the demands of upper management and the feelings of rank-and-file employees"). Or you might write what journalists call an **essence quote**, which captures the essence of the statement and perhaps employs a particularly vivid word you recall the interviewee saying (for example, "Once, she said, she got 'french fried' by her boss when she published a particularly critical letter in the company newsletter").

- How did the interview end? Was it cordial? Did the interviewee invite you to ask more questions later if you had them? Were promises made to get back to the interviewee to check further facts or to share a story or report you may be writing? It is imperative that you make notes reminding yourself of any such agreements.

Do not delay or compromise on following through with delayed note taking if you were unable to take notes or record the interview. It's your only chance to be systematic. With every passing minute after the interview ends, you'll forget or—sometimes worse—misremember more details.

Delayed note taking (especially if you're as good at it as Capote was) has the following advantages:

- It is particularly useful in atypical interview situations, such as in a car on the way to an airport or a concert, or an interview "on the move" during a factory tour.

- It requires the interviewer to process impressions as well as content, so nonverbal details of context are often better recalled.

- It reduces the possibility that interviewees will practice a scripted set of sound-bites to deliver intact; when they see that the interviewer is not recording exact wording, they're likely to talk more conversationally, in vernacular.

- It reduces the chances of signaling special interest in a point. Although interviewing is not usually full of competitive game playing, a social worker, for example, would not want to cue a father that what he's just said contradicts what his daughter described yesterday; or an ethnographic researcher would prefer to participate fully in the bowling tournament rather than call attention to another bowler's juicy turn of phrase. With the right training and reminders, the researcher will remember to record the comment later.

Disadvantages of delayed note taking are also worth noting.

- It likely sacrifices interviewers' confidence in direct quotations.

Trying Out Your Skills

Tape record a television or radio celebrity profile interview, perhaps conducted by Charlie Rose of PBS or Barbara Walters of ABC. Imagine yourself in the role of the interviewer who has to write an essay about this interview, but do not take notes while the tape is playing. Then, immediately following your viewing, give yourself thirty minutes of uninterrupted time to practice delayed note taking skills:

- List everything you believe to be important for your article, which will appear, you hope, in *Rolling Stone* or *Vanity Fair*.

- Make notes about the emotional tone of the interviewee's disclosures. Was he or she excited to be interviewed? Bored? Preoccupied with nitpicking the questions?

- Make notes about topics you'd like to return to in a follow-up interview.

- Write down any striking quotations—short or long—that you remember.

Then, replay the tape and check out your memory. What do you need to work on to enhance your skill at delayed note taking? (This exercise will also assist your ability to take notes during the interview.)

- It discourages interviewers from using **probe notes**—those notes an interviewer jots down as reminders of questions or topics to bring up later in the interview.

- Its success depends upon a certain skill of memorization that many people find hard to develop (although with practice it becomes much easier).

- It eats time. Interviewers need to schedule not only the interview, and perhaps the transportation to and from the interview, but also an extra significant block of time to be alone.

- It entails, for some interviewing tasks, very significant violations of interviewees' frames and expectations. Lewis Dexter (1970), in analyzing the problems of interviewing specialists and experts in a field (specifically, male lawyers in the study cited here), is dubious about relying too much on delayed note taking:

> Many interviewers can train themselves, apparently, to get significant parts of an interview simply by recording it afterwards from memory. However, in the type of interviewing we are here describing, this seems needlessly risky. Most professional men will appreciate an interviewer's need to take notes, and taking notes will give an excuse for looking back and reflecting if an interview takes an unexpected turn. (p. 86)

Many interviewers value thoroughness enough to combine taking brief or sketchy notes in the interview with delayed note taking. This minimizes the negatives and accentuates the positives. In addition, as you will see, there are good reasons to set aside this extra note taking time even if you tape the interview. Although your tape picks up the words, it will miss your important and shifting impressions and your all-important gut feelings about relevance, truthfulness, and interest. Those need to be recorded, too.

Tape Recording

World-famous author Gabriel Garcia Marquez (1997) is an outspoken critic of contemporary journalism. As he considers today's journalists in all corners of the world, he sees "more [concern] with a 'scoop' than with any kind of story. And . . . one of the demons in this drama is the tape recorder" (p. 32). What is the problem?

> Before the tape recorder was invented, the job was done well with only three elements of work: the notebook, foolproof ethics, and a pair of ears for listening to what the sources were saying. Somebody needs to teach young reporters that the recorder is not a substitute for memory but simply an evolved version of the notebook, which served so well when the profession first started.
>
> The tape recorder is the guilty party in the vicious magnification of the interview. Radio and television, because of their own natures, turned the interview into the journalist's ultimate goal, but now even print media seem to share the erroneous idea that the voice of truth is not the journalist's voice but the voice of the interviewee. . . .
>
> The tape recorder listens and repeats—like a digital parrot—but it does not think; it is loyal, but it does not have a heart; and, in the end, the literal version it captures is never as trustworthy as notes taken by the journalist who pays attention to the real words of the interlocutor and at the same time values them with his intelligence and qualifies them with his morality. Maybe the solution is to return to the lowly little notebook so that the journalist can edit intelligently as he listens and relegate the tape recorder to the role of witness. (pp. 33–34)

The Garcia Marquez statement, bluntly (and courageously?) included in a 1996 speech presented to the International Press Association, vibrates with implications. We could disagree with him on several points (when did an entire profession ever have ethics that were "foolproof"? the technology of tape is a "demon"?), but it's more important to underscore several of his fundamental points.

First, he's suggesting, we think, that the ultimate goal of an interviewer is not to get the interview itself, but to apply the information or insight from the interview to some useful purpose. In other words, the larger frame for interviewing should always be *further* communication, and neither interviewer nor interviewee should forget this. Journalists and writers are interviewing someone in order to accomplish something else, such as to write an honest account of a far-off military maneuver, to interpret the motivations of city council members for readers who cannot attend their meetings, or to give us more insight into how a president makes decisions. Too much reliance on the tape recorder puts the interview itself on a pedestal, almost as if it's a stand-alone package of meaning.

Second, Garcia Marquez implies that taping can make journalists lazy if its effect is to substitute a machine for the human effort of listening and interpreting. Understanding is a matter of framing, as we have seen, and the tape machine never frames anything—it only reproduces talk. Third, and very significantly, he does *not* ask interviewers to avoid tape recording their interviews. He agrees that the machine should be used but relegated to the "role of witness." By doing so, interviewers can be alert listeners and still have corroboration and extra context for their interpretations if they need it.

Some forms of interviewing never involve taping, such as brief survey research interviews conducted in malls or at the workplace, or telephone interviews inquiring about customer satisfaction with products or services. They rely on clear-cut or forced-choice responses that the interviewer simply marks on an interview report or score sheet. Other forms inherently involve taping, and the taped record they produce is invaluable. For example, ethnographic interviewers and discourse analysts conduct interviews for the express purpose of generating transcripts of talk that they will analyze later. Courtroom questioning of witnesses by lawyers is preserved by an official transcript produced by a machine or court reporter/transcriber whose exact transcript serves the same purpose as a tape recorder. Oral historians use tapes to construct sensitive narrative portraits from a person's memories, using the interviewee's own words. But most interviewers face a clear decision in planning for their meetings. To tape or not to tape?

Consider these advantages of tape recording interviews:

- It creates an artifact of the interview that can be referred to later, for clarification, support, or documentation. Although no interviewer plans on being sued, litigation is a constant spectre in today's culture, and professional interviewers understand that the tape can serve as an insurance policy.

- It gives interviewers increased flexibility and versatility in noting contextual and nonverbal factors, as they do not have to listen precisely for how things are worded. That can always be double-checked later. More attention can be paid to the interviewee's speech style, the ways the interviewee dismisses criticism, the development of central ideas over longer periods of time, and personal quirks and idiosyncracies.

- It flatters some interviewees, who are pleased that an interviewer might value their words so much as to keep them. Similarly, it reassures interviewees who are concerned that a listener might miss something along the way.

- It helps interviewers operating under adverse conditions such as extreme cold or bad lighting, when it may be impractical to take thorough notes.

- It particularly assists interviewers listening for quotes in reproducing the exact wording a person chooses. Professional writers know, along with their editors and supervisors, that quotations propel a story and pique a reader's interest (see Box 5.4).

- It provides interviewers and interviewees with a valuable educational tool. They can review tapes to hear the progress they're making as communicators and to analyze their mistakes.

Taping does not create only advantages, as you have seen from Marquez's objections. Here are some of the problems and dilemmas faced by interviewers who tape their conversation partners:

- It intimidates some interviewees. Oriana Fallaci (1963), an interviewer famous for her conversations with celebrities, found that "getting them to talk in front of a

BOX 5.4   **INTERVIEWERS IN ACTION**

Michael Schumacher

"One of the main characteristics of shoddy or 'yellow' journalism is the out-of-context quotation. Fortunately, . . . this type of out-of-context quoting is not a standard—or even common—occurrence in the writing business.

"Of more concern is another out-of-context issue, this one finding the writer giving complete, accurate quotes that are not properly framed. There is a huge difference, for example, between a convicted killer's saying 'I'm so mad I could kill him' and an angry or frustrated actress's saying the same thing. Part of the difference can be found in the character of the speaker, and part in the context of the remark.

"Interviewees make outrageous or provocative remarks all the time. Interviewers, always quick to notice a pay-off line when it's delivered, will not only take note of these remarks, but they will encourage the expansion of them. They'll egg the person on, encourage further discussion, fake empathy in an effort to keep the conversation going. Then, when the conversation is finished, they will rush to their typewriters or word processors and build a story around the comments.

"There is some debate as to whether these words should be reprinted at all. Should hundreds, thousands, or even millions of readers hold an interviewee accountable for remarks made in the heat of the moment? Is this fair play—even if the person knows he or she is being interviewed? What is the value of words spoken during a crisis situation? Should interviewers quote or not quote as a result of judgments based on context? Should journalists even act as such judges?

"There are no easy answers to these questions. It is important, however, that you be fair in whatever action you choose to take. You cannot isolate quotes from their contexts, nor can you bend or reshape the context to suit the purpose of your article. You must properly frame the quotes you intend to use."

Source: Schumacher, 1990, p. 175

machine that is recording every pause and every breath is, in 50 percent of the cases, fraught with tension" (p. ix). In other words, it creates an overriding "I'm being taped" frame for these interviewees.

- It can discourage candid disclosure. It's natural to believe that if someone is recording your speech exactly, then your misstatements and mistakes could come back to haunt you. Politicians, lawyers, arbitrators, and others who are either carefully monitored or often in the public eye are particularly sensitive to taping. They may not avoid your questions if a recorder is turned on, but you can be sure their answers will either be practiced or worded with exceptional deliberation. One public figure we interviewed for a book on journalistic interviewing told us, "I end up talking to the tape recorder instead of the reporter."

- It isn't selective. The tape may be an hour long, with only two or three minutes of relevant material dispersed throughout in different sections. This material can be difficult and time consuming to locate.

- It can, as Marquez says, encourage laziness. Some interviewers fall victim to the "I can always find it on the tape" syndrome.

- It can be unreliable. The well-known Murphy's law says that if something can go wrong, it probably will. At the crucial moment in a hard-won interview, batteries will fail or the cassette will jam.

Effective taping involves a series of specific decisions (see Box 5.5).

✿ BEYOND THE BASICS

There are many possible extensions and elaborations of the framing concept. Students of interviewing could examine its implications, for example, for conflict management in the interview, for the detection of deception, and for self-understanding. However, the conceptual umbrella of frame analysis provides a particularly apt setting for exploring one issue in particular: how the current cultural controversy over language choice and multiculturalism might affect interviewers and interviewees.

Political Correctness, Language, and Interviewing

Much of interpersonal style depends upon nonverbal cues, but this does not alter the fact that people usually interview each other to obtain verbal information. We tend to frame interviewing, in other words, as a primarily linguistic event. It is a focused encounter that is presumably or ideally cooperative, for the purpose of generating additional information or insight for one or both parties. Language is not only a medium of communicative exchange but also a reality-defining environment in which we exist; it is not only what we say to each other but also the basis for our critical thinking and the interior dialogues that enrich our lives. With flexibility of language comes flexibility of thought, flexibility of planning, and—perhaps most important of all—flexibility in considering how different the worlds of others might be. Language allows us to *decenter*, or transcend ourselves in imagining a cooperative society. Interviewers should carefully consider its potential.

In recent years, two trends have dominated popular social dialogue about language, especially in the United States, Western Europe, and Africa. Although there are many more than two positions in this dialogue, and although many of our distinctions will fail to capture the complexity of the argument, it might be helpful to highlight two basic positions. The first trend, which has been termed *multiculturalism,* or at times *cultural pluralism,* emphasizes that language (among other things) sends powerful messages about the cultural identities of all who speak and write. Society, according to the multiculturalist perspective, must listen well to be able to respect and accept the positive contributions

BOX 5.5   **R E M I N D E R S**

The Nuts and Bolts of Tape Recording for Interviewers

- Inform your interview partners that you would like to tape, and request permission. Concealing the tape recorder or "wearing a wire" may be necessary for undercover cops, and deception certainly makes for an exciting movie plot, but it is not normal practice for professional interviewers. The professional literature in communication and related fields often includes debates about exceptions based on a so-called watchdog philosophy of journalism, for example, but the majority of interviewers in organizational, governmental, and personal life should not even consider deceptive taping as an option, in our opinion.

- Keep the taping as unobtrusive as possible. Use the smallest tape recorder you can find, and put it a couple of feet off to the side of the conversation, where you and your partner will not fixate on it. It will probably need no further adjustment. Today's built-in microphones are quite sensitive and generally omnidirectional. They should pick up the entire interview, plus some ambient room sounds. Your best taping strategy after setup is to have no strategy; forget the machine except when you need to turn over or change the tape.

- Check to be sure the recorder works before arriving at the interview. Use new or fully charged batteries unless you're certain that an electrical outlet is handy.

- Take **tape-sensitive notes.** That is, use your notebook to write important points about where on the tape a comment or interchange might be found. For example: "Most concerned re $: t/1, s/2, 1st 5" could be your note reminding you that the interviewee was most concerned about his salary increase in a comment you will find on tape 1, in the first five minutes of side 2.

- After the interview, decide how you'll process or keep the recording. You have several options, five of which are described here. Use **transcription**—when you need or want to turn the entire taped interview into printed text for later analysis. This involves laborious hours alone for you (or someone who owes you a favor!), listening carefully to get the wording transcribed exactly. Use **selective transcription** to listen with your goals and maybe your interview schedule in mind, transcribing only those sections of the interview (usually only from the interviewee's turns) that are directly relevant to your purposes. In **reduced note taking** you listen to the tape while reading the notes you took during the conversation, in effect using the tape to "reduce" the interviewee's words so that you can fill in gaps in your existing notes. With **quote searching,** you listen to the tape until you hear interviewee quotes that will assist in meeting your goals that stimulated the interview in the first place. Finally, **archiving** means you simply label the tape clearly (who you interviewed, when, where, why) and keep it, along with any pertinent notes, in a safe place.

---

each group, with its identity, can bring to the overall culture. Each identity brings with it a particular linguistic way of being in the world. The problems and successes of intercultural communication, therefore, are framed in terms of linguistic versatility and respect. Multiculturalists believe (see the next section) that language is not a neutral tool or medium for conveying thought, but that language is inevitably charged with multiple points of view and can never be completely neutral. Multiculturalists interested in interviewing, for example, might suggest that interviewers and interviewees, especially if they represent relatively privileged social groups, keep the following guidelines in mind:

- *Decenter* from their own unique perspectives while acknowledging that language is an important expression of cultural identity. That is, anticipate how you'll be understood or misunderstood by others with different linguistic habits.

- *Familiarize* themselves with different language styles and labels. That is, you are responsible for becoming informed about how various other cultural groups might be employing language.

- *Choose language with respect and sensitivity,* in order not to inflame or insult other cultural groups unnecessarily.

An alternative perspective, which we might call **linguistic conservatism**, contests the assumptions of a multiculturalist philosophy of language. In the sense we're using the term, *conservatism* does not refer to conventional politics but to the goal of preserving—or conserving—language as a commonly shared experience that each person can assume all others will employ in similar ways. Linguistic conservatives believe language is essentially a neutral medium for communication and that the goal of speakers and writers is to achieve accurate interpretations in listeners and readers. Effective communication is achieved when communication becomes, in this way, more efficient: Can you predict accurately what the other's meanings will be as a result of your word choices? Language is thought to be a system of meanings legislated by the acceptance of usage guidelines from its most educated elite speakers and writers. Linguistic conservatives interested in interviewing would offer different advice to interviewers and interviewees:

- *Learn and use language as the "common coin of the realm."* That is, the best policy is to educate yourself to speak "right," "call it as you see it," and then expect others to understand you.

- *Avoid linguistic compromise.* That is, ultimately, the best mark of respect is to judge others by their ability to meet the same standards you hold for yourself.

- *Regard various cultural groups' objections to some labels as oversensitivity.* That is, according to this view, interviewers and interviewees both are hindered by being constantly concerned with whether they are offending others by their speech, and we should all become less defensive about language.

Linguistic conservatism disdains what has come to be called **political correctness,** a belief of some critics that society is increasingly controlled by the political agendas of minorities. By charging political correctness, linguistic conservatives and their allies assert that multiculturalists unfairly try to enforce certain ways of speaking upon everyone, whether others want to use them or not. Some regard political correctness as a relatively benign way of joking with ourselves about our sensitivity to language (witness the many greeting cards and jokes about the "PC" term and the popularity of the vigorous television show "Politically Incorrect"). In some quarters, this phenomenon is not described in a lighthearted way. A 1990 *Newsweek* cover, for example, warned us to "Watch What You Say" because the thought police were monitoring everyone. Further, the charge implies this enforcement is unfair to the majority of people who are not in favor of thinking of society only in terms of its subgroups (see D'Souza, 1992).

Then-President George Bush's commencement address in 1991 at the University of Michigan made serious claims:

> The notion of political correctness has ignited controversy across the land. And although the movement arises from the laudable desire to sweep away the debris of racism, sexism and hatred, it replaces old prejudices with new ones. It declares certain topics off-limits, certain expressions off-limits, even certain gestures off-limits. What began as a cause for civility has soured into a cause of conflict and even censorship. Disputants treat sheer force—getting their foes punished or expelled, for instance—as a substitute for the power of ideals. Throughout history, attempts to micromanage casual conversation have only incited distrust. They've invited people to look for insult in every word, gesture, action. And in their own Orwellian way, crusades that demand correct behavior crush diversity in the name of diversity. (quoted in Wilson, 1995, p. 8)

The president's speech, in fact, ignited more controversy, with a spate of television shows and newspapers editorializing about the repressions inherent in acknowledging diversity by changing our ways of speaking about it. Critic John Wilson (1995), representing a more or less multiculturalist or cultural pluralist point of view, replied by analyzing the language of Bush's charge itself. He notes that the president's speech denies the reality of prejudices: "which are called 'old' prejudices, as if no one believes them anymore" (p. 8). It dismisses racism: "which no longer exists except as 'debris,' since charges of prejudice are created by hypersensitive minorities who 'look for insult'" (p. 8). And it suggests that ". . . the danger to freedom comes not from racists (who can be dealt with using 'reason') but from the 'political extremists' who 'roam the land, abusing the privilege of free speech, setting citizens against one another on the basis of their class or race.' In this turnabout, it is not racists but leftists who abuse free speech (which has suddenly been transformed from a right into a privilege). When Bush said that 'such bullying is outrageous,' he referred not to those who use racial epithets to abuse other people but to the 'extremists' who criticize racism" (pp. 8–9).

Both sides engage in volatile rhetoric, and this issue tends to divide people. Each side accuses the other of political motives and bullying. Even bringing up the controversy in a textbook could be seen as inappropriate by some. However, closing your eyes to the disagreement will not make it vanish. Your very presence as interviewer or interviewee cannot help but make some kind of statement about endorsing cultural pluralist or linguistic conservative positions. With that in mind, and without entrenching ourselves in the anger of conservative versus liberal, right versus left, are there ways students of interviewing can acknowledge the controversy while still negotiating their way through the jungle of language decisions they must make?

We believe that understanding the process of framing provides a key. With the concept of framing, you can create a personal style of interview communication that respects a cultural pluralism that is not artificially or tyrannically politically correct. In our opinion, no position on language or interpersonal communication can afford to dismiss the increasingly pluralist character of our cultural landscape. You may, if you choose, ignore or disagree with some arguments from the multiculturalist interpreters of language, but it is difficult to deny that the world itself is becoming increasingly multicultural. It is no longer possible to presume there is only one "right" way of speaking.

Framing and Acceptance-Oriented Language

In this book, we frame our ideas and examples as much as possible in terms of gender-neutral or culturally sensitive language. We do so out of a sense of inclusiveness and fairness (you can assume we're multiculturalists in this way). But political correctness, narrowly defined, is not our concern. We aren't trying to conform to what someone told us we'd better do, or else. Rather, we are pursuing a more mundane and easily identifiable goal: We simply want to communicate understandably with as many readers as possible, as much of the time as possible. We have tried to choose language that "lets you in" consistently and shuts no one out. We may fail more often than we'd like to imagine—most speakers and writers are only dimly aware of their own biases, and much racism and sexism resides in the unexamined nooks and crannies of everyday figures of speech. Yet our attempt to craft meaningful ideas using language that excludes no one is exactly what we suggest as the interviewer/interviewee's most reasonable path through the choices of linguistic framing.

Beyond our own language choices, though, you will read many quotations in this book that reflect language assumptions of an earlier era. Authors have used "he" or "mankind" to refer to anyone or everyone, even if female. Intelligent authors from history have also referred to ethnic, racial, gender, socioeconomic, or sexual preference groups in ways that were customary in their time, but in ways those groups would not approve of today. Do we go back to revise the quotations by inserting "he or she" and "human" for "he" and "man"? No. Do we avoid using the quotations? No. Do we adopt the increasingly common practice of inserting "[sic]," as though we've discovered the author had made an error that appeared in the original writing? No (it wasn't a mistake to the author). We'll trust readers to understand our point about inclusiveness and diversity without revising linguistic history.

At the same time, we all should realize that words always create consequences. What we call something or someone frames how we see and hear that thing or person. When previous generations were using "he" and "man" virtually universally as generic words, they were inadvertently making it more difficult for women to see themselves as actors in the wider social world of our lives. If we insist on using government-generated terms such as "Hispanic" instead of cultural groups' own designations for themselves, we inadvertently suggest that such groups have less voice in determining their own fate. If mature African American men continue to be called "boys" when speakers typically do not refer to European Americans of the same age in the same way, should we be surprised that such references are heard as condescending and offensive?

Some people respond, "Wait a minute. Aren't we getting too sensitive here? These are only words, after all. It doesn't really matter what I call you, as long as it's not a put-down and I treat you with respect." As comforting as this sounds, it does not square well with the findings of twentieth-century research in communication, linguistics, psychology, and sociology. For example, in gender relations, there is significant evidence that ". . . clearly indicate[s] that *man* in the sense of male so overshadows *man* in the sense of human being as to make the latter use inaccurate and misleading for purposes both of conceptualizing and communicating" (Miller & Swift, 1991, p. 28). In experiments, for instance, both men and women, young and old, tend to draw pictures of males when such language is used, indicating that in their minds the terms are far from truly generic. Whether or not speakers who use a supposedly generic "man" mean for it to refer equally to women, it is not interpreted as such *within the listener's frame.* To listeners, such words appear to refer primarily to male experience, with the expected feelings of exclusion.

Just as multiculturalists are rankled by the refusal to use people's preferred terms for their own group or their own experiences, linguistic conservatives are rankled by what they perceive as warped and awkward neologisms to achieve politically correct inclusiveness. Perhaps the most common object of derision is the "-person" designation in gender relations, and some people get quite upset about it. They believe women can reasonably be thought of as "chairmen," "postmen," and "freshmen" with little or no fuss. It does sound odd to say "postperson" or "freshperson," and many jokes are premised upon such awkward constructions, so one could admit that a change creates a new problem while solving an old one. Yet when people are offended by a term, does it make sense to continue the offensiveness just because a change sounds unusual? (All linguistic changes sound strange at first hearing.) What about reframing the controversy from an I win—you lose situation to a usage that's just as clear, with neither set of emotional baggage? In interviews, we suggest you find alternate terms that are just as accurate. For example, you might refer to neither chairmen nor chairwomen, or even chairpersons, but to "chairs" (it means the same thing); similarly, you can avoid "postman," "postwoman," and (echh) "postperson" by using "mail carrier" (see Box 5.6).

Summary

In this chapter we've asked you to take a macroscopic look at how interview communication might be perceived. Far from being a simple activity of speaking and listening, or questioning and answering, interviews also involve interpreting people and information. The process of framing, originally discussed by Gregory Bateson (1972) and Erving Goffman (1974), helps interviewers and interviewees get their priorities straight. Those who do well at asking questions and providing good answers may not automatically do well at glimpsing the larger pattern in which those questions and answers must be understood.

Effective interviews involve skillful framing. This chapter suggests some abstract skills and appreciations but concentrates on presenting practical and concrete suggestions for

BOX 5.6   R E M I N D E R S

Acceptance-Oriented Language for Interviewers and Interviewees

- Read widely in popular newspapers and magazines (for example, the *Washington Post, Newsweek, Harper's*) and in academic or professional journals in your field (for example, public relations, advertising, training, fund-raising) to get a feel for the acceptable ways of referring to people and groups. Virtually all publications now are gravitating toward inclusive and gender-neutral language that recognizes diversity. If such inclusive constructions as "he or she" sound awkward to you, current style manuals list good strategies for recasting your words to achieve clarity without making references to gender.

- Whenever you perceive a contradiction between a term that seems comfortable and one that appears to exclude or perhaps offend persons because of their gender, race, ethnic affiliation, or sexual preference, choose the inclusive term even if it sounds awkward. Remember, awkwardness is in the experience of the listener, too. If you know that a specific term or label runs the risk of offending even some women, some people of color, some gays and lesbians, or some older citizens, why would you want that result in even some of the cases? Even if a black woman does not prefer the term African American, it is unlikely that she'd find it offensive.

- Remind yourself that inclusive language tends to be technically more accurate. For example, even if you choose to say "chairperson" or "chairwoman," these are accurate terms (at different levels of generality), although a generic "chairman" is inaccurate whenever it refers to a woman in that position.

- Perform a personal bias check. Ask yourself: Which groups do you often make fun of? Which groups do you just not understand at all? Which groups appear to have clear-cut characteristics that you dislike? In the answers to these questions lie clues to your pattern of bias and to your frames for communicating with individuals who may be members of such groups.

- Before embarking on a series of important interviews, do a "language check" on yourself. Interview several of your friends in informal settings to get their reactions on the following questions: With what terms do you customarily refer to women? To men? To those from ethnic or racial groups other than your own? To controversial groups in political and social life?

- Sensitize yourself to "red flag" messages that signal (perhaps unintentionally) either that you're insensitive to another group's experience, or that you consider large numbers of people to have essentially similar lives. For example, Marsha Houston and Julia Wood (1996) identify a list of phrases that can be "'red flags' when used by members of privileged classes and ethnic groups in conversation with members of nonprivileged classes and ethnic groups":

"What's the black perspective on this?"

"I've suffered discrimination too."

"I know how you feel about racism/classism."

"I think of you as just like me."

"You're really exceptional."

"Your people . . ."

"It's remarkable how far you've come."

"Personally, I've never discriminated against Hispanics, Asian Americans, working-class people" (and so on).

"I've experienced sexism, so I understand racism." (p. 53)

- Consult published guidelines for more specific advice and answers to specific problems. We mention several of them in "The Interview Bookshelf" at the end of this chapter.

- Return to the beginning of the chapter and review the extended example of the employment interview between Barbara and Rose. If you were Rose, the interviewee, would you be tempted to metacommunicate? To offer an account? If so, (1) how would you do so, and (2) in your opinion, at what point in the interview would it be most appropriate?

- Journalists and research interviewers are often tempted to tape interviews and conversations when interviewees are unaware of the recording, which creates obvious frame disparities. Yet this tactic has generated significant controversy. Consider the following two policies from the codes of ethics of daily newspapers.

From the *Beaumont (Texas) Enterprise*:

It is acceptable for a reporter to use a tape recorder both during in-person interviews and on the telephone without notifying the party being interviewed so long as the reporter has identified himself or herself as a reporter to the source.

From the *Detroit Free Press*:

Except in rare and justifiable instances, we do not tape anyone without that person's knowledge. To do otherwise violates a general policy of treating people as we would want to be treated. An exception may be made only if we are convinced the recording is necessary to protect us in a legal action or for some other compelling reason, and if other approaches won't work. Such instances require a managing editor's approval in advance.

(Black, Steele, & Barney, 1993, p. 119)

If you were a working journalist applying for jobs at these two papers, with which policy would you feel most comfortable? Suppose a managing editor from each interviews you, asking how you feel about the taping policy. What would you say to each editor?

- With the stipulation that no one necessarily fits any category completely, do you consider yourself primarily a multiculturalist, when it comes to language frames, or a linguistic conservative? Imagine that you have been asked to conduct a series of interviews in Catholic churches throughout a major urban area (think about your nearest large city in order to respond to this question), for the purpose of determining parishioners' attitudes toward the local archdiocese. How do your feelings and impressions about political responses to language affect how you'll prepare?

improving your awareness of how interview partners work within coconstructed patterns of meaning. Four fundamental skills of framing are described in "The Basics": metacommunicating, contextualizing, offering accounts, and reframing. These skills are then placed in the practical interviewer-oriented context of how to record and recall what you've learned in the interview. Your choices of note taking and taping often dictate how your interviewee will choose to frame his or her comments. In "Beyond the Basics," we ask you to consider a framework for understanding the contemporary controversy about political correctness and then apply that framework to making language choices that will signal your acceptance of others' perspectives and their humanness.

The Interview Bookshelf

On the basic concept of framing

Goffman, E. (1974). *Frame analysis.* New York: Harper Colophon.

The source on the concept of framing. Although written at a fairly high level of sophistication, Goffman's work is enjoyed by a wide range of readers because he includes so many great examples. One of the most stunning and provocative works in the past three decades of social science writing.

On an interview study of framing in everyday life

Belenky, M. F., Clinchy, B. M., Goldberger, N. R., & Tarule, J. M. (1986). *Women's ways of knowing: The development of self, voice, and mind.* New York: Basic Books.

An eye-opening book about how women's frames, and ways of communicating about them, are often different from men's. Many narratives are presented in the unique voices of thoughtful women, and the authors relate the interviewees' stories to other research in psychology, communication, and politics.

On how storytellers develop their narratives in different contexts of listening

Bauman, R. (1986). *Story, performance, and event: Contextual studies of oral narrative.* Cambridge, UK: Cambridge University Press.

Bauman studied Texas storytellers for over fifteen years and found that much of their art depended upon how context—what we call frames—could signal what was heard as truth, what was heard as playful deception, and what was heard as tall tale.

On how an interviewer could establish a new frame

Hartshorn, N. (1996). *Catch: A discovery of America.* Denver, CO: MacMurray & Beck.

The author threw some ball gloves and baseballs into his car trunk along with a tape recorder and notebook, then hit the road to interview people "in search of a conversation." Along the way, he found the extraordinary in "ordinary" people and the accessible sides of several celebrities. His method? To ask folks to talk while they played catch with him—an unusual frame that enabled some fresh kinds of communicating.

On inclusive language

Dumond, V. (1990). *The elements of nonsexist usage: A guide to inclusive spoken and written English.* New York: Prentice Hall Press.

Schwartz, M., & The Task Force on Bias-Free Language of the Association of American University Presses. (1995). *Guidelines for bias-free writing.* Bloomington, IN: University of Indiana Press.

These two books help chop through the thicket of difficult language choices that interviewers and interviewees face. Dumond includes a variety of options that avoid offending others while expressing your intentions succinctly and a glossary of alternative, nonsexist terms. Schwartz's book (although we wonder if any communication can literally be bias free) goes beyond gender to suggest practical ways of becoming sensitive to differences of race, ethnicity, citizenship and nationality, religion, disabilities and medical conditions, sexual orientation, and age. Also valuable is Schwartz's annotated bibliography of other books on inclusive language.

References

Agar, M. (1994). *Language shock: Understanding the culture of conversation.* New York: William Morrow.

Bateson, G. (1972). *Steps to an ecology of mind.* New York: Ballantine.

Bateson, G. (1980). *Mind and nature: A necessary unity.* New York: Bantam.

Bateson, G. (1991). *Sacred unity: Further steps to an ecology of mind* (R. E. Donaldson, Ed.). New York: Harper-Collins.

Bauman, R. (1986). *Story, performance, and event: Contextual studies of oral narrative.* Cambridge, UK: Cambridge University Press.

Belenky, M. F., Clinchy, B. M., Goldberger, N. R., & Tarule, J. M. (1986). *Women's ways of knowing: The development of self, voice, and mind.* New York: Basic Books.

Berkow, I. (1997). *To the hoop: The seasons of a basketball life.* New York: Basic Books.

Black, J., Steele, B., & Barney, R. (1993). *Doing ethics in journalism: A handbook with case studies.* Greencastle, IN: The Sigma Delta Chi Foundation and The Society of Professional Journalists.

Dexter, L. A. (1970). *Elite and specialized interviewing.* Evanston, IL: Northwestern University Press.

D'Souza, D. (1992). *Illiberal education: The politics of race and sex on campus.* New York: Vintage.

Dumond, V. (1990). *The elements of nonsexist usage.* New York: Prentice-Hall.

Fallaci, O. (1963). *The egotists: Sixteen surprising interviews.* Chicago: Henry Regnery.

Goffman, E. (1974). *Frame analysis.* New York: Harper Colophon.

Gorden, R. L. (1980). *Interviewing: Strategy, techniques, and tactics.* Homewood, IL: Dorsey Press.

Heritage, J. (1988). Explanations as accounts: A conversation analytic perspective. In Antaki, C. (Ed.), *Analysing everyday explanation: A casebook of methods* (pp. 127–144). London: Sage.

Houston, M., & Wood, J. T. (1996). Difficult dialogues, expanded horizons: Communicating across race and class. In J. T. Wood (Ed.), *Gendered relationships* (pp. 39–56). Mountain View, CA: Mayfield.

Killenberg, G. M., & Anderson, R. (1989). *Before the story: Interviewing and communication skills for journalists.* New York: St. Martin's Press.

Laing, R. D. (1967). *The politics of experience.* New York: Ballantine.

Garcia Marquez, G. (1997, July). The roving recorder. *Harper's Magazine, 32–34.*

Mendelsohn, J. (1985). *Being liberal in an illiberal age: Why I am a Unitarian Universalist.* Boston: Beacon Press.

Miller, C., & Swift, K. (1991). *Words & women: New language in new times* (Updated ed.). New York: HarperCollins.

Nelson, R. P. (1979). *Articles and features.* Boston: Houghton Mifflin.

Rogers, C. R. (1967). Some learnings from a study of psychotherapy with schizophrenics. In C. R. Rogers & B. Stevens, *Person to person: The problem of being human* (pp. 181–192). Lafayette, CA: Real People Press.

Schumacher, M. (1990). *Creative conversations: The writer's complete guide to conducting interviews.* Cincinnati, OH: Writer's Digest Books.

Schwartz, M., & Task Force on Bias-Free Language of the Association of American University Presses (1995). *Guidelines for bias-free writing.* Bloomington, IN: Indiana University Press.

Smith, M. J. (1975). *When I say no I feel guilty.* New York: Bantam.

Tannen, D. (1986). *That's not what I meant! How conversational style makes or breaks relationships.* New York: Ballantine.

Tannen, D. (1990). *You just don't understand: Women and men in conversation.* New York: William Morrow.

Terkel, S. (1967). *Division street: America.* New York: Pantheon.

Watzlawick, P., Weakland, J., & Fisch, R. (1974). *Change: Principles of problem formation and problem resolution.* New York: W. W. Norton.

Wilson, J. K. (1995). *The myth of political correctness: The conservative attack on higher education.* Durham, NC: Duke University Press.

✿ 6 Interviews for Employee Selection

One of the ironies in employment practice is the emphasis that is placed on the relatively unstructured, face-to-face interview to arrive at selection decisions within organizations, despite the interview's questionable validity in predicting job success when compared to other selection techniques (i.e., biographical information, work samples, pencil & paper tests). Recent literature reviews have suggested that low interview validity is likely the result of both passive and active judgment errors made by interviewers as they gather, retrieve, and process applicant information.

—Robert Eder and Gerald Ferris, *The Employment Interview*

LEARNING GOALS

After reading this chapter, you should be able to

- Define the employment interview and its major components and processes
- Understand why employment interviews can be analyzed as collaborative rhetorical communication
- Prepare for, and conduct, employment interviews by assuming the role of interviewer
- Prepare for, and conduct, employment interviews by assuming the role of interviewee
- Understand the legal context for employment interviews and its underlying philosophy of fairness

Most people can swap stories about bizarre job interviews. Applicants tell of interviews conducted on the run, in which an interviewer was troubleshooting a factory crisis, running from department to department, while the luckless interviewee hustled breathlessly behind, trying to get a word in edgewise. In other cases, interviewers have used the occasion to flaunt their power, ask for dates, brag about their own accomplishments, and spend most of the time telling each applicant how good the others have been.

Personnel managers and other job interviewers also tell nearly unbelievable tales of what some interviewees do and say. *Listservs* on the Internet (electronic mailing lists that appeal to subscribers with particular interests) currently circulate several versions of stories about applicants who have shocked organizational representatives. In one instance, the applicant wore a Walkman with headphones and said she could listen to music and pay attention to the interviewer at the same time. Another supposedly asked for the interviewer's resume to see if he or she was qualified to judge the candidate's credentials, while a third proceeded to unpack a sack of hamburgers and fries during the interview because the interview was scheduled for the middle of the day. Although the authenticity of some of these stories may be questionable, there is enough truth in them to suggest that many people aren't aware of others' expectations in this ticklish situation or of how their own actions might be interpreted.

Yet this isn't just any mundane ticklish situation. Interviews have potentially life-changing consequences for both sides. It is a make-it or break-it occasion for many with families to feed and careers to launch, seen from one perspective, or for organizations to run smoothly or customers to be served with integrity, seen from the other. The appropriate match of personality to position, and skills to jobs, can—if done well with the fullest possible exchange of information—create a halo of satisfaction all around. This success also extends far beyond the job location and the hiree's individual responsibilities to enhance and enrich families, neighborhoods, careers, corporate responsiveness, client satisfaction, and a variety of other outcomes.

Robert Eder and Gerald Ferris (1989) mention in this chapter's opening quotation that employment interviews are notoriously weak in predictive validity; that is, a supposedly "good" interview is not a consistently good predictor of an employee's subsequent success in the workplace. Although this may seem discouraging for would-be interviewers and interviewees, we should consider carefully the reason they give for this problem. Surveying the research, Eder and Ferris suspect that interviewers just are not skilled enough or insightful enough to know what makes an interview encounter effective or "good." Although recent trends deemphasize the kind of unstructured interview procedures Eder and Ferris critique, interviews are still too often prepared for haphazardly by both sides. Perhaps one of our most basic tasks as communication specialists is to convince both organizational representatives and applicants that interviewing should be taken seriously, prepared for carefully, practiced intensively, and followed up systematically.

Surprisingly, considering the typical frustrations and the crucial importance of successful job interviewing for both applicants and organizations, many students seem to believe that employment interviewing is merely a matter of common sense. They believe they don't need to research much because the demands of interviewing are so obvious, and, in fact, "everyone already knows" what to do in an interview, how to dress, and what to say. Many want to trust blindly in the occasionally apt but often misleading advice to "be natural" or "just be yourself."

In this chapter we will survey many reasons why this is dangerous advice if taken too literally. First we'll look at basic considerations of interview communication from what we call a rhetorical perspective. We will consider the employment interview as a focused form of interpersonal and organizational assessment based upon evidence gathered, shared, and adequately analyzed by both parties. The distinctive personal goals of the interview will be described from both standpoints—interviewer and interviewee—and put in the perspective of shared goals that can emerge from the interchange. In "Beyond the Basics" you will build on your understanding of the interview as communication to consider two other detailed issues: how the legal context of employment interviewing serves as a valid constraint on what can, and can't, be said in the interaction; and how the principles of employment interviewing extend to other contexts of interviewing where selection is the goal.

Beyond "Just Being Yourself": Defining the Employment Interview as Communication

THE BASICS ✿

Don't get us wrong. Being yourself is a fine thing to be. If, by "being yourself," you mean that you're comfortable with your own identity and personality, that you're reasonably confident as a communicator, and that you trust yourself to adapt to a variety of circumstances, then all of these are certainly helpful for communicators.

However, trusting yourself to respond spontaneously is necessarily limited by the contexts and specific challenges in which you find yourself. Does it, for instance, seem to be good advice to be yourself when you've agreed to be a best man or maid-of-honor in someone else's lavish wedding ceremony? Does it seem to be good advice to be yourself when thinking about how you'll act when sitting down to take the Graduate Record Exam or LSAT? For that matter, is it a good thing simply to be yourself when you're expected to play a certain position on a soccer team or a certain role in a play? There are many ways to express your unique personality, but in none of these other contexts would it make sense to trust your personality and what you already know about yourself in lieu of specific preparation for how to merge your talents with those of others. You might also expect big problems with trusting yourself to be a good interviewee or interviewer in employment selection situations.

The **employment interview** can be defined as an encounter between a potential employee and an organizational representative or representatives for the purpose of mutually exploring information relevant to subsequent hiring or selection decisions. Several features of the definition are especially important to stress in the beginning of the chapter.

First, the employment we are talking about may go beyond the normal definition of a job. Many organizations use the techniques of employment interviewing to select interns, volunteers, and other representatives; and certainly college admissions—especially for graduate school and professional programs—use these same approaches to choose people (see Klitgaard, 1985). Second, note that not all employment interviewing conforms to the stereotype of a single applicant entering an office to face a stern personnel manager sitting behind a massive desk. Some interviews are conducted in the specific work context that is relevant for the employee function, and some (especially in follow-up interviews) involve more than one organizational interviewer. Third, we stress a *mutual* selection process. Because both parties engage in interviewing, it is a bit misleading to say only that the employer interviews the applicant. Once the interview is framed or understood primarily in such a limited unidirectional way, many communicative aspects of interviewing become submerged in real or imagined power relationships, and otherwise assertive interviewees turn timid and fail to get answers to their questions about the organization. Although for the sake of simplicity we will continue to identify applicants as "interviewees" and organizational employers as "interviewers," any good employment interview must provide at least some opportunity for applicants to interview organizational representatives.

For an employment interview to be effective for both sides, the communication has to be transactional, to use our term from Chapter 1. Each party must acknowledge how it is affected by, and how it affects, the other. Finally, notice that the interview is an occasion for gathering and processing information and impressions, but this information is only useful if it leads to subsequent decision making. An employment interview is not the time to make rock-solid decisions but instead is a time to generate information and interpretations that can be used later to shape fair decisions. From the interviewee's perspective, "Does the company want me? Did I get the job?" is only one of these decisions. Another, often just as important, is, "Do I want to work here?" Or, if an applicant is enthused, "Should I follow up with requests for more information about benefits before making a final choice?"

In any case, this definition of the employment interview suggests that it is a communication exchange, an event with mutual implications, rather than just a trial in which a powerful party tests a powerless party. Both sides have influence, but they are different forms of influence that are enacted differently.

The main practical message of this chapter, succinctly stated, is "Get out of yourself." Note that we are not saying, "Forget yourself" or "Don't capitalize on your own uniqueness." We are saying that interviewees and interviewers cannot stay *within* themselves and hope to accomplish the valid transactions that must occur in a successful interview. "Get out of yourself" suggests that you expand your focus to include the needs and goals of the other person. Interviewees cannot frame the situation selfishly, because organizations won't select employees (or graduate students, interns, or other applicants) altruistically. Similarly, interviewers cannot frame the situation in terms of organizational demands and take-it-or-leave-it attitudes, because the best potential employees will avoid such positions, leaving such interviewers only subpar applicants to interview.

Consider this "get out of yourself" problem as it confronts both interviewee and interviewer. Employment consultant Tom Jackson once conducted a workshop attended by one of the authors. His message, detailed in his helpful book, *Guerrilla Tactics in the Job Market* (1978), warns that too many job applicants frame the selection interview entirely as their own opportunity. "Why do you want this job?" the personnel manager might ask. "Because I've been out of work for so long. I need a job," replies the applicant. Think about it. This is an honest reply; the interviewee is "being himself." But, to paraphrase Jackson, "The employer doesn't give a damn if you need a job." (Actually, his words were much more colorful, but you get the idea.) Interviewers are not necessarily callous or unfeeling, but their problems transcend the interviewee's need for a job. The interviewee who came before needs a job, too, as does the next, and the next. An organization wants to hire you not to add value to your life, but to add value to its own life—to enhance its own functions. Organizational interviewers want to hire people who will make their own jobs go more smoothly. Therefore, as Jackson and other savvy interviewing consultants will stress, employers see you in terms of the value you bring to the job, not in terms of the value the job brings to you (see Box 6.1). To the greatest possible degree in interviews, you should define yourself—and communicate about yourself—in this same way. In other words, get out of yourself, and see yourself in the context of the organization's goals and needs.

The same reminder applies to the interviewer, who has to consider the organization's needs in the context of the particular employee's satisfaction. In a sense, the organization

BOX 6.1   INTERVIEWERS IN ACTION

Personnel Managers

In Yana Parker's (1983) book, *The Damn Good Resume Guide,* several anonymous personnel managers evaluate resumes and react to applicants' habits and attitudes more generally. Their conclusions confirm Tom Jackson's suggestion that interviewees must adapt to others' needs. Here are some especially appropriate quotes:

- *"Be ready for the interview.* Most people are *not.* You need to do a . . . good deal of research about yourself. Get ready for the interview by:

  knowing what the job is about

  knowing why you're applying

  knowing how you're qualified"

- *"Be prepared for the interview.* Be ready to answer the question, 'Why do you want to work for this company?' In our case (large bank) a major question I ask is, 'Do you think you'd be comfortable working in a large corporation where things would be fairly structured?' A lot of young people nowadays are turned off by that, but it's important for people to feel at ease at work, so they should ask themselves that question."

- *"Rank your strong points.* Come in knowing that, and it saves a lot of energy."

In his book, Jackson (1978) also interviewed experienced employment interviewers to obtain their perspectives. Although their complaints don't apply to the best of today's more sophisticated job seekers, the reminders remain valid. For example:

- "I'll swear that this woman I interviewed didn't even have the first idea of what we *did.* She spent most of the time trying to find out about the benefits."

- "Seventy-five percent of the college kids we interview never get around to letting us know what they can do for us. They do a good job telling about their future interests and goals, but they forget to relate it to us."

- "Please tell people, particularly if they are just entering the job market for the first time, to read up a bit on what the employer does so they can at least show that they care a little."

---

that wants to hire the best possible workers with the best possible fit must also decenter (in communication terms), must also "get outside itself," to anticipate the experience of potential (and current) employees. Turning Jackson's hypothetical question around, an applicant might ask, "Why would I want to work for you?" If the organizational interviewer can only respond, "Because we need someone who can sell a whole range of new customers on the need for cellular service," then the organization has not "gotten outside itself" and may lose an excellent candidate. Skillful interviewers who instead translate the organization's goals into the life goals of the applicant help create a bond that bolsters both sides. Effective communicators know themselves and the perspectives they represent, but they transcend those perspectives, too.

Success in employment interviewing comes from the perception that the participants are primarily interested in communicating and not merely engaged in testing someone, in selecting someone, in trying out for the team, or in having an audition. Although the interview contains elements of these other tasks, don't assume that they are the major frames for what is going on.

Interviews conducted to match applicants with organizational positions feature a curious clash of objectives that create a rhetorical encounter—a communication situation in which each party approaches the other with relatively clear, but often idiosyncratic, goals. **Rhetoric,** as practiced by Aristotle, is the study of how persons discover the available means of persuasion in their communication with others and then seek to implement persuasive strategies to influence the others. In this classical sense, rhetoric is not the same as manipulation (which involves unfair control of information or consequences), and it is also not the same thing as empty public talk (the "mere rhetoric" politicians often accuse opponents of using). Ideally, rhetoric is informed and ethical communication in which participants test ideas with their talk and writing. Yet because it often involves at least a comparison of different objectives, the rhetorical encounter can be intensely ego involving, emotional, and therefore, difficult. Opportunities for misinterpretation lurk around every corner.

We stress a rhetorical approach to help you anticipate some of the dangers inherent in the interview situation and prepare for them. Think about three specific rhetorical concerns that apply to any selection interview: *context* (the social, cultural, and physical situation in which you communicate), **persuasive proofs** (the means of persuasion with which you attempt to communicate effectively), and *ethics* (the value bases of right and wrong that help you choose how to communicate). Some researchers (Kirkwood & Ralston, 1996) imply that effective employment interviewing can reflect all three concerns—it can be adapted well to context, be persuasively oriented, and be ethical—and that even such a persuasive situation can and should be a "collaborative dialogue":

> We believe teachers are obliged to aquaint students with a vision of what employment interviewing ought to be: a collaborative dialogue that acknowledges and supports the needs of employers and applicants to make informed decisions about whom to hire or which offers to accept. If not in the university classroom and interviewing texts, where else will students confront this possibility? Even were one to view this approach to interviewing as hopelessly idealistic (a view we do not share), it is incumbent on communication educators to raise the possibility for students. (pp. 175–176)

Context

What is the context for the employment interview? Think of context as a description of the background or backdrop for the content of the message participants attempt to articulate with each other; messages exist within contexts that in turn influence how the messages are interpreted. For example, a joking remark by an interviewee about her awkward handling of a personnel conflict might be appropriate and reasonable in the context of a follow-up interview in which a strong rapport has been established with the interviewer, yet the more formal context of an initial interview would make such a lighthearted approach unlikely. Surely, too, you have noticed how certain offices and placement of chairs and desks tend to formalize conversations (Is there a huge desk separating the communicators? Are the chairs eight feet apart?) or how some conversations in midafternoon have a slower pace than morning meetings. To imagine a different kind of context, think of interviewing a new applicant right after you've had an argument with your own boss, or think about going to a job interview when all that is really on your mind is how long you'll suffer from this migraine headache. These are examples of the many different kinds of contexts that should be analyzed as you make decisions about how to communicate in the interview.

1. *Situational/social context:* What kind of situation is it? What do the communicators understand about why they are talking? If two people are talking smoothly face-to-face, how does an onlooker change the dynamics of the conversation? The goals and interpersonal rules of certain social situations might change an otherwise taboo behavior into something permissible. One university career center (Saint Louis University Career Center [SLU], 1997) asks students to consider how they might want to—and be expected to—act differently in the following diverse, but typical, interview situations:

- **One-on-one interview** (individualized attention, with one organizational representative talking with an applicant).

- **Panel interview** (several organizational representatives take turns asking questions and bringing up issues).

- **Meal interview** (a complex social setting often involving lunch or dinner, in which an interviewee's social and conversational skills, and the ability to concentrate informally on the questions of one or more interviewers, are paramount).

- **Behavioral interview** (an increasingly common situation in which an interviewee is "asked to complete a variety of tasks including handling a crisis situation, demonstrating a particular skill, role playing or preparing a response to a case study" [SLU, 1997, p. 22]). This situation is based upon what researchers call *behavior description theory* (Janz, 1989), which presumes that interviewees' descriptions of actual past behaviors provide excellent clues to their prospective behaviors in new jobs. In fact, this research found only four key types of interview information: credentials, experience descriptions, opinions, and behavior descriptions. Of these, "Only behavior descriptions offer practical, clear data on which to base predictions of future performance" (p. 159).

- **Second interview/On-site visit** (a follow-up interview often for the purpose of further investigation and familiarization with the actual work setting; applicants will likely meet many potential coworkers in a short time and under actual organizational conditions).

2. *Temporal context:* What has happened before? How long have the participants known each other? What time of day is it? Although many people don't recognize how profoundly time affects their relationships, "time talks," as anthropologist Edward Hall

(1959, pp. 128–145) put it. Think about the situational context of a meal interview and its temporal elements. For example, it's most likely to be at a certain time of day (noon), more likely to be a second interview (with memories of the first already planted), and very likely to be of a certain predictable duration (it takes at least an hour to order, be served, converse, and conclude).

3. *Immediate nonverbal context:* How is the furniture arranged? Is the other person's speech hard to listen to because your attention is drawn so often to the odd way he or she is dressed? Does the brightly painted wall distract you? Although this type of context can't *cause* or *determine* what is said, it's safe to assume that it always will influence what is said.

4. *Psychological/physiological context:* Do you expect to succeed? To be believable and persuasive? If so, such contexts may create *self-fulfilling prophecies* that make positive outcomes more likely for competent communicators. In a self-fulfilling prophecy, what you think will happen becomes more likely to happen. Of course, negative expectations may become self-fulfilling as well. What are you worried about during the interview, and how might that distract you? If your fear of having a bad interview experience is excessive, you might be making a negative experience more likely—by distracting yourself from the very choices under your control that could make it better.

Although it seems almost self-evident to say so, job interviews take place only when there is a contextual convergence of goals: one person or organization wants to fill a position while another person wants to achieve a position. Although each side is motivated, the extent to which they realize that the motivation is mutual may not be readily apparent to either party. The applicant may be too entangled in personal fears of not getting a job to realize that the employer *needs* to find someone; the employer faced with a loss of productivity or with dissatisfied coworkers who have taken on extra duties to make up for a job vacancy may not realize fully the candidate's sincere motives. Thus the most successful interviews are ones in which both sides collaborate to share information in dialogue, even if a hiring is not the result.

In spite of the fact that the physical context is usually determined by organizational interviewers and applicants/candidates usually feel less powerful and more ill at ease, researchers into the social context of employment interviews still stress the mutual influences of dialogue (Howard & Ferris, 1996, p. 112). Further, recent experience has shifted the traditional emphasis on the interviewer's perspective to a fresh interest in interviewees' perspectives (p. 125). However, the factors of context—especially how they affect interviewers' decision making—are relatively underresearched (pp. 113, 125).

Persuasive Proofs

Classical rhetorical theorists have described the three basic ways communicators influence audiences: **ethos** (the persuasiveness that comes from the force of character), **pathos** (the persuasiveness that comes from appeals to emotion), and **logos** (the persuasiveness of logical appeals). What is the relevance of persuasive proofs used in the employment interview?

Ethos   In contemporary life ethos is usually discussed as "credibility" and, according to researchers, involves two major characteristics, expertise and trustworthiness, and a minor one, dynamism. That is, highly credible job applicants (those high on an "ethical proof" scale) are more likely to be hired when they know what they're talking about (are expert), are seen as being ethical, honest, and reliable (are trustworthy), and are perceived as enthusiastic and animated (are dynamic). How can applicants accomplish this? We'll discuss how in more detail later, but the expertise element of ethos is why interviewees want to have solid resumes that describe accomplishments well; trustworthiness is why they are sure to relate stories about positive performance appraisals of attendance, thoroughness, and honesty in past jobs; dynamism is why they want to use as many action words as possible and beware of an excessively low-key monotonic style of speech.

Pathos   Pathos is usually a less relevant and less examined factor in employment interview rhetoric, possibly because the process is presumed to be such a highly rational one. Interviewers and interviewees aren't expected to make decisions based on emotions. Yet this fact does not mean that emotions play no part in interviewing. Indeed, some evidence (Frank & Hackman, 1975) suggests that similarity between interview partners and perceived personal attractiveness play an important role in who is hired.

Logos   Logos, or logical proof, involves careful and systematic reasoning that demonstrates why your assertions are true: examples are appropriate, reasoning "hangs together," and the evidence used pertains directly to the claims it is supposed to support. An interviewer asks, "How do you know you can handle the kinds of workers and cultural tensions we have here at OneWorld Electronics?" The respondent says, "I set up a training program for similar workers three years ago at Dynamico and have studied conflict management ever since I was in college." Without saying so directly, the answer implies that these facts are not only to be taken as good evidence, but it should be assumed that they indicate an ongoing capability to accomplish the same results at OneWorld.

Ethics

What are the primary ethical issues of the employment interview? Recall in Chapter 1, we discussed both a deontological ethic, which ideally stresses principles and duties that should apply to everyone all the time—such as truth telling—and a teleological ethic, which ideally looks to the consequences of acts to evaluate how much good for humans can come out of those actions. Of course, life isn't lived "ideally" but in a world where important choices are rarely as clear cut as we'd like. For example, to sketch a hypothetical situation, what would you put in your resume about managing an office when you know that you were given the lion's share of such duties in your previous employment, but officially, "office manager" was someone else's job title? If you put "office manager" on that line, are you being truthful? Some would say yes, arguing that in truth you managed the office, so the label is appropriate. Others might argue that since the title was never yours, you have no right to claim it. Even if you consider the claim to be literally a lie, can it be morally justified at some level?

One particularly helpful ethical principle for employment interview participants is what Sissela Bok (1979) calls the "test of publicity." It asks

> . . . which lies, if any, would survive the appeal for justification to reasonable persons. It requires us to seek concrete and open performance of an exercise crucial to ethics: The Golden Rule, basic to so many religious and moral traditions. We must share the perspective of those affected by our choices, and ask how we would react if the lies we are contemplating were told to us. We must, then, adopt the perspective not only of liars but of those lied to; and not only of particular persons but of all those affected by lies— the collective perspectives of reasonable persons seen as potentially deceived. We must formulate the excuses and the moral arguments used to defend the lies and ask how they would stand up under the public scrutiny of these reasonable persons. (pp. 98–99)

Boiled down to its basics, the **test of publicity** suggests that when confronted with moral choices, you can apply this criterion: Is the action I am tempted to take one that I would feel comfortable making fully public, if need be, to a wide audience of reasonable people? Do I believe I could explain my choice successfully? Not all moral dialogue has to be publicized, Bok believes—you don't need to call attention defensively to your resume item about "office manager" in each interview, for example—but moral decisions have to be "*capable* of being made public" (p. 97; emphasis added).

Over the next several sections of this chapter, we survey rhetorical goals from the standpoint of both interviewee and interviewer. We will not separate these discussions very far from each other, even though each will be somewhat detailed. You probably will find yourself in both roles in your professional career, and the rhetoric of each should help you understand the dynamics of the other.

Interviewers' Rhetoric and Goals

The interviewer's role can be distinguished by many factors, including depth and breadth of knowledge about the anticipated position; directive control over the interview setting; a perception that the interviewer is representing an organization in a legal sense; a heightened responsibility for encouraging a comfortable relationship with the interviewee; and the added decision-making responsibility of acting as a filter, narrowing the pool of interviewees the organization will be able to evaluate subsequently. Interviewers enact dual responsibilities to the applicants and to the organization, but the organizational responsibilities seem more politically motivating for many interviewers. The complicated nature of balancing all these tasks makes it necessary that interviewers prepare carefully in advance. Before the interview(s), interviewers should ensure they are prepared in the following ways:

- *Know why you're conducting the interviews.* Have a clear idea why the interviews in question are taking place, and verify with superiors their role in the selection process. For example, will a given round of interviews result in a hire (**primary selection interviewing**), or will these be preliminary interviews primarily serving to select a group of applicants who will be interviewed in more depth later (*two-stage screening interviewing*)? The length of the interview, its detail, the type of notes you would keep, and other decisions would hinge on an understanding of the basic purpose of the interview.

- *Know how to describe the available position.* In many cases you'll simply be given a predetermined description of the position from superiors and will be expected to shape your interviews according to its demands. If, however, you have a voice in defining the position, make the most of it. First, prepare a **needs assessment**—a systematic description of what the new hire will need to do and to know—for the position you want to fill. Be sure you have a clear, and easily communicated, definition of the position. It will help to develop both a **surface description version** (streamlined into one sentence) and a **depth description version** (a more specific account, perhaps with handouts, for applicants who request more information).

- *Know the work setting.* At a concrete everyday level, you must understand the actual work environment in which new hires will begin; you will be a primary informant, if not the only source, for your interviewees. Visit the workplace in which the successful applicant will work, and, if necessary, briefly interview supervisors and coworkers there to get a good sense of what the job involves. Even if your superiors do not ask you to do so, develop two documents for yourself: First, write out a **profile of essential skills** that would enable someone to excel in the job setting. This profile might be used to construct a second list, a **criteria checklist,** to supplement your interview guide, and on which you could take notes during the interviews.

- *Know the law.* Familiarize yourself with all laws and regulations that affect the questions you can ask and the way you conduct the interview. In "Beyond the Basics" we will provide more specific information to support and guide employment interviewers in making the difficult choices involved in questioning and responding to applicants. For now, however, you should know that a common term among those who discuss the practical and legal implications of employment interviewing is the acronym **BFOQ.** In general, interviewers need to focus their interviewing on **bona fide occupational qualifications**—those qualities and qualifications that are clearly and demonstrably related to how well a given job will be performed. An interviewer can't just ask anything that arises from native curiosity; some questions, if they suggest the possibility that an employer might base a decision illegally on race, gender, age, or other forms of discrimination, are unlawful.

- *Seek training opportunities.* Don't assume that because you know more about the job requirements and the organization that you'll be able to communicate with applicants without much preparation. Inexperienced interviewers are just as susceptible to interpersonal blind spots and missed opportunities as anyone else, and structured training in interviewing will help you understand your own style in more depth. There are even more practical reasons for training: researchers have found that interviewers who have been trained systematically in the process are more alert to, and less influenced by, interviewee "self-promotion" behaviors (Howard & Ferris, 1996, p. 131).

Planning will probably be invisible to interviewees if the interviewer does her or his rhetorical job smoothly; the interview will be experienced as conversational and natural. Competent interviewers convince applicants that it is OK, comfortable, and reasonable to disclose why they can do the job well, and this result serves both sides' interests. Yet one important difference from everyday conversation is that most conversations don't entail this much forethought. Remember: The interviewer's primary job as a communicator is to work hard ahead of time and behind the scenes to set the stage on which spontaneous, satisfying conversation can emerge, but the interviewer cannot force that talk, nor is there any guarantee that all such talk will be productive. Aside from the ultimate goals of hiring and being hired, each party mainly needs the interview to meet the goal of providing useful information. How can interviewers structure the rhetorical encounter so that both sides will meet their informational goals? We'll look at some ways to do this in the next section.

Creative Forms of Interviewers' Questioning, Listening, and Framing

Remember that interviewing involves three fundamental processes—listening, speaking, and framing. Because employee selection interviewers typically take a directive, inquiring role, let's start with speaking. Speaking is an initiating process, listening a process of active reception/conception, and framing an overall process of helpful appropriate interpretation, understanding, and attribution of meaning. The employment interviewer speaks primarily as a questioner, listens primarily as an organizational representative who attempts to answer candidates' concerns, and frames information primarily as a decision maker.

Questioning from the Interviewer's Perspective

Employment interviewers are responsible for planning the basic structure of the interview. They must, therefore, be proactive on some issues that interviewees can afford to approach with a wait-and-see attitude. The interviewer's best proactive tools are a knowledge of the typical stages of employment interviews and a clear schedule of relevant questions adapted to those stages.

Most experts divide the basic selection interview into a few standard stages of development. Because the stages really are the essential tasks accomplished by both interviewer and interviewee, each appears to demand its own particular type of questioning: stage 1, opening and rapport building; stage 2, interviewer inquiries; stage 3, interviewee inquiries; and stage 4, closing and clarifications.

• *Stage 1: Opening and rapport building.* What is rapport? Some scholars conceive of it as involving "coordination," "mutual attentiveness," and "positivity" (Tickle-Degnan & Rosenthal, 1990). They mean that in a condition of **rapport,** communicators create a relationship that ideally is coordinated but not manipulated, and one in which they respond attentively to each other in creating a positive tone. Rapport is *emergent* in the sense that it emerges from how two people talk with each other, and it cannot be considered something to be forced, inoculated, or triggered by techniques (Jorgenson, 1995). Rapport does not necessarily mean that participants are buddies or that they're in love, but that they become mutually and, to some extent, positively cofocused on the task at hand.

Rapport tends to be built in situations of relatively informal but genuine small talk. It is a conversational style that emphasizes personal comfort and simply "being with" each other over the literal exchange of information. Typical topics of this type of **phatic communion,** as some communication theorists refer to small talk that serves mainly to humanize relations, are weather, traffic, a particularly interesting (but noncontroversial) news event both parties have heard about, the immediate surroundings of the interview, and the like. Family topics may be tempting, though discussions about the interviewee's family life run the risk of violating privacy and may veer into territory that is technically illegal, as we shall see in a later discussion of the legal context of interviewing. Although it seems trivial at first glance, rapport building has an enormous impact on later stages of interviewing, because people use this opportunity to size up how safe it is to disclose personal details and feelings, be honest about reservations and weaknesses, and assess their own abilities. If you are uncomfortable interviewing others, it is absolutely essential that you practice the conversational styles of rapport building.

• *Stage 2: Interviewer inquiries.* These tend to be questions and comments about the interviewee's knowledge, skills, abilities, and appreciations. (See Box 6.2 for the questioning tendencies of one experienced interviewer.) Much of your interview of a job applicant will be guided by an interview schedule, which (you'll recall from previous chapters) is a list of questions or topics with which you structure the interview. Think of your schedule as the verbal skeleton of the interview, the solid inner framework by which you'll ensure that the other person has an equal and fair chance to impress you, and by which you'll also be sure to get all the information you've determined you need. Having a schedule of questions does not mean that you can't explore side issues or explore interesting leads with probes (follow-up questions). It only means you have a preplanned structure to return to when the exploration has taken its course.

BOX 6.2   INTERVIEWERS IN ACTION

Nancy Austin and Mary Kay Haben

Nancy Austin, a noted management consultant, summarizes the experience of another experienced employment interviewer, Mary Kay Haben of Kraft Foods. Note the emphasis on realistic questioning that should deflect the game playing that undermines many interviews, and note also that this is a slightly different approach from the behavioral interviewing described earlier, although both rely on narrative conversation.

"Old-fashioned recruiting and selection methods can't keep pace with corporations' rapidly changing needs. That's why Mary Kay Haben, executive vice president of the pizza division at Kraft Foods, spends so much time thinking about the questions she and her managers ask. 'We work hard to focus our questions on the job that has to be done,' she says. That means lots of open-ended inquiries to get beyond the canned responses that, let's face it, applicants are sick of giving and interviewers are sick of hearing. . . . Haben quizzes candidates on mini case studies: 'I'll describe a situation and ask, "How would you handle this?"' In other words, she lays out a real live business problem, then steps back and watches the prospect tackle it. She also relies on 'multiple data points,' reactions from five or six Kraft managers who individually interview the same roster of candidates, then meet later to compare notes. 'In the old days,' she says, 'everybody followed the resumes and asked exactly the same things.'"

Source: Austin, 1996, p. 24

In the past decade most researchers on employment interviewing have stressed the need for structuring the situation more carefully to obtain the kinds of applicant selections that will ultimately profit the organization. To believe that the best interviews are wholly spontaneous is to squander opportunities for information. Further, it keeps you from being able to compare candidates and their skills systematically when the interviews might be separated in time and space.

Interview schedules do not need to be elaborate (although for some positions they may need to be much more detailed than our examples here). Box 6.3 presents one suggested basic format, in which an interviewer interested in hiring registered nurses for a clinical setting develops a sequence of questions to guide an interview after the basic personal data has been exchanged.

The sample schedule in Box 6.3 combines behavioral interviewing questions with mini–case studies to provide opportunities for candidates to describe themselves. In addition, the emphasis on more generalized questions at the beginning and on more open-ended inquiries will presumably invite candidates to adapt their explanations to the specific position being discussed (or, if they don't, that's important information, too).

Corporate consultant Arnold Kanter's (1995, pp. 85–89) advice to employment interviewers on questioning is especially relevant in the context of Chapter 4, on questioning styles. Here we will summarize his seven basic types of questions that are asked of applicants; you will see that they aren't equally effective by any means.

BOX 6.3   INTERVIEWERS IN ACTION

A Sample Interview Schedule For a Critical Care Nurse Position

Why are you considering/desiring Surgical Critical Care?

What are your future goals—personal/professional?

What were the circumstances concerning your leaving your last job?

Did you like your last job?

Did you encounter stressful situations?

How did you handle those situations/what did you do?

What aspects of your job (schooling) did you find most satisfying? Least satisfying?

What clinical experiences have you had?

Scenarios:
  Patient complaint: Clinical situation:

On any given shift, what is your goal with patient care?

Explain what "empowerment of patients" means to you.

Describe one of the best nursing care experiences you've ever encountered.

Describe the worst nursing care experience you've ever encountered.

What unique services do professional RNs provide that other health care workers do not?

What is your comfort level with the Nursing Process? (What is the Nursing Process?)

What adjectives would you use to describe yourself?

How would you describe your last manager?

How would you describe your previous co-workers?

Are you interviewing elsewhere? Where?

Source: Shiparsky, 1996, p. 32F

- *Open-ended questions* are effective as conversation starters and help keep the spotlight on the interviewee. (Most experts suggest interviewees should probably talk, on average, two to three times as much as interviewers.)

- *Closed-ended questions* can be effective in eliciting specific details or keeping pressure on a respondent (if that's your goal), but they are usually not well suited to maintaining the conversational flow sought by most interviewers. They lend a staccato tone to interviews, encouraging short answers interspersed with terse questions.

- *Leading questions* are those in which the question itself telegraphs the desired answer ("Wouldn't it be better to work in a big-city atmosphere like Atlanta?"). For most purposes, leading questions are ineffective because they don't encourage either candor or further disclosure.

- *Broad-brush questions* like, "Tell me about your work experience last summer" (p. 87) are open and inviting, perhaps effectively so, but may be so imprecise that the

1. Review the sample interview schedule in Box 6.3.

- Although the questions aren't overtly divided into topics and groups of issues, what is the overall organizational pattern? What are the major divisions of the organization Shiparsky is recommending? Are they similar to the stages recommended in this chapter? If so, how? If not, why not? What is recommended in this chapter that does not appear in the schedule?

- This schedule (an actual document, not a hypothetical suggestion) was obviously designed for a fairly long interview. Try to rewrite it to fit a twenty-to-thirty-minute interview opportunity. Which questions could be eliminated? Which could be combined into questions that cover topics more rapidly?

2. Write a schedule of eight to ten questions appropriate for interviewing applicants for the latest job you've held. Try to:

- Move from general to more specific questions
- Write at least two questions with behaviorally based emphases
- Word questions unambiguously
- Cover all relevant job skills

candidate has to request clarification of terms or intent. Use these kinds of questions when you're reasonably certain the interviewee knows your intent.

- *Compare and contrast questions* have certain advantages because you can see the person's mind at work in a problem-solving mode ("Compare and contrast two types of feedback—oral and written—in their ability to encourage meaningful behavior change in workers"); be ready, though, with reasonable probes to check on what the interviewee might mean by the response.

- *Self-appraisal questions* allow interviewees to account for why their achievements were so impressive, or mitigated, or mixed. With these questions, you learn not only about their accomplishments or their opinions about them but also about their theories of personal achievement or cause and effect.

- *Multiple questions*—asking several things all wrapped up in one inquiry—usually only confuse respondents and give you squishy information at best. Avoid them. Imagine being asked in a nerve-racking situation, "Who, if any, were the most effective teachers you had at the university, what were their most interesting classroom techniques, and what did you learn about your own training style as a result of interacting with them?" Huh?

- *Stage 3: Interviewee inquiries.* These tend to be questions and comments to satisfy the interviewee's curiosity and interest concerning the description of the position and the organization. Many interviewers unintentionally hog the available time with their own questions, relegating interviewee's inquiries to an afterthought. This is one of the bigger mistakes you could make. First, your best-qualified interviewees will be consistently counseled, in classes, workshops, and career centers, to ask relevant questions and will come to interviews prepared with them. The day of interviewee-as-victim has passed. If this opportunity to inquire is denied them, they may tend to wonder about the overall responsiveness of your organization and may look elsewhere. Second, you can learn a great deal about the professional savvy, personality, and qualifications of candidates by the kinds of questions they ask. For example, if you are asked, "What are the major subsidiaries of your company?" or "Who are your major competitors in the Minneapolis market?" you can be sure that this person has not spent much time researching readily available public sources of information.

As a general rule, plan to set aside about a quarter of your total time for the interviewee's inquiries about such issues as working conditions, interpersonal environment, promotion potential, travel, evaluation procedures and criteria, and other matters of interest to candidates. Some interviewees might not have this many questions. In that case, you might bring out a set of questions in a kind of "contingency schedule" or find a graceful way to move to the interview's closing phase.

• *Stage 4: Closing and clarifications.* As the name suggests, this stage serves two functions. First, many human events are experienced in terms of a narrative structure in which beginnings, developments, and endings play important parts. It's as if we wish our lives to be dramatic stories that, no matter how satisfying as they develop, need a satisfying sense of closure. Think of the times when people complain about having unfinished business with someone or think they've left something hanging in an encounter. Interviews are no different. Without a sense of closure in an interview, all participants experience at least some discomfort of ambiguity, in which they're more likely to recall the unanswered questions than the answered ones. Second, beyond the satisfactions of psychological closure lie more pragmatic concerns of ambiguity; even when there is a noticeable conclusion to the conversation, the interviewee may not know what the next step of the process is (or should be). Nor does he or she necessarily know how long it will take to be notified about the results of the organization's search process.

Interviewers can do a great deal to finalize the interview in a way that's satisfying for both sides:

• Summarize in general terms the obvious strengths and potential the candidate demonstrated in the interview. Be careful to avoid appearing so enthusiastic that false hopes are raised, and keep your comments relatively unspecific. Leave conversational space for a reply in which the interviewee can also summarize impressions of your organization and the job fit.

• Describe the next step(s) in the organizational selection process, including relevant time frames.

• Discuss with the interviewee any follow-up information to be shared. Is either party going to send supplementary information, and if so, when should it be expected? Is there a preferred form for such information (phone, e-mail, fax, or post)?

• Thank the interviewee, reinforcing the goodwill and rapport established in the interview.

Listening from the Interviewer's Perspective

In Chapter 3 we defined listening as "the active process through which communicators process aural (sound) stimuli, interpret them as messages, and use them to construct meanings of speech, speakers, and contexts." Listening, as this definition suggests, not only functions as the outcome of speech but also enables speech in the first place. We don't speak meaningfully to each other unless we expect to be listened to, and if, while speaking, our listener's attention or interest wanders, we quit speaking. Speech is so thoroughly directed to an anticipated listener, in fact, that we could say that in many ways listening styles *regulate* speech styles.

If, as an interviewer, you develop the impression that a particular candidate is unenthusiastic, could it be that she's given up on your ability to listen carefully and is just going through the motions, instead of acting as enthused as she feels? If you develop the impression that an applicant doesn't know any details about the computer program he claims to know intimately, it could be that your listening style has given him no evidence that you can process such detail, and he simply has chosen not to include it.

So, considering the sobering thought that interviewers may actually be contributing to artificial problems that others may experience, how can their interviews give maximum opportunities for applicants to show what they know and what they can do? Here are some basic principles of listening for employment interviewers: wait, demonstrate, verify, clarify, record. Let's look at them one by one.

Wait   Remember that interviewees are usually more nervous than you are, and typically, more rides on the outcome of the interview for them. After you ask a question or introduce an idea, don't assume that a hesitation means your partner is having trouble answering. She or he may be balancing several effective responses but just hasn't chosen one of them yet.

Remember from Chapter 4 that one of the skills taught in teacher education programs has to do with what's called wait time—maintaining sufficient silence after a question for respondents to decide how to answer. Inexperienced teachers may ask a class, "Who were the early leaders of the civil rights movement?" and, when they get no immediate response, assume that no one has the answer. Wrong. Often, when timed, teachers discover they've waited barely a second or two before moving on. Many in the class may have a good response, but it takes time to form an answer that commits the speaker to public positions that will be judged. Interviewing is a similar challenge, and interviewers should use silence similarly—allow enough open time for the respondent to formulate a meaningful answer.

Demonstrate   Double-check your listening style to analyze how you appear to your partner while listening. Are you attuned primarily to the conversation at hand rather than shuffling through other papers, taking phone calls, or looking at your watch? Remember from Chapter 3 that listening, when done well, is much more than a psychological or cognitive process; skillful listening looks like listening on the outside, too. You can demonstrate your listening by practicing **attending behaviors** (nonverbal cues that reliably indicate a listener is paying attention). Nod affirmatively at points made by your partner (this kind of nodding is generally perceived not as agreement but as an indicator of interest, saying, in effect, "I'm with you, go on"). Lean forward at times to increase the sense of immediacy between the two of you. Maintain appropriate eye contact, but more isn't necessarily better in this case. Generally, directing your gaze at your partner during especially important points helps to convince him or her that you're listening; staring constantly, however, is not an indicator of interest or of listening. All these things are impossible to quantify, of course, and to turn them into precise prescriptions raises more questions and problems than it resolves. In the final analysis, we emphasize this: If you fail to demonstrate your listening overtly, don't be surprised if the interviewee leaves feeling disconfirmed at best and, at worst, with an abiding distaste for your organization.

Verify   Listen actively and, to the extent possible for you, empathically. A basic goal of listening is to convince interviewees that they've been given a full and fair hearing, as we pointed out in Chapter 3. One way to accomplish this is to reflect their own words back to interviewees, along with your developing interpretations of their meaning, at crucial points in the interview. This gives your partners a chance to tell you when they've been misunderstood.

You could overdo this style of listening and turn it into a rote technique. Every statement doesn't need to be reflected and verified, and if you try to do this in an information sharing interview, the flow will be damaged irreparably. However, skillfully applied and well timed, active listening can unlock many further disclosures. Here's how it works:

INTERVIEWEE: "When hired at my last job I became concerned that people had their own agendas and failed to work together. I thought they needed more structure."

INTERVIEWER: "Things were in disarray at first."

INTERVIEWEE: "Yeah. They didn't say so, but it was almost as if they brought me in to tighten up policies."

INTERVIEWER: "So that's what you did?"

INTERVIEWEE: "It took me a year or more, but I worked to simplify things at meetings. But in between our department meetings, I met with people separately and tried to clarify with them what they expected from themselves and what I expected of them."

INTERVIEWER: "It sounds like you didn't want to remove all of their own agendas, or erase their feelings of autonomy, but just wanted each of them to get a better sense of the whole. Is that right?"

INTERVIEWEE: "Absolutely. After that first year, productivity went way up, too."

Notice that the interviewer is not trying to question, or pry, or even to clarify what the interviewee is saying. The goal is only to verify that his or her listening is more or less accurate—that the other is not feeling misunderstood. Even if you're wrong about the inferences you make, if you are wrong out loud, your partner can reply to it with a "Yes, but . . . ," or a "That's almost it. But beyond that . . . ," or "I didn't mean to suggest that." It's verification, plain and simple. But it's content verification that serves an interactional process purpose as well.

Clarify   Use your "listening spare time" (see Chapter 3) to compare and contrast what the interviewee tells you with other information you have collected. You may sense a contradiction between a story about previous employment and what the applicant put on a resume. You may recall that early in the interview the applicant said she always gets along well with superiors but now is talking about her tension with the boss's directive style. You believe the applicant when he says that as a leader he works subtly and effectively behind the scenes, but you wonder if that claim is contradicted by the three formal complaints he filed against others in his previous job.

In listening to clarify, your role is not like a prosecuting attorney who must interrogate the interviewee. In some instances, you simply use your discriminative listening skills (the skills that let you notice differences between phenomena) to note the possible areas of misunderstanding. Some of them you will not even want to bring up. But in fairness to the interviewee, many potential misunderstandings are averted by effective discriminative listeners who are alert to the need to clarify and who are willing to broach the subject openly.

Record   Review the rationale and the techniques for recording information while listening. Take notes relevant to the criteria and job description you prepared beforehand. Probably the simplest way to do this is to turn your schedule or criteria checklist into a one- or two-page form for note taking. Reconsider, for example, the schedule earlier in this chapter for interviewing nurses; this is not simply a list—think of it as also being a criteria form, complete with blank spaces in which to record your impressions, brief quotes, and questions for follow-up. And don't forget the follow-up, either. In addition to listening well within the interview to the applicant, listen well afterward to your own reactions. If your gut feeling is that a candidate is better than the paperwork shows, or better than your notes reflect, this is a signal for you to reconsider the notes carefully. If possible, compare your notes with someone else in the organization who has interviewed this person or others for the designated position.

Interviewees might get nervous if you don't take a few notes. They also might get nervous when you *take* notes, thinking you're only registering flaws, problems, gaps, and gaffes. Interviewees naturally tend to be nervous. Try not to cause them more nervousness unnecessarily. Take the kind of minimal notes that will remind you later of what's crucial, and demonstrate your interest in remembering salient points, but not so many notes that you're distracted from the conversation. A rule of thumb: If you're writing so much that the interviewee often has to pause in the conversation for you to finish, then your eye contact, as well as your listening, is probably going to suffer. This decreases the naturalness of an interview setting that is probably too artificial already.

Framing from the Interviewer's Perspective

Sociologist Erving Goffman (1974) thought that framing involves a more or less basic question: "I assume," he wrote, "that when individuals attend to any current situation, they face the question: 'What is it that's going on here?'" Interviewers should apply this question to behaviors in selection interviews. Framing is much more complex than this question (see Chapter 5), but it provides a useful starting point for sharpening our analysis here.

Interview partners never act randomly but adapt their social messages to each other, creating patterns of behavior. Those patterns will not be seen or understood in the same ways by different people, however. At best, communicators develop similar interpretations as they attempt to explain to themselves what is going on. But instead of just shrugging our shoulders and assuming this divergence of interpretations is inevitable, communication specialists want to figure out what these differing frames mean for the ongoing interaction. Let's consider a series of questions employment interviewers could ask about their own framing in relation to interviewee framing.

1. Are our frames highly incongruent? What are the implications if (for instance) I define the situation as a conversation, but the applicant defines it as an audition or a test? If I start to kid the interviewee and she or he takes it as criticism? What—to apply Goffman's question—is really going on here?

It might be helpful for you to discuss your own frame assumptions in the opening of the interview. (Don't use the word *frame;* despite its usefulness in explaining the concept in a textbook, it will probably sound like jargon and give you something else to explain.) You might say something like, "I know interviews often feel like nerve-racking tests, but I really just want this to be a friendly exchange. When it's over I want us both to have the kinds of information we'll need to make better decisions. OK?" Don't be naive. This won't calm everyone, but it gives the other person an opening to discuss potentially different frames or prior experiences that weren't as comfortable.

2. How do the different roles make our frames even less congruent? What are the implications if I expect natural and "real" answers, but the applicant has been primed to provide "stock" answers? What is really going on here?

It's probably not necessary to make the roles more obvious than they already are. In most employment interviewing, for example, you are the one with the job or the one who is working where the other wants to work. That provides a political or power dimension to the talk that is hard to miss. Simply be aware that most applicants these days have received some sort of training, workshop, or mock interviewing experience in which they practiced "good" responses to common interview questions. College career counseling offices, for example, typically hand out lists of the 75, 100, or even 200 FAQs (frequently asked questions). Chances are, you'll hear many stock answers (ones that sound right but aren't personalized) and many individually canned answers (ones that tell of personal experience but have been practiced or rehearsed so much that they sound stale). In situations like these, try reframing (see Chapter 5) to get the two of you out of your predesigned roles. Insert a mini–case study or a hypothetical situation in which you both could imagine yourselves, perhaps, as coworkers. Reframing, though it is often discussed as an approach to relational and psychological health (Watzlawick, Weakland, & Fisch, 1974), is also a simple way to change some conversational ground rules—thereby perhaps leveling the playing field. In general, it's usually helpful to minimize the role differences, although this will probably never be fully successful, and, we should acknowledge, some positions demand a more rigid sensitivity to roles.

3. Do my habits of attribution create problems of communication? Do our different attributions keep us from understanding each other? What is really going on here?

Attribution theory has been developed by social psychologists and interpersonal communication researchers to describe how we attempt to explain other people's behaviors (see Kleinke, 1986, pp. 184–199, for a clear summary). With our great faith in cause-and-effect relationships, humans want to know the source of actions—the reasons why people do what they do. This is true even though researchers tell us that social events depend on multiple causes and prior effects, and are situationally embedded. We still strain for a clean-cut explanation, or cause, to which we can attribute someone else's actions. Attributions become minitheories and in effect are explanation frames. For example, Molly quits her job as a copywriter for an advertising firm within two months of beginning work. From Molly's point of view she might not be able to pinpoint one reason, but it seems right to resign for a multitude of reasons that don't necessarily relate to performance quality, but they do relate to strained relations with new colleagues, dissatisfaction with the daily demands for creativity, a desire to spend more time with family at home, the possibility of a new job closer to home, and so forth. The personnel interviewer, however, won't even suspect most of these things; she will simply see this as a hire that didn't work out. Why?

Most commonly, such attributions are made by assuming internal or external causation. That is, we find explanations to support a belief that someone was motivated internally ("Molly quit because she wasn't creative," for example, or, "She's a quitter"). Or we find explanations that relate the action to external stimuli ("Sexual harassment has always been a problem in that department. They drove her out"). In either case, the explanation is probably too simplistic, but each attribution frame creates a particular kind of reality that shapes future communication. As an interviewer, be especially careful about the **fundamental attribution error,** which is the tendency to regard others as motivated internally, by their "real nature" perhaps (whatever you think that is), while you tend to assume that you, and others like you, are motivated by the circumstances in which you find yourself. Here's the danger: In the example of Molly, it's too easy for you (as the interviewer) to believe that you wouldn't have quit, that you have what it takes, that your own problems are attributable to unforeseeable problems out of your control, while Molly's problems might be explained (too easily) by character flaws or personal traits. Do you see how this could create a tendency toward unfair judgment on the part of interviewers? Humans' tendency to make fundamental attribution errors feeds the unfair stereotyping by which narrow-minded people are tempted to think, "All women are . . . ," "I knew I couldn't trust a man to do that . . . ," or "Asians have trouble with . . . ," for example.

4. How do biases and stereotypes influence my frames? What are the implications if we each let our stereotypes govern the interaction? What is really going on here?

We described the fundamental attribution error as a "tendency to regard others as motivated internally, by their 'real nature' perhaps . . . , while you tend to assume that you, *and others like you,* are motivated by . . . circumstances. . . ." We emphasize these words here to highlight common problems in cross-cultural communication—bias and stereotyping. Humans will probably never erase all vestiges of cultural biases, but education in their effects will help us diagnose the problem. The fundamental attribution error is closely related to **ethnocentrism**—the sense that your own cultural group is the standard by which others must be judged (*ethno* means "people"). People often jump to the conclusion that another's abruptness, rudeness, lateness, or decision-making style can be attributed to their so-called natural characteristics as a representative of a particular culture, race, gender, sexual orientation, age group, or socioeconomic group. Ethnocentrism creates a reality of "us" (a group that does things normally, naturally, and reasonably) and alien realities of "them" (groups that demonstrate a range of irritating, wrong, irresponsible, dangerous, or unproductive behaviors).

Stereotyping, the "pictures in the head" that predict and explain others, is not always or necessarily negative. If you let your stereotypes calcify, however, your perception of a group won't let you acknowledge individual uniqueness fully. Not all people are equally prone to negative ethnocentric stereotyping, but we all probably exhibit aspects of it. This is enough to remind you to seek out what might be the interviewee's frame(s) for the interview and to take alternate definitions of the situation into account with sensitivity and empathy. For more information on similar issues, review Chapter 5's discussion of framing in interviewing.

Interviewees' Rhetoric and Goals

Our goal in this chapter is to provide a mix of classic references and the freshest, up-to-the-minute sources and insights into employment interviewing. The territory we survey here is too vast for comprehensive coverage, yet we should emphasize especially the changes in employment interviewing that have become noticeable over the past decade or so.

As we suggested at the beginning of the chapter, many early studies of the validity of employment interviewing found that the interviews didn't do much good—at least in the traditional sense of efficiently predicting who would be effective employees. What was wrong? Employers and academics alike theorized that interviewers probably hadn't taken their task seriously enough, weren't structured enough, and were too focused on opinions, claims, and what has loosely been termed "experience" (has the applicant performed a task before?). These analysts have created a remarkable revolution in the structure and techniques of these interviews, as you read in the previous sections on interviewers' goals and rhetoric. Box 6.4 summarizes some of the changes we've noted from a variety of authors and sources. The changes have particularly important implications for interviewees because they demand adjustments in your rhetorical preparations.

Overall, what should guide the interviewee's choices in preparing for the successful interview? What are the most important rhetorical roles and goals? Answers vary, and no one has a lock on the correct ones. You probably should be wary about trusting anyone (much less textbook authors you've never met) to prescribe answers that you'll automatically accept. The job search process is your responsibility. Many, if not most, choices in it must be based on situational knowledge that generalizations will never cover. Therefore, we don't want to intrude artificially by telling you what you should do. (We're not reluctant to make valid-but-general suggestions for you to consider, as you've seen.)

The interviewee's goals necessitate certain ways of thinking about role adjustments. For example, many people think an applicant's overall goal is to get a job. That's an easy answer, one that comes to mind the fastest. But on more careful consideration, would you be satisfied with *any* job? Or *equally* satisfied with a broad range of jobs? Probably not. You don't just want *a* job—you want the job that's right for you at this moment in your life, one that allows you to use the skills you know you have, and use them in a satisfying way with coworkers who cooperate readily with you. Most likely, too, you have in mind something that advances you along a career path. A *career path* approach is a way of recognizing that each job has to be seen in the context of its unique contribution to your extended professional life. At a given point in that flow of professional development, it may be better for you to turn down a job when you have only one offer (if you're afraid, for example, that it will lock you into a schedule or duties that will make it harder to develop the most important skills for your overall career). So it's not a job you're after, and many interviewers, you'll find, are people you don't even need to worry about impressing. You won't know that until you do your research and interviewing, but acknowledging your role as a career-planning professional should take off a great deal of pressure. Each interview is a new opportunity to learn whether this is the right job for your career.

Therefore, your role as an interviewee, when obvious surface differences are boiled away, is remarkably similar to the interviewer's. Both of you are learners and both are decision makers. You're not begging and pleading. You're deciding (see Box 6.5). If you are especially good at what you do, the employer will be fortunate to hire you, and the interviewer, in fact, may have to do quite a good selling job to get you. The learning/decision-making role of interviewees is not meant to indicate that it doesn't matter how persuasively you present yourself. Nor should it instill a false or strident arrogance. Simply reassure yourself that you, as well as the other person, have some decisions to make as a result of the interview process.

The job search is not easy; in fact, according to many who have been through it, job seeking is like a full-time job itself. Before the interviews come, the ground must be

BOX 6.4　　REMINDERS

How Employment Interviews Have Changed: Implications for Interviewees

- *Interviews are much more structured.* You're less likely to get "tell me about yourself" questions that meander into a twenty-minute chat. You can expect interviewers to exercise quite a bit of control over the direction and content of topics.

- *Interviews are much more focused on actual behaviors from your past.* Interviewers try to elicit your personal account of how you solved problems successfully in previous jobs and organizations through **behavior-based interviewing** (now known as **BBI**). Interviewers are less likely to be impressed with the fact that you were a training supervisor and more likely to ask, for example, how your training program in communication skills helped to resolve interracial conflict on the assembly line. The fact that you got a performance award for excellence in 1994 may be nice, but the interviewer is more likely to be interested in how you handled actual complaints in your department.

- *Interviews are much more dependent upon your abilities as a storyteller.* This is an outgrowth of behavior-based interviewing. Interviewees are now expected not only to remember incidents but also to frame them as interesting and relevant narratives. A much wider range of oral communication skills has become relevant.

- *Interviews tend to be longer.* Interviewees in a former era could expect interviewers to screen candidates, relying on resume information intensively and forming fairly rapid impressions on the basis of personality. But employers no longer trust rapid first impressions; they want to see how you communicate in a sustained interaction.

- *Interviews more often involve multistage and multi-interviewer sequences.* Consistent with the trends toward more structure and longer interviews, employers now are proactively "protecting their investments" by interviewing strong candidates more than once. They are conducting follow-up interviews and panel or series interviewing, in which you meet a sequence of different people in different settings, each of whom will be looking for different things in what you bring to the organization.

- *Interviews more often involve pre-interview testing or screening.* According to one account (Neuborne, 1997), preemployment testing, which often starts as a screening process before the interview stage, "has boomed into a more than $2 billion industry and has seeped into almost every job category, from tow-truck driver to chief financial officer" (p. B1). Although it is controversial in its potential for civil rights abuses and possible discrimination, employers argue that by using such tests they match people to positions much more efficiently, with significant savings and satisfaction all around. These may be psychological tests assessing personality characteristics or straightforward skills tests designed to measure particular job-related abilities. Somewhere in the interview process of serious candidates, many employers now conduct screening investigations that verify employment history, credit history, legal troubles, professional and academic credentials, licenses and degrees, and so forth. Civil libertarians are right to be worried, as these tests and investigations peel off another layer of privacy from our society. Still, they are a fact of contemporary professional life, especially for managers, decision makers, and those charged with the welfare of others. You would be wise to prepare yourself accordingly, although genuinely well prepared candidates always have had little to fear from such procedures.

BOX 6.5   INTERVIEWERS IN ACTION

Bernard Milano

Bernard Milano, partner in charge of recruiting at KPMG Peat Marwick, offers this advice for college students preparing for employment interviewing:

"If you think you're going to college to land a job after graduation, maybe you should think again. Hopefully, the work you're doing now in school will serve as a down payment to the career that you ultimately want—not just a job.

. . . Career counseling, job fairs, on-campus recruitment and employment ads in newspapers, trade publications and the Internet are all good and useful things, but the selection process is about what you choose, not about who chooses you. You may use those tools as guidance, but you should be the principal actor in the decision-making process. It's not hard. It just involves viewing the whole job search procedure from a different perspective.

. . . Remember who's in charge here. It's your life, your career. Passivity is not an option. The same enthusiasm and skills you develop while positioning yourself for the job you want are the characteristics that will move you up each rung of the career ladder."

Source: Milano, 1997, p. 7

prepared and cultivated with care. You're wise to see yourself as a comprehensive communicator involved in a many-faceted campaign that integrates analysis, self-assessment, implementation, and feedback thoroughly at every stage.

Preparing carefully increases your chances of getting the kind of interviews that will clear a satisfying career path. That preparation involves self-assessment, position research and assessment, persuasive cover letters and resumes (the plural forms here are significant, as you will see), planning for nonverbal impressions, and role-playing.

Self-Assessment

None of us knows for certain, at any particular moment, what we're capable of accomplishing. We vaguely recall what we've done, where we've been, and what we've enjoyed, perhaps, but that is not enough for the specificity even of a job search, much less the daunting task of beginning to chart a career. Yet it's possible to turn those vague recollections and feelings into a sharper self-portrait if you're willing to do a little legwork (see Box 6.6).

The real question becomes, "What do I know I'm good at?" And its corollary is, "What evidence demonstrates my effectiveness at accomplishing these things?" Because we suspect you're immersed in ideas about interviewing while reading this book, why not try interviewing as a route to learning more about yourself? But besides asking yourself the questions, choose the person who knows you best in each of these slices of your life: friendship, on-the-job or volunteer work efforts, academic achievement, family, organized

BOX 6.6   INTERVIEWEES IN ACTION

Elsa From

One woman's experience as a job seeker illustrates the importance of honest self-assessment.

"When I got back home I sat around for a few weeks still feeling sorry for myself, wondering what kind of job I could do or wanted to do. It was hard to focus on it. Jobs all seemed alike. I didn't have a clue about them.

"My friend Bob . . . invited me to New York City for a week and I went. I had to get away to clear my mind. While I was there Bob set me up with this friend of his who is a career counselor, and I had a couple great sessions with her. One of the things she had me do was go through this five-page thing she had, an exercise I guess you call it, or a process. Very interesting. I had to make lists of things about myself, what did I like to do, what didn't I like, what were my skills, my interests, where did I want to live. I got to find out a lot of things about myself. Stuff I already knew, but better organized. Fascinating. I don't understand why we never did this in school. You know most of us never really look at ourselves, we just do what someone else tells us. Someone's mother wants them to be a nurse so they are, or a kid gets an erector set and his dad praises him for something he builds, and twenty years later he's a famous bridge builder.

"Anyway, this woman and I went over these lists of things about me, boiled it down, and came up with a half-dozen things to look for in a job. I don't remember the list now but working with my hands was one thing, direct contact with people was another. Something about sales. Several other things."

"Anyhow, I came up with a long list of jobs that fit in with things I liked to do, boiled it down to some job targets, and started to look."

Source: Jackson, 1978, p. 25

sports, or avocational groups. Add to this select group a couple of professors or previous employers who are familiar with your work over the past couple of years, even though they may not have in-depth knowledge about you. Tell each person that you're doing an organized self-assessment, and ask them to volunteer five or more adjectives or descriptors that in their opinion characterize your communication skills and work habits. Don't spend time arguing with them if you think they're wrong, or basking in glory if they're complimentary, or even asking them to come up with reasons for their impressions. Simply write down the adjectives they mention. Later, after talking with all your "informants," sit down with an "honesty partner"—someone who knows you well enough to help you tie together the other strands of feedback.

The next self-assessment step is to trace the adjectives back to the likely evidence each person used in forming this impression of you. For example, the professor for whom you served as a research assistant calls you "reliable." Considering this carefully, you recall that in an entire academic year you never missed a meeting with her, and every time she sent you to the library to find a source citation to back up a point, you always came back with two or more. Through this trace-back strategy, you are not only building a backlog of skills and skill descriptions but also stockpiling some stories you could tell in a conversation with an employment interviewer.

While this is not the only kind of self-assessment you can do profitably, it is one good alternative. Its advantage is that it employs what we call **relayed feedback.** You're not saying these things about yourself (that might be perceived as boasting). In a later interview you'll simply be reporting that these are impressions you are *relaying* from the people who have worked closely with you. If you're like most people, you simply need to be reflective and systematic in order to come up with a surprisingly long list of good descriptions and evidence. When referring to relayed feedback, you pass along others' perceptions of, and responses to, your work. For example: "My final performance appraisal as an undergraduate TA said that I put in more hours assisting the COMM 100 students than any other TA my faculty advisor could remember." Such a statement is much more meaningful and concrete than your personal claim that you're "a hard worker."

Position Research and Assessment

When you become interested in interviewing for a job, don't just apply and hope the employer will find you qualified. You can take some of the guesswork out of the process by doing your homework. Several types of research are especially helpful:

- On virtually any four-year college campus, you will find a career center that maintains up-to-date resources: dozens of directories and books that detail the organizational structure and status of major businesses, goals and activities of nonprofit organizations, representative job descriptions and listings, and so on. Check these out for every organization that (you hope) will interview you.

- At your library, do database searches for articles in prominent publications that mention the organizations you've identified. Reference librarians will help you locate the print sources most relevant to your quest. Database availability may vary with your library and may change over time, but look especially for such sources as ABI/INFORM, *Trade and Industry Index, BusinessWire, PR Newswire, Standard & Poor's News, Standard & Poor's Corporate Descriptions,* and *Standard & Poor's Register.* Pay especially close attention to newspapers in the city or town where you'll interview, but don't forget to check the hometown paper of the corporate headquarters as well. If the organization has a national or international profile, it's wise to check the national newspapers that are known as **papers of record** (those that try to keep track of all important national and international political, social, and economic trends). Papers of record in the United States are usually considered to be the *New York Times, Washington Post, Wall Street Journal,* and *Los Angeles Times.*

- Take advantage of the Internet resources devoted to career information. Martin Yate (1996) suggests several and counsels that many more sites are being added constantly. The following is excerpted from Yate's book:

Career Mosaic (http://www.careermosaic.com/cm/cml.html) lists profiles and job listings for top technology companies.

CareerWEB (http://www.cweb.com/) also lists available job openings, but gives you the opportunity to apply on-line. The CareerWeb features the Career Fitness Test and Career Fitness Center, so that you can test and improve your career skills. You will also find the CareerWEB Library, with a list of job-search tools.

E-Span's Interactive Employment Network (IEN) (http://www.espan.com/) lists job openings from thousands of clients nationwide. Included are interactive interview questions, job-search practice exercises, and research resources. The career fair calendar provides a geographic listing of career events.

The *Monster Board* (http://www.monster.com/) is a collection of job-search utilities that includes job opportunities, on-line resume submissions, employer profiles, a "cyberzone" for students, and a listing of career events.

Online Career Center (http://www.occ.com/occ/) also offers thousands of job opportunities and a comprehensive resume database. The career assistance center is worth investigating, as is the recruiter's office. OCC On Campus provides assistance to students, and OCC also keeps members abreast of career events.

To search for other sites, go to (http://rescomp.stanford.com/jobs.html). This helpful listing is sponsored by Stanford University. (pp. 295–296)

Persuasive Cover Letters and Resumes

A **resume** is a summary of the skills and experience that presumably qualify you for a particular job. It is usually sent or given to an organizational representative along with a **cover letter,** a narrative description of why you believe you are a good fit for the job and can meet the organization's needs. Contemporary resumes are still delivered in traditional ways (postal delivery, hand carried), but increasingly, resumes are sent in electronic versions on-line. Not long ago, the conventional wisdom for job candidates was to spend a great deal of time and energy crafting a resume and making it unique so that it would draw the right kind of attention. Then the candidate would take the typescript to a printer and have scores of resumes printed so they could be sent out over the next weeks and months to potential employers.

Resumes, like a lot of things, aren't what they used to be. First, preparing only a single version of a resume these days is not practical, given the different kinds of jobs and career niches for which candidates will be considered. The ready availability of word processing programs and laser printers means that resumes can be—indeed, are often expected to be—tailored uniquely for almost every submission. Second, it is usually no longer necessary or desirable, if it ever was, to have a glitzy eye-catching resume that uses a variety of cute or unusual fonts, colors, or shadings. (Actually, "cute" choices were never effective, according to most experts in the field.) According to Yate (1996), 78 percent of companies surveyed in 1993 used computerized resume-tracking programs; the figure is probably considerably higher today. As you would predict, these programs scan for keywords or buzzwords, often the same nouns that appear in the original listing describing the position. The new trend toward electronic resumes, therefore, stresses the same approach: a straightforward, clean, direct style that emphasizes keyword labels or phrases to establish qualifications without ambiguity. According to one brochure distributed by a large campus career center, sample or representative keywords that characterize advertising/communication positions are "booth development," "image campaign," "promotional materials," "sales promotion," and "cable television." Keywords appropriate for compensation specialists, on the other hand, might include "equity review," "incentive plan," "job classification," and "salary structure." What are some keywords that reflect the kinds of jobs you're likely to apply for? In the same brochure (SLU, 1997), career consultant Marilyn Moats Kennedy is quoted as saying, "It is important to alter your resume to fit a particular job. One of the biggest mistakes people make is that they do not pick up on the keywords in job postings and advertisements and include them in their resumes" (p. 15).

Research reinforces the importance of establishing a strong first impression with interviewers. Part of this suggestion is based upon how interviewers respond to carefully prepared written materials, well-understood skills, and clear descriptions of qualifications. A form of self-fulfilling prophecy seems to be at work, in which interviewers who read of strong credentials use a subsequent interview to confirm that positive first impression, rather than to poke holes in it (Dipboye, 1982). In one study, researchers (Dougherty, Turban, & Callender, 1994) found that interviewers' positive first impressions "were followed by interviewers' use of confirmatory behavior and styles, including a positive style of interviewing, selling the company, providing job information to applicants, less information-gathering from applicants, more confident and effective applicant behavior, and more rapport of applicants with interviewers." Further, there was, under this self-fulfilling prophecy, more sharing of job information with applicants and, most important perhaps, "a favorable orientation toward job offers" (p. 663). Freely translated into everyday language, it pays down the road to be thorough with your written materials up front.

Advising job hunters about resume and cover letter strategies has become a cottage industry, in which experts relay a vast array of hints and prescriptions, some of which seem contradictory. We can only scratch the surface here, synthesize some of the more helpful suggestions that emphasize the mutual learning that comes from such written messages, and then refer you to career guides, such as those mentioned at the end of the chapter, for more detailed information.

Think of a cover letter as a kind of ideal introduction to who you are in relation to the organization's needs, stressing your skills and strengths. The best cover letters are succinct, narratively interesting, motivating, and directed to a specific organizational representative. Choose the content for the cover letter by asking, "If someone were to meet me for a couple of minutes, what would I want to be sure to say, and how, ideally, would I want to say it?" Although cover letters are often skimmed rapidly, many personnel managers do read them, but they develop impressions in a matter of moments, or minutes at best. Your cover letter, then, should emphasize short, direct sentences and paragraphs with concrete and vivid language. It should tell a story that may not be told fully in your resume—why, for instance, you've decided to commit to a career change at this moment in your life, or why the importance of studying public relations has crystallized for you because of recent events in the news. Finally, the cover letter should lead the reader directly to a careful study of the resume: "As you will see . . ." statements can create such a bridge. Many cover letters reflect a three-part goal, with major paragraphs devoted to each section: State your relationship to the position or anticipated position, including why you are interested in it; state how your resume indicates your qualifications for this position; state your willingness to stay in touch (see Figure 6.1).

Resumes tend to be either chronological or functional. A **chronological resume**—almost always a reverse chronology—charts your personal experience from job to job, from school to school, from experience to experience, from responsibility to responsibility. Within each heading, your skills are stressed. A **functional resume,** alternatively, organizes your qualifications around the functions you can fulfill for the new organization and the skills you bring, grouping your previous jobs and experiences underneath them. See the resumes in Figures 6.2 and 6.3 for representative hints on shaping your own resume. Some additional suggestions will help you put together a clear, communicative resume:

- A one-page resume is often counseled in the literature, but do not shy away from a second page if your background and accomplishments genuinely warrant it.

- Stay away from "cute" techniques such as decorative fonts, wide variation in print size, excessive boldfacing, elaborate shading, and the like; let your message be the main message.

- Remember the **DPFP sequence:** draft, proof, feedback, proof. (1) *Draft stage* (start by brainstorming about your skills and responsibilities and by reconstructing your employment history; turn your sloppy notes into a draft document). (2) *Proofreading stage* (eliminate all unnecessary words, and ensure there are no typographical mistakes, misspellings, or grammatical glitches). (3) *Feedback stage* (share the proofread draft with colleagues, career professionals, and friends, and systematically note their responses and suggestions; tell them your goal is credibility, which—you recall from the rhetorical approach—includes proof of expertness, trustworthiness, and dynamism). (4) *Second proofreading stage* (after revisions, go through your resume again to catch errors introduced during the process).

- Omit the following information from your resume unless it is directly and unequivocally relevant and helpful for your desired position: physical description and health information; ethnic, religious, or cultural connections; hobbies; military service (except for job-related experience); part-time positions; expected salary; why you left previous positions; names and addresses of your references. (An exception might be made if one or more of your references is likely to be recognized as particularly important or influential by your potential employer.)

- Omit any statement about yourself that could be interpreted as self-serving ("I am a strong motivator of people" or "I have high ethical standards"). Readers readily dismiss such rhetoric. Let your record speak for you.

219 South Jefferson Avenue
St. Louis, MO 63108

April 15, 1998

Ms. Francine J. Wilshore
Director of Human Resources
Storm Consulting, Inc.
1417 Ninth St. North
Kansas City, MO 64154

Dear Ms. Wilshore:

This letter is a response to your advertisement for an Organizational Skills Trainer that appeared in several recent editions of the *Kansas City Star*. I would like to assure you of my interest in this position and my ability to do an excellent job for Storm Consulting.

As the enclosed resume demonstrates, this is the type of position I've envisioned since becoming a communication major during my sophomore year. I originally declared this major after taking an exciting course in public speaking, but rapidly began to appreciate the theory and practice of leadership, persuasion, interpersonal communication, media technologies, and journalistic writing. I still enjoy the times I speak to audiences, but have come to appreciate clear and succinct writing, as well.

With the help of committed faculty, I was able to achieve Dean's List standing throughout my junior and senior years and was elected as the first president of a recently established campus organization for communication students. My internship at Anheuser-Busch gave me a wide range of experience with everyday training activities, including computer-assisted learning and the publication of a new training manual in interviewing strategies.

My resume will tell you much more about my qualifications. Still, I would appreciate the opportunity to discuss the position with you in person. I will be contacting your office in the near future to discuss the status of the Storm Consulting search. If there is further information I could supply, or if you would like to contact me to discuss the position further, please notify me. I appreciate your consideration.

Sincerely,

RoseAnn M. Fernandez
314-977-3196
<rosean@cytrack.com>

Enclosure

FIGURE 6.1   Sample Cover Letter

DARYL F. YOUNG

Before May 15, 1997
Reinert Hall, Room 234
Saint Louis University
St. Louis, MO 63103
314/768-2368

After May 15, 1997
83 Chouteau Drive
Collinsville, IL 62065
618/872-5932

Career Objective

To obtain an entry-level position in the private accounting industry utilizing education and experience in accounting.

Education

Saint Louis University, St. Louis, Missouri
Bachelor of Science in Business Administration, May 1998
Major in Accounting
GPA: 3.65/4.00

Indiana University, Bloomington, Indiana
Completed 30 hours toward a Bachelor of Science degree, August 1984 to May 1995

Experience

Office Assistant (August 1996 to May 1997, August 1997 to May 1998)
Registrar's Office, Saint Louis University, St. Louis, Missouri
• Supported the Assistant Director with various office responsibilities including typing, filing, and generating monthly reports.
• Processed transcript requests.

Intern (Summers 1996 and 1997)
Judy P. Krantz, C.P.A., University City, Missouri
• Assisted a private accountant with routine accounting procedures serving over 400 clients.
• Reviewed payroll tax report forms to insure accuracy and verify calculations.
• Implemented a new computerized accounting system to expedite income tax returns.
• Designed an automated system to handle accounts payable and receivable.

Extra-Curricular Activities

Accounting Club, 2 years
• President
• Fund-raising Chair
Pi Kappa Phi social fraternity, 4 years
• Vice President for Alumni Affairs
• 1995 Homecoming Program Chair
University Choir, 2 years

Honors

Dean's List, seven semesters
Recipient of three academic scholarships
Who's Who Among American Colleges & Universities

Interests

Enjoy golf, fly fishing, chess and cooking

FIGURE 6.2   Sample Resume: Chronological Style *Source: Employment Guide 1997–1998,* p. 12, Saint Louis University Career Center. Reprinted by permission of CASS Recruitment Media / CASS Communications, Inc.

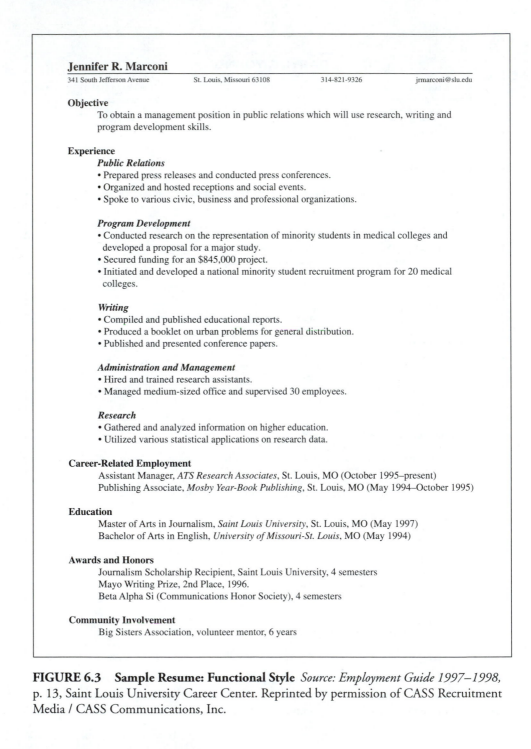

Jennifer R. Marconi

341 South Jefferson Avenue   St. Louis, Missouri 63108   314-821-9326   jrmarconi@slu.edu

Objective
> To obtain a management position in public relations which will use research, writing and program development skills.

Experience
> *Public Relations*
> • Prepared press releases and conducted press conferences.
> • Organized and hosted receptions and social events.
> • Spoke to various civic, business and professional organizations.
>
> *Program Development*
> • Conducted research on the representation of minority students in medical colleges and developed a proposal for a major study.
> • Secured funding for an $845,000 project.
> • Initiated and developed a national minority student recruitment program for 20 medical colleges.
>
> *Writing*
> • Compiled and published educational reports.
> • Produced a booklet on urban problems for general distribution.
> • Published and presented conference papers.
>
> *Administration and Management*
> • Hired and trained research assistants.
> • Managed medium-sized office and supervised 30 employees.
>
> *Research*
> • Gathered and analyzed information on higher education.
> • Utilized various statistical applications on research data.

Career-Related Employment
> Assistant Manager, *ATS Research Associates*, St. Louis, MO (October 1995–present)
> Publishing Associate, *Mosby Year-Book Publishing*, St. Louis, MO (May 1994–October 1995)

Education
> Master of Arts in Journalism, *Saint Louis University*, St. Louis, MO (May 1997)
> Bachelor of Arts in English, *University of Missouri-St. Louis*, MO (May 1994)

Awards and Honors
> Journalism Scholarship Recipient, Saint Louis University, 4 semesters
> Mayo Writing Prize, 2nd Place, 1996.
> Beta Alpha Si (Communications Honor Society), 4 semesters

Community Involvement
> Big Sisters Association, volunteer mentor, 6 years

FIGURE 6.3   Sample Resume: Functional Style *Source: Employment Guide 1997–1998,* p. 13, Saint Louis University Career Center. Reprinted by permission of CASS Recruitment Media / CASS Communications, Inc.

- Include a job objective statement that directly reflects or mirrors the position description. This means your resume will be adapted in different ways to each different position. Some students think this is dishonest or deceptive—how can you have so many different objectives at one time? Think of it differently by reframing the issue. Your life doesn't have one simple and overriding objective (is it your life's objective to have a good family life, or warm friendships, or a satisfying professional life? Aren't all these objectives relevant simultaneously?) The same is true of your job search. Everyone has a mix of different objectives all the time, in all arenas of life. Each position you decide to apply for thus invites you to articulate a new kind of objective.

- Include many keywords (the job category and titles typical of positions you're applying for, for example). See the discussion at the beginning of this section for more details.

- Stress action words along with specific evidence when describing your skills. Reduce the level of abstraction and allow readers to visualize the kinds of changes they could expect after hiring you. In other words, don't just suggest that you "have" a skill called "coordination"; make the resume vivid and active by creating lists of details describing the what, when, how many, or where of things or people you coordinated. For example, in your work as an assistant manager for a sporting goods store, you may have

    trained twenty new employees over the past three years;

    resolved over twenty-five customer complaints to the mutual satisfaction of customer and company;

    designed weekly product displays for maximum impact; and

    communicated employee feedback to management during monthly staff meetings.

Planning for Nonverbal Impressions

How you'll be perceived by interviewers is never a purely rational process of evaluating credentials, skills, and reasons. In fact, as you've learned from earlier chapters and other coursework in communication, all relationships are influenced by a blend of verbal and nonverbal messages. Each form of message, in a sense, creates the context for the other. What you claim to be true, for example, is often disregarded or dismissed because it appears to conflict with your nonverbal messages. I tell you I'm confident, but my voice quavers and you see the sweat breaking out on my forehead. Communication scholars researching the effects of such situations have called these contradictions between verbal and nonverbal message systems **mixed messages.** You don't want to display mixed messages any more than you have to, although some will probably arise in any extended interpersonal situation. So, rather than leaving your nonverbal presentation entirely to chance, we suggest you prepare for crucial elements of it.

Trying Out Your Skills

Write a rough draft of a resume, and use it as the basis for role-playing exercises for practicing your ability to talk about yourself. Give a printed version of your resume to three different partners—a close friend at about your same level of job experience, one of your communication teachers or graduate students, and a representative of your career center. Ask for their reactions to how well your resume characterizes you. Compare their advice, and attempt to account for any differences in what they tell you. Revise the resume and arrange role-plays with each of them.

Ask yourself the following questions about this experience:

• With which role-play partner did you feel most comfortable?

• Which partner was most direct with you and/or gave you the most constructive feedback?

• Which partner knows the most about the career objective you plan to pursue?

• Are you still uncomfortable explaining any parts of your resume? Either revise your resume or continue to practice your explanations of them.

The most commonly researched aspect of planning for nonverbal communication in interviews is the problem of how to dress. Clothing is a nonverbal indicator that could undermine your desired image as someone who is serious, attentive, and responsible. In other words, inappropriate choices of elements of your appearance can create mixed messages. Pat Mahony, a human resources program manager, says, "I look at the way [job applicants] are dressed and figure that that's the best they're going to look. If their clothes do not look good on the first day, then you know [their dress] will only be more relaxed once they come on board" (quoted in Eng, 1998, p. G20). Recent changes in the on-site cultures of many companies, however, have been moving toward a more relaxed style, thus creating confusion for applicants. Do you plan to "dress up" even in situations where you suspect a much more casual look is the norm? No one can answer this question definitively, but a more conservative approach will usually be safer. Since the days of John Molloy's best-selling *Dress for Success,* first published in the 1970s (see Molloy, 1988), a certain kind of prescription has predominated in the literature—dark suits for men and women, solid and traditional colors, subdued hairstyles, and subdued makeup for women. We suggest you consult one of the specialized interview preparation books or professional career consultants on your campus for more specific ways to adapt your own look to the expectations for the professional setting you anticipate.

Unfortunately, according to researcher Richard Ilkka (1995), "attention to dress and grooming often dominate to the exclusion of other areas" of nonverbal communication in advice to applicants, and ". . . it is not surprising when selection interviewing education promotes appearance as a product to be attained, yet minimizes study of the judgmental process" (p. 12). This is true; you should probably also prepare for other nonverbal messages such as timing (ensuring you are punctual), posture (demonstrating attentiveness and interest), and gestures (for appropriate emphasis). However, one especially important factor, Ilkka suggests, is that early impressions appear to be decisive in many interview interactions (p. 13), and nonverbal cues of appearance and dress are crucial.

Role-Playing

Putting all the elements of preparation together can be a difficult process of coordination. You can't do it by yourself. You need teammates—people willing to interact with you as you try out all the things you're learning and considering. You don't want to be, or appear, phony or too practiced. But you know from such other aspects of your life as musical performance or sports that a discipline of practice increases your awareness of your own potential. What others can do for you is to supply extra sets of eyes and ears, giving you feedback. For instance, does your pause before answering a question come across as an insecure and hesitant stalling tactic or as a measured and thoughtful approach to answering fully? If the former, what would help you make the impression match the confidence you actually feel?

Creative Forms of Interviewees' Framing, Listening, and Questioning

Framing, listening, questioning: Alert readers will notice that we have reversed the order of the three skills of interviewers' interaction in this section. In doing so, we are emphasizing the different perspectives of the two participants. While interviewers typically approach the interview's structure first as an opportunity to probe the candidate's suitability for the position, then as a chance to answer the interviewee's questions, and finally as a task of assessing the overall process, the interviewee's experience is quite different. He or she enters a situation in which the frame is largely influenced by the interviewer's context, needs, and directive control. How to respond to that preexisting interpretive frame is perhaps a more basic interviewee interactional problem than the actual responding or questioning. Then, in terms of sequence, the majority of the interview will focus on answers to the employer's questions. Finally, the opportunity for asking questions of the interviewer usually comes toward the interview's conclusion.

One other preliminary reminder. As we suggested before, it's especially effective to take a both-sides approach to understanding the interview. Although the problems of being the interviewer and the problems of being interviewed are usually treated separately in textbooks and the popular media, our position is that the two are intimately connected, and thus we discuss them in the same chapter. You will learn how to be interviewed only by a full recognition of the interviewer's role and vice versa; the two roles are mutually interdependent.

Framing from the Interviewee's Perspective

Surely the interview feels like a desperate trial at times. The successful applicants we've known, though, have defined the interview as

- an opportunity rather than a test;

- a learning experience rather than a demonstration; and
- a dialogue rather than a monologue.

If you define the interview in these more inclusive and less threatening ways, you're more likely to perceive opportunities to "get out of yourself," as we put it early in the chapter. Every comment and question can be seen not only in terms of what it does to you, or in how you hear it, but also from the perspective of the other person. Communication theorists have termed this **decentering**—the ability to see things from other perspectives than your own—and it's closely related to empathy. Never forget that if you are genuinely qualified, the employer will want to select you. But you have to understand the reasons, and the reasoning, that could lead to that decision.

Listening from the Interviewee's Perspective

Listening skill declines as perceived threat increases. The adrenaline flows and so does ego-involvement. We are potentially at our worst as listeners when we are placed in pressure-filled situations. Therefore, communicative interviewees pay special attention to listening skills and styles. The following reminders pinpoint some ways to do this.

• *Decenter, to understand the interviewer's context.* Perhaps the most important reminder, consistent with flexible framing, is to hear the questions in the context the interviewer asks them. Interviewers don't need to know how much you need a job or what a good job could do for your family or self-esteem. In fact, they are only indirectly impressed with what your skills have done for someone else, except inasmuch as they can translate it directly into the present selection process. They ask the questions to elicit insight not into what you can do, but into what you can do *for them.* Therefore, listen so carefully that you can phrase your responses with this slant:

INTERVIEWER: "What qualifies you to be an editor of a major newsletter?"

INTERVIEWEE: "When I was at Consolidated, I was the person everyone consulted about their copy, because they thought I could catch all the grammar and syntax problems. I know your newsletter, *The Coyle Call,* needs that kind of close attention from an editor. We can't afford to offend intelligent readers with sloppy publications."

Notice that the interviewee does not frame the response wholly in terms of personal qualities. To do so would miss an opportunity. Instead, the answer gives extra concrete information succinctly, relates it to the employer's need, and even begins to identify with the process as a professional colleague ("we"). Even if not hired for this position, perhaps because she hasn't held the title of editor before, the interviewee has positioned herself as an intelligent listener who hears things from another's perspective. The best case scenario is being hired; the next-best case scenario is being remembered positively. Many interviewers who are impressed in this way will make a note to call someone else in the organization to see if the applicant fits there.

• *Verify inferences and meanings.* Do not answer a question unless you understand fully the terms of the question. Your prior research into the job, the employer, and the professional jargon should have prepared you to understand the basic terminology and duties about which you're likely to be asked. However, something will usually come up that you did not anticipate. Instead of looking quizzically at the questioner and saying, "What's that?" practice your active listening by bringing your inferences into the open:

INTERVIEWER: "Are you willing to come on board as an adjunct for a year or so?"

INTERVIEWEE: "I think by an 'adjunct' position you mean someone who isn't technically going to be full time, but who will qualify for most of the same benefits. Is that right?"

You may be wrong, or you may be right, according to the interviewer's meaning. However, you will not be answering the wrong question after the interviewer clarifies things for you. Additionally, you may impress the interviewer with your assertiveness and willingness to check things out thoroughly. Despite possibly being wrong, you position yourself as a learner, in other words.

• *Listen for openings that allow you to highlight or clarify your skills.* Many sincere and well-intentioned people are so afraid of sounding boastful that they wear their modesty like a badge. Communication trainers and teachers often stress *assertiveness* skills, by which they mean achieving that middle ground between an *aggressive personal style* (disregard for or dismissal of the rights or abilities of others) and an *acquiescent personal style* (disregard or dismissal of one's own rights or abilities). In a job interview, you are expected to be assertive; you should neither dismiss your own achievements nor imply that others deserve no credit. You want to be seen as both a personally influential force in an organization and, at the same time, a team player. This is an admittedly delicate balance, but interviewers are taught to listen for it. For example:

INTERVIEWER: "Why were you so successful as editor of the university's student paper?"

INTERVIEWEE: "I'm not entirely sure, but I think it was partially because I paid so much attention the year I was copy editor. I saw what the previous editor did to solidify new readership, but I also saw firsthand the problems she had with the administration. I cut back on our emphasis on columnists, increased coverage of student organizations, and policed some writers' confrontive attitude about President Smythe. I wouldn't have been able to do this without strong support from Dr. Jacks and my staff. We really worked well together."

• *Regard even relatively closed or terse questions as invitations for elaboration.* For example, what's wrong with this interchange?

INTERVIEWER: "Have you ever supervised a department with more than a dozen employees?"

INTERVIEWEE: "Yes, of course."

INTERVIEWER: "When?"

INTERVIEWEE: "Well, it was a few years ago."

Each answer is responsive at one level but turns the interviewer's role around to your disadvantage. Even if she or he is a poor interviewer, it's to your advantage to keep the talk from becoming an interrogation. Elaborate on what you assume to be the relevant details concerning the question's topic, and you will smooth out the conversation:

INTERVIEWER: "Have you ever supervised a department with more than a dozen employees?"

INTERVIEWEE: "I sure have. Several years ago, Martinez Manufacturing asked me to take over the public relations office on an interim basis while they searched for someone with ten years' or more experience. At the end of that three-month period, they hadn't found someone they liked from outside, so they asked me if I'd be interested in the job—even though I'd only worked there for a year and a half."

INTERVIEWER: "That's interesting. I wonder if they'd ever done that before. . . ."

In her research, Lois Einhorn (1981) found that "elaboration of information" was a significant factor that distinguished successful from unsuccessful interviewees: "Usually the unsuccessful applicants did not expand their answers. Fifty-eight percent of one . . . applicant's responses, for example, contained less than ten words; 29% consisted of 'um hum,' 'no,' 'okay,' or 'yeah.' By contrast, all of the successful applicants used extensive detail, treating their experiences and abilities thoroughly" (p. 223). Certainly, all elaborations won't be equally effective, and more talk isn't necessarily better talk. To talk for five minutes could quash your chances as easily as it could solidify them. Still, the questions employment interviewers ask usually should be taken to imply that they want extra information, even if you're not literally asked for it. Try for a style of focused elaboration, and look for nonverbal signals that tell you to conclude your story (fidgeting, glancing at a watch or clock, removing eye contact).

Questioning from the Interviewee's Perspective

Toward the conclusion of your time together, most interviewers will ask you whether you have questions for them. At this point the roles shift, but they shift a little bit more subtly than many interviewees believe they do. You might be tempted to assume that you can breathe a figurative sigh of relief, now that the pressure is largely off you. You'd be wrong. The responsibilities have shifted, but one crucial factor has not changed: You are still being evaluated. The kinds of questions you ask, and your style of asking them, will be noted and scrutinized with care by the organization.

In her study of interviews conducted by representatives of two firms, Einhorn (1981) found that questioning behaviors were one of the differences between successful interviewees and people the companies could do without. She writes:

> The successful applicants' communication was specific and comprehensive in questioning as well as in answering. These applicants asked the interviewers specific questions about a wide variety of subjects, and the questions tended to be focused. The following questions to the Lazarus interviewer are typical: "What brands/makers do you carry in the junior size of women's wear?" "What is the reason for your extensive point-of-purchase displays and are they means of motivating customers to start becoming innovative?" "How often do you have promotional activities?" Both successful and unsuccessful interviewees often asked questions about the companies' training programs and expansion plans, but as a group, the successful applicants asked about other matters, too, such as the organizations' clientele, turnover rates, and recruiting procedures. They also asked pertinent questions about the interviewers' and the companies' backgrounds and often phrased their questions in the first person. For example, instead of asking, "What are the duties and responsibilities of the job?" the successful interviewees asked, "What would be my duties and responsibilities?" By wording questions in the first person, these applicants indirectly expressed confidence in receiving offers from Lazarus and Keller Crescent. Psychologically, this phrasing also forced the interviewers to imagine the applicants in the jobs. (pp. 223–224)

With so much riding on the tone of the interview, regard your questioning period as a further opportunity to solidify a relationship of mutual respect with the organizational interviewer:

- Be sure to have questions. Prepare a general list ahead of time (this is your own mini–interview schedule), and carefully monitor as the conversation progresses which questions have already been answered. Presumably, details such as when and where you will work are important. Beyond those, however, ensure that your prepared questions address all the areas you consider crucial in workplace quality of life, such as interactions, evaluations, autonomy of judgment, and creativity.

- Be careful about asking picky, hyperdetailed questions, especially on a preliminary, or **screening,** interview. Interviewers expect more detailed questions in follow-up interviews when both sides know they are more serious about each other. (Follow-up or second interviews are sometimes specifically termed **selection** interviews, even though that word also applies to the employment interviewing process as a whole.)

- Preface your questions with expressions of interest or curiosity that put your skills in context. For example: "I've never been a part of an organization that put such a premium on monitoring the press! You must have workers who stay on top of the news by reading papers and magazines all the time. How many people do that?"

- Be sure your questions don't betray your ignorance in areas where you shouldn't be ignorant. You can't realistically be expected to know everything, and to ask questions is usually better than remaining ignorant. But some questions have such obvious answers that your interviewer will wonder why you didn't do the most elementary homework: "Where is your corporate headquarters?" "I wasn't sure your company had expanded into the radio station market yet. Has it?"

- Don't act like a shopper. We've encouraged you to frame the experience as learning and decision making, but if employers see you only in this way—as if you could get job offers so easily you merely have to choose among them—this suggests an arrogance most organizations would likely shy away from. Beware, in other words, of the "grocery store mentality" that characterized the unsuccessful interviewees in Einhorn's (1981) research (see also Box 6.7).

- Use questions to demonstrate your knowledge, not simply to inquire about issues and trends. For example: "In the *Phoenix Business Journal* last month, Lon Mathers speculated about a quantum leap in Internet connection and file transfer speeds through ordinary phone lines. What do you think that will do to the industry if it develops?"

✿ BEYOND THE BASICS   The Legal Context of Employment Interviewing

This chapter has concentrated on describing the aspects of employment interviewing that have a direct bearing on the immediate dialogue as it develops between interviewers and interviewees. In our experience, students are clearly interested in learning new skills and appreciations for this dialogue, and herein lie the most crucial needs to be addressed in preparing for the job searches that are most prominent in the minds of most students. Students' future professional roles also necessitate learning about the face-to-face interview from the standpoint of an interviewer, a role most will play often in professional life.

Behind all the interactional challenges of interviewing, however, stands another set of challenges that are often just as important. Certainly, all employment interviewing has been affected profoundly in recent decades by a legal environment of increasing governmental attention to fairness, to opportunity, to access, and to justice. Employers have a significant amount of power over their own organizational policies (which is normal and expected), and they also have power over their employee's lives (some of which might be unreasonable and illegal for good reason).

Whether your immediate role is interviewee or interviewer, you should be aware of relevant laws governing appropriate interaction and practices in interviews. Kanter's (1995) book reviewing employment interviewing factors lists eight principal federal statutes "bearing on non-discrimination in employment" (p. 209): the Civil Rights Act of 1981, the Age Discrimination in Employment Act of 1967, the Veterans' Reemployment Rights Act, the Glass Ceiling Act of 1991, the Americans with Disabilities Act of 1990, Title VII of the Civil Rights Act of 1964, the Rehabilitation Act, and the Pregnancy Discrimination Act. In most circumstances, only legal counsel for organizations need to

BOX 6.7   R E M I N D E R S

What Do Successful and Unsuccessful Interviewees Do Differently?

Earlier, we cited Lois Einhorn's 1981 study of two employers' perceptions of college student applicants. She taped and analyzed on-campus interviews but also asked company interviewers to complete questionnaires before meeting the interviewees, based only on application materials. After the interviews, interviewers filled out other questionnaires about their impressions of interviewees. "Candidates were classified as successful if the interviewers' perceptions of them improved considerably and as unsuccessful if the interviewers judged them more negatively after the interviews" (p. 218). You might question whether some interviewees might have been "unsuccessful" not because of their behavioral strategies but because they perhaps found these companies less desirable to work for. Still, the study gives a valuable glimpse into the inner dynamics of job interviewing as it "really" exists—in the relational realm. In this summary, we have paraphrased Einhorn's findings.

Differences in Identification with Employers

Successful interviewees emphasized or expressed

- clearer career goals
- career goals consistent with the position applied for
- concern for careers over jobs
- preference for the workplace over graduate school
- specific interest in working for these firms
- reinforcement of interviewers' ideas
- understanding of how employers' job descriptions related to them
- more context and rationale for the "negatives" in their records

Differences in Support for Arguments

Successful interviewees used

- more evidence, especially factual and hypothetical illustrations, comparisons, statistics
- less reliance on personal experience and explanations
- more elaboration of stories of personal qualifications
- more comprehensive and focused questioning of interviewers

Differences in Organization

Successful interviewees used

- more of the time set aside for the interviews
- more speaking time within the interviews
- summary statements when interviewers moved to terminate interviews
- forward-looking comments to inquire about subsequent decision making

Differences in Style

Successful interviewees used

- more active and concrete language
- more positive descriptions of experience (fewer words of negative connotation such as "no," "awful," "difficult," "dull")
- more technical jargon appropriate to the employers
- more coherent sentence structure
- fewer grammatical errors

Differences in Delivery

Successful interviewees spoke

- with more animation and vocal variety and forcefulness
- with more precise articulation
- with more natural accompanying gestures
- with fewer nervous habits (inappropriate laughing or shaking the foot)
- with more positive nonverbal cues (smiling, nodding affirmatively)
- with better eye contact and more expressions of interest

Differences in Images Conveyed

Successful interviewees were perceived as

- more dynamic, active, and enthusiastic
- more professionally competent and knowledgeable
- more assertive

know all the ins and outs of these laws, as well as relevant state and local statutes that also affect the legality of communication behaviors. There is no need in the context of this chapter to review the laws one by one. However, some general principles need to be understood.

The statutes are generally intended to address the power differences between hiring organizations—often large systems of people and practices backed by significant resources—and the individuals who apply, and are in some ways vulnerable, to them. When an applicant is interviewed, he or she has no reasonable way of knowing whether the interviewer's characterizations of the organization, promises about hiring and decision making, and procedures are accurate. Prior research will help you, as an applicant, put promises and procedures into perspective. But it will rarely uncover all you'd need to know, or, in fact, the depth of detail the organization could discover about you in just a few minutes if it wanted to do so. Legal statutes restrict an organization's ability to mislead you, lie to you, or treat you by different standards than they would treat another applicant, thus cheating you out of time, energy, and money. We are not suggesting that most organizations do these things as a matter of course, but it is reassuring to note that such procedures are subject to legal action.

Closely tied to the power issue is the fundamental matter of fairness. Employers expect and deserve a wide latitude of choice about who can best fill their own positions. After all, such concerns as company profits, organizational reputation or prestige, and even survival of an organization depend upon who works there. Hiring ineffective people is not only unpleasant and inefficient, but costly. Millions of dollars are spent retraining workers or hiring new ones to replace "bad hires"; no wonder corporations, government agencies, and nonprofits are investing money up front to improve their ability to identify productive workers. However, this concern for who is hired should not translate into institutional patterns of discrimination or prejudice. All kinds of people can do all kinds of jobs. They deserve access to the jobs they can thrive in, regardless of the color of their skin, their ethnicity, their sexual orientation, their age, their gender, their marital status, their physical appearance, or their physical disabilities.

Unfortunately, we do not yet live in a society that fully values or encourages diversity. Many organizations use the power inherent in the hiring process to practice unfair discrimination against certain groups, including—but not limited to—African Americans, Latinos, and other ethnic groups; women; gay, lesbian, and bisexual persons; applicants who are "too old" by an organization's arbitrary standard; or those physically challenged in non-job-related ways.

If you doubt that job discrimination happens often, consult newspapers and newsmagazines over the past five years; you'll find a case in which the highest executives of one of our largest oil companies allegedly used their boardroom discussions to ridicule and tell racist jokes about African Americans; you'll find another case in which major national chain restaurants counseled their personnel officers not to hire blacks or homosexuals; and another major chain in which there was a systematic mistreatment of minority customers. Broadcast newsmagazines have also done notable stories recently about the difficulty physically disabled applicants have in even obtaining interviews, despite the fact that they were exceptionally well qualified for the positions by all objective measures. According to one of the leading diversity consultants in contemporary management, Marilyn Loden (1996), "... in a 1995 study conducted by a bipartisan congressional committee, [white men were] found to hold 95 percent of senior management positions in industry despite the fact that they represent 43 percent of the American workforce. According to the same study, despite three decades of affirmative action, glass ceilings were still firmly in place for women and people of color above middle-management levels" (p. 23).

Interviewing professionals and researchers speak of *bona fide occupational qualifications* (increasingly referred to as BFOQs), which are those attributes and abilities that can reasonably be considered essential to a high-quality performance within the designated job. For example, a mute person (someone who has no ability to vocalize) could not reasonably expect to perform as a telephone telemarketer, and a company could not be criticized for failing to consider the applicant for that position. However, telemarketing firms have hundreds of other jobs for which this person would be fully qualified. Kanter (1995) offers a striking example of a Texas law firm that "not too many years ago" asked for the following information from applicants in interviews:

1. Are you married?   Spouse's name:

2. Do you plan marriage soon?   Fiance(e)'s name:

3. Where did you grow up?

4. Where did your spouse/fiance(e) grow up?

5. What does your spouse/fiance(e) do?

6. Where do your parents live?
   (a) Mother
   (b) Father

7. Where do your spouse's/fiance(e)'s parents live?
   (a) Mother
   (b) Father

8. What do your parents do for a living?
   (a) Mother
   (b) Father

9. What do your spouse's/fiance(e)'s parents do for a living?
   (a) Mother
   (b) Father

10. How do you and your spouse/fiance(e) feel about living and working in the area?

(1995, p. 171)

It's not hard to imagine some of the motivation behind these questions, none of which come close to indicating BFOQs for lawyers or law clerks. Using such questions, interviewers who are prone to discriminate unfairly could ascertain—or obtain strong clues about—such things as personal plans, private family decisions, ethnic affiliations, age, social class backgrounds, and other irrelevant issues. Or if applicants reasonably objected to sharing such personal information, they could be disqualified virtually without cause.

Statutes and case law, along with Equal Employment Opportunity Commission enforcement, have established a variety of areas in which unlawful questions occur. Some general principles will help you recognize especially troublesome areas in interview questioning and responding, although they are no substitute for professionals familiarizing themselves with the actual laws that define legally defensible interviewing:

- *Race:* Requests to identify someone's race, or even to produce a photograph, are unlawful.

- *Gender:* Inquiries about marital or relationship status, physical data such as height and weight, and similar questions are unlawful. Neither can interviewers inquire into child care arrangements, birth control, or pregnancy issues.

- *Religion:* Questions about styles of worshiping, affiliations with religious groups, or membership in organized religions are unlawful.

- *Disability:* Inquiries about diseases or conditions, or the experience of being disabled, are unlawful, as are probes into possible adjustments or accommodations an applicant might think he or she will need if hired. A recent article (Halvorson, 1997) illuminates this problem of interviewing and suggests ways that classes can become more sensitive to the Americans with Disabilities Act.

- *National origin:* Asking where someone was born, or about their native language, or about the details of their U.S. citizenship are unlawful.

You may be thinking that some of these things could reflect areas of relevance in the hiring process. You're right; they *could* be relevant somehow, if relevance is defined broadly enough. Yet the danger for unscrupulous or even unwittingly prejudiced interviewers to abuse such questioning situations is great—great enough for agencies and courts to try to protect applicants from their unfairness. How can you avoid these pitfalls, then, as an interviewer? How can you respond reasonably as an interviewee if unlawful issues come up?

Several recommendations are particulary important for interviewers and organizations who value fairness (see Campion & Arvey, 1989, pp. 66–67). First, organizations should have clearly defined job descriptions from which clear performance criteria can be developed. No interview can be totally objective, but certain pitfalls of unexamined subjectivity can be avoided if the criteria are clear. Second, organizations should select and train interviewers and interview teams appropriately. All-white and all-male teams, especially when they're inexperienced, can too easily lead to discrimination. Third, questions should not only be relevant to the job criteria but should also be asked of *all* candidates. This highlights one of the obvious dangers of unstructured interviewing. Fourth, organizations should review the work of their interviewers, and when necessary, counter negative results of subjective discrimination with multiple- or panel-interview designs. Fifth, organizations and interviewers should keep accurate records of selection interview procedures. Sixth, the results of past interview practices should be monitored for fairness across groups. With this kind of organizational introspection, the fate of all interviewees will be in better hands.

What about the practical dilemma of being asked an unlawful question when you're the interviewee? Most authors of job interviewing guidelines would counsel you to be direct in responding, but not to answer questions with which you're uncomfortable. Martin Yate (1996, p. 183) suggests that you remind yourself that many unlawful questions may come from innocence or naïveté and not from racism, sexism, ageism, or other forms of blatant bias. Be as polite as you can, but move the conversation on to what you know are your genuine employment qualifications. Later, analyze what happened. Another strategy is to attempt to understand the interviewer's reason or motive for asking the unlawful or questionable question and then reply to that concern if possible. For example, if an interviewer appears to veer into illegal questioning about a woman's family life, this may be due to a fear that employees with strong family ties might avoid working overtime when the company faces deadlines. (It may be due to the chauvinism of the male interviewer, too, but calling attention to this fact doesn't serve many useful purposes.) A possible reply might give the benefit of the doubt and focus on job-related issues: "Family is always important to me. But if the company needs me to work overtime, I'll find a way to do that. I always have in the past."

The organizational interviewer's form of questioning can become another bit of evidence you use in making your own decision about where to work. If an interviewer persistently pries into your private life or your cultural beliefs ("How many children do you intend to have, anyway?" or "What do you, as a black man, think about feminism and the 'glass ceiling'?"), consider the possibility that he or she may represent the organization's culture, and perhaps reflects it in ways you wouldn't like later. At times, you may simply choose to say, "I'm uncomfortable talking about that with someone I've just met. Can we move on?"

Extensions of Selection Interview Principles

The principles of selection interviewing considered in this chapter are most commonly applied in employment interviews between two persons, in which one elicits information about the possible hiring of the other. It might be useful, however, to think in a wider frame about selection interviewing. Let's consider several areas of contemporary life that demonstrate similar problems and practices.

Service Providers

Companies, school boards, youth groups, military service groups, and many other organizations often ask service providers to make presentations before a selection group makes a decision. For example, two or more food service companies may appear before a university committee that is charged with making a recommendation on who will provide food for the new student union. Each company provides preliminary written materials describing its qualifications for handling the responsibilities, each appears in front of the committee to make its best presentation, and each answers questions about its services. Undoubtedly there would be opportunities, as well, for the providers to question the committee about the plans for the student union, projections for student enrollment over the next decade, the kinds of entree selection the committee envisions, and so forth. After interviewing "applicants," the committee makes its decision. This process is remarkably similar to an individual's experience when applying to a company.

Elite Selection

Although the words "elite selection" may seem odd, they are often used to refer to the situation in which a limited number of people are selected for special training. If you want to attend an Ivy League university, a graduate school, law school, or medical school, or if you hope to be chosen for a special fellowship or prestigious award, you will go through a process of elite selection, conducted perhaps by individual preliminary interviewers, a screening committee, and a final selection board. Although the end result may not be a job, the kinds of questioning you receive and the kinds of nervousness you experience will resemble elements of a job interview.

One of the clear differences, though, between elite selection and the job hiring process is that in the former, most applicants are at what Robert Klitgaard (1985) calls the "right tail." That is, many employment interviews attract a typical "bell curve" of applicants. (Visualize a curve in the shape of a bell, rising from the left where there are very few totally unqualified applicants, peaking dramatically with a large number of "average" applicants, then falling off to a very few completely qualified candidates.) The "left tail" is the unqualified side, the "right tail" the highly qualified side. However, in elite selection, almost all candidates represent the right tail—those who are all technically qualified for high accomplishment. When slots are few, it becomes a more difficult and much more subtle task to make fine distinctions between people. Then, too, when choosing educational elites, decisions also are made on the grounds of other factors that affect the learning environment for all. This is why Harvard, for example, has never chosen its student body wholly on a purely meritocratic basis of grades or test scores but also considers such factors as geographical location, leadership and student activities, and racial and ethnic diversity. Although face-to-face interviews have never been a highly regarded means of predicting later accomplishment among such elites, the interview is an extra opportunity for applicants to impress selection agents.

The Informational Interview

As you near the time when you must take job hunting seriously, you would be wise to set up a number of informational interviews. This type of experience is technically not an employment interview but is closely related. In a sense, it's a preemployment interview or an employment reconnaissance interview. Most large organizations have personnel departments that are familiar with, and welcome, this kind of contact with students and people who are considering a career shift to a new type of job. With a commitment to informational interviews, organizations become well known in a community and are able to spot exceptional candidates early in the process, sometimes long before they graduate. Occasionally, informational interviews with personnel directors result in internships or other formal ongoing involvement with the organization. More often, an informal friendship or mentorship is forged, and the two people stay in touch. At the very least, setting up several informational interviews will give you insight into organizational cultures and realistic but relatively low-pressure practice in conducting yourself in an interview situation. Personnel managers who conduct these kinds of interviews often give out informational packets that help you evaluate entire job categories and industries.

Many interviewing classes feature out-of-class exercises in which you are asked to interview professional interviewers. Our advice is to take the opportunity to meet interviewers in your tentative career choices. They could give you excellent advice, not only on interviewing but also on working in complex organizations. In informational interviews, your goal should be to make an impression primarily as a listener—but as a listener with excellent preparation, communication skills, and potential. Do not try to force employment possibilities into the conversation artificially. Do a good job of investigating a career or a company, and you'll be doing something even more significant at this stage of your development.

The Persuasive Interview: A Preview

Clearly, the employment interview is a site for persuasion. People's attitudes, values, and beliefs are affected by what they learn there. In addition, much research into the employment interview process is premised on such topics of interpersonal persuasion as

- Refer back to the sample employment interview schedule of questions (Box 6.3), which was written to select a registered nurse for a surgical care facility. The last item the interviewer plans to bring up is an inquiry about whether the applicant is interviewing elsewhere and, if so, where. What is your first impression of this question? If you were an applicant interviewing for the position, how would you respond?

  Give yourself the luxury of thinking this out fully. Still hypothetically assuming you're the applicant, you know you've been invited for two other interviews next week. Write out one possible realistic response to this question based on your situation.

  Now write out an alternative response that you think is also appropriate, but one that takes a different approach.

  Which of your responses is more accurate? More honest? More general? More noncommittal? Does such a question seem fair? Compare and discuss your responses with others in your class. Why do you think a respected interviewer actually recommends this approach?

- Imagine a hypothetical situation in which you're asked by your boss to interview a large number of prospective employees for a crosstown delivery and messenger service. Following the reasoning that this is a high-pressure business, she asks you to make the interviews as stressful and uncomfortable as possible for interviewees. She wants you to hire only those candidates who do not buckle under the pressure.

  First, what do you suppose she means by a high-stress interview? What would she want you to do? Be gruff, rude, and distant on purpose? Demand rapid responses? Work into your conversation a demanding tone? Insults? Take a position on the advisability of such an interview strategy. Would it, in your opinion, yield the results she expects? Why or why not? Analyze her suggestion in terms of frame analysis; that is, how would interviewees frame such an approach?

- Hypothetical: You are an African American applicant for a job in the human resources department of a major brewery. The interviewer, a white male, has made several friendly remarks about how the company has been attempting to increase the number of minority employees, "to let the rest of us know how to communicate with blacks and minorities because they, you know, don't buy our beer much." He says he thinks affirmative action is a good thing. He then turns to you and asks, "Are you in favor of affirmative action yourself?"

  How do you respond? Does this question seem lawful to you? Appropriate? If so, why? If not, why not?

impression management, compliance-gaining, exchange theory, self-monitoring, cognitive consistency research, and the like (see, for recent examples, Dougherty, Turban, & Callender, 1994; Miller & Buzzanell, 1996; Stevens, 1997; Stevens & Kristof, 1995). In Chapter 11 we'll discuss "persuasive interviews" as a label usually applied to other one-on-one interactions where attitude change is the goal—such as sales or negotiation. However, remember that all interviews have rhetorical elements in them, and all are thus persuasive in some sense.

Summary

Contrary to the approach of most writing on employment interviews, we decided to integrate the perspectives of interviewer and interviewee into one long chapter, rather than separate what interviewers do from what interviewees do. At times we must focus on one or the other, of course, but generally it is the relationship between the rhetorical roles and goals of interviewer and interviewee that interests us. To be effective, each must share a knowledge of what the other is worried about, what the other is trying to accomplish with the encounter, and how a collaborative relationship can provide an especially effective basis for deciding about careers and positions.

A recent study (Peterson, 1997) underscores the importance of studying and practicing interpersonal communication skills and appreciations in achieving employment goals. Both interviewers and interviewees should be aware of its findings. In the study, over 98 percent of personnel professionals responding to the researcher's questionnaire marked either "strong agreement" or "agreement" that oral and nonverbal skills were significant in influencing hiring decisions. Further:

> Respondents were asked to report whether job applicants displayed adequate communication skills. Compared with their overwhelming agreement that communication skills were important, only 59.68% of respondents indicated agreement that current job applicants displayed adequate communication skills. . . .
>
> Interviewers were also asked to identify the most prevalent communication inadequacies. These data identified the five most prevalent oral and nonverbal communication skill inadequacies as (a) eye contact, (b) topic relevance, (c) response organization, (d) listening skills, and (e) response clarity. (p. 289)

The topics of this chapter are at the core of your ability to improve as an interviewer or as an interviewee. We have discussed how a relational approach to interviewing can help establish an environment of collaboration. Within that environment, although rhetorical goals might differ—creating conflict of purpose at times—both sides have a similar overarching goal. Both need to have more information to make an intelligent decision; thus, both need adequate motivation and preparation to become learners. Both need to listen carefully and to frame their knowledge in a wider context.

In "Beyond the Basics" we introduced you to the relevant issues of legal context. This context, while it may not directly affect all the preparation strategies that interviewees and interviewers undertake, nevertheless influences many of the outcomes of interviewing. We suggest that legal issues are not cut-and-dried, "do this, don't do that" stipulations that must be memorized (although organizations and individuals do need a heightened awareness of them). Instead, there are good reasons for fairness, reasonableness, and equity that we all should consider carefully in the workplace. Finally, we have described how many of the same principles of selecting candidates and jobs can apply to other situations of selection interviewing.

The Interview Bookshelf

On the basic research that illuminates the employment interview

Eder, R. W., & Ferris, G. R. (Eds.). (1989). *The employment interview: Theory, research, and practice.* Newbury Park, CA: Sage.

Probably the best single-volume academic introduction to the classic studies of employee selection. Contains literature reviews in the areas of impression effects, interviewer decision making, context, information search strategies, applicant impression management, interpersonal dynamics, and other important areas.

On a balanced, "both sides of the table" approach

Kanter, A. B. (1995). *The essential book of interviewing: Everything you need to know from both sides of the table.* New York: Times Books.

Kanter writes an informal, anecdotal account that is fair to both interviewers and interviewees. Although many popular books opt for easy advice and gimmicks, Kanter usually attempts to explore how subtle the interview can be as a communication meeting. Yet he does so with unusual clarity and graceful writing.

On the job search process

Bolles, R. N. (1998). *The 1998 what color is your parachute? A practical manual for job-hunters and career-changers.* Berkeley, CA: Ten Speed Press. [updated annually]

Yate, M. (1996). *Knock 'em dead: The ultimate job-seeker's handbook.* Holbrook, MA: Adams. [updated annually]

There are dozens, if not hundreds, of books written to help insecure job seekers prepare for the interview process. All give advice on what to research, how to craft a resume, how to anticipate tough interview questions, and so forth. Many are helpful, but some seem little more than collections of quick-fix techniques. Relatively few books assist the interviewee in performing realistic self-reflection about his or her communication style and career goals, or encourage interviewees to see the interview as communication. Here are two veteran authors whose tried-and-tested books, through multiple editions, have proven especially helpful.

References

Austin, N. K. (1996, March). The new job interview: Beyond the trick question. *Working Woman,* pp. 23–24.

Bok, S. (1979). *Lying: Moral choice in public and private life.* New York: Vintage.

Bolles, R. N. (1998). *The 1998 what color is your parachute? A practical manual for job-hunters and career-changers.* Berkeley, CA: Ten Speed Press.

Campion, J. E., & Arvey, R. D. (1989). Unfair discrimination in the employment interview. In R. W. Eder & G. R. Ferris (Eds.), *The employment interview: Theory, research, and practice* (pp. 61–73). Newbury Park, CA: Sage.

Dipboye, R. L. (1982). Self-fulfilling prophecies in the selection-recruitment interview. *Academy of Management Review, 7,* 579–586.

Dougherty, T. W., Turban, D. B., & Callender, J. C. (1994). Confirming first impressions in the employment interview: A field study of interviewer behavior. *Journal of Applied Psychology, 79,* 659–665.

Eder, R. W., & Ferris, G. R. (1989). Preface. In R. W. Eder & G. R. Ferris (Eds.), *The employment interview: Theory, research, and practice* (pp. 11–14). Newbury Park, CA: Sage.

Einhorn, L. J. (1981). An inner view of the job interview: An investigation of successful communicative behaviors. *Communication Education, 30,* 217–228.

Eisenberg, A. M. (1979). *Job talk.* New York: Macmillan.

Eng, S. (1998, January 18). Company culture sets dress for job interviews. *St. Louis Post-Dispatch,* p. G20.

Frank, L. L., & Hackman, J. R. (1975). Effect of interviewer-interviewee similarity on interviewer objectivity in college admission interviews. *Journal of Applied Psychology, 60,* 356–360.

Goffman, E. (1974). *Frame analysis.* New York: Harper.

Goodale, J. G. (1989). Effective employment interviewing. In R. W. Eder & G. R. Ferris (Eds.), *The employment interview: Theory, research, and practice* (pp. 307–323). Newbury Park, CA: Sage.

Hall, E. T. (1959). *The silent language.* New York: Fawcett.

Halvorson, S. (1997). Interviewing: Role playing to help understand the Americans with Disabilities Act (ADA). *The Speech Communication Teacher, 11,* 1–3.

Howard, J. L., & Ferris, G. R. (1996). The employment interview context: Social and situational influences on interviewer decisions. *Journal of Applied Social Psychology, 26,* 112–136.

Ilkka, R. J. (1995). Applicant appearance and selection decision making: Revitalizing employment interview education. *Business Communication Quarterly, 3,* 11–18.

Jackson, T. (1978). *Guerrilla tactics in the job market.* New York: Bantam.

Janz, T. (1989). The patterned behavior description interview: The best prophet of the future is the past. In R. W. Eder & G. R. Ferris (Eds.), *The employment interview: Theory, research, and practice* (pp. 158–168). Newbury Park, CA: Sage.

Jorgenson, J. (1995). Re-relationalizing rapport in interpersonal settings. In W. Leeds-Hurwitz (Ed.), *Social approaches to communication* (pp. 155–170). New York: Guilford.

Kanter, A. B. (1995). *The essential book of interviewing: Everything you need to know from both sides of the table.* New York: Times Books.

Kirkwood, W. G., & Ralston, S. M. (1996). Ethics and employment interviewing. *Communication Education, 45,* 167–179.

Kleinke, C. L. (1986). *Meeting & understanding people.* New York: W. H. Freeman.

Klitgaard, R. (1985). *Choosing elites: Selecting the "best and the brightest" at top universities and elsewhere.* New York: Basic Books.

Loden, M. (1996). *Implementing diversity.* Chicago: Irwin.

Milano, B. J. (1997, September 5). Preparation proves productive. *The University News,* p. 7.

Miller, V. D., & Buzzanell, P. M. (1996). Toward a research agenda for the second employment interview. *Journal of Applied Communication Research, 24,* 165–180.

Molloy, J. T. (1988). *John T. Molloy's new dress for success.* New York: Warner Books.

Neuborne, E. (1997, July 9). Employers score new hires. *USA Today,* pp. 1B, 2B.

Parker, Y. (1983). *The damn good resume guide.* Berkeley, CA: Ten Speed Press.

Peterson, M. S. (1997). Personnel interviewers' perceptions of the importance and adequacy of applicants' communication skills. *Communication Education, 46,* 287–291.

Saint Louis University Career Center (1997). *Employment guide: 1997–1998.* St. Louis, MO: Author.

Shiparski, L. (1996). Successful interview strategies. *Nursing Management, 27,* 32F, 32H.

Stevens, C. K. (1997). Effects of preinterview beliefs on applicants' reactions to campus interviews. *Academy of Management Journal, 40,* 947–966.

Stevens, C. K., & Kristof, A. L. (1995). Making the right impression: A field study of applicant impression management during job interviews. *Journal of Applied Psychology, 80,* 587–606.

Tickle-Degnan, L., & Rosenthal, R. (1990). The nature of rapport and its nonverbal coordinates. *Psychological Inquiry, 1,* 285–293.

Watzlawick, P., Weakland, J., & Fisch, R. (1974). *Change: Principles of problem formation and problem resolution.* New York: W. W. Norton.

Yate, M. (1996). *Knock 'em dead: The ultimate job-seeker's handbook.* Holbrook, MA: Adams.

❀ 7 Interviews in Organizations

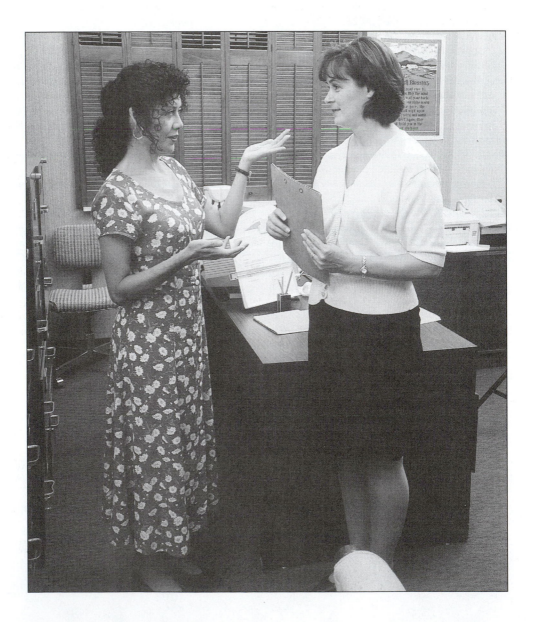

Communication is more than an important organizational function. It reflects corporate values, maintains them, and even creates them. Communication can build or shake morale. While some see it as only one part of the organizational structure, others understand communication as the network by which the organization is held together. Organizational life is constituted by means of communication.

—Margaret Whitney, in *Corporate Communication*

LEARNING GOALS

After reading this chapter, you should be able to

- Describe the role played by interviewing within contemporary complex organizations
- Prepare thoroughly for conducting appraisal interviews
- Communicate skillfully within appraisal, intervention, exit, and termination interviews, as both interviewer and interviewee
- Explain how conflict, trust, and supportive climates play positive roles in effective organizational interviewing

The management of the Marriott Marquis on Times Square, flagship hotel of the international chain, thought its 400 housekeeping employees enjoyed a nearly perfect work environment of good pay, generous benefits, and satisfying work conditions. But a survey revealed a different story. Given a chance to speak out, the employees said they wanted respect and appreciation, which they felt they weren't getting. "When you see us in the elevators, don't ignore us. You know our name. We're wearing it," they told managers. "And can we get some uniforms that don't look goofy?"

Marriott learned an important lesson, according to motivational expert Bob Nelson, author of *1001 Ways to Energize Employees* (1997). Good communication helps organizations prosper. Effective interviewing contributes to good communication.

Organizations put great stock in selection interviews. Hiring competent employees is at the core of organizational decision making, as you learned in Chapter 6. Interviews, however, remain essential to the continuing success of organizations, particularly those that conscientiously promote and value face-to-face communication. Over time, successful managers will use interviewing occasions to assess, discipline, promote, assist, reassign, or terminate employees.

But in a broader, proactive application, such face-to-face talk helps organizations gather information, boost morale, solve problems, improve performance, develop talent, examine issues, explore new ideas, and interact with the public. Framed as communicative "inter-views," they help management and staff collaborate in identifying, refining, and accomplishing personal and organizational goals. Interviews also enable organizations to listen and learn from workers, promote a sense of ownership and pride among them, and treat them as persons, not just as interchangeable cogs in a machine.

This chapter begins with an overview of communication in corporations and organizations, within the contemporary climate of increasing emphasis on managing change, promoting teamwork, sharing information, and seeking excellence. These are hallmarks of many progressive, successful organizations.

The appraisal interview receives major attention in "The Basics" because of its primacy as a channel of communication in organizations. Interviewing skills and appreciations are also essential in the sensitive and challenging intervention and termination interviews managers must conduct, and many basic appraisal skills apply equally well to these other contexts of evaluation. Please note, as well, that interviewing within organizations includes helping, information-gathering, and persuasive applications, which are covered in detail in other chapters.

"Beyond the Basics" relates organizational interviewing to two interdependent areas of research and theory—conflict management and defensive/supportive climates of communication. Here you'll see how conflict and trust aren't necessarily contradictory elements of organizational communication.

THE BASICS

Communication in Today's Organizations

Communication is the lifeblood of organizations, especially large, far-flung ones with a diversity of employees. Communication occurs inside the organization, as it defines and constitutes itself, and outside, as it extends, amplifies, and clarifies its messages to shareholders, clients, and the public at large. The means of communication include annual reports, Web pages, memoranda, press releases, publications, public forums, training videos, advertorials, and focus groups.

The face-to-face interview, however, isn't always seen as an important element of organizational communication and, as a result, is underutilized at times. But with today's emphasis on change in organizations, the value of interpersonal communication, including interviews, appears to be greater than ever. ". . . [E]arly in most organizational changes, no one may know what these changes will mean to the individual," according to management specialist James Champy (Hesselbein, Goldsmith & Beckhard, 1997). "Concerns cannot be met by one-way forms of communication. We must mobilize managers to have conversations with people across the organization about the drivers and implications of the change program. It's in the give and take of discussion that people will discover the truth about what's likely to happen" (p. 15). Conversational approaches to organizational change are increasingly influential (see, for examples, Senge, 1990; Shotter, 1993), and they do not involve interviewing in only its information-gathering or its interrogative connotations. As Winograd and Flores suggest, "The most essential responsibilities for managers . . . can be characterized as participation in conversations for possibilities that open new backgrounds for the conversations of action" (quoted in Shotter, 1993, p. 148).

Dozens of social, political, economic, and technological forces buffet contemporary organizations, churning up problems and challenges over such issues as layoffs, customer relations, quality control, employee empowerment, equity, and ownership. Traditional models and theories have given way to approaches that depend on effective communication. Two figures, in particular, have influenced change in organizational life: W. Edwards Deming, guru of the Total Quality Management (TQM) movement, and Douglas McGregor, creator of the Theory X and Theory Y dichotomy of leadership styles.

Deming studied and amplified the management philosophy that rebuilt the Japanese economy after the devastation of World War II. In his classic book, *Out of the Crisis* (1988), Deming sought to reshape American industry, in both manufacturing and service components, by applying the best notions of the Japanese model, emphasizing increased productivity through improved quality. Deming's proposals for change depend on effective communication throughout the organization—especially, though, *from* and *between* employees. His view credited workers with **intrinsic motivation**—an inner drive to learn, take pride in their work, improve, and experiment. By its strict devotion to achieving quotas or objectives, traditional American management, Deming thought, stifled intrinsic motivation among employees and, worse, bred fear, rivalry, and inferior performance while simultaneously damaging teamwork and morale (1988, p. 102). The culmination of Deming's philosophy, the **total quality management** approach, requires commitment and teamwork by everyone in the organization. TQM and comparable programs that guide organizations falter when communication is denied, discouraged, or dreaded.

Douglas McGregor (1960) set the stage for many of Deming's ideas with his theories of management based on perspectives of human nature and human behavior. **Theory X management** assumes that workers are inherently lazy and shun responsibility. Managers operating from assumptions like these adopt an authoritarian, top-down mentality that distrusts employees, figuring they work best when closely directed, monitored, supervised, and forced to perform. **Theory Y management,** on the other hand, assumes that most workers are self-motivated and can take on responsibilities. Theory Y hypothesizes that people generally look for ways to do satisfying work, rather than looking for ways to avoid work. If shown ways to help create such productive satisfaction, employees respond well. Theory X and Y types both rely on communication, but their motivations and methods differ dramatically. McGregor's ideas have been so successful that when a special twenty-fifth anniversary edition of his book was issued, Warren Bennis, an influential organizational theorist, wrote, "When I say that *The Human Side of Enterprise* created a 'new taste,' I'm dead serious, since this book, more than any other book on management, changed an entire concept of organizational man and replaced it with a new paradigm that stressed human potentials, emphasized human growth, and elevated the human role in industrial society. . . . Much of the work that goes on now could not have happened if this book hadn't been written" (Bennis, 1985).

The Deming and McGregor theories have generated both devotees and detractors. We introduce their ideas not as an unqualified endorsement but rather as evidence that leading voices in organizational management stress vertical (top-to-bottom and vice versa) and horizontal (across and between departments) communication patterns that rely on effective interviewing. Effective interviews energize individuals, organizations, and the larger community in which they work.

Appraisal Interviews

Organizational **appraisal interviews** are conducted to share insights and information between superiors and subordinates. Generally, they have served two functions: (1) the *feedback function,* in which managers and supervisors use the interview to provide employees with evaluative information that they could use to revise their behaviors and attitudes, and to encourage feedback from the employees; and (2) the *goal-setting function,* in which superiors and subordinates collaboratively translate their current understandings into behavioral plans for the future.

Reports and anecdotal evidence suggest that employees are wary of appraisal interviews because of their reputation as an uncomfortable critique of one's work and worth (Half, 1993). That is especially true in organizations with inadequate opportunities for communication between management and staff. Unsure of where they stand, employees enter the interview with thoughts like these: "Am I valued?" or "Am I in trouble?" If the interview goes as they fear, with an emphasis on what is wrong and little on what is right, most employees will slink back to their desks or workplaces filled with resentment and hurt feelings instead of a renewed sense of worth and a commitment to do better. If viewed as a negative experience, employees assume defensive postures: "I'm here to prove I'm a good employee. I'm ready to defend my record. I don't deserve criticism." Even when the experience isn't negative, too few appraisal interviews are seen as positive or uplifting.

A poorly conducted appraisal stimulates a variety of reactions. For many employees it confirms what they already know. The interview, which caps the appraisal process, is often pro forma, and it says, "Keep on doing what you're doing"—a verbal pat on the back that might frustrate creativity or foster complacency. Based on preconceptions and past experience, disillusioned employees may consider the appraisal interview a waste of time: "What's the use of busting my tail when no one seems to care?" Others take a more introspective view: "Surely, there is something I can do better." At times even highly motivated employees, with positive attitudes about themselves and the organization, learn to their surprise that a new manager doesn't share their rosy assessment. In the end, many workers suffer in silence, frustrated with their work and relationship with management but afraid to say so to a superior who's blissfully unaware of that frustration.

BOX 7.1　　INTERVIEWERS IN ACTION

Dorothy Leeds

Management consultant Dorothy Leeds describes what she learned about how organizations conduct appraisal interviews:

"The performance appraisal is one of the manager's best tools for motivating people, yet it is seldom, if ever, exploited to its full potential. As typically handled, performance appraisals are virtually meaningless. When 200 managers in a large New York company were asked about their own last performance appraisal, only 10 of them said they had received a thorough give-and-take appraisal interview. Some had received no more than a token pat on the shoulder and a charge to keep up the good work. Others had been subjected to a harangue and a long list of gripes."

Source: Leeds, 1987, pp. 183–184

In situations like these, employees won't see the appraisal as an opportunity for growth and satisfaction, in part because the boss doesn't see it that way either. From the perspective of some supervisors, it's a chore, not an opportunity to accomplish productive goals. Perhaps they don't like to judge any more than employees like being judged. Perhaps they don't approve of the appraisal process, finding it of little practical value or misguided in its intent. Moreover, they may not have a say in improving the process, so, they conclude, why take the interview seriously? If that weren't enough, there are the occasional legal worries of delivering bad news in a litigious society. See Box 7.1 for one researcher's findings on appraisal interviews.

Despite its reputation as a ticklish and often uncomfortable situation, the appraisal interview is an important moment, and in effective organizations it can neither be avoided nor written off as a routine exercise. Besides its obvious career consequences, the appraisal interview often amounts to the organization's primary, but far-from-complete, evaluation of an employee's performance and, more important, ability. When done well, an appraisal encourages dialogue and sets up the potential for future improvement.

Why Appraise?

Government and the military services developed appraisal instruments in the early 1900s as a systematic, objective method to determine promotions. By the 1950s, organizations and businesses had widely accepted the need for appraisals, but the methodology remained relatively unsophisticated. The Civil Rights Act of 1964 and the Equal Employment Opportunity Commission (1970) moved organizations toward clearer, more structured, and better documented procedures and guidelines by which managers could justify and defend the legality of decisions to hire, fire, promote, or demote.

Executives and managers still often conduct appraisals as an obligatory part of running an organization, fulfilling, to one degree or another, the traditional purposes of critique and performance review. However, appraisals not only help motivate and nurture employees, stressing strengths as well as weaknesses; but they also can improve relations between management and staff by bridging differences in male-female, black-white, young-old, white-collar–blue-collar communication, and other cross-cultural settings. Inadequate opportunities for discussion between employees and their supervisors, on the other hand, are the root of misunderstanding, resentment, low morale, and, ultimately, overall dissatisfaction with the job. Appraisal interviews, conducted by competent professionals, encourage both supervisors and subordinates to be diagnostic and introspective; participants more clearly sense how they can be more communicative problem solvers and troubleshooters in their careers.

Job Satisfaction and Communication

One method of assessing job satisfaction rests on a **Quality of Work Life formula** (QWL) of eight factors (from Bruce & Blackburn, 1992):

- fair and adequate compensation
- a safe, healthy place to work
- opportunities to develop human capacities through meaningful work and role in new ways of doing jobs
- growth, such as opportunities to improve skills, knowledge, and, security—a sense that job is safe
- social integration and interaction with coworkers and management
- fair play and recognized rights, with respect for equity and equal opportunities, in a setting free of harassment
- consideration for *total life space,* which entails the ability to balance the demands of work, home and family
- a sense of social relevance, leading to pride in both the job and employer. (p. 15)

Notice how many QWL factors on this list depend on frank, consistent, and open communication, which even the best organizations sometimes lack. "We are always surprised at the reluctance of managers to provide regular feedback to their employees," according to organizational researchers (Bruce & Blackburn, 1992, p. 22). Further, "[b]y not communicating regularly with those who work for them they hamper job satisfaction and impede performance. . . . [T]hey do not give their employees the opportunity to maximize performance and satisfaction" (p. 22).

Certain themes and phrases resonate in studies of employees' attitudes about work and employers: respect, chances to be heard, a stake in interesting work, appreciation for a job well done, opportunities to make a difference. Quality of Work Life and other methods of determining job satisfaction rest on mutually attentive interpersonal communication. The appraisal interview constitutes a valuable opportunity to communicate and thereby advance individual and organizational goals (see Box 7.2).

Approaches to Appraisals

The interview often is the last step of an organization's appraisal process, but its effectiveness depends on a consistent, clear, reliable, and fair appraisal system, with accompanying evaluative criteria and data. An organization that takes appraisals seriously carefully develops the standards, methods, and objectives of its appraisal system.

Four considerations influence the appraisal process: (1) the philosophy and operating principles of the organization, often expressed in a mission statement, core values, and policies; (2) the particular requirements of employment, including the individual employee's job skills and personal traits; (3) the performance expectations, or goals, set for the employee by supervisors, colleagues, and others who depend on the employee's performance; and (4) concrete performance results, measured by standards set by the organization, ideally in consultation with employees.

Philosophy   An organization that translates its ideals into behaviors and accomplishments can be expected to select and assess its employees on how well they advance those ideals. If customer service is the hallmark of the company, then appraisals are bound to assess how employees handle complaints or correct mistakes. In addition to their direct application to the job, organizational ideals, such as a commitment to social responsibility, might carry over into employees' civic lives. Ben & Jerry's ice cream company, for example, practices "caring capitalism" that considers the impact of its business decisions on the community, and its employees are encouraged, in their own ways, to act as responsible citizens (Cohen & Greenfield, 1997).

Job Requirements   From building cars to handling insurance claims, job requirements usually spell out the skills, abilities, and traits needed for success in a particular line of work and, therefore, influence the content and method of appraisal. A job that requires outstanding writing skills might also call for someone with the temperament to accept criticism and keep cool under deadline pressure. Traits and performance aren't always compatible, however. A personable, cooperative, and loyal worker might be slow and sloppy at completing assignments; the office grinch might be a perfectionist whose work surpasses that of all others. We might prefer to work alongside someone with a sense of humor; but that trait, while pleasing in certain contexts, could be a detriment in work that calls for serious attention and resolve. Obviously, there are traits essential to a job as opposed to traits with which we feel comfortable.

Expectations   Appraisals sometimes go beyond critiques of performance—such as how sales representatives fulfill day-to-day tasks—to establish and then assess the attainment of more far-reaching goals. The ideal here is that simply satisfying the norm might not be enough in organizations that stress expectations for growth and development by employees or staff. Further, expectations can be, and usually are, highly individualized. The six-month goal set for a national sales representative, for example, might be to increase the number of units sold by 5 percent; in another department of the same organization, the production manager's goal might be to reduce defects by half. Expectations are also related to personal growth, as evidenced by, say, a willingness to take on additional responsibilities, an ability to adapt to a new operating procedure, or a willingness to undergo remedial training. Appraisals, then, examine the fit of individuals within the larger organization—especially in organizations where change is continuous and creativity, advancement, and improvement are not only valued but also are an integral part of the job expectations. As we will see later, this entails taking a systems approach to organizational life. A *systems* perspective suggests that one part of a complex organization cannot be considered apart from its connections to other parts.

Performance   The bottom line for most organizations still amounts to actual performance within the culture and standards of the organization. Using various means, organizations measure results. Task-oriented appraisals focus on accomplishing concrete assignments—the quantity and quality of output as compared to quotas or standards or comparisons with others. Traditional ways of measuring results include recorded tallies of results or consequences, such as accident rates, absences (sick days, tardiness), sales figures, and other quantifiable measurements of productivity. While appraisals focus on individual performance, they often account for the individual's role in a *performance chain* across the organization. One worker's deliberate pace, for example, can hamper the work of others along the line, whether auto makers or claims processors. In certain jobs, though, particularly those dependent on a special craft or talent, haste wouldn't be an issue.

No two organizations approach performance appraisals in the same way, but most examine, in one combination or another, how well individuals in the organization adhere to operating principles, exhibit traits essential to the work at hand, produce quality work according to organizational expectations, and accept constructive criticism for improvement. Organizations commonly use narrative, ranking, or rating methods in their appraisal systems, and each influences the content and conduct of the interview that follows.

Narrative Methods Among the oldest—and most subjective—appraisal methods employed by appraisal interviewers is the **narrative**, a form of written, anecdotal evaluation. There are numerous variations on a narrative approach, but it usually is guided by some predetermined structure, such as a question or series of questions to guide appraisers. Typically, narratives are unconstrained by precise categorizing, which is why narrative appraisals sometimes take the form of **global essays**, which are narratives that respond to the supervisor's generalized, or global, impressions of a worker's performance. A global essay might be stimulated by the appraiser's response to open-ended questions such as, "Please provide an overall evaluation of this employee's performance for the period January 1, 1999–December 31, 1999."

The narrative approach tests the evaluator's compositional talents. A facile writer can produce a devastating or dazzling appraisal readily. An inexperienced writer might struggle to find words to describe an employee's strengths and weaknesses accurately. Strong employees who are evaluated by weak writers may come off relatively weaker than they really are. Yet this is not the only problem with a thoroughly narrative approach to appraisals. With the current emphasis on litigation, managers are reluctant to produce a critical written report that could be used against them in court. Therefore they choose safe, nondescript language that might camouflage deeper reactions. Some writers of appraisal narratives often anchor their appraisals in an overall, ambiguous label of some sort, such as describing an employee as "excellent" or "outstanding," but without providing criteria or examples to justify such generalities. Effective, focused appraisal interviews can provide the specifics to enliven and support the written narratives.

Narrative accounts can also include employees' **self-evaluative essays.** They, too, usually leave great leeway for literary exposition. The employee may produce what amounts to flattering miniautobiography—a portrayal based more on fancy than fact. On the other hand, self-evaluative essays can provide a useful counterpoint to a manager's essay and stimulate a productive discussion to reconcile differences in their narrative descriptions. If employee narratives are the norm, and if they are taken seriously by the organization, this invitation encourages employees to see how their own stories can fit within the larger narrative or culture of the organization. Not surprisingly, people who expect to be heard have more to say; thus, interviews based on such evidence can be quite fruitful.

Another type of narrative account, the **critical incident report,** focuses more concretely on details and examples. It documents, through observation and note taking, occasions when the employee excelled or stumbled. Just as behavior-based interviewing conducted by employment interviewers will ask about specific moments in the applicant's work history and the stories that emerge from them, critical incident organizational appraisal turns on stories of organizational life. An "incident" might be an employee's exceptional speed in completing a task well, or it might be an unsolicited letter from a customer describing that same employee's attentive service "beyond the call of duty." As paper-trail documentation, the critical incident report helps organizations create a tangible record to justify performance rewards, or to justify demotion or other punitive action. However, a

- Write a first draft of a one- or two-paragraph global essay appraising the work of a coworker or covolunteer whose situation and job you know well. (Do not attach the person's name to the appraisal, but write your essay with an actual person in mind.)

- Edit and revise your essay to insert at least one detail, illustration, or example for each evaluative statement you've made.

- Are there unstated criteria that you used to evaluate job performance? If so, try to articulate them. Is everyone in the workplace equally familiar with these criteria? Particularly important: Ask yourself if the criteria guiding your appraisals are clear to the worker whose performance you're evaluating.

- Would the worker be surprised to read your essay? If so, why?

- If you shared it with him or her, would it provide a useful basis for a subsequent appraisal interview? See if you can create a brief interview schedule from the information in your essay. Later, compare your results in this exercise with what you'll learn about structuring the appraisal interview.

collection of critical incidents risks a disproportionate emphasis on isolated deficiencies and inconsequential foul-ups rather than on continuing accomplishments, if supervisors are not careful.

Supervisors may have difficulty deciding what is critical (what is an important indicator of skill). An evaluative system that wholly depends on the evaluator's personal idiosyncrasies is worthless. Even when critical incidents are categorized by headings such as "delegating authority" or "initiative," the evaluator still must decide, preferably systematically and ahead of time, how the behavior is critical and how it contributes to the organization's mission. Although meant to be objective, the method—like other evaluative procedures—rests on subjectivity.

The **field review,** another narrative method, usually involves a manager or representative of the human resources or personnel office visiting factory, office, or department to observe workplace activity and collect information to use in a narrative report. The field review takes two common forms. In one, the personnel representative asks the employee's immediate supervisor questions and elicits details to assist the evaluator in producing a narrative appraisal; in the second, the person responsible for the field review writes the report from direct observation.

As a rule, narratives emphasize generalities more than specifics. They tend not to assess with uniform, well-understood standards and criteria, and thus can be seen as arbitrary. A good appraisal interview offers the opportunity to discuss the narrative, and for the employee to respond, challenge, and even amend it. But if the interview gets bogged down in a debate over the content of the narrative—the story told by one person about another—it prevents a productive examination of problems and solutions. The narrative involves, to some degree, two egos potentially in conflict. To the evaluator, the words count; they represent his or her version of the truth. To the evaluated, it's a portrayal that can attack one's being.

Narrative methods, even though they are variable and subjective, are especially valuable when used in conjunction with other appraisal methods and when they result from a collaboration between appraiser and appraisee.

Ranking Methods   In general terms, **rankings** are quantitative assignments or estimates that compare a person or thing directly to other persons or things on the basis of some stated criterion. As opposed to rating systems, which we will describe next, a ranking pits whatever is evaluated against others by direct comparisons: "In our small department, Jan is our best writer, LaToya our second best, and Robert our weakest." Of course, Jan, LaToya, and Robert may all be ineffective, or wonderful, writers—thus you can see a problem with ranking systems. Direct comparisons sometimes ignore other measures of competence. Does it mean much to be the best writer in a department where all the employees have grammar and syntax problems? On the other hand, if you're ranked as the least effective trainer in an award-winning department, your skills may far surpass the best trainer in an ineffective one.

Among the first complex organizations to use rankings systematically were the military services, especially in officer candidate training, as means of identifying leaders for command positions. In any ranking system, though, someone has to define the attributes, aptitudes, and behaviors that differentiate one employee from another. In the military, aggressiveness and decisiveness are considered signs of leadership; in another type of organization, the ability to compromise marks the best leaders.

One common version of ranking asks an evaluator to assess an individual in terms of important characteristics, such as "communication skills" or "problem solving," along a percentile: top 10 percent; upper 25 percent; middle 40 percent; lower 25 percent, for example. In some ranking forms, the last entry asks the evaluator to calculate, supposedly by averaging and weighing rankings on preceding questions, an "all-purpose," cumulative, or "overall" rank.

Rankings might require that managers create a **forced distribution** to show where individuals fit within an assessment of all employees in a department or operation. By this method, the evaluator divides a group of employees into specific performance categories, usually broken down into poor, below average, average, above average, and exceptional. In some organizations, an evaluator's rankings that fall outside a normal distribution might be met with skepticism or derision: "Can you believe McIntyre has nothing but perfect employees working for her? Who's she kidding?" If that is the organization's response, it could force evaluators to rank some exceptional employees into an inappropriate pattern expected by management.

Another method, **peer ranking,** illustrates how colleagues view a fellow employee. Often the ranking categories deal with collegial elements such as compatibility, teamwork, and work ethic. Peer rankings may help reveal a problem undetected by the boss, who finds her administrative assistant a model employee; peers, though, see the assistant as a menace. Personal relationships can't help but enter into the thinking of peer evaluators, even though the ranking category might have nothing to do with the person's physical or personality traits. Perceptions, however, do count, and the peer ranking, although rarely used as a principal method of appraisal, contributes to a broader picture.

Rankings tend to be more focused than narratives, but may not be much better at specifying criteria. Asking someone, for example, where an individual ranks on factors such as maturity or creativity doesn't provide much guidance. Is maturity exhibited in manner of dress, deportment, or hairstyle? ("She dresses like a teenager." "Why doesn't he act his age?") Is maturity characterized by wisdom or good judgment? Perhaps it's a mellow demeanor or a quality of age, like "mature" wine?

There is nothing wrong with striving for improvement or excellence. But a judgmental, competitive approach to ranking people can create problems. To be average usually isn't acceptable in organizations. But what is average? Aren't 50 percent of people in all categories of employment—whether clerks, pilots, teachers, or electricians—below average by definition? Nonetheless, *average* suggests a condition of blandness or dullness. When rankings constitute the core of an organization's appraisal system, care must be taken to avoid making people feel incompetent for being average or below average.

Rankings relate to and sometimes work in tandem with rating systems of appraisals, the next group of appraisal methods.

Rating Methods   Even though all evaluation is by definition subjective, in some formats ratings come closer to the goal of objective fairness. **Ratings** ask evaluators to describe and assess employees' skills in terms of a series of carefully defined categories, often with examples or specific criteria. If rankings ask evaluators to compare workers with each other, ratings ask them to compare workers with behavioral standards that are closely matched to work success.

Graphic rating scales are among the most frequently used methods of appraisal in organizations. The rating criteria reflect presumably important qualities for the job—generally a selection of traits, behaviors, and attitudes such as "resource utilization," "flexibility," "customer relations," "cooperation," "interpersonal communication"—accompanied by one or more definitions or examples of what each category means. In nursing, for example, important health care tasks would certainly receive priority in a rating, such as prompt, accurate administration of medications or careful maintenance of medical records. But less easily defined traits or behaviors, such as interpersonal warmth, could warrant ratings, too.

Rating forms range from a single page to booklets covering hundreds of categories and questions. Rating boxes or checklists ask evaluators to distinguish the level of performance or degree of compliance, such as outstanding, satisfactory, or needs improvement, or, in another variation, exceeds, meets, or fails to meet standards. A range of ratings might be included, as well; for example, a scale on how an employee follows instructions might offer these choices: always, usually, about half the time, seldom, and never.

Some rating forms, now called **360-degree appraisals,** collect feedback from everyone whose own productivity and performance depend on the employee under review. For example, at a newspaper, the person responsible for supervising the printing presses works with employees in nearly every operation—news, circulation, advertising, and production. A late-breaking event, such as a World Series game, might mean starting the presses forty-five minutes later than usual to ensure that the home-delivered edition contains a full account of the game. The sports editor depends on the pressroom supervisor's cooperation, and so do others who must coordinate their tasks with the printing of the newspaper.

Because a single supervisor might not be able to provide a comprehensive picture of the employee's effectiveness, the approach of a 360-degree appraisal is to "circle" the employee's contributions with impressions from coworkers who may encounter her or him from different perspectives. These comprehensive ratings work especially well when flexible interaction is important to the success of the organization, which is usually the case. A 360-degree appraisal also stresses the importance of team as well as individual performance. With input from several angles, composite ratings might reveal an inconsistent pattern of strengths and weaknesses. The employee's immediate superior sees only a piece of the operation and judges the performance "strong." But colleagues in another department find room for improvement on their ratings. It's an approach that can add balance and context to typical ratings conducted within the employee's own sphere by a single supervisor.

Many organizations encourage employees to conduct a **self-rating.** A choice might be involved: Add your own rating to your supervisor's, or be rated only by the supervisor. In another variation, both supervisor and employee independently complete the rating form, then meet to compare and discuss results. Self-rating lets employees assess their work according to defined organizational criteria, not by how they might define the job idiosyncratically. When the employee's appraisal parallels the supervisor's, there shouldn't be resentment or disagreement. If their appraisals contrast, it's not likely to be on all accounts; there will be some agreement, and disagreements can be discussed at the appraisal interview.

Although popular in organizations, rating forms have disadvantages, especially when used to the exclusion of other methods. Despite appearing to be precise in measuring traits and performance, ratings are subject to the shifting attitudes and maybe the biases of the managers who define the categories and standards. At times, evaluators find themselves trapped into assigning ratings for categories they consider irrelevant or insignificant as indicators of ability or performance. Finally, trait ratings aren't automatically designed to encourage improvement or to develop better work relations. How, for example, does one become more creative when rated low in that category? Unless accompanied by a thorough discussion of solutions, a trait rating may diagnose without proposing a treatment.

A special form of rating was developed, in part to offset supervisors' tendencies toward leniency in assessing employees. The solution, called a **forced-choice rating,** uses four behavioral statements—two that seem favorable to the employee and two that seem unfavorable. But the rating incorporates several wrinkles. First, one favorable statement and one unfavorable statement aren't designed to discriminate between an effective or ineffective worker. The evaluator must choose one statement that best fits the employee's performance and one that least fits it. Second, a value is assigned to each statement, but the evaluator does not know the value; the human resources office scores the forms.

In another attempt to refine ratings appraisals, industrial psychologists developed the **behaviorally anchored rating system** (BARS). The BARS approach differs from typical ratings in how the form is developed; BARS incorporates prior consultation with a large number of evaluators and, in some cases, the evaluated. Developing a BARS instrument involves a thorough analysis of the job and its requirements. A guiding question to BARS development asks, "What must an employee do on this job to be considered proficient?" Based on answers to the question (or similar questions), dimensions of the job are identified; then a set of anchors—expressed in behaviors for that dimension—are described and assigned a numerical value along a continuum, ranging from high to low performance. In a sample BARS for department store sales associates, for example, one dimension of the job might be "response to customer questions," with the following set of anchors:

7—always responds with useful information in a prompt and courteous manner

6—provides useful information but lacks warmth

5—responds cheerfully but sometimes can't answer basic questions about products

4—well informed about products but occasionally responds with impatience

3—informed and respectful but doesn't go beyond the basics in answers

2—prone to disagree or argue with customers

1—frequently unable to answer questions or act courteously

Before implementation, BARS scales go through stages of pretesting and revision, again, with input from both raters and those who will be rated, to determine the validity of dimensions, anchors, and numerical values. Presumably, a BARS system, once complete, constitutes agreement among employees, supervisors, and management about evaluative criteria. Moreover, participation in creating the ratings gives people a personal stake in the system—a sense that the appraisal reflects *us* (employees and supervisors) and not just *them* (management).

The BARS philosophy is an extension of the advice for job candidates in Chapter 6: always think of your skills and abilities in terms of behaviors and actions that translate into the organization's benefit, not, first and foremost, your own.

No appraisal method is perfect. A BARS, while more participatory and precise than other approaches, takes time and money to develop; it also might require frequent modification, as jobs and job demands change in an organization. The BARS may be somewhat better than other ratings, but it still goes only so far in providing feedback for change and improvement by employees.

Goals   Appraisals that concentrate on a critique of performance amount to a report card. Here is how you did: A for dean's list, B for "good," C for average, D for deficient, and F for failure. A different management philosophy avoids the psychological implications of gradelike procedures and emphasizes a goals orientation preferred by organizations that embrace an approach called **management by objectives** (MBO).

MBO combines a management strategy with a type of appraisal. The goals usually start with top management setting the organizational objectives. At various levels within the organization, managers determine department and unit goals and action plans to accomplish them. Eventually, the goal setting extends to individual employees, who, in collaboration with superiors, agree to goals for themselves. An MBO strategy directly depends on communication within the organization, as management and workers collaborate in forming organization, department, and individual goals. Instead of relying on inflexible standards that are presumed to be valid, MBO relies upon a more local approach. Supervisors and subordinates collaborate on setting mutually agreed upon objectives by which they will be evaluated later. Ideally, appraisals are based on the degree to which goals were achieved. Often an MBO program assigns priorities to different goals and weighs them by degree of difficulty. The interview is the communication laboratory in which these decisions are made.

In summarizing the research in **goal-setting theory,** Eric Eisenberg and H. L. Goodall, Jr., (1997) suggest that intelligent and communicative managers don't set the goals themselves and then hope to motivate employees to achieve them, but instead work with employees to help them set reasonable motivating goals that the employees then are more likely to meet. In this way, subordinates develop a sense of ownership with respect to goals that reflect their own voices. Further, Eisenberg and Goodall present this advice, consistent with goal-setting research:

1. Set clear and specific goals, which have a greater positive impact on performance than do general goals.

2. Set goals that are difficult but attainable; they will lead to higher performance than will easy goals.

3. Focus on participative rather than assigned goals.

4. Give frequent feedback about the goal-setting and work processes. (p. 245)

A related appraisal-management strategy is called a **performance plan.** William Swan (1991) endorses a continuous process of performance management, which includes appraising employees by how they follow through with and meet the performance plan. Swan includes supportive activities toward meeting goals, including coaching (see Box 7.3), feedback, and monitoring. The performance plan should be not only specific and challenging but also realistic and measurable.

Goals-based appraisals usually involve a combination of self-improvement and performance objectives. These objectives may be formulated from the results of other methods of appraisal, particularly graphic scales or BARS. Based on an appraisal or another form of assessment, a plant manager, for example, agrees with his supervisor on three self-improvement goals for the coming year: complete an environmental-safety course, serve on the board of a professional organization, and publish a report in an industry periodical. (The individual goals, of course, benefit the organization as well.) The plant manager and

BOX 7.3   R E M I N D E R S

Coaching for Performance Enhancement

- *What is an organizational coach?* The word *coach* in sports conjures images of a charismatic authority figure who throws tantrums over bad calls, bears down on players in practice sessions, and motivates through force of will. Coaches may be good or bad, but we like to assume that they care not only about success but about people. In organizations, coaching implies some of the same characteristics but without some of the connotations of emotional intensity. Organizational **coaching** is defined here as a mutual activity in which one person helps another change behavior, solve problems, or develop plans, with the ultimate goal of improved performance.

- *What does a coach do?* Organizational coaching is similar to sports coaching in its emphasis on practicing fundamentals, then progressing to higher levels of achievement. All coaching focuses on actual behavior and its consequences: "When you do this, that happens." "Why do you suppose that happens?" "Do you want it to happen?" "Why not change your approach and see what happens then?" The coach acts as a particularly committed observer who continually offers concrete and specific feedback about input/ output relationships. Unlike some coaching models, however, organizational coaching isn't primarily based on ordering, lecturing, scolding, correcting, arguing, threatening, or cajoling (although in a given relationship, elements of each may develop). While not usually viewed as a formal interview, coaching typically relies on interview techniques, especially listening and questioning.

- *How might a coach listen and question with a worker?* The questions focus on obtaining details and descriptions of how someone works or performs, with the coach alert for flaws and potential problems in execution. The listening helps the coach decide how to provide feedback and suggestions for change. Most coaches attempt to help employees move from easy to more difficult tasks, using **microgoals** (Waldroop & Butler, 1996)—a series of systematic small steps into which a task has been divided. For example, consider microgoals in a news reporter's attempt to turn a batch of facts into a story. Writing coaches Roy Peter Clark and Don Fry (1992) believe simple questions help the coach and writer work together on improving a story:

How do you feel about the story so far?

What's the story about? Have you found a focus?

What's your best quote?

What does the reader need to know?

Who are the most interesting people in your story?

Questions like these help the writer find the strengths and weaknesses of the story without the coach necessarily passing judgment. A successful coaching relationship relies on rapport, trust, and praise. Impatience, negativism, and distance mark an unsuccessful experience.

- *How is coaching related to performance appraisal processes?* Coaching is related to the performance appraisal process in its interviewlike interchange of questions and responses, but it should be a distinct activity. If you are a manager or supervisor, don't wait until a predetermined appraisal occasion to begin coaching; early diagnosis and attention can save you many headaches later. If you are an employee who wants to succeed, you can request a coaching relationship in many situations. Coaching is a road to development that benefits both the individual and the organization. Generally, however, it doesn't work well as a one-time or sporadic occurrence. In certain situations, especially in the early stages of learning a new job, it might be a daily routine.

supervisor also agree on several production-performance-related goals, among them to install a computer-driven inventory system by midyear.

MBO and performance plans encourage advancement and growth in a climate of dialogue. Appraisal based exclusively on accomplishment of goals poses problems when those goals aren't met satisfactorily but the organization remains successful. Does that mean the employee is a failure or that the mutual goal-setting process is off target? Goals must be realistic, considered within the framework of anticipated real conditions and institutional support. As Swan observes, an organization shouldn't demand higher achievements without providing appropriate incentives and support.

Whatever appraisal method is used, the interview itself should ensure that employees are heard and given a chance to act upon the appraisal (see Box 7.4).

Conducting Appraisal Interviews

Remember that the appraisal interview process involves both a feedback function and a goal-setting function. In other words, it is a communication situation in which interviewer and interviewee look both backward and forward, and must do so cooperatively. Done well, the appraisal interview requires sound objectives, preparation, knowledge, strategies, and attitudes.

Objectives   Planning starts with setting objectives for the meeting—what the participants hope to accomplish. The allotted time for interviews, often ranging from thirty minutes to an hour, both dictates and limits the objectives. Although participants may already be friends, or would rather stretch out in a friendly rambling chat, a focused, purposeful discussion usually results. Objectives vary but management consultant Eric Skopec (1990, p. 134) suggests six distinct topics, three of which focus on performance critique (feedback):

- Review of individual's job
- Review of standards of evaluation or appraisal
- Review and discussion of current levels of performance

The other three deal with performance planning (goal setting):

- Discussion and agreement on plans for improvement
- Deciding on support the supervisor or organization can provide
- Development of long-term prospects

That is substantial ground to cover in the brief time available for a typical interview. Separate critique and planning interviews might work better, as long as a thorough review of feedback can also be integrated into the primary discussion of goal setting in a follow-up interview. Some experts also recommend splitting salary and promotion

BOX 7.4 INTERVIEWERS IN ACTION

James Autry (I)

James Autry, former president of the Meredith Magazine Group and a prominent speaker and writer on humane management, writes often about the paradoxes of the business world. He captures much of what it is like to be "in charge," often evaluating others' behavior, and at the same time to be a caring human being.

"A young manager friend asked me to 'list the paradoxes of management' sometime. I've usually avoided doing it because I don't think I know all the paradoxes of management and because I think some of them are not just restricted to management. But fools rush in, so here I go:

"The leader must:

- "be long-term and short-term at the same time, assuring that the quarterly earnings of the company meet the financial requirements set by the board while often sacrificing short-term earnings in order to assure the long-term growth and development of the company and its stakeholders

- "be in touch and aware of what's going on without looking over people's shoulders

- "inspire and often direct people in accomplishing the vision and mission and purpose of the organization while empowering people to manage themselves and make their own decisions

- "accept and perform the role of spokesperson for the company, and the person in the spotlight, the person upon whom much attention is showered while letting go of ego and control and becoming a resource for the employees

- "encourage and support the rights and the growth and the independent thinking of individual employees without sacrificing the rights and growth and interdependence of the community of employees

- "care for people and fire people, sometimes the same people

- "encourage risk-taking and reward successes while preventing any mistakes that could jeopardize the survival of the enterprise

- "embrace with full commitment the demands and responsibilities, as well as the rewards, of the job with all its paradoxes while embracing with full commitment the demands and responsibilities, as well as the rewards, of being a parent and spouse and friend."

Source: Autry, 1994, pp. 265–266

discussions from those involving employee development. James Goodale (1982), for example, suggests that organizations conduct performance critiques approximately three months before salary budgets are set for the coming year. Once the budget is determined, schedule another interview to explain, justify, and discuss salary and promotion decisions.

Preparation   For interviewers, preparation encompasses a range of details, although a single guiding principle applies: stay focused on the individual. For legal reasons, interviewers will want to conduct all performance appraisals according to a consistent set of guidelines, to ensure that some employees are not given favored or special treatment, either intentionally or inadvertently. However, a one-size-fits-all interview is simply not realistic or productive. To be effective, interviewers must (1) develop their overall approach so that it consistently and fairly gives all employees equal opportunity; and (2) develop a personalized approach that gives each employee the sense that he or she is uniquely important. This responsibility for dual preparation is the special ethical challenge for appraisal interviewers.

Interviewers prepare by thoroughly reviewing the interviewee's performance and traits, drawing on personal observation, employee records, and appraisal reports. They analyze these materials for distinguishing features of the employee's personality, performance, and potential. How, for example, does she respond to criticism? What motivates him to leave early so often? Are there any hidden or underdeveloped strengths? Additional homework might be necessary, such as asking discreet questions of others to fill in missing pieces or complement inconclusive records.

Interviewees should prepare, too, by assessing the interviewer, especially in terms of communication style, such as listening behavior, and by reviewing topics expected to be covered in the interview. In some cases, organizations encourage or assist employees in preparation. For example, the employee might receive appraisal information before the interview or complete a self-evaluation form or narrative as a basis of discussion at the interview. In addition, both participants should draft—or at least anticipate—goals for improvement, which can be discussed at the appraisal interview or a follow-up session.

Preparation for both interviewer and interviewee also includes attention to scheduling details: reasonable notice, along with date, time, and place of the interview session. A detailed letter or memo about the interview should be sent well in advance; that notice should give the interviewee realistic choices for scheduling the meeting. Don't assume the date, time, and place are inconsequential considerations. For the interviewee, an interview might fall on the anniversary of a spouse's death, with disastrous emotional results. For the interviewer, it might come in the middle of a family crisis, to the detriment of an interviewee who could suffer the unintended negative consequence of a terse conversation. Conditions like these may warrant rescheduling.

Also consider the communication implications of when a meeting is scheduled during the day. Do you interview an assembly-line worker at the end of a twelve-hour shift? Should a supervisor schedule an appraisal interview right after a long, draining meeting with department heads? There may be no choice, but whenever possible, the interview should be scheduled for a time when each participant is emotionally and physically alert.

The setting can influence the success or failure of an interview. Certainly, appraisal interviews should be conducted where privacy and minimal interruptions are ensured. In addition, the setting should invite relaxed conversation. Many such interviews are conducted in supervisors' offices, but supervisors should attempt to reduce the power differential inherent in the setting, by choosing similar chairs, for instance. An interviewee coiled in a straightback chair, confronted with the boss looming from a tall cushy chair behind her desk, may experience what is meant as a conversational sharing of goals more as an inquisition or interrogation. The employee's discomfort doesn't serve the boss, either, if she values a shared approach to problem solving. There are no perfect places for appraisal interviews; too many variables and individual preferences intervene. But surroundings matter, and they should be considered as a nonverbal factor of preparation.

A final component of preparation is training and practice. Often those entrusted with appraisal interviews learn by trial and error. A serious-minded organization prepares employees who must conduct appraisal interviews with videos, exercises, readings, and communication skills workshops, then follows up with critiques of the evaluator's performance in interviews, using ratings and feedback from interviewees themselves. An organization's commitment to preparation in appraisal interviews pays off in many ways. Primarily, preparation helps ensure the fullest participation by interviewer and interviewee, enabling them to communicate with comfort, clarity, purpose, and, in the end, results. Without mutual preparation, the odds of a disappointing, counterproductive outcome increase.

Attitudes   **Attitude,** an abstract term we use to refer to someone's predisposition to behave in certain ways, takes concrete, identifiable forms in practice. Attitudes are expressed and interpreted through words, body language, and actions. An awareness of attitudes is important for both participants in an appraisal interview, but the interviewer—usually the interviewee's boss or superior—generally sets the tone. For interviewers, the attitude of empathy should prevail above all else. If it does, it encourages other supportive attitudes, such as courtesy, open-mindedness, and collaboration.

Empathy, described in more detail in earlier chapters, is a sincere effort to identify with another person's experiences, emotions, and motivations—even while you realize you can never completely give up being yourself. Empathy is not mind reading, although efforts to be empathic can be perceived as more or less accurate by the other person in the relationship. An appraisal interview can be a threatening and momentous event in an employee's life, with serious financial, psychological, and physical implications. Empathic interviewers imagine what it's like to be appraised; it can be a humbling, tense experience. Knowing that, an empathic interviewer tries hard to reduce stress and strain, through, for example, a sign of respect, such as standing to greet and welcome the interviewee. Empathic interviewees imagine the discomfort experienced by evaluators who don't enjoy critiquing others' behavior.

Empathy also involves withholding judgment and setting aside assumptions. A willingness to listen and learn enhances nearly all interviews, but it's crucial in appraisal interviews. The interview isn't an occasion for personal vendettas or personalized favors. Supervisors and evaluated employees alike must resist letting feelings distort their listening and overall response to the other person ("Henderson's such a jerk"). What people do (performance) is one thing; who they are (personality) is another. Effective appraisal interviewers and interviewees separate the two as much as possible, following psychologist Carl Rogers's (1961) insight that positive regard can still be extended to people whose behaviors we dislike.

A potentially negative attitude that permeates many interviewer-interviewee relationships is the matter of control. That attitude naturally applies to interviews between superiors and subordinates. In appraisal interviews, there must be a willingness on the interviewer's part to give the interviewee an opportunity to talk freely. The interviewer, in other words, should temporarily step down as boss. It's the interviewee's moment.

Approaches   An appraisal interview calls for a deft, sensitive touch because the discussion often strikes close to what most of us hold dear: our pride. Although this topic is usually discussed in terms of an unfeeling and powerful interviewer victimizing an interviewee, many reminders here apply to the evaluated employee as well. Accusations flung at interviewers also raise the level of defensiveness. An appraisal interview marked by gruff criticism or a tone of aggressive dismissal invites defensiveness. Sometimes interviewees under pressure exhibit **flight behavior** (withdrawal-oriented choices) rather than **fight behavior** (confrontational choices), preferring to back off by speaking more softly or acting passively. Certain methods help offset defensiveness and promote discussion: I-messages, active listening, and questioning.

- *I-messages.* A nonjudgmental approach to discussing deficiencies or problems of performance involves use of I-messages that address specific behavior. To say, "You are too selfish with your coworkers" accuses the employee. To say, however, "I'm noticing that you often borrow software and office materials without sharing them with coworkers so they can be more productive too," helps an employee understand your position while sounding less blaming and less judgmental. It leaves room for discussion of the interviewer's observation and leaves open the possibility that the interviewer may be wrong.

- *Active listening.* In an appraisal interview, active listening (see Chapter 3) is useful because it's responsive yet nonjudgmental. If an employee reacts to criticism by saying, "Why is it always *my* responsibility to be nice to the other guy?" an active listening response might be, "You believe it's unfair for me to ask you to get along better without reminding the others that they should do that, too." Active listening often involves mirroring essential elements of the interviewee's message as, first, a sign of the interviewer's engagement; second, a way to check perceptions and correct misunderstandings; and third, a means of supporting communication with positive outcomes.

    The responsibility for active listening falls primarily to the interviewer, who should concentrate with an open mind on the interviewee's messages, interpreting them for meaning and responding appropriately. Employees often believe that they aren't heard accurately in the organization; an active demonstration of listening skill sends a powerful message about the organization as a whole. A major study of "perceived supervisor listening behavior" and its relationship to employee commitment was conducted within a large utility company. Its authors (Lobdell, Sonoda, & Arnold, 1993) discovered that when supervisors are perceived as effective listeners, the results help everyone:

Supervisors are then perceived as more responsive generally, increasing job satisfaction.

Supervisors' effective listening is presumed to represent the entire organization positively—the organization is perceived as more open and effective.

Employees begin to feel more empowered, with more control over their job conditions.

Employees feel more committed to the organization.

- *Questioning*. Asking good questions should be a goal of all interviews, but in appraisal sessions, interviewers should expect to devote far more time to listening than questioning. Interviewers are better advised to create an interactional space in which their partners feel comfortable in sharing candid evaluations. When appraisal interviewers do question, often it will be to probe, to clarify, and to build upon the interviewee's comments. It isn't a time to gather information about performance, except for necessary clarifications, as that should have been done well ahead of the appraisal interview. It is a time to confirm perceptions, seek explanations, and explore solutions through light-handed probes and questions.

  Of particular value are questions that help the participants understand mistakes and achievements by asking and answering "What happened?" In examining a critical incident, for example, the question might simply be, "What made the good (or bad) results possible?" Exploratory questions build a broad foundation supporting improved performance within the organization. But remember, direct questions are often not as effective as acknowledgement of your own willingness to be surprised. For example, can you hear the difference in the tone of these two interviewer comments?

INTERVIEWER: "Why did you cut back on production, just when we were getting a foothold in that market?"

INTERVIEWEE: "What makes you think I didn't have a good reason for cutting back? There's a lot you don't know about my operation."

INTERVIEWER: "I noticed you cut back on production when it seemed we were getting a foothold in that market."

INTERVIEWEE: "Right. I bet that surprised a few people. Let me tell you why I did that. . . ."

Organization   No standard script or instruction manual exists for appraisal interviews. Nonetheless, most appraisal discussions show a progression of topics, starting with an opening that frames the interview as a positive event, with benefits for all concerned. Recall Skopec's six objectives for the appraisal; if blended a bit, they suggest an effective organizational structure for a single appraisal interview. After a rapport-building opening, a review of the job responsibilities and standards for evaluating the employee's performance in it sets the stage for a discussion of performance levels. Then the participants turn to the crucial task of mutual planning for future job responsibilities and how to meet them more effectively. Although different approaches are possible, we analyze the prototypical appraisal interview in five major stages that trace employee behavior in a roughly chronological manner, from previous acts and evaluations (past), through the current dialogue engaged in by the interview (present), toward an agreement about performance goals (future).

1. *Opening.* The first few moments of any interview set the tone for what follows. The organizational supervisor should take responsibility for defusing, as much as possible, the threatening character of the interview and for establishing a conversational tone of mutual respect. In appraisal interviews, both participants might experience jitters. A smile and warm greeting can help calm everyone:

INTERVIEWER: "Tom, it's good to see you. Please have a seat. Would you like some coffee?"

INTERVIEWEE: "Thanks. It's colder out there than I thought when I left home. Will we ever get out of this snowy pattern?"

INTERVIEWER: "Probably so. Spring has to come soon, doesn't it? Do you still drive in across that dangerous bridge? . . ."

There is usually little need to engage in small talk for more than a few minutes. In fact, too many niceties might heighten anxiety. It's best to move ahead, with the supervisor, at first, taking the lead. For example:

INTERVIEWER: "Well, you know we set aside time to talk one-on-one with staff every three months. This is a good opportunity for us to go over how things are going for you and discuss some things that could benefit both of us. I hope we can help each other define what we have to do for the next quarter."

INTERVIEWEE: "Good. I'd like that, too. There are quite a few matters I'd like to bring up later. Some unexpected things happened in my shop, but overall, it's felt like a good year so far."

The interviewer's opening conveys an important message: This isn't just about you; it's about me, too. Indeed, the person responsible for an appraisal interview should judge his or her own performance on the basis of how well the discussion goes and what is accomplished in the short and long run for all concerned.

Even when the interview's purpose seems self-evident, reviewing what is going to happen serves as a helpful reminder and guide. Here, the interviewer covers the main points of discussion and expectations:

INTERVIEWER: "Tom, I hope we can accomplish three things in this session: review records and ratings of your performance, talk about it together, and then agree on where we go from here. I'd like to give you plenty of opportunity to discuss anything that comes up."

2. *Review.* In the second stage, participants exchange insights and perceptions to see if they are defining the position and criteria similarly. For instance:

INTERVIEWER: "My notes show that last spring we agreed you would be evaluated on three primary goals—one for each of your areas of responsibility. We would look at the outcomes of your training programs— how many trainees were rated higher on communication skills. We would also look at the new database system you put in place and how satisfied office personnel were with it. Finally, we said we'd look at whether you and the PR people have started to get along more smoothly. Was there anything else?"

INTERVIEWEE: "Well, yes and no. Those were the main areas, all right. But I remember being a bit more specific about the PR side of that equation, too. I think we tied that goal to the feedback/complaint incident forms. And didn't we say we would reassess my budget based on the high evaluations my people have been receiving in workshops and seminars?"

3. *Evaluation/critique.* Interviewers disclose how they apply criteria to evaluate employees' performance. Interviewees disclose how workplace conditions, including support from relevant personnel and materials, have affected their performance. If employees seem reluctant to supply this information, interviewers may have to invite it overtly.

In most cases, interviewers won't go over every appraisal item or finding. As part of preparation, they should identify and highlight major strengths and weaknesses. It's important to acknowledge achievements and contributions to the organization; unfortunately, some supervisors feel compelled to stress weaknesses, with a few rationalizing, "We pay you to do a good job. Let's spend our time talking about the areas where we need to see improvement." A sprinkling of praise followed by detractions draws the discussion too soon into the negative zone and irritates most people being evaluated. Genuine strengths can be found in virtually all employees; highlight them to reinforce effective behavior. People can't feel too secure about the areas in which they're competent. Positive feedback— that which supports existing trends—can be crucial in averting future problems.

Interviewers and interviewees should leave ample time for feedback, because the quality and substance of feedback will determine whether the interviewee finds the experience beneficial or a waste of time. People enter an appraisal interview with different objectives and expectations in mind, but few expect to listen to a supervisor's monologue. An appraisal interview, above all, should invite both sides into an exchange of feedback relevant to the interviewee's job performance. After all, it's the interviewee's career at stake. Competent, conscientious employees usually have a lot to say and relish an opportunity to react, reflect, confirm, question, discuss, and plan when it comes to matters concerning them and their jobs.

4. *Goal setting.* Participants cooperate in exploring ways to maintain the levels of effective performance or strengthen levels of substandard performance. At times, a brainstorming atmosphere will predominate at this stage, as the two attempt to solve mutual problems together. At other times, interviewers will have to emphasize unambiguously

what the employee must do to improve. As this stage develops, interviewees might want their behavior to reflect a **bargaining model** (Grigsby, 1983). Chris Argyris (1960) contends that workers and organizations always maintain **psychological contracts** with each other in addition to official work agreements. These psychological contracts involve usually unstated expectations about what should be exchanged between an organization's members—for example, what employees expect to give to, and receive from, the organization; how organizations expect to support employees; and what support organizations expect in return. Because of the power differential in appraisal interviewing, Grigsby suggests that ongoing appraisal provides an appropriate context for employees to clarify the psychological contract and perhaps to bargain new terms for it. For example, consider what an early implementation of this could do for the appraisal process:

> Bargaining approaches can also ensure a continuing dialogue. Subordinates could be encouraged to think of their relationship with the organization as an exchange relationship (i.e., what am I giving to, and what am I receiving from this organization?). Supervisors would also be asked to evaluate each subordinate in these terms. As a part of each new employee's orientation procedure, the manager would present his or her expectations. The aim here is to make explicit those aspects of the psychological contract that are rarely, if ever, acknowledged. The new employee would then be encouraged to evaluate these comments and respond to them. The ensuing dialogue would form the basis for working out a mutually satisfactory superior/subordinate relationship.
>
> Managers and new subordinates might meet periodically and review this exchange relationship. This approach would be especially useful where employees possess highly valued skills they might use as a basis for establishing bargaining power in the organization and where successive increments in productivity are measurable. (pp. 329–330)

In this sense, bargaining shouldn't be thought of as a win-or-lose game in which managers and subordinates try to win resources the other will be denied or in which a gain for one will be a defeat for the other. Rather, as experienced negotiators know, satisfying solutions often lie in the "between region" of relationships—solutions that allow each side to win at the same time but would never be considered in a wholly competitive model of dialogue. Grigsby is right to stress that such bargaining is dialogic, even when the perceived power differential is significant.

5. *Closing.* In the final stage, participants acknowledge or ratify the understandings they've reached together and, if appropriate, discuss how and when they will meet again. At this stage, neither interviewer nor interviewee should be unsure of whether the appraisal tone has been positive, negative, or neutral; neither party should be unsure of the next step in this process (will there be a follow-up meeting? allocation of additional resources to assist the employee?); neither party should be unsure about the criteria governing the next evaluation. Because appraisal interviews can involve interpersonal tension if not conflict, the closing stage is an especially important time for reaffirming and supportive messages from the evaluator.

Box 7.5 provides tips for both interviewers and interviewees in appraisal sessions.

BOX 7.5 **REMINDERS**

Conducting Appraisal Interviews

Interviewers

- *Prepare adequately.* Take responsibility for giving the person evaluated a fair hearing. That requires a thorough review of the record, with a focus on individualized performance, not simply on how she or he compares to coworkers. The interview isn't a time to leaf through files, trying to catch up and figure out what's going on. It's time to pay careful attention, not do something that should have been done well before the interview.

- *Set aside assumptions.* You'll have access to a stack of evaluative materials. They represent a piece of a larger picture. The interview involves learning what goes beyond the record. Try to enter the interview with as few assumptions as possible.

- *Listen more, talk less.* As a supervisor, you may talk more than you need to. Consider an appraisal interview from the reverse perspective—as the employee's opportunity to be heard. Guide the interview, but allow time and opportunity for the employee to determine content and direction also. At times you'll need to encourage those who find disclosure difficult. Some research into a construct called **willingness to communicate** (WTC) suggests that many otherwise exceptional workers will rarely decide to volunteer their ideas and feelings openly within organizations (Richmond & Roach, 1992).

- *Reserve judgment.* At first, interviewees may react with defensiveness, anger, resentment, and other spoken or nonverbal expressions that sting interviewers. Don't take it personally, unless you are part of the problem. People need to ventilate. You won't be able to listen and learn if you're caught up in your own emotions.

- *Remember, no one is perfect.* Yes, you may consider Ms. Excel a model employee and wish everyone in your department could be like her. They can't. She isn't perfect either. Give each employee fair, full credit for accomplishments and refrain from comparisons with Ms. Excel.

Interviewees

- *Prepare adequately.* Gather all the documents and evidence ahead of time that can help you be introspective and realistic about your own performance. Don't try to guess what the supervisor will tell you, but familiarize yourself with the materials that may be considered in the interview.

- *Be self-critical.* Try to acknowledge areas that need improvement—do a reality check. Ask colleagues before the interview to help you see yourself more clearly. Enter the interview with an open mind and realistic perspective. It doesn't do any good to delude yourself.

- *Stay calm and controlled.* Prepare for criticism. If you lose your composure, you won't be able to listen and inquire. Keep a clear head, so you'll be able to respond appropriately and well.

- *Comment substantively, not emotionally.* When being evaluated, it's natural to be tense, and undue tension usually clouds judgment. Your goal is to avoid the appearance of defensiveness, but you do have a position you want to represent clearly and assertively. Prepare for possibly unfair adverse judgments with counterevidence—details, examples, records. Demonstrate your point, don't just argue it.

- *Think about goals systematically.* Supervisors may appreciate what you've done, but that was yesterday. What are you going to do tomorrow and beyond? Whether it's requested or not, reflect on what you might do better and ask your supervisor for his or her opinions. When engaged in mutual goal setting, take notes (including relevant quotes) that will help you remember later what the two of you decided. Don't trust your memory when you're in an emotionally involving context.

Intervention Interviews

Occasionally, supervisors find it necessary to take action in order to help others do their jobs more effectively. An employee may become embroiled in an ongoing conflict with another, a personal habit has begun to have negative consequences for customers, or productivity has dropped abruptly for no apparent reason. Perhaps a health problem or other personal emergency has deflected the employee from the kind of concentration the job demands, creating dangerous or disruptive consequences for all concerned. In such situations, responsible supervisors must take action, and the best first step is a series of conversations designed to get information from the employees' perspectives.

An **intervention interview** may be defined as a face-to-face organizational meeting between superior and subordinate for the purpose of understanding or managing a crisis or problem more fully. At one end of the continuum, an intervention interview may be a friendly inquiry; at the other extreme, it may be an occasion for disciplining or terminating the employee.

This discussion is limited to forms of *first-level interventions,* in which supervisors diagnose and begin to address problems that are essentially interpersonal or organizational in nature. More significant actions, *second-level interventions,* are sometimes called for, and everyone in the organization should be aware of them. For example, many organizations have **employee assistance programs** (EAPs) that address serious emotional, medical, or behavioral problems. A trainer who consistently but unexpectedly cancels workshops and conference trips may arouse suspicions of substance abuse. If reasonable inquiries confirm that this is true, a second-order intervention is called for. Usually as part of a benefits package, employees can be referred to EAP-based drug and alcohol awareness training or treatment, psychological counseling, and a variety of other health-related services. Although managers need to be able to communicate responsibly about such programs, and direct employees effectively to them, most supervisors are not personally qualified to act as counselors, social workers, doctors, or specialists in labor-management negotiation. Here, we discuss first-level interpersonal interventions that occur outside the cycle of regularly scheduled performance appraisal.

Performance Problems, Performance Solutions

Performance problems, which include excessive absences, errors, uncooperativeness, broken promises and deadlines, cheating, and overt conflicts, to name only a few, can signal the need for intervention. A decline in performance ought to be demonstrable and sustained, not a temporary slump, before intervention occurs. However, certain single instances, such as a complaint about sexual harassment or a complaint of racial discrimination, are so important that they should be addressed immediately on their own merit. Here the normal procedures of appraisal interviewing are inappropriate, and managers have to become detectives in order to become skilled helpers. Generally, an intervention interview—whether it is with a supposed problem person, a supposed victim, or a supposed observer/third party—accomplishes two things:

- *The intervention interview is a site of inquiry, fueled by curiosity.* That is, the manager seeks to discover what has happened in as much detail as possible. To do this, he or she tries to avoid preframing the situation with personal expectations. (Even though Jake has a history of not getting along with customers, in *this* incident, the customer may in fact be exaggerating and distorting the facts unfairly in the complaint against Jake.) Open questions, frequent perception checks, and behavioral demonstrations of active listening are particularly crucial in encouraging interviewees to elaborate with their own stories. All things being equal, intervention interviewers encourage the fullest possible opportunities for all concerned to give their side of the story. They ask the journalist's questions: who? what? when? where? why? how? what else? The last question—the clearinghouse "what else?"—is particularly crucial.

- *The intervention interview is a site of problem solving, fueled ideally by a spirit of cooperation.* It not only diagnoses and identifies what is wrong, but in it participants proceed to consider what can be done. It is a context potentially fraught with emotion or controversy. A worker may feel she is unfairly blamed, and branded by a double standard, for how she talks and dresses. Although the interviewer might not be directly involved in the original incident, he or she becomes a part of the complex emotions with which the woman thinks about the unpleasant interchange. Asking questions that seem neutral can be interpreted by participants as taking sides, and an attempt to reach a well-intentioned compromise can be perceived as a cop-out, a sellout, or a personal put-down. Consider the example in Box 7.6 for a case of how interventions could take place in volatile interpersonal circumstances. What if Joan comes to you and asks for your opinion about this double standard? What if you are informed that she's filed a grievance for sexual harassment on the basis of being constantly "propositioned"? Are interventions of any sort called for? (See "Making Your Decision," at the end of this chapter, for other questions about Joan's experience.)

Exit Interviews

The term **exit interview** refers to interviews with employees who resign or retire from an organization voluntarily. The goal of this form of interview is to create a sense of closure for the interviewee, to request and obtain valid feedback about the organization, and to facilitate the transition for both worker and organization. Leaving a job isn't an easy step. Though it may be the employee's choice, there still may be confusion, anger, resentment, victimization, or other unresolved feelings.

The employee about to leave an organization can provide a quality of insight rarely obtained from ongoing employees. When good employees quit, it is time to determine reasons, to take stock of the situation (see Box 7.7). What makes other options or other companies more attractive? In a sense, managers conduct exit interviews to "debrief"

BOX 7.6   I N T E R V I E W E E S   I N   A C T I O N

Joan

"I worked in an office where sexual innuendo was commonplace, and I never thought anyone really took it seriously. I mean, you should hear some of the filthy jokes that we passed around. Anyway, my girlfriend Cathy used to say 'Joan, you are *such* a slut' to me after I told a joke, and everyone would laugh. Then the trouble started. Men stared at my legs, my chest, looked longingly into my eyes, that sort of thing. I know I'm attractive, so I didn't pay any attention at first. But then the subtle propositions started, and that's when I got confused. Why me? Was it because I told some dirty jokes? Men do that sort of thing all the time and nobody thinks them bad or easy because of it. But it came to me that Cathy's 'innocent' little statement and all that silly laughter was really just a cover for a reputation that I didn't deserve but was getting anyway. But I learned the lesson too late; during my first appraisal I was informed that my behavior was 'distracting' to other workers. I knew what was meant. I only wish that I had known what was really going on before I was made a victim of it."

Source: Goodall & Phillips, 1984, p. 133

people who are leaving. Let's survey the three basic functions of exit interviews and the kinds of issues and questions that characterize them.

- *Closure.* If you're the interviewer, your expressed interest and your listening style encourage the interviewee to discuss this moment as a turning point defining a time period in his or her life and in the life of the organization. Here are sample topics that can create a sense of closure in exit interviews: What successes did you achieve while you were here? What were the high points? Which were the most important projects? Which people did you most enjoy and profit from meeting or working with? Was anything important left finished? If so, what? How do you propose we continue the work you started here?

  If you're the interviewee, you'll also want to create closure for yourself. If the parting is amicable, ask about such things as how your role was perceived, what organizational advances were made with you in the position you held, and what plan the organization has in mind to fill your role.

- *Feedback.* If you're conducting an exit interview, encourage the interviewee to help you assess the organization as a communication environment. With this information, you could make positive changes that will support others. Here are sample topics to encourage employee feedback in exit interviews: What did you see as the pluses and minuses of this organization from your point of view? Do we do a good job performing our central mission? Rewarding outstanding performance? Ensuring a fair, diverse, and nondiscriminatory workplace? What held you back from doing a better job? Resources? Interpersonal rivalry? Low expectations for your performance? Unreasonably defined job descriptions?

BOX 7.7   **R E M I N D E R S**

Why People Quit

- Limited opportunities for advancement
- Lack of recognition
- Unhappiness with management
- Inadequate salary or benefits

- Boredom with job
- Unfair workplace discrimination or bias
- Interpersonal conflict

As an interviewee, inquire about evaluative feedback that will assist you in your next position(s). What were your particular strengths? Deficiencies? On which dimension did you make your greatest progress during your stay?

- *Transition.* As an interviewer, encourage the interviewee to think about what skills, knowledge, and attitudes learned in this organization can be utilized elsewhere. What will he or she take to the next position? What new skills and practices will be more important there? Does the employee want to keep in touch with people in this organization? All such topics will help even somewhat disgruntled employees experience you, and the organization you represent, as caring and concerned.

As an interviewee, discuss how this experience has prepared you for further skill building, and disclose whatever you're comfortable sharing about future plans. Solicit the reactions of your interviewer.

Termination Interviews

Being told you're out of work is one of life's most deflating and devastating messages. "You're fired," is one blunt way it could be said. These days, you're more likely to be downsized or laid off, but the effect is the same.

Perhaps you could imagine those words coming from Dagwood Bumstead's boss, Mr. Dithers, in the long-running cartoon "Blondie." If the task fell to us, we'd probably find a gentler way to break bad news (or so we'd like to think). But being terminated from a job isn't always a painful, shocking experience. It might be expected, with the employee wondering, "What took them so long?" It might signal a new beginning for someone who can't, for various reasons, admit the job was never a good match.

Dismissing an employee, no matter what the circumstances, ought to be done face-to-face, usually with the immediate supervisor taking responsibility. A dismissal interview may not be pleasant, but it's a necessity for practical, ethical, and legal reasons (see Box 7.8). If there was ever an occasion in which clarity and support were important, this is it. In the termination interview, several interpersonal skills are necessary:

- *Rapport skills.* Difficult messages must be delivered in a context where others have the resources to process them fully and not be devastated by them. Managers who

BOX 7.8   INTERVIEWERS IN ACTION

James Autry (II)

"No one ever believes he or she is justly fired. There must be some sort of immune system that protects us from facing the reality of our own failures.

". . . I want people I've fired to know why and to decide for themselves what might have been done. I want them to learn what to do next time. And I want them to realize that they still have a future, and they will grow enormously in embracing that future.

"But I don't expect ever to convince anyone of that, and when indeed a person I've fired does learn and grow and make a better life, I don't expect to be thanked.

"Nevertheless, I have the satisfaction of knowing that only one or two people did not go on to better things after I fired them. The rest of them have done well.

"The nagging question, of course, is if they've done well somewhere else, why didn't they do well for me?

"It's a question that can keep me awake nights."

Source: Autry, 1991, p. 207

must terminate employees are wise to discuss the circumstances that made the decision advisable or necessary, and to discuss such conditions in light of the relationship between the two people. Here is one way to start: "Marva, a number of us have had a long and productive relationship in this department, with almost no turnover. We've had good times and bad. The past six months, maybe you'll agree, haven't been pleasant—at least since our budget was cut. . . ." Remember that rapport is not a *product* that people have but a *process* of constantly attended-to mutual interest in each other.

- *Statement skills.* Avoid ambiguity as much as possible. After introducing the topic, stay away from euphemisms (words or labels with which we attempt to put a more attractive spin on negative things). Stay away from indirect messages that can easily be misinterpreted, such as, "Bottom Line Products has struggled recently to solidify our acceptance in department stores, and your department has had a particularly tough time. We think a change would be better for all concerned." A nervous employee might think at first, "Whew. I thought she was going to fire me. I've wanted changes in this unit for years, myself." Subsequent clarification will be embarrassing for both parties. A clearer, cleaner message, though still tactful, would be, "Although this is difficult, I need to tell you, Jane, that Friday has to be your last day at Bottom Line Products. I wish we could extend you until after Christmas, but the budget base just isn't there."

If the termination is tied to substandard job performance, you are doing no one a favor by disguising that fact: "We have decided to hire a marketing director who is more activist, more research oriented, and more connected with the way store managers make their decisions." In addition, termination interviews need a balanced, both-sides approach. If negative factors make the termination necessary, this is also a good time to outline clearly the positive contributions made by the employee.

- *Facilitation skills.* Terminations evoke strong emotions. Through the invitational nature of your verbal and nonverbal messages, interviewees should find it possible to ventilate emotions and to discuss what this action means to them. They might want to express the frustration they feel, the perceived unfairness, the anger, or perhaps the unexpected exhilaration of newfound freedom. Consider using silence productively; after you express whatever regret or other genuine feelings you are experiencing, you need not fill the air with apologies, expressions of sadness, surface compliments, or reassurances you can't back up. Most recipients of emotionally charged news simply need a little time and space to process what it means for them.

- *Clarification skills.* The next steps to be taken by the employee and the employer should be clear at the end of the interview. What should the employee do between now and Friday? How will the e-mail account be handled? Is there severance pay? Outplacement benefits? Many organizations in corporate life provide a wide range of services for downsized (talk about euphemisms!) and other terminated employees, including job search seminars, resume assistance, and access to phones and e-mail accounts for specified time periods. As the interviewer, tell interviewees about all benefits. Make sure they know what kind of help they might expect from you personally; some supervisors actively help employees look for new opportunities. Often, terminated employees are unclear about what kind of recommendation they can expect on the basis of the current employment. After all, if they're fired, how good can they be in the organization's eyes? If appropriate, clarify for employees what kinds of helpful and positive commentary on their performance the organization could provide for future employers.

✤ BEYOND THE BASICS

Organizational interviews typically focus on encounters in which people's reputations and prestige, if not their egos, are directly affected. What one person wants can be perceived as directly opposed to what another thinks is best; yet not only must they work together somehow toward a common goal, but person A is often charged with evaluating the performance and contributions of person B, as we've seen.

Dialogical approaches to organizational life, such as MIT's dialogue project (see Isaacs, 1993, 1997; Senge, 1990), presume that a wide variety of conflicts can not only be absorbed effectively within healthy organizational life but also are, in fact, essential for its continued vitality. As William Isaacs (1997) observes, "Dialogue is a way by which better inquiry, better confrontation and clarification of thinking can come out" (p. 7). Dialogue presumes that we must take each other into account as fully as possible, that we must address ourselves to the uniquely different persons we encounter rather than to some label or stereotype, that collaboration and even conflict can produce outcomes none of us could enact separately, that genuinely open listening helps create more genuine speech, and that human life is ultimately founded on trust.

Conflict in Organizational Interviewing

Janice Hocker and William Wilmot (1991) define conflict from a communication perspective as "an expressed struggle between at least two interdependent parties who perceive incompatible goals, scarce resources, and interference from the other party in achieving their goals" (p. 12). Several things about the definition are interesting for the purposes of studying interviewing behavior. First, conflict is expressed somehow. People may feel resistance or dislike for each other, but it becomes conflict as it is reflected in their message behaviors. We are in conflict, in other words, when we act like it, and when we communicate in a certain way. You could say, then, that conflict is always to a certain extent *shared,* as communication is shared, transactionally.

Second, conflict is based upon perception. If interviewers and interviewees believe they are in conflict, and act as if they are, they *are.* It isn't reasonable for a third party to waltz in and glibly say, "You two aren't really in conflict; you agree on many issues." Rather, they are engaging in conflict by virtue of how they are communicating. The third party may justifiably believe they shouldn't be in conflict, or that they don't adequately perceive a common ground that is possible, or that they are overlooking a potential for agreement. Nevertheless, the conflict is real to the participants.

Third, perceptions change, often as a result of communication. Thus people in conflict may become less antagonistic, or more so. Communication does not automatically resolve conflicts, as some optimists might like to presume. But better communication could well supply the information upon which a thicker, denser conflict might be built. Communication, and therefore dialogue, does not solve problems nearly as efficiently as it helps to frame them, shape them, and define them. For example, an interviewer is living in a fantasy world if she believes that her subordinates would shape up if they would only allow themselves to understand her communication style. In fact, they may already dislike the interviewer's goals and perceived interference because they understand the style in question very well.

Fourth, not all conflict is bad. At times it can energize groups, organizations, and cultural groups and help them construct new possibilities for themselves. Conflict challenges us to examine assumptions and reevaluate strategies. The appraisal interviewer who too readily perceives "being a team player" or "acting like a good company citizen" as positives to be rewarded may be undercutting the vitality of the organization. Instead, the troublemaker or gadfly, who nevertheless works hard and values the life of the group, may be a radically effective employee who deserves recognition, not suspicion.

Yet, despite the fact that some outcomes of conflict have value, interviewers and interviewees are confronted daily with forms of conflict that are unproductive. Consider a

BOX 7.9   REMINDERS

Anger in the Workplace

"Going postal" has replaced "going ballistic" as a way of describing someone whose anger crosses over into violence. The expression refers to a series of violent acts committed by employees of the U.S. Postal Service a few years ago. But anger and violence can be found in insurance offices, banks, advertising agencies, factories, and any other place people work. Sometimes, in fact, people arrive at their jobs already angry, ready for a slight nudge to send them hurtling into unproductive conflict.

Seth Allcorn offers advice for those consumed by anger, and advice for those trying to deal with the anger of others in organizational interviews of all types. When angry (as an interviewee in an appraisal or intervention interview, for example), Allcorn suggests these steps (p. 47):

• Do not put off communicating anger for long periods.

• Think through what you want to say.

• Do not withdraw into silence.

• Avoid using strong words; do not accuse or attack.

• Be open to criticism.

• Keep focused on the problem.

• Look for a solution.

Of course, anger distorts perceptions and undermines reasoning. Following Allcorn's advice when you are angry might be difficult. It should be easier, however, for someone facing an angry person to follow these steps (p. 56):

• Do not be defensive.

• Sit back and listen.

• Sift and sort, separating facts from feelings and fantasies.

• Directly discuss the anger.

• Discover your role in the anger.

• Do not accept blame for the anger in others, even if you did provoke it.

• Remember, anger isn't bad, and it may be necessary for growth, development and improved relations.

• Help the person focus on solutions rather than merely ventilating.

Source: Allcorn, 1994

foreperson on the assembly line who curses new employees before they have a chance to learn their routines. Consider conflict that arises from a male vice president's persistent put-downs of women's capabilities. Conflict that results in polarization, conflict that results in ritualized competition, conflict that results in increased dehumanization and violent inclinations toward the other side—all these define conditions in which managing conflict is desirable. In fact, the conflict experts suggest (Grove, 1991; Hocker & Wilmot, 1991), much of the time it's better to manage conflict rather than to seek to resolve it. Use it, understand it, deal with its assumptions, keep it from escalating into hate or distrust, but don't banish it (see Box 7.9).

Trust and Defensiveness

Organizational interviewers who know how to use conflict effectively realize its relationship to trust. Years ago, group and organizational theorist Jack Gibb (1961) synthesized much of what researchers knew about trust into a typology of what he called defensive and supportive climates. To him, defensiveness developed (as in employees) in relatively threatening communication situations, just as the likelihood of feeling supported and understood grew in an essentially different climate. Within Gibb's typology is a wealth of advice for interviewers and managers. **Defensive climates** are those that emphasize:

- *Evaluation* (the assumption that attaching value is, and needs to be, common)
- *Control* (the assumption that people are basically untrustworthy and need to be told how to act)
- *Strategy* (the assumption that persons in social situations need to plan carefully how to persuade and dominate others)
- *Neutrality* (the assumption that leaders, for example, need to be essentially uninvolved and dispassionate in order to be objective)
- *Superiority* (the assumption that leaders can act as if they are better persons than the persons they "lead")
- *Certainty* (the assumption that leaders must be decisive, sure of their decisions, and unbending in implementing policies)

To Gibb, these climates of organizational and group life were certain to create conflict because they were built on mistrust. A supervisor who counted on these characteristics to inform a managerial philosophy could be assured of a series of confrontational encounters in interviewing employees, even though many employees would simply acquiesce to the demands of the situation by resigning, by leveling their productivity, or by withholding the kind of vital energy it takes to build a cooperative organization. When workers communicate defensively, they communicate unproductively.

Gibb had studied other organizations that were more successful, though. Many of them had facilitated climates relying on completely different communication assumptions. **Supportive climates** are those in which people tend to feel secure enough to communicate honest reactions more directly; they do not feel the need to defend themselves either from attack or someone's disinterest. In his typology, Gibb created direct contrasts for purposes of illustration and diagnosis:

- Instead of *evaluation,* substitute the supportive climate of *description* (the assumption that a thorough emphasis on careful noting of behaviors and reactions is more helpful, and less threatening, than judging people constantly)
- Instead of *control,* substitute the supportive climate of *problem orientation* (the assumption that a collaborative approach to problem solving and goal setting yields greater job satisfaction and better results)
- Instead of *strategy,* substitute the supportive climate of *spontaneity* (the assumption that group members appreciate leaders who can be immediately "present" in the situation, without facades or game playing)
- Instead of *neutrality,* substitute the supportive climate of *empathy* (the assumption that leaders do not have to be uninvolved in the organizational lives of group members, but can attempt to immerse themselves in the world as others experience it)

- Instead of *superiority,* substitute the supportive climate of *equality* (the assumption that, as people, leaders are no better and no worse than other group members—even though their achievements merit respect)

- Instead of *certainty,* substitute the supportive climate of *provisionalism* (the assumption that anyone's solutions are open to question and can be changed)

Note how well Gibb's supportive climate categories contribute to the kind of dialogue described earlier. Although he understands that such concepts as neutrality and evaluation may at times be inevitable and serve valid purposes (we cannot eliminate evaluation from an appraisal interviewing process, for example), they do not need to be emphasized unduly in interviewing. One review of relevant research reports that criticism by appraisal interviewers "resulted in greater defensiveness, more negative attitudes toward appraisals and less improvement in subordinate performance." Yet when that criticism "was revised into goals, subordinates' performance improved" and, with more coparticipation in goal setting, defensiveness diminished (Krayer, 1987, p. 277).

When we stress in this book that interviewing can be a dialogue, we do not mean that it is without roles or status, or that it should happen without planning. Roles are inevitable and preparation is vital. We merely suggest that a higher quality of interaction develops when the trust of supportive dialogue links communicators, even in conflict. With that quality of interaction comes better information and insight for interviewers and interviewees.

Summary

In the working world, much of the quality of your life is defined by your professional experience in organizations. Careful attention to listening, questioning, and framing practices in organizational interviewing can improve that quality of life significantly, because through interviews you begin to process the feedback you need in order to improve.

After a brief discussion of recent trends in organizational learning, we describe the mechanics and dynamics of appraisal interviewing in detail. Building on that base, we extend the same philosophy to intervention interviews, exit interviews, and termination interviews. Finally, "Beyond the Basics" takes a deeper look at the communicative aspects of conflict and how conflict can be managed effectively if interviewers and interviewees are aware of the influence of supportive and nondefensive conversational climates.

The Interview Bookshelf

On the organizational context surrounding interviewers and interviewees

Eisenberg, E. M., & Goodall, H. L., Jr. (1997). *Organizational communication: Balancing creativity and constraint* (2nd ed.). New York: St. Martin's Press.

A comprehensive description of the contemporary complex organization, with special attention to how organizations are changing to become more dialogic and culturally sensitive.

Trying Out Your Skills

- After reading the following intervention interview excerpt, list what you believe to be problems in the communication choices made by the interviewer. Be specific; what would you say and do differently?

- If you were the interviewee, would you take a more assertive stance? A less assertive stance?

- What roles do the following play in this conversation: empathy, conflict management and anger in the workplace, defensive/supportive climates, appraisal methods, problem-solving attitudes, and dialogue.

INTERVIEWER: You know, this place wasn't always this much fun. Used to be that we didn't coddle employees the way we do now. Did you realize that?

INTERVIEWEE: Since I only started last year, Sir, I wasn't aware of what happened before that.

INTERVIEWER: Well, it's true. It seems to me that there's no discipline any more among workers, no self-pride in doing good work. No sense of pride in the company. It's discouraging. How many times have I had you in here to talk to you about making all your private phone calls during the business day? Lots. Everybody's doing this behind my back, thinking I don't know what's going on. But I do. I really do.

INTERVIEWEE: I wasn't sure what this was about. It's about taking phone calls? This is the second time you've mentioned it to me. But it's the first time you've called me into your office. I'm really sorry. When I started working here, my little girl was sick. Remember? And she or the baby-sitter wound up calling me several times every

day. You even let me take some time off. I just kind of thought it was OK then, and if it was OK then, using the phone might still be . . . er . . . acceptable if . . .

INTERVIEWER: That's what I mean. "I just kind of thought." "I just kind of thought." Businesses don't work that way, Miriam. I'm telling you now, I want it to stop. And if it doesn't, we'll have to find someone else who can give us their full attention.

INTERVIEWEE: So I'm not supposed to call anyone at work . . . I know that.

INTERVIEWER: Right. No calls.

INTERVIEWEE: I'm sorry. I'm confused. It's not clear about taking calls. What should I do if someone calls me, like in an emergency or something? I need my job. I'm scared to lose it and don't want to. I shouldn't take any calls any more?

INTERVIEWER: Miriam, I'm going to say this one more time. No calls. Which word isn't clear? "No" or "calls"? *No* calls.

INTERVIEWEE: Even in an emergency? I've got three kids.

INTERVIEWER: Would you please get back to work?

INTERVIEWEE: Yeah. Will this go in my file?

INTERVIEWER: Will what go in your file?

INTERVIEWEE: Are you going to write me up in a report? Because if you do, I'd like you to know that you haven't called me in here several times about the phone calls, or whatever you thought. Maybe it was somebody else.

INTERVIEWER: Just get to work. I'll deal with this later. . . .

- An employee you have just had to terminate comes to you and asks for advice on how to take negative feedback, thinking this will be useful in her next job. In fact, you did believe she reacted somewhat defensively over the past three or four performance appraisals. Based upon your general understanding of the feedback process, and your understanding of how and why people become defensive when being evaluated, create a list of specific recommendations for how an interviewee should listen and respond to negative feedback. Be sure to include suggestions on what to do if the feedback seems undeserved, unnecessarily abusive, or otherwise off the mark.

- Your superior, the managing editor of the newspaper at which you work as a reporter, has just finished an appraisal interview with you in which she said you have no problems whatsoever. She's pleased with your initiative, your stories, and your pleasant personality around the office. The interview appears to be finished after only five or six minutes. However, you know that you both marked off thirty minutes for the meeting, and you'd like to know more details. What questions or approaches would you use to "interview the interviewer?" Devise a rough schedule of things about which you'd like to get more detailed feedback and perhaps discover some less-than-positive reactions to your work.

- "Joan" (see Box 7.6) approaches you and asks you to talk with the men in her department about what constitutes sexual harassment. She is tired of the treatment she's getting from them. It's clear to you that all claims of sexual harassment need to be taken seriously. However, beyond that sincere concern: (1) What details of her department's situation would you want to get from Joan, so you can assess the depth of the difficulty she's experiencing? (2) Where would you find good definitions and discussions of this issue, assuming your organization has drafted no formal sexual harassment policy? (3) What do you tell her about your plans? Will you schedule interviews with each man? (4) Would you set a time frame within which you'll get back to her with your findings?

On the demands of performance appraisals

Bruce, W. M., & Blackburn, J. W. (1992). *Balancing job satisfaction and performance*. Westport, CT: Quorum Books.

Leeds, D. (1987). *Smart questions: A new strategy for successful managers*. New York: Berkley Books.

These two practical accounts deemphasize theory while still placing organizational interviews in a coherent framework. Consult these books for a variety of excellent examples.

On the dilemmas of a CEO who must balance humane caring with productivity

Autry, J. A. (1994). *Life & work: A manager's search for meaning*. New York: William Morrow.

Autry is a storyteller, whether he is illustrating a point with an anecdote or a poem (he's a published poet who has been profiled by Bill Moyers on PBS). His stories show a variety of ways to be successful in organizations by emphasizing communication. "The companies," he writes, "that concentrate on the relationships are the ones most likely to achieve quality in everything they do" (p. 50).

References

Allcorn, S. (1994). *Anger in the workplace.* Westport, CT: Quorum.

Argyris, C. (1960). *Understanding organizational behavior.* Homewood, IL: Dorsey Press.

Autry, J. A. (1991). *Love and profit: The art of caring leadership.* New York: Avon.

Autry, J. A. (1994). *Life and work: A manager's search for meaning.* New York: William Morrow.

Bennis, W. (1985). Foreword. In D. McGregor, *The human side of enterprise* (25th anniversary printing, pp. iv–viii). New York: McGraw-Hill.

Bruce, W. M., & Blackburn, J. W. (1992). *Balancing job satisfaction and performance.* Westport, CT: Quorum Books.

Champy, J. A. (1997). Preparing the organization for change. In F. Hesselbein, M. Goldsmith, & R. Beckhard, (Eds.), *The organization of the future.* San Francisco: Jossey-Bass.

Clark, R. P., & Fry, D. (1992). *Coaching writers.* New York: St. Martin's Press.

Cohen, B. R., & Greenfield, J. (1997). *Ben & Jerry's double-dip.* New York: Simon & Schuster.

Deming, W. E. (1988). *Out of the crisis: Quality, productivity, and competitive position.* Cambridge, MA: Massachusetts Institute of Technology Press.

Eisenberg, E. M., & Goodall, H. L., Jr. (1997). *Organizational communication: Balancing creativity and constraint* (2nd ed.). New York: St. Martin's Press.

Gibb, J. (1961). Defensive communication. *The Journal of Communication, 11* (3), 141–148.

Goodale, J. G. (1982). *The fine art of interviewing.* Englewood Cliffs, NJ: Prentice-Hall.

Goodall, H. L., Jr., & Phillips, G. M. (1984). *Making it in any organization.* Englewood Cliffs, NJ: Prentice-Hall.

Goodman, M. B. (Ed.). (1994). *Corporate communication: Theory and practice.* Albany, NY: State University of New York Press.

Grigsby, (1983).

Grove, T. G. (1991). *Dyadic interaction: Choice and change in conversations and relationships.* Dubuque, IA: W. C. Brown.

Half, R. (1993). *Finding, hiring, and keeping the best employees.* New York: John Wiley & Sons.

Hesselbein, F., Goldsmith, M., & Beckhard, R. (Eds.). (1997). *The organization of the future.* San Francisco: Jossey-Bass.

Hocker, J. L., & Wilmot, W. W. (1991). *Interpersonal conflict* (3rd ed.). Dubuque, IA: W. C. Brown.

Isaacs, W. (1993). Taking flight: Dialogue, collaborative thinking, and organizational learning. *Organizational Dynamics,*

Isaacs, W. (1997, August). Restoration of common sense: An interview with William Isaacs. *Executive Excellence,* p. 7.

Krayer, K. J. (1987). Simulation methods for teaching the performance appraisal interview. *Communication Education, 36,* 276–283.

Leeds, D. (1987). *Smart questions: A new strategy for successful managers.* New York: Berkley Books.

Lobdell, C. L., Sonoda, K. T., & Arnold, W. E. (1993). The influence of perceived supervisor listening behavior on employee commitment. *Journal of the International Listening Association, 7,* 92–110.

McGregor, D. (1960). *The human side of enterprise.* New York: McGraw-Hill.

Morin, W. J., & Yorks, L. (1990). *Dismissal.* New York: Drake Beam Morin.

Nelson, B. (1997). *1001 ways to energize employees.* New York: Workman.

Richmond, V. P., & Roach, K. D. (1992). Willingness to communicate and employee success in U.S. organizations. *Journal of Applied Communication Research, 20,* 95–115.

Rogers, C. R. (1961). *On becoming a person.* Boston: Houghton-Mifflin.

Senge, P. (1990). *The fifth discipline: The art and practice of the learning organization.* New York: Doubleday.

Shotter, J. (1993). *Conversational realities: Constructing life through language.* London: Sage.

Skopec, E. W. (1990). *Communicate for success.* Reading, MA: Addison-Wesley.

Swan, W., with Phillip Margulies. (1991). *How to do a superior performance appraisal.* New York: Wiley.

Waldroop, J., & Butler, T. (November/December, 1996). The executive as coach. *Harvard Business Review,* pp. 111–117.

Weiss, D. H. (1995). *Fair, square & legal.* New York: Amacom.

Whitney, M. A. (1994). Analyzing corporate communications policy using ethnographic methods. In M. B. Goodman (Ed.), *Corporate communication* (pp. 185–197). Albany, NY: State University of New York Press.

✿ 8 Interviews in Journalism

It is possible, of course, for reporters to overdo their reliance on interviews—to believe that unless something is said during an interview it isn't real. . . . Still, "interviewing" in the broadest sense involves a reporter's immersion in new information that will shape his views. Through the process of listening, learning, testing assumptions, and letting themselves be surprised by new evidence, reporters decide what they think is true enough to write.

—James Fallows, *Breaking the News*

LEARNING GOALS

After reading this chapter, you should be able to

- Compare and contrast traditional images and methods of interviewing with emerging concepts of the journalistic interview as a form of discovery through dialogue
- Recognize the differences among various types of journalistic interviews
- Understand the facets of interviews in journalism, from purpose to postinterview assessment
- Explain the different types of record keeping by reporters
- Discuss the ethical concerns journalists and their interviewees face in interviews

A few years ago, baseball Hall of Fame legend Willie Mays went to Clearwater, Florida, mainly to sign autographs at $10 apiece. By early afternoon he'd obliged more than 1,000 fans. Afterward, he agreed to an interview with several local news reporters. By most accounts, it didn't go well.

Mays declined to answer many questions, saying, "I will not talk about anything controversial." He insisted that four witnesses stay in the interview room. Then a reporter asked a seemingly innocuous question about Mays's illustrious career: Any regrets? "Regrets? What do you mean?" Mays snapped. "That was my life for twenty-two years. All I wanted to do was play baseball. I loved it. How can I play for twenty-two years and regret the things I do?"

Mays bristled when another reporter asked him whether a rookie ballplayer looked like "the next" Willie Mays. "I don't understand why (the media) starts calling somebody 'the next Willie Mays' when he has only been in the major leagues for a few months. There have been four guys in the last four years you guys have been calling 'the next Willie Mays.'"

"How about comparing today's ballplayers with those of your era?" a reporter asked. "That would be talking against people, and I don't do that," Mays said.

Evidently Mays was dissatisfied, as were the reporters. What, if anything, went wrong? The Mays episode is not typical of what happens in news interviews, but even first-time interviewees frequently gird themselves against a reporter, fearing the encounter will be unpleasant. People's impressions of the news interview often are influenced and skewed by Hollywood stereotypes and limited experience, such as watching a movie like *The Paper* or observing Leslie Stahl at work on "60 Minutes."

Some reporters act aggressively in interviews because they tend to frame their work as a quest for hard-won truth—a fact-finding mission in the name of the public's right to know. At times, reporters cloak themselves in the First Amendment, unrealistically concluding that everyone owes them an answer because they're doing democracy's work. The reporters try mightily to carry out an important, honorable role. Their interviewees maintain a wary guard, mindful of how some reporters might appear: nosy, rude, and arrogant. Not surprisingly, when neither side expects a comfortable, productive experience, the results can be a self-fulfilling prophecy.

Some news interviews may indeed be adversarial, with both sides contributing to an unprofitable outcome. But most journalistic interviews go well. Given the predispositions of both sides, the challenge is often for journalists and news sources to work together, even in hard-news situations. In "The Basics," we discuss the traditional view of journalistic interviewing and compare it with recent forms. We'll present an inventory of interview types that will help you understand how news is made by interviewing. In the last section of "The Basics," you'll learn about the fundamentals of news-related interviewing, insights that can be applied to a wide variety of information-gathering tasks expected of nonjournalists as well.

"Beyond the Basics" focuses on the complicated ethics of journalistic interviews, concluding with an overview of the satisfactions of doing journalism well.

✿ THE BASICS

Tradition and the News Interview

The interview has served as a basic tool of journalists since the early 1860s. News, after all, is shaped by the words of legislators, judges, police chiefs, celebrities, athletes, and all others deemed newsmakers. In journalism, the adage that actions speak louder than words should be rethought; reporters and editors know that words *are* deeds. Michael Schudson (1994) describes the remarkable influence of the news interview when he writes

> The interview is the fundamental act of contemporary journalism. Reporters rely overwhelmingly on interviews; according to a study of Washington reporters in the 1980s, journalists depend so heavily on interviews that they use no documents at all in nearly three-quarters of the stories they write. (p. 565)

Journalists use interviewing to satisfy the imperative of the news story: answering the who, what, when, where, why, and how of events and issues. Journalists deal in attributed facts, and interviews provide attribution. The interview also goes beyond the facts, drawing emotions, opinions, and speculation from news sources, often in their own words. These revelations form the essence of news.

The traditional formula of the news interview puts journalists in control. The reporter asks questions, and someone the journalists call a news "source" responds. The interview appears to belong to the reporter; the interviewee is expected to provide what the journalist needs. In its bare-bones form, the news interview is economical, expedient, and valuable; it can also, given this formula, be impersonal, manipulative, and unproductive.

Many journalists learn interviewing on the job and, if graduates of a journalism school, through their teachers and textbooks. In either case, journalists' knowledge of interviewing typically rests on anecdotes, folklore, and trial and error. Rarely are they aware of the research and theory of interviewing.

Many journalists also assume interviewing comes naturally, and for some, it does seem natural. But even those with an instinctive talent for interviewing are exposed to questionable advice in some newsrooms and classrooms. Here is an example from a leading textbook for reporting students: "When you have to ask tough questions, blame someone else." That kind of tactic isn't going to go over well with most people, who will readily recognize it as a ploy. It suggests that the reporter is playing games and not being forthright; it reinforces stereotypes. Journalists have enough troubles with reputation as it is.

Writer Janet Malcolm (1989), in a controversial observation that polarized the community of journalists, helped reinforce that reputation: "Every journalist who is not too stupid or too full of himself to notice what is going on knows that what he does is morally indefensible. He is a kind of confidence man, preying on people's vanity, ignorance, or loneliness, gaining their trust and betraying them without remorse" (p. 38). Malcolm exaggerated, intentionally perhaps, in making a point that reporters will go to extremes for a story, because the story—their story—is of paramount importance. The *Washington Post's* Bob Woodward, an icon of investigative journalism for exposing President Nixon's role in the Watergate scandal, fits Malcolm's description, his critics say (Anson, 1996). One of them, Judy Belushi, widow of comedian John Belushi, claims Woodward betrayed her in writing the book *Wired,* a devastating account of her husband's drug and alcohol abuse. "[Woodward] seemed so honest," she said. "He would say, over and over, 'John was a wonderful man. We must tell his story.'" Expecting a warm portrait, Judy Belushi helped open celebrity doors for Woodward. "I was like a Pavlovian dog," she said (p. 136). For another story, Woodward allegedly told colleagues how he would get the girlfriend of Washington, D.C., Mayor Marion Barry to cooperate: "I'll play with her kid," he said. His colleagues said he did just that, and the mother, charmed, opened up to him.

The criticism of Woodward might ring true to a public accustomed to stereotypes. In fairness to Woodward and all journalists, one-sided criticisms like these often come from disgruntled celebrities or politicians with ulterior motives. Talking to children and building rapport aren't inherently bad methods of interviewing. Journalism, however, suffers from an image of manipulation. Reporters are often driven by an overarching commitment to get to the truth, to tell the story. How far a journalist should go for a story remains a subject of sharp disagreement within the profession. A larger question, however, hasn't been as thoroughly addressed: Is there a way to get the story and do it by collaborating with, not exploiting, interviewees?

The News Interview Revisited

Increasingly, the take-charge, pump-'em-with-questions style of interviewing is yielding to the interview-as-conversation, an approach fine-tuned by veteran writers such as Studs Terkel and Charles Kuralt. "I realized quite early in this adventure," Terkel (1970) said, "that interviews, conventionally conducted, were meaningless. . . . The question-and-answer technique may be of value in determining favored detergents, toothpaste, and deodorants, but not in the discovery of men and women. It was simply a case of making conversation. And listening" (p. 21). Kuralt's (1985) vivid and multifaceted portraits of ordinary people in everyday places developed in a similar way. "I have tried to go slow, stick to the back roads, take time to meet people, listen to yarns," Kuralt said, describing how he found his "On the Road" reports. Both journalists acknowledge their work does not involve deadline stories of crime, disasters, and political intrigue. Kuralt once joked, "If I come upon a real news story, I call some real reporters to come cover it" (p. 14). Kuralt and Terkel know that not all interviews lend themselves to informal conversational styles. But Kuralt's and Terkel's respect for people and willingness to hear them out apply in nearly all news interviews.

Veteran editor and writer James Fallows (1996) sees interviewing as a conscientious, thorough trip of discovery, not a systematic regimen of questions and answers. "Through the process of listening, learning, testing assumptions, and letting themselves be surprised by new evidence, reporters decide what they think is true enough to write," he said (p. 58). And ". . . [you] must sometimes ask questions whose answers you think you know, so as to confirm what you have heard and to compare answers from several sources. But the main working of reporting involves asking questions whose answers you don't know, simultaneously exposing your ignorance but opening up the possibility of learning something new" (p. 143).

Fallows, Kuralt, and Terkel understand that news doesn't grow on trees, ready for plucking. Often the stuff of news emerges from the dialogue between two people. News, then, becomes a cocreation of journalists and those they interview. The quality of the story often depends on how well the two communicate. Complete openness is an unrealistic goal, even if it were possible. However, if trust, candor, and other qualities of open talk are missing, the interview probably won't achieve much depth, texture, or insight. The reporter will come away with a story, but not one that has reached its fullest potential.

Reporters who communicate effectively with interviewees often practice empathy, which we discussed in Chapter 3 and elsewhere as the ability to imagine another person's perspective on the world while recognizing that such educated guesswork can never be completely accurate. Empathy in an interview requires journalists to take seriously the other person's feelings, values, goals, and points of view. Journalist and writing instructor Don Murray (1988) has seen empathy work well for interviews. "If we can get out of ourselves and enter into the lives of those we interview then we may ask perceptive questions and may receive perceptive answers" (p. 2). To empathize is not to agree, nor is it an emotionless neutrality. Empathy in a news interview rests on the reporter's willingness not to be limited by his or her own experience. Genuine empathy is usually evident to the interviewee and can overcome reluctance to talk candidly. Without empathy, news interviewees might assume the worst—the reporter is either uncaring or out for personal gain.

Reconsider the Willie Mays episode—an interview seemingly gone awry—with empathy in mind. Was Mays's request to stay away from controversial issues unreasonable? Was Mays merely protecting his image? Did the reporter, reacting to the ballplayer's "attitude," decide to show him who's boss? Was Mays's "attitude" the by-product of unhappy encounters with other reporters who put their story ahead of his? Is it possible that relatively few reporters have taken the time and effort to understand Mays as he understands himself?

No one is required to give an interview, even public servants. Most people, though, readily cooperate with journalists, at least until they get burned. Those interviewed for a news story put themselves in a vulnerable position when they allow a journalist to quote, paraphrase, or explain their views. If the journalist makes them look stupid, evasive, calculating, insensitive, careless, rude, or any one of a hundred misrepresentations that will be read, heard, or viewed by thousands of others, it is experienced as a betrayal. The betrayal rarely is calculated; more likely it will be the result of the reporter's inability or unwillingness to understand what is at stake for the interviewee. It's a betrayal that extends beyond the consequences for the interviewee; it's a betrayal of the fundamental responsibility of journalists to get the story right.

Interviews based on empathy and a listen-to-learn attitude seem more productive than the old model of treating an interviewee as a means to an end (see Box 8.1). Journalists depend on people for the news; they can't do the job well without the help of others.

Types of News Interviews

Journalists specialize in information-gathering interviews, and the tasks they face are shared by all other interviewers who care about learning new and interesting insights. Even if you do not plan a career as a reporter or editor, and even if you hope never to make "Hard Copy" with your fifteen minutes of fame, you'll be interviewing like a journalist whenever you are verifying information on your company's policies with the vice president

BOX 8.1　　　INTERVIEWERS IN ACTION

William Blundell

W illiam Blundell, author and feature writer for the *Wall Street Journal,* describes the difference between treating the interviewee as a human being as opposed to a "lemon we are trying to squeeze dry in as few minutes as possible":

"I know reporters who are chronically nagged by their failure to get good quotes. The people in their stories appear wary, blandly cautious in their statements, unwilling to show themselves. I suspect they're reacting to a quick squeeze by the reporter, who is conducting his interviews as cold, businesslike transactions when they should be conversations."

Source: Blundell, 1988, p. 90

for human relations or gathering the facts necessary for a brief article in your organization's newsletter. You're a news person in many ways if others in your organization treat you as an opinion leader. Virtually any leadership role can be enhanced by the skills and appreciations of journalistic discovery.

However, we will focus here on how career journalists and their sources conduct interviews. News interviews might last only a few minutes; in fact, many of them do. A few may extend over a period of days. Although certain interviews are routine, all are potentially important in providing a context for news. Each type of interview serves a particular function, helping reporters verify facts, reconstruct events, gather quotable reactions, probe feelings, and clarify ambiguity.

In the course of doing a story, a reporter might employ a variety of interviewing methods, each with different advantages and limitations. News interviews don't fit into neat categories. Here, though, we discuss eight relatively discrete types that reflect the variety of news-gathering techniques journalists regularly employ and the situations in which they're used.

Screening/Verification Interviews

A reporter's daily work includes collecting hundreds of bits of information, most of which never go on the air or into print. Sometimes it's a quick telephone call to confirm a fact, such as the date of a meeting or the school district's enrollment figures. A more involved inquiry might be needed to get a city official to explain arcane language in a proposed ordinance.

Reporters conduct numerous mini-interviews in the course of a day, trying to track down someone who can provide useful, reliable information for a story, and who is willing to talk for publication or broadcast. Other quick-hitting inquiries by reporters help determine whether a tip deserves consideration as a news or feature item. The fate of hundreds of potential stories rests on snap decisions by journalists exercising news judgment. A farmer might phone to say he's grown the largest pumpkin in Crawford County, but a few questions by the reporter who takes the call determines that another farmer set the record weight a year ago; a potential human-interest story doesn't pan out. The same reporter, with adroit questioning of a woman distraught about her mother's death from a "routine" gallbladder surgery, detects the makings of a compelling story.

These are not necessarily exhaustive, carefully planned interviews, but they are important in getting to the heart of the news, leading perhaps to more substantive interviews at later stages of developing stories. They put a premium on spontaneous talk that opens out into significant disclosure.

Background Interviews

Some stories require reporters to take a crash course on a special topic. Reporters are assigned to cover conferences, business transactions, legal cases, scientific developments, and public policy issues without necessarily having any expertise in these subjects. It's imperative that they ask enough questions for basic understanding of a subject before they translate a complex matter for the public. This is a frustrating fact of life for reporters. Few like going into a story cold, and in practice, news editors try to assign the best prepared, most knowledgeable reporter to the story.

The background interview exposes a common deficiency among journalists: They can't be specialists on every story they cover. However, they can act as intelligent translators for experts and can help them share what they know with a general audience. The right questions put to a professor who is an expert on federal taxation can help a local reporter understand and report on a subject of interest to thousands of people in the community, even though the expert's name never gets publicized.

News Gathering Interviews

The term *news gathering*—although widely used in journalism—is curiously misleading. News is not so much what journalists find and "gather" but more often what they help to shape and even create through their communication skills. News is a complex phenomenon in which journalism plays a formative role. But instead of coining an entirely new term, we will simply redefine the existing one. By *news gathering,* we mean the attempt to discover facts and create opportunities for the expression of opinions, relevant to an event or issue that needs explanation.

Reporters usually don't get to witness a news story unfold from start to finish. It happens occasionally, when a crime or disaster plays out over time and journalists arrive at the scene quickly. More often, reporters must rely on the eyes, ears, and memories of others. They must reconstruct what happened by learning from participants, witnesses, and those with essential information, such as emergency crews. A looming deadline may require a quick succession of basic questions: What's your name? What happened? What did you see? Often there is not time or the need to build close rapport. Everyone may be pumped with adrenaline and ready to talk immediately about the dramatic episode they lived through.

Aside from their necessity in breaking stories, news-gathering interviews constitute the crux of journalistic activity. At city hall, police headquarters, the courthouse, and other traditional sites for news, interviews go on in businesslike fashion by people accustomed to being questioned and providing answers that reporters need. Of course, a routine interview can be lulling, like relying on an autopilot mechanism. Journalists must stay alert and listen carefully while also encouraging interviewees to resist similar complacency.

Reaction Interviews

When the governor vetoes a bill, the Supreme Court issues an opinion, or the president intervenes in a strike, reporters scurry about for "reaction" comments. Wire service reporters or national correspondents produce the big stories out of Washington, D.C., or the state capitol. Reporters around the country typically localize these stories, often going to experts at local universities or organizations who can lend a local flavor or angle to a national story.

Reaction interviews frequently focus on social and political conflict. Reporters and experienced news sources understand how competing sound bites or quotes enliven a story, pitting one side against the other. When reporters value clever comments over substantive ones, however, the danger cuts both ways, with spokespersons quite willing and able to play the quoting game. Quotemeisters—glib practitioners of wordplay—are in great demand, but their comments may shed relatively little light on the conflicts in question.

A special type of reaction story is difficult for all sensitive journalists—interviews with victims or survivors of tragic accidents. Despite stereotyped images to the contrary, most reporters detest prying into personal tragedies; they are not callously trying to upset people already in pain. It might seem heartless when a reporter with a microphone asks a mother whose child just died in a DUI accident, "How do you feel?" In practice journalists seldom ask such blunt questions, and they certainly avoid them at the start of an interview. Sensitive reporters, practicing empathy, gently elicit information, and sometimes they explore the feelings of grief or anger or guilt, which help dramatize the intense human cost of auto accidents, drownings, drive-by shootings, drug overdoses, suicides, and other daily heartbreaks. Box 8.2 offers a checklist for reaction interviews.

In-Depth Interviews

Apart from the frantic pace of breaking news coverage, journalists occasionally enjoy the time to conduct lengthy, expansive interviews that reveal people, places, and predicaments in sharp, intimate detail. With this goal, in-depth interviews create what are called **personality profiles** of both public and private figures. News organizations seldom pay a celebrity

BOX 8.2   R E M I N D E R S

Conducting a Brief Reaction Interview

Opening

- Introduce yourself and whom you represent.

- Explain your request clearly in terms of your story and goals. ("People are curious about the strike's effects on the town. Since you are a store owner, I'm interested in your opinion about short-term and long-term effects.")

Focused Listening

- Listen for quotes—statements that are pertinent, succinct, and vivid.

- If appropriate, share previous quotes and facts with respondents to stimulate reactions.

- Verify the quotes in your notes by reading them back to the interviewee.

Closing

- Express your personal appreciation for the help.

- Invite the interviewee to contact you later with further reactions, if appropriate.

---

or politician for an interview; it's even more uncommon to allow the interviewee any form of approval over the final product. Journalists, though, sometimes accept conditions in return for a hard-to-get interview. Moreover, writers who want a fair, accurate, and complete portrayal may review their work with the subject prior to broadcast or publication, although some conditions might make such an arrangement an unacceptable threat to the interviewer's independence. What is "right" in these situations will vary. Personality stories put journalists and interviewees into an intense, often symbiotic relationship, with each party heavily invested in the outcome. Complications are bound to arise.

Journalists also conduct in-depth interviews for *immersion reporting*. For example, reporters writing about drug abuse, poverty, AIDS, or prison life depend on interviews, conducted over a period of time, to tell their stories powerfully and well. *Washington Post* reporter Leon Dash (1996) used in-depth interviews spread out over four years in "Rosa Lee's Story," the account of a 58-year-old inner city matriarch and her family's life of crack cocaine, prostitution, crime, and poverty. His series won a Pulitzer Prize and was subsequently published as a book. The investment level for all parties to this type of interview is quite high, and winning prizes doesn't ensure that everyone will be pleased with the experience. Thousands of people who read about Rosa Lee complained to the *Post* about what they considered a disturbing, depressing, invasive story. Journalism, however, contributes to our awareness of important human conditions through penetrating accounts like Dash's. In a PBS interview months later, Rosa Lee, in tears of gratitude, told Dash, "You listened to me and you heard me."

Broadcast Interviews

Broadcast journalists interview people for the same reasons print journalists do, but they often work under more trying conditions. They usually have less time to collect stories, rushing with camera crew and technicians from one event or interview to the next, with little opportunity to air more than a few seconds from the interview. When doing live interviews, of course, they have no opportunity for retakes or corrections. Broadcast reporters not only must inform; they also must perform. How they look and sound over the air can be as important as the information they provide—a fact of professional life most accept reluctantly.

Broadcast interviews serve as a centerpiece of talk shows, newscasts, and broadcast newsmagazines. Each context has its differences and complications.

Live News   The live, on-the-scene interview is broadcast journalism's version of the roulette wheel. Instant coverage of breaking news is broadcasting's great advantage over print news, but because of the risks inherent in live interviews, broadcast reporters rarely snatch someone off the street and put them on the air. More often they play the odds, relying on well-informed public officials, such as a fire chief; or they prescreen interviewees to assure that they have something safe and sound to say. Nonetheless, when the camera rolls and people start talking—especially recounting a confusing, breathtaking event—they may blurt reckless or profane or misinformed comments before the reporter can cut them off. Even experienced journalists swept up by a dramatic story can go overboard. The competition among broadcasting outlets to "bring you the news first" increases the pressure for frequent use of live interviews. It's not a job for excitable, rash types, either behind or in front of the microphone.

Taped and Edited News   Broadcast journalism is especially dependent on human voices —excerpts of which create *actualities* for radio or *sound bites* for TV. Reporters or their producers spend a good part of their day lining up people who can provide the words and visuals needed to complete a story. Such interviews rarely last longer than a half hour, and many are completed in far less time. Although longer stories are now more common on evening newscasts, the typical news report seldom exceeds five minutes, with many no longer than ninety seconds. Interviews conducted for local or national newscasts yield only a quote or two. Knowing how the process works, savvy news sources prepare for an interview by compressing their knowledge and opinions into quotable nuggets. Less compelling remarks get cut as reporters and editors construct a tight audiovisual news package.

Newsmagazines   "60 Minutes" established the commercial and journalistic value of broadcast newsmagazines. With a few exceptions, "60 Minutes" and its progeny, such as "Dateline," "20/20," and "48 Hours," produce high ratings at costs far lower than those for prime-time entertainment and drama programs such as "Seinfeld" or "NYPD Blue." Newsmagazine programs face stiff competition, among themselves and against the rest of the prime-time TV lineup and rivals on cable, as well. The stories these programs air must be as polished and compelling as anything coming from the entertainment division. Stories short on emotional electricity don't get told; interviewees lacking human-interest

BOX 8.3   INTERVIEWEES IN ACTION

Stephen Hess

Washington, D.C., think-tank expert Stephen Hess frequently hears from TV news outlets looking for a source:

"A producer calls to check me out, asking enough questions to know whether I am likely to say what they are after. If I do not respond appropriately, they say they will get back to me. Which means they will not. This is a big city and someone else is sure to have the magic words they are looking for."

Source: Hess, 1996, p. 103

---

appeal or high drama don't get on the air; and the stars of these programs don't earn million-dollar salaries for mediocre performances. With much at stake, news producers go through considerable screening and fieldwork to find the right stories and the right people to tell them, even to the point of auditioning interviewees (see Box 8.3).

Broadcast news creates an illusion, intentionally at times, that Morley Safer or Diane Sawyer conducted every interview for a report. However, many interviews are done by field producers and other staff people, off camera. The high-priced "talent," as TV's heavy-hitters are sometimes called, often fly in later for the taped segments, after the groundwork is completed.

Talk Shows   Entertainment has become a significant element in much of what passes as news these days, especially in political talk shows. Few television talk shows are live, but many are taped live with little opportunity for extensive editing. As a result, interviews must be crisp, sharp, and, above all, entertaining—filled with emotion, humor, and satire. The hosts and their guests are chosen for their ability to be incisive, controversial, smart, or quick with quips.

Critics say that on talk shows, in particular, and broadcast news in general, interviews are more about performance art than news gathering. On a larger scale, the critics believe broadcast interviews encourage argumentation, not dialogue; that they value mere quotability over substance; and that they reduce complicated issues to two-sided diatribes or a horse race mentality. In fairness, some print interviews deserve similar criticism. But the problems seem more serious in broadcasting.

Complicating the broadcast talk show interview is the juxtaposition of words and visual images, demonstrated by close-ups, camera angles, and background scenes competing with the interviewee's comments. Most communication intended for broadcast is rehearsed to some degree or another, and this can create an artificial climate. Most interviewees are probably excessively self-conscious about what they're saying and the context of their talk. When talking on the record to any journalist, especially when on air or camera, communication can be especially strained. But natural, conversational interviews do occur in broadcasting, and they can be quite absorbing. Watch how Oprah Winfrey, for example, puts interviewees at ease through her skillful attention, her self-deprecating good humor, and her conversational speech style.

Telephone Interviews

The telephone is both a major advantage and a major compromise in communication. Although it impressively extends the immediate reach of our messages, it sacrifices the ability to observe many subtle cues of communication while we listen. However, telephone interviews are undeniably efficient and indispensable for journalists. The telephone is most often used by print reporters, who use it to do much of their "legwork" from the office. Broadcast journalists need faces for their reports, so, with the exception of radio reporters, they seldom use the telephone other than for background or screening interviews. The telephone has always been a good way to get to busy people; the popularity of cellular phones has enhanced access. Voice mail and other ways of depositing and retrieving messages allow reporters to bypass a secretary and leave detailed messages. A reporter's recorded message, in turn, gives a news source opportunity to formulate an answer before calling back. In the interest of saving time and meeting deadlines, news sources can leave answers on the reporter's voice mail.

The telephone clearly has its advantages and uses, but it cannot be a direct equivalent to a face-to-face interview. In a direct encounter, interviewer and interviewee can detect and assess nonverbal messages; face-to-face, they have a better chance of engaging in conversations of substance. Box 8.4 offers advice for interviews conducted by telephone.

Cyberspace Interviews

The latest way of conducting interviews is by e-mail, chat room, or computer bulletin board system conversations. Some of these interviews are done in real time, which approximates interviews by telephone but without the benefit (with most current technologies) of hearing actual voices. E-mail is also like the telephone in that messages can be left and answered at the convenience of all parties. Still, e-mail creates problems for interviews. In cyberspace talk, symbols sometimes substitute for what the speaker's tone of voice or facial expression would convey. For example, the use of ALL CAPITAL LETTERS for a word or sentence is considered equivalent to shouting and is discouraged. The etiquette for on-line talk is still evolving, and most of it isn't absolute or even generally agreed upon. As a result, cyberspace talk poses dangers you won't confront in everyday speech.

Cyberspace interviews are often like a long-distance chess match: I make a move, you respond and wait for my next move. Although spontaneity suffers, e-mail interviews afford more time for reflection and consideration than interviews by phone or in person. Sometimes, in fact, it's easier to obtain an interview by e-mail than by conventional means. *New*

BOX 8.4   R E M I N D E R S

Tips on Telephone Interviews for Participants

- Ensure that you have enough time and adequate concentration. You don't want to talk to someone who is distracted or rushed because other pressing business is on the desk or on the mind. A reporter, for example, who is trying to do several things at once while on the phone risks flawed results; an interviewee who is preoccupied won't be engaged enough to do justice to the interview. Both participants must recognize what is at stake and set aside other tasks and thoughts. If that is not possible, then a phone interview isn't appropriate.

- Focus on clarifying one major question if possible, with its appropriate follow-up probes and responses. A telephone interview is not an optimal occasion to process complex information, so avoid complicated schedules and convoluted answers.

- Speak slowly, distinctly, and precisely, remembering that phone talk isn't as complete and clear as face-to-face communication. Telecommunication still poses hearing difficulties in addition to the listening difficulties that typically accompany any interview. The hearing difficulties could be physical due to an auditory disability by one or both participants; technical due to static or a bad connection at one or both ends of the line; or verbal due to rapid, mumbled, or otherwise garbled speech by one or both parties.

- Avoid conducting important interviews by phone just because it's convenient. Phone interviews involve too many trade-offs. They offer a quick way to gather and exchange basic information but have inherent limitations for interviewers and interviewees. Interviewing by phone is generally one dimensional, with no visual or sensual context. Consider the possibility of using the phone only for **pre-interviews**—short interchanges that set up and coordinate longer interviews and perhaps exchange very basic personal data.

- Don't interrupt or talk over the other person's remarks. While interruption is common and expected in everyday talk, many of the cues to signal its appropriateness are visual.

- Summarize and repeat crucial information to ensure it has been understood. Both parties benefit from reassurances that their conversation has produced mutual understanding. In a restricted-channel situation like telephone talk, you won't have access to many cues of attentiveness. Double-check important details, such as dates, spellings of names, and telephone numbers.

Yorker writer John Seabrook (1994) based much of his portrait of Microsoft guru Bill Gates on e-mail interchanges. Seabrook thought that Gates, of all people, would be approachable through the information highway. Seabrook sent a brief e-mail message, identifying himself and explaining the story he was doing, ending the message with a question: "What do you think is unique about e-mail as a form of communication?" (p. 48). Eighteen minutes later, Gates responded. Their e-mail interview continued intermittently for a month. A productive e-mail interview can even set the stage for an eventual face-to-face meeting. Although Seabrook was successful with what we could call an emergent or developmental e-mail interviewing strategy, we suggest a bit more planning for the beginning interviewer (see Box 8.5).

BOX 8.5   **REMINDERS**

Conducting a Brief E-Mail Interview

- Contact the respondent ahead of time—by phone or e-mail—to invite his or her participation and to agree upon a time frame for responses and follow-up questions.

- Use the preliminary contacts for building rapport and informing the interviewee of your purpose.

- In the first content-oriented e-mail posting in which you pose questions, reiterate briefly the basic understandings previously reached by the two of you.

- Don't use Internet jargon or *emoticons* (also known as *smileys*—the visual representation of facial expressions portrayed by colon, semicolon, slash, and parenthesis keys), unless you're certain your partner is comfortable with such conventions.

- Unless the interview is in real time (as in a chat room setting from an on-line service), concentrate on just a few (between three and six) open-ended questions, to which the interviewee can respond at a comfortable level of disclosure.

- Use probes (follow-up questions) to check out or verify possible misunderstandings or express unusual interest or surprise. Otherwise, assume the interviewee has told you what he or she desires to reveal.

- When replying, use your e-mail system's edit or reply features to highlight the precise statements to which you're replying. Do not reply in such a way as to resend the interviewee's entire message.

- A follow-up post thanking your respondent would be appropriate and appreciated.

Fundamentals of Journalistic Interviewing

The journalistic interview takes on a unique life of its own and rarely follows a standard, predetermined pattern. Nearly all news interviews, however, include several fundamental considerations, which we will summarize as purpose, preparation, questioning, listening, record keeping, assessment, and analyzing conditions.

Purpose

Any journalist pursuing the news must answer the question "What is the story?" Usually this is answered early in a news assignment, which is what you'd expect. But journalists don't always do the expected; news emerges in strange ways at times. Occasionally, journalists don't find the story, or at least not the one they expected to find, until well into interviews and information gathering. There is a risk in answering "What's the story?" too quickly, thus predetermining the outcome and precluding the discovery of something truly new and unexpected. Operating without a story in mind, however, doesn't help either. Most reporters, based on initial information, leads, experience, and instinct, tentatively define the story. Beyond that, they must be prepared to be flexible.

The initial conception of a story influences who must be interviewed and which goals will guide the interview. Here decisions can get tricky, especially if the story is potentially controversial, harmful, or embarrassing. Let's say the reporter's purpose is to investigate an apparent conflict of interest involving the mayor and her brother-in-law, whose company received an exclusive, lucrative contract to make repairs on all city vehicles. Journalism's role as a watchdog involves such investigations. But what happens when the interviewer's purpose clashes with that of the interviewee? Is it realistic to envision their interview as a partnership? It probably wouldn't be a congenial partnership. Nonetheless, collaboration, to some degree, often yields better results than confrontation. The reporter can stand pat on her objective to investigate; the mayor's brother-in-law can pursue his purpose of explaining and defending his business with the city. Together, they can, if willing, find a common purpose of producing a story that is as truthful and fair as possible.

Even with far less volatile stories, reporters are wise to share the purpose of the interview. Revealing the purpose usually helps in obtaining an interview. Reporters often must overcome a respondent's reluctance to talk. People generally want to know what a reporter wants from them, and why. People resent being misled or kept in the dark, and a resentful interviewee isn't going to be too interested in talking.

Determining the purpose helps both journalists and their respondents prepare for their common task. Consider the problem of determining purpose from the differing standpoints of both roles. As the interviewer, ask yourself the following questions:

1. *Why do I need to know more about this topic or person?*

2. *What is the story?* If you don't have much sense yet of the shape of the story, you should plan more exploratory questions.

3. *Who will be reading or hearing my account? What will they want to know?* Reporters are expected to ask about what audiences want to know, not simply to follow up on their own curiosity. Therefore, a degree of sensitivity to the public's concerns is part of the job.

4. *Am I most interested in context or in detail, or both?* In deciding, don't underestimate the importance of accurate details even in nonpivotal areas. Most people are rarely if ever mentioned in print, and journalists shouldn't underestimate the disappointing, discouraging feeling respondents experience when they see their names misspelled, or their beloved family business misidentified, during a perhaps too-brief moment of public recognition. Remember, too, that getting a name wrong may mean an innocent person will be associated inadvertently with a misdeed.

5. *How can I keep my mind open for new purposes that might emerge from the interview?* Although each story probably begins with hunches and hypotheses, good interviews often give interviewers reasons to develop new hunches along the way while dropping their old ones.

As the interviewee, ask yourself the following questions about the interviewer's purpose:

1. *Why does the interviewer want to talk to me? What motivates the interview from his or her side?* You might want to do some research if you know the interview is imminent. For example, if you're a recently elected president of the student

government about to be interviewed by the editor of the campus newspaper, wouldn't it be worthwhile to review last year's editorials and stories to determine the editor's priorities and possible hot topics?

2. *What is my basic motivation for talking to this person? How do I want to be seen, heard, and interpreted? Are there potential pitfalls in how I talk about a topic?* Ask yourself if your main purpose is to relay information or facts, or to be perceived in a certain way, or both.

3. *Will I want or need to set any limits for the interview? Is any information out of bounds?* The reminders later in this chapter concerning record keeping, assessment, and conditions will help put these questions in perspective. For now, though, consider carefully what boundaries you need or want to define, given your own purpose.

4. *Who will be reading or hearing the journalist's account? What will they want to know? How could they reward or penalize me?*

Preparation

When time permits, reporters prepare for interviews by using a combination of research, reading, listening, hanging out, and reflection. To rush in with a hastily scribbled list of questions undermines an interview in several ways. First, experienced interviewees measure a reporter's credibility by the questions asked. Are they bright, provocative, thoughtful? Are they far too obvious—ones that an ill-prepared, rookie reporter would ask? In the eyes of many interviewees, a reporter's preparation reflects his or her professionalism. Preparation is also a sign of respect that says to the interviewee: I care enough about you to learn who you are and not to burden you with questions whose answers I can get in a reference book or newsroom library. Preparation not only impresses and inspires the interviewee; it also heightens the reporter's confidence.

In the interest of a better story, good reporters try to give interviewees an opportunity to prepare. Of course, full disclosure by the reporter might give an evasive or devious news source a chance to prepare an orchestrated, calculated response, instead of one that is spontaneous, unrehearsed, and candid. In most situations, giving an interviewee time to prepare is worth the risk. Preparation is especially helpful when seeking specialized information from an expert. Even experts cannot know or remember every particular of their work; sometimes, too, afforded time to prepare, an interviewee rethinks a subject, coming up with fresh insights.

Again, consider the preparation choices from both sides of the interview encounter. As the interviewer, remember these points:

1. *Research the interviewee's interests if possible.* Ordinarily, you will need to understand the basics of the topic you will be exploring with the interviewee. Although there are exceptions (broadcast interviewer Larry King, for example, claims he rarely does preliminary research on interviewees' interests because he doesn't want

to stifle spontaneity and a fresh style), most interviewers will be more comfortable knowing possible directions the interview might take.

2. *Anticipate vocabulary.* Become familiar with the interviewee's speech habits, special jargon, or unique styles of phrasing things.

3. *Investigate the context in which someone's information might be placed.* For example, before interviewing a Texaco executive about possible racial bias within the company, you might want to do an on-line search about other recent cases in which large corporations have been charged with discrimination, or about Texaco's recent record in affirmative action compliance.

From the other perspective, that of the interviewee, remember these points:

1. *Anticipate misunderstanding.* Interviewers rarely have enough time to prepare fully for the interview; therefore, they might not have as clear or as sophisticated a purpose for the occasion as you do. Anticipate how an interviewer, although sincere, might still misunderstand your ideas and might even frame the interview in a radically different way than you would. For example, a journalist might plan to interview you for a personality profile, while you know your company has just made a major pharmaceutical breakthrough that could make news. Wouldn't you want to talk about that, even if the reporter didn't ask?

2. *Police your jargon.* Remember that in many situations your *jargon*—the specialized language and references commonly used within your own job, hobby, or cultural position—will not be shared by the journalist's audience. Plan ways to explain or frame your ideas in accessible language.

3. *Clarify the interviewer's purpose.* You have a right to inquire about the purpose of the interview. Reporters are accustomed to interviewing under different conditions and using the information they receive in varying ways. You can influence some of their interview purposes by requesting that your name not be used or that the information you supply will be used only as context for the journalist's pursuit of other information, not as news in and of itself. Journalists use several terms to describe ground rules for interviews. Please note, though, that there is no universal agreement on what these terms mean. We define **not for attribution** to mean that the source of the information can be identified by a general description ("a Capitol Hill insider tells *Newsweek* that . . ."), but not by name. **On background** means that what a source says will not itself be a part of the story but will be used by the journalist to understand the subject better and possibly track down additional information. **Off the record** means the journalist will not use the information in any way. In the absence of precise definitions for these terms, we recommend that you establish beforehand exactly how the information you provide will be used and attributed. Without such clarification, the interviewer might incorrectly assume that anything you say is fair game.

4. *Stay alert for interviewer strategies.* Remember that although journalists aren't necessarily trying to be sneaky or deceptive, they probably know a thing or two about tactical communication. What appears to be the drift or main focus of an interview may not in fact turn out to be the real purpose. For example, a journalist may spend twenty minutes talking casually about the day-to-day operations of the rural school where you work, only to ask at the end of the conversation, almost as an aside, how much time the principal spends away from the school on trips and consultation visits. What you thought was an interview preparing for a light feature about the personalities of people at your school, you later discover to have been an investigation of how some administrators rip off the district. This doesn't mean journalists are devious and deceitful—they have a responsibility to the public as well as to individual interviewees. It only means that interviewees are well advised to be alert and consider (realistically) that the most obvious purposes may not be the most important ones.

Questioning

As you have read in earlier chapters, interviewing isn't all asking and answering questions. The question-and-answer exchange often tends to discourage natural conversation, but sometimes it's the most efficient way to collect information. Journalists need to decide which questions to ask, as well as when and how to ask them. A few reporters make long lists, but most rely on a few primary or starter questions. They develop additional questions based on the ebb and flow of the interview. For inexperienced journalists, a question list is a security blanket, which is OK. But strict adherence to such a list will result in a stiff give-and-take routine. Experienced reporters take a conversational approach to interviews, working in questions unobtrusively.

An important part of journalists' questioning is follow-up. People seldom answer a question fully on their first attempt. They need time and help in fleshing out initial remarks. Reporters sometimes repeat a question in several forms until an answer emerges, or they might simply say, "Tell me more" or "That's interesting" while they wait for additional detail. In reconstructing a news event or encouraging an anecdote, reporters ask a series of "what happened" questions, such as, "What did you do when you heard the shots?" or "After the gunfire stopped, what did you do next?" In stages, the interviewee provides a detailed account.

Remember that a probe is a type of follow-up question or response that seeks clarification, elaboration, or confirmation. A *reflective probe,* for example, might have a reporter asking, "Let me repeat what you said to make sure I understand you." Silence on the reporter's part might serve as a probe that nonverbally says, "Keep talking" or "Take your time in answering."

Veteran editors often tell beginning reporters to ask the questions readers or viewers would ask. People want to know how a story affects them. If it's about a pending teachers' strike, working parents will want to know, among other things, "What would I do with my kids?" That basic question might not occur to an unmarried, childless reporter. Journalists are the public's surrogate in finding answers to questions; they are also our surrogate listeners.

In focusing on questioning, interviewers need to remember several important issues:

1. *Prepare a schedule.* As a reminder about thoroughness, and as a backstop for an interview that doesn't develop much conversational flow, prepare a *schedule,* or tentative agenda of basic questions to which you can refer easily if necessary. At times it may not be necessary. At the end of the interview, briefly review your schedule to ensure you haven't forgotten something crucial. Few things are as embarrassing for professional journalists as the need to recontact someone because they overlooked a question. Typically, journalists are taught the importance of a checklist approach to anything they cover: who? what? where? when? why? how? These are the sacred *5 w's and an h* of journalism. Though they needn't be asked in this order, readers, listeners, and viewers do want to know these things about events. In addition, at the end of each interview, consider *the sixth w:* what else? Get into the habit of asking something like, "Is there anything else you think you'd like me to know? Anything you think I've forgotten to ask or have overlooked?" This simple, concluding probe could spare you recriminations and torment later.

2. *Sequence your questions and topics appropriately.* Plan a tentative sequence of questions adapted both to the interviewee and to your purpose for the interview. Typical journalistic patterns are **topical** (move from issue to issue), **chronological** (move from older to more recent events), **funnel** (move from general to specific), or **inverted funnel** (move from specific to general). In addition, if some areas of the interview are likely to be ticklish or tense, you might not want to lead with those and risk having the entire tone of your conversation affected by the emotional responses those questions might trigger.

3. *Anticipate defensiveness.* Remember that certain questions will likely provoke defensiveness in interviewees. For example, "Why did you promote Ramsey after the complaint was filed against him?" would rarely be heard as a neutral request for a reasoned rationale. Interviewees are more likely to interpret your question as a commentary on the action. This might not always be bad (journalists are interested in how some interviewees might respond under fire, after all), but you should always be aware of it as a possible outcome of the interaction.

4. *Probe often.* Remind yourself that all answers are not equal, nor will all respondents think of everything on the first pass. Review the uses of probes described in detail in Chapter 4. These useful follow-ups get behind or beyond the first response to explore it further. Some probes are overtly for clarification and are meant as checks on your listening.

5. *Be aware of how your questions invite answers.* Remember that different kinds of questions invite different kinds of responsiveness and thus different qualities of answers. In many situations where collecting accurate information is primarily important, journalists avoid *leading questions*—those whose phrasing projects the kind of answer the questioner appears to want or expect ("You never intended to keep that plant open after acquiring it, did you?"). In other contexts, a leading question can be an effective technique to stimulate an interviewee's emotional responses and a series of interesting statements as well.

Consistent with the forms of questions discussed in previous chapters, journalists think of questions as being relatively open or closed, or relatively direct or indirect. Open-ended questions invite the interviewee to be expansive, and they assign a significant degree of control over the interview to the respondent. Think of the differences between these two questions, asked of the new board member of the Scranton Art Institute:

A. "When you go to the art gallery, which sections do you gravitate toward?"
B. "Do you appreciate modern art?"

In some cases, the two questions might yield similar answers; the interviewee might tell you that he visits the Mondrian collection because he enjoys experimentation in modernist approaches, for example. Yet question A invites him to think in a more open and exploratory way and in no sense structures the ground rules (at least about art) to which the respondent would have to reply. He has room to move, in other words. The second question, which is more closed, constrains the reply more to conform to the interviewer's goals. Additionally, can you see how the two questions also differ in their degree of directness? An interviewer interested in how the other person feels about modern art could either approach that curiosity directly (question B) or relatively indirectly with the possibility of follow-up probes (question A would be a good entree).

6. *Questions can be counterproductive.* Because interviews are conversations, they do not have to rely on a string of questions. Although questions are important, your interviewee will also respond if you characterize events in a certain inviting way. For instance, while interviewing the volleyball coach, you might say, "Well, coach, your opponent, Morgan State, looks tough again this year. . . ." The coach will take your comment as a cue to talk about the upcoming game, or to prognosticate about final conference standings, or perhaps to conjecture about how Morgan State's best players are overrated. Although this can be a helpful interviewing style if it's not overdone, don't be surprised if a contrary interviewee occasionally tries to trip you up: "I'm sure it looks that way to you media types. You always give them too much ink."

When you find yourself being interviewed by a journalist, remember these points about questioning:

1. *Verify the question.* It's wise to make sure you understand questions fully before answering. It's in a journalist's nature to listen for quotes, not only for information. Editors and readers expect quotes in stories, and the more striking or unusual the better. The problem for an interviewee is having a response wrenched out of the context of the rest of your message. Nothing can guarantee this won't happen, but interviewees who request clarification often are less likely to get themselves in quote trouble.

2. *Don't take offense if a reporter doesn't seem to accept your answers to questions at face value.* It's in a reporter's survival kit to be skeptical and to dig underneath the surface. It's usually nothing personal or suspicious that keys them to do this.

3. *Ask your own questions.* You might ask for example, "Who else are you interviewing on this matter?" "How is the story shaping up?" "Will this be part of a larger piece about school board policy, or is it possible that the story will be only about my actions?" Although journalists may not be at liberty to respond fully or may not know the answer to your question, many times they'll try to clarify things.

4. *Recognize the dynamics of "no comment."* Understand that a "no comment," although it's technically a neutral response, will still be interpreted by journalists and their audiences as meaning something (that you have something to hide? that you don't know an answer and are avoiding embarrassment? that you've been told by someone else not to talk about something?). Use this response sparingly, if at all.

Listening

Listening, to journalists, should be much more than passive attention that simply registers comments and questions. Listening sustains and creates communication; how we listen influences how others answer our questions and what we say next in response. Writer Gay Talese (1995) learned to listen as a boy, hanging around his mother's dress shop, where customers would try on clothes and discuss their lives. He observed the importance of listening patiently. "I learned to listen with patience and care, and never to interrupt even when people were having great difficulty in explaining themselves, for during such halting and imprecise moments . . . people often are very revealing—What they hesitate to talk about can tell much about them" (p. 80).

Reporters listen carefully for details in interviews. They also listen for context, using mind, eyes, and other powers of assessment to comprehend what they hear. The best journalists attempt to set aside attitudes and influences that might impair their ability to listen in a way that is willing and prepared to learn something new. They listen unselfishly, attuned to the interviewee's needs as much as their own.

Reporters who don't listen, and show it, can expect to get caught. A TV reporter interviewing celebrities arriving for the 1997 Academy Awards ceremony questioned Winona Ryder while looking over her shoulder to catch the eye of another Hollywood actor. After answering his question, Ryder cocked her head and said in exasperation, "Why, you're not even listening to me." The interview ended there.

As a journalistic interviewer, remember these important points about listening:

1. *Build rapport by demonstrating your listening acuity.* In other words, active listening is crucial in convincing the interviewee to trust you. Remember that active listening means the verbal and nonverbal behaviors by which a listener proves a message has been understood in the way the speaker hopes it would be. Psychologists Carl Rogers and Richard Farson (1957) note—in a message with special relevance to journalists—that "while it is most difficult to convince someone that you respect him by telling him so, you are much more likely to get this message across by really behaving that way by actually having and demonstrating respect for this person. Listening does this most effectively" (p. 11). Active listening could take several forms, but the most common is a verbal checking back—what we earlier called a clarification probe. Journalists could inquire, "I heard you say two things a while ago. One is that you believe the truck driver cut off the pickup. Then later, you said 'maybe,' and seemed less sure about who cut off whom. Do I have that right?" Thus, at the same time you're complimenting the interviewee by paying careful attention, you're inviting a more thoughtful, and maybe a more accurate, response.

2. *Remember that listening is identified with visual cues.* Listening is not just a way of registering meanings cognitively and not just a physiological process. It's also a recognizable set of observable behaviors that members of a culture will interpret in relatively predictable ways. Listening, in other words, has an appearance. In typical North American cultures, listeners tend to maintain persistent—though not total—eye contact. They nod and give other verbal and nonverbal encouragement for speakers to continue, they lean forward often to indicate a kind of immediacy with speakers, and they introduce no unnecessary barriers between speakers and themselves. Journalists should do a self-inventory of listening habits

to isolate problem behaviors, even if they're good listeners cognitively. Do you really need those sunglasses? Are there times when burying yourself in the notebook or scanning the horizon for other interesting people might cause someone to break off an interview prematurely?

3. *Let yourself be surprised by what the interviewee might say.* Journalists often have deadlines that encourage them to write much of the story in their heads before finishing the information-gathering process. Monitor your own habits of framing and interpreting to ensure that you're not just listening through the filters of your prejudices and previous assumptions.

4. *Anticipate the effects of context.* Be aware of how different contexts and settings can affect listening. If you interview a doctor in the office at midday, don't be surprised if her listening is divided or diffused between your concerns and the perhaps more immediate demands of patients or her colleagues.

As a journalist's interviewee, remember these points about listening:

1. *Don't leave active listening to the interviewer.* Active listening is just as relevant a skill for you as it is for reporters. Openly express what you think the question is, from the interviewer's perspective: "You seem to want me to evaluate how easy it was to work with Barbra Streisand. Is that right?" Another active listening approach is to verify a level of accurate interpretation by asking the interviewer for a reflective or paraphrased response. If you're a public health worker, you could say: "We've been talking for ten minutes now about the HIV virus and I'm wondering what you think is my strongest recommendation."

2. *Assist the interviewer's listening by providing him or her with informal definitions.* You can help the interviewer listen if you insert brief definitions of specialized terms you have to use. For example, you might say, "I get a lot of my information by searching Lexis/Nexis, the on-line database you can access in most research libraries." (Don't assume that all journalists know all about various electronic search options, although most do.)

3. *Monitor nonverbal signals of interest or understanding from your interviewer.* Watch for indications that the interviewer is confused, especially curious, or losing interest. Did he start to look at his watch or yawn? Did she quit taking notes and sigh deeply? Or did he start leaning forward expectantly, with more eye contact? You'll want to adapt your comments accordingly. It would be nice to imagine that all journalists will be skilled, sensitive, and experienced, but your common sense tells you the opposite. Some interviewers will be rookies and others, arrogant know-it-alls who clearly don't care about your positions. Remember that your story has to be told not just *to* them but *through* them, whatever their attitudes and skills, so help them listen by anticipating problem areas. Repeat significant information and slow down when introducing material that might be unfamiliar.

Record Keeping

Journalists keep a record of most interviews because it's risky not to. A clear record of notes or tapes will not only reassure editors and interviewees alike but also help jog memory later. Many reporters keep their notes and, less commonly, their tapes of important interviews for later reference, perhaps as context for further stories.

Sometimes, reporters delay taking notes or activating the tape recorder until they feel the interviewee is comfortable and ready to talk. Although it's difficult to keep verbatim quotes and specifics, attention to such details tells interviewees that the journalist is committed to accuracy. A careful, complete record of interviews is essential as a reporter puts together a story. It's also important if questions arise later, in the newsroom or courtroom, over the truthfulness of the story.

Record keeping involves a surprisingly complex set of choices. Reporters who focus too intently on taking notes may collect the details but not the larger context and meaning of messages. Those relying on a tape recorder may relax, confident a machine is keeping track of every word. They mentally drift, and later, when replaying the tape, they realize they weren't altogether "there" for the interview and thus can't adequately put what they hear in context. Whether taking notes, using a recorder, or employing a combination of both, reporters ought to balance careful note taking with concentrated mental engagement (see Box 8.6).

Assessment

Information must be analyzed and synthesized in terms of the interview's purpose. Part of any reporter's postinterview assessment involves confirming what has been heard, what has been learned and what gaps might remain in the story. At times, this is as simple as going over notes, deciding what to use and what to discard. Reporters seldom use a majority of their notes in a story; they cull the immediately useful from the extraneous information. Basically, reporters prepare to write a story or put together a broadcast report by asking themselves What do I have? What does it mean? How can I best tell this story? What is missing? After this round of assessment, a reporter could conclude there is more to be learned or cleared up. Another round of interviews follows.

A deeper period of assessment involves the larger picture: What's been accomplished by this interview? What's my journalistic purpose? Has it been served? How does it mesh or clash with what I perceive as the interviewee's purpose? Questions like these may lead into an ethical self-examination by the reporter or a discussion involving others in the newsroom.

Conditions

Reporters seeking interviews sometimes must submit to an interviewee's preconditions or rules. Reporters usually resist attempts to control an interview or subsequent story. However, the competition for exclusive interviews, particularly with celebrities, makes it hard

BOX 8.6   R E M I N D E R S

Record Keeping for Journalists

Decide which form your record keeping for a given interview will take: direct notes, delayed notes, or tape recording. Review Chapter 5 for an expanded discussion of these alternatives.

For most brief and straightforward journalistic interviews of less consequence, *direct notes* are not only fine but are expected by interviewees. The interviewer simply jots down important points while the respondent is talking. A small notepad is especially appropriate, but watch out for the tendency to pay more attention to the notes than to the speaker.

In some interviews, such as with an excitable or highly emotional interviewee, note taking would feel intrusive, or it could detract from your ability to notice the nuances of nonverbal reactions. Some reporters prefer a *delayed notes* method in which they take very few if any notes during the conversation but then set aside a time immediately following the interview for scribbling as many details as they can remember. With practice in delayed note taking, even many short quotes can be recalled, although relying too much on memory is chancy. Don't restrict yourself only to what was said, though. Record your estimate of how the context might have affected the interview, how the tone changed after you introduced a certain topic, when the interviewee was especially forthcoming or expansive; and definitely note whatever promises you made to him or her about calling back, when or how the story will run, whether a recheck on quotes is to be expected, and so forth. Be aware of the dangers of delayed note taking as well as its benefits. For example, journalists may overestimate their ability to remember and introduce mistakes unintentionally; in addition, some news interviewees will get nervous if they don't see you taking notes, and your credibility will plummet.

Another alternative is *tape recording,* an increasingly common choice. Some years ago it seemed the majority of everyday interview subjects became squeamish and uncommunicative at the sight of a recorder, but now with the advent of tiny and unobtrusive microcassette recorders, the technology seems relatively unthreatening to most people.

If you decide to tape, ensure that the interviewee understands exactly when a tape recorder is on. Hidden taping, although a topic of intense debate among high-profile journalists covering big stories for major networks and papers, should not be controversial at all for most journalists. Because undisclosed taping keeps interviewees from a full range of choice about their own talk, it's simply unethical in virtually all everyday journalistic occasions. A public that believes this practice is common is a public that won't trust the institution of journalism. Perhaps some stories about dangerous practices are so protected and insulated, and the people involved so despicable, that some rare deception could be justified. Yet this isn't journalistic "business as usual." "Beyond the Basics" considers journalistic ethics in greater detail.

to take an inflexible stance. Box office stars and others in the public eye have the leverage to make all sorts of demands, including who is assigned to do the interview and what subjects are out of bounds. A reporter or editor might decide that a conditional interview is better than none at all. On the other hand, public officials and politicians tend to seek interviews rather than dodge them. But even these talkative types are likely to set ground rules for certain stories, such as speaking "off the record" or "not for attribution" or "on background only" (see discussion earlier in this chapter). Those arrangements allow reporters to gather quotes or inside information with the typical proviso that the speaker's identity cannot be revealed. In journalism, though, credibility and authenticity suffer

• See how well you interview in two respects: accuracy and note taking. Interview a friend or classmate about a vivid anecdotal experience, such as a first date or first car. Develop a very brief schedule of primary questions to bring forth the anecdote, and probe to encourage the sharing of vivid details. A five- or ten-minute interview will be sufficient. Tape your interview to produce a precise record, but also take careful notes of the interviewee's experiences. Then, without listening to the tape, reconstruct as much of the story as possible by creating a first-person account (as if in the interviewee's words) *based only on your notes.* (*Note:* This will be difficult, and no one should expect to do it perfectly.) Sit down with the interviewee and review the "transcript" together as a first stage of assessing your accuracy in note taking. Then compare the transcript to the tape, listening to it together, alert for lapses or errors in your note taking.

• If you want to check your framing and listening skills, use your notes to produce a brief story based on the interviewee's anecdote. Then go over the story with the interviewee, assessing both its factual and contextual accuracy.

when words and opinions are attributed to nameless sources. See Box 8.7 for some tips if you are the interviewee.

BEYOND THE BASICS

Ethics

Journalism ethics covers everything from plagiarism to conflicts of interest. The ethics of news interviews receives less attention than broader issues, such as the use of hidden cameras and undercover reporters on "Prime Time Live" to document unsanitary practices at Food Lion supermarkets. The ethics of interviewing deserves fuller consideration because of the interview's importance in creating news. Finding common ethical ground, though, is difficult. Years before her involvement in the Food Lion episode, Diane Sawyer ("Diane Sawyer," 1988) talked about ethics in journalism: "You cannot form an exact science of ethics. . . . You can talk about it, but you can't teach it because in the end it derives out of the whole human being" (p. 2). We cannot conclusively say of journalism ethics, "This is right and that is wrong," even in the debate over the "Prime Time Live" incident. But we can explore several key ethical turning points commonly found in journalistic interviews.

Obtaining Interviews Ethically

Reporters occasionally lie to get an interview. In some cases they use masquerades, disguises, and impersonations to gain access and get people talking. At other times, rather than use outright deception, reporters withhold their identity, at least early on, and strike up a conversation, hoping the news source assumes they're not a journalist. Another form

BOX 8.7   R E M I N D E R S

Being Interviewed by a Journalist

As the interviewee, here are some points to remember:

- *Disregard tape recording technologies as much as possible.* You needn't worry too much about talking directly into the microphone of the recorder, if the interviewer is taping. Almost all recorders now have built-in omnidirectional microphones that pick up sounds throughout a room. Remember, though, that when the microphone is on, everything you say is being recorded and might be used. Sometimes, for example, as TV reporters conclude an interview, the sound, even as equipment is being put away, may remain on. If you keep talking, the interview isn't "over."

- *Remember that you can choose to speak without being recorded.* If an interviewer doesn't ask your preference but begins to tape the conversation, you can request that the recorder be turned off.

- *You can inquire about the interviewer's record keeping.* Many reporters are willing to share the contents of their notes. Although the reporter isn't likely to give you the notes, don't hesitate to ask about what they contain in the form of quotes, statistics, descriptions, and the like. It's to the advantage of both interviewer and interviewee that these things are reported accurately, and you might be able to catch a mistake on the scene.

of lying involves misrepresenting the purpose of the interview because the interviewee might cooperate for one type of story but have reservations about another.

Whenever journalists use trickery or lies to get a story, they deny the interviewee freedom of choice about talking in public. An interview obtained by dishonest means has little hope of achieving a partnership. A reporter's dishonesty also invites countertactics by the interviewee, with implications for the journalist's primary imperative, the pursuit of truth. Is lying to obtain an interview, or other forms of deception, always unethical? That's an open question, and to answer it ethically requires thoughtful, careful deliberation. Some words of wisdom from reporter Mitch Albom of the *Detroit Free Press* apply: "Never assume that you can pull the wool over anybody's eyes, just because you're a reporter and they're an average person," he says. "I always say, 'Here's why I'm calling.'" He adds, "Somebody once wrote that there's no more seductive sentence in the English language than, 'I want to hear your story,' and maybe they're right. Because often you don't have to do any more than just say that" (quoted in Scanlon, 1996, p. 56).

Conducting Interviews Ethically

Several tricky issues arise in journalistic interviews. One is the use of hidden recorders. The motives of reporters who secretly record interviews vary. Some seek candid, off-the-cuff comments, uninhibited by the presence of a tape recorder. Others hope to induce a news source to say something incriminating, snaring the source later with a smoking-gun tape. Are all secret or surreptitious recordings unethical? That, too, cannot be answered easily; important stories of major public interest have been told through secret recordings. The circumstances and consequences must be considered.

BOX 8.8   INTERVIEWERS IN ACTION

Connie Chung

In a two-hour taped interview, network reporter Connie Chung induced Kathleen Gingrich, mother of House Speaker Newt Gingrich, to comment on her son's opinion of the First Lady. "I can't tell you what he said about Hillary," Mrs. Gingrich said at one point. "You can't?" Chung said. "I can't," Mrs. Gingrich replied. Chung leaned toward Mrs. Gingrich and said, "Why don't you just whisper it to me, just between you and me?" Mrs. Gingrich took the bait, saying, "'She's a bitch.' That's about the only thing he ever said about her" (p. 1A). CBS aired the interview, opening what one account called a Pandora's box of difficult ethical issues.

Source: "Pandora's Box," 1995

Skilled reporters ask good questions. Where do they draw a line separating ethical and unethical questions? Forceful, direct inquiries are common in journalism; loaded, leading questions meant to trap or ambush an interviewee are not. Such questions might get results, but at what cost? The notion of partnership in interviews won't survive in an adversarial, aggressive climate. Moreover, what is the ethical responsibility regarding the subjects broached, such as asking a candidate for president, "Have you ever committed adultery?" Ethical journalists ask questions of themselves as a guide: What is the journalistic purpose of my questions? What might be the consequences of asking certain questions? Can I justify asking questions that have the potential to upset or hurt someone?

Skilled reporters also possess a talent for getting people to speak openly, sometimes contrary to their best interests, which is especially true of people unaware of how reporters operate. Should reporters issue a warning similar to the Miranda warning used by police: "Don't tell me anything you wouldn't want publicized; what you say may be held against you in ways neither you nor I can anticipate"? Trust and compassion enhance communication. Manipulation and ruthless pursuit of information do not. A reporter's intentional exploitation of interviewees is hard to justify. Compassionate reporters also know that for various reasons people don't always exercise good judgment in what they say, and thus reporters might give an interviewee a second chance to reconsider ill-advised remarks (see Box 8.8).

Using Interview Results Ethically

Interviews are seldom printed or broadcast in their entirety. A period of editing generally follows, with parts of the interview retained and others discarded. The journalist's primary ethical obligations are to use interview material accurately and fairly. A degree of license must be allowed because journalists are not mere stenographers, taking down all that is said and conveying it to the public. They are expected to analyze, assess, weigh, work with words and observations and create a story. But they must not distort or misrepresent what an interviewee said. Beyond that, as journalists put the story together, they must not use rhetorical sleight of hand, such as quoting out of context or selective use of words. A reporter, for example, may have good reason to use a fraction of an interview. But motives count. Did the reporter select a particular quote because it confirmed her perceptions of the interviewee as a nitwit?

When the interview is conceived and conducted as a partnership, a reporter cannot escape the responsibility to consider the story a collaboration whenever possible. Interviewees put themselves at the mercy of journalists, and most journalists respect the power they hold and use it honorably.

Public Dialogue

Some critics argue that traditional journalism faces a major image problem: its practice of one-way, take-it-or-leave-it, conveyor-belt news is out of touch with the needs and concerns of ordinary Americans. To the critics, journalism repels people with its detached, aloof, elitist manner, sending people to such inviting, user-friendly media as on-line information services or call-in talk programs.

Journalism plays an important role in our shared civic experiences and knowledge. It sets local and national agendas, legitimizes what it explains, and helps us connect with other people and places. Today, a movement called **public journalism**, or *civic journalism,* has many news organizations reporting stories and sponsoring activities in an attempt to become more integrally involved in their communities. A central goal of public or civic journalism is to go beyond reporting the news and attempt to help people think and act more as citizens. Newspapers have sponsored public forums on issues such as race relations, and they have given people opportunities to raise questions and offer solutions to local problems. As a result, there is greater emphasis in journalism on communication, which might sound ironic. In the traditional and important journalistic role of informing, some elements of communication, particularly listening and conversation, might be deemphasized in newsrooms. In some redefinitions of journalism, news is seen largely as a by-product of communication by and between people. The journalistic interview, therefore, assumes a major role in the public dialogue because it constitutes much of what is news. Journalists function in interviews as public surrogates, conversing, listening, and learning so that the rest of us in the larger community might converse, listen, and learn as well.

Challenges, Rewards

Mike Patterson, a character in the comic strip "For Better or for Worse," attends journalism school, where he's discovered that reporting involves responsibilities that aren't always clear. In a series of daily strips, Mike wrestles with his conscience over a feature about Mr.

- Sherry Johnson, an attractive, popular high school senior, disappears on her way to school. She stopped at an ATM for $50; that is the last record of her whereabouts. Sherry's on the honor roll, sings in the church choir, and plans on becoming a teacher. Her parents and the police fear she's been abducted. You're assigned to cover this developing story, reporting on the girl, her family, and her fate.

  How far would you go in finding out about Sherry from classmates, friends, family, and church members? Would you ask about her mental health, her romances, her home life? Would you interview her parents? Her ten-year-old brother? Her former teachers? An ex-boyfriend? What would you ask those you interviewed? What would you consider out of bounds?

  What if several of Sherry's classmates told you they think she's a runaway? What if someone called you anonymously and said, "Sherry ran away from home because her father's abused her." Would you investigate? If so, how deeply would you probe, and whom would you interview?

  How would you define your relationship with the worried family? Would you console them as well as question them? Or would you remain purely professional, suppressing any emotional involvement?

As you grapple with these questions, keep in mind the divided responsibilities journalists face. This is a difficult story to report, and it presents numerous ethical issues in how to conduct interviews. You might want to conduct mock interviews with friends or classmates, asking them to play assigned roles.

- You're a reporter for a city's daily paper, engaged in your first interview with a major political official. Midway through the interview with Mayor Dooley, she evidently begins to have second thoughts about her disclosures several minutes ago about City Hall financial records. She stops in midsentence and says, "I'll keep talking with you, but only if you call me this afternoon and let me change any quotes you're going to print."

  You want to continue the interview, but wonder about the advisability and ethics of giving the interviewee this much control over your story. Consider the dynamics of this interview situation and the implications of her ultimatum for future interviews. What do you say to her at this moment?

- Revisit the Willie Mays episode that opened this chapter. Although it's easy to criticize a reporter when an interview goes sour, what, if anything, would you have asked or done differently if you'd been sent by a daily paper to get quotes from Mays?

Bergner, a quiet, dignified custodian at Mike's university. Mike talks to Mr. Bergner one day and finds his life story fascinating. Mr. Bergner reluctantly agrees to an interview. The result is a touching story that pleases Mike, and the campus newspaper accepts it for publication. Unfortunately, the custodian was under the impression the interview was for a class project, not publication. "I don't think I want it in the paper," he says. Mike blurts back, "It's a great story!" "Yes," says Mr. Bergner, "and whose story is it, Mr. Patterson? Yours or mine?"

The question dogs Mike, but he finally decides to withdraw the story. He tells the custodian, "Maybe I'm not tough enough to be a journalist." He's told in reply, "It's not 'tough' that makes a good journalist, Mr. Patterson. It's integrity." Journalists quickly learn they face multiple responsibilities. Overall, they have a responsibility to the truth—at least to the degree that it can be determined. The encounter between Mike Patterson and Mr.

Bergner reveals other responsibilities as well. Journalists are in the business to disclose information, not withhold it. Mike brought a good, worthy story to life; should he now kill it? He has responsibilities to his audience, too, and not only responsibilities to be accurate and fair. He must also measure the public's stake. Is he duty bound in the public interest to tell the story? Then there's Mr. Bergner. If the news amounts to a cocreation of reporters and their interview partners, then it's difficult for any reporter to say, "It's my story, not yours. I can do with it what I want."

Reporters seldom enjoy the luxury of simply "doing journalism," free from nagging concerns like these. The stakes usually are too high for journalists to pretend that getting the story ends their responsibilities. A reporter's mistakes and misunderstandings, even those that seem slight, can reverberate into the community and lives of people. Journalists meet their responsibilities in different ways. Veteran reporter Richard Clurman (1990) says he operates from a formerly heretical view that sharing a story with its principal characters prior to broadcast or publication can only help journalists do a better job. "It can be the final step in reporting to test interpretations, facts and conjectures with those about whom the journalist is writing." Clurman seeks "new illuminations and nuances that otherwise would have escaped even careful reporting and checking" (p. 11). Journalistic interviewees get arguing rights, not editing rights, Clurman says. A news story can be viewed as the intricate interplay of journalist, interviewee, and public audience; it certainly isn't something a journalist produces alone.

Considerable emotional strain accompanies the work of caring journalists. But most would say the rewards outweigh the pressures. There is great satisfaction in knowing that through your efforts, people are heard, understood, and helped. Not all stories have happy endings. Journalism reflects the world in all its dimensions and qualities, both good and bad. Journalists, however, who find and tell stories that inspire hope, offer solutions, build community life, and right wrongs probably enjoy the greatest satisfaction.

Summary

Journalists and, in turn, the public rely on interviews as a major source of news. The techniques and tasks of journalistic interviewing apply to nearly everyone responsible for gathering reliable, important information and distributing it to others. Accuracy is the primary goal of information-gathering interviews.

Journalists use interviews in various ways to fit various situations, from quick-hitting news reports to longer, textured profiles of people. But certain fundamentals apply to most interviews in journalism: purpose, preparation, questioning, listening, record keeping, and postinterview assessment. In addition, interviews can involve conditions set either by the interviewer or interviewee, such as off-the-record agreements.

Interviewees often approach journalists with wariness. In part, they react to stereotypes of journalists as prying, insensitive, and aggressive. In truth, most reporters approach their jobs with compassion and seriousness of purpose. Ethics is an important concern in contemporary journalism. While interviewing ethics hasn't received as much attention as other aspects of the journalist's work, certain guidelines and duties set standards of behavior. As in other fields, though, there are no ethical absolutes. Journalists often must weigh and balance the responsibilities and obligations of their profession against the consequences of their reporting. It is a job full of challenges and rewards.

The Interview Bookshelf

On the journalist's experience

Brady, J. (1976). *The craft of interviewing.* Cincinnati, OH: Writer's Digest Books.

Without a doubt the best known interviewing book among journalists. Brady tells interesting and wise stories about resourceful journalists and the problems they solve.

On practical problems and solutions in journalistic interviews

Killenberg, G. M., & Anderson, R. (1989). *Before the story: Interviewing and communication skills for journalists.* New York: St. Martin's Press.

An attempt to describe the journalistic interview as everyday talk and the journalist as an interpersonal communicator.

On ethics in journalism

Black, J., Steele, B., & Barney, R. (1993). *Doing ethics in journalism.* Greencastle, IN: Sigma Delta Chi Foundation and The Society of Professional Journalists.

A thorough and challenging analysis of actual cases, along with applications from actual journalistic codes of ethics.

Klaidman, S., & Beauchamp, T. L. (1987). *The virtuous journalist.* New York: Oxford University Press.

With both concrete and philosophically informed examples, this book asks journalists to consider carefully the harms they might cause by sloppy communication.

On public/civic journalism

Charity, A. (1995). *Doing public journalism.* New York: Guilford Press.

This book reinforces our emphasis on listening and shows how a new kind of journalism has to depend on a profound respect for interviewees and audiences.

On being interviewed by journalists

Hilton, J. (1987). *How to meet the press: A survival guide.* New York: Dodd, Mead and Company.

Although the interview isn't a war or even a competition, it can sometimes feel unequal to interviewees. Hilton helps anyone prepare to meet professional journalists on their own terms and with more confidence.

References

Anson, S. A. (1996, June/July). Off the record. *George,* pp. 110–114, 134–140.

Blundell, W. E. (1988). *The art and craft of feature writing.* New York: Plume/Penguin.

Clurman, R. M. (1990). *Beyond malice.* New York: New American Library.

Dash, L. (1996). *Rosa Lee: A mother and her family in urban America.* New York: Basic Books.

Diane Sawyer: Conscientious voice of "60 Minutes." (1988, May). *In Touch,* pp. 1, 2.

Fallows, J. (1996). *Breaking the news: How the media undermine American democracy.* New York: Pantheon.

Hess, S. (1996). *News & newsmaking.* Washington, D.C.: Brookings Institute.

Kuralt, C. (1985). *On the road with Charles Kuralt.* New York: G. P. Putnam's Sons.

Malcolm, J. (1989, March 13). The journalist and the murderer. *New Yorker.*

Murray, D. (1988, January). Writing on writing. No. 3, *Boston Globe,* pp. 1, 2.

Pandora's box of an interview. (1995, January 5). *St. Petersburg Times,* pp. 1A, 12A.

Rogers, C., & Farson, R. (1957). *Active listening.* Chicago: University of Chicago Industrial Relations Center.

Scanlon, C. (Ed.). (1996). *The best newspaper writing of 1996.* Chicago: Bonus Books.

Schudson, M. (1994). Question authority: A history of the news interview in American journalism, 1860s-1930s. *Media, Culture & Society, 16,* 565–587.

Seabrook, J. (1994, January 10). E-mail from Bill. *New Yorker,* pp. 48–61.

Talese, G. (1995, December). The art of hanging out. *Writer's Digest,* pp. 80, 61–64.

Terkel, S. (1970). *Division street: America.* New York: Avon Discus Books.

✿ 9 Interviews in Social Science and Humanistic Research

Meaning is not merely elicited by apt questioning nor simply transported through respondent replies; it is actively and communicatively assembled in the interview encounter. Respondents are not so much repositories of knowledge—treasuries of information awaiting excavation—as they are constructors of knowledge in collaboration with interviewers.

—James Holstein and Jaber Gubrium, *The Active Interview*

LEARNING GOALS

After reading this chapter, you should be able to

- Describe the philosophy of research interviewing
- Understand the logic of different stages of research planning
- Compare and contrast quantitative and qualitative research methods
- Plan and conduct basic versions of four survey interviewing methods: the survey interview, the focus group interview, the oral history interview, and the ethnographic interview
- Discuss ethical implications of research interviewing from the perspective of the interviewee

When he's not writing steamy, best-selling novels, the Rev. Andrew M. Greeley oversees studies for the National Opinion Research Center (NORC) in Chicago, one of the country's most famous research institutions. NORC conducts polls and surveys of major issues such as drug abuse, sexual relations, homelessness, and mental health. Its research taps into the attitudes, beliefs, and behavior of the American public, and NORC's findings flow into a river of survey data used in decision-making situations ranging from marketing dog food to conducting foreign policy.

Social science and humanistic research methods extend beyond public opinion interviews to include studies in anthropology, communication, geography, history, linguistics, psychology, and sociology. Although definitions of the social sciences and the humanities are debated by researchers, and although the distinctions are rarely clear cut, the term **social science** generally refers to attempts to discern and describe relatively precise patterns of human behavior, in both individual and group contexts, as exhibited in many studies in sociology, psychology, economics, and other fields. The **humanities** are generally thought to be those lines of research—among them, literature, philosophy, history—that attempt to discover the qualities and values that make humans particularly human. Many communication researchers stand in a fertile middle ground emphasizing both social behavior and humanistic values. A wide range of social science and humanistic researchers use interviews to re-create the past, understand the present, and predict the future. Interviewing is vital work, helping to expand knowledge and, at times, offering solutions about such important subjects as teenage smoking habits and suicide rates among the elderly. Social science and humanistic researchers play a major role in uncovering, investigating, and explaining human experience.

Unfortunately, although interview researcher Charles Briggs (1986) estimates that perhaps 90 percent of all studies in the social sciences use data from interviews (p. 1), most of the articles and books examining interviewing techniques ". . . are of the 'cookbook' type, providing recipes for better baking using interviews yet without seriously considering the nature of the interview or its inherent weaknesses" (p. 2). Despite thousands of studies, he can conclude that "we still know very little about the nature of the interview as a communicative event" (p. 2).

In a sense, we're all researchers as we go about the everyday tasks of shopping, traveling, reading the paper, and voting. As everyday researchers, people sample opinions, test hypotheses, ask questions, and conduct informal interviews. However, many who do research as a calling or career elevate the collection, interpretation, and application of their inquiries to a level of science. A dedicated professional researcher relentlessly and systematically pursues a kind of truth—at least the best attainable version of the truth. Others who use interviews in their work, such as journalists or social workers, don't always engage in precise scientific inquiry or see themselves as researchers. They might collect anecdotal evidence from interviewees and weave it into literary or nonfiction forms that portray reality in a less precise but more involving narrative way.

Yet even in the deadline-driven world of reporting, a level of science applies—or should apply—when news organizations administer polls and analyze data, engaging in what some call *precision journalism* (Meyer, 1991). It could be argued that anyone in the pursuit of knowledge should at least respect, and often act within, the spirit of scientific inquiry. Physicist Lawrence Cranberg (1989) observed that trained researchers "seek to discover hidden facts and arrive at elusive truths," and they share a "skilled determination to get at them" (p. 47). The journalist and scientist, he added, "march to the same orders and serve the common need of mankind for shared knowledge and understanding" (p. 46). Although different people define facts differently, and although facts are not objects that can be discovered whole, Cranberg's basic sentiment applies to a wide variety of knowledge seekers.

In this chapter you'll be introduced to the fundamentals of research interviewing. The conclusions reached by analyzing interview data contribute to both quantitative and qualitative research. **Quantitative research** transforms experience into information by creating countable categories and units that can aid future decision making. **Qualitative research,** as the name implies, focuses less on quantities than on the qualities of data—their meaning or value. Both types of research can make scientific contributions (although science is occasionally identified more with quantitative studies), and many research projects combine quantitative and qualitative methods to help explain communication more systematically. We'll discuss more of the differences in "The Basics" section. But for now, we'll define **scientific research** as a systematic, public, and verifiable path toward practical human knowledge. Scientists use a variety of methods of inquiry and measurement, and social scientists, in particular, rely on various formats of interviewing—questionnaires, telephone surveys, and in-depth conversations, for example.

After an introduction to the philosophy and characteristics of scientific inquiry, we'll look at a form of quantitative research—the survey—and then move to qualitative intricacies of focus group, ethnographic, and oral history interviews. In "Beyond the Basics," two ethical issues of research are discussed. First, the idea of qualitative research as a collaborative activity (a persistent theme of this book) is applied to the interaction of interviewers and interviewees. Second, we describe why it's important for ethical researchers to obtain the informed or implied consent of respondents.

Philosophy of the Research Interview

THE BASICS ✽

How do we come to know something? This question propels **epistemology,** the study of how human knowledge and insight develop. Fred Kerlinger (1986) describes four ways humans come to know: tenacity, intuition, authority, and science. *Tenacity* relies on repetition and ingrained beliefs. Often it's something drummed into us as children: "If you go outside with wet hair you'll catch a cold" or "Lightning doesn't strike twice in the same place." Such knowing is part of our socialization, but knowledge based on tenacity often lacks proof. It's more folklore than fact. *Intuition* relies on common sense and gut feelings. A police officer, for example, employing *anecdotal* and *impressionistic* evidence, concludes violence depicted on TV instigates real-life violence. Intuition has its value, and sometimes what we know intuitively corresponds with findings of valid research. Intuition, however, can lead researchers astray because it isn't grounded in carefully collected and analyzed *empirical* data from controlled, systematic observation or experimentation. When tenacity or intuition fail at supplying an answer, there is *authority,* such as a report in a reputable publication or the words of an expert in a specialized field. In the best of circumstances, an authority provides valid, sound information and opinion. Of course, the voice of authority, while sounding sure and exact, might merely echo flawed intuition or untested hypotheses.

That leaves *science,* a word most of us associate with the solid "truths" of life. The other means of knowing can be haphazard and unreliable, but Kerlinger says science gives us something based on proof—something to count on. Keep in mind, however, that we learn in combinations of ways. In fact, scientific investigations often spring from creative hypotheses gleaned from intuition, authority, or tenacity. Moreover, scientific knowing can be flawed, too; when framed differently by various audiences, it can, and usually does, produce conclusions that are misleading, ambiguous, inconclusive, fragmentary, or even dishonest. An automatic reverence for scientific method is being critiqued by a variety of researchers whose orientation is described variously not only as qualitative, but as interpretive or naturalistic. Yvonna Lincoln and Egon Guba (1985) observe that despite the successes of science, "cracks have begun to appear in science's magnificent edifice as new 'facts' are uncovered with which the old paradigm cannot deal or explain. Normal science . . . is becoming more and more difficult to sustain. Serious challenges are being mounted from the perspective of alternate paradigms that suggest new and different answers" (p. 7).

These challenges do not suggest that traditional science is dead or irrelevant. Rather, its brands of cause-and-effect structure and data-based usefulness are not the only ways we can know the world. Steinar Kvale (1996) identifies a number of epistemological positions relevant to qualitative interviewing but which aren't based upon traditional science (pp. 38–50). Each philosophy depends on the researcher's recognition that human beings create meaning through their relations, that new information emerges from communicative interactions, and that people see, interpret, and understand in different ways.

For example, to illustrate the most important of Kvale's categories, researchers who embrace **postmodern** thought are a varied group, but many operate from the philosophy that knowledge doesn't necessarily correspond to or mirror reality in a direct one-to-one relationship. Rather, some postmodernists contend, knowledge amounts to a *social construction*. In other words, knowledge grows anew as people continuously interpret, negotiate, and renegotiate the meanings of the social world. In postmodern thought, the interview serves, in Kvale's words, as a "construction site" of knowledge (p. 42). Postmodernists perch on only one branch of social science and differ in outlook from social scientists who reason with presumably "hard" data that they claim directly corresponds to the reality it represents.

Knowledge can be considered factual in a scientific sense, of course, but it is also created through people communicating with each other. Thousands of perceptual details and experiences are stored within us—our personal data bank. A survey questionnaire can tap that data bank through questions such as "When were you born?" "How much do you weigh?" and "Who was your first-grade teacher?" Beyond readily recalled facts and statistics of our lives, though, inquiry depends on mutual understanding and cooperation. For example, consider these questions:

"What was the world like when you were born?"

"Do you like your appearance?"

"Did your mother's heritage influence you?"

"What was your first-grade teacher like?"

Here communication gets far more complicated, and meaning is at stake. An interplay of questions and answers is likely to result. The question like "What was the world like when you were born?" might lead to this response, "Do you mean, 'How did we live?' or 'What was it like socially?'" But even then, little is really specified. An exploration gets under way, and the destination remains in doubt as interviewer and interviewee work together toward understanding. The interview constitutes research, although it is far from approximating the precision of physical science with its test tubes, chemical equations, and precise measures.

Researchers distinguish between two principal types of investigation—quantitative and qualitative. A researcher usually chooses one or the other basic type for a specific study, although overlap and integration of the two approaches is also possible. The difference between the two, according to one authority (McCracken, 1988), lies partly in scope. "The quantitative researcher uses a lens that brings a narrow strip of the field of vision into very precise focus. The qualitative researcher uses a lens that permits a much less precise vision of a much broader strip" (p. 16).

Quantitative researchers in the social sciences try to generate, categorize, and account for numerical data by using instruments such as questionnaires or survey interview *guides* (schedules). The findings reflect the mathematical precision of the research, and interpretation becomes a way of explaining or qualifying what the numbers show.

Qualitative researchers concentrate on the less tangible qualities of experience that characterize social action. Their methods include field study, focus groups, in-depth interviews, and participant observation. The researcher becomes an "instrument" for collection of data, using powers of communication, observation, and interpretation to conduct the inquiry. A qualitative approach requires a personal, hands-on relationship with the data collected. Narrative explanations and findings dominate qualitative research, not numbers or charts.

Russell Bernard (1988) helps us further understand the relationship of quantitative to qualitative research with this explanation:

> . . . [A]ll quantification is not science, and all science is not quantified. Searching the Bible for statistical evidence of the existence of God, for example, doesn't turn the enterprise into science. By the same token, at the early stages of development, any science relies primarily on qualitative data. . . . As sciences mature, they come naturally to depend more and more on quantitative data and on quantitative tests of qualitatively described relations. For example, qualitative research might lead us to say that "most of the land in Xakaloranga is controlled by a few people." Later, quantitative research might result in our saying "76 percent of the land in Xakaloranga is controlled by 14 percent of the inhabitants." The first statement is not wrong, but the second statement confirms the first and carries more information as well. (p. 24)

In political science, for instance, a qualitative project might rely on in-depth interviews of voters talking about their own political beliefs and experiences, or their evaluations of the political system. In a quantitative study, instead of face-to-face in-depth interviews or observation of political actors, the research draws on a representative sample of voters and asks carefully constructed and administered survey questions to collect information that not only describes the voters' political beliefs and experiences but also accounts for variable influences of, for example, age, gender, religion, education, and income. From that data, the quantitative research predicts, within a range of confidence, how, say, white males between the ages of twenty-five and thirty-five will vote on a school tax referendum. Box 9.1 outlines the basic structure of a research project.

Survey Interviews

Researchers use quantitative and mixed quantitative/qualitative surveys for descriptive, explanatory, exploratory, and analytical purposes. In marketing, for example, surveys

- *Select the problem.* A researcher becomes curious about a problem that can't be explained sufficiently by existing research and theory. He or she tentatively decides the problem is worthy of study and considers practical and ethical implications of a possible project.

- *Review the literature.* A **literature review**—a careful written analysis of existing research and data on the proposed subject—helps narrow the study and leads to establishing a hypothesis or research question.

- *Frame a hypothesis or a research question.* A *hypothesis* is a tentative prediction about a population being studied. A *research question,* appropriate for studies that are less associated with the traditional scientific method, asks specifically how two or more concepts or variables are related.

- *Select a methodology.* Once a hypothesis or research question is set, the researcher selects a methodology appropriate for testing the hypothesis or exploring the research question. The methodology undergoes a pretest before data collection begins, if feasible. For example, a smaller pilot study might help the researcher determine whether a proposed survey instrument (question-

naire) contains confusing, ambiguous, or inappropriate questions.

- *Collect data.* In most qualitative projects, the researcher personally collects data through interviews, participant observation, and other methods. In a quantitative study, trained assistants might help the researcher administer surveys or collect data in other systematic ways.

- *Analyze data.* Qualitative research involves personal reflection and scrutiny by the researcher; however, there is usually a pattern or system to the analysis, such as comparisons of interview responses in identifying emergent themes. In quantitative research, the data often undergo statistical analysis based on coding of the responses from surveys or data, such as census figures.

- *Present results.* Once analyzed and checked for error, the findings, including conclusions based on them, are shared with other researchers through scholarly publications or released to the public through a report or other method of dissemination. Increasingly, qualitative researchers are sharing tentative results with interviewees and other respondents whose cooperation helped produce the insights in the first place.

---

explore and explain consumer behavior and attitudes, helping companies introduce new products or improve existing ones. In politics, surveys gauge public opinion on policy and campaign issues, and candidates often adjust their positions based on survey results. Academic researchers find surveys useful for a variety of projects, such as identifying attitudes of parents toward court-ordered school busing or determining the decision-making criteria of editors and other media gatekeepers.

For the sake of **validity** (whether a method assesses what it is supposed to assess) and **reliability** (whether it assesses the same phenomenon whenever the method is used), surveys can't be haphazardly designed or administered, unless someone doesn't want to know the truth or hopes to hide the truth. In survey research, reputations suffer when results go sour. Validity and reliability are expected, and falling short of those standards isn't acceptable.

Surveys succeed or fail to the extent that they meet three basic criteria: Do they get people to respond *honestly, accurately,* and *completely*? A survey ideally will allow and

Jean Converse and Howard Schuman

Converse and Schuman, experienced interviewers at the Survey Research Center of the University of Michigan, trained and supervised many student interviewers. Their book collects and analyzes interviewer reactions after research projects were completed. Here are some excerpts:

> "Interviewers come to know a 'cross-section' of Americans in a way that many of us never do. We gather our collection of friends and acquaintances from the people we find in our own small worlds—at work, in the neighborhood, in the church group, the bowling league. Even when we get to know those strange and inexplicable people, the friends of our friends, we have not usually ventured very far from our accustomed ways of talking, dressing, being busy or lazy, or trying to think about things."

> ". . . Interviewers venture out of their own small worlds. They meet people they would never otherwise meet, and they often find a degree of reflectiveness, personal candor, and genuine talk that is not even an everyday occurrence among close friends. They occasionally encounter indifference or suspicion, but they leave many an interview with the experience of a fleeting but genuine friendship."

> ". . . The variety of scenes and situations to which the interviewer is admitted is richer than most of us gather up in a few days or weeks within our own small worlds. The process is one of sampling not only people but moments of lives being lived."

Source: Converse & Schuman, 1974, p. 1

encourage forthright responses, even when exploring sensitive subjects such as drug use or mental problems. The survey must avoid any ambiguity that could undermine the accuracy of its findings; if one person defines "well off" in terms of salary, but the next respondent defines it in terms of neighborhood safety, are they really answering the same question? Finally, the survey must gain respondent cooperation that is as complete and thorough as possible. The design or format of a survey can either discourage or encourage participation. A survey can't accomplish its objectives if people won't participate willingly and conscientiously. Box 9.2 offers some relevant experiences from survey interviewers.

Types of Surveys

Three types of research surveys supply information under different circumstances, with corresponding advantages and limitations: self-administered questionnaires, telephone surveys, and interviewer-conducted surveys. Each survey approach involves compromises. Knowing their strengths and weaknesses, however, allows you to select a method that best meets your goals.

Self-Administered Questionnaires   Researchers distribute survey questionnaires by mail or other means of delivery, such as computer disk. The researcher surrenders face-to-face administration of the survey in return for efficiency—reaching a large number of respondents at a reasonable cost. Although people asked to complete a survey might set it aside, turning their attention to other business, the self-administration allows them to participate anonymously and at a time and place convenient for them. Several companies also provide mailing lists of potential respondents divided by specific demographic or lifestyle characteristics; a self-administered survey based on such a list has obvious advantages.

Self-administered surveys constitute a kind of interview-at-a-distance, with predecided questions posed and answered. As a communication process, it lacks the advantages of immediate feedback and interactive context. Respondents cannot clarify the meaning of the overall instructions or of a particular question. Context problems include researchers' uncertainty over who completed the survey; it might not be the person to whom it's addressed. Another disadvantage is the return rate; it's too easy to toss a questionnaire in the trash, although reminders help encourage returns. The collection of data through the mail can be agonizingly slow. Moreover, to ensure a response, mail surveys cannot be too long—usually no more than a couple of pages. That, of course, also reduces the amount of data collected.

Recent evidence (Tourangeau & Smith, 1996) suggests that **computer-assisted self-administered interviewing** (CASI) and **audio computer-assisted self-administered interviewing** (ACASI) have advantages over other more personalized interview forms in one crucial respect. In exploring topics of sensitive importance to respondents, such as illegal drug use or sexual habits, answering questions administered by computer (especially in the ACASI mode with an accompanying voice) increased reports of possibly embarrassing acts. Roger Tourangeau and Tom Smith (1996) write, "We believe that the two self-administered modes foster a greater sense of privacy of the collection process. . . . It is also possible that, by letting the respondent interact directly with the computer, ACASI and CASI help convince respondents of the legitimacy and scientific value of the study" (p. 301). Other possibly sensitive topics such as racism, personal hygiene, or reading habits might be explored more effectively with research using ACASI and CASI.

Telephone Surveys   Most people are accessible by telephone, and when you reach them voice-to-voice—rather than counting on them to open mail and complete a questionnaire—they are less likely to ignore or put off your request for assistance. As a result, the response rates with telephone interviews generally run higher than those of mail surveys. Researchers also have the opportunity to establish a connection with the respondent and to provide feedback. A longer list of questions might be appropriate, as well.

On the other hand, in an age with pervasive telemarketing, many people are wary of being asked to participate in a telephone survey. Occasionally, a "survey" turns out to be a sales pitch. Many of us will hear the word "survey" and abruptly dismiss the caller ("I'm too busy to talk right now"). The prevalence of answering machines also works against telephone surveys. Even when home, people use answering machines and other technologies such as Caller ID to screen calls.

Although more personal than a piece of mail, the telephone still cannot provide much nonverbal context for interviewers to evaluate whether a survey is being taken seriously. Is the respondent, for example, watching a TV program or looking after a baby while answering? Such preoccupation can affect the reliability of surveys. Telephone surveys also cost more to administer than surveys sent by mail. Recruiting and hiring bright, reliable telephone interviewers isn't easy, and training sessions increase the costs.

Interviewer-Conducted Surveys   The most desirable of all survey approaches, the interviewer-conducted survey, also tends to be the most expensive and time consuming. Its chief advantage is the use of face-to-face interpersonal communication, which allows for a more detailed, fuller response on a human scale, with the opportunity for rapport between interviewer and interviewee. Every respondent is asked a set of questions from a highly standardized schedule, but this method still encourages a more personal quality of communication.

Face-to-face communication also can produce disadvantages, particularly if, instead of rapport, the interviewer and interviewee find communication strained and unpleasant. Some literature (for example, Converse & Schuman, 1974, p. 54) even identifies **over-rapport**—the occurrence of interviewer bias as a result of excessive closeness or cordiality—as a hindrance to survey interviewing. To survey a large number of people, the researcher usually enlists a field staff of interviewers. Even with thorough training, they will communicate differently and, further, might fail to suppress biases or follow instructions to maintain neutrality. There is no such interviewer effect in mailed surveys.

Planning and Administering Surveys

Most survey research involves five separate but mutually supportive steps: setting a research objective; selecting a sample of respondents from the target population; constructing the survey questionnaire or instrument; administering the survey; and analyzing the data. Designing a survey-interview project is a complex and creative task, and we don't want to mislead on that point by suggesting it's a simple, paint-by-numbers process. Survey researchers usually possess an extensive background in statistics, probability sampling, and the use of analytical tools. Many are highly paid for their talents; it's not a job for dilettantes. What follows is a basic summary of common survey activities, not a definitive set of instructions.

Research Objective   A series of preliminary questions often helps a researcher fine-tune the focus of the survey and determine what to ask and how to ask it. Will the survey collect descriptive data, such as who reads supermarket tabloids or watches soap operas? Will the survey include questions seeking explanatory data as well, such as why people say they watch soap operas? Will it compare demographics, such as rate of viewership by age, race, income, and gender, to further understand who watches and why?

The Sample   John Allen Paulos, author of *A Mathematician Reads the Newspaper* (1995), is concerned about the too-often blurred distinction between scientific surveys and informal ones:

> Too many stories (usually local) are prefaced with something like, 'This is not a scientific poll, but a sampling of your friends and neighbors who called our special 900 number. . . .' A more accurate prologue might be, 'Here is what a few of the most fervent people in your community think about this issue.' Confidence intervals for such 'samplings' should be quite broad to accommodate their considerable hot air. (p. 153)

After a research objective has been firmly set and defined, survey researchers, contrary to Paulos's characterization of quick-fix popular media polls, systematically study a **sample**—a group of respondents of necessary size and type to represent the larger population. Even this is a compromise. A researcher who surveys *all* members of a given population, such as the congregation of a church, conducts what is called a **census.** Usually, though, researchers study only a segment of the membership and attempt to generalize with confidence from results provided by that sample. At times, the number of respondents used in survey research seems to the everyday citizen to be almost too small for drawing conclusions, but sampling procedures can be so sophisticated that results are remarkably representative and helpful. For example, the A. C. Nielsen Company, a worldwide leader in market research, uses a basic sampling of 4,000 individuals to determine what 260 million Americans watch on TV, and although its methods aren't perfect, no one has managed to supplant Nielsen as the accountant of audience size and preferences.

Survey samples fall under two broad categories: probability and nonprobability. **Probability surveys** use various mathematical guidelines to ensure a representative sample of the population. The guiding principle of probability is that all members of a target population have an equal chance of being selected for the sample. **Nonprobability surveys** do not follow mathematical guidelines of probability, so their usefulness as an accurate, reliable predictor is limited. However, they can be helpful in collecting preliminary data or in investigating a small or select population. Note the following fundamental differences between the two.

Probability surveys use mathematical guidelines to draw a representative sample of a particular population. With a probability survey, every member of a population has an equal chance of being chosen, a condition sometimes referred to as **random selection.** One researcher (Stacks, 1992) illustrates the process with an analogy of a jar holding 10,000 marbles—8,000 red and 2,000 blue (p. 179). You could select a sample by mixing the marbles and selecting 10, one at a time, but replacing each marble after noting its color. By chance, you could draw 10 marbles of the same color. Odds are better, though, that you'd come closer to a sampling percentage that reflects the population (several times as many reds as blues). But how close? A random sample of 100 would likely come closer to the actual 4:1 ratio, and 1,000 closer still. Probability surveys also permit estimates of **sampling error,** that is, the degree to which a given sample statistic will likely fail to correspond to the actual characteristics of the population. Formulas help researchers compute the sampling error; once computed, the rate of sampling error allows researchers to determine the degree to which the findings can be accepted as reflective of the population.

Types of probability sampling include simple random sampling, systematic sampling, and stratified random sampling. Use of a **simple random sample** depends on knowing and numbering the complete roster of the population. If you wanted to survey a sample of 50 professors out of a population of 500 in your city, you would assign each a number from 1 to 500. Then, locate a table of random numbers (included in many books on research methods); this table contains columns of grouped numbers arranged in a random pattern. Pick an arbitrary starting point on the table, perhaps by closing your eyes and dropping a pen point on a column. Also arbitrarily, decide whether to go up or down in columns if you don't select a number in your sample the first time. For example, your pen might land on 77,832, but 778 is higher than any of the numbers you've assigned to the population. Because you've decided to go down the columns, say, you move to the next number down, perhaps 00789; Professor No. 7 (007) becomes the first person selected to be surveyed for your random sample. Then select the remaining 49 numbers by moving through the table in the same way. Other approaches include using a computer program to select a random sampling—or literally putting the numbers in a hat and drawing 50 (while returning drawn numbers to the hat).

The **systematic random sample** resembles a simple random sample with a different selection method, one in which every nth part or unit of the population gets selected. To get a sample of 20 from a population of 100, every fifth number would be picked, starting with a number selected at random, say, 9, and then moving at intervals of five (14, 19, 24, and so on). Systematic random sampling works well when the population comes from a directory or yearbook. Researchers are careful, though, when using a telephone book or other reference that might not include all members of a population.

Earl Babbie (1992), an expert on social science research, notes that **stratified random sampling** offers a greater degree of representativeness and a lower degree of sampling error than the other approaches. A stratified sample allows for study of subsets of a population and, therefore, enables the researcher to account for and compare variables within the population. Working with a human population, those variables might include age, gender, education, occupation, and geography (place of residence), for example. The units of a population then are separated by common characteristics into homogenous groups (strata) before drawing a sample. To study voters as a population in a stratified sampling would mean looking at subsets of voters, say, by age but also, for example, by region or religion.

Nonprobability surveys do not seek to guarantee a representative sample of the population and thus could utilize a variety of other methods of sampling, including a **convenience sample** (also called an **available sample**). In a convenience sample, respondents are chosen to participate in a research project because they can provide useful data and because they are simply available. For example, professors and peers sometimes involve college students in surveys that have nothing inherently to do with campus life; students are a group hardly known to be representative of larger social trends of political or economic participation, but as a group they are quite easily tapped. A **snowball sample** is composed of a group of respondents who then identify more respondents, who identify others, and so on. Another type uses a **quota sample** of respondents chosen to match, for example, known percentages in the larger population. Election records of a precinct might show that 40 percent of the voters are registered Democrat, 50 percent Republican, and 10 percent independent. You could, then, draw a sample that reflects those percentages; if known, variables of age, race, and other factors could also be included in the sample.

Question Design and Construction   The bare bones of a survey, whether administered on paper or orally, includes a sequence of standardized questions preceded by an introduction and instructions. (See Box 9.3 for one particularly influential survey question sequence.) The introduction typically explains the nature and purpose of the survey; the instructions help both interviewer and interviewee reduce the likelihood of misunderstanding or error. Introductions and instructions should be kept short, simple, and, above all, clear.

Typically, standardized survey questions require respondents to choose among several possible answers or ranges of response. The most common survey questionnaire employs either scales or multiple-choice selections. Often the opening questions seek demographic information—place of birth, age, occupation, or residence, for example. For coding and comparison purposes, these questions sometimes reflect groupings, as in this example:

What is your age?

___ 18–25

___ 26–40

___ 41–55

___ 56–70

___ above 70

Certain scales work well with particular information-seeking objectives. For example, in measuring attitudes, a **Likert-type scale** (named after its originator, Rensis Likert) offers a statement and asks the respondent to indicate a choice from a range of approval or agreement:

Police should be able to conduct car searches during routine traffic stops.

___ Strongly agree

___ Agree

___ Undecided (or neutral)

___ Disagree

___ Strongly disagree

Various forms of rating scales often include number references as codes for later calculation and analysis of the survey data:

What's your opinion of the news coverage in the *New York Times*?

Objective ___ ___ ___ ___ ___ Biased

  (5) (4) (3) (2) (1)

One Common Survey Question Structure—Gallup's Quintamensional Sequence

George Gallup and the American Institute of Public Opinion have developed over the past half century a sequence and structure of questioning that establish how much information respondents might have, and how much thought they've given to a topic, before they provide significant opinions. The quintamensional sequence, as it's known, also increases survey validity by checking whether respondents understand the questions in roughly the same ways. William Foddy exemplifies the five-part sequence in this way:

1. "A general question to establish whether respondents have the required information concerning the topic. (e.g. Have you heard of X? yes ___ no ___)

2. "An open question to get at respondents' general perceptions or feelings about the topic. (e.g. What are your views about X?)

3. "A dichotomous question to elicit perceptions or feelings about a specific aspect of the topic. (e.g. Do you favour or not favour Xi? favour ___ not favour ___)

4. "An open question to get at reasons for responses toward the aspect of the topic specified in step 3. (e.g. Why do you favour [not favour] Xi?)

5. "A rating question to allow respondents to indicate the strength of their responses toward the aspect of the topic specified in step 3. (e.g. How strongly do you feel about this?: Very strongly, Fairly strongly, Not at all strongly.)"

Source: Foddy, 1993, p. 62

Semantic differential scales, similar to the preceding example, ask for a series of choices, along a continuum, between opposite descriptions. Semantic differential scales probe the rater's subjective connotations—inner semantic meanings—for the item or object being rated. Varying the placement of presumably positive and negative concepts can help prevent respondents from slipping into a pattern of answering, as line two in the following example illustrates.

The president's foreign policy:

Active ___ ___ ___ ___ ___ ___ Passive

Weak ___ ___ ___ ___ ___ ___ Strong

Confident ___ ___ ___ ___ ___ ___ Worried

In determining behavior, there is often need for a **frequency scale**, which provides specific data on behavioral occurrences.

How often do you eat at a restaurant?

___ 5 or more times a week

___ 2–4 times a week

___ once a week

___ less than once a week

___ never

BOX 9.4   **REMINDERS**

Categories of Difficult Questions

In *Constructing Questions for Interviews and Questionnaires,* William Foddy summarizes research into questions that created problems for respondent interpretations (listed from most common to least common):

1. "Two questions presented as one (e.g. 'Which brand do you use or do you change brands frequently?').

2. "Questions with a lot of meaningful words (e.g. 'How many of each sized packet have you bought?').

3. "Questions which include qualifying phrases or clauses (e.g. 'Have you bought any chocolate in the last 7 days, not counting today?').

4. "Questions with multiple ideas or subjects (e.g. 'Which have you heard of or shopped at?').

5. "Questions that contain difficult or unfamiliar words.

6. "Questions that contain one or more instructions (e.g. 'Do not include X in your answer').

7. "Questions that start with words that are meant to soften them (e.g. 'Would you mind . . .').

8. "Questions with difficult phrases.

9. "Hypothetical questions.

10. "Questions that are dependent upon prior questions for meaning (e.g. 'Q1/ Did you buy a copy of X?' 'Q2/ Where is it now?').

11. "Questions with negative elements.

12. "Inverted questions (e.g. 'The ones you bought last time—what were they?').

13. "Questions including either 'if any' or 'if at all' (e.g. 'Which of these, if any, have you bought?').

14. "Questions that are too long.

15. "Questions that include both present and past tenses.

16. "Questions in which singular and plural cases are used."

Source: Foddy, 1993, p. 51

We've introduced elementary examples of common scale types, but other more sophisticated methods are available as well. If you plan to conduct complex survey research, we suggest you consult a handbook in social science survey methods (for example, Bouma & Atkinson, 1995; Foddy, 1993), or take a survey research class. In large-scale projects, those researchers responsible for constructing the survey instrument itself may hire professional interviewers to administer the surveys.

The basic rules of constructing and asking questions apply in survey interviews, so review our discussion in Chapter 4. Yet standardized social science interviewing demands, if anything, an even greater attention to the wording of questions, according to Foddy in Box 9.4, where he illustrates previous research into complex questioning.

Foddy (1993, p. 51), after reviewing the literature, recommends that researchers adhere to the following principles in wording questions (paraphrased here):

- Brevity
- Grammatical simplicity
- Specificity
- Concreteness

The principle of **brevity** reminds researchers to edit their questions to eliminate unnecessary words. A question that violates the principle of brevity is "When considering the overall political and judicial scene in Washington, do you find yourself encouraged or discouraged?" Researchers achieve **grammatical simplicity** by removing "complicating phrases and clauses" and by phrasing questions in positive form. Phrasing questions with complex grammar and negative constructions can involve too many interpretations that muddy the intended question. A question that violates the principle of grammatical simplicity is "What, given the public's recent preoccupation with healthy alternatives, does not worry you about the following foods?" **Specificity** implies that researchers choose words that have as few meanings as possible for the intended audience. A question that violates the principle of specificity is "Which educational experiences have been important for you recently?" Finally, by conforming to the principle of **concreteness,** researchers provide tangible, easily understandable choices, examples, or illustrations. A question that violates the principle of concreteness is "Would you say you go to see movies often or seldom?" Concreteness is closely related to specificity, but the emphasis in specificity is to choose words that respondents will interpret in the same way ("educational experiences" is so ambiguous that one person could call a basketball game educational, while another might limit the term to classroom learning). The emphasis in concreteness is not only on specificity of terms but also on providing empirical definitions for respondents ("often" and "seldom" can be made empirical by substituting scales for how often they attend movies). Box 9.5 takes you through decisions for a typical survey interview.

Focus Group Interviews

What Is a Focus Group?

According to Thomas Greenbaum (1993), focus group methodology is used more frequently than any other type of qualitative research (p. 4). He cites research industry estimates that about 110,000 focus groups were conducted in 1990 in the United States alone (Greenbaum, 1993, p. 143). In the years since, focus groups have grown even more popular, as consultants in marketing, education, politics, and other applied fields attempt to learn more about those they serve, and researchers into more general cultural and social trends use interviewlike procedures in focus groups to develop insight into the dynamics of human decision making. Why all this popularity?

A **focus group** is an artificial group recruited by researchers to discuss what draws participants to certain attitudes, preferences, or products, in addition to why and how they make their social decisions. Focus groups are particularly useful for determining buying or shopping habits, assessments of product packaging, product development and positioning factors, candidate images, and assessments of advertising or marketing campaigns. Focus groups also might be valuable for organizations wanting a structured approach to developing innovative ideas.

BOX 9.5 **REMINDERS**

Administering Survey Interviews

You might be asked to serve as a survey interviewer as part of your job or as a volunteer for an organization. You'll likely receive detailed instructions on how the organization wants you to administer the survey, but here are some general reminders:

- *Rehearse.* Go over the questionnaire or survey instrument carefully. Be familiar with the language used; if you're not, consult a supervisor or dictionary for definitions or explanations. Be aware of the proper pronunciation of unfamiliar words, too.

- *Establish a supportive climate.* Introduce yourself and the project cordially and sincerely. Don't tell jokes that make light of the task at hand. It should be treated as serious, significant business, but a smile and pleasant demeanor are appropriate. Dress for the occasion, as well, choosing a wardrobe that fits the circumstances. Although many interviews are reasonably formal occasions, field interviews in a factory probably shouldn't be conducted in a suit and tie.

- *Stick to the question schedule.* Don't ad lib or vary the questions. Your alterations could negatively influence the results. In asking questions, try to maintain a steady, consistent tone. In particular, avoid inflections or pitch that could artificially lead or suggest a response.

- *Record responses accurately.* Problems of **coding** (deciding how to place responses into categories) are common even for research designs that allow for little respondent choice. If questions are closed, or if respondents must choose from a list they don't appear to understand, an interviewer must, in some cases, engage in what survey researchers call training the respondent. That is, the instructions should be explained again and the list reread for the respondent. Do not interpret a respondent's answer yourself, or give an ad hoc explanation; to do so would alter the comparability of results. Coding problems are much more serious for open-questioning designs, because individual responses must be coded into one or more classifications of the interviewee's or interviewer's devising. If questions are open, any evidence of misunderstanding is potentially more serious, and interviewers must probe for increased clarity. In such situations, practitioners (Fowler & Mangione, 1990) suggest that you reread the question and concentrate on only three basic types of probes: (1) "How do you mean that?" (2) "Tell me more about that." (3) "Anything else?" (p. 41). The less intrusive the probe, the better.

- *Take your time.* Rushing through a survey might save a few minutes but at a high cost. You want respondents to be comfortable and confident with their answers. If they have the time to respond fully and carefully, you have the time also.

- *Reaffirm a supportive climate at the conclusion.* Close the interview with a well-phrased expression of appreciation. If appropriate, you might offer to share a summary of your overall findings with the respondent.

The group is facilitated by a moderator, and a record of the interaction is produced and subsequently analyzed for its content. At times, third-party sponsors are present as observers, perhaps behind one-way glass. These observers may in some cases communicate with the moderator in order to have him or her follow promising threads of discussion, ask new questions, request clarifications, and the like. Focus groups have become so popular that variations on the methodology have proliferated, and there are now literally hundreds of different styles and models from which to choose (see Greenbaum, 1993; Hayes & Tathum, 1989; Krueger, 1994; Morgan, 1993).

A researcher (Calder, 1977) who takes a "philosophy of science" perspective on focus groups highlights three approaches to such research. First, in *exploratory* focus groups, the emphasis is on generating discussion that will define for researchers the specific constructs people use in explaining their worldviews. The group will be successful if researchers emerge with a clearer, more scientific, and more systematic notion of the categories people use in making everyday decisions. In *clinical* focus groups, the purpose is to use group interaction to provide content that can be interpreted later by an analyst trained to look for designated patterns. Whereas exploratory groups are fueled by an overtly scientific motive, the clinical group instead provides interpretive and highly subjective evidence. Even more subjective is the third type, the *phenomenological* focus group, whose sole purpose is to generate data by which researchers can try to experience the inner world of a decision maker or consumer relative to an idea or product.

Thomas Greenbaum (1993) presents focus group methods as a qualitative interview-like alternative to other qualitative interview research designs such as *one-on-ones* (traditional depth interviews with a single respondent), *dyads* (an interview/discussion between an interviewer and a pair of respondents, such as a wife and husband team), and *small-scale quantitative research* (small studies designed to obtain specific "directional" clues from respondents without any attempt to generalize to a larger population).

What Is the Communication Process of a Focus Group?

Greenbaum (1993, Chapter 3) encourages researchers to prepare their focus group studies in a clear and systematic manner. Although we don't have the space in this chapter to provide a comprehensive handbook for focus group studies, you should understand that such studies, like other research, must be guided by clear research questions that reflect the focus of the design. Sponsoring researchers or clients must also consider such crucial planning factors as whom to hire and train as moderator; where and when the groups will meet; and how participants will be recruited and, in most cases, screened with a brief questionnaire verifying that they belong to the specific demographic or sociocultural groups probed by the study.

More directly related to interviewing and interpersonal processes, however, is the actual interactional role of the moderator. Focus group moderators create blended roles in a sense, combining some expectations of an interviewer with the expectations of a small group facilitator or task leader. Certainly, the moderator does not act straightforwardly as an interviewer who asks a series of questions, each of which is answered before moving on to the next. Nor does a moderator ask individual respondents in turn to answer questions about their decisions, attitudes, images, or product choices. Instead, using a guide, or schedule, similar to other qualitative research interviews, the moderator skillfully defines a task, then opens up areas of dialogue in which the group focuses on the designated topic (see Box 9.6).

Moderators must take into account the most difficult challenges facing focus group validity and negotiate between group members' own influence patterns. For example, a focus group of eight to ten people (common for a *full group* rather than a *minigroup* study) runs the risk of having two or three highly verbal and highly opinionated participants who will dominate the group. Moderators must be effective enough listeners and framers to discern when other members may be intimidated or even silenced by these behaviors; gentle probing and invitational inquiries should be distributed throughout the group to give all a chance to contribute. At the same time, the goal of the group is not to have respondents react primarily to the moderator but to each other. The tensions introduced by this subjective process have given focus group critics their most potent ammunition—the research often is based upon group interaction dominated by a few highly opinionated or ideological members.

Oral History Interviews

What Is Oral History?

Oral history creates a rich documentary record of an interviewee's firsthand perceptions, through the collaborative relationship of interviewer and interviewee. Eva McMahan's (1989) succinct definition refers to "interview/conversations designed to record the memorable experiences of people" (p. xiv). Oral history emerges from conversations in which both parties focus mutually on elaborating the stories of the interviewee. Although this may sound at first like a simple activity that is hardly deserving of the label "research method," skillful oral history interviewing has produced some of the most involving and influential literature and history of our century.

Studs Terkel (1985) won the Pulitzer Prize for *The Good War,* an oral history of women and men swept into the turmoil of World War II. Terkel's impressive collection of interviewees—among them a Red Cross volunteer, an atomic bomb scientist, a combat photographer, a gay Marine, and a Japanese schoolboy—reconstructed and relived the 1940s through their emotionally powerful stories. Few histories offer such a vivid overview of World War II from personal recollections.

Oral history, whether it's on Terkel's large scale or on the personalized family scale described by Paul Friedman in Box 9.7, yields a rich lode of remembrances, anecdotes, and insights from living people talking about their pasts. Historians traditionally have relied on documentary evidence, examining deeds, ledgers, diaries, court records, birth certificates, census data, and other tangible facts, and dismissing, by and large, oral testimony from people who have lived through the events themselves.

The Moderator Guide in Focus Group Research

Prominent focus group consultant Thomas Greenbaum recommends the following structure for a well-run schedule of activities and questions for moderators:

- "*Introduction.* Here the moderator will introduce him or herself to the participants, briefly explains the purpose of the session, and alerts them to the microphones or video cameras that are recording the sessions and the one-way mirror through which observers watch the session. Finally, the participants introduce themselves.

- "*A warm-up.* Here the participants are asked to discuss very general issues related to the topic. For example, if a group is being held to expose people to a new concept in dog food, the warm-up would be used to learn basic information about the participants' dogs and how they feed them, including how often and the types of dog food they purchase. The moderator guide identifies all the topics that are to be covered in this warm-up discussion.

- "*A details section.* Here discussion is intended to identify important information about the product category. In the dog food example, the moderator might have the participants discuss the advantages and disadvantages of the dog [f]oods they currently buy, and what a manufacturer could do to make the optimal dog food. The moderator guide identifies in outline all the points the moderator should cover in this section of the group.

- "*A key content section.* In this part of the group, input will be gained from the participants about the research topic itself. In the dog food example, the participants are exposed to several different concepts for new types of dog food. The guide identifies the areas that the moderator probes during this section in order to ensure that the discussion of the topic is thorough.

- "*Summary.* The summary section gives the participants an opportunity to share any information about the topic that they may have forgotten or otherwise omitted. A common way to elicit this information is for the moderator to ask them to give 'advice to the president' about the topic."

Source: Greenbaum, 1993, pp. 39, 43

Over time, however, historians came to value evidence collected from the fertile grounds of human memory. Some early oral histories attempted to preserve the wisdom of "great men and women" before they passed on. Today, oral history encompasses a diversity of voices underrepresented in history books that concentrate on the rich, famous, and politically powerful. Oral testimony enriches and expands our sense of culture, for it enables those who might feel they are without expository ability, confidence, or opportunity to add their chapters to a vibrant ongoing human narration.

Tape recording now allows family members to construct oral histories with important people in their lives and to pass them on to future generations like portraits or heirlooms. Oral histories also feed a growing interest in genealogy, inspired, in part, by Alex Haley's phenomenal best-seller, *Roots,* and the television miniseries based on the book. But if this possibility sounds appealing to you, realize that people do not narrate their lives simply on call. They perhaps are willing to talk, but often only under conditions in which they're convinced their conversation partner is listening.

Trying Out Your Skills

Read the following conversational excerpt in which Audrey, a college student, interviews an older neighbor who was a student activist in the 1960s. She has an assignment to do an oral history interview and wants to know more about that era. Reconsider the basic skills of journalistic interviewing (Chapter 8), and decide for yourself what makes Audrey's talk with Leon different from, or similar to, a journalistic interview.

AUDREY: . . . Were the sixties a time when you felt energized?

LEON: Energized? Yeah, I guess. It was more like I never had to stop and think about things in terms of being energized or not. Everything was charged up, not just me, at least at KU, where I went to school. You wouldn't think a vanilla place in the Midwest like that would be real politicized—and a lot of it wasn't, I guess—but it was hard for me to go anywhere and not meet dozens of people who were socially conscious.

A: "Socially conscious." What forms did that take?

L: Well, I don't know. Folks cared. It's hard to describe to students nowadays, who seem to me, at least, to be so concerned with slotting themselves for jobs. You had students then who would boycott classes to protest the presence of the National Guard, even though it would hurt them in their programs, directly. Kept a lot of 'em from graduating. Graduating didn't . . . Anyway, I remember that there was this girl in my poli-sci class that was a senior, writing her honors thesis and all. She told me about this time when there was a march that she wanted to be in— felt she had to be in—and her prof had scheduled her to present the thesis to a three-person panel or something. She went in the conference room only long enough, she said, to fold the cover page into a paper airplane and float it at them, then she was out the door while it was still in the air! Man . . . I hadn't thought of her in a long time. I wonder if she ever graduated. Probably. Sometime.

A: There were troops on campus part of the time in the late sixties, right? What were you doing then?

L: I was . . . I was . . . (gulps) . . . barely hanging on. Barely. I don't want to get into it here. The atmosphere was charged, like I said, but a lot of us didn't have a clue what we were doing. I kinda crashed and burned a couple of times, lost a couple of friends. Painful . . . Maybe some other time, okay?

A: That's OK. No problem. Do you want to end our session today and pick it up tomorrow? Or do you want to just move on to another time? What did you think when the president resigned? . . .

Issues and Problems of Oral History Interviewing

Can human memory be trusted? Different forms of this deceptively simple question are often debated among historians and others who gather oral testimony. It certainly is an extremely meaningful question if oral testimony is the only source of detailed information about a historical event (see Sypher, Hummert, & Williams, 1994). Yet this is rarely the case. The oral historian employs the interview as an occasion for interaction, not as a test

BOX 9.7   INTERVIEWERS IN ACTION

Paul Friedman

Communication professor Paul Friedman has written a manual describing "life stories interviewing," a form of oral history for families. Here are some excerpts:

". . . Although my primary concern was to connect better with my father, I didn't want to wait for my once- or twice-a-year trips to his home to do this. I wanted to develop an approach to visiting with all persons in his generation in ways that would be meaningful and stimulating to us both, to make connecting with older persons a more regular part of my life. . . ."

"I was . . . surprised to learn that many of the elders with whom I visited had not . . . as yet shared these accounts with their own children. At those times I often wished that I had a tape recorder available, so that our conversation could be made available to their family members, as well.

"Closer to home, I thought how wonderful it would be to record my own father's stories of his youth for my children. By then, however, it was too late. He had passed away, as my mother had fifteen years earlier. That opportunity was gone forever. His loss moved me, nevertheless, to launch the project that culminated in this handbook."

Source: Friedman, 1983, pp. 1–3

of memory. Questions are not designed to elicit only accurate and verifiable facts, but a person's life as he or she remembers living it, the memories that persist, the experiences that continue to shape a unique life.

The oral historian uses the interview as a primary instrument of learning and knowing. Oral histories do unearth facts, but they also produce social meaning and a context that color the documentary facts of history. Records (box scores, photographs, newspaper clippings), for example, can prove beyond a reasonable doubt that "Cool Papa" Bell played center field for the St. Louis Stars and Pittsburgh Crawfords of the old "Negro Leagues" from 1922 to 1946, compiling a .338 lifetime batting average. The records, however, fail to capture the experience and the stories of a talented athlete reflecting on why he played on fields of relative obscurity instead of Yankee Stadium or Fenway Park. Could an interested and committed interviewer help put flesh on the skeleton of statistics and events? How would an interviewer with this goal define the task?

First, an oral historian would *emphasize the present in probing the past.* Charles Briggs (1986) asserts that ignoring this "deeper issue" is a common mistake for interviewers:

The goal of oral history is to elicit information about past events. Researchers have noted the selectivity of memory. Yet a lack of awareness is apparent with respect to the fact that oral history interviews produce a dialogue between past and present. Interviewees interpret the meaning of both the past and the present, including the interview itself. Each query presents them with the task of searching through their memories to see which recollections bear on the question and then fitting this information into a form that will be seen as answering the question. Oral history interviews are thus related to the present as systematically as to the past. (p. 14)

Second, an oral historian would *emphasize conversational teamwork.* The oral history interview is a "conversational narrative" that is "jointly created by the interviewer and the interviewee" (Grele, 1994, p. 2). The interviewer knows two things: first, that the interviewee's story is paramount; second, that the interviewee's story would likely not exist in its present form were it not for the continuing attention, curiosity, and stimulating questions of an interviewer. Narratives are not just stories *told,* but stories *heard.* The opportunity for a fresh and active listener creates the essential energy for oral history.

Conducting an Oral History Interview

Much of our specific advice for oral history interviewing is consistent with suggestions by James Hoopes (1979) in his *Oral History: An Introduction for Students.* In addition, most reminders for journalistic interviews also apply to oral historians (see Chapter 8), if the more elaborate time frame of oral history interviews is taken into account.

Establish an Authentic Relationship   In many kinds of interpersonal encounters, such as employment interviews, it is not enough to be advised to "be yourself." You should work to be your best professional self. Hoopes believes "be yourself" is still good advice for interviewers in this highly personalized task, in which trust is essential. If the task of oral history hinges on relational meanings, give the interviewee a real person—not a cardboard persona—to react to.

Match Your Dress, Language, and Behavior to the Context   Are you interviewing the mayor downtown? You'll probably want to wear a suit. Are you traveling to Boomsville to interview a retired factory worker at a rural cafe? Wear comfortable clothes that both reflect your personality and will not be seen as out of place at the Eat-Rite. Drop all academic jargon in interviews in favor of an informal conversational style; remember that the best interviewers familiarize themselves with the interviewee's language habits without trying to mimic them.

Seek a Location with Minimal Potential for Interruption   Although it may be tempting either to give the interviewee a choice of where to be interviewed, or to conduct the interview in a place relevant to the memories that might be evoked (such as a busy factory), a somewhat private environment is probably best for most interviews in the long run.

Explain Your Purpose and Procedures Clearly   Don't assume that respondents will remember what you told them last week, or in an earlier phone call. Refresh their memories and redescribe your interest in their stories, perhaps while setting up and testing your tape recorder. Briefly mention why it's important to tape personal narratives (it ensures you won't miss the importance of all their words, even if you're distracted momentarily by a particularly fascinating or funny story). Briefly discuss the overall reason for the study, the benefit for the interviewee in having his or her words remembered, and the purpose to which their stories will be put. Many interviewers will want to offer their partners a taped copy of the interview narratives.

Take Notes, but Not Compulsively   Even if you are recording, the notes will orient you to important insights and will ultimately save time. Judicious note taking is a reminder to you to listen carefully and a tangible demonstration to the interviewee that he or she is saying interesting things to you. Overzealous note taking subtracts you from the conversation.

Curb Your Tendency to Judge or Evaluate   Interviewers can elicit content such as racist jokes or accounts of interviewees' cruelty or violent behavior. Although the "be yourself" dictum might make you want to respond with an argumentative reply, remind yourself that this is not your role. Evaluative responses create defensiveness, and your partner may simply clam up. See if you can probe and listen actively to "get inside" the other person's attitudes even further. You may find that although the interviewee uses language you don't appreciate, or has done some unsavory things, there are good-hearted touchstones of his or her humanity also. In some extreme cases, you may need to tell the interviewee that you are so uncomfortable with the language or stories that the discomfort interferes with your listening.

Word Questions as Neutrally as Possible   Although your empathy is an important addition to the interview, this does not mean that you have to load your questions with positive emotional agreement ("You were right to lash out at your father. Was he as violent after that?") or lead the interviewee toward some conclusion that might not have been reached except for your question. ("He was really a poor excuse for a parent, wasn't he?" is inappropriate except as a paraphrase or perception check of something the interviewee has already said.) Your goal, with primary questions or probes, is to create an open space within which the other person can move, psychologically speaking.

Proceed Along Both Vertical and Horizontal Dimensions   This concept is borrowed from Paul Friedman (1983), who suggests that an excellent organizational "spine" for the interview is a chronological progression; think of this chronology as the **vertical dimension** of the interview's contents. However, at each point in this vertical, chronological

BOX 9.8   **R E M I N D E R S**

Conducting an Oral History Interview

- Establish an authentic relationship.
- Match your dress, language, and behavior to the context.
- Seek a location with minimal potential for interruption.
- Explain your purpose and procedures clearly.
- Take notes, but not compulsively.

- Curb your tendency to judge or evaluate.
- Word questions as neutrally as possible.
- Proceed along both vertical and horizontal dimensions of the interviewee's narrative recollections.
- Review the record for narrative insight.

progression, different things were happening in different parts of the interviewee's life. He worked in a factory and organized a new union under adverse circumstances. At the same time, he coached Little League and participated in a wide variety of civic organizations. At the same time, he experienced a disintegrating marriage and contentious family life. At the same time, he secretly donated 15 percent of his already meager wages to the church for an orphan-relief program overseas. Each of these areas waiting to be explored exists in a **horizontal dimension** relative to the vertical chronology from infancy through old age. This distinction suggests a fruitful starting point for putting together a schedule of questions or topics. See if you can identify ahead of time certain landmarks that would help the interviewee place your question "vertically" and then help you follow up with "horizontal" explorations. For example, the outbreak of World War II might be such a landmark for a storyteller: "I'm curious where you and your family were living in late 1941, when Pearl Harbor was attacked." A series of well-chosen landmarks can give your interview a stimulating and workable structure.

Review the Record for Narrative Insight   After the interview or interview series, interviewers ideally have a tape recording and notes that indicate important ideas, possible kernel quotations, turning points, or other especially interesting expressions from the interviewee. Depending upon your purpose, you can choose from three levels of action that might be appropriate next: (1) The *secondary notes level:* For some projects and some interviewees, it is sufficient to review the tape along with your in-process notes immediately, simply looking for overall patterns of thought and adding new notes or pages of notes written in ink of a different color and keyed to the date on which the new notes were written. Some interviewers call this "enlarging" the notes. It is particularly appropriate for preliminary or exploratory interviews or for interim analysis when several interviews must be conducted in a brief period. (2) The *notes and quotes level:* Review tape and notes by doing the first level, but transcribe significant quotes accurately and add the quotations to your notes. You may want to type your notes at this stage; in doing so, many interviewers make connections they wouldn't otherwise see. (3) The *full transcript level:* Review tape and notes as in level 1, but then transcribe the entire interview. You then might edit and

You could conduct a mini-oral history interview by following the guidelines in Box 9.8 in interviewing either an older member of your extended family, such as a grandfather or grandmother, or an older member of your neighborhood or community who has a particular skill or who has made a difference over the years in people's lives.

- Contact the person, describe what you'd like to learn, and ask permission to talk. *Important note:* Choose a person you are sincerely interested in knowing better, not someone you're picking just to complete the assignment. Assure the interviewee of your genuine interest, even though it may be a course assignment.

- Agree upon the ground rules of interviewing (such as the best location or whether there are any taboo topics the interviewee would like to avoid).

- If acceptable to the interviewee, a sequence of two or three separate shorter interviews will be more effective for your purposes than one lengthy interview.

- In addition to taping (if acceptable to interviewee) and note taking, test your skill in delayed note taking (see Chapter 5) immediately after each interview. Analyze your own style of encouraging helpful disclosures from the interviewee.

- Do not forget a follow-up thank-you to the interviewee. Many respondents will also enjoy receiving a copy of the tape you make.

- Write a brief paper relating what you learn about your oral history interviewing style through this experience.

---

shape the different stories from the interview(s), with the help of the interviewee, into a seamless overall narrative, to produce a documentary record of the person's experience in his or her own language and voice. (See Box 9.8 for a summary of how to conduct oral history interviews.)

Ethnographic Interviews

The oral historian attempts to enter an interviewee's personal narrative world and assist in its articulation. This is a world of subjective involvement, a world of qualitative research, and a world of relationship development that is very different from the traditional scientific goals of achieving increasingly precise knowledge of causality and greater predictability and control over future events. Another form of qualitative interviewing, done within the ethnographic tradition, typically travels even further from traditional scientific or quantitative criteria.

What Is an Ethnographic Interview?

In one of the clearest introductions to the qualitative research methods of **ethnography**, Michael Agar (1986) defines the term and goes on to differentiate it from other forms of research:

The social research style that emphasizes encountering alien worlds and making sense of them is called ethnography, or "folk description." Ethnographers set out to show how social action in one world makes sense from the point of view of another. Such work requires an intensive personal involvement, an abandonment of traditional scientific control, and improvisational style to meet situations not of the researcher's making, and an ability to learn from a long series of mistakes. The language of the received view of science just doesn't fit the details of the research process very well if you are doing ethnography. (p. 12)

In ethnographic studies, the researcher seeks to encounter a different culture or subculture on its own terms, by participating within it and describing its ways of experiencing reality. Although ethnographers engage in participant observation and unobtrusive methods that do not necessarily involve interviewing, one noted researcher (Fetterman, 1989) claims "the interview is the ethnographer's most important data gathering technique. Interviews explain and put into a larger context what the ethnographer sees and experiences" (p. 47).

Issues and Problems of Ethnographic Interviewing

The handbooks by Fetterman and Agar, among others, do not create a step-by-step formula for conducting ethnographic interviews, because much of the ethnographic experience must be based upon spontaneous improvisation. Interview occasions often arise unexpectedly, and the window of opportunity for them might be of uncertain duration.

For example, Felizia, an ethnographer studying the culture of university faculty, may be attending each of the open meetings of the faculty senate for an entire academic year. After the September and October meetings, the room cleared quickly. After November's meeting was adjourned, however, a brief disagreement erupted among several stragglers over the definition of *collegiality* in tenure discussions. Felizia hung around at the door until the faculty members had almost finished, then turned to go. Fran fell into step with her. "What did you think of all that?" Fran asked. "Well," Felizia said, "I'm just here as an observer to see how faculty make decisions, and I'm not a faculty member, but frankly, I had no idea what they were talking about." "You're right. It's unclear to me, too, and I've been teaching here for ten years. You want to know what I think? . . ." While walking to the parking lot, Felizia engages Fran in an "interview of opportunity." (See "Making Your Decision" at the end of this chapter for a follow-up question to this scenario.)

Although many ethnographic interviews are informal and relatively unstructured in this way, most ethnographers also try to schedule more structured interviews in which the purpose is to question the other person in an attempt to make what is strange or even incomprehensible more familiar. David Fetterman (1989, p. 48) advises that the more formal interviews conducted by ethnographers tend to be "verbal approximations" of survey questionnaires with specifically worded and sequenced questions.

In general, ethnographic interviewers must be alert for differences between known culture and the new one being freshly experienced, and they must be open to the possibil-

BOX 9.9   **INTERVIEWERS IN ACTION**

William Foote Whyte

I n his classic study, *Street Corner Society*, sociologist William Whyte worked with a resourceful, trusted "informant" named Doc, who introduced the researcher to people in the neighborhood. When Whyte started asking sensitive questions about gambling and payoffs to police too early in his research, Doc admonished him, "Go easy on that 'who,' 'what,' 'why,' 'when,' and 'where' stuff, Bill. You ask those questions, and people will clam up on you."

Whyte said he learned a valuable lesson about interviewing:

"I did not abandon questioning altogether, of course. I simply learned to judge the sensitiveness of the question and my relationship to the people so that I only asked a question in a sensitive area when I was sure that my relationship to the people involved was very solid."

Source: Whyte, 1955, p. 303

ity that the differences are radical, not slight redefinitions or alterations of basic elements of the known system or culture. Ethnographers' listening becomes attuned for what Clifford Geertz (1983) calls **local knowledge**—understandings that are specifically relevant for the local and immediate context in which they are communicated. At times those differences can involve cultural idiosyncrasies so striking that interviewers are thrown off stride.

Even the notion of a communicative event labeled an "interview," as we've stressed, is a culturally specific idea, the characteristics of which aren't found in the same forms in all cultures. The interview plays better in cultures that are relatively individualistic in orientation. Cross-cultural interviewers may find that the whole interviewing enterprise has unfamiliar and perhaps contradictory meanings in different cultural contexts. After all, the notion of a stranger inquiring about one's business and expecting truthful and full replies seems a poor bet for universality. Irwin Deutscher (1973, pp. 156–166) and others report that some cultures have a "courtesy bias" in response to strangers' questioning, while others normally respond with deception or a "sucker bias" (pp. 158–159). For one interviewer's experiences, see Box 9.9.

Whatever is discovered, the ethnographic interviewer must make sense of his or her experience. This is done not only through the normal forms of note taking and possibly recording (discussed in previous chapters), but through extensive observational **field notes**. In field notes (some authors merge the words: *fieldnotes*), the interviewer/ethnographer systematically records not only what is said but also contextual observations that help to infuse cultural communication with meaning. Although we cannot do justice to this task in just a few paragraphs, and although there are probably as many types of field notes as there are ethnographers (see Berg, 1989; Emerson, Fretz, & Shaw, 1995), three basic stages help beginners to understand the process.

In the first stage of field notes the ethnographer records as many details about the interaction as possible, including its context. It may be necessary to write some of these notes during times when the researcher is not in direct interaction. The goal is to produce a descriptively rich and dense **note set**—unrefined data as complete as possible—with no regard to what the details might mean theoretically and without thinking about how they might be analyzed later. Afterwards, in an inductive second stage often termed **open coding**, interpretations and labels are added to the margins of field notes to aid the researcher in analysis. "In open coding, the ethnographer should not use preestablished categories to read fieldnotes; rather he should read with an eye toward identifying events described in the notes that could themselves become the basis of categorization. . . . The ethnographer should seek to generate as many codes as possible, at least initially, without considering possible relevance either to established concepts in one's discipline or to a primary theoretical focus for analyzing and organizing this ethnography" (Emerson, Fretz, & Shaw, 1995, p. 152). Finally, after many readings and rereadings of field notes and their tentative codings, the researcher will begin to observe themes in the data. He or she is then ready for a third stage of **focused coding** (Emerson et al., pp. 160 ff.), in which the researcher restudies the data with an eye toward noticing as many links between codes and themes as possible.

At various times throughout the process of research, ethnographers train themselves to write brief theoretical notes to themselves and others that they call **memos.** These memos simply describe the state of the researcher's understanding at any given moment. They are typically kept in a notebook (loose-leaf binders are most efficient) along with original proposals for the research, any relevant organizational agreements, financial records, field notes, and miscellaneous observations. By keeping and consulting a series of memos, the researcher checks on his or her interpretive progress as it develops.

❀ BEYOND THE BASICS

One persistent theme of this book has been a concern for the ethical implications of interviewing. In a variety of ways we've tried to suggest that ethical decision making helps both interviewers and interviewees to ground their communication. In "Beyond the Basics," we want to explore two important issues related to the ethical involvement of interviewees in research. First, we will examine why interviewees need not be treated as research "subjects" but instead can be seen as full-fledged "participants." Second, we include a warning against dehumanizing manipulation, which can occur if researchers aren't aware of issues of consent.

Interviewees as Coparticipants

Research interviews are situations in which roles are crucial. The researcher, usually with relatively high prestige and institutional support, approaches individuals, often called subjects or informants, to probe their beliefs, attitudes, values, and behaviors. When the information is obtained and analyzed, the researcher writes up "his" or "her" study, constructed with the resources supplied by respondents. What's wrong with that?

Well, nothing is necessarily wrong with the data or the conclusions, but something seems at least faintly disturbing about the process. If the labels are any indication, the research enterprise tends to cast interviewees (as neutral a term as we can think of) in a decidedly one-dimensional and powerless role. Although in philosophy, "subjects" are considered to be thinking and deciding entities, being a subject also implies other less complimentary connotations. When people are subjected to a condition or treatment, they come under its influence; when people are said to be subjects of a monarchy, they are subservient to it. Calling interviewees informants, as some ethnographers do, similarly slots their role in a unidimensional and somewhat trivializing way. It's as if providing information is their only useful function when, in fact, most ethnographies emerge from interviewer-interviewee relationships that are far more richly nuanced and even emotionally based than this. An analogy in journalism is when reporters refer to a "source," who turns out to be a person whose knowledge and insight provide the basis for a story.

Students of language know that it matters what we call things. Names and labels change perceptions. Why wouldn't we assume, knowing this, that if we apply labels that objectify and dehumanize, we might start treating subjects, informants, and sources as less-than-human objects? We can't justify manipulating *persons,* ethicists suggest, but *objects* are manipulated all the time.

Elliot Mishler's (1986) book on research interviewing devotes an entire chapter to the question of "a striking asymmetry of power" (p. 117) and to several projects designed to "empower respondents" in nonmanipulative ways. He wants "to shift attention away from investigators' 'problems,' such as technical issues of reliability and validity, to respondents' problems, specifically, their efforts to construct coherent and reasonable worlds of meaning and to make sense of their experiences" (p. 118). In other words, if an interview provides significant information for an interviewer, it provides a no less significant experience, potentially, for an interviewee. The interview is a collaboration within which each side has the opportunity to grow and discover something important, but Mishler points out that standard social science interview formats tend to alienate respondents.

Although the trend is far from a landslide, more contemporary interview researchers are experimenting with changes to the prevalent vocabulary of subject or informant. Thinking of interviewees as coparticipants or research participants adjusts and recalibrates the power relationship. Perhaps with this change will come a new respect for the potential interviewing has to change and help interviewees, not just interviewers.

Consistent with this trend, much of the newer interpretive or naturalistic approach to qualitative research advocates a methodological move called the **member check** (Lincoln & Guba, 1985, pp. 314–316). In this strategy, interviewers and other researchers take tentative conclusions and interpretations of data back to the interviewees, recognizing that without their participation the study would have been impossible. Member checking increases the credibility of the study by performing the following purposes, paraphrased here from more detailed descriptions in Yvonna Lincoln's and Egon Guba's work (1985, p. 314):

- it provides a way to ascertain whether respondents intended the messages researchers heard;

- it lets respondents correct errors of fact and obviously inaccurate interpretations;

- it stimulates recall further and can encourage disclosure of extra information;

- it ultimately aligns respondents with researchers' interpretations, by inviting them to coparticipate in evaluating results;

- it provides an occasion for summarizing data accurately;

- it provides respondents the opportunity to assess overall adequacy of the study.

Research, Informed Consent, and Implied Consent

The history of social science research is partly an unpleasant record of deceit and deception (Korn, 1998). Some researchers misled or lied to participants in attempting to observe their behavior in unusual circumstances. In other studies, researchers never informed participants that they were being observed systematically at all. Some unsuspecting people may have believed they were in stimulating conversations with potential friends, while in fact they were being interviewed by trained researchers who would use them as data sources and never see them again. At times, research participants were placed at risk, psychologically or socially, while the researcher proceeded to publish the study and reap professional rewards. Although interviewing studies were hardly the worst culprits, contemporary research organizations and institutions of higher education have attempted to ensure a more ethical research environment.

On campuses, for example, **institutional review boards** or **human studies research committees** made up of faculty and administrators are charged with reviewing proposed research projects in which people might be exploited, harmed, or even unduly embarrassed. Research that involves human respondents should be screened carefully for potential dangers, and researchers must be reminded to obtain consent from interviewees and other participants. Ideally, *informed consent forms*—usually single-sheet descriptions of the study and any conceivable risks—should be completed and signed by participants whenever feasible; some campuses and other organizations have printed standardized forms for such purposes.

In some studies, signed consent forms may be impractical or inappropriate (a large number of respondents to a mail survey questionnaire, for example, or a small number of passersby stopping for a survey at the food court of your local mall). In these instances, **implied consent** may be obtained simply by the respondent's obvious willingness to participate. Even then, the instrument itself, or whoever administers it, should describe any risks or setbacks a participant could experience by being in the study. Another form of implied consent occurs in interview research. Interviewers introduce the consent issue orally with a brief description of potential risks (or the absence of them) and then ask if the participants understand the statement. Continuing participation signals an implied

- Review the example in this chapter of Felizia, a nonacademic ethnographic researcher studying faculty decision making. She talked to Fran, a faculty member, about her perceptions of the "collegiality" argument. Reconsider this interchange in the context of the notions of informed consent and implied consent. In your opinion, was Felizia clear enough in her statement describing her involvement? Did Fran get an accurate idea of the kind of involvement she was agreeing to by talking with Felizia?

- Hypothetical situation: An unknown benefactor has given you a grant of $10,000, which requires you to conduct an interview research study of your own choosing. Which quantitative or qualitative interviewing methodology in this chapter would you use? What made that one seem more attractive than the others? What research question or hypothesis would you investigate? Why?

- A market research company has asked you to be a moderator for a series of three focus groups discussing college students' use of cellular phones. Do an introspective self-survey of your interpersonal skills, and compare them to the demands of moderating focus groups. Do you take the job? If so, are there any necessary skills that you'd want to practice before moderating the groups? Which ones?

- A prominent social science survey researcher is giving a speech in which she justifies her methods and tells a number of humorous anecdotes. You are in the audience. You hear her say, at one point, "Social scientists have to remain neutral at all times. Although ethnographers get a lot of interesting stories, we shouldn't kid ourselves into thinking that they actually contribute to reliable new knowledge. Their subjectivity taints all of their experiences." Based upon what you've read in this class and others, take a tentative position on her assertions. During the question-and-answer period, you have a chance to ask a question of her. What do you ask, and why?

consent on the part of interviewees. Bruce Berg (1989) points out that this approach also retains the advantage of preserving anonymity and confidentiality of respondents, an important issue in many research projects (pp. 138–139).

Summary

Interviewers and their interviewees, working together to make their relationship meaningful, have produced a great deal of what we know about human behavior. Whether this knowledge comes from traditional social science philosophies that often emphasize quantitative research methods, or whether it is shaped by humanistic philosophies that utilize qualitative methods, many basic principles of interviewing remain the same. Advertise your willingness to listen, and invite the other's speech. Help the interviewee focus on what you want to know, using carefully worded questions. Create an environment in which relationships and meanings are coordinated flexibly. Check back with the interviewee's meanings to ensure you haven't misinterpreted messages. Frame messages from a variety of possible perspectives in addition to your own. Record the interchange systematically, so it might be analyzed more thoroughly.

This chapter has examined four basic types of research interviews, each of which has its own unique advantages. Survey interviews offer the advantage of generating a large amount of data through highly standardized questions—data that allow ready comparison across groups and conditions. Focus groups help researchers probe preferences and habits of a specified group of people. Oral history interviews supplement factual knowledge with narrative knowledge, deepening our understanding of the past. Finally, ethnographic interviews stress active immersion in settings where the interviewer may be in some sense a stranger—they create open possibilities for glimpsing and understanding different worldviews and cultural patterns.

The Interview Bookshelf

On the role of questions in surveys

Foddy, W. (1993). *Constructing questions for interviews and questionnaires: Theory and practice in social research.* Cambridge, UK: Cambridge University Press.

Provides a thorough introduction to the linguistic and methodological issues researchers must deal with in designing questions. Very practical and also grounded in interpersonal communication research.

On classroom and home projects in oral history

Sitton, T., Mehaffy, G. L., & Davis, O. L. (1983). *Oral history: A guide for teachers (and others).* Austin, TX: University of Texas Press.

An explanation and discussion of oral history that moves into an interesting collection of oral history activities for teachers, students, and families. It's more than a how-to book; the authors provide an easy-to-read theoretical and practical context for conducting oral history.

On basic introductions to qualitative research interviewing

Holstein, J. A., & Gubrium, J. F. (1993). *The active interview.* Thousand Oaks, CA: Sage.

Mishler, E. G. (1986). *Research interviewing: Context and narrative.* Cambridge, MA: Harvard University Press.

Two books that capture the excitement of interviewing. *The Active Interview* is shorter and tightly written, with excellent examples. *Research Interviewing* is possibly the best book in its field, but challenging reading if you haven't taken a communication theory course recently.

References

Agar, M. H. (1986). *Speaking of ethnography.* Newbury Park, CA: Sage.

Babbie, E. (1992). *The practice of social research* (6th ed.). Belmont, CA: Wadsworth.

Berg, B. L. (1989). *Qualitative research methods for the social sciences.* Boston: Allyn & Bacon.

Bernard, H. R. (1988). *Research methods in cultural anthropology.* Newbury Park, CA: Sage.

Bouma, G. D., & Atkinson, G. B. J. (1995). *A handbook of social science research: A comprehensive and practical guide for students* (2nd ed.). Oxford, UK: Oxford University Press.

Briggs, C. L. (1986). *Learning how to ask: A sociolinguistic appraisal of the role of the interview in social science research.* Cambridge, UK: Cambridge University Press.

Calder, B. J. (1977). Focus groups and the nature of qualitative marketing research. *Journal of Marketing Research, 14,* 353–364.

Converse, J. M., & Schuman, H. (1974). *Conversations at random: Survey research as interviewers see it.* New York: John Wiley & Sons.

Cranberg, (1989). "Plea for recognition of scientific character of journalism," *Journalism Educator, 43,* 46–47.

Deutscher, I. (1973). *What we say/what we do: Sentiments and acts.* Glenview, IL: Scott, Foresman.

Dunaway, D. K., & Baum, W. K. (1984). *Oral history: An interdisciplinary anthology.* Nashville, TN: American Association for State and Local History.

Emerson, R. M., Fretz, R. I., & Shaw, L. L. (1995). *Writing ethnographic fieldnotes.* Chicago: University of Chicago Press.

Fetterman, D. M. (1989). *Ethnography: Step by step.* Newbury Park, CA: Sage.

Foddy, W. (1993). *Constructing questions for interviews and questionnaires: Theory and practice in social research.* Cambridge, UK: Cambridge University Press.

Fowler, F. J., & Mangione, T. W. (1990). *Standardized survey interviewing: Minimizing interviewer-related error.* Newbury Park, CA: Sage.

Friedman, P. G. (1983). *The life stories interview: Creating a portrait on tape.* Lawrence, KS: University of Kansas Department of Communication Studies.

Grele, R. J. (1994). History and the languages of history in the oral history interview: Who answers whose questions and why? In E. M. McMahan & K. L. Rogers (Eds.), *Interactive oral history interviewing* (pp. 1–18). Hillsdale, NJ: Lawrence Erlbaum.

Greenbaum, T. L. (1993). *The handbook for focus group research* (Rev. and expanded ed.). New York: Lexington.

Hayes, T. J., & Tathum, C. B. (1989). *Focus group interviews: A reader* (2nd ed.). Chicago: American Marketing Association.

Holstein, J. A., & Gubrium J. F. (1995). *The active interview.* Thousand Oaks, CA: Sage.

Hoopes, J. (1979). *Oral history: An introduction for students.* Chapel Hill, NC: University of North Carolina Press.

Kerlinger, F. N. (1986). *Foundations of behavioral research.* New York: Holt, Rinehart & Winston.

Korn, J. (1998). *Illusions of reality: A history in social psychology.* Albany, NY: State University of New York Press.

Krosnick, J. A., & Abelson, R. P. (1992). The case for measuring attitude strength in surveys. In J. M. Tanur (Ed.), *Questions about questions.* New York: Russell Sage Foundation.

Krueger, R. A. (1994). *Focus groups: A practical guide for applied research.* Thousand Oaks, CA: Sage.

Kvale, S. (1996). *Inter-Views: An introduction to qualitative research interviewing.* Thousand Oaks, CA: Sage.

Lincoln, Y. S., & Guba, E. G. (1985). *Naturalistic inquiry.* Beverly Hills, CA: Sage.

McCracken, G. (1988). *The long interview.* Newbury Park, CA: Sage.

McMahan, E. M. (1989). *Elite oral history discourse: A study of cooperation and coherence.* Tuscaloosa, AL: University of Alabama Press.

Meyer, B. (1991). *The new precision journalism.* Bloomington, IN: Indiana University Press.

Mishler, E. G. (1986). *Research interviewing: Context and narrative.* Cambridge, MA: Harvard University Press.

Morgan, D. L. (1993). *Successful focus groups: Advancing the state of the art.* Newbury Park, CA: Sage.

Paulos, J. A. (1995). *A mathematician reads the newspaper.* New York: Basic Books.

Sitton, T., Mehaffy, G. L., & Davis, O. L. (1983). *Oral history: A guide for teachers (and others).* Austin, TX: University of Texas Press.

Sypher, H. E., Hummert, M. L., & Williams, S. L. (1994). Social psychological aspects of the oral history interview. In E. M. McMahan & K. L. Rogers (Eds.), *Interactive oral history interviewing* (pp. 47–62). Hillsdale, NJ: Lawrence Erlbaum.

Stacks, D. W., & Hocking, J. E. (1992). Essentials of communication research. New York: HarperCollins.

Terkel, S. (1985). *The good war: An oral history of World War Two.* New York: Ballantine.

Tourangeau, R., & Smith, T. W. (1996). Asking sensitive questions: The impact of data collection mode, question format, and question context. *Public Opinion Quarterly, 60,* 275–304.

Whyte, W. F. (1955). *Street corner society,* 2nd ed. Chicago: University of Chicago Press.

✣ 10 Interviews in Helping Professions: Diagnostic, Therapeutic, and Counseling Contexts

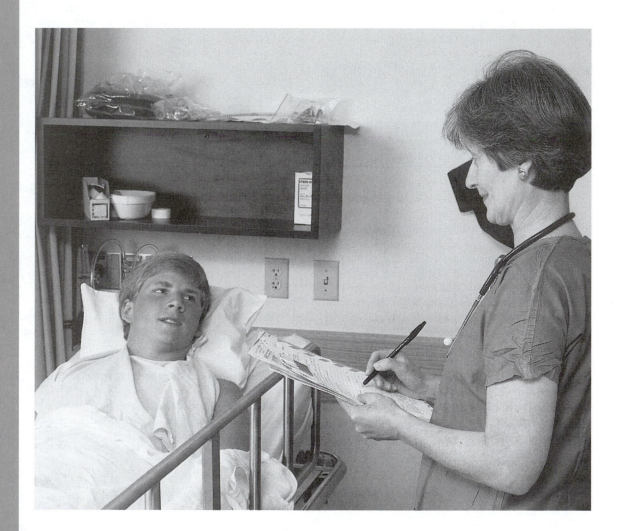

"Sacks, you're unique," the [doctor] said. "I've never heard anything like this from a patient before."

"I can't be unique," I said, with anger, and rising panic. "I must be constituted the same way as everyone else! Perhaps (my anger was getting the better of me now), perhaps you don't listen to what patients say, perhaps you're not interested in the experiences they have." "No, indeed, I can't waste time with 'experiences' like this. I'm a practical man, I have work to do."

"Experience aside, then, the leg doesn't work." "That's not my business."

"Then whose business is it? . . ."

—Oliver Sacks, *A Leg to Stand On*

LEARNING GOALS

After reading this chapter, you should be able to

- Define essential elements of a helping philosophy
- Communicate effectively as interviewer or interviewee in diagnostic, therapeutic, and counseling interviews
- Recognize when sincere attempts to help can turn unhelpful
- Demonstrate effective empathy verbally and nonverbally
- Discuss the ethical implications of helping contexts

As a resident in psychiatry at Massachusetts General Hospital in Boston, Dr. Robert Coles (1989) came under the spell of Dr. Alfred O. Ludwig, an "affable old gent," but a "bit slow on the draw, perhaps over the hill" (p. 5). Hard of hearing, Dr. Ludwig forced Coles to speak up and speak loudly, and the older man spent far more time listening to his younger colleague than "teaching" him.

At first, Coles resisted Ludwig's unusual methods of patient care. Over time, though, Dr. Ludwig's ideas about listening and learning from patients inspired Coles to encourage patients to tell *their* stories, and Coles discovered how important a role communication played in medicine. "The people who come to see us bring us their stories," said Dr. Ludwig, whose words followed Coles over three decades of practice. "They hope they tell them well enough so that we understand the truth of their lives. They hope we know how to interpret their stories correctly" (p. 7).

317

Despite Dr. Ludwig's sage advice, Coles found himself conflicted. "Was I to 'treat,' or was I to listen carefully, record faithfully, comprehend as fully as possible?" (p. 25). The answer seems obvious: To treat someone who wants or needs help means listening, recording, and comprehending. The interview, then, becomes a means of helping, a means of treating.

All interviews ought to help in some way, certainly in terms of advancing knowledge or understanding. But when people suffer from illness, anxiety, or other conditions that they cannot deal with alone, the interview can be an essential instrument of hope and, if all goes well, of successful results.

Not everyone undergoing therapy, counseling, or treatment participates voluntarily. A teenager who cannot control her anger or a spouse who demands a divorce might resist, at least at first, any efforts to intervene. They carry bottled up emotions and concerns that effective communication can release. People in need often face intense feelings of vulnerability, fear, or self-doubt that may either explain or exacerbate their problems. Sometimes reassuring, empathic communication alone brings relief.

A helping interview begins with a period of discovery—a diagnostic stage. Its first application, then, involves gathering information about both facts and feelings, in a mutual enterprise if possible. From there, the interview often assists as a means of treatment. Its therapeutic use applies widely—for a professional athlete coping with Hodgkin's disease, a middle-aged executive mired in depression, or a teenager haunted by memories of sexual abuse.

Interviewing in all contexts involves ethical and legal responsibilities. But the seriousness of helping situations requires a heightened commitment to listen, learn, understand, and act. In certain cases, the process of helping means a deft and delicate touch, like handling a piece of fragile china or defusing a ticking bomb.

This chapter cannot thoroughly educate you in medicine, psychotherapy, psychiatry, social work, marriage and family counseling, or other helping professions. Generally, a professional who listens well in order to diagnose, offer advice, and recommend action completes years of training and study symbolized by a license to practice. Helping, though, is a human impulse, not just a professional duty, and each of us is asked often to lend a hand, or sympathetic ear, perhaps to ease someone's disappointment or despair. We don't need a license to encourage positive communication; as helper or helpee, interviewer or interviewee, better relationships tend to increase personal satisfaction. One brief warning, though: Don't overreach. A familiarity with skills of the helping interview will not make someone a therapist, nor does it necessarily provide reliable insight into people's inner dilemmas. Empathic listening, for example, often has therapeutic effects, but thoughtful professional helpers understand that it takes extensive knowledge and training to understand the consequences of empathy in a given situation.

"The Basics" begins with an overview of helping attitudes and philosophies. From there, we explore ways to ask, listen, and learn as part of *diagnosis* in a wide range of helping contexts, including medical interaction between patients and health care personnel. The section on using interviews in various *therapy* settings is increasingly relevant in a contemporary culture where therapeutic communication is widely discussed even in popular media. The helping role of *counseling*, which is sometimes seen as a form of therapy, focuses on everyday problems more often addressed by interpersonal communication skills rather than by extensive mental or behavioral treatment. "Beyond the Basics" explores those times when attempts to help may create unintentional limitations for people. Finally, we highlight crucial ethical aspects of helping interviews.

The interview isn't a wonder drug of conversational cure but a functional form of communication with limits of application and usefulness. Moreover, other helping methods, including medication, exercise, and diet, may build on what the interview accomplishes. But the interview does enable professional helpers to explore, examine, and assess; most significantly, it helps patients and clients participate *together* in determining what's wrong and what to do about what's wrong.

Helping: Philosophy, Attitude, and Activities

THE BASICS

In an exceptionally clear summary of helping skills, Pedersen and Ivey (1993) write that "interviewing or counseling is the most frequently used method for supervising and/or managing people in most, if not all, cultures" (p. 88). Interviewing contributes to coping and defining self and others, although how it does so varies significantly from culture to culture. Not surprisingly, when people confront crises of coping and interpersonal definitions, it is to the interviewing process that they usually turn for help.

No single preferred or ideal approach to helping exists, and effective interview styles vary as well. A surgeon with a curt, clinical style of communication might lack interpersonal warmth, but she's your first choice for a gallbladder operation. A blunt, direct therapist might succeed in cutting through the defenses of a difficult client, where his partner's softer empathic style fails. Many models can guide helping interviews. A helper, for example, might apply alternating yet complementary styles of confrontation and empathy when conditions warrant. Every case is unique, and how each plays out depends on a unique, unreproducible mix—the personalities, needs, and attitudes of its participants. Indeed, some people find it exceedingly hard to accept or admit they need help, and others just don't have much experience in accepting it. No one can force a gift of help on others.

As Oliver Sacks suggests in the opening quotation, people bring their unique stories, but we have much in common in our desire to be understood.

Philosophy, Attitudes

Given a choice of approaches, a growing segment of the helping professions attempts to work in *partnership* with patients and clients. In medicine, for example, a **patient-centered philosophy** appeals to some practitioners as ultimately more helpful than disease-centered and doctor-centered models (Stewart et al., 1995). Patient-centered medicine is characterized by concern for the whole person, with the doctor and medical staff exploring both the disease and the *illness experience*. A patient who suffered a life-changing heart attack and bypass surgery comes to his doctor sad and fearful that he can no longer participate in outdoor sports with the family. A disease-centered response might be to interpret the man's feelings as depression and prescribe medication; a doctor-centered response might be to interpret his feelings as normal and dismiss them. A patient-centered response acknowledges the man's experiences thoroughly, recognizing that feelings count. As Moira Stewart and her colleagues note: "Dealing with this patient's *experience of illness . . .* may be helpful by alleviating fears, correcting misconceptions, encouraging him to discuss his discouragement, or simply by 'being there' and caring what happens to him" (p. 41). The patient-centered method encourages helpers to let people help themselves toward a solution.

Influencing the patient-centered model and other strategies of helping is the philosophy of **client-centered therapy** developed by psychotherapist Carl Rogers (1961), a term he later modified and generalized into the *person-centered approach.* Although he used different labels for concepts at various points in his career, his work focused on three basic processes. Rogers and others building on his ideas (for example, Carkhuff, 1969; Muldary, 1983) identified three **facilitative conditions** effective helpers create with clients: respect, genuineness, and empathy.

- *Respect,* which Rogers sometimes called positive regard or acceptance, means recognizing that every human possesses inherent dignity and is potentially worthy of being valued. In helping, it's important to accept the value of the whole person without reservations. It's not necessary, however, for the helper to approve of all that the helpee does or represents. Many times the behavior of others is so dangerous, bizarre, or antisocial that it can't be encouraged or held in respect; but the person is more than the sum of his or her behaviors or ailments or shortsightedness. This distinction, according to many helpers in social work, psychology, and counseling, is crucial for a helping philosophy.

- *Genuineness,* which Rogers sometimes called congruence, means that it is usually helpful for a communicator to match inner feelings and attitudes with what one says or does in the relationship. This doesn't mean that everything a helper thinks or feels is blurted out indiscriminately. Instead, it's based on the premise that people who pretend, mask their feelings, or deceptively exploit others show disrespect for the other person. Feigned regard isn't genuinely helpful.

- *Empathy* is consistent with, and supports, attitudes of respect and genuineness. Those who practice empathy do their best to understand the experiences of another person—to see the world through the other's perspective—while still recognizing that the empathizing communicator can never merge completely with this other perspective or understand it fully. When you empathize, you try to imagine what it's like to "stand in both places," knowing who and where you are, but attaching great importance also to sensing the stance of the other person. Practicing empathy also includes communicating through words and actions the sincere attempt to understand. Your empathy, though based on respect and genuineness, must also be apparent—a message in itself that "I care."

People in need don't always find a doctor, therapist, or counselor with helping attitudes. An everyday example illustrates two contrasting styles regarding the attitude of respect.

SON: "I don't know how I'm going to get all these assignments in on time for my teacher. He's so demanding."

FATHER: "Well, what do you expect me to do about it? You've had all term to get them done. Don't blame others for your lack of self-discipline."

SON: "I'm not asking you to do anything about it. What makes you think I'd ask you, anyway? I was just talkin'. No reason."

FATHER: "All right, then. Get to work."

Consider this alternate approach:

SON: "I don't know how I'm going to get all these assignments in on time for my teacher. He's so demanding."

FATHER: "It sounds like you're really pressured and worried. More than last year, that's for sure."

SON: "Yeah. I blew the whole first half of the semester. I knew this was a tough class, but I just went ahead and dug a deep hole for myself anyway."

FATHER: "It's like you've got to do 15 weeks' work in the next 6 or 7."

SON: "I can do it. I've just got to get to work."

Any fictionalized dialogue can be concocted to produce a predetermined result, so be wary about this one. However, ask yourself if the patterns here reflect your usual behavior. Rogers believed that people are constantly looking for ways to take responsibility for themselves, and to grow as communicators, but they're occasionally thwarted. The facilitative conditions or attitudes are his attempts to remove these blocks in a relationship, so the other person can glimpse new possibilities.

In the first exchange, the father doesn't empathize with his son's feelings and experience but, instead, replies with an inference (the son didn't *say* he was blaming the teacher) and a judgment. The son defends himself with a counteraccusation, and the problem itself is not addressed; it's unlikely he will, in fact, now "get to work." In the second exchange, the father withholds judgment, reacts simply by showing he's listening, and thereby opens a door of opportunity for the son to explore his own problem. The logic of the conversation encourages responsibility on both sides, and the son himself decides to work on the class projects. Rogers doesn't suggest that people *always* should withhold criticism of others, only that if help is the goal, listeners should demonstrate accurate understanding first. As a matter of fact, it's only after a conversation in which we feel respected and understood by another real person that we are really open to their feedback. This approach is the basis for the skills of active listening and perception checking suggested by many interviewing specialists, described throughout this book (see Box 10.1).

Rogers is realistic enough to know that the act of unselfish giving sometimes might mean taking the personally difficult path of assertive intervention if that is in the interviewee's

BOX 10.1   INTERVIEWERS IN ACTION

Alfred Benjamin

Benjamin, a writer and teacher of interviewing, claims

"Help is an enabling act. The interviewer enables the interviewee to recognize, to feel, to know, to decide, to choose whether to change. This enabling act demands giving on the part of the interviewer. He must give of his time, his capacity to listen and understand, his skill, his knowledge, his interest—part of himself. If this giving can be perceived by the interviewee, the enabling act will involve receiving. The interviewee will receive the help in a way possible for him to receive it and for it to remain meaningful to him."

Source: Benjamin, 1974, p. xii

best interests. He doesn't advocate passive acceptance of all behavior. We can accept *people* but still might express our problems with their *behaviors*. In fact, it's consistent with the condition of genuineness for the interviewer/helper to express consistent negative feelings and perhaps even to confront directly. You might imagine, therefore, that the father in the second example will be better able to share his discomfort or irritation with the student's behavior.

Helping Activities

Many kinds of professionals provide help to others—hospice nurses, social workers, clergy, school counselors, and psychologists, to name a few. The lines separating fields and functions aren't always precise; roles often intersect. Moreover, not everyone in these professions would define themselves as helpers. Rather than distinguish among helping roles by job description, we examine three common helping activities that involve interviews: diagnosis, therapy, and counseling.

- *Diagnosis:* To help someone, it's essential to figure out where and how help is needed and to determine tentatively the best course of action. The **diagnostic interview** is a focused inquiry into symptoms, conditions, and feelings, for the purposes of assessing an individual or situation and determining what can be done to provide help. As you'll see, it's a potentially complicated step to offer help.

- *Therapy:* In some cases, the interview constitutes the heart of therapy—it *is* the therapy. Certainly, therapeutic uses of the interview support other means of treatment of physical or mental ailments. Therapy covers a broad spectrum of treatment in response to emotional, cognitive, and behavioral issues. It often unfolds over extended periods of time, as interviewer and interviewee remove layers of defenses and buried feelings in a series of interviews. The **therapeutic interview** assists in systematically revising someone's behavior, thinking, or psychological state. Obviously, in an overall sense of therapy, diagnosis is an integral first step in an ongoing therapeutic process. We make the distinction here merely to distinguish between basic types of interviews, not to suggest that diagnosis isn't a part of therapy.

- *Counseling:* Counseling, too, relies heavily on effective communication but differs from therapy in scope and focus. The **counseling interview** helps people by discussing advice and strategies that could assist them in making sound decisions or working out problems in their lives. Therapists usually need licenses to practice because they deal, at times, with life-and-death situations; counselors are typically well trained but generally don't continue to work with someone exhibiting serious psychological or behavior problems. If they do encounter something outside their expertise, they'll refer a client to a specialist.

Defining these helping activities doesn't mean they're mutually exclusive. Diagnosis often leads to counseling or therapy, and therapy might lead to follow-up counseling. Sometimes books or speakers use *therapy* and *counseling* interchangeably, because these helping professions use comparable methods. In certain instances, all three interview activities combine to accomplish helpful results.

Diagnostic Interviews

In a helping situation, careful and thorough diagnosis can isolate a general problem area and begin to define possible responses to it. Making a diagnosis isn't always easy because people sometimes do not see how to reveal the truth of their situations, or will simply refuse to reveal essential aspects of the problem. The diagnostic stage means looking into places and issues that the interviewee may fear exploring. The person needing help might be torn by ambivalent urges to disclose or deny. "Do I want to know what's wrong? Can I face it? Have I the strength to confront this problem? Will I succeed?" Formidable concerns like these might require attention before an accurate and helpful diagnosis can be made. On the other hand, the diagnosis might be strikingly evident, and merely the opportunity to talk about a problem with someone who can listen with care and understanding leads toward a "cure." While it's natural to associate the word *diagnosis* with medical care, it's a process that launches nearly all helping interventions. The preparatory and execution steps of a diagnostic interview apply to a wide range of fields. In social work, for example, the diagnostic interview assesses, in one application, eligibility for social services. Broadly defined as it is, diagnosis plays a part in nearly all helping circumstances, although some therapists and counselors, following Rogers (1961), believe that too many helpers overemphasize the precision of diagnosis while too often ignoring efforts to establish an accepting, empathic relationship.

Several issues are particularly important for diagnostic interviewers to consider. You will want to create optimal circumstances for the sharing of accurate information and helpful interpretation and framing of experience.

Comfort Zone

Visit a doctor's office or counselor's suite and you'll often see a pleasant setting built with wall art, aquariums, comfortable furniture, soft lighting, or soothing color schemes. The comfort zone of helping sets the stage for productive talk but can never guarantee it. When people make the decision to go outside themselves to seek help with a problem, they may be anxious or embarrassed already and don't need additional threats or discomforts. A welcoming environment in effect states, "This is a place where you can feel secure." Providing a place where privacy is assured should also be a major consideration.

Preparation

Time set aside for the interview shouldn't be used to collect basic information that could be obtained easily in other ways. In many interviews, particularly in a doctor's office, patients fill out a medical history questionnaire. Occasionally, an assistant conducts a screening interview for those seeking help to ensure that the problem can be addressed effectively in depth by another professional. Questionnaires and other means of collecting data probably won't lead directly to a diagnosis, but they assist in ruling out problems or in providing clues, such as a family history of depression or pattern of tardiness.

Perceptions

People seeking help can appear needy or even pathetic to listeners. Check your own perceptions. Ask yourself how perceptions influence your assessment of others. Do you find a classmate with a model-thin figure disgustingly self-absorbed? Do you think someone who can't stop smoking doesn't care about living or about how this action affects his or her family? Do you find yourself afraid of close contact with an AIDS patient? Think of perceptions based on biases and stereotypes that lead you to judge or classify people. Who are you seeing and how are you seeing them? Then consider how those perceptions might affect you in a role as helper. In all helping activities, helpers must accord respect and maintain an open mind. To do otherwise risks tainting the diagnosis and everything else that follows.

Getting Started

If the diagnostic interview marks a first encounter between helper and helpee, introductions are crucial, including perhaps a brief exchange of names and small talk. Typically, the diagnostic interview begins without much delay.

Going to a doctor or lawyer with a vague but troubling problem usually stimulates a rapid-fire series of questions. A recent study (Branch, Levinson, & Platt, 1996) estimated that the typical physician conducts over 100,000 clinical interviews in a career but never gets much beyond what they call the "Find it—Tell What to Do model" (p. 69). In order to "find it" (the problem), the interviewer asks and the interviewee answers. The relationship of many helping situations centers on diagnosis; because this is seen as an interview motivated by efficiency, the questioning emphasizes collecting facts rather than eliciting stories or experiences. It's also a relationship that reinforces the professional's position of authority and control.

To avoid dominating the interview, and to include the interviewee in the diagnostic process, helping professionals should focus on learning core information with which they can address a touchstone of the process—a question asked of themselves: "How can I help?" From there, questions can and should invite the patient's involvement:

> INTERVIEWER: "Tell me what you want to talk about. Let me know how you feel as we go along."

Starting out can be the hardest part. Where do you begin? It's not realistic to expect the interviewee to initiate communication, although some will. However, don't expect reticence either. No matter how it begins, a diagnostic interview can take a while to unfold. Many medical interviewers (Branch et al., 1996) suggest starting with a broad or global question to give your partner plenty of rhetorical room to move. Robert Smith (1996) writes that the open-ended beginning question should follow "immediately after summarizing the agenda" and could sound something like, " 'Given what you've told me, how are you doing (. . . how are things going)?' One links the question to the agenda to start developing the story" (p. 33). Thus, the so-called funnel sequencing of questions seems broadly applicable to diagnostic interviewing. Here's a simple, common way to start:

> INTERVIEWER: "How are you feeling today?"

> INTERVIEWEE: "Oh, OK, I suppose. Maybe a little down these days."

When the patient (or other helped person) accepts this invitation, he or she is establishing an agenda that the helper is wise to note carefully. Branch and colleagues suggest that the interviewer probe to specify this agenda early in the interview and double-check to be sure the full agenda is laid out. At times, people will start with describing a single problem, only to be cut off by the assumption that it is the only thing on their minds. Doctors and other diagnosticians are wise to ask, in several different forms, the "what else?" clearinghouse question: "What else has been bothering you about this?" "Is there anything else I should know about it?" "Are there even more side effects that you haven't described yet?" These kinds of questions will frame the problem not as a single issue, waiting to be treated, but as a difficult, multifaceted experience. In traditional practice, however, some helping professionals frame such a question as a disease- or problem-centered inquiry, asking, in a sense, "Why are you here? What's wrong mentally (or physically)? What are your symptoms?" as if there were only a single stimulus.

In the following list, Putnam (1996, p. 78) summarizes recent evidence about the medical interview with geriatric patients. The "strategies" suggested by the evidence apply to other diagnostic interviewing also, especially in the "getting started" stages of discovery.

- Convince the patient that you are interested in him or her, that is, that you want him or her as a customer.

- Establish the patient's agenda by eliciting his or her major concerns.

- Elicit the patient's specific requests.

- Elicit the patient's understanding of the illness.

- Look for clues of the patient's feelings and elicit them if appropriate.

- Elicit appropriate background information about the patient, that is, the social setting of the illness.

- Build and use the relationship with the patient to carry out the data-gathering and treatment functions of the interview.

- Give information after first finding out what the patient knows and then filling in the gaps.

- Finally, find out what the patient expects for treatment and negotiate a plan.

Similar advice about diagnostic interviewing comes from Lehrman's (1995) experience as a lawyer interviewing clients who have suffered domestic violence. Although she doesn't use the word *agenda,* she makes it clear that legal interviewers in such sensitive situations must

BOX 10.2   INTERVIEWEES IN ACTION

Norman Cousins

Editor and medical school professor Norman Cousins, author of *The Healing Heart*, helped young medical students learn about the human side of treating patients. Cousins drew on his experiences as a heart attack patient in describing the communication style he believes creates an "environment of healing." Here is what patients want from their physicians beyond medical competence:

> "They want to be looked after and not just looked over. They want to be listened to. They want to feel they are in the doctor's thoughts. In short, patients are a vast collection of emotional needs."

> *Source:* Cousins, 1983, p. 136

First, use everyday language.

Second, ask specific questions.

Third, assume nothing. (p. 39)

Because her diagnosis often must be reached with women who, for self-protection, deny the events at one level, or perhaps even blame themselves, specificity is crucial after the initial rapport:

> Most clients will tell you their story twice: once to pour out their pain and a second time to answer your legal questions. As you listen, try to picture every detail in your mind. Be careful not to assume anything. For example, if your client says, "He hit me in the face," you may assume he slapped her across her cheek. But she did not say that; perhaps he punched her in the nose.
>
> Consider yourself a film director who is planning a movie of the violent incident. Every detail must be accurate. To find out exactly what took place, you might ask: Where was he? Where were you? How close to you was he? What did he do? How did he do it? How hard did he hit you? With his open hand or fist? What did it feel like? What did he say? What were his exact words? Were you afraid? Did he use a weapon? How big was the knife? Was anything in the room broken? Were there others present or within range to see or hear? What did they do? (p. 39)

Listening

Competence at listening affects every type of interview. In helping, though, careless or incomplete listening is especially damaging—there is too much at stake (see Box 10.2). Listening conscientiously and attentively comes with the territory of helping. In diagnostic interviews, though, it's especially important to listen *interpretively:* What is being said and what does it mean? Two levels of interpretive listening apply in helping interviews—content-oriented listening and feeling-oriented listening.

Listening for content focuses on statements of fact or belief, such as a teacher's remarks about his tension headaches:

> INTERVIEWEE: "These headaches are killing me. Nobody seems to be able to help
>   me. I don't feel stressed out, but I guess I am. I'm really feeling down about it all."

His words represent facts, or content, including the statement about "feeling" down. We often use the word *feel* to introduce a statement of fact or belief. The facts of the headache sufferer's comments suggest follow-up questions and another round of interpretive listening.

Listening for feelings focuses on verbal or nonverbal indicators embedded in or implied by statements, such as an angry tone of voice or excessive hand-wringing. Interpreting what these signs mean requires additional exploration, often through active listening (see Chapter 3; see also Coulehan & Block, 1992, for an application of Rogers's respect, genuineness, and empathy in the medical interview context). Active listening assists helpers in responding appropriately and nonjudgmentally.

> INTERVIEWER: "It sounds as if you're frustrated by not finding a cause or
>   solution to your headaches."
> INTERVIEWEE: "Well, yes. I haven't been able to lead a normal life since they started."
> INTERVIEWER: "Tell me about that, would you? I wonder when they did start."

Empathic listening remains crucial in diagnosis. It communicates a sincere effort to understand, and it reduces the possibility of helpers listening only through their own perceptual filters. Instead, they enter the patient's world of experience, where they're most likely to be able to build a collaborative diagnosis (see Box 10.3).

Asking and Answering

Our analysis of questioning (see Chapter 4) will apply to most helping interviews. In particular, effective probes bring vague or abstract statements into sharper focus, such as someone saying she's feeling "blue" or "down." Helpers working toward diagnosis, then, probe for purposes of confirmation, verification, and specificity.

One type of problem question looms large in diagnostic interviews—the leading question. Some people habitually defer to the judgment and suggestions of the professional; so when a doctor says, "You don't think your anxiety is anything to worry about, do you?" the patient's own assessment (or the ability to reach one) is undercut. Used improperly, leading questions pose problems in all interviews. But they can seriously impair an accurate diagnosis because people in need often want to be led or can't manage to resist a professional's suggestions.

During a diagnostic interview, questioning, listening, and interpretation ideally coalesce. Careful listening and note taking facilitate effective probes; effective probes facilitate interpretation, which, in turn, ought to lead to tentative diagnosis. A helping professional

BOX 10.3   **R E M I N D E R S**

Empathy and Attending Skills across Cultural Differences

Sometimes in classes, we hear people say, "I know exactly what you're going through" or "All people are basically the same." Although they are almost always well intentioned when saying these things, both of these conclusions are demonstrably inaccurate. No one knows exactly what my pain has been, or yours. And although people everywhere share much in common, the cultural differences are far from superficial for communicators trying to understand each other. Empathizing is tough, but cross-cultural empathy is even tougher. Consider the following research findings:

> "Derald Sue and David Sue (1990) describe differences in communication styles between Native Americans, Asian-Americans, Hispanics, European-Americans, and African-Americans to demonstrate the likelihood of miscommunication across these ethnic and racial boundaries when inadequate attending skills are used. They describe Native Americans as speaking more slowly and softly, using indirect gaze when listening or speaking, interjecting less and encouraging communication less, more likely to use silence or delayed auditory response, and using a manner

of expression that is more low-keyed and indirect. Asian-Americans and Hispanics are characterized as speaking softly, avoiding eye contact when listening or speaking to high-status persons, depending on similar rules, using moderate delay in verbal response, and being low-keyed and indirect. African-Americans are characterized as speaking with affect, using prolonged direct eye contact when speaking but less when listening, interrupting or turn-taking when they can, being quicker in verbal responses, and being affective and emotional in their interpersonal responses. European-Americans are characterized as speaking loudly and rapidly in a controlling manner, using greater eye contact when listening, using head nods and nonverbal markers a lot, being quick in responding, and being objective and task-oriented. The contrasting and conflicting patterns of communication are obvious. It is easy to see how the same behavior by different ethnic groups might lead them to misinterpret that behavior."

Source: Pedersen & Ivey, 1993, p. 103; see also Sue & Sue, 1990

---

may want to remind the interviewee several times that questions can be directed to the helper as well. Surely no experienced diagnostic interviewer assumes that the absence of verbalized questions means that *inner* questions aren't nagging the interviewee; questions that are invited sincerely are more likely to be voiced and, therefore, answered.

Asking and answering should be a two-way proposition. Talking out concerns and options facilitates later treatment, if it's required. Discussion should be based on an exchange of information, not just the helper's supposedly expert assessments.

Keeping a Record

Memory fails us at times, particularly when trying to juggle dozens of tasks and activities over the course of a day or week. Taking notes aids in recall and signals that someone is listening, which is why good record keeping supports many kinds of interviews.

The purpose of note taking is not only to record the other person's comments, though this is a surprisingly common misapprehension of beginning interviewers. It also involves recording personal reminders to the listener to follow up or strike out in another direction, prompted by a speaker's response. There is always a danger that focusing on notes diminishes interpretive listening; to reduce that possibility, doctors often take skeletal notes but flesh out details on a tape recorder immediately after the diagnostic interview. That allows them to listen intently and reconstruct what transpired before memory dims.

Resistance

Diagnosis in the face of denial and defensiveness complicates an already challenging task. Respect, genuineness, and empathy on the helper's part alone may not suffice to break through barriers of resistance. Extra effort may be necessary, coupled with an awareness of the source of denial or defensiveness. Fear of the unknown often fuels denial. But signs of defensiveness might mean the helper's attitude needs fine-tuning; it might also, though, reflect the interviewee's natural feelings of loss of control over the situation. Without cooperation, the diagnosis cannot achieve partnership. Realistically, helpers cannot always achieve cooperation no matter how hard they try.

To Withhold or Disclose?

A perennial debate among health care professionals centers on how much information is shared with patients. The debate extends, to a lesser degree, into other areas of helping. Typically, the debate pits those favoring full disclosure and the patient's self-determination against those favoring strategic disclosure based on what the helper considers best for the patient's overall well-being. Indeed, some patients don't want to know everything the doctor knows. Ethical concerns rise to the forefront, requiring that helpers define and prioritize both consequences and duties. The duty to tell the truth, especially when truth in human conditions is never exact, might result in more harm than good in the helper's ethical reckoning.

We cannot tell you what to do; we can stress that rigid and automatic adherence to one approach over another usually isn't good practice. The helper's presumption probably should lean toward disclosure, with any exceptions made for good reasons the helper might be able to identify; phrased in terms of classical ethics, this is a largely teleological and utilitarian position.

What Happens Next?

Closing a diagnostic interview certainly warrants as much care as opening one, perhaps even more. A closing should result in closure, leaving no serious questions and concerns unanswered. Loose ends could compound problems, increasing stress and doubt.

The closing is also a time of reassurance from the helper. Unless the diagnosis verifies that there is nothing to worry about, the patient or client will wonder what lies ahead.

BOX 10.4   R E M I N D E R S

Diagnostic Interviews

Interviewers

- *Help the interviewee establish an agenda early in the interview.* Open-ended questions help get the process started, but specifics must be probed for the agenda setting. Then other open-ended questions can bridge to further concerns.

- *Listen for stories people tell.* Humans use narratives to define and redefine themselves. A helper shouldn't cut short storytelling, fearing that there is no time for diversions. Far from superfluous, narratives contain evidence and explanations. Let them surface, then identify and empathize with their inner logic.

- *Avoid a snap diagnosis.* Initial perceptions and instant reactions act powerfully on people, including helpers. Remind yourself to guard against letting potentially inaccurate, skewed perceptions affect your ability to listen and understand. This is where Rogers's notion of respect (regard or unconditional acceptance) helps helpers.

- *Be thorough.* An accurate diagnosis takes time and concentration. Thoroughness includes keeping written records of the interview for immediate and follow-up reference. Rushing through an interview invites errors of omission and commission.

- *Don't lead.* As helper, you're an authority figure to many who seek your assistance. Let them speak fully and freely, and involve them in speculating about the diagnosis. Directing and focusing the interview isn't the same as leading it.

Interviewees

- *Prepare.* You do yourself no favor by passivity; take an active role in monitoring your life. If you're voluntarily seeking diagnostic help, prepare a list of questions you want answered. Do some homework as well. An on-line search engine will gather a collection of references and Web sites where you can educate yourself about what you're experiencing. Remember your responsibility to your own well-being.

- *Persist in getting answers.* No matter how busy or distracted a helper might appear to you, be sure he or she understands you. Repeat important points, and persist in seeking a response to your concerns. If necessary, request that the helper listen actively by paraphrasing your concerns. You'll be able to hear where the helper has misheard or misinterpreted your words, and you can correct them.

- *Listen actively, with notes.* Check your own perceptions and meanings with the interviewer, especially if they involve technical jargon, or if you're feeling so emotional about the conversation that listening is difficult. Stated simply, this helps the helper help you.

- *Talk over what lies ahead.* Don't suffer in silence. Explore the future. Remember, too, that a helper rarely knows with certainty what is going to happen to you or anyone else. Various possibilities and options almost always exist with any diagnosis. Explore them with your helper.

Normal questions include, "How is this going to change me or my life?" and "What can I expect in terms of getting better?" Although reassurance has limits, especially if the prognosis looks grim, a sense of control and hope fortifies people who are experiencing problems; there's a restorative power in knowing something is being done. The mind can do wondrous things when called upon. If all the answers aren't evident by the time the interview ends, at the very least there should be follow-up encouragement. "Let's meet again and see if the diagnosis bears out." Helpers aren't omniscient, but their words can be empowering. Box 10.4 reviews key steps in diagnostic interviewing.

BOX 10.5   REMINDERS

Cognitive Therapy and Self-Interviewing

A branch of therapy stresses using cognitive processes as means to solving problems of depression or low self-esteem.

- The goal in cognitive therapy is to break habits of irrational perceptions and replace them with realistic but positive thoughts, although some patients require medication for severe symptoms.

- The method of cognitive therapy delves into how people perceive the world, with its combination of positive, neutral, and negative conditions. We subject our observations and experience to an internal dialogue as we attempt to integrate them. The feelings and moods that emerge reflect the conscious meaning we assign to them. David Burns (1992) identifies cognitive distortions common to our thinking. One, for example, is "fortune telling" or jumping to conclusions. Fortune-telling individuals, in effect, look into a crystal ball that only foresees misery. Those haunted by negative feelings, Burns says, lock themselves in a prison of emotions (p. 48). Self-examination and treatment provide a key to escape. The process includes writing down negative or self-critical thoughts as they pop up, asking yourself what distortion they represent and then talking back to them with realistic, positive thoughts.

Therapeutic Interviews

Therapy encompasses an array of problems and treatments, but in nearly all cases, the interview constitutes a primary method of therapeutic helping. Interviews enable therapists to uncover feelings, search for meaning, and find root causes. Usually the interview ventures from shallow emotional waters into the depths of feelings and experiences. Unlike a diagnostic interview that might reach the conclusion that all's well, a therapy interview means there is a problem that requires attention.

Successful therapy depends on open, trusting communication; getting to that point, however, is rarely easy. Part of the challenge involves helping therapy patients think clearly and attentively so they can listen, understand, and inquire and thereby collaborate in the therapy. Therapists cannot accomplish much otherwise. People facing therapy carry in one hand heavy baggage of heightened uncertainty, anger, fear, embarrassment, or a host of concerns associated with the idea of treatment; in the other hand, they carry the problems that initiated the need for therapy in the first place. Therapists might have to identify and unload the first set of baggage before progressing to the primary problem. Some forms of *brief therapy,* however, are specifically not focused on identifying underlying problems but instead help clients develop behavioral solutions through questioning techniques (see deShazer, 1985).

Three types of therapy-based interviews predominate in the field: behavioral, cognitive, and psychotherapeutic. The *behavioral interview* centers on breaking a cycle of behavior, such as situational panic attacks. The **cognitive interview** attempts to accomplish change by replacing negative thoughts with rational thoughts (see Box 10.5). **Psychotherapy,** a broader term that can include cognitive approaches, focuses on investigating and confronting disabling psychological conditions, such as deep-seated depression or anxiety. Each form of therapy moves ultimately toward a goal of change.

The advice under diagnostic interviews relates, as well, to therapeutic sessions. A comfortable, inviting setting, adequate preparation, purposeful yet delicate questioning, and record keeping fit a majority of helping interviews. The delicacy, responsibilities, and stages that distinguish therapy sessions from other interviews, however, merit special attention.

Knowledge for Helping

Helping through therapy begins with a crucial determination on the helper's part: Who is my patient or client? A patient-history questionnaire ascertains certain particulars—age, occupation, marital status, medications, alcohol use, and sleep patterns. It won't reflect characteristics and traits; nor will a history reveal who the person is at that moment. We are different from situation to situation, exhibiting, as Deborah Tannen (1986) observes, various sides of the same person. Certainly, a psychologist or psychiatrist sitting in an armchair in a book-filled office and facing a stranger seems a far different person from the one who sits in her own living room, bouncing a grandchild on her lap.

Those in therapy often grapple with a list of debilitating forces, including a bundle of material and psychological losses—loss of a job, loss of a loved one, loss of control, loss of privacy, loss of coping ability, for example. Knowing the degree and type of loss lets therapists begin assembling an answer to who is the person seeking their help.

Role for Helping: Who Is Responsible?

Alfred Benjamin (1974) creates a pragmatic context for the issue of responsibility in helping interviews. He tells the story of a stranger who once asked him for directions but, when given them, went the other way. "You're going in the wrong direction," Benjamin shouted. The man replied, "I know. I'm not quite ready yet" (p. 1). People who ask for help may not be "quite ready" to accept it. It's a mutual process that also engages the responsibility of the "helped."

The therapist also remains responsible. Entering into a therapy relationship obligates the helper like an oath or contract to provide the highest possible quality of dialogue and responsiveness. Backing out isn't professionally acceptable or ethical unless continuing the relationship risks harm. Therefore, the therapist cannot give up easily or shirk responsibility when a case proves especially frustrating or upsetting. Therapist Harlene Anderson (1997) describes how client and therapist bring different characteristics to the interview, each with responsibilities of expertise:

> A client brings expertise in the area of content: a client is the expert on his or her life experiences and what has brought that client into the therapy relationship. When clients are narrators of their stories, they are able to experience and recognize their own voices, power, and authority. A therapist brings expertise in the area of process: a therapist is the expert in engaging and participating with a client in a dialogical process of first-person story-telling. It is as if the roles of therapist and client were reversed: The client becomes the teacher. A therapist takes more of an "I am here to learn about you from you" stance.

As one young client said to her student therapist when the therapist stumbled, made mistakes, misunderstood, and did not know, "When you are as famous as Freud, you will have to tell them that I was your teacher." (p. 95)

Therapeutic interviewers, Harlene Anderson believes, need to approach clients they interview as expert witnesses on their own lives and as persons with whom a dialogical relationship is possible.

In addition to fidelity to the client, the therapist assumes a responsibility to maintain a professional distance and demeanor at all times. The vulnerability and needs of the therapy patient should never be exploited by the therapist, a point developed more fully in "Beyond the Basics."

Stages of Therapy Interviews

Many therapists find it difficult to specify a structure or sequence of questions or topics for the therapeutic interview. Therapists assume they usually will be conducting **nonscheduled interviews,** by which they mean that specific questions and topics cannot be set in advance. The creativity and spontaneity of dialogue is the overriding criterion: "The structure of the therapy conversation is spontaneous, determined by moment-to-moment exchanges that zigzag and crisscross. It does not follow a predetermined script such as a structured question guideline or sequenced actions. I cannot know my questions ahead of time; I cannot choose words to produce a specified outcome. . . . Hence, the conversation may appear disorganized to an outside observer or one who has a preconception of what the conversation should look like" (Anderson, 1997, p. 126). However, even though individual therapists don't predetermine structure, some research has disclosed a general set of tendencies that characterize many therapy interviews.

Openings in therapy interviews differ from those in diagnostic interviews, mainly because clients know, to a degree, what they're facing. For example, a medical doctor diagnoses moderate to severe depression, referring the patient to a psychiatrist. The client recognizes that the symptoms—crying, lack of energy, irritability—support the doctor's diagnosis. The opening, then, signals the first of three common stages (Carkhuff, 1969; Gazda, Childers, & Walters, 1982) of therapeutic helping. That first stage—*facilitation*—starts with the therapist typically trying to practice empathy, establish rapport, and build trust. A *transition,* or *exploratory,* stage moves into an examination or analysis of what is causing the depression, usually proceeding from surface feelings to underlying issues. An *action* stage usually involves talking through possible solutions or strategies for change. Rarely does a single session encompass all three stages; therapy often requires multiple sessions at each stage or step.

Assuming the therapy extends over several interviews, openings sometimes involve reviewing what happened at the previous session and what happened to the client in the meantime. Closings often preview the goals or subjects of the next interview. In therapy, a path toward progress might mean retracing steps and incrementally reaching toward a form of progress that is mutually defined. Ending a session usually will not be a time for closure as much as for reflection and reorientation.

Sensitivity

When in need of help, people want their immediate concerns addressed. They may raise their concerns, but when the professional dismisses them as insignificant or irrelevant, clients don't usually disagree, argue, or persist. The helper in therapy interviews must resolve to listen intently to clients, especially those who meekly submit when the therapist interprets or suggests. Let's say a patient (P) sounds willing but uncomfortable about taking an antidepressant medication, and that concern generates the following response by the therapist (T).

P: "I guess taking medication is OK, but do you think I'll experience side effects?"

T: "Look, every medication has side effects. Your situation requires medication. We have to get you out of this depression; the side effects are secondary."

A sensitive therapist probes signs of unease:

T: "It sounds as if you're worried about side effects. Let's talk about them and see what we can do to allay any fears."

A sensitive attitude isn't enough. Sensitivity refers, as well, to the ability and willingness to remain alert at all times for the needs of the patient or client, picking up on faint signals of concern, not only booming ones. Patience, too, is part of the helper's commitment to sensitivity.

Another facet of sensitivity in therapy interviews centers on providing a sense of security for the client through a method called **holding** by some experts (Tolor, 1985). In therapy, holding isn't a physical act. The therapist, through supportive talk, communicates that the client can feel safe in sharing painful or shameful details. Holding serves a figurative, verbal purpose, somewhat like a reassuring hug from a father calms an upset child.

Counseling Interviews

In a world of confusing choices and complicated problems, people need knowledgeable, helpful advisers. High school students rely on guidance counselors for advice on everything from birth control to scholarships; job seekers unsure of what work best fits their attributes seek vocational counseling; managers and supervisors in companies must help employees resolve problems and grievances through counseling skills (see Chapter 7 and its emphasis on organizational appraisal and intervention interviews); people with dependencies join organizations that help them break destructive habits. Counseling occurs in prisons, offices, homes, and locker rooms. People train in specific fields of counseling, or they study counseling as part of their career preparation, as clergy or teachers do. We all do some counseling, even without a shingle or special training. Remember that counseling tends to have different goals than therapy, although the line dividing them can be indistinct. Whereas therapy attempts to establish a relationship in which behavior change is the focus, most counselors try to help by enabling or facilitating the client's own decision making and feelings associated with self-worth and inner control. Counseling takes various forms, but the focus here is on fundamental issues common to many forms, followed by examples of special circumstances.

Counseling Principles

Authorities on counseling (Litwack, Litwack, & Ballou, 1980) suggest that counselors orient themselves by a set of guiding principles as they venture into neighborhoods and other settings to deal with families and individuals with a diversity of problems. Three principles stand out from their list (pp. 25–28):

- *Principle No. 1: There is no single, correct way to counsel.* Using a standard formula in counseling won't succeed because of the differences among people even when they go through comparable problems, such as a crumbling marriage. One couple's marital problems aren't the same as another's. Each case doesn't require reinventing one's counseling repertoire, but each case does require an individual assessment followed by an individualized approach.

- *Principle No. 2: It's not the counselor's role to preach, moralize, or impose values on clients.* As professional helpers, counselors see behaviors that may strike them as wrong, reckless, or unwise. Satisfaction and fulfillment, like clothing, come in assorted colors and sizes. A counselor's expectations shouldn't be imposed on others. Principle No. 3 offers a partial explanation.

- *Principle No. 3: Individuals possess inner resources to help themselves.* In other words, the counselor shouldn't assume all the responsibility for a client, even though sorely tempted to take charge. Social workers, for example, frequently find themselves drawn into the plight of a family struggling to provide for themselves. Counselors, though, must resist the temptation to let others lean on them—unless, of course, there is the possibility of imminent danger if they fail to intervene to support a client.

Setting

Counseling occurs in sun-filled offices; it also occurs on windy street corners, front porches, in nursing homes, and classrooms. Sometimes counselors have no control over the environment. The counselor's case assignments, for example, may require monitoring and advising clients in their homes. Even when there is a choice of settings, there are trade-offs. Counseling someone in convenient, familiar surroundings also might mean constant interruptions from phone calls or crying children. An office, while private and quiet, remains an institutional, perhaps impersonal, place. Weighing advantages against disadvantages makes sense; often the need for privacy determines where to counsel.

BOX 10.6   INTERVIEWERS IN ACTION

Maria Vesperi

In *City of Green Benches,* a study of the elderly in St. Petersburg, Florida, anthropologist Maria Vesperi observed outreach workers interviewing candidates for adult day care. One of these candidates was Mr. Dawson, 82, a large man who walked with the aid of a cane. As the outreach worker interviewed him, Mr. Dawson remained polite but guarded. The outreach worker tried to pin him down about a date for the center's minibus to pick him up, and Mr. Dawson evaded an answer and seemingly moved into irrelevant details about his life. The worker grew impatient and abruptly ended the session with, "Well, I'm sure. We'll look forward to seeing you starting Monday morning, OK?"

Vesperi followed her account of Mr. Dawson with this cogent point:

"The Messrs. Dawson of this world seem doomed to be abandoned in mid-sentence. Others invariably find them tedious, difficult to follow, boring. At worst they are labeled 'Wanderers,' that is, incapable of remembering the original context of a conversation. I would suggest, however, the tendency to tune out this type of monologue is a central factor in our cultural construction of old age. Perhaps if we listen a little more closely, we can understand why Mr. Dawson and the well-meaning outreach worker failed to communicate."

Source: Vesperi, 1985, p. 55

The "Who" of Counseling

Conditions requiring a counselor's help often sweep couples or whole families into their vortex. Incest and spousal abuse are obvious examples. But when an individual suffers from a consuming problem, such as an addiction, it's likely family, friends, and associates suffer as well. In counseling terms, a spouse or parent exhibits *codependency,* a psychological condition characterized by manipulation and control by the person with the addiction. Counselors look for signs that those other than the principal subject need their help.

Being Aware of Differences

Astute counselors learn to account for differences in culture, age, health, and social status. Those who aren't astute stumble along, failing to understand what they see and hear, which, in turn, prevents them from providing effective assistance. In the worst instances, their lack of awareness hurts rather than helps clients. Increasingly, for example, counselors encounter elderly clients, whose behavior and attitudes can perplex and irritate someone who is uninformed and insensitive about their lives (see Box 10.6). A counselor cannot take people for granted or interpret them and their problems in terms of what the counselor defines as normal. To do so is a recipe for failure.

Crisis Intervention

A crisis tests the counselor's ability under fire because an acute condition demands direct help, not tomorrow or next week, but immediately. In a casual sense, a flat tire on a 15-year-old family car, particularly for a laid-off, single parent on food stamps, spells "crisis." In a counselor's world, however, a crisis isn't something as "ordinary" as a flat, a two-pack-a-day smoking habit, or credit card debt. Most of us think of crises as a suicide threat, loss of a job, or inconsolable grief over a loved one's death; then again, while potentially serious, not all suicide threats, job losses, or tragedies escalate to crisis proportions. A crisis is a serious threat to an individual's well-being that the individual alone cannot escape or solve without outside help.

A crisis isn't necessarily defined by an event; more often it's constituted by an individual's response or perceptions, which puts the counselor under pressure to judge accurately when and when not to intervene. When it happens at work, or when work performance is affected, an organizational representative may need to appraise the situation as important enough to intervene. The employee may be referred to an *employee assistance program*—treatment opportunities offered as part of a benefits package by many employers (see Chapter 7 for more on appraisal and intervention interviewing in organizations).

Some crises are so serious and immediate that telephone intervention *hotlines* have been established at counseling centers. These allow distressed people to call and engage a responsive and trained listener (usually a volunteer) at times when they have no one else to turn to. Sandra Fish (1990), building on the work of other researchers and therapeutic communication theorists, emphasizes an appropriate model for counselors who talk with such anonymous callers by breaking a more complex model into four sequential stages. First, the counselor must simultaneously diagnose the seriousness and urgency of the call and begin to build a relationship of mutual trust with the caller. Second, the counselor helps the caller articulate the nature of the problem—what has stimulated the call, in other words. Third, the counselor helps the caller discuss and "mobilize" (Fish, 1990, p. 158) strengths and weaknesses. Fourth, the counselor and caller attempt to reach a plan of action based upon the information shared. This complex blend of therapeutic communication and counseling approaches must be formulated in *minutes*. Often, experts have found (p. 159), callers place great emphasis on receiving clear information, confidently communicated, even when there is little time to develop sustained empathy. Hotline counselors must be able to provide information, not just be sympathetic people who understand that the callers are troubled.

An interpersonal crisis doesn't necessarily erupt with sobs or violence; it can build quietly and gradually. Skilled counselors look for certain signs, including a precipitating event, vulnerability, and loss of control. The **precipitating event** poses a hazard or threat—news of a child's death or a spousal beating. **Vulnerability** accounts for emotional or physical conditions. Does the precipitating event threaten to push someone over the brink of despair? Does the individual's history suggest a strength to endure or rebound? **Loss of control** manifests itself in different ways, such as a retreat into depression or a plunge into anger. When a vulnerable person cannot maintain stability or equilibrium to cope with a perceived or real threat, she or he needs rescue.

Crisis intervention requires sensitive skill in listening and diagnosis, combined with the courage to take a stand. In life-threatening crises, involuntary confinement in a health facility might be warranted, and the counselor in direct contact with clients may either request that step or recommend it to family members. Dealing with less severe situations, counselors use soothing talk and empathy to evaluate, investigate, and act on the crisis, enlisting the individual to draw on strengths and resources in search for resolution. The importance of supportive, calming talk cannot be overemphasized. People in crisis cry out, by words or deeds, for help; they've reached the bottom of an emotional well, and it's dry. Talk can replenish and sustain them while the counselor and other helpers try to help them find a way out of crisis.

Social Work

Teachers, police officers, and ministers engage in social work, although the brunt of those duties fall to a cadre of state and local government employees working for social agencies. Depending on particular assignments and agencies, social workers supervise child-custody cases, assist unwed teenage mothers, oversee welfare programs, and monitor boarding homes, for example.

Social workers find interviews useful for familiar purposes: information collection, evaluation, and investigation. The distinguishing feature of the social-work interview, however, is its emphasis on the relationship between clients and their place in the social system and its demands. Social workers deal with cases assigned by their agencies, which explains why they're sometimes called *case workers*. The job varies, but primarily social workers either address how individuals relate to the system or how the system relates to individuals. For example, in one case, the social worker visits parents who have been accused of child abuse by an anonymous caller to a hotline. If the accusations bear out, the social system responds on behalf of the children.

In one observer's words (Kadushin, 1972), the social-work interview generally takes place "with troubled people or people in trouble" (p. 14). There are exceptions, of course. The focus on problems, though, is an escapable aspect of social work, and the parade of problems can drain anyone's energy and emotions. A social worker's assessment of situations that an interview intervention cannot resolve can lead to life-changing recommendations, such as taking a child away from her parents or closing an assisted-living center and relocating a dozen frail residents. Interviewing skills cannot solve certain problems, but certainly such skills serve social workers in making crucial yet wise decisions.

BEYOND THE BASICS

Is Help Sometimes Hurtful?

Ram Dass and Paul Gorman's (1985) book on service to others contains this powerful warning: "Caught up in the models of the separate self . . . , we end up diminishing one another. The more you think of yourself as a 'therapist,' the more pressure there is on someone to be a 'patient.' The more you identify as a 'philanthropist,' the more compelled someone feels to be a 'supplicant.' The more you see yourself as a 'helper,' the more need for people to play the passive 'helped.' You're buying into, even juicing up, precisely what people who are suffering want to be rid of: limitation, dependency, helplessness, separateness" (p. 28). Here is yet another demonstration of a skills-plus approach. "Helping" itself is not contained in a skill or a role; in fact, the skill or role may be counterproductive if you use it too zealously or too selfishly. The basis of helping is not doing something for someone else, but respecting in dialogue their own potential for accomplishing things (see Box 10.7).

340

Not everything done in the name of helping is helpful. Help, for example, can be too directive, leaving the helpee little opportunity for self-determination. It involves the therapist offering a prescription for treatment, without the full participation of the client. To complicate matters, a directive, dominant approach does little for the client's self-esteem or coping skills. Not all practitioners believe it's wrong or unhelpful to exercise professional dominance, and certainly assertive intervention might be necessary to accomplish helpful outcomes. The degree to which the expert takes charge constitutes another one of those fuzzy lines that professional helpers must recognize and then decide where they stand.

A therapist can also cross a comparably fuzzy line from empathy to sympathy, which jeopardizes the helper's ability to remain clearheaded about treatment. Moreover, a client could interpret a therapist's sympathy as a sign of pity, thus exacerbating problems instead of easing them. Empathy involves a keen sensitivity to the other person's condition; sympathy, however, results in one person presuming to judge the feelings of another, as if from a superior position. It's difficult if not impossible for anyone to make hard but helpful choices when guided primarily by feelings of sympathy. Intense emotional involvement in the client's problems also takes its toll on the therapist, perhaps to the point of compromising the treatment of other clients.

A trusting, collaborative relationship between client and therapist enhances treatment. When the relationship tilts toward detrimental dependence, however, the helping potential diminishes. Without trying, a therapist can become the center of a client's existence— guru and savior rolled into one. The answers to problems rest in the client, not the helper, but when dependency develops, the helper frequently dominates the relationship. This is generally not a helpful situation, but there is such a thing as constructive dependence (Purtilo, 1990), which refers to mutual respect and collaboration between therapist and client (p. 101), a form of dependence by partnership.

Another form of unhelpful help is what Dean Barnlund (1990) calls "quick and dirty" therapy. The quick-fix approach indicates a selfish quality to the therapy. It also limits the individual's freedom to exercise problem-identifying and problem-solving strategies. In Barnlund's estimation, "The key to therapeutic communication [is] . . . the ability to engage individuals in liberating and cathartic interaction that enhances individuals' personal insight, vigor, problem-solving resolve, and satisfaction with themselves" (p. 31).

Ethics of Helping

"Do no harm." This is the ethical principle that looms over helping interviews. Avoiding harm means recognizing what forms of harm or injury can happen in the name of helping. Injury or harm can be a calculated act by helpers; most often it happens by accident or because of neglect or indifference.

Helpers face competing ethical choices of duty and consequence (see Chapter 1). An ethical duty of truth telling can, on occasions, cause harm. But so could withholding the truth. Medical professionals often confront that dilemma. The truth about an illness can complicate recovery, and withholding the entire truth could spare patients anxiety and accompanying problems, such as high blood pressure. Telling the truth, though, gives patients options and opportunities to address the truth of the illness as they see fit. Therapists confront dilemmas, too, over ethical duty to an individual or society. For example, is it ethical to break a pledge of confidentiality if you have evidence that a client has committed a crime or might hurt someone? The dilemma also might involve deciding whose interests come first, the counselor's or the client's: My family vacation and mental health come first; Mr. Simon's problems will have to wait.

The following ethical concerns arise in helping contexts. As is often the case, no absolute answers seem feasible when people try to act ethically in complex webs of feelings and goals. Knowing where ethics intersect with practice can, however, lead to informed, sensitive consideration of the right thing to do.

Protecting Privacy

Helping interviews depend on a climate of trust, and trust leads to disclosure. Confidentiality and privacy mark nearly all helping situations. Privacy, on one level, means care in protecting records, notes, and other documents involving the patient or client. Only people with a legitimate need to know should ever have access to records. Confidentiality means self-restraint on the helper's part not to discuss cases with others, unless they have a need and right to know.

A breach of privacy or confidentiality might go without incident. On the other hand, disclosure of confidential matters can do great harm to the people involved. Teachers, for example, shouldn't be allowed uncontrolled access to students' counseling files. It might be tempting for a teacher to go over a child's records, but the consequence could be preconceptions affecting how the child is treated in the class.

Fiduciary Responsibilities

Helpers often assume an obligation to help those who cannot help themselves. That's particularly true with clients in vulnerable positions because of physical or mental impediments. Fiduciary refers to holding something in trust; applied to helping contexts, fiduciary responsibilities resemble a guardianship, like a family member assigned or chosen to look after a child's welfare.

There are limits to fiduciary responsibilities. But at a minimum, a helper must monitor the condition of those who can't help themselves and, if warranted, serve as an advocate to ensure their well-being.

Clear and Present Danger

Counselors deal with people with violent tempers and reckless tendencies. Despite the professional standard of respecting and protecting privacy, there may come a time when a helper must go against the wishes of a client or put the interests of others ahead of those of the client. The point isn't usually reached until the helper believes a clear and present danger exists to either the client or someone the client might hurt. What is "clear" and what is "present' will depend on circumstances and indicators that the helper must weigh. But if warning bells ring, the ethical helper cannot ignore them.

Safety Precautions

Safety precautions relate directly to the dictum guiding many health professionals: Do no harm. Helpers cannot ethically engage in unnecessarily risky experiments or endanger clients by methods of treatment. Using human guinea pigs was denounced long ago, but the practice perhaps continues in subtle ways if clients are not kept informed of the potential range of consequences in the relationship. In the interest of helping someone else who needs help, clients sometimes agree to try out unconventional or experimental treatment, but in those instances, the helper should secure informed consent beforehand. A helper who embarks on a questionable course of treatment or therapy without the client's knowledge might say, "The ends justify the means." That can be an exercise in ethical rationalization.

Beyond avoiding clearly unsafe practices, the helper's responsibility extends to every facet of care. Helpers must ask continuously: Is there any danger in what I'm doing, or not doing, in my relationship with the client? The ethics of helping demands diligent attention to safety considerations.

In most of the preceding situations, legal implications also arise. Unethical conduct can result in litigation against helpers. Even when well meaning, carelessness or moral shortcuts on the helper's part invite malpractice suits. Conscientious care remains the hallmark of the helping professional.

Summary

Helping others places great demands on professional therapists, doctors, teachers, supervisors, managers, and all those whose jobs and responsibilities include caregiving and counseling. The fragile condition of people who need outside help for their problems requires both a deft and delicate touch in nearly all aspects of helping.

The interview serves helpers by facilitating communication, building rapport and trust, exploring problems, and collaborating in finding solutions. The techniques and principles generally associated with effective interviewing apply to helping interviews as well. Special circumstances, however, require heightened concentration and sensitivity by helpers as they listen and interpret what transpires in interviews and other communicative encounters.

Diagnosis begins many helping interventions, followed, when needed, by treatment, various forms of therapy, or counseling. Therapy often enters into people's emotions and psyches, and the helper's responsibilities increase with the severity and depth of problems. Counseling helps people deal with common but real, even serious problems of family life

Imagine someone coming to you and saying, "I need help." It happens frequently enough in our lives, although the request isn't always so direct. But by a friend's behavior and words, the message comes across, "Help me." Here's a situation in which any of us could be called upon:

> Over coffee in the university commons, a friend confides in you about her growing discomfort over a professor's behavior toward her. Although your friend doesn't act overtly concerned on the surface, you sense something more serious is bothering her. The fact that she initiated the conversation suggests to you she wants and needs your input.

What next? What kind of listening and responding would be appropriate in her case? Do you encourage her to get into particulars about the professor? How deeply do you delve? What do you do if she reveals apparent instances of sexual harassment but attempts to pledge you to confidentiality? How do you advise her, if at all? Where do your primary responsibilities lie?

Work through this scenario, incorporating what you know about helping interviews.

and individual conditions. Dealing with the problems of others can be stressful to helpers; they also run the risk of getting too involved in their clients' lives.

Ethical and legal issues further complicate the helper's work. In short, helpers face major challenges, but the rewards often make the effort and complications worthwhile.

The Interview Bookshelf

On the philosophy and practice of the helping interview

Benjamin, A. (1974). *The helping interview* (2nd ed.). New York: Houghton Mifflin.

Full of metaphors, personal experiences, and story-quality examples, the author lays out a philosophy of helping along with practical advice.

On therapy and counseling

Rogers, C. R. (1961). *On becoming a person.* Boston: Houghton Mifflin.

Anderson, H. (1997). *Conversation, language, and possibilities: A postmodern approach to therapy.* New York: Basic Books.

Bohart, A. C., & Greenberg, L. S. (Eds.). (1997). *Empathy reconsidered: New directions in psychotherapy.* Washington, DC: American Psychological Association.

Of these three books on therapeutic dialogue, one work is an old standby in the field and the other two are recent additions. Carl Rogers's "technique," according to some people, was "reflecting feelings" through active listening. But Rogers himself disavowed the whole notion of relating to others by techniques; he simply wanted to let others know they could be understood, no matter how unusual their experiences might seem. Harlene Anderson respects clients and their difficulties, and this is clear from her sensitive descriptions of therapeutic conversations. Her writing has many examples and insights about language and empathy, a topic explored in depth in the APA-sponsored anthology.

On medical interviewing

Coulehan, J. L., & Block, M. R. (1992). *The medical interview: A primer for students of the art* (2nd ed.). Philadelphia: F. A. Davis.

Smith, R. C. (1996). *The patient's story: Integrated patient-doctor interviewing.* Boston: Little, Brown.

Both books are highly practical introductions to interviewing that avoid overgeneralization and prescription. Highly recommended.

References

Anderson, H. (1997). *Conversation, language, and possibilities: A postmodern approach to therapy.* New York: Basic Books.

Barnlund, D. C. (1990). Therapeutic communication. In G. Gumpert, & S. L. Fish (Eds.), *Talking to strangers* (pp. 10–28). Norwood, NJ: Ablex.

Benjamin, A. (1974). *The helping interview* (2nd ed.). Boston: Houghton Mifflin.

Bohart, A. C., & Greenberg, L. S. (Eds.). (1997). *Empathy reconsidered: New directions in psychotherapy.* Washington, DC: American Psychological Association.

Branch, W. T., Levinson, W., & Platt, F. W. (1996, July 15). Diagnostic interviewing: Make the most of your time. *Patient Care,* 68–70, 75, 79–83.

Burns, D. D. (1992). *Feeling good: The new mood therapy.* New York: Avon Books.

Carkhuff, R. R. (1969). *Helping and human relations: A primer for lay and professional helpers, Vols. 1 and 2.* New York: Holt, Rinehart & Winston.

Coles, R. (1989). *The call of stories.* Boston: Houghton Mifflin.

Coulehan, J. L., & Block, M. R. (1992). *The medical interview: A primer for students of the art* (2nd ed.). Philadelphia: F. A. Davis.

Cousins, N. (1983). *The healing heart.* New York: W. W. Norton.

deShazer, S. (1985). *Keys to solution in brief therapy.* New York: Norton.

Fish, S. L. (1990). Therapeutic uses of the telephone: Crisis intervention vs. traditional therapy. In G. Gumpert & S. L. Fish (Eds.), *Talking to strangers: Mediated therapeutic communication* (pp. 154–169). Norwood, NJ: Ablex.

Gazda, G. M., Childers, W. C., & Walters, R. P. (1982). *Interpersonal communication: A handbook for health professionals.* Rockville, MD: Aspen.

Kadushin, A. (1972). *The social work interview.* New York: Columbia University Press.

Lehrman, F. L. (1995, February). Strategies for interviewing domestic violence clients. *Trial,* 38–43.

Litwack, L., Litwack, J., & Ballou, M. (1980). *Health counseling.* New York: Appleton-Century-Crofts.

Muldary, T. W. (1983). *Interpersonal relations for health professionals.* New York: Macmillan.

Nightingale, F. (1969). *Notes on nursing.* New York: Dover.

Pedersen, P. B., & Ivey, A. (1993). *Culture-centered counseling and interviewing skills: A practical guide.* Westport, CT: Praeger.

Purtilo, R. (1990). *Health professional and patient interaction.* Philadelphia: W. B. Saunders.

Putnam, S. M. (1996). Nature of the medical encounter. *Research on Aging, 18,* 70–83.

Ram Dass, & Gorman, P. (1985). *How can I help?: Stories and reflections on service.* New York: Alfred A. Knopf.

Rogers, C. R. (1961). *On becoming a person.* Boston: Houghton Mifflin.

Sacks, O. (1984). *A leg to stand on.* New York: Summit Books.

Smith, R. C. (1996). *The patient's story: Integrated patient-doctor interviewing.* Boston: Little, Brown.

Stewart, M., et al. (1995). *Patient-centered medicine.* Thousand Oaks, CA: Sage.

Sue, D. W., & Sue, D. (1990). *Counseling the culturally different: Theory and practice.* New York: John Wiley & Sons.

Tannen, D. (1986). *That's not what I meant!* New York: Ballantine.

Tolor, A. (1985). *Effective interviewing.* Springfield, IL: Charles C. Thomas.

Vesperi, M. D. (1985). *City of green benches.* Ithaca, NY: Cornell University Press.

✤ 11 Interviews in Persuasive Situations

. . . When a professional salesperson makes a presentation, he or she will listen more than speak. In a presentation, you should listen— with the prospect speaking—at least 55 percent of the time. If you're doing more than 45 percent of the talking, it's time to pull back on the reins, talk less, and listen more. You just aren't going to persuade the prospect with your brilliant oratory. On the contrary, you persuade the prospect by getting him or her to talk. And you do that through the skillful use of questions in the sales interview. Yes, questions rather than statements. And, even though it's called a "presentation," presenting is only part of it. To be effective, a presentation is really an interview, involving a two-way dialogue between you and your prospect.

—Bob Kimball, *AMA Handbook for Successful Selling*

LEARNING GOALS

After reading this chapter, you should be able to

- Participate in, and define, persuasion as a helping relationship
- Enact the stages in a generalized process of persuasive interviewing: opening, discovering, matching, choosing, and closing
- Relate the goals of personal selling to an interpersonal ethic of communication
- Explain the fundamental skills of negotiation and interrogation/advocacy interviews

THE BASICS

The title of this chapter is both highly accurate and somewhat misleading.

It is accurate in the sense that you will indeed read about skills and appreciations that are especially important in certain kinds of interviews we call "persuasive situations." These situations include, among others, the typical sales encounter, the negotiation context, and the legal situations of courtroom or law enforcement advocacy and interrogation. These contexts have in common the intention of one or more parties to affect the beliefs, attitudes, values, and behaviors of other people. That motivation to affect someone else is the genesis of the many definitions of persuasion throughout the centuries, even though people often change beliefs, attitudes, values, and behaviors without the conscious attempt of another person to motivate them. **Persuasion** is usually defined, therefore, as the attempt of one communicator or group to influence the beliefs, attitudes, values, and behaviors of others.

The previous paragraph also hints at how the chapter title can be misleading as well. Perhaps the public defines persuasion too narrowly at times. In the popular mind, persuasion seems to be identified almost exclusively with situations in which someone is consciously and directly trying to "sell" something, such as a bar of soap, a used car, or a senatorial candidate. Or people think they are target audiences for persuasion when someone speaks in the residence hall as a recruiter for student organizations or when a minister, rabbi, or priest suggests values appropriate for moral decision making. However, in a sense, all human interaction depends upon at least *implicit* requests that we adapt our behaviors and attitudes to each other. We gain cooperation with our points of view in close friendships just as politicians do in their congressional campaigns; we persuade in informal conversations with parents and children just as much as when we're haggling with a salesperson at the car dealer down the road. It's the goals that differ. If you consider persuasion in a broader everyday sense, almost all human interactions involve persuasive goals of some kind.

As we consider persuasion in this chapter, remember that the "attempt of one communicator or group" to influence others often won't take the form of a conscious plan to get them to change in specific or predetermined ways. Informal persuasion often works in everyday conversation at an implicit, almost background level. We might be talking about homework or health care, but we want others to think well of us; we might be shopping together for trivial items but still want companions to take our suggestions seriously. Consider the following examples of persuasion, representing the other categories of interviewing treated in this book:

- In interviews for employee selection, most applicants hope to convince interviewers of their suitability for the defined position and to establish a personal image of competence; personnel interviewers wish to maintain the credibility of the organization and persuade excellent candidates that this job is a good match for them.
- In interviews for organizational decision making, such as appraisals and interventions, employees want superiors to see their productivity within the organization; the superiors hope to convince employees to adopt mutually agreed-upon strategies to increase effectiveness and teamlike cooperation.

- In interviews in journalism, interviewers hope to persuade interviewees that it is in their best interest to share information and insight about newsworthy topics; news sources often hope to influence the ultimate shape of the story so they don't look ill informed, incompetent, or uncaring.

- In interviews in social science and humanistic research, interviewers persuade respondents that they make valuable contributions through their participation in the researcher's study; interviewees often have a story to tell (or a set of facts to relate) that they hope will be compelling and interesting to a wider audience.

- In interviews in helping professions, effective helpers persuade clients, patients, and others that certain actions, skills, styles, or treatments will result in positive outcomes; those interview partners typically want to be seen in certain ways (for example, as sincere, as helpless victims of circumstance, as knowledgeable partners in developing treatment, or in a variety of self-serving ways).

Therefore, *all* interviews could be thought of as persuasive interviews, if you consider persuasion's literal broad definition. Still, some interviewers consciously put persuasion front and center. Although personal selling is the most obvious form of persuasive interview, two other types of persuasive interviews are also especially prominent: negotiation and interrogation/advocacy interviews. A salesperson offers an audience goods or services but often must interview to determine the desirability or suitability for the audience. A negotiator engages in a give-and-take in which different positions could become reconciled to each other. An advocate or interrogator interviews often by probing an interviewee's well-defined point of view or version of reality to ensure its accuracy or to test its possible bias.

"The Basics" will survey principles of persuasion, while noting how persuasive factors affect interviewing choices. We suggest that persuasion is ideally not a relationship of manipulation or intended manipulation but a much more benign human relationship. Then, referring often to sales contexts as a prototypical persuasive situation, we will examine how people are influenced in persuasive interviews. In "Beyond the Basics" you'll find descriptions and suggestions to help you interact in the two other common persuasive interviewing contexts—negotiation and interrogation/advocacy interviewing.

Persuasion as Helping, Not Manipulation

Some people are afraid of persuasion and want nothing to do with it. Small wonder, given the extravagant—even threatening—claims made for it. After searching for Web sites devoted to sales and persuasion, a recent "hit" yielded these claims from a practitioner marketing his system of skills (capitalization, boldface, and punctuation in original):

"Imagine being able to Sell, Persuade or Talk
ANYONE into ANYTHING, ANYTIME!

Further, the author suggests that "armed with [his] skills you'll find that". . .

Your Business Profits Skyrocket.

Your Associates Beg Your Counsel.

Your Adversaries Flee.

Your Lovers Vow Eternal Loyalty.

Your Children Instantaneously Obey.

All this sounds extraordinarily handy if you're inclined, say, to rule the world; it's less wonderful if you think you might accidentally encounter someone with this magical power. Although you may want to believe no reader takes such claims for skills programs seriously, we know that many take them very seriously indeed. Such a philosophy espouses an underlying ethic of manipulation with which many people paint the entire process of persuasion itself. To be a persuader, they think, is to be a manipulator or an invader of other people's lives. But somewhere between the extremes of renouncing persuasion on one hand and coveting it on the other is a balanced account of persuasion in human interaction.

Even if you consider yourself a "live-and-let-live" person, you don't need to apologize for attempting to be persuasive. Only the most disinterested, asocial, or isolated humans literally do not care how they are perceived by others or whether their interests are considered by others. In other words, people generally hope to make a difference in each other's lives, and there is nothing wrong with that. It's consistent, we believe, with the attitude that others have a right to their opinions, attitudes, beliefs, and values. Responsible persuasion does not *limit* other people's rights as much as it *expands* them. Responsible persuasion lays the groundwork for change but does not demand that change from others, nor does it seek to fence people in, limiting them to a particular point of view. It is not a matter of "looking out for number 1" or getting what you want no matter what the cost. It doesn't depend upon a dog-eat-dog model of the world, as many people wrongly assume. That doesn't mean there aren't selfish, deceptive, or even deceitful persuaders in the world who are ready to line their own pockets by cheating others. Recognizing their existence, however, does not make unethical persuasion the norm.

If James Craig's point, described in Box 11.1, is correct, we could expect caring communicators to be responsible for telling each other what they want in their relations with others. The best way to "let live," in other words, is to give other people sufficient information about the expectations they are coming up against in your reactions. To do less is to turn communication into more of a guessing game than it already is. This is not manipulation as much as it is clarity. Still, we must be careful in considering the manipulative potential for this kind of helping.

The persuasive interviewing context is one in which a persuader attempts to facilitate something the interviewee wants and vice versa. Although both interviewers and interviewees can be persuaders, most literature in the field tends to assume the persuader is the interviewer and the interviewee is the person whose attitudes or behaviors may change. Interviewers often miss the mark, but this concern for the other person is—or should be—

BOX 11.1   INTERVIEWERS IN ACTION

James Craig

"I recently discovered that I have a long history of going around dissatisfied with contributions to joint efforts made by other members of my family, by colleagues, and by people who work for me. Either they didn't do what I wanted them to do, or they didn't do it the way I wanted it done. I generally communicated my dissatisfaction to them, either directly, or, more frequently, indirectly. I thus polluted the atmosphere of my relationships. But I now realize that I seldom got very clear with myself *in advance* as to exactly what I did want from the others. And, consequently, I seldom let them know what I expected of them. That is, until I would find that they had failed to meet my previously *unvoiced* criteria.

"I now know that I had been putting other people in untenable positions. I had given them great freedom to figure out what to do and how to do it. I had left them with the false impression that *whatever* they might choose to do would be o.k. with me. And then, *unless* they chose exactly what I would have chosen *if I had taken the trouble to figure it out*, I would be dissatisfied with them, and would let them know of my dissatisfaction in one way or another. . . .

"Now that I'm aware of what I had been doing I take the responsibility for figuring out what I want, and for communicating it to the other people in my relationships. That doesn't mean that I dictate to them. (They wouldn't accept it if I tried to.) And we may or may not settle on a specific course of action designed to satisfy me. But we all know where we stand and what our various expectations are. People are kept out of mystery. And the atmosphere stays much clearer."

Source: Craig & Craig, 1979, p. 75; emphasis in original

their guiding light. The most practical ethical approach to this problem, we believe, is to consider persuasion as a helping relationship (Anderson & Ross, 1998, p. 224), consistent with many of the suggestions in Chapter 10. In most of our examples, we'll assume that sales interactions provide a prototype for understanding persuasive interviewing.

Interaction in the Persuasive Interview

In Box 11.2 the first two points describe pre-interview factors that are extremely important but do not directly reflect the interaction of interviewer and interviewee. The remaining three, however, directly translate into a generalized chronological sequence for conducting the persuasive interview. Although any professional in persuasive interviewing could note hundreds of exceptions, the core of most interviews will be shaped by these concerns: discovering, matching, and choosing. When considered alongside the necessity for opening and closing the interview, they form the model for persuasive interviewing laid out in Box 11.3.

BOX 11.2   REMINDERS

Responsible Persuasion in Interviewing

- *Knowledge/research:* The persuader inventories available resources thoroughly before approaching the interview. Resources could include products, services, delivery systems, or personal experience, but the responsible persuasive interviewer is familiar with what is being offered, sold, provided, or advised and, perhaps even more important, believes in it himself or herself. Remember that *credibility* is based primarily on perceived *expertise* and *trustworthiness,* both of which are bolstered by solid research and knowledge in your area. (Potential respondents or interviewees are well advised, too, to do their own homework; especially in today's on-line culture, it is becoming much easier to research the backgrounds of those who would try to persuade, along with their goods and services. For purposes of streamlining this discussion, however, we will concentrate on responsibilities of persuaders, because by understanding them, you can infer the responsible behaviors of interviewees' roles as well.)

- *Audience analysis:* The persuader has researched and analyzed the audience members in advance, attempting to determine the valid needs, wants, and interpersonal styles that might characterize their decision making.

- *Focus on Discovery:* The persuader uses the interview to discover the unique ways that this particular other person (the interviewee, for example) could potentially benefit from the resources. This step of the process involves virtually all the skills of informational interviewing used by journalistic, research, and helping interviewers.

- *Matching:* The persuader matches resources to individual needs in responsible and thoughtful ways, and communicates the qualities of such matching to the interviewee.

- *Respect for choice:* The persuader to this point has created the conditions under which an informed choice might be made by the interviewee. Here, the persuader must "create a space" in which the other's choices genuinely reflect his or her own judgment, not the persuader's judgment or the persuader's techniques.

Opening

The opening of a persuasive interview draws upon the willingness of participants to speak with each other informally. As with most interview openings, it is relatively brief and stresses the task of building rapport. *Rapport building,* a topic covered in more detail in earlier chapters, (1) clarifies the basis for the relationship between communicators, (2) puts the communication situation on a less formal basis, and (3) ideally establishes a foundation of pleasant interaction in which, no matter how difficult the designated topic of the interaction, the interviewer and interviewee at least will like or appreciate each other. Think of rapport not as a product of a relationship but as a certain process of relationship in which the communicators are actively and pleasantly adapting themselves and their messages to each other.

Other than rapport building, an opening often designates the purpose for the discussion and sets the ground rules for interaction:

BOX 11.3   **REMINDERS**

A Model Sequence for Interaction in Persuasive Interviews

- *Opening* (clarification, rapport, personalization)
- *Discovering* (understanding the other, developing bases for decision making)
- *Matching* (exploration of links between persuaders' resources—ideas, products, and so forth—and audience beliefs, attitudes, values)
- *Choosing* (creating a full opportunity for significant choice)
- *Closing* (facilitating a decision, commitment, or change)

INTERVIEWER (financial consultant): "Good afternoon, Ramona! How are things? I appreciate your calling me about that mutual fund we talked about for your dad. I've put together a few brochures and ideas here that should only take us about fifteen or twenty minutes to go through. But first, how's that shortstop of yours doing? Is he leading the league in hitting and dirty caps again this summer?"

This greeting gives the interaction an informal feeling and lets the interviewee know that talking about personal things won't be considered a waste of time. It both personalizes the conversation by demonstrating that Ramona's life is important enough to remember, and it signals her about how much time to expect the interview to take. Presumably the interviewer, Marion, has budgeted at least thirty minutes for the meeting.

INTERVIEWEE (coming to an appointment set up to obtain preliminary information for her father): "Hey, I don't know his average, Marion, but he's sure loving his new coach. Did your boy have Jess Zamora as coach when he went through the program? Jess really works well with the kids."

INTERVIEWER: "Yeah, sure I know Jess—ever since his parents lived on St. Louis Street, just down from us. His parents did business with me for years, too, before they moved to Birmingham. Maybe you didn't know that Jess and my older daughter were quite an item for a while?"

INTERVIEWEE: "Now that you mention it, I did hear that. Wow, things really change around here, don't they? Just a few years ago, Mom and Dad were riding herd on me, and now here I am having to run all kinds of errands for Dad. Kind of ironic."

INTERVIEWER: "How's he doing since your mom's accident?"

INTERVIEWEE: "Well, it's hard on him, and he's not doing real well with making decisions. That's why I'm here, trying to pull some things together for him to decide. What about that mutual fund plan? Money's really on his mind these days."

INTERVIEWER: "I've got it right here. Let's go over the company's reputation first, OK? . . ."

The opening serves to relate person with person, at one level, and persons with task, at another level. It should serve as a clarifier, both emotionally and interactionally, for participants.

Discovering

Successful persuasive interviewers do not simply sell a product or a point of view to a waiting audience, despite the rich lore in many professions about supposedly surefire sales pitches. Persuasion essentially doesn't work from the outside in, as if an incoming message unlocks some secret place in people's decision making, and the outcome is then assured. *No one else persuades you,* you might say; instead, *you persuade yourself* by combining the reasons, materials, and ideas of another person, and then mixing these externally supplied ideas creatively with a personal awareness of your own goals and desires. External persuaders can certainly influence you at this stage, but only if they discover enough about how you frame your own situation. How can they do that? In discovering what is necessary for persuasion, interviewers ask, encourage, listen, and frame.

- Interviewers ask questions that provide the most helpful base of information, probably using more or less a funnel sequence. Concentrate on neutral **what-questions** (for example, "What meals do your family members look forward to the most?" "What is the ideal percentage of attention a senator should give to foreign affairs compared with domestic?") rather than on **why-questions** (for example, "Why do you cook so much pasta?" "Why do you give more attention to foreign policy?"). With this information, interviewers can shape and frame their suggested solutions to the problems faced by the interviewee or suggest the most helpful courses of action.

Remember that questions can backfire if an appropriate reason for them hasn't been established by the opening. If the information is seen as irrelevant, the questions will be perceived as evidence of a prying or nosy attitude. Many people in the contemporary information culture that dominates, especially in Europe and North America, don't mind being asked questions about their personal affairs, but many others (justifiably) still do. We suspect that privacy issues may become even more controversial as some aspects of information retrieval and widespread database dominance become more entrenched. Consider carefully whether you actually need the information before you request it.

Further, assume that in some cultural contexts, the request for specific information may do more harm than good unless it is handled with great tact and sensitivity. As Harry Triandis (1994) suggests, cultures and cultural groups that value **collectivist** communication styles (in which group identification is more important than individual feelings and goals) do not usually respond positively to outsiders' inquiries for personal information, even though that information would be readily discussed within a family. "Collectivists," he wrote, "are especially opposed to 'washing the family's dirty laundry in public' and go to extremes to hide unfavorable information about in-group members from outsiders" (p. 230). Further, collectivists tend not to disclose information easily to strangers (p. 231), although interviewers may benefit from what is called the **passant phenomenon.** In such an interaction, many people—collectivists and individualists—will disclose information if they believe the listener is a reliable person they are unlikely to meet again, that is, if the interviewer is just a conversation partner "in passing" (p. 232).

• Interviewers mix into the conversation strategic comments that encourage elaborations from the interviewee. Conversational interviewing is especially desirable in persuasive settings because the most influential messages are those perceived as nonpurposive; that is, to the extent that a persuader is seen as being merely or primarily self-serving, respondents will tend to become defensive if not resistant. The exclusive use of questions might suggest that the interviewee is being pumped or grilled, a feeling most of us would avert if possible. Much information comes from informal responses to interviewer observations but without some of the baggage of defensiveness. In their article "Interviewing by Comment: An Adjunct to the Direct Question," Snow, Zurcher, and Sjoberg (1981) discuss the dynamics of such an approach. They found that "questions, in contrast to comments, characteristically call forth, circumscribe, and imply answers. That is, questions 'frame' the response or talk of the interviewee" (p. 288). On the other hand, "interviewing by comment" (their phrase) "facilitates the process of discovery . . . generally associated with the creation and development of knowledge" (p. 287).

Interviewing by comment can be discerned in the following examples of nonquestions that nevertheless could elicit important information: "That real estate agent really seemed to irritate you"; "The world's getting crazy when so much of our scarce free time goes into maintaining and fixing gadgets"; "It's hard for two people to agree completely on something that costs as much money as a college degree"; "You want the contract, but you don't want it if it threatens those gains you made last year." Do you see how each of these comments invites—almost necessitates—a response that could provide extra information and insight?

• Interviewers encourage interviewees to tell stories about their lives, their dilemmas, and their own successes. They invite accounts of how people have been successful in their previous experiences. If you're selling cars, for instance, it's usually a good idea to elicit and then not to interrupt an enthusiastic story about how much the buyer loved a previous car manufactured by a competitor. Your first impulse might be to try to change the subject— move the speaker away from memories that might not help your cause. But the enthusiasm and his or her willingness to express it to you is a much more important positive sign than the story's content itself is a negative sign. From the story, you will discover what this person enjoys about cars and what goals will motivate the next purchase.

• Interviewers listen carefully to interviewee responses to their questions and comments, discerning the specific points about which there is most ambiguity or doubt—or specific points that might be missed by other listeners. Your listening must not only be accurate, but it must be demonstrated overtly, perhaps in the form we earlier termed active listening. For example, if you are attempting to mediate between two powerful civic groups in order to get an agreement about new parking regulations downtown, you might find yourself in an interchange like this:

> INTERVIEWER (mediator/negotiator): "John, when someone from your side talks, things are usually expressed in terms of what's going to happen down the road, in the future. Yet, at the same time, Janeece's group sounds more concerned with the short-term implications for shoppers downtown. Have I got that right? I'm wondering if I could invite more long-range observations from Janeece, or someone who'd like to speak to that, and more discussion about immediate consequences of the change from John or somebody who agrees with him."

> INTERVIEWEE (JANEECE): "I'm sorry. I thought our position on long-term changes for downtown was obvious. [JOHN: (muttering) 'Nope. . . .'] Let me backtrack a bit. . . ."

At times, listening for discovery will necessarily take a different form. Remember that part of listening is trying to figure out what is *not* being said and why the speaker is overlooking or avoiding those comments or observations. Listening for what is not said could lead you to observe, perhaps, if you were a traveling representative for a pharmaceutical company: "Doctor Fernandez, I heard you say several times you 'haven't been unhappy' with the responsiveness of the people from Ross. But I haven't heard you say that a change is out of the question. Are there things they aren't doing, maybe, that you wish could happen?"

Is the emphasis on listening for discovery effective? When one major company had a portion of their sales personnel participate in a training program called "Selling by Listening," they discovered that one of the divisions that received training increased sales by almost 34 percent, but a comparable group that didn't receive the training increased only by about 3 percent (Anderson, 1995, p. 169).

• Interviewers attempt to develop a frame for the decision (or issue, or idea) that is congruent with the interviewee's frame. Despite the obvious occasional deceiver or manipulator, most successful persuaders in the long term are highly empathic communicators who can glimpse what the world looks like to the other person(s). What beliefs are held about how the world works? (Interviewees are unlikely to think of alternatives outside the boundaries of these beliefs.) What attitudes predispose them to evaluate options or act in certain ways? (They may not immediately understand or respect attitudes they consider inconsistent with their own.) What are the operational values that they carry with them from situation to situation? (They're unlikely to make many decisions inconsistent with longstanding values.)

Then, from within the imagined alternate frame, persuasive interviewers more completely understand the kinds of information and the forms of reasoning they must provide—or elicit—to clarify the decision-making process for the interviewee. This step is impossible, of course, without the speaking and listening skills that precede this stage.

Some commentators, notably Rolph Anderson (1996), have tried to project how persuasion will change for salespersons as new electronic media and on-line database research takes hold of our lives even more firmly in the coming century. Notice, however, in the following comment, how many times he places in the foreground the expected and traditional responsibilities of audience analysis, even though they are draped in new clothing:

> High-technology can never fully replace the salesperson's ability to establish trust with customers, respond to subtle cues, anticipate customer needs, provide personalized service, nurture ongoing relationships, and create profitable new business strategies in partnership with customers. However, salespeople must take on new roles and revitalize some old ones in serving customers—e.g., (1) learning more about their customers' businesses and taking responsibility for customer profitability, (2) helping customers create long-run competitive advantages, (3) learning how to use their company resources to create added value for customers, (4) building good relationships with their own headquarters support team, (5) devoting more attention to intelligence gathering as the "eyes and ears" of their companies, (6) making use of the latest technology to increase customer contact and service while reducing costs, and (7) developing long-term, mutually profitable partnerships with customers. (p. 30)

New technologies are increasingly removing any excuse a persuader might have had in years past for not discovering essential facts and background about the audience. The amount of information available to communicators is staggering, in fact. We suggest you consult the many new sources designed to guide communicators in their on-line research (see Courtright & Perse, 1998, for a manual written especially for communication specialists and students).

Matching

Information gained in the discovery stage is useful only if you have a suggestion, a product, or a new perspective that is perceived as genuinely helpful for the interviewee, and then only if you explain it well enough to create an obvious link between the interviewee's current situation and the improved future situation. No idea or product sells itself by its inherent attractiveness; indeed, we "buy" based upon presumed future outcomes that adopters or customers consider to be desirable or necessary.

In a complex world, though, we often are confused or even intimidated by the vast array of choices we confront. Most people are knowledgeable about a number of topics, but few of us are competent to move comfortably from diagnosing engine troubles with an auto mechanic to asking a corporate lawyer sophisticated legal questions about the lawsuit filed last month by a coworker. You may know how to tell whether your computer's memory is inadequate for new software the boss wants you to run but not understand enough about operating system distinctions to ask intelligent questions of outside vendors in the department heads' meeting deciding on technology upgrades. We all have somewhat different bases of knowledge and competence, but we have to make decisions in many areas of relative ignorance. In the matching stage of persuasive interviewing, an interviewer shows he or she is credible enough—expert enough and trustworthy enough—to assist an interviewee through an informational maze, even when the decision maker feels overwhelmed by the task. Obviously, this is a responsibility that potentially invites misrepresentation, distortion, and selfishness. But effective persuaders understand that such tactics are ultimately counterproductive. Not only are they ethically wrong (as we will discuss in more detail later), they are ineffective. When one's needs are not matched well with a product, a service, or an idea, that mismatch becomes painfully obvious soon enough, and the persuader who urged the decision is discredited in that relationship.

How do people change their minds as a result of messages they can match and align with needs and wants? A particularly revealing classic explanation is provided by the social psychologist Herbert Kelman (1966). He distinguished three processes of social influence: compliance, identification, and internalization.

Compliance occurs "when an individual accepts influence from another person or from a group because he hopes to achieve a favorable reaction from the other. He may be interested in attaining certain specific rewards or in avoiding certain specific punishments that the influencing agent controls" (p. 152). Compliance conditions are those, for example, in which a person claims to agree with a comment because agreeing serves a more important need at that time than arguing the point. As soon as a given listener might leave the scene, the agreement (and the presumed influence) would evaporate. Compliance also suggests that people's reactions are sometimes based more on how they want to be seen by others than by intrinsic attraction of the product, the idea, or the service under discussion. "What the individual learns, essentially, is to say or do the expected thing in special situations, regardless of what . . . private beliefs may be. Opinions adopted through compliance should be expressed only when the person's behavior is observable by the influencing agent." Thus, a persuader's matching of a particular goal to systems of interviewee beliefs, attitudes, and values becomes quite dependent upon the continued presence of the persuader or some similar persuasive agent. Compliance-based social influence, therefore, is transitory unless the relationship from which it springs is continually sustained. For example, some influence might be based upon compliance in an ongoing superior-subordinate relationship (see Chapter 7), but when a new boss is hired, the employee wouldn't necessarily act the same way. Used car salespersons could not rely upon compliance-based influence because theirs is rarely a persistent relationship with buyers.

Identification is a somewhat more lasting process of social influence. In his specialized use of the term, Kelman means that people sometimes adopt other people's behaviors or preferences because doing so aligns them with the desirable others. In essence, they mimic other people. Advertisers and marketers have long understood that a "me, too" or a "bandwagon" aspect motivates some consumer behavior. We buy things because we want to be seen as the kind of person who buys those things. The fashion industry operates on this basis, and it is the reason why many people wouldn't be caught dead wearing the wrong brand of jeans, even when they realize intellectually that "their" brand may have been assembled in the same factory, by the same workers, and using the same materials, as a cheaper brand they disdain. Still, identification operates at a deeper level than this, Kelman believes. We change or modify a wide range of beliefs and attitudes on the basis of how they will be perceived by these significant others defined as important in our lives. In a sense, identification describes our desire to see a self not only psychologically but also socially—but socially in terms of a specific other person or group with whom we want to identify.

Although compliance and identification are similar in some respects (the actual content of the idea or adopted behavior is not the primary stimulus for the influence, for example), identification differs in that it means the person is influenced in both public and private situations, whereas compliant influence is usually shown only in public or when certain others are physically present. Identification works as long as the person's presumed role relative to the other is operative. For example, the ordinary role of a car salesperson relative to you may be very specifically defined and contained only in those moments when you're buying a car. But if she or he can establish a strong enough bond with you, later sending you Christmas cards and calling you occasionally to see how the car is working out for you, perhaps you'll define the role differently. It may become a more ongoing and persistent feature of your life. Instead of being only "the woman who sold you that car," she becomes—perhaps—"your friend who also works for a car dealership." That new role—friend—persists, and your identification with her as a friend has probably changed some of your attitudes, for example, about the kind of car she sells. The relationship frames the product, through identification.

Finally, Kelman describes the deepest and most lasting process of social influence— **internalization.** This develops when people discover that proposed changes are genuinely congruent with their value systems and become rewarding for that reason. Although Kelman believes that internalization is often understood in terms of rational or systematic attempts at persuasion, it doesn't necessarily operate that way. The key to internalization is that the person influenced integrates the new decision (beliefs or behaviors, for instance) into a larger pattern of values so that it makes a kind of intuitive sense.

A persuasive interviewer who hopes to have a lasting influence will value the process of internalization most highly, because it doesn't depend upon the continued presence (Kelman calls it "surveillance") of the influencer, nor does it depend upon a particular continuing role definition between communicators. It presumes precisely those conditions that persuasive interviewers attempt to facilitate in this stage of their task—that interviewer and interviewee mutually work to match what is useful about the suggested change with what is important to the prospective adopter. These links can't be decided beforehand and *told to* the adopter, but must be *explored* together through skillful and sensitive give-and-take of interviewing. (See Box 11.4 for how two professionals describe this process of exploration.) Let's try an example well suited to student decisions to attend a college or university: the interaction between a college recruitment representative and a student with her or his parents. Here are some particularly useful topics and questions for exploring a potential match:

BOX 11.4   **INTERVIEWERS IN ACTION**

Maxine Dennis and Susan Fu

Maxine Dennis

"My job involves meeting with professors and discussing their textbook needs with them. Prentice-Hall publishes a huge variety of texts, so chances are we've got a book that will fit the professor's needs in either a lower- or higher-level course. My basic objective is to get a commitment from the professor that she or he will use a Prentice-Hall textbook in a particular course for the coming semester. Professors are smart people; they appreciate open, honest communication without any pushiness. And because most major textbooks are revised every three years or so, I am interested in cultivating long-term relationships with my professor-customers so that they will consider future editions of the books I sell. I listen carefully to their evaluations of the current editions of Prentice-Hall and competing texts and communicate their comments and critiques to our home office marketing and acquisitions staff people. To us, the professors' input is just as important as their choice of books, and I try to make sure that they realize this."

Source: Anderson, 1995, p. 155

Susan Fu

"In a marketing class I took, I remember the lecture about professional selling. Like many people, I thought you had to be a smooth talker and quick on your feet to be a salesperson. But my professor stressed that the best salespeople are first and foremost excellent listeners who are sincerely interested in helping the customer fill a need or solve a problem. That sounded like something I could do well, so, after graduating in 1983 with a B.S. in Computer Science and a minor in Business, I interviewed with several firms for technical sales positions and decided to go with Hewlett-Packard as a staff sales representative. . . . On any one day, I may be on face-to-face customer calls all day, or hosting customers for a demo at our sales office, attending a trade show to generate leads, or prospecting by phone."

Source: Anderson, 1995, p. 313

- *Learning styles and personal preferences.* (For example: "What have been your most successful educational experiences in the past?" "Is it important to you that teachers get to know you personally?")

- *Long-term goals.* (For example: "Have you decided to focus on any particular career track, as of now?" "What do you see yourself doing in ten or fifteen years?")

- *Short-term goals.* (For example: "You played in the band in high school; is it important for you to keep up with your music, even though you're shooting for a career in international diplomacy?" "It sounds like you want to continue to play soccer. Do I have that right?")

- *Other drawbacks or advantages.* (For example: "Lexington is a surprisingly cosmopolitan city, but we've found that some students prefer a more urban environment. Have you thought about this question?" "We haven't discussed tuition, which looks pretty steep on paper. I was wondering if you'd already researched what a high percentage of students get significant scholarship assistance.")

By inquiring about such things, the recruiter is not actively attempting to get a commitment from the student to enroll. Instead, the responses will provide information with which both parties can clarify and assess whether a certain decision is right for them. The interviewer wants to suggest matches that make sense to the student and parents in meeting their own goals.

Choosing

In persuasive situations, all communicators are participants, but at the choosing stage, the primary attention turns to one person—the interviewee, the one for whom a change or a new decision is being suggested. Sales professionals refer to him or her as **the prospect** to emphasize the contingent nature of decision making. Despite your best efforts to represent your idea, yourself, or your product accurately, and despite a seemingly close fit between someone's desires and the suggested change, the final choice is not yours. Both parties typically frame a persuasive interview as leading toward the goal of choice, and in some ways, that choice will be necessarily one sided. To see how this works, let's revisit the overall process again, leading up to the choice stage. (See if you can highlight prominent features of opening, discovering, and matching in the following example.)

One of the authors and his wife recently invited a representative of a large local construction and home improvement company into their home to investigate the possibility of new or refurbished kitchen cabinets. Because we'd never done this before, we expected a short visit, perhaps with someone taking measurements and leaving some brochures. What happened, however, was a completely different experience. We were interviewed thoroughly by a very skillful young woman who had clearly gone through a training program that stressed the careful sequencing of topics, questions, and answers.

Seated at the kitchen table with us, she talked about how much she liked "neat old houses" like ours and how important kitchens were to the life of a family. Switching gears subtly, she asked what we knew about the company she represented. We'd heard of it through ads and because of some friends' experience using them for cabinetry work. She wondered how we felt about the negative image some home improvement companies had developed in our area. We'd heard about some of that, we said, but since we'd avoided having major work done, we had no direct experience with such fly-by-night operations. This was an opening for her to discuss the many decades this company had maintained its leadership and how good its reputation was with the Better Business Bureau. Presumably, we were left to conclude, a company that did shoddy work or a company that cheated people could never stay in business fifty or sixty years in the same local area.

Next, she took out an official-looking three-ring binder with a series of pages containing detailed pictures, product dimensions, and—most important of all—questions about how we use the kitchen, what we store on the shelves, how pleased we were with the present configuration of cabinets, what we had hoped to spend if we decided to do the shelves with her company, and so forth. With each answer, she paraphrased the response to ensure she had written down its essence. At no time did she say anything that sounded like a sales pitch or an appeal to buy. No reasons to choose one product over another were ever given, nor did she even hint about whether she concurred that the existing cabinets needed replacement or remodeling.

From other pages in her notebook, she produced detailed comparisons of various plans that would presumably accomplish our goals. She encouraged us to eliminate plans and options that clearly did not meet our goals or our budget. She didn't make these decisions but progressively invited us to state a series of seemingly small judgments that kept us focused on our own goals as they matched, or failed to match, the company's options. Using the main criteria we supplied—budget, appearance, configuration, and minimum intrusion of workers, among others—we eliminated several plans while narrowing choices to two or three. There was a glitch, however. A particular wood we wanted wasn't listed in the package deals we'd identified. Would that be a problem? How big a problem? She replied frankly that she didn't know the answer to our question. A phone call to the company was unsuccessful, as our conversation took place after normal business hours, but she promised to get back to us very shortly, which she did. (A kept promise, no matter how tiny, is one of a persuader's best advertisements!) Although she might have lost credibility with some people for not knowing the answer, the effect was the reverse with us. She gained credibility by responding in what we perceived as a direct manner and by reacting with a very human sense of embarrassment at not knowing all the appropriate information. Consider the frame: If she'd been seen as incompetent before this issue came up, her ignorance might have been judged as laughable or intolerable; within the context of her previously won credibility and competence, we framed the very same behavior as honest and trustworthy.

Thus, the stage had been set for choice. We had all the information we needed (or thought we needed) about the company, and about its cabinets and workers. She had all the information she needed about us, our budget as we saw it, and our goals for a different kitchen. It was time to choose. The best strategies for the choice stage of persuasive interviewing are the ones she implemented:

- *Signal the choice.* (For example: "Well, that's about all I know. What I've tried to do is to help you clarify the decision. The ball's where it should be—in your court.")

- *Invite further questions, comments, or issues.* (For example: "If you have any other thoughts about this, or if questions come up that we didn't cover, feel free to call me any time, even at home. OK?")

- *Retreat to give the other person room to decide.* In some programs encouraging dialogue among competing groups, for example, facilitators have found that they can't force dialogue to occur, but that if a space is created in which it *can* develop, with appropriate invitation it often *will* develop. Choices operate by the same principle. If you're the interviewer, you hope for a commitment that remains influential—one that's internalized, in Kelman's terms. (For example: "I'm going to leave you alone now. Take as long as you want." Or, "I'll tell you what. I've got another call to make today. Talk it over between the two of you and get back to me in a day or so. If I don't hear, should I take that as a no?)

The choice stage presents many ethical dilemmas for persuaders. Many unscrupulous persuaders are tempted to use overt or covert pressure to limit others' choices. Or they actively misrepresent the choices themselves. Before participating in persuasive interviews, communicators might want to anticipate some of the ethical points that are involved in typical influence attempts. Our purpose is not to increase the level of cynicism in contemporary society (that is high enough, thank you) but to ensure that we're dealing realistically with the kinds of challenges that arise for both interviewer and interviewee. Almost by definition, attempts at persuasion, especially if the stakes are high, are full of opportunities for ethical compromises in which the end is presumed to justify the means.

Neither is this chapter the place for a full discussion of philosophies guiding ethical communication; that topic has been presented earlier in different chapters. However, Charles Brown and Paul Keller (1979; Keller & Brown, 1968) have described an especially fruitful approach to analyzing the ethics of interpersonal persuasion. Keep their criterion in mind when deciding (1) how to frame your invitations for choice making of others; (2) how to listen to influence attempts when you are the interviewee; and, in anticipation of our next stage of persuasive interviewing, (3) how to speak and listen during the all-important closing stage, whether you are interviewer or interviewee.

Brown and Keller (1979, Chapter 11) survey several approaches to interpersonal ethics that emphasize the content of what is said and focus on the accuracy, truthfulness, and strategic effects of words. Without denying the value of this approach, they decide to take a more relational approach, as we have in this book. Their interpersonal ethic "is more concerned with the attitude a speaker and a listener show toward each other" (p. 276). More specifically:

> A's communication is ethical to the extent that it accepts B's responses; it is unethical to the extent that it is hostile to B's responses, or in some way tries to subjugate B. The ethic can best be put to a test when A discovers that B rejects the message A is sending. (p. 276)

Brown and Keller's **interpersonal ethic,** based on the criterion of whether one's messages maintain or expand others' choices, has clear and demanding implications for persuaders (see Box 11.5).

BOX 11.5   REMINDERS

Implications of the Interpersonal Ethic for Persuasive Interviewers

Brown and Keller suggest the following implications for persuaders (paraphrased here except as noted):

- "Whatever enhances the basic freedom of response . . . is more ethical; whatever either overtly or covertly attacks that energy is less ethical" (p. 279).

- Persuaders help create and maintain the full and free range of listener choices relevant to the topic at hand. Internalized attitude change happens when people realize that they've considered all reasonable options and chosen the best one (for them) on appropriate grounds.

- Persuaders know that lies, misrepresentations, distortions, and strategic omissions tend to limit the choices of listeners and are, in most cases, unethical.

- Persuaders have to be as willing *not* to make the sale, or *not* to convince the listener, as to sell or convince others. This does not mean that advocates for positions shouldn't care whether they are successful. It only means that when listeners choose otherwise, persuaders accept the result as something that might be better for the listeners, from the listeners' frame of reference.

- Persuaders avoid assuming they can be certain about what is right or good for other people. They can be strongly committed but cannot get inside someone else's life to know what is best for them.

- Persuaders who limit the choices of others are behaving unethically toward themselves, as well. Brown and Keller write that coercive communication is not just unethical because it injures the other person, but "it is unethical for the user also, because it gradually cuts a person off from his or her own creative growth. The constant effort to exercise power over others makes one increasingly dependent on getting defeated responses from others. If the desired responses are not forthcoming, the effort to persuade must be redoubled. And this preoccupation closes the door to one's own personal development."

Source: Brown & Keller, 1979, pp. 277–278

Closing

Claire Kerr, a division major account manager with the NCR Corporation, describes the simplicity of what she calls her "selling style": "I find that presentations are most effective when they are clear, concise, and simple. The same rules apply to the close. Customers respect salespeople who are direct and come straight to the point. I don't use 'ulterior motive' closes, play games, or use tricks" (quoted in Anderson, 1995, p. 191). Her statement indicates the special meaning most sales professionals have in mind for this final stage of the persuasive interviewing process.

A **close** is, in this specialized jargon, not just the finishing touches on the interview, or the last few things an interviewer has to say. It becomes the moment of decision itself, the psychological turf where persons commit to something. Although it's often assumed to be the time when the "prospect," the "customer," or the "decision maker" commits, it's also when the persuader commits to something—a fact missed in many discussions of selling and persuasion. The representative from the home improvement company did call us back with extra information about the availability of the wood we wanted, as she'd promised. She did ask when we'd like to meet again with her, suggesting the final phase of

BOX 11.6   R E M I N D E R S

Kimball's Five Steps for Closing

1. "Ask questions and get the prospect to talk to identify needs, problems, and buying motives.

2. "Confirm understanding with a reflective summary statement.

3. "Present features of your product and translate those features into benefits which address the prospect's attendant buying motives.

4. "Ask questions to have the customer confirm the benefits. It *may be* true if *you* say it. It *is* true if *they* say it.

5. "Make a request for action."

Source: Kimball, 1994, p. 171

her pragmatic relationship with us, the close. Then, presumably, she would have initiated a discussion of how we could order the work and get the whole process started. As you will see, there are many approaches for doing that.

Instead, however, she graciously accepted our different decision. We had by that time changed our minds about the work, and we still live contentedly with the old cabinets. Though this was not the closing outcome she had wished for, it was still a clarification and an unambiguous decision. Some might think she failed with us. No. She achieved for herself and her company a qualified success. We decided not to order the cabinets, but she had earned our trust and goodwill enough to warrant a call to the same firm in the future, in all likelihood. Although it sounds unusual to say so, she also earned stories like this one, which have been told to several friends complete with the name of the firm.

The noted leadership consultant Paul Hersey (1988), in his book *Selling: A Behavioral Science Approach*, emphasizes the importance of closing:

> Our studies indicate that the behavior of top performers is significantly different than that of average performers when closing sales. Average performers tend to become pushy and directive. But top performers recognize customer apprehension and engage in supportive behaviors instead. By enhancing the match between customer needs and product benefits, involving the customer in the decision process, and acknowledging customer objections as needs, top performers significantly increase the probability of a successful close. (p. 189)

Hersey's statement connects the closing stage to earlier responsibilities of persuaders in the stages we've labeled discovering, matching, and choosing. He justifiably emphasizes the sensitivity to listeners' cues and the ability to support the listeners' needs rather than only satisfying their own. By being creatively and ethically unselfish, then, many persuasive interviewers not only satisfy ethical criteria but also actually increase their productivity and the quality of their communication. Instead of framing what they do as meeting their own needs, successful sellers and other persuaders define themselves as ". . . problem solvers attempting to meet other people's needs, wants, and desires" (Woodward & Denton, 1988, p. 313).

Box 11.6 presents five basic suggestions for successful closing, as described by an experienced salesman. Bob Kimball (1994) doesn't dwell on ethical concerns in this list and consequently could be perceived as advocating gimmicks. However, each of the suggestions builds on a valid insight on persuasion research which, if blended with ethical sensitivity, could be as helpful for interviewee as for interviewer. Note, too, how the close in some ways recapitulates the overall process of persuasive interviewing in a microcosm.

Try not to think of closing as a series of techniques. Techniques are those behavioral strategies that practitioners know will work for them and which they try to package for others. Sometimes they'll work for you and sometimes they won't. It's not the technique that really works (or not) but you, speaking effectively with a unique audience that responds uniquely. You're better advised to learn basic principles of persuasion and ethics, then blend what you know with your own style within your own contexts. Staying alert to consequences and feedback will help you refine your style; maybe someday, you'll be able to recount hundreds of your own stories. But persuasive interviewing is a process that is too dialogically based to be reduced to a list of gimmicks. Once you recognize that, however, it doesn't hurt to listen to others' stories.

There are probably as many cute names for closing strategies as there are different people telling stories about closings. Some are clearly ethical and mutually helpful, while others cut some ethical corners. For example, in what Anderson (1995, pp. 321–329) calls the **assumptive close,** the seller/interviewer assumes that the respondent has already agreed to buy the product or service, thereby making it much more difficult for a "no" response. A **standing room only close** implies, if not states, that the respondent must act now or forever lose the opportunity to get something he or she wants (even if this isn't true). These are examples of ethically suspect tricks of the trade that responsible communicators should not have to rely upon. Other closing strategies make much better ethical sense. A persuader using a **testimonial close** simply attempts to seal a deal with a strong supportive statement about the product or service, preferably a statement from someone the respondent finds highly credible or similar to himself or herself in relevant details. A **choice close** reminds the respondent of available options and lays them out clearly so that a decision seems like a clearer, cleaner step (some unethical persuaders, of course, might artificially or unfairly limit the choices in order to trick listeners). A **counterbalance close** seeks to counter a respondent's valid objection with an equally valid or greater advantage that offsets the objection, then opens discussion of decision making.

We have used the sales interview encounter as a prototype, or representative example, of the problems involved in persuasive interviewing. Although only some of us become salespeople by trade, everyone attempts to sell things occasionally. We not only sell cars and old bikes, but we also persuade others every day at work to give our ideas a careful hearing. Familiarity with basic concepts of persuasive interviewing will also help you, as a respondent or interviewee, to understand the approaches of professional persuaders you'll encounter at a motivational speakers' seminar, your local furniture store, or the muffler repair shop.

The traditional sales encounter is far from the only kind of persuasive interview. In "Beyond the Basics" we will survey briefly two other contexts for interviewing and point out their distinctive characteristics and skills.

Assume you have just been hired by your college or university as a "student ambassador" whose responsibility is to give campus tours to prospective students and parents (see a similar example earlier in this chapter). Such students are expected to be guides, information providers, representatives, and persuaders. Consider carefully:

- What do you think the dean of student affairs would tell you your primary goal should be? What do you think it should be?

- Which specific skills described in this chapter would most help you accomplish this job?

- Which aspects of your personality would be your biggest assets in this job? Your biggest drawbacks?

- Every campus wants to put its best foot forward. Yet prospective students and their parents often ask difficult questions that will test your responsiveness and Brown and Keller's *interpersonal ethic* (see earlier discussion). *Hypothetical instance:* Assuming you know that student assistants in residence halls often look the other way on alcohol violations, and that several instances of alleged date rape have been largely ignored by campus officials, how do you react to this parent's inquiry: "Martha wants to come here, but we'll be 500 miles away. How would you describe the safety of dorm life and the disciplinary system?" Write out the best response you could give. Is it persuasive? Is it fair to the parent? To the school? To Martha? Does it meet the criterion of the interpersonal ethic? If so, how? If not, why not?

Negotiation Interviews

BEYOND THE BASICS

Management consultant Gerald Nierenberg (1987) understands the pervasiveness of negotiation in everyday life: "Nothing could be simpler in definition or broader in scope" than this process, he believes. In fact, "every desire that demands satisfaction—and every need to be met—is at least potentially an occasion for people to initiate the negotiating process. Whenever people exchange ideas with the intention of changing relationships, whenever they confer for agreement, they are negotiating" (p. 4). Parents negotiate about how to raise children. Employees negotiate pay raises for themselves with their companies. Union and management representatives negotiate collective bargaining agreements. Reporters and celebrities negotiate to determine how the results of their interviews will be presented, and in which forum.

Therefore, we will define a **negotiation interview** as any situation in which parties (1) are expected to communicate intentionally and persuasively, (2) are expected to function as both interviewer and interviewee, and (3) are expected to seek agreement or consensus. After examining each of these stipulations, we will look at negotiation in terms of interviewing's three basic processes—speaking, listening, and framing.

- *Parties are expected to communicate intentionally and persuasively.* In negotiation contexts, there are "sides," even if there is no overt conflict. One person's (or group's) goals and background are presumed to be different from another's, and this is often seen as a positive, energizing force behind negotiations. Successful negotiators value differences and seek to exploit them to discover new forms of effective relationship. In other words, negotiators are not afraid of conflict.

- *Parties are expected to be both interviewers and interviewees.* In most interview forms, the roles of interviewer and interviewee are at least relatively fixed. People generally know whose responsibility it is to initiate communication, who should take responsibility for the context, whose information is the focal point for interaction, who asks the questions, and who determines when the interaction has run its course. In negotiations, each party takes responsibility for asking questions, and each must answer them as well. Because negotiations are this kind of mixed-role interview situation, some logistical decisions become complicated: Who schedules the meeting? Who speaks the most? Who requests behavior changes first? How long does the meeting last? and other questions do not have automatic or easy answers in many negotiation sessions.

- *Parties are expected to seek agreement or consensus.* Many interactions in daily life do not need to lead to a mutually agreed-upon conclusion, but negotiation does feature this expectation. The basis for negotiating is a presumed relationship of some sort from which neither party wishes to escape. In anticipating future communication, then, one or both parties advocate a different form of relation.

Speaking

A prime goal of negotiation is to establish a *win-win outcome* in which each side can see that it has gained from the encounter. When one party wins (monetary, relational, physical, or psychological rewards, for example) but the other clearly loses, the resulting bitterness can undercut even normal communication functions. While not all suggestions or demands can be settled in a win-win manner, negotiators owe it to each other to explore the possibility of such thinking.

Speech in negotiation interviews, therefore, best contributes to success if it has the following characteristics:

- *Clear statements of position.* No one will stay in dialogue with you for long unless you're at least somewhat clear about what you want and why you're talking with this specific other person about it.

- *Contingent language.* Some words cut off replies from others. For example, "I know you're going to profit from exploiting these workers" is an accusation that leaves no "breathing room" for the other person. He or she can be expected to react defensively in a way that could close off future possibilities for talk. Much better (though less rhetorically flashy) would be something like, "I think the workers' predicament shouldn't lead to extra profits for the company."

- *Invitational language in questioning.* No techniques or tactics are always successful in human relationships. Yet in the midst of emotional negotiations, nervous communicators often forget one of the most effective of communication "openers," which is to ask simply, "What do you think?" There are many versions of "What do you think?" questions: "How does that sound to you?" "Would your departments be able to live with that policy?" "I've talked a long time now; I want to make sure I get your point, too." Invitational language is not the language of weakness, as some people suppose, but a language of strength. Only people who feel secure in their own communication styles develop the strength to invite others to contribute significantly.

- *Assertive language.* Inviting other opinions does not mean you have to agree with them. Remember that *assertiveness* is defined as the ability to stand up for your own rights while also respecting the rights of others. If you habitually speak clearly, contingently, and invitationally, then those times when you have to state positions strongly will be particularly effective. Otherwise, an unswervingly aggressive stance will dilute others' listening just as much as a persistent acquiescence (an "I'll accept anything" stance) will.

Listening

The goal of listening in negotiation contexts is to create opportunities for others to influence you, while giving yourself the type of information and insight you need to make better decisions. Consider these characteristics of listening:

- *Using reflective perception checks.* Active listening skills are crucial in negotiation, and one especially helpful demonstration of them is the reflective *perception check:* "I want to make sure I heard your suggestion correctly. I think you said that instead of my current office I could count on one of those two around the corner, provided that Jane retires this year." Use as many of the other person's words as you remember, but phrase your understanding in your own words too (it's your perception, after all). Active listening doesn't parrot the other's words but simply attempts to verify your understanding of them. Effective perception checks give your negotiation partners a chance to hear their thoughts in relational context and gives them the further opportunity to correct misperceptions.

- *Holding your fire.* Complicated negotiations often turn emotional, and the potential for blaming others is therefore always with us. While listening, remind yourself constantly that (1) the other person may not mean to offend you by his or her language choices; (2) you can wait to get more information before concluding that a particular phrase or strategy is meant as a put-down or an insult; (3) you can almost always respond appropriately to a negative comment later, as well; and (4) you can compartmentalize your reactions. In other words, even though the other person offends you, for example, it may be that your overall goal is better achieved by not making the offense into an overriding issue. Listen to it to be sure, but interpret it in a broader context.

- *Corraling your biases.* Review Chapter 3 and its suggestions for performing a listening self-analysis. We all have biases that interfere with effective, contextualized, and accurate listening. Get to know your own biases and how they might hold you back. If necessary, interview friends, coworkers, and acquaintances about your listening biases before entering a significant negotiation. Negotiations aren't battles, but they often feel so much like them that it's hard to analyze your own behavior calmly within the stress of the conversation.

Framing

The goal of framing in negotiation is to understand the potential for agreement in a way that is fair both to yourself and to other negotiators. Although inferences are inevitable, your understanding should be based upon available facts and must be realistic. Consider the following characteristics of framing:

- *Avoidance of mind reading.* Remind yourself constantly that you can know what other negotiators are saying and doing (if you train yourself to pay close enough attention), but you can't know what they are thinking or what their motives are.

- *Awareness of attribution processes.* Try to avoid what communication and social psychology researchers call the *fundamental attribution error*—assuming that others act as a result of some fundamental human characteristic ("who they really are," for instance) while your own actions are attributable to situational factors ("anyone would have acted this way if they'd been in my situation," for example). It's too easy to assume that your boss fired your friend because the boss is a vindictive person, but when you fired someone, it was obviously because your employee's poor performance gave you no choice. As far as we know, people act all the time as a result of a mix of personal and contextual factors.

- *Benefit-of-the-doubt thinking.* Remind yourself that your frames for another's behavior will never be congruent with theirs. Actively imagine what their frames *might* be. Don't leap to the conclusion that someone won't understand you, or won't believe you, or won't concede a point to you. Despite your inability (we presume) to mind read, you can be creative in imagining multiple frames that might be persuasive for the other person.

Some situations demand a special form of negotiation interviewing called **mediation**, in which a third-party communicator enters negotiations that are especially difficult or challenging—perhaps because of conflict—to employ appropriate interviewing skills. According to one research team, "Mediation may be defined as the intervention of a neutral third party who, intervening at the request of the parties, assists the parties to find a resolution that fills their needs" (Evarts, Greenstone, Kirkpatrick, & Leviton, 1983, p. 2). The mediator's persuasive goal is to find the areas of potential agreement that are obscured by the conflict or mistrust separating participants. At first, neither side may be convinced that anything other than their own demands or goals would be acceptable, but effective interviewing by non-ego-involved mediators can create surprisingly fertile common ground. One of the most effective mediators and dispute experts in the field of communication is John (Sam) Keltner. See Box 11.7 for his suggestions on how mediators should try to function in their roles as persuasive interviewers.

Interrogation/Advocacy Interviews

The public now seems infatuated with the entertainment potential of the legal system, as demonstrated by the O. J. Simpson murder trial, the Oklahoma Federal Building bombing trials, the 1998 lawsuit against Oprah Winfrey by Texas cattle owners, the investigation into the JonBenet Ramsey murder case, the aggressive investigations of Independent Counsel Kenneth Starr into President Clinton's personal background, and other prominent cases. During recent years, the ascendance of "Court TV," the popularity of "People's Court" and "Judge Judy" daytime shows, and the attempt of prominent CNBC host Geraldo Rivera to have the "program of record" in covering high-profile legal cases have made it clear that popular culture appreciates legal drama, if it is not at times obsessed by it.

Most citizens will be interviewed in either a law enforcement or a courtroom context at some point in their lives. The interviewer will either be an interrogator (a police officer, for example) or an advocate for a particular point of view. Although their purposes vary, interrogators and advocates are both persuasive interviewers. Respondents might be suspects, witnesses to an event, litigants in a lawsuit, members of a family under suspicion of child abuse, or just people who have talked with those who fit these categories.

The principal purpose of interrogators is to persuade an interviewee to disclose all relevant facts fully, even when full disclosure might not be in his or her best interest. To do this, the skillful interrogator combines the sensitive insight of counselors and social workers with the critical and analytical evaluations of a selection interviewer. Interrogators concentrate on questions, sometimes fairly aggressive or intrusive ones, in attempting to spotlight what needs to be discovered. J. T. Dillon (1990) discusses a number of what he terms "human relations" qualities that help interrogators do their jobs, such as empathy, congruence, respect, and sincere concern for the other person. However, the overriding quality he emphasizes is "non-judgmental response" (p. 76). If an interviewer already seems to have made up his or her mind, what is the point of talking if you're the interviewee? Almost anyone will be more likely to disclose information to a questioner they believe to be fair, open, and willing to be persuaded.

Even given the obvious advantages of talking to a fair-minded person, respondents to interrogations have many reasons not to talk, or to talk deceptively. They may want to hide something that signals some form of legal or social guilt. They may be withholding or concealing embarrassing facts about themselves. They may be trying to protect a loved one. But beyond these obvious roadblocks, interrogators contend with the following problems, paraphrased here from Dillon (1990, pp. 78–79). The respondent might

- have faulty perception;
- not remember the issue in question;
- not understand what is being asked or requested;
- believe the information requested is not relevant or important enough to mention;
- consider the issue "too distasteful, frightening, or taboo" to discuss;
- be affected unconsciously by bias or prejudice.

Dillon reminds us that many interviewees, in fact, may ". . . agreeably be telling you what you seem to want to know. They confirm your view without your even realizing it. Then you think you have discovered the facts about this matter. But nothing has been discovered, certainly no facts" (p. 79).

Interrogators have to dig deeper. In such circumstances, Dillon and others suggest (p. 80), patience is one key. Interrogators must not rush the process by imposing artificial time limits or by failing to pause significantly after questions and answers. A second key is persistence: Interrogators may ask about a fact or issue, get one kind of answer, and then later in the interview return to the same basic inquiry by phrasing the question differently. They want to see if the response frame is different the second (or the third) time around. A characteristic of persistence is usually a nonaccusatory questioning tone, something consistent with a nonjudgmental attitude. How do most interrogations progress, then?

Questioners often start with nonthreatening topics, in order to relax informants and let them adapt to an often threatening situation. Before direct and specific questioning begins, interviewers tend to ask what Dillon (1990, p. 85) calls a **free narrative question**—one that lets the interviewee create a free-form personal account, with no structuring from the questioner. For example, a police officer might ask, "When you were standing on the corner, a white car pulled up. Could you tell me what happened then?" After a series of probing direct questions to ascertain the degree of truth or falsity in the free narrative, the questioner attempts to cross-check the earlier answers, asking often about seemingly unrelated details to test the consistency of an interviewee. To close the questioning, the interviewer often will ask a "what else?" question similar to the "sixth W" we advocated for journalists in Chapter 8. "Is there anything else you'd like me to know?" a questioner might ask. Finally, experienced interrogators understand that after the tape recorder has been turned off and the notebook closed, interviewees often relax and provide useful and informative nonverbal cues, not to mention offhand comments that pertain to their earlier answers.

Examination of witnesses in a courtroom employs similar styles of interviewing. However, lawyers who engage in such interviews operate under very different constraints imposed by the official physical presence of onlookers (a jury, a gallery of observers, sometimes even cameras broadcasting or taping trial proceedings). In addition, courtroom participants must act within a set of rules that govern their communication; for example, certain kinds of leading questions are permissible in a cross-examination of a witness that are not permitted during direct questioning. Many legal systems throughout the world recognize that truth can emerge from the systematic clash of positions and proofs, each side presented by an advocate whose responsibility is to point out the flaws in the other side's reasoning. Interviews conducted within courtrooms, then, often take the form of demonstrations of reasoning—demonstrations that are a mixture of planning and spontaneity. Observers may be frustrated with the results of a given case, or with the ethical cross-pressures exerted on interviewers and interviewees who are asked to become advocates, but the overall system has been proven remarkably effective at producing just results.

Advocacy interviewers, in court for example, frame their questions and comments in order to encourage listeners toward a certain conclusion. By the nature of the context, they are systematically and predictably biased, in other words. Yet the courtroom advocate need not become negative, as an acquaintance of the famous lawyer Rufus Choate recalled in this account:

> Commenting once on the cross-examination of a certain eminent counsellor at the Boston Bar with decided disapprobation, Choate said, "This man goes at a witness in such a way that he inevitably gets the jury all on the side of the witness. I do not," he added, "think that is a good plan." His own plan was far more wary, intelligent, and circumspect. He had a profound knowledge of human nature, of the springs of human action, of the thoughts of human hearts. To get at these and make them patent to the jury, he would ask only a few telling questions—a very few questions, but generally, every one of them was fired point blank and hit the mark. His motto was: "Never cross-examine any more than is absolutely necessary. If you don't break your witness, he breaks you." His whole style of address to the occupants of the witness stand was soothing, kind, and

BOX 11.8   *INTERVIEWERS/INTERVIEWEES IN ACTION*

Clarence Darrow and William Jennings Bryan

The following excerpt is from the famous Scopes evolution case, tried in Dayton, Tennessee, in 1925. Defense attorney Clarence Darrow was defending Thomas Scopes, a high school teacher accused of violating a state law forbidding the teaching of evolution. On the stand was William Jennings Bryan, a fundamentalist religious leader and politician:

DARROW: Have you an opinion as to whether—whoever wrote the book, I believe Joshua, the Book of Joshua, thought the sun went around the earth or not?

BRYAN: I believe that he was inspired.

D: Can you answer my question?

B: When you let me finish the statement.

D: It is a simple question, but finish it.

B: You cannot measure the length of my answer by the length of your question. (Laughter)

D: No, except that the answer be longer. (Laughter)

B: I believe that the Bible is inspired, with an inspired author. Whether one who wrote as he was directed to write understood the things he was writing about, I don't know.

D: Whoever inspired it? Do you think whoever inspired it believed that the sun went around the earth?

B: I believe it was inspired by the Almighty, and He may have used language that could be understood at that time.

D: Was —

B: Instead of using language that could not be understood until Darrow was born (Laughter and applause)

D: So, it might have been subject to construction, might it not?

B: It might have been phrased in language that could be understood then.

D: That means it is subject to construction?

B: That is your construction. I am answering your question.

D: Is that correct?

B: That is my answer to it.

D: Can you answer?

Source: Weinberg, 1964, pp. 196–197

reassuring. When he came down heavily to crush a witness, it was with a calm, resolute decision, but no asperity—nothing curt, nothing tart. (quoted in Welman, 1948, pp. 209–210).

- Some observers have argued that it is unrealistic to think salespersons and other persuasive interviewers should actively promote the freedom of choice of prospective buyers and other interviewees. Ethics demands only (the argument goes) that sales personnel not blatantly lie, but beyond that, everyone knows that their intention is to mislead. In this view, stretching the truth, making extravagant claims, intentionally distracting interviewees from registering serious objections, and withholding the negatives of one's product or service are all accepted and expected tactics. We have taken the position in this chapter that promoting freedom of choice is not only ethical but realistic. What, in your opinion, is the best argument against our position? The best argument for it?

- Negotiation and sales interviews are not necessarily separate interviewing experiences, as you know from the last time you haggled with a used car dealer. Negotiation, however, is an uncomfortable experience for many buyers. One expert in sales research notes that a current trend in the marketplace, therefore, is an upswing in "fixed price dealers" and the increased use of "buying representatives" such as Autovantage, Autobytel, and Consumers Car Club (Anderson, 1996). Survey your communication skills and interests introspectively. What would you gain from avoidance of negotiation? What would you lose? To what extent would your distaste for negotiated buying (if present) be alleviated by more confidence in your skill in interpersonal interviewing?

- Many lawyers are told in law school they should never ask a witness a question to which they don't already know the answer. Yet early in this book we suggested that genuine questions are those to which you don't already know the answers and that effective interviewers should always be willing to be surprised. Are these positions contradictory? If so, how and why? Analyze the Darrow-Bryan exchange in Box 11.8 with regard to whether, and how, Bryan surprised Darrow with his answers.

Thus, two major differences between normal interrogation and courtroom advocacy become clearer: The interrogator seeks accurate accounts without necessarily judging them as for or against external positions, while an advocate elicits accounts to prove or disprove positions in a two-sided conflict; the interrogator is patient and persistent, ideally taking as much time as necessary for the interview, while the advocate searches for the pointedly dramatic moments in which a question or answer can best support an argument. The advocate interviewer must use responses to help frame a specific interpretation for a listening judge or jury, while recognizing, as Choate's observer reminds us, that too much hostility will stimulate listeners to react psychologically against the too-aggressive questioner. In Box 11.8, does the lawyer, Clarence Darrow, balance these concerns effectively, in your opinion?

Summary

The major idea of this chapter can be stated simply: Although "interviewing" sometimes suggests a neutral pursuit of information, understanding persuasion—as a potent non-neutral force—can be crucial for interviewers and interviewees.

We begin by introducing persuasion as an interpersonal activity that occurs constantly in various types of interviews. We are constantly attempting to change others' beliefs, attitudes, and values. Even if we weren't trying to do so, such change would happen anyway as a result of natural processes of human accommodation and adjustment. Some people, however, think that intentionally trying to change another's mind is an attempt to manipulate or to trick someone into serving the persuader's interests but not their own. Manipulation is possible. Yet persuasion in interviewing can also be conceived as a helping relationship, a mutual process in which a persuader seeks to help the other person achieve his or her own desired goals for the mutual benefit of persuader and the one to be persuaded. This, we suggest, is clearly the rationale of ethical sales attempts, but it is the basis of other persuasive forms as well.

Using personal sales as a prototypical persuasive situation, we have developed a five-stage model for interviewers: opening, discovery, matching, choice, and closing. Communication skills are discussed in their cultural and ethical contexts, with the goal of explaining why persuasion is so complex.

In "Beyond the Basics" we look at two additional important forms of persuasive interviews that involve millions of people each year: negotiation (including mediation) and interrogation/advocacy interviews. Although these are distinct from each other, and the two of them considered together have different premises than sales interviews, the basic principles of persuasion operate in them all.

The Interview Bookshelf

On the possibilities of being fooled by persuaders

Crossen, C. (1994). *Tainted truth: The manipulation of fact in America.* New York: Simon & Schuster.

Read this book if you think you're much too sophisticated to fall for the sleazy tricks of manipulative people. Most of us even fall for shoddy reasoning that persuaders don't *intend* to be manipulative.

On a general appreciation of persuasion research, principles, and practices

Johnston, D. D. (1994). *The art and science of persuasion.* Madison, WI: Brown & Benchmark.

Many excellent books on persuasion research and practice are available. This is a recent and clearly written text that emphasizes dialogue, taking the perspectives of both persuader and the person to be persuaded.

On a basic approach to sales interviewing

Anderson, R. (1995). *Essentials of personal selling: The new professionalism.* Englewood Cliffs, NJ: Prentice-Hall.

Rolph Anderson has provided a lively mix of stories, research, and strategies. Among the strengths of the book is its exceptional readability and its many excellent first-person accounts of interviewing.

On different forms of persuasive interviewing

Keltner, J. W. (1987). *Mediation: Toward a civilized system of dispute resolution.* Annandale, VA: Speech Communication Association.

Nierenberg, G. I. (1987). *Fundamentals of negotiating.* New York: Perennial Library.

Wellman, F. L. (1948). *The art of cross-examination* (4th ed.). Garden City, NY: Garden City Books.

We could have included an even greater variety of suggestions here. Keltner, in the vanguard of teachers who developed academically respectable and humane interpersonal communication classes in the 1960s and 1970s, has turned his attention to consulting and dispute resolution. His book is an impressively practical account of how to help others come to agreement by using interviewing skills. Nierenberg's book is widely cited in organizational life. He helps you understand why rigid cause-and-effect thinking is not always helpful for communicators trying to reconcile different positions. Wellman's treatise on cross-examination is also a classic of sorts, but we should warn you that it's dated and veers toward racist and sexist stereotypes in many examples. His appreciation of the power of language in the legal profession, however, is impressive.

References

Anderson, R. (1995). *Essentials of personal selling: The new professionalism.* Englewood Cliffs, NJ: Prentice-Hall.

Anderson, R. E. (1996). Personal selling and sales management in the new millennium. *Journal of Personal Selling & Sales Management, XVI(4),* 17–32.

Anderson, R., & Ross, V. (1998). *Questions of communication: A practical introduction to theory* (2nd ed.). New York: St. Martin's Press.

Brown, C. T., & Keller, P. W. (1979). *Monologue to dialogue: An exploration of interpersonal communication* (2nd ed.). Englewood Cliffs, NJ: Prentice-Hall.

Craig, J. H., & Craig, M. (1979). *Synergic power: Beyond domination, beyond permissiveness* (2nd ed.). Berkeley, CA: ProACTIVE Press.

Courtright, J. A., & Perse, E. M. (1998). *Communicating online: A guide to the internet.* Mountain View, CA: Mayfield.

Dillon, J. T. (1990). *The practice of questioning.* London: Routledge.

Evarts, W. R., Greenstone, J. L., Kirkpatrick, G. J., & Leviton, S. C. (1983). *Winning through accommodation: The mediator's handbook.* Dubuque, IA: Kendall-Hunt.

Hersey, P. (1988). *Selling: A behavioral science approach.* Englewood Cliffs, NJ: Prentice-Hall.

Keller, P. W., & Brown, C. T. (1968). An interpersonal ethic for communication. *Journal of Communication, 18,* 73–81.

Kelman, H. C. (1966). Three processes of social influence. In M. Jahoda & N. Warren (Eds.), *Attitudes* (pp. 151–162). Baltimore: Penguin.

Keltner, J. W. (1987). *Mediation: Toward a civilized system of dispute resolution.* Annandale, VA: Speech Communication Association.

Kimball, B. (1994). *The AMA handbook for successful selling.* Chicago: American Marketing Association / NTC Business Books.

Nierenberg, G. I. (1987). *Fundamentals of negotiating.* New York: Perennial Library.

Snow, D. A., Zurcher, L. A., & Sjoberg, G. (1981). Interviewing by comment: An adjunct to the direct question. *Qualitative Sociology, 5,* 285–311.

Triandis, H. C. (1994). *Culture and social behavior.* New York: McGraw-Hill.

Weinberg, A. (Ed.). (1964). *Attorney for the damned.* New York: Simon & Schuster.

Wellman, F. L. (1948). *The art of cross-examination* (4th ed.). Garden City, NY: Garden City Books.

Woodward, G. C., & Denton, R. E., Jr. (1988). *Persuasion and influence in American life.* Prospect Heights, IL: Waveland Press.

✿ 12 Understanding and Analyzing Interviews in Popular Media Culture

Broadcast news should aim to stimulate its audiences to take up its information and insert it into the culture of their everyday lives. It should aim to be talked about, which means it must discard its role of privileged information-giver, with its clear distinction between the one who knows (the author) and those who do not (the audience), for that gives it the place and the tone of the author-god and discourages popular productivity. Rather, it should aim to involve its viewers in making sense of the world around them, it should encourage them to be participants in the process, not recipients of its products: it should . . . aim to make them readers rather than decipherers. Instead of promoting a final truth, then, it should promote discussion . . . or disagreement.

—John Fiske, *Reading the Popular*

LEARNING GOALS

After reading this chapter, you should be able to

- Understand the extent to which popular culture relies upon information obtained through interviews
- Describe how broadcast interviews differ from other forms of professional interviewing, because of overhearing audiences, dramatic requirements, the need for illustration, pervasive streamlining, and transitory content
- Conduct a basic broadcast-type interview as interviewer or interviewee
- Analyze broadcast interviews by observing how interviewers and interviewees enact identity codes, situational codes, verbal codes, and nonverbal codes
- Adapt broadcast interviewing styles and skills to other interview situations

Chances are, most of what you know about your favorite celebrity was learned from an interview. Do you follow the career of Michael Jordan or Lisa Leslie, professional basketball players deluxe? Singers Madonna or Ray Charles? Film stars Denzel Washington or Jennifer Lopez? If you do, it is because of information you would have missed if not for a raft of zealous interviewers. Have you looked up advice recently about, say, how to break into network news? In all likelihood, that advice—from interviewers Diane Sawyer, Bernard Shaw, or Tom Brokaw, for example—was obtained through interviews. Interviews help us learn about intriguing people and issues.

Your book collection might include an autobiography of a celebrated musician. Perhaps you don't realize that many "autobiographies" of famous people are not produced by the star writing down memories but by another writer who has interviewed the celebrity and shaped the recollections into a coherent and engrossing narrative. Even if you read only novels, interviews are also crucial for writers of fiction. Listen to them talk about their research (on an interview talk show, for instance), and you'll hear how often they had to interview public defenders or judges or court reporters before adding the nuances of detail to that courtroom thriller you admire. Interviews support our literature by giving it a structure of vivid facts and details.

You might enjoy listening to or watching talk shows on radio or television; if so, you should realize that most shows Oprah Winfrey presents (or Montel Williams, Sally Jesse Raphael, Howard Stern, Regis Philbin and Kathy Lee Gifford, Jerry Springer, Rush Limbaugh, Don Imus, and others) are little more than occasions for one-on-one or group-on-one interviews in front of an audience. Some shows are morally uplifting (Oprah interviewing Elie Wiesel or Maya Angelou, for example), and others can be dispiriting (someone learning via a Jenny Jones or Ricki Lake interview that a spouse is having an affair, for example). Infomercials for MasterThyThighs or PersuasoMastery tapes, or whatever the current craze might be, feature testimonials from satisfied customers told breathlessly to a rapt Suzanne Somers, Fran Tarkenton, or Jacqueline Smith. Interviews entertain us, shock us, and provide revealing glimpses into the human condition.

Do you respect the mayor or school board president, or do you consider them self-serving and overly political? Without information gleaned through public and quasi-public interviews, you would have virtually no evidence to support your attitudes. Imagine a political campaign without popular media interviews on television and radio. You'd have to attend each speech, and follow each candidate around, to gather your own idiosyncratic information. You have neither the time nor the inclination to do that, even if you had the money or curiosity. Interviews streamline our decision-making process.

A calamity strikes Florida, such as a hurricane or series of tornadoes. Within minutes, network and local reporters are talking with people who thought just this morning that their lives were ordinary. Now, they're transformed into heroes, fools, victims, and storytellers by resourceful questioners with microphones. The president flies to Orlando to visit the tragic scenes, and the public observes him talking to survivors, asking about their resources and provisions, eliciting stories of their courage. Here is yet another kind of interview. After Air Force One takes off, a press secretary briefs reporters and the assembled citizens on the president's impressions and then invites questions in a group interview. We're symbolically assured, whether in Waukegan or Waikiki, not only that Floridians are going to be well taken care of, but so will we all if such tragedies happen in our communities. Interviews are occasions of social order, and we use them to reassure ourselves that at least some events can be orderly and predictable, somehow knowable and manageable.

These are only a few of the ways our popular culture exists in and through interview styles that help create and sustain a mediated reality. Although some critics bemoan this technological condition, it makes little sense to ignore it. Instead, this chapter will look at the assumptions behind interviews in popular media culture, to see what they reveal about culture generally. Here, we are less concerned with the behavioral skills you can develop as an interviewer or an interviewee and more concerned with the analytical skills you can develop to understand how interviews function in popular culture. Studying interviewing is closely linked with other skills in a communication curriculum, such as those taught in media literacy, persuasion, public relations campaign, or rhetorical criticism courses.

"The Basics" will examine media assumptions about how interviews should be conducted; we'll try to take you behind the scenes and encourage you to think about interviews in a new way. For purposes of clarity and focus, we've decided to concentrate on broadcast interviews rather than discuss all popular culture media forms. These broadcast forms include interviews that are live and taped, in front of a studio audience and without a studio audience, in one-on-one or panel settings, on radio or television. In "Beyond the Basics" we ask you to become a critic in accomplishing two tasks. You'll discover new ways to listen to and observe broadcast interviews more systematically and will develop strategies for importing or adapting broadcast styles for your own improvement as interviewer and interviewee in other interview situations.

Learning and Interviewing

Most interviews in everyday professional life are motivated by interviewers who have a clear and immediate learning goal: They need to gain information or insight someone else possesses. For example, social science researchers, oral historians, journalists, medical personnel, and salespersons all do their jobs by developing a solid understanding of the other person's perceptions, even if they have to start from a base of little or no knowledge.

Most media interviews, however, especially in the broadcast media, make very different demands upon participants; interviewers already may know the other person's basic message (or they think they do), and they attempt to elicit an interesting or dramatic articulation of it for a proposed audience. Ken Metzler (1997) suggests a number of other differences between broadcast interviewers and their cohorts in other professions. Broadcast interviewers "tend to dive for what glitters" in "short, provocative, usually superficial interviews." They emphasize the dramatic and "colorful" response, often in a scene or location that itself is designed to suggest a message to an audience. They "[cut] quickly to the essence of a situation," with a "firm and narrow sense of purpose" that often can be achieved in four to six minutes. They encourage respondents to adopt a "performance attitude," because opportunities to impress an audience are fleeting (pp. 145–146). Such characteristics leave little room for the kind of learning attitude stressed throughout this book. Broadcast interviewers must be flexible enough and prepared enough to know

**THE
BASICS** ✿

before the interview what the content is likely to be, yet at the same time be skilled enough as a listener to follow unexpected threads of meaning that arise (see Box 12.1). Interviews in popular media culture are indeed a different animal, but ignoring their demands can be a big mistake for communicators who justifiably seek a wider audience for their ideas and goals.

Interviewers in any situation can learn important insights about technique from skilled broadcast communicators. However, broadcast interviewers have some different goals that are distinctive from, if not contradictory to, those of other interviews. The nature of the goals and the assumptions that guide them will make a big difference in analyzing the interviewing process. Beware of simply trying to import media interviewing styles into your other interviewing tasks in businesses, schools, or in such specialized communication tasks as fund-raising, training, public relations, personnel management, or sales. A given strategy or technique might appear to work for Oprah, but few of us play in her league, or with her rules.

Media Assumptions about Interviews

Five assumptions, or tendencies, seem to drive media interviews. They are interrelated, and careful observers will notice exceptions to all of them, but they help us see the media in ways that tend to be overlooked in the everyday bustle of tuning in to our favorite television and radio programs (and, more recently, our favorite Web sites).

Interviews Must Be Framed for an Overhearing Audience

Larry King (1989) is an unusual interviewer. The CNN talk show host, who also has been a dominant force in radio talk over the years, says he never wants to read the books of authors before he interviews them. To read the book, he thinks (p. 136), is to reduce the element of surprise he wants to feel when the author starts explaining plots, characters, and ideas. He tries to enter the situation as the "typical" audience member who, in all likelihood, is unfamiliar with the book but might want to read it. He tries to ask the audience's questions, in other words. Most interviewers want to give the appearance of insiders who are probing with the author into deep issues, but King is even unafraid to appear ignorant about those issues at times.

Although his methods are uncommon, King's approach exemplifies one of the most basic assumptions of media interviewing—the always-present audience. His interview style is informed not by his own curiosity alone, and perhaps at times not by his own curiosity at all, but by *an inferred curiosity of others* that he wants to represent. This condition in some ways frees him to ask different questions from different perspectives than he otherwise would if the interview were a private one-on-one affair. Just as newspaper reporters are often substitute listeners for the rest of us as they write about news events,

BOX 12.1   I N T E R V I E W E R S   I N   A C T I O N

Susan Stamberg

Noted radio host Susan Stamberg, renowned for her public affairs interviews, offers advice on the relationship between planning and spontaneity in broadcasts:

"I think it's good to go in with a sense of what it is you want to happen in the course of the conversation. . . . What points do you want to get made? What information do you want to elicit? Then you have to be ready to abandon that at any moment if something comes up that you hadn't thought about before, but that strikes you as far more interesting.

"The biggest mistake is coming in with a list of 10 questions and then not paying any attention to the answers that are being given. . . . The guest may get off on a tangent, but it can be much more interesting than anything you've got on paper."

Source: Biagi, 1992, p. 116

media interviewers are surrogate inquirers for the public when they have access to celebrities, stars, athletes, and politicians.

However, King and other media interviewers also are constrained by the presence of the unseen audience. He has to speak at least partly with our vocabulary and language habits rather than his own, and he must be ready at a moment's notice to rephrase subtly an interviewee's lofty rhetoric into everyday vernacular. Although he might be weary personally of a prosecuting attorney's account of a president's legal trouble, King knows he'll have to ask anyway.

The presence of the audience might mean at times that interviewers adopt pretenses of not knowing. "When did you write your first book?" for instance, would be an odd and possibly insulting question to ask if you were interviewing a well-known writer such as Mary Higgins Clark for the college literary magazine. You would be expected to know such basic facts before you arrive for the interview; you should have done your homework on her career. Yet if she hears the same question during a radio interview downtown, she is unlikely to think anything unusual has been asked. Rather than assuming the interviewer to be lazy or ignorant, she'll assume the question is designed to help the overhearing audience orient themselves toward her work.

The sociologist Erving Goffman (1981) refers to the audience in broadcast situations as a **ratified participant**, even though it's one that will not assume a speaking role. He means that the audience is taken into account as if it were participating but without ever actually being able to participate. In cases like " 'on the spot' interviewing," he writes, "the announcer may turn from . . . fellow participants at the microphone and acquaint the audience with background matters. He may even go so far as to let the audience know what has already transpired between the talkers just prior to the broadcast. . . . In these ways the audience can appear to be brought into the conversation as it unfolds, knowing enough to follow the talk, in principle no less knowledgeable than the platform listeners themselves as to what is about to be said" (pp. 234–235). The "ratified participant," the audience that might participate only tangentially, is nevertheless in charge throughout the interview, in a sense: John Heritage and David Greatbatch (1991) conclude that ". . . the footing of news interview talk as oriented towards the overhearing audience is managed at all points over the course of the talk and not merely at those points where an overt reference to the audience . . . takes place" (p. 109). In other words, both interviewer and interviewee implicitly understand throughout the interview that they are ultimately making their remarks to and for the audience—even when they aren't mentioning the audience (see also Heritage, 1985; Livingstone & Lunt, 1994).

Interviews Must Be Dramatic

Because broadcast interviews in popular culture are framed with large unseen audiences in mind, what those audiences expect becomes paramount. It's not as though the listeners have made a large commitment of time and energy to attend an event, as they would by purchasing a ticket to a show, driving to a theater, parking, and sitting down for an hour or more of performance. The interview can vanish from the tube or the radio in a flash if a listener gets bored. Physical presence presumes a continuing attention to talk that electronic presence does not.

Thus, interviewers and interviewees in media contexts know that audiences must be caught, enticed, given emotional and dramatic reasons to continue a psychological commitment to listening (see Box 12.2 for a vivid example). They must frame the event almost from the start as relevant. The best way to ensure this kind of commitment, interview participants know, is to lead with dramatic, surprising, shocking, or at least highly involving aspects of a narrative. Then participants work to intersperse other such interesting moments throughout the course of the interview. This requirement, of course, usually makes for a very different interview structure than so-called "ordinary" interviewing.

An example of one form of media interviewing that particularly exploits drama is the daytime talk show on television. According to Joan Shattuc (1997) in her analysis of one of Phil Donahue's shows, such programs

> stage a highly standardized drama of the disenfranchised. The *Donahue* program sets up veiled class, education, and gender distinctions as the image, primarily of women, the working class, and ethnic people exploited by powerful male lawyers. The power polarities are usually not so clearly portrayed as in this program . . . , but talk shows always build a sense of a victim (someone who has been cheated, emotionally hurt, physically beaten, or otherwise mistreated) and a perpetrator (boss, parent, husband, lover) into the conflict. (p. 80)

BOX 12.2   **INTERVIEWERS IN ACTION**

David Frost

British interviewer David Frost negotiated to interview ex-President Richard Nixon in 1976 about the Watergate issues and other aspects of his presidency:

"'Ah,' said Nixon as I entered his office. 'The Grand Inquisitor.'

"'No, no,' I said, 'just your friendly neighborhood confidant.'

"In fact, of course, I knew I would probably have to play both those roles, and several more besides. But then that's one of the things that interviewing is all about. We discussed makeup and how his office could be effectively lit.

"'It's the way you look that I'm really worried about,' Nixon said almost playfully. Then he added, 'After all, *you've* got a whole career ahead of you. . . .'" (pp. 70–71)

"We would, with Nixon and myself as the alchemists, be using our own raw material to provide a better quality of source material for journalists, historians, and political scientists to ponder. Some questions which we knew would produce news stories might never be asked. Others, unless of overriding importance, might be edited out. News per se was not our first priority. Insight into the man and his administration was. . . .

"I would remain ever alert, of course, for targets of opportunity, for moments of potential openness, such as would occur months later when Nixon himself introduced the topic of his alleged foreign bank accounts and his rumored love affair with a European countess. But that was different. That was seizing the moment. In our general preparation, the thrust of every line of questioning had to grow out of that which we already knew. A proper foundation for each line of questioning was critical." (p. 41)

Source: Frost, 1978

Shattuc amplifies her point:

Talk radio offers a set of traits similar to those of the TV talk show in that the format combines call-in shows on social issues, interview shows, and psychological advice shows that provide the range of topics found on the latter. Talk radio also stages controversy to create dramatic appeal. Additionally, talk radio is wholly dependent on audience participation by means of listener call-ins. (p. 7)

Although we certainly find many differences among the different forms of broadcast talk shows, all of them introduce drama and controversy through the mechanism of a host or expert who *interviews*—that is, who interprets a topic and explores it through questions phrased for a guest, a panel, a studio audience, a call-in audience, or in some cases, all of these.

BOX 12.3   INTERVIEWERS IN ACTION

Jim Loughman

Loughman, a longtime host on the prominent Chicago talk radio station WGN, discusses his best and worst guests:

• The best guests: "Basically, I wanted interesting people with strongly held views. All the better if they were newsmakers. . . . The best guests I interviewed were not necessarily ultra-high-profile. It gets back to what I mentioned a moment ago about strongly held views. The other side of the coin is the willingness, even eagerness, to express and defend those views; to mix it up with friends and foes alike; to be stimulating and provocative."

• The worst guests: "They were the ones who acted like all they had to do was show up; people who rested on their press clippings, or put on airs, or spoke condescendingly to the audience. Politicians come to mind. Lots of them."

Source: Hilton, 1987, p. 76

Interviews Must Illuminate or Illustrate

Face-to-face interviewing, as we have seen, usually involves the interviewer communicating with an interviewee, each with separate goals of learning or discovering something new. Media interviewers know that if the interview is defined in this way, genuine learning can become a recipe for risky, boring, and possibly dangerous broadcasts (for one host's experience, see Box 12.3). Why is this true?

Media interviews feature a peculiar kind of unspoken collusion or teamwork between interviewer and interviewee. This form of teamwork is not when the two people get together beforehand and decide on a script or set up answers artificially. Instead, on an informal basis and often without deciding overtly on how it will happen, the two adapt their behaviors mutually to a commonly understood purpose and set of roles. Heritage and Greatbatch (1991) found that on broadcast news shows, interviewees naturally allocate certain rights to interviewers, such as opening and closing shows, deciding when topics will shift, and making conversational interruptions.

On the other hand, Stephen Claflin (1979) notes that many interviewers typically will not press interviewees on how their talk conflicts with that of other public figures or even how it conflicts with their own prior statements. Despite the absence of formal planning, in other words, interviewers and interviewees appear to collaborate in saving face and carrying off the event without a hitch. Interviewers will ask questions in such a way that interviewees will be able to meet at least some of their objectives and vice versa. Because interviewers are often at least public figures who are potentially "known quantities" before the conversation takes place, interviewees understand what kind of communication to expect, even if they do not know the exact questions that will arise. And because interviewees are usually chosen because of their notoriety or celebrity or newsworthiness, they also are at least somewhat predictable communicators to interviewers.

To use prominent examples, a scientist/researcher working for a tobacco company who will be interviewed on successive days by Katie Couric of NBC's "Today Show" and Mike Wallace of CBS News' "60 Minutes," has access to a backlog of similar interviews conducted by the two interviewers. The executive will understand that Couric's style is folksy and informal, with "fastball" questions often framed by a cushion of seemingly pleasant conversation. Wallace's style is known to be more tenacious, as he often launches a series of probes bluntly phrased to illuminate flaws in reasoning. What kind of "teamwork" can the researcher expect if an interviewer presents such threats? How does this qualify as teamwork? The answer is that the media interview is usually a transaction in which an interviewer, producer, program, or station negotiate a trade with an interviewee. The station gets a dramatic event to fill time, make news, and interest an audience. The interviewee gets access to the program's audience and therefore obtains exposure for his or her ideas, explanations, or self-defense. This is not to say there aren't double crosses and ambush interviews occasionally. Yet in virtually all radio and television interviews—even with accused child abusers and traitors—audiences will hear interviewers creating a relatively open and congenial space for interviewees to frame their actions. Some research even shows that interviewers are constrained by the situation to be, in Heritage and Greatbatch's (1991) term, "neutralistic" in much of the conversation. They're not expected to argue or nitpick answers the respondent provides. Interviewees, by the same token, do not normally complain that interviewers' questions put them on the spot too much or are too unfair. The rules are mutually understood, and the roles are mutually agreed upon.

Therefore, for all these reasons, media interviews are not about interviewers learning something as much as they are concerned with illuminating, illustrating, or representing something of consequence to an audience. Media interviews are not just about news, but they actually make news. Therefore, we should not be surprised at the following comment about talk show conversations, offered by Ronald Berman (1987), former chair of the National Endowment for the Humanities:

One might imagine that the talk show would be interested in the eccentric individual, but it really is more concerned with groups. It tries to find issues to discuss that have some public shape—and that already have attracted constituencies. Although the talk show *displays* many individuals, some of them deviant or eccentric or different in other ways from the mass audience ideal, it tries to associate them with general conceptions. No matter how outlandish, they are representative of something. Talk shows will have on hand participants who belong to associations or coalitions. Their audiences will be picked to match or oppose interests. And one can hardly appear on a talk show without being presented as a symbol: A woman becomes a Woman on the spot. (p. 43)

When Berman says that the issues must have "some public shape," he suggests that media interviews fulfill a demonstrative role. An individual, speaking as an individual person, is rarely interviewed. Rather, he or she is interviewed as a representative of a point of view, an organization, or a cultural group. This factor became obvious in the media attention focused on the O. J. Simpson trials by a variety of talk and interview shows. It would be naive to assume that interviewees and experts were chosen simply on the basis of what they had to say or on the merits of their legal qualifications. In addition to such criteria, most shows also tried to ensure they interviewed a mix of legal commentators: women and men, African American and white, defense attorneys and prosecuting attorneys, and perhaps even conservative and liberal critics.

Stephen Claflin (1979) wants to increase dialogue in the public sphere. The current conventions of interviewing encourage politicians and advocates of all stripes to advertise their positions in the media without having to defend them against authentic and heartfelt disagreement. News interviewers, for example, are too docile for Claflin's taste; they allow respondents to make unsupportable if not ludicrous claims and get away with this tactic. Instead of allocating the responsibilities of interviewing to media representatives who don't sufficiently press public figures on the implications of their positions, he offers a "radical proposal" for dialogic free speech in public discourse: Why not have advocates on different sides of controversial issues interview each other in public? The public would learn much from such interchanges, not the least of which is who can phrase a clear and fair question, who listens well to opposing positions, and who respects the other side enough to frame it as a serious possibility. None of these types of information is generally a part of the puzzle that voters, for example, piece together at election time.

Now, as Claflin quotes *New York Times* media critic John J. O'Connor, "most (television) panel formats are carefully designed to protect the interests of the guest. When questions are rotated among a group of journalists, the results are virtually guaranteed to be superficial. A questioner getting close to the core of one subject will find that his time is up. Another questioner takes over and, more often than not, begins to pursue an entirely different subject. The reason for this standard routine is purely practical. Without some built-in safeguards, prominent politicians, the kind most courted for television, would simply refuse to appear on panel shows" (p. 12). O'Connor's observation is not recent, and the 1990s have bred a more contentious press corps. Still, the complaint will be confirmed to a disturbing degree by watching next Sunday morning's network political interview programs or the president's next press conference, as Claflin explains:

> Most influential people seem to want to express opinions publicly but show much less enthusiasm for discussing opinions publicly with someone who may disagree. Most seem to favor use of free speech only if it is easy and free of risk, only if they don't have to get involved in asking or answering any questions except the "news conference" kind which usually play leapfrog with various topics without dealing with any subject at any length.
>
> Why shouldn't influential people who make public statements explain them? Why not explain their ideas? Most of the rest of us have to do this. Why not talk publicly to people of opposing views? In private conversation, in family matters and in business affairs most people have to talk to others they disagree with every day. (pp. xii–xiii)

Although popular media culture has not adopted Claflin's suggestion of expert spokespersons interviewing other expert spokespersons in public, we have perhaps moved somewhat further in that direction since his book appeared. News and public events talk shows now feature a more rigorous interaction among different representatives, as on ABC's "Politically Incorrect." Unfortunately, participants almost always talk over each other's words, competing for air time with loud and rapid speech. Claflin's innovative suggestion for media reform in which disagreements are explored through clearly framed interviewing roles has not been tried seriously. If it were to be tried, it might create a new version of public dialogue in which genuine learning could take place among interview participants, not just the representation of positions they wish to illustrate or illuminate.

Interviews Must Be Streamlined

Media interviewers often experience a series of time management problems that set their context apart from other interview situations. One analyst (Cohen, 1987) describes how:

> . . . time constraints pose a special problem in television interviewing. Getting to a story and setting up the interview is logistically more complex in television than in any other medium. More equipment is needed to record the interview and to transmit it, both in live or in prerecorded formats. Also, television scheduling is very precise, more so than in any other mass medium (mainly in the United States). As a result, the timing of the interview, live or recorded, and the editing process must all be done with careful consideration of the program context in which the interview will be telecast. Despite what appears to be a tendency for shrinking news-holes in newspapers, it is likely that newspaper editors are still more flexible in deciding to allocate more space to a particular story if they deem this necessary. In the television industry, however, given the more severe constraints, comparable decisions are more complex and, therefore, less likely to be made. (p. 27)

A factor influencing the relative brevity of media interviews is that a wide variety of technicians and planners must be on the job to support the occasion. Another is that time equals space in the broadcast industry, and few shows can afford to allocate sufficient space to long-form interviews with individual respondents (although exceptions such as Charlie

Rose, Barbara Walters, and Brian Lamb come to mind). Longer interviews, therefore, are either discouraged or are edited to highlight their juiciest, most newsworthy, most conflictual, or most embarrassing moments.

Savvy interviewees realize that if they can say something memorable in a brief interview, it probably will be shortened even more if it is re-reported. The media tend to quote and requote *sound bites,* those short sloganlike statements that supposedly capture longer and more complex modes of thought in a few words. In 1968, network newscasts ran uninterrupted quotes from presidential candidates that averaged 42.3 seconds; by 1988 that figure had dropped to 9.8 seconds (Davis, 1993, pp. 58–59). Such a trend can't continue much further, although it could become even more entrenched. Currently, media consultants like Jack Hilton (1987) *train* political and corporate interviewees to speak in sound bites in the first place:

> Extemporaneous speech combines . . . composition and presentation . . . simultaneously. Because that's fraught with peril for a speaker much of my work as a consultant is aimed (yes, manipulatively, but not sinisterly) at separating the two.
>
> This kind of forethought and preparation was demonstrated . . . in the second TV debate in 1984 between President Reagan and Walter Mondale. After the President's frankly doddering performance in the first debate two weeks previously, senility became an issue in the campaign, and the Reagan brain trust anticipated a question from someone on the panel of reporters about the President's age.
>
> On stage in Kansas City, they were accommodated in spades before 80,000,000 television viewers by Henry Trewhitt of the *Baltimore Sun.* And Mr. Reagan ad-libbed his reply just as he had written it on a legal pad several days before, flawlessly and verbatim: "I will not make age an issue in this campaign," he said. "I'm not going to exploit for political purposes my opponent's youth and inexperience."
>
> Twenty three words, or about eight seconds at my rate of speech (not including the audience's explosive response). I'll wager $50 that you saw it on the late-evening newscasts of October 21st, unless you were visiting the Australian outback. An additional $25 says that you'll see it replayed on television every four years until the tape wears out. (p. 39)

Interviews Must Produce Transitory Content

Perhaps because of the brevity of media interviews, their content is usually short-lived and ephemeral. Although the occurrence of an interview—the fact that it was arranged—is undoubtedly important, what is said usually has a short shelf life. Think about what kinds of talk qualify for newsworthiness or requoting: the juicy comment, the accusation, the characterization so intense or unusual that it shocks audiences, an expressed conflict with another public figure, a statement so embarrassing or difficult to explain that listeners' attention becomes drawn to it. While all of these comments will raise eyebrows, they rarely have impact over a sustained period, and they rarely come to characterize someone's career.

We expect other speech occasions and genres to produce memorable quotations, but expectations for the broadcast interview appear to be lower. From a speech, for example, we gather presumably significant statements about a person's future, or plan for a campaign, or the potential for larger cultural change. Interviews are important but usually not as a source for these types of statements. Another speech genre, testimony, also creates serious content to which we expect public figures to adhere closely.

The typical broadcast interview, however, is considered by audiences to be a creative mix of information, entertainment, public relations, and advertising motives. It is quickly forgotten or dismissed. If you doubt this, track the talk show appearances (on "Meet the Press," "Face the Nation," "The Geraldo Rivera Show," or "The Charles Grodin Show," for examples) of a prominent and controversial spokesperson for a point of view such as cultural critics William Bennett or Tavis Smiley, or lawyers doing daily analysis of extended cases such as the Rodney King case in Los Angeles. Surely most analysts do not attempt to lie or deceive in their commentaries. But neither do they go out of their way to explain or reconcile inconsistencies between what they said last night and what they asserted last week, last month, or last year. They assume—rightly—that because of how the public listens to media interviews, their observations are valuable for the moment in which they're uttered but become disposable almost immediately. Unless they are formalized as part of a speech or testimony of some sort, the statements enter what Wayne Booth (1988, p. 184) calls the "meaning chopper" of the news, never to be heard of again in their appropriate context.

Some observers (for example, Postman, 1988) have suggested that this lack of concern for historical context is a function of the broadcast medium itself, which supposedly trivializes genuine knowledge. Television, and to a lesser extent, radio, encourages us to think primarily in terms of a brief and generally ahistorical perspective. You don't have to agree fully with critics like Neil Postman to acknowledge that electronic media have helped to change some human perceptual habits. Electronic media, especially television, have made it possible to reach vast audiences with crucial information and interesting entertainment possibilities. It is senseless to lash out at a medium of our own devising. It is not senseless, however, to note that it might have some specific effects on a particular communication context, such as interviewing.

Bill McKibben (1993) watched an entire day of television taped (with the help of friends) from over 90 channels on the Fairfax, Virginia, cable system. McKibben wrote a book describing the important and trivial messages he saw and their relationship to his life. One of the things he noticed most was how much television deals with itself and other transitory messages, and how much it glorifies its own historically brief time period of the past four decades or so. "Which is fine—but nothing," according to McKibben, "that comes *before* television is covered in any detail at all" (p. 64). Some exceptions, such as Ken Burns's PBS series on the Civil War, baseball, and the Lewis and Clark expedition come to mind, but in general, "The brightness surrounding the last forty years blinds us to all that preceded it—and forty years is a very short time, even to an individual" (pp. 64–65). Further:

> Bob Hope, for instance, came on the J. C. Penney shopping channel to hawk his new book. We know Bob Hope from years of specials, from footage of him entertaining the troops. But he is an old man, too. He's talking about World War II, and tells a joke

about how FDR trained his dog Fala on the *Chicago Tribune*. The interviewer brays—convulses—but it's hard to believe he has any idea about Colonel McCormick's feud with Roosevelt; Bob might as well tell Saint Thomas Aquinas jokes. The past fills our minds, but only the past of the last four decades. As a result, those four decades seem utterly normative to us, the only conceivable pattern for human life. (p. 65)

The plight of the hapless interviewer in McKibben's example capsulizes the place of media interviews in our culture, in which the fact that the interview took place overshadows the content of what is actually said. Though McKibben strongly suspects the interviewer doesn't get the joke (which depends upon remembering a historical relationship between two men now long dead), that is not the important thing. The important thing is that Bob Hope—a comedian whose career spans generations—is *on*. The important thing is that he has told a joke on the air, and a distant audience expects laughter. No one needs to understand, much less remember, the joke, but the interviewer wants to avoid the immediate impression that a respected comedian told a joke that got no response. So he plays out a charade, representing "our" appreciation of Bob Hope. If McKibben had not been chronicling his experience for a book, no doubt he would have forgotten where and when he saw Bob Hope, what he said, and why he appeared. Most media interviews are produced, in other words, with the assumption that they'll be transitory.

In a general sense, media interviews serve three masters: information, entertainment, and recognition. They must be informative and entertaining while they ensure that certain spokespersons and their issues become recognizable. Ideally, the interview threads these three functions together, as interviewer and interviewee cooperate to produce informative and memorable entertainment (or entertaining and informative memories, or impressive and entertaining information). Box 12.4 reviews ways participants in media interviews can acknowledge and include the audience.

❁ BEYOND THE BASICS

In this section we will suggest ways to build on the foundation of your understanding of interviewing in popular media by exploring your interests in the context of radio and television interviews. So far, the focus has been on differences between forms of interviews and other interviewing tasks and functions, but it's also important to acknowledge the similarities. Interviewing is so pervasive in popular culture, with so many positive and negative models available, that we shouldn't overlook this interesting learning opportunity.

Observing Broadcast Interviews Systematically

In a survey of professional studies of television news interviews, Akiba Cohen (1987, pp. 49–63) organizes the literature under these headings:

- General Preparation and Control
- Identity Codes

BOX 12.4   R E M I N D E R S

Practical Tips for Media Interviews

For the Interviewer

- *Remember the audience:* Ask their questions, and translate answers so they will understand the issues; prepare carefully, even though you want to let yourself be surprised by some disclosures. Make sure you have all the facts straight (titles and qualifications of interviewees, for example).

- *Help the interviewee to dramatize:* Unearth conflicts, contradictions, disagreements, choice points, problems of analysis, and threats to audience members; if appropriate, encourage two or more interviewees with strong opinions to "interview" each other and state the others' interpretations fairly. Most experienced interviewers believe it's fair to brief interviewees on the projected topics (to allow them to prepare too), but they will not share specific questions.

- *Streamline the interaction:* Ask brief, well-focused questions; redirect the discussion if the interviewee gets off track or too long-winded; cover ground, but do it economically. Remind interviewees ahead of time that short, punchy examples help audiences relate to them but that extended narratives usually fall flat. Don't be timid about interrupting long-winded talkers.

- *Help the interviewee to emphasize a point or case:* Although you may disagree, defer your disagreement until you're sure the point has been stated clearly.

- *Summarize the interview's major points and contributions:* If it's important to do so, create a historical context for the interviewee's ideas, to counteract the tendency for audiences to forget the content of broadcast interviews.

For the Interviewee

- *Remember that you're both* talking to, *and* talking through, *the interviewer:* By engaging in an illuminating conversation with him or her, you're reaching many more people in an unseen audience.

- *Answer the questions, but also use them to* bridge *to other points you want to make:* Your reason for appearing may be different from their reason for choosing you to interview, and a good **bridge** is a transition to new conversational territory. Sometimes you'll have to create your own openings. For example: (after an answer) "You know, a similar question arose when Marge Kennedy was mayor, and nobody paid attention. She and I believe. . ."

- *Dramatize and streamline your ideas with direct examples:* Audiences won't follow lengthy chains of reasoning, and they tend to get lost in a thicket of statistics. Though it might offend your sense of subtlety, try to boil down ideas to striking comparisons: "Harvard's endowment *increase* for last year alone was more than four times the *total* endowment of our university." Relate the unfamiliar to the familiar in brief stories, and the audience is more likely to remember your idea because of this reframing.

- *Show, don't smother, your personality:* Audiences recall impressions much more clearly than content. Often a person who makes a mistake or is nervous comes across as more believable and likable than the slick operator who has everything figured out and states a case with glibness. We're not suggesting that you "be yourself" as much as we're encouraging you to be conversational and avoid trying to be someone else.

- Situational Codes
- Verbal Codes
- Nonverbal Codes

For this activity, you will need two partners, a video camera and blank tape, a VCR, and monitor.

- Assume that a series of interviews from ten to fifteen minutes long will be broadcast on a local cable channel, on a show titled "The American College Student Today: Direction and Drift." Thus, it is important for interviewers to be professional in demeanor and interviewees (as themselves) to be personable and full of opinions.

- Tape a round of interviews (A interviews B with C as observer/critic; B interviews C with A as observer/critic; C interviews A with B as observer/ critic). Each interviewer must take the broadcast nature of the occasion into account in conducting the interview, but beyond that you can focus on any aspect of college life that you think illustrates the show's theme. Be creative in asking questions and equally creative and thoughtful when answering them. See if you can approximate broadcast-quality appearance and interestingness.

- Afterwards, discuss the activity from the standpoint of your roles as observer/critics. How did interview participants talk differently compared to other interview assignments during the semester? How did you act or move differently? What accounts for the differences?

These five categories provide an effective checklist for observing and analyzing broadcast interviews systematically. Let's look at each of them in turn, exploring their potential for understanding the process and structure of interviewing.

General Preparation and Control

The **literature** (what professionals and scholars call the body of knowledge in any given phenomenon or process) focuses on the role of interviewer and is full of advice about being prepared and maintaining control of the interaction. Interviewers are told to familiarize themselves fully with relevant topics, of course, and also with backgrounds of the people they'll interview. Cohen appears surprised at how often the interviewer is assumed to be in the position of controlling the action, almost like a general in a battle among troops.

When observing media interviews, try to answer these questions about preparation and control:

- How does an interviewer signal—consciously or unconsciously—the level and quality of preparation he or she has done?

- What is the interviewer trying to accomplish by discussing this preparation? (Alternatively: What does the interviewer inadvertently suggest about the interview if he or she betrays a lack of preparation?)

- What are the control mechanisms of the interview?

- Who states the purpose and topic of the interview?

- Who introduces topic changes?

- Who interrupts whom?
- Who summarizes?

Identity Codes

The use of *code* here doesn't mean a series of direct linguistic correspondences, as in wartime codes or ciphers that keep the other side from understanding your messages. Rather, a **code** in communication scholarship is an organized and interlinked set of conditions that characterize a situation. To study this type of code is akin to getting inside the logic of a situation in order to understand more completely how it works. When you analyze codes, you are not trying to be ultrasensitive to single instances, nor are you seeking to assign blame to persons. You are looking for patterns of behavior that may be so woven into the fabric of interviews that they are hard to see at first glance.

Cohen analyzes interview **identity** (who someone is, in terms of their perceived characteristics) in three ways: demographics, social roles, and relationship to the story. **Demographics** refers to gender, age, ethnic group, and similar characteristics. **Social roles** are the positions interviewers and interviewees are assumed to hold, along with the behaviors associated with them. Roles in society range from specific elected jobs, such as senator, to family roles, such as parent. Different roles provide potentially different levels of credibility for speakers. **Relationship to the story** is Cohen's term suggesting that some people are more closely tied to certain topics by virtue of their interests, their skills, or their background experiences.

When observing media interviews, try to answer these questions about identity codes:

- Why was *this* interviewer selected to conduct this interview? Who else could have been chosen? What might this choice say about the relationship between the sponsoring organization (TV station, for example) and the story? Between the organization and the interviewee? Who decided to match a particular interview assignment with a particular interviewer?

- How might the interviewer be tied to the topic or interviewee through demographics, social roles, or relationship to the story? Are there possible patterns of special insight, expertise, or bias? Are some identity code decisions made with audience appeal in mind? (For example, is the ex-athlete sportscaster more likely to interview Tiger Woods or Martina Navratilova when they come to town, even if their appearance is for a news event like a charity ball? Is the station's African American reporter dispatched automatically to black neighborhoods to cover a teachers' strike?)

- What criteria may have determined that *this* interviewee would be chosen to answer questions? Have some individuals become identified as "experts" primarily because they've made themselves available often to answer questions? Consider professional qualifications: Why are journalists experts on governmental affairs, and why are they interviewed more often than political scientists by other journalists? Consider race, gender, and class issues: Note, for example, the number of times the same white males turn up to comment as "experts" on prestigious interview shows like "Nightline." Consider what you know about interviewers: Is it possible that some interviewees are selected because they are easy to find, because their ideologies are highly predictable, or because they are friends of the interviewer or producer?

- How is the interviewee's identity framed and represented by the interviewer? Race, gender, and class issues are relevant here also. Can you identify differences between how women and men, homosexuals and heterosexuals, blacks and whites, or rich and poor are addressed by interviewers (by first names or honorific titles, for example)?

Situational Codes

Researchers of nonverbal communication understand that where an interview takes place has a profound effect on participants. On-location interviews are sometimes quite brief not because the interviewer planned them that way but, for example, because it's cold or wet, and there are no chairs. Less obvious, perhaps, is the effect on an audience. The situation and how it is handled tells the audience how to take the interview—whether they should take its statements as definitive, tentative, emotional, objective, reasoned, or spontaneous. NBC correspondent Arthur Kent and CNN correspondent Peter Arnett became famous during the Gulf War through their interview reports in Israel or Baghdad conducted with missiles passing overhead, and explosions going off nearby. Although participants rarely refer directly to their surroundings in more normal circumstances, some sort of context is always available for audiences to interpret. Situational codes are particularly pronounced on television, of course, but they also become surprisingly influential in radio interviews: National Public Radio producers, for example, often have their field producers on location tape interviews with indigenous background sounds such as crickets or crackling fire, to suggest the experience of "being there."

When observing media interviews, try to answer these questions about situational codes:

- What is in the background, visual or aural, of the interview conversation? Presuming that participants had some choice of time and place, what made this situation attractive?

- What clues within the interview might indicate whether the site was chosen by interviewer, interviewee, both, or neither?

- How does the situation reinforce the content of the interview? How does the situation detract from it? Do the participants appear to be aware of these influences?

- Do contextual design factors symbolize or represent the status of interviewer or interviewee, perhaps affecting your estimate of other codes? For example, if an interview is held in an executive's office, does he or she sit behind a massive mahogany desk, symbolizing power, prestige, and distance? What does this suggest about the meaning of the interaction and about what topics are more, or less, likely to come up?

- Is the interview conducted live or taped for later broadcast? At one extreme, live interviews suggest immediacy, involvement, and a high level of implied importance of an event for an audience, such as covering a hostage crisis after a bank robbery. At the other extreme, live interviews might simply be a choice of convenience, such as an anchorperson on the midday news interviewing a cookbook author on a publicity tour.

- How has a taped interview been edited, if at all? Look for shifts in background, clothing, camera angle, and facial expressions, to name only a few cues. Most editing is benign and necessary to fit complex messages in tight broadcast schedules. It's not unheard of in the broadcast world, however, for a less prestigious employee to conduct a personality profile interview, only to have the respondent's words later interlaced with edited-in reaction shots of a star interviewer. Such practices validly raise ethical concerns. If the interviewer or producer is willing to shortcut the process in this way, what else might have been shortchanged?

- Are situational codes mixed with identity codes in predictable ways? Does a station only interview African American adolescent males, for example, in gyms? Teenage girls only when they are cheerleading or sitting in honors classes? Retired people only in nursing homes? What's the message here? What do such examples tell you about media perspectives on these groups?

Verbal Codes

Specialized rules appear to guide interviewers and interviewees in their talk. Although broadcast interviews are commonly conversational, they are often only distantly related to everyday conversations as you might have them around the cafeteria table, or while at a ball game, as we have shown earlier in the chapter.

When observing media interviews, try to answer these questions about verbal codes:

- What rules guide the phrasing of questions? When are they broken and by whom? What happens after the violation? Generally, given the brevity of this type of interview, questions will be short and direct. When, if ever, does an interviewer ask a lengthy question—say, a hundred or more words—and achieve a helpful and positive response? Further, how are questions "formulated" (set up, introduced, signaled)?

- What does the interviewer disclose about himself or herself? Why, and to what purpose, is the disclosure included? What effect does interviewer self-disclosure have on the interviewee?

- How are the especially meaningful questions or answers "marked"? That is, when and why do interviewers say things like, "Now we're getting to the crux of the matter," or interviewees say things like, "If there is one thing I want you to understand about me, it is . . ." In your opinion, what motivates communicators to mark their speech in this way?

- Are there discernible verbal turning points, or critical incidents, after which the tone of the talk changes significantly? These might be breaches of etiquette, real or imagined insults, or misunderstandings of words or stories.

- Whose vocabulary predominates? Does the interviewee adapt to the linguistic habits of the interviewer, or vice versa, or do you perceive evidence of mutual adaptation? What might such observations tell you about the relationship that develops between them?

Nonverbal Codes

The study of nonverbal codes is too vast to explore in much depth here. Cohen (1987, pp. 59ff.) highlights three areas that have clear relevance for interviewing—space, artifacts, and "filmic procedures." By **space**, he means that the way people choose distances for communication and how they sit or stand relative to each other send their own set of messages in interviewing. **Artifacts** are objects we display intentionally or unintentionally that might contribute to interpersonal meaning. **Filmic procedures** are conventions that tell us how to interpret other messages. Filmic issues are examples of the importance of framing in interviewing, because through them an audience understands important aspects of a communicator's intent. Cohen's interest in televised interviews leads him to stress visual cues rather than the nonverbal **paralinguistic** vocal cues (inflection, pitch, rate, volume) that are discernible in radio interviews as well as on television.

Researchers of nonverbal communication warn that it is futile to try to decide what a behavioral message "means," as though it carries a single certifiable meaning. Instead, nonverbal messages are perceived within patterns of other nonverbal and verbal messages. Within a given context, a message might be seen or heard as consistent or inconsistent, but it never means only one thing. Thus, as with the rest of communication, analysis has to be contingent; it is based on a great deal of guesswork.

When observing media interviews, try to answer these questions about nonverbal codes:

- How do participants manipulate the space between them? How much space is maintained, and do you notice differences between interviewers? Between an interviewer and his or her different interviewees? Between an interviewee and his or her different interviewers? What motivations might lie behind these differences? Does the spatial arrangement shift when a topic, or emotional tone, changes? If so, how? Are there times when a participant literally retreats or advances spatially?

- How do participants use posture or other spatial messages to indicate interest or willingness to change topics? For example, turning away might be seen as consistent with a desire to change the subject, while a respondent who leans into a question at least appears to be anxious to answer it. Normal conversation is usually conducted at a slight angle between conversants—not straight-on or (obviously) not turned away. Deviations from this usually unstated expectation might be an interesting signal for analysts to consider.

- How do participants use eye contact, or the absence of it, to indicate closeness, truthfulness, confirmation, or willingness to answer?

- Do participants use props to signal their intentions, affiliations, or allegiances? If so, how? And if so, does the interview partner call attention to it? On March 11, 1998, NBC's "Today" anchor Matt Lauer interviewed Casey Martin, a professional golfer whose lawsuit stimulated the sport's governing association to change its rule forbidding players to use carts in sanctioned tournaments. Martin, whose painful and chronic leg condition would keep him from competing otherwise, was discussing how pleased he was to be able to continue on the tournament circuit. Late in the interview, Lauer said he couldn't help noticing the "swoosh" (the Nike logo) on a couple of articles of clothing Martin wore. He asked a difficult, but fair, question invited by Martin's display of these artifacts: Did this controversy, however unpleasant, open some economic doors for Martin that would not have been possible considering only his skill at golf?

- How are the participants portrayed in the two filmic codes that Cohen (1987) emphasizes: "the angle of the shooting of the interview" and "the closeness of the shot" (p. 60)? Most broadcast interviews longer than a sound bite feature one or more **establishing shots**—visuals in which both participants are shown interacting together, within an identifiable context, sometimes with a **voice-over** (explanatory commentary added to the tape later). This tells viewers both what is taking place and where. In the interview you choose to analyze, what is established in the establishing shot?

    Further, what seems to be the rationale by which producers vary the three major kinds of shots of interviewees and interviewers? A **medium shot** depicts what conversants know as a "social distance," including most of the body and some of the background context in which the person speaks. The **head and shoulders close-up** conforms more to "personal" distance, bringing the viewing audienc[e] equivalent of touching distance of the speaker. The **tight shot** (extr[e] brings the viewer to a hyperintimate distance uncharacteristic of ord[inary] sation. Assume that each time you see a certain shot, it's a result of some[.] Some changes in shots are undoubtedly to increase variety and interest[,] other camera changes, rhetorical purposes might dictate the shift. Wha[t] producer be trying to "say" by zooming in on forehead perspiration, someone off camera, a smirk, or an eyelid twitch?

Adapting Broadcast Interview Styles for Your Own Interviewing Goals

Clearly, many communication choices that are appropriate and necessary for broadcast interviewers do not translate well to other interview tasks. You would have a hard time adapting Rosie O'Donnell's loose and friendly talk show banter to a survey or oral history interview or to a serious attempt to address an employee's problem behaviors in an intervention interview. Ted Koppel's or Bryant Gumbel's approach to exposing inconsistencies in the rhetoric of public officials and Barbara Walters's warm personality profiles of celebrities are effective within their own contexts, but they provide largely disastrous models for employment interviewers to emulate.

At the same time, let's recognize that these famous interviewers have become successful for reasons that make sense. Many aspects of popular broadcast interviewers' communication can be incorporated effectively into general interviewing styles if we are careful in making the connections. Read the following descriptions as *tendencies;* they are behavioral styles that tend to be appealing in the broadcast context and could have a wider application too. To make that application, interviewers must be both knowledgeable about the process and introspective about themselves.

Effective broadcast interviewers must be extraordinarily flexible communicators. Look for ways to adapt each of their strengths to whatever interviewing task you're asked to perform. Interviews differ significantly, but all depend to some degree on these general skill areas. Broadcast interviewers can teach all of us something about being conversationalists, sensitive time managers, comprehensive listeners, contextualizers, and culturally sensitive communicators. Consider each in turn.

Conversationalists

Broadcast interviewers tend to be appropriately informal and spontaneous, or they find another line of work. This does not mean that they like to "wing it" in interviews, although some undoubtedly must work without a net at times. Being a conversationalist means that interviewers look for openings to put others at ease with everyday language, informal gestures, and perhaps well-placed humor. Conversations tend to be "locally managed" interactions, according to communication researchers, which means in everyday terms that the talk is experienced as having an immediate importance for the communicators. Despite the advantages of preparation, no one can script a genuine conversation. Effective interviewers are as fully "with" interviewees as possible.

Sensitive Time Managers

Broadcasters develop excellent time-management skills. They often work live, so they accept the responsibility for regulating the interchange to produce a seamless occasion. Even when interviews are taped for later broadcast, they work to ensure all relevant topics are covered within a target time frame, so that intrusive and perhaps expensive editing isn't necessary. Although other interview occasions may not be as time sensitive as broadcast interviews, many participants unfortunately forget, or become oblivious to, the expressed time constraints of an interview partner. Many interviewers, therefore, could profit from observing how broadcasters make transitions from topic to topic ("You know, that's an unexpected side of you that we don't often see; I'm curious whether your parents encouraged you to take that direction. What was your early life like?"). Similarly, interviewers in other professions could study how broadcasters close interviews with respect and appreciation for their partner's contribution ("Thanks so much for talking with me today. I learned not only about your commitment to the industry but also about your concern for the culture as a whole. You've put things in a fresh perspective. Is there anything else you want to add before we go?").

Comprehensive Listeners

Interviewers in popular media tune themselves as listeners to nuances of wording and nonverbal context. Through experience, they learn to tell when someone is getting uncomfortable or tired, or when they've just disclosed something unintentionally. Working in tight time constraints fine-tunes their diagnostic abilities in communication, and they develop fairly accurate assessments of others' internal frames of reference. This comes from an immersion in a special kind of interviewing that most of us don't experience, however; interviews aren't everyday occasions for most other professional interviewers, who can be at least as nervous or ill at ease as their interviewees. Nervousness impedes their listening skill, because listening involves a kind of relaxed concentration on a variety of cues, both verbal and nonverbal. Pay attention to how broadcast interviewers pick up on small cues and use them to check out possible meanings ("A while ago you said you were 'happy' with your career. Just now, though, you started to say 'happy' but changed it to 'happier.' It's like you're moving in the right direction, but might not be there yet. Am I sensing an ambiguity here?").

Contextualizers

Successful broadcast interviewers learn to place interaction in a wider context. They understand that the interview is only a small slice of someone's life and an atypical one at that. Its importance may come as much from what *isn't* said as from what *is* said. Interviews are often important, in other words, in their relationship to the rest of someone's life and not in and of themselves. The contextualizing perspective is particularly useful for journalistic and employment interviewers who encounter others every day in situations that are much more uncomfortable for the interviewee than for the interviewer. Is Tamika Jones a nervous person because she acts nervous around a reporter? Is Robert Hawkley a forgetful or unreliable person because he neglects to mention his experience as a supervisor at Walgreen's, even though it's listed in his resume?

Culturally Sensitive Communicators

Because broadcasters are constantly thinking of potential audience responses to what they say and do, interviewers must develop culturally flexible communication styles. This does not mean that they have learned to mimic different groups' cultural speech practices and can do so on demand. Nor are we referring to the ability to do accents or dress in trendy ways. These usually are perceived as affectations. Rather, many broadcasters analyze audiences well and can anticipate the most troublesome or offensive zones in communication. This ability relates to the use of sensitive language discussed in Chapter 5. The principle is relatively simple: Discover what labels or styles potentially offend people, and then avoid these messages whenever possible.

Summary

This chapter has taken a slightly different approach than others in the book. Most chapters have introduced you to basic skills of interviewing or to the application of those skills to a particular professional context. It is possible that you will enter a profession in which one or more of these well-defined applications is necessary for the daily performance of your job. You need to know not only the how-to aspects of interviewing in professional life but the "why to" aspects and at least some of the research and theory that support the skills.

This chapter and the next attempt to expand the skills-application context to a wider social context. All professions and all careers are affected by an increasingly global popular media culture. All informed citizens hear hundreds of interviews on television or radio each week and are often influenced deeply by their style and content. It's tempting at times to think that we can learn something about interviewing from these unique personalities, who are public celebrities in their own right. Students bring to class examples of Oprah Winfrey's interviewing style, or Howard Stern's, or Leslie Stahl's, and they are understandably intrigued. Can we learn from them? Of course we can, with reservations.

In this chapter we've attempted to place this culturewide obsession with interviewing into professional perspective. The differences between broadcast interviewing (where most influential popular culture interviews occur) and other interviewing occasions are enormous. At the same time, certain prominent skills of broadcast interviewers are clearly

- Imagine you are a producer for a network news show like "Meet the Press" or "Face the Nation." The head of the news division has suggested that the show include more video clips of politicians' speeches, entrances, photo ops, and the like, and fewer "talking heads" sitting around a table arguing. Do you agree that this is a good move? It will surely cut down on the opportunities for extended interviews of political figures and for roundtables—the interviewlike discussions among political analysts. What is your position? What arguments would you put in a memo to support your position?

- Several scenes in the film *Broadcast News* illustrate the ethical dilemmas associated with how to broadcast videotaped interviews. In controversial situations, how much of the interview could be considered fair context if the segment presents a negative criticism of the interviewee? Is it ethical to intercut reaction shots from the interviewer that were taped outside the actual interview? View the film and keep a log of each "decision point" that involves an ethical choice about in-terviewing. For each, ask yourself: (1) Why did the character(s) make a particular choice? (2) What would I have done, given similar situations, responsibilities, and pressures?

- Larry King, the famed broadcast interviewer, once wrote: "I try to follow a few other rules for interviewing. For openers, I ask short questions. The longer you take, the less the audience is learning. Good questions start with the words *Why* or *How?* Bad questions start with the words *Did* or *When*. With *Why* or *How* questions, I can get some elaboration from the guest. With the others, I'm inviting one-word answers, which everyone hates" (1989, p. 135). In your opinion, is King right about "Did" and "When" questions? Imagine yourself in King's position, interviewing celebrities and politicians. Pick a celebrity you'd like to meet, and prepare several "Did" and several "When" inquiries. What would the interviewee likely answer? Are there occasions in which "Did" or "When" questions are helpful?

transferable. After reading this chapter, you should have a more balanced view of our interview-immersed media culture.

The Interview Bookshelf

On how television has become its own reality

McKibben, B. (1993). *The age of missing information.* New York: Plume.

McKibben wondered what it would be like to watch all available programming that was aired on a single day in the nation's (then) largest cable system—all the sitcom repeats, all the infomercials, all the local interviews, all the cooking shows. His book contrasts what he learned from the screen with what he learned from a day alone in the Adirondacks.

On planning broadcast interviews

Biagi, S. (1992). *Interviews that work: A practical guide for journalists* (2nd ed.). Belmont, CA: Wadsworth.

Biagi's excellent discussion of broadcast interviewing points out similarities and, more important, differences between broadcasters' jobs and other journalists' goals.

On the inside track of broadcast interviewing

Joyce, E. (1988). *Prime times, bad times.* New York: Anchor.

Hilton, J. (1987). *How to meet the press: A survival guide.* New York: Dodd, Mead.

Joyce, a former president of CBS News, takes us behind the scenes of network news, often including fascinating, if gossipy, portraits of well-known interviewers. Hilton fancies himself on the other side. As a former broadcaster and political commentator for ABC, he now trains public figures to "get their message across" even when talking to ignorant, hostile, or incompetent interviewers. Both books probably will make you wince and worry about ethics at times, but both at least help us know what to trust—and fear—in an interview-driven culture.

On critiques of television culture

Livingstone, S., & Lunt, P. (1994). *Talk on television: Audience participation and public debate.* London: Routledge.

Mander, J. (1978). *Four arguments for the elimination of television.* New York: Quill.

Postman, N. (1985). *Amusing ourselves to death: Public discourse in the age of show business.* New York: Penguin.

Mander and Postman offer polemics—extended arguments advancing a position. Be careful when reading them, but read them. Ad executive Mander's book is often simplistic, and many communication scholars frankly hate its tone. Still, it's been quite influential in the wider cultural discussion of media. Postman is much more scholarly and subtle in supporting his warnings. Livingstone and Lunt have a position, too, but it is more hopeful about the future of public dialogue.

References

Berman, R. (1987). *How television sees its audience.* Newbury Park, CA: Sage.

Biagi, S. (1992). *Interviews that work: A practical guide for journalists* (2nd ed.). Belmont, CA: Wadsworth.

Booth, W. C. (1988). *The vocation of a teacher: Rhetorical occasions 1967–1988.* Chicago: University of Chicago Press.

Claflin, S. T., Jr. (1979). *A radical proposal for full use of free speech.* New York: Philosophical Library.

Cohen, A. (1987). *The television news interview.* Newbury Park, CA: Sage.

Davis, D. (1993). *The five myths of television power.* New York: Simon & Schuster.

Fiske, J. (1989). *Reading the popular.* Boston: Unwin Hyman.

Frost, D. (1978). *"I gave them a sword": Behind the scenes of the Nixon interviews.* New York: William Morrow.

Goffman, E. (1981). *Forms of talk.* Philadelphia: University of Pennsylvania Press.

Heritage, J. (1985). Analyzing news interviews: Aspects of the production of talk for an overhearing audience. In T. A. van Dijk (Ed.), *Discourse and dialogue (Handbook of discourse analysis, Vol. 3)* (pp. 95–117). London: Academic Press.

Heritage, J., & Greatbatch, D. (1991). On the institutional character of institutional talk: The case of news interviews. In D. Boden & D. H. Zimmerman (Eds.), *Talk and social structure: Studies in ethnomethodology and conversation analysis* (pp. 93–137). Berkeley: University of California Press.

Hilton, J. (1987). *How to meet the press: A survival guide.* New York: Dodd, Mead.

Joyce, E. (1988). *Prime times, bad times.* New York: Anchor.

King, L., with Occhiogrosso, P. (1989). *Tell it to the king.* New York: Jove.

Livingstone, S., & Lunt, P. (1994). *Talk on television: Audience participation and public debate.* London: Routledge.

Mander, J. (1978). *Four arguments for the elimination of television.* New York: Quill.

McKibben, B. (1993). *The age of missing information.* New York: Plume.

Metzler, K. (1997). *Creative interviewing: The writer's guide to gathering information by asking questions* (3rd ed.). Boston: Allyn and Bacon.

Postman, N. (1985). *Amusing ourselves to death: Public discourse in the age of show business.* New York: Penguin.

Postman, N. (1988). *Conscientious objections: Stirring up trouble about language, technology, and education.* New York: Alfred A. Knopf.

Shattuc, J. M. (1997). *The talking cure: TV, talk shows, and women.* New York: Routledge.

⌘ 13 Wrapping It All Up: Listening to Learn as a Professional

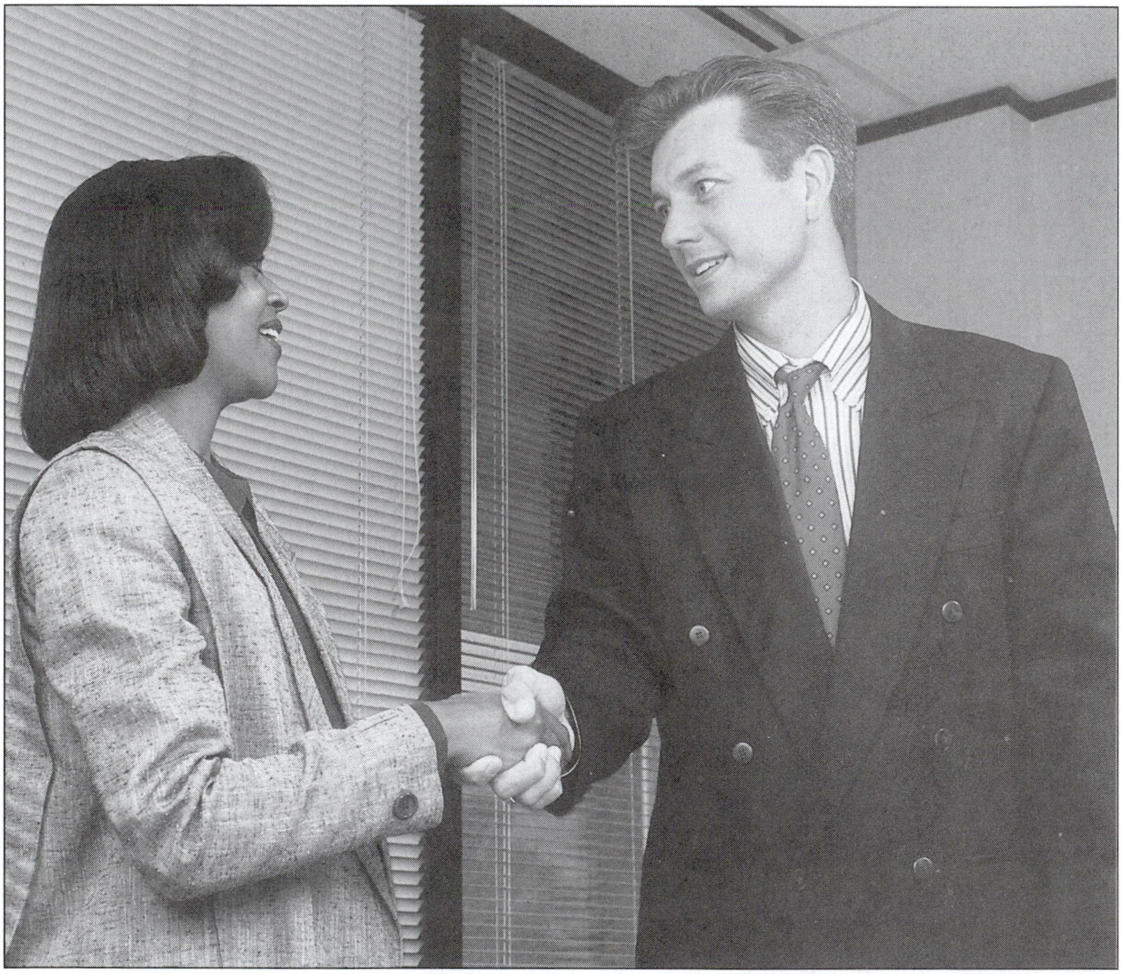

If we are to understand the process of interaction between interviewer and respondent, we cannot concern ourselves only with the mechanics of the interviewing process, nor can we be satisfied to study the interview as a series of discrete stimulus-response episodes. We must be concerned instead with the goals, attitudes, beliefs, and motives of the principals in the interview.

. . . Influence between the interviewer and the respondent is by no means a one-way process. The relation is reciprocal, with the psychological fields of both interviewer and respondent constantly in process of modification because of cues each receives from the other. Most students of interviewing recognize that the motivation of the respondent depends to a considerable extent upon interviewer characteristics and behavior. It is less frequently recognized, however, that the interviewer's behavior depends in part upon the respondent. . . .

—Robert L. Kahn and Charles F. Cannell, *The Dynamics of Interviewing*

LEARNING GOALS

After reading this chapter, you should be able to

- Summarize the philosophy and rationale of *Interviewing: Speaking, Listening, and Learning for Professional Life*
- Describe four focal points for skills-plus interviewing—focused conversation, curiosity, skills, and continuing learning
- Explain why listening, questioning, and framing are the basic skill areas for interviewers and interviewees
- Choose among many strategies for continued learning in interviewing after reading this book

There are many new things under the sun. However, in a classic early interviewing text published more than 40 years ago Robert Kahn and Charles Cannell (1957) highlight important issues that are still crucial. They stress how a supposedly straightforward communication act is in reality a complex system of interwoven psychological and sociological processes. Interviewing isn't what one person does to another but a process that develops when two interdependent communicators collaborate in a quest for information and insight. Simplistic research methods and prescriptive training just won't do if an interview is to fulfill its promise.

407

The Centrality of Interviewing

As an effective interviewer and interviewee, you have found the front door for entering the social conversation about information, organizational decision making, and public policy.

In an era in which many compete to make your decisions for you, interviewing skills (and the appreciations supporting them) allow you to find out answers for yourself. They let you go to the source, to test solutions, to check information, to personalize your particular professional quest. Interviewing lets your learning be firsthand and personalized, rather than a batch of warmed-over ideas received from others. It lets you take charge of more of your own learning in many of the most crucial arenas of professional life.

Rather than prescribe answers or make your decisions more automatic, we've tried to suggest a two-sided approach to problems of obtaining more information and insight. First, learning about interviewing in this book will help to clear the muddy waters of interpersonal hesitation, apprehension, and fear. Many of us are justly afraid of encountering others face-to-face or through other forms of direct and immediate contact. Interviewing involves learning the fundamental skills of interpersonal communication. Second, studying interviewing will muddy some waters that might have previously seemed clear. This is a good thing. That is, without overcomplicating things, we've tried to show how this topic, which some presume is straightforward and nonproblematic, is actually more complex than it is often assumed to be. Throughout this book, therefore, we've encouraged interview participants to see themselves not only as speakers and listeners enacting skills but also as thinkers. Effective interviewers and interviewees prepare carefully, diagnose and troubleshoot possible problems, assess their experiences, project the probabilities for future success, and adjust accordingly. They need a familiarity with the broader psychological, social, and cultural contexts of interpersonal relationships. They frame their experiences in ways that are not always observable in the simple behaviors people demonstrate for each other.

Some kinds of learning tend to close people down, while others can open people up. Think about a poetry teacher who teaches poetry writing by having you memorize and copy Shakespeare's sonnets. Surely your time wouldn't be wasted, because Shakespeare is worth studying and you can learn much about rhyme and meter by modeling and emulating his work. But the outcome of this learning isn't likely to help you glimpse the wider range of functions poetry can serve, nor will it necessarily help you develop your own creativity as a poet. Something enlightening has happened, but you've been closed down, in one sense, by the imposition of someone else's experience on your own. Experiencing other poems, other poetries—including your own first attempts in your own voice—would develop your own artistic abilities. Keep Shakespeare, or rhymed poetry, but not as your sole focus. Skills help, but you go beyond them to other appreciations and applications in order to open yourself up to a new area like poetry.

Interviewing is a bit like learning poetry in this sense. We encourage you to develop a wide range of appreciations and curiosities to go along with your basic communication skills. Trust the advice of experienced practitioners, but don't swallow it whole and indiscriminately. We've included many boxes in which practitioners discuss real-life dilemmas they face, and you'll notice they don't all agree on what to do about these problems. We've included many boxes asking you to make your own decisions in hypothetical and real cases. An education in interviewing involves not only learning how to speak and listen but also how to think.

Learning Skills-Plus Interviewing

We have framed this book as a skills-plus approach for a good reason. It's important to know what to do, which is the focus of a skill-building approach. But it's equally important to know why it works and to be flexible in atypical situations. Don't shirk either the "What?" or the "Why?" questions in studying interviewing. Without a broad base of behavioral and cognitive skills, you won't be able to perform competently in everyday interview situations. You won't have the raw materials to build with. But on the other hand, if you *only* stress such skill building, you miss much of the context in which those skills exist. You'll be able to deal with the so-called normal situations but will be shocked or immobilized when creativity is necessary.

We divided each chapter into both basic issues and other ideas that build on or extend them—"The Basics" and "Beyond the Basics." Experts might disagree about some of these choices and believe we've relegated some truly basic information to the ends of chapters. In no sense are the "Beyond the Basics" sections impractical, marginal, or dispensable. Rather, they describe issues that, in our opinion, might be addressed best with the rest of the chapter's content firmly in mind. We thought it would aid your reading to defer some topics until a baseline understanding of terms and concepts was built. In some cases instructors will assign entire chapters, while other instructors might assign only "The Basics," leaving the later topics for other courses or for your personal reading.

The major themes of a complex subject are difficult to summarize. However, a final chapter is a good place to attempt to boil things down. When you think back over all of what you've read, what basic ideas seem most relevant across contexts? Regardless of what specific interview contexts or roles in which you might find yourself, we can think of just a few basic principles that all interviewers and interviewees should keep in the front of their minds.

Remember That Interviewing Is Focused Conversation

Chapter 1 defined an interview as "an interpersonal or public communication situation in which one or more persons seeks information and insight from another or others." Although interviewing is occasionally described as a one-sided activity of extracting information, the best interviews tend toward conversational talk in important ways. The term itself discloses a clue to the potential of interviewing: Interviews can become "inter-views." By interviewing, we learn what we have in common with others, what they have to share with us, and vice versa. "Inter-view": Views can become shared between (inter-) communicators, just as in conversations.

However, interviewing is not the same as having everyday spontaneous conversations; if it were no more difficult than that, taking classes in it wouldn't be necessary. Instead, an interview is a *focused* conversation. Interviewers and interviewees build on the skills of normal talk, whether they are discussing a possible job or a possible new treatment for a hospital patient, a product preference in a brief mall survey or a campaign commitment from a politician talking to a reporter.

Let Curiosity Guide You

People presumably want to interview because they want to learn something new, and they consent to be interviewed because they have something to say. Both of these insights rely on a faith in our human capacity for speech to improve our relationships. When we need to know about something, we usually seek out someone to ask; when asked, we tend to respond. This reciprocal relationship, so often at the heart of friendships and families, is also at the core of career success for communication professionals. Having good questions and being willing to respond appropriately are in many ways the hallmarks of professional success in any career.

Nurture Dialogic Skills and Appreciations

Dialogic skills and appreciations ideally motivate interview communicators. This means that each respects the uniqueness of the other person, and each attempts to create occasions in which both go beyond what they already know to achieve new insight. It means that the best interviews are prepared for carefully but not prefabricated or scripted. It means that the participants value their differences as much as their similarities. It means that each side tries to imagine the reality of the other, communicating empathically even when intimate communication is not involved. It means that each communicator speaks ethically and authentically to preserve the range of choices of the other. The three dialogic skills emphasized in this book are listening, questioning, and framing.

Listening Sets the Stage   Listening is the baseline skill that lets an interview develop between two or more people. Concepts of listening and speech cannot be separated easily in everyday life, even for analytical purposes. However, one insight does clearly suggest the importance of listening. Without the expectation of being heard and, at a deeper level, listened to, we don't even begin to consider the possibility of asking questions. Speakers who are self-absorbed don't progress very far in any human endeavor. Instead, the more common experience for speakers is to imagine their partner's style and capacity of listening and then fit speech to that estimate.

Listening, as we've stressed it in this book, is an active process of understanding and checking meanings with others. It is not merely a passive reception of others' messages.

You listen actively by paying attention, to be sure, but also by reflections, paraphrases, and perception checks that let others know when they've been misunderstood. With effective listening, questioning and framing become meaningful.

Questioning Fuels Learning   As we intend the term, questioning implies both the act of asking questions and the attitude of checking reality. Genuine questioning in an interview demonstrates how you want to learn, when you have a desire to learn, and why you're willing to inquire. A friend of the authors intersperses his conversations, about topics large and small, with a simple verbal habit—every so often he'll ask, "What do *you* think?" Then he waits to hear what you'll say. It's surprising how many good ideas he hears and how good people feel about being asked. Of course, not all questions operate that way; some questions can be taunts, or manipulations, or sarcastic comments, or attempts to embarrass others: "What makes you think *that*?" "I got an A, just like last week. What did you get?" "You don't like Senator Hudson's vote on schools, do you?"

Questioning, as we've stressed it in this book, is an open invitation that convinces others that you're going to listen carefully to how they respond. But beware of too much, or too little, reliance on questions. Without them, interviews don't seem like interviews. But with only questions, interviews seem like interrogations and cross-examinations.

Framing Creates Perspective   People don't just accumulate information, as if facts were packages of meaning that they need to gather. Interviewers sometimes overgeneralize by referring to "information gathering" as though the information was sitting only slightly under the surface of life, "out there" somewhere waiting to be found by an industrious truth seeker. In fact, as evidence cited throughout our book verifies, communicators never collect information neutrally in that sense; they are forever interpreting, tingeing perceptions with feelings, investing them with connotations of good or bad, perceiving their importance in light of this or that goal.

Framing, as we've discussed it in this book, probes how interviewers and interviewees interpret information in their own contexts and put it to their own uses. The question becomes: How can we recognize and gain access to others' frames? Interviewers experience this problem, for example, when they decide how to establish rapport and open up conversations—where is this other person coming from? Interviewees experience this also when they try to figure out, often with fragmentary clues, what a questioner really wants to know.

Continue to Learn

When concluding a class, many students pack up their notes, sell the textbook back to the bookstore, buy a new notebook, and start thinking about next semester. This might be one class where you should keep your notes and books handy and the ideas in the front of your mind. In addition to their obvious relevance for professional careers, interviewing skills and appreciations are extraordinarily helpful and applicable in completing assignments in college classes.

You're fishing for a good term-paper topic in your Persuasion class; interviewing a political science, law school, or media ethics professor could lead you to some interesting controversies in government-media relations—prior restraint of publications, definitions of hate speech, political implications of pornography definitions, for example. Or you're having trouble in your Philosophy of Communication class and need to ask your teacher specifics about how Wittgenstein relates to conflict management. Or you are studying for your first exam in Communication Research and realize you need a refresher or two in qualitative interviewing skills. Or your Public Affairs Reporting class requires you to spend a day at the county courthouse and write at least two stories; is it possible you'd want to talk to lawyers or police officers? Or the Women's Studies Program is being reviewed by the campus administration, and you'd like to survey recent graduates to discover their impressions of the faculty and curriculum.

To keep your learning about interviewing fresh, we suggest you do the following:

- Keep an informal interviewing log in which you note especially good examples of effectiveness in interviewers or interviewees. Who are the best interviewers in popular media? What are their strengths? How can you build those strengths into your own interpersonal style? Who are the least effective interviewers in popular media? What are their weaknesses? How can you avoid those weaknesses in your own style?

- Read more about famous interviewers, such as Barbara Walters, Ray Suarez, Charles Kuralt, Studs Terkel, or Terry Gross.

- Volunteer for any interviewing tasks that come up in your student activities group, civic or neighborhood club, or political action group.

- Interview several interviewers to see if their experiences match ideas and advice you've read in this book and other textbooks or articles. One particularly practical suggestion is to conduct informational interviews with several successful professionals in the career area you're considering. Ask them not only for opinions but also for stories—anecdotes that illustrate the centrality of effective interviewing in their jobs. Find out from them firsthand whether interviewing skills are practical in the world of work.

- Write at least two forms of your resume, and update them regularly whether you're applying for jobs or not. This personal habit will remind you to be systematically introspective about your qualifications and your communication skills. Work with the career center on your campus to stay current with new expectations employers might have about resume format and content, including on-line innovations.

- Schedule role-play employment interviews with career center personnel and with several professors in your department who understand the career for which you're preparing yourself. Make sure they feel comfortable giving you both positive (reinforcing) and negative feedback and that they have enough time to coach you fully on options for adapting your behavior.

Summary

Studying interviewing can be based on conversational dialogue, we suggest. Although this approach might sound nonthreatening, it does put your ego on the line. Interviews are collaborative, but their participants encounter each other as unique individuals too.

This book has been written for performance courses that combine practice in professional tasks with insights about interpersonal communication. It has asked you to monitor your communication competence in front of other people and to practice better ways to listen, speak, and frame information in order to learn. In doing so, you integrate skills with attitudes, theory, and research in the best tradition of communication studies disciplines.

References

Kahn, R. L., & Cannell, C. F. (1957). *The dynamics of interviewing: Theory, technique, and cases.* New York: John Wiley & Sons.

❦ Glossary

account   A statement offered to make your frame clear and explicit in response to a possible misunderstanding with a communication partner. See **framing**.

acknowledgment cluster   In **confirmation theory,** a group of statements or behaviors that indicate a willingness to follow or remain engaged with someone's words, expressed through verbal or nonverbal signals.

acquiescence   When communicators passively accept whatever happens or is said, acting as though they have no right to exert control in the situation.

active listening   A style of responding in which the listener is willing to test his or her interpretation aloud, with the intent of enhancing and refining communication. Active listening often is expressed by a communicator saying, for example, "I'm hearing that your main idea is . . . ," followed by a paraphrase of the speaker's meaning.

affective/behavioral inference response   A listener's verbalized attempt to note and interpret a speaker's behavioral or nonverbal messages.

aggressiveness   When communicators attempt to prevail or control communication, with little or no regard for the feelings or rights of other participants.

amplification probe   Follow-up questions or comments that ask for an expansion of a response to a primary question.

appraisal interview   An organizational interview designed to allow a superior to assess and communicate with a subordinate through mutual feedback and goal setting.

appreciative listening   Listening to enjoy the creative or aesthetic features of a message.

archiving   Labeling a tape clearly, with date, place, and subject, and keeping it, along with written notes or other interview material, in a safe place.

artifacts   Objects people display intentionally or unintentionally that are meaningful in a relationship. An executive's desk, for example, is an artifact that may symbolize status, while the photographs displayed on that desk may suggest commitment to family life.

assertiveness   A midpoint between **acquiescence** and **aggressiveness** in communication, when speakers act or express themselves in ways that protect their own rights while respecting the rights of others.

assumptive close   When a seller in a persuasive encounter concludes the interview by assuming the respondent has made a commitment to buy, complicating the process if there is a "no" response.

attending behaviors   Nonverbal cues that indicate a listener is paying attention.

attitude   A person's predisposition to behave in certain ways.

attribution theory   A description of how people attempt to explain, or "attribute," behaviors to either internal or external causes.

audio computer-assisted self-administered interview (ACASI)   A form of survey research interview in which the interviewee, working at his or her own pace, privately responds to questions from a computer program that includes an interviewer's voice. See **computer-assisted self-administered interview (CASI)**.

bargaining model   An approach to appraisal interviews in which an employee reacts to a supervisor's stated goals by attempting to clarify through dialogue the **psychological contract**—those subtle expectations that bind an organization's members together.

behavioral interview   In selection settings, an interview in which the interviewee is asked either to describe handling a crisis situation or to demonstrate a skill—an approach based on the presumption that past behavior often predicts future performance. Known also as *behavior-based interviewing (BBI)*. In therapy settings, a behavioral interview centers on breaking a cycle of behavior.

behaviorally anchored rating system (BARS)   A form of appraisal rating that assesses workers' performance according to standards based on a thorough analysis of job requirements.

blindside questions   Questions the interviewer knows the interviewee will not expect; used to surprise and either test reactions or obtain an unrehearsed answer.

bona fide occupational qualifications (BFOQ)   A legal term used to describe the qualities and qualifications demonstrably related to effective performance in a given job.

breaking the frame   When one of the two or more communication partners violates shared assumptions regulating their interaction.

bridge   A phrase or question used to make a transition to another conversational subject.

census   A group of survey respondents that includes all members of a given population.

choice close   A method of closing a persuasive interview by laying out options to help the prospective buyer reach a decision.

chronological organization   An interview style in which questions move from past toward recent or current events or details.

chronological resume   A **resume** that summarizes an applicant's qualifications, experience, and other attributes from most to least recent. See **functional resume**.

clarification Similar to **paraphrasing**—a skill of critical listening that helps communication partners ensure that each understands the other.

clarification probe A type of follow-up question or comment that assists understanding by enabling communication partners to test perceptions and listening acuity.

clearing The psychological and physiological process of eliminating distractions that could interfere with the ability to listen.

clearinghouse questions See **wrap-up questions**.

client-centered therapy To Rogers, a term for a therapeutic relationship focusing on nonjudgmental listening and **empathy** rather than on a therapist's behavioral or analytical techniques.

close A term for the final stage of persuasive interviewing when a commitment or binding decision occurs.

closed questions Sometimes called closed-ended questions, they seek specific information and limit the range of a respondent's answers. See **open-ended questions**.

coaching A mutual activity of one person helping another improve performance through changing behavior, solving a problem, or developing a plan.

code In the context of communication studies, an organized and interlinked set of conditions that characterize a situation; the internal logic of a context that may sometimes be difficult to see.

coding A system researchers use to place responses or collected data into categories.

cognitive interview A therapeutic approach that focuses on helping a client replace negative with rational thoughts.

communication The complex process of developing shared meaning through messages, both verbal and nonverbal, between persons in a relationship.

communication competence Knowledge, skills, and motivation to behave appropriately in communication relationships.

communication noise See **noise**.

communication rule An implicit social agreement that helps people decide what behavior is obligated, preferred, or prohibited in certain social contexts.

compliance The process of accepting the influence of another person in the hope of achieving a favorable reaction from that person.

comprehensive listening Listening to comprehend a speaker's meaning or intention.

computer-assisted self-administered interviewing (CASI) A form of survey research interview in which the interviewee, working at his or her own pace, privately responds to questions from a computer program. See **audio computer-assisted self-administered interviewing (ACASI)**.

concentration The ability to filter out the effects of distractions when listening.

confirmation theory Suggests that communication quality often depends on the acknowledgment and recognition people receive from others.

confirmative probe A follow-up question or comment that attempts to test or challenge the reliability of answers.

connotation The range of informal meanings words acquire in everyday usage.

content inference response A way of telling a speaker that you have both heard and attempted to understand what has been said.

contextualizing Acknowledging for yourself, and perhaps for your communication partner, the full context in which communication is occurring.

convenience (available) sample In research interviewing, a sample group of respondents selected on the basis of availability or convenience rather than representativeness.

conversational maxims Four factors—quantity, quality, relevance, and manner—that help conversants determine when and how they need to be flexible.

cooperative principle The presumption that each speaker should contribute appropriately to the purposes and directions of a conversation.

counseling interview An interview context in which professionals help clients discuss strategies that might assist them in making sound decisions or working out problems.

counterbalance close A persuasive interviewing strategy that sellers use to encourage acceptance of an idea or product by matching a respondent's reservations with an offsetting benefit.

cover letter A narrative description to introduce yourself and explain why you're qualified and a good fit for a job.

credibility In communication, a listener's estimate of a speaker's expertise, trustworthiness, and, to a lesser extent, dynamism. See **ethos**.

criteria checklist A list of qualifications and other employment considerations that help selection interviewers supplement a list of essential skills. See **profile of essential skills**.

critical incident report A narrative assessment that focuses on concrete examples of a worker's ability to carry out job responsibilities.

critical listening Listening that focuses on judging the worth and quality of messages.

decentering The ability to see things from perspectives other than your own; closely related to **empathy**.

defensive climate An interpersonal context, often stimulated by unnecessary judgment or criticism, that encourages communicators to react as if they are protecting themselves from attack.

delayed note taking A style of recording interview information that relies on memory to collect details and later recall an interview; used when on-the-spot note taking isn't possible or advisable.

demographics Characteristics such as gender, race, or age used by researchers to define or identify segments of a population.

denotation The literal meaning of words as defined, for example, in dictionaries.

deontology An ethical orientation that stresses strict adherence to rules or duties in one's behavior and decision making.

depth description version A detailed position description for job applicants.

diagnostic interview A focused inquiry into the possible causes of a physical or psychological problem; takes into account symptoms, conditions, and feelings for the purpose of assessment and possible treatment.

dialogue Moments of communication that depend on mutually interactive, reciprocal relationship, not technique or strategy. In dialogue, communicators become partners in producing insights and understanding of each other and the topics they explore.

direct questions Questions that are blunt, to the point, and specific.

discriminative listening   Listening to determine types and subtleties of differences in messages.

disqualifying response   In **confirmation theory**, when a communicator dismisses, trivializes, or disparages the words and ideas of others.

doubled-barreled questions   Questions with two or more parts to them, making them difficult to answer.

DPFP sequence   An abbreviation for the *draft, proof, feedback,* and *proof* method for creating, refining, and checking a resume.

egoism   A branch of ethics that emphasizes an individual making the decisions most likely to produce the greatest good for that individual.

emotional sensitivity   The ability to infer from a speaker's words and behaviors the emotional state of mind behind messages.

empathy   Sensing someone else's world accurately, as they sense it, without leaving your own. In part, both an attitude and an ability to detect and appreciate another person's feelings, emotions, and concerns.

employee assistance programs   Programs sponsored by, or contracted by, large corporations in which employees can find help for serious emotional, medical, or behavioral problems. These options are often recommended during intervention or appraisal interviews for employees whose work may be suffering temporarily.

employment interview   An encounter between an applicant and an organizational representative for the purpose of mutually exploring information and subjects relevant to hiring or selection decisions.

endorsement cluster   In confirmation theory, a group of statements or behaviors that accept and treat a speaker's messages as important or OK.

epistemology   The study of how human knowledge and insight develop.

establishing shots   Visuals used in television or video to help audiences see how participants are oriented physically to each other within a context.

ethnocentrism   The attitude suggesting that all cultural groups should be judged by the standards of the perceiver's own culture.

ethnography   A form of research in which an interviewer or participant observer attempts to experience as directly as possible a different culture's expectations, values, beliefs, and behavioral patterns.

ethos   In classical rhetoric, one of three ways communicators persuade others (see **logos** and **pathos**). Ethos is persuasiveness that comes from force of character; often known in contemporary communication studies as **credibility**.

euphemisms   Presumably inoffensive words used as replacements for words that are considered unpleasant or offensive.

exit interview   An interview by an organizational representative with an employee who resigns or retires; conducted for purposes of closure, feedback, and assistance with the transition to new jobs and tasks.

facilitative conditions   To Rogers, the qualities of respect, genuineness, and empathy found in effective relationships between helpers and clients.

field notes   An ethnographer's detailed, written record of cultural communication, including contextual observations, that can make unfamiliar cultural patterns more meaningful.

field review   A narrative assessment conducted by a manager or supervisor who observes a worker's performance on the job and uses those observations for a written report.

fight behavior   A confrontive reaction to criticism.

filmic procedures   Broadcast decisions involving how to film or videotape interaction, such as televised interviews; these decisions key audiences to how they should frame or interpret that interaction.

flight behavior   Withdrawal and passivity in the face of criticism.

focus group   An approach to research in which respondents are recruited by a researcher to discuss in groups what draws them to certain attitudes, preferences, or products. Moderators in such studies are, in effect, group interviewers.

forced-choice rating   A special type of rating system designed to channel raters' responses into a limited number of categories.

forced distribution   A ranking approach that requires managers to show where individual workers fit within categories in relation to an assessment of all employees of a particular department or operation.

frame (framing)   The complex inner process of interpreting and evaluating patterns of messages according to the contexts in which they occur.

free narrative question   An inquiry that allows a respondent to create a personal account with no structuring from the interviewer.

full mental focus   A skill of **comprehensive listening** that capitalizes on the "spare time" created by the difference between the rate of speech and the rate of thought.

functional resume   A **resume** that organizes an applicant's qualifications around the functions of a particular job, such as "office management" or "writing skills." See **chronological resume**.

fundamental attribution error   The tendency for an interviewer or other communicator to regard others as motivated by internal forces while assuming his or her own motivation is determined by the circumstances at hand.

funnel organization   A method of interviewing that begins with general, open-ended questions and moves to increasingly specific and narrow ones.

global essay   A form of narrative assessment by which a supervisor writes generalized, or "global," impressions of a worker's performance.

goal-setting theory   A concept based on the belief that managers and workers should jointly identify and seek attainment of a set of performance objectives.

head and shoulders close-up   A camera perspective that brings the audience within the equivalent of touching distance of the speaker.

hearing   The physiological or biological process by which sounds are perceived by the human ear and auditory apparatus. Compare with **listening**.

high-flex communicator   Someone who understands, appreciates, and adapts to both the context and the process of **communication rules**.

highly scheduled interview   A structured interview planned in advance that follows a detailed and prescribed organization.

holding   A therapeutic method that employs supportive talk to make a client feel safe in sharing painful or embarrassing details.

horizontal dimension   In oral history interviewing, areas or branches of an interviewee's life to explore relative to the **vertical dimension** of chronology.

human studies research committee   See **institutional review board**.

hypothetical question   A form of question that creates a dramatic or narrative situation and asks respondents to react as if they were participants.

identification   In the process of social influence, how people sometimes adopt the behaviors or preferences of others they admire or model.

I-message   A nonjudgmental way of responding to a speaker's statements without raising defensiveness. An I-message indicates only that the speaker believes or feels something, without implying that someone else necessarily is responsible for causing that state.

immediacy theory   Explains how face-to-face communication that is verbally and nonverbally close and direct increases communicators' satisfaction. Nonverbal immediacy can be increased, for example, by more eye contact or by reducing interactional distance; verbal immediacy can be increased by substituting personalized phrases such as, "I am pleased with your department's work this quarter, Jeanne" for, "The marketing department is improving this quarter."

impervious response   When one communicator, such as an interviewer, acknowledges the presence of another but fails to act as if the other person could make a significant difference in the relationship.

implied consent   A research interviewee's unstated but obvious willingness to participate in a study. See **informed consent**.

impression management skills   The ability to adjust talk and nonverbal messages successfully to meet the demands of a communication situation and to present an appropriate image to others.

indifferent response   Words or actions by which someone suggests he or she doesn't care about a speaker or the speaker's words.

indirect questions   Questions, often marked by introductory phrases or qualifiers, that allow the respondent to infer intentions and meanings rather than be confronted directly.

inflection   How speakers emphasize certain words over others by varying vocal volume or pitch.

informational interview   An interaction that focuses on learning something specific from another person or group.

informed consent   In an interview or other research setting, the oral or written assurance that participants understand the risks and benefits of answering questions.

institutional review board   A body charged with reviewing research proposals and sometimes monitoring research that involves potential risk to participants. Known by other names, such as *human studies research committee*.

internalization   The process of social influence in which people conclude a proposed change fits within their value systems and adopt it for that reason.

interpersonal ethic   An ethical approach that weighs the implications of one's messages for their impact on the communication rights of others. In general, an interpersonal ethic is guided by the maintenance or expansion of choices available to communicators.

interrogation interview   An interview designed to persuade an interviewee to disclose all relevant facts fully even when disclosure may not be in the individual's best interest.

intervention interview   A face-to-face meeting between a superior and a subordinate in an organization for the purpose of dealing with a crisis or problem attributable to the subordinate's behavior.

interview   An interpersonal or public communication event in which one or more persons seek information and insight from another or others.

interviewing by comment   A means of using comments or statements to elicit important information.

intrinsic motivation   A concept describing workers' inner tendencies to learn, improve, and experiment.

inverted funnel organization   A method of interviewing that progresses from narrow, specific questions and widens to broader, general ones.

jargon   The "inside" language of particular fields, professions, or interests that is often unfamiliar to outsiders.

leading questions   Questions that suggest by their form the kind of answers desired by the questioner.

Likert-type scale   An instrument to measure attitude; it asks respondents to consider an issue or statement, then indicate where they stand on a scale of approval or agreement.

linguistic conservatism   The attitude that society should preserve or "conserve" language as a commonly shared experience; this perspective assumes that words should be applied and understood in similar ways by communicators, whatever their cultural backgrounds. See also **multiculturalism** and **political correctness**.

listening   The holistic activity of processing aural stimuli, interpreting them as messages, and using them to construct meanings of speech, speakers, and contexts.

literature   The current body of knowledge in any field of study.

literature review   A careful written analysis of existing research and data on a proposed topic to be studied.

loaded questions   Questions that plant a questioner's emotional presumption within the wording, often using judgmental or accusatory language.

local knowledge   In ethnography, understandings specifically relevant for the local and immediate context in which they are communicated.

logos   In classical rhetoric, one of three ways communicators influence audiences (see **ethos** and **pathos**). Logos refers to persuasiveness that comes from appeals to logic.

management by objectives (MBO)   A management philosophy that values attainment of organizational goals.

meal interview   A complex interview setting often scheduled for lunch or dinner, in which an applicant's ability to converse and interact with one or more interviewers is tested by the need to divide attention among several different tasks.

mediation   An interaction that involves a neutral third-party interviewer to help settle difficult negotiations.

medium shot   A camera perspective that approximates what is considered the proper social distance for interpersonal communication.

member check   A qualitative researcher's method of asking interviewees from researched groups to review tentative interpretations and conclusions to guard against errors.

metacommunication The process by which communication partners address the state of their communication through either implicit, silent commentary or explicit verbal analysis.

metamessages Messages (often tone of voice or visual clues, like a wink) used to tell others how to interpret other messages.

microgoals A series of small steps systematically leading to the attainment of a major goal.

mirror response Reflecting or repeating a speaker's statement to help verify and note that the speaker has been heard accurately.

mixed messages Perceived contradictions between verbal and nonverbal messages sent by a communicator.

moderately scheduled interview An interview that mixes standard, preestablished questions with improvised and individualized ones.

multiculturalism A term with various meanings, it particularly suggests an emphasis on how language and mannerisms can communicate powerful messages about or affecting cultural identities. Multiculturalists, therefore, tend to conceive of language as an arena to effect cultural change. See **linguistic conservatism** and **political correctness**.

narrative The human tendency to tell and appreciate dramatic stories. Also, an appraisal method based on an anecdotal evaluation, written either after, or as the basis for, an appraisal interview.

needs assessment A systematic description of what a job calls for in terms of a new employee's skills and knowledge; an aid in selection interviewing.

negotiation interview Any situation in which competing parties function as both interviewer and interviewee in exchanges expected to result in agreement or consensus.

noise Any psychological or physiological interference with a listener's attempt to attend to messages.

nonjudgmental response A listening approach that avoids attacking or otherwise judging a speaker's words or actions.

nonprobability survey In interview research, a sample population selected without the use of mathematical guidelines of probability.

nonscheduled interview An interview interaction determined by moment-to-moment exchanges rather than questions and topics set in advance; nonscheduled interviews are common in many therapy situations and on-the-scene journalistic settings.

not for attribution An understanding in a journalistic interview: When an individual, usually a public figure, agrees to an interview on the expressed condition that he or she will not be identified in a reporter's story as the source of the information. See **off the record** and **on background**.

note set The raw, dense collection of interview data that the researcher later refines by analysis.

off the record An understanding in a journalistic interview: When someone supplies a journalist with information with the stipulation that it is not to be published. See **not for attribution** and **on background**.

on background An understanding in a journalistic interview: When someone agrees to provide a journalist with off-the-record information with the agreement that it will not be published or broadcast, or attributed to the source. It may, however, be used by the journalist to discover further relevant information about a story. See **not for attribution** and **off the record**.

open coding Interpretations and labels added in the margins of field notes to aid the qualitative interviewer in later analysis.

open-ended questions Questions that invite respondents to choose their own direction, depth, and context for answers. See **closed questions**.

oral history A rich documentary record produced from an interviewee's firsthand perceptions or memories.

pace The timing and tempo of questions.

panel interview A form of selection interview in which several organizational representatives take turns asking questions and seeking information from an applicant.

papers of record Periodicals, such as the *New York Times*, considered authoritative sources on political, social, and economic information.

paralinguistic cues Nonverbal vocal variations, such as pitch and volume, that influence how a speaker's message will be interpreted.

paraphrasing The repetition of a speaker's ideas or statements in a listener's own words to verify accurate listening.

passant phenomenon A condition in which people will disclose highly personal information to a stranger they do not expect to meet again.

pathos In classical rhetoric, one of three ways communicators persuade others (see **ethos** and **logos**). Pathos is persuasiveness that comes from appeals to emotion.

patient-centered philosophy An approach to helping interviews in medicine; characterized by concern for the whole person, with medical personnel exploring the illness experience from the patient's perspective.

peer rankings A method of appraisal that evaluates an employee or group member on the basis of colleagues' assessments of his or her work relative to the performance of other colleagues.

performance plan An outcome of organizational interviews that help employees set realistic goals for attaining measurable improvement.

personality profile A journalistic article or report on an individual based on in-depth interviewing.

persuasion The communication process in which beliefs, attitudes, values, or behavior are influenced by others' messages.

phatic communion Small talk that serves mainly to humanize relations.

political correctness A term describing a belief that society is increasingly controlled by political agendas of various cultural groups, particularly efforts to enforce rules about acceptable language and behavior.

postmodernism A philosophy suggesting that knowledge and truth are social constructions that shift as people continuously interpret, negotiate, and renegotiate meanings of the social world. Therefore, in this view, meanings (such as an interviewee's intention) are not eternal or fixed, waiting to be discovered; they must always be acknowledged as situational, ever changing, and, to some extent, unspecifiable.

pre-interview A short interchange that sets up or coordinates longer interviews.

preparatory questions In an interview, communication that helps show hospitality, establish rapport, or screen information in a nonthreatening way.

primary questions Interview questions whose purpose is to open areas of inquiry and discover basic information. See **probes**.

primary selection interviewing   A single round of interviewing intended to identify and select a particular employee for a particular position.

probability survey   Interview research using a sample population drawn by mathematical guidelines to represent a larger population accurately.

probe notes   An interviewer's written reminders to help recall questions or topics he or she wants to address later in the interview.

probes   Questions or inquiries that confirm or amplify information elicited by **primary questions** or by previous probes. Also called probe questions.

profile of essential skills   A document that lists the main qualities and qualifications necessary to excel in a given job. See **criteria checklist.**

psychological contract   Unstated expectations about appropriate behavior or attitudes shared by members within an organization.

psychotherapy   Treatment that focuses on investigating and confronting disabling psychological conditions, such as deep-seated depression; typically, psychotherapy is conducted in face-to-face interview settings.

public journalism   A movement that stresses greater involvement by news organizations in community life and resolution of community problems.

punctuation   The mental act by which people attribute causes and effects, stops and starts, and other indicators of meaning to what they see and hear.

qualitative research   An inquiry, often using interview methods, that concentrates on less tangible qualities of experience that characterize social action. See **quanitative research.**

Quality of Work Life formula (QWL)   A method of assessing job satisfaction according to a set of criteria.

quantitative research   An inquiry to generate, categorize, and analyze statistical data by use of instruments such as questionnaires and surveys. See **qualitative research.**

quota sample   A group of respondents selected to match, for example, known percentages of subsets found in a larger population.

quote searching   Listening to a taped account of an interview until you hear the quotes that best meet your goals.

random selection   A mathematical method of ensuring that every member of a population has an equal chance of being selected for a **sample.**

rankings   Quantitative assignments or estimates that compare a person or thing to other persons or things based on a stated measure. In ranking procedures, each member must be designated as first, or second, or third, and so on, in a given group. See **ratings.**

rapport   Positive, natural, and mutually attentive talk and behavior that encourage further talk by creating an environment of comfort and cooperation.

ratified participant   A concept that accounts for the silent, but fully recognized and important, participation of the audience in broadcasts.

ratings   Evaluations that assess persons or things on the basis of a series of carefully defined performance criteria. Ratings differ from **rankings** in that they reflect individual performance quality, while rankings reflect performance quality in direct comparison with other persons or things.

recognition cluster   In **confirmation theory,** a group of statements or behaviors that indicate direct engagement with, and focused attention on, a speaker.

recognition skills   In **discriminative listening,** attentiveness to verbal, vocal, and behavior cues of meaning.

reduced note taking   Reading the written notes of an interview while listening to the taped conversation, comparing the two, and filling in gaps in the notes.

reframing   Consciously developing a new context in which to interpret phenomena; often involves recasting a potentially negative or unhelpful frame to one that is positive and helpful.

regulation skills   In **discriminative listening,** being sensitive to and acting on cues that signal turn taking and other behaviors that govern conversation.

relayed feedback   A skill that allows job applicants and other interviewees to pass along positive assessments others have made of them without appearing boastful.

reliability   Whether a research method measures the same phenomenon whenever it is used. See **validity.**

resume   A succinct summary of the education, work experience, and skills that qualify a person for a job. See **chronological resume** and **functional resume.**

rhetoric   The study of intentional communication, often involving how people implement strategies to influence others.

rhetorical questions   Questions for which the answer is so obvious that they don't need to be answered at all.

rhythm   A comfortable, harmonious order and progression of an interview.

sample   A group of respondents for an interview or study that represents a larger population.

sampling error   The degree to which a given sample statistic will likely fail to correspond to the actual characteristics of a population.

schedule   An interviewer's planned organization of questions or topics.

screening interview   Preliminary interviews designed to determine whether a job applicant meets requirements and warrants a fuller **second interview** or follow-up interview.

second interview/on-site visit   A follow-up interview often for the purposes of exposing an interviewee to the work setting and meeting potential coworkers under actual organizational conditions.

selection interview   An interaction designed to determine whom to hire for a job or select for an honor or award; the term is sometimes used to describe the employment interview process as a whole.

selective transcription   Transcribing sections of a taped interview most relevant to the interviewer's purposes.

self-evaluative essay   A type of narrative assessment based on a worker's personal portrayal of his or her performance.

self-fulfilling prophecy   A phenomenon in which prior perceptual habits and expectations at least partially determine what people find in new situations, thereby "fulfilling" their own expectations.

self-rating   An employee's appraisal of personal performance, based on criteria or standards on a rating form provided by the organization.

semantic differential scale   A measurement instrument that asks respondents to consider a concept along a continuum, ranging from one quality to its opposite: hot-cold, active-inactive, and so forth.

simple random sample   A sample based on assigning each member of a population a number and then choosing a sample from a table of random numbers.

skill   The ability to adapt behaviorally to meet the demands of different contexts.

skills-plus approach   Communication that emphasizes skills in the context of the values and motivations of the people using them.

snowball sample   A sample developed as a group of respondents identifies more respondents, who identify others, and so on.

social roles   The positions assumed by interviewers and interviewees along with behaviors associated with those positions.

sound bites   Short, sloganlike statements that supposedly capture longer, more complex ideas in a few quotable words; often used in media coverage.

standing room only close   A tactic used by sellers to imply or state that a respondent must act now or forever lose the opportunity to buy something framed as desirable or wanted.

stereotyping   Using mental pictures or expectations to predict and explain others.

stratified random sample   A sample that takes into account and studies various subsets, such as age and occupation, of a random sample.

stress questions   Questions expressly designed to make respondents uncomfortable so the interviewer can observe reactions.

suitcase questions   Questions crammed to overflowing with implications or details.

supportive climate   An interpersonal atmosphere or context that encourages communicators to seek ways of supporting each other. See **defensive climate**.

supportive questions   Questions or probes that help direct and advance interviews by bolstering, setting up, or following up primary questions.

surface description version   A concise statement prepared by an organization for applicants, describing a job position.

surplus of seeing   To Bakhtin, the idea that each person in a communication relationship sees, hears, and thus contributes perspectives that the other partner cannot.

symbolic interactionism   A theoretical perspective that explains human interaction by how communicators ascribe meaning to their own and others' acts, constructing a symbolic world they then inhabit verbally.

systematic random sample   A method of selecting a sample based on every nth part or unit of a population.

tape-sensitive notes   Notebook entries an interviewer uses to remember important points or statements and specify where they can be found on the tape.

teleology   An ethical orientation that emphasizes the importance of outcomes and consequences in actions and decisions.

test of publicity   An ethical principle based on asking whether a communicator would feel comfortable in publicizing an action to a wide audience of reasonable people.

testimonial close   A seller or persuader's strategy to close a deal by introducing a statement from someone a potential buyer finds credible.

testing   A skill of critical listening that involves a constant willingness to detect and assess communication problems and discuss them openly.

Theory X management   To McGregor, a management orientation that assumes that people work best when closely directed, monitored, and forced to perform. See **Theory Y management**.

Theory Y management   To McGregor, a management orientation that assumes workers are self-motivated and can take on responsibilities. See **Theory X management**.

therapeutic interview   A means of assisting someone in need to systematically revise behavior, thought, or psychological state.

therapeutic listening   Listening to help others accomplish their goals through supportive styles and behaviors.

360-degree appraisal   An appraisal method based on collecting feedback from everyone whose productivity and performance depend on the employee under review.

tight shot   In television or film, an extreme close-up of a speaker; displays for the audience a perspective uncharacteristic of ordinary conversational distance.

topical organization   A pattern of questioning that moves from issue to issue.

total quality management (TQM)   To Deming, a management concept that emphasizes improved productivity through improved quality.

transaction   A relationship in which participants mutually and simultaneously influence and define one another; because interviewers and interviewees assume roles that define each other, and because their talk is interdependent, interviewing is a good example of a transactional process.

transcription   Converting the entire taped record of an interview into a printed account that can be more easily analyzed than extensive replaying of the tape.

utilitarianism   An ethical approach that stresses concern for consequences of acts, particularly favoring those acts that produce the greatest good for the greatest number.

validation   Acknowledgment through words or actions that there has been a sincere, cooperative exchange of views.

validity   Whether a research method measures what it purports to measure. See **reliability**.

vertical dimension   In oral history interviewing, the chronological progression of an interviewee's recollections.

vulnerability   In crisis intervention, the degree to which an individual can rebound from or endure a difficult condition or event.

wait time   A significant pause of several seconds used to elicit fuller, richer answers by giving a respondent time to think through the implications of a point.

what-questions   Neutral, information-seeking inquiries used in interviews to help frame suggested solutions or courses of action.

why-questions   Inquiries that focus on explanations and justifications rather than information useful in working out solutions or courses of action.

willingness to communicate (WTC)   This concept concludes that many otherwise exceptional employees will rarely volunteer their ideas or feelings openly within organizations.

wrap-up questions   Known also as *clearinghouse questions,* these give the respondent a final word or opportunity to supply information the questioner has not covered.

you-messages   Judgmental responses that tend to cause a defensive reaction, such as, "You made me mad."

❦ Index